Y0-CMN-608

THE PATE CHRONICLE

THE PATE CHRONICLE

Edited and translated from
MSS 177, 321, 344 and 358 of the
Library of the University of Dar es Salaam
by Marina Tolmacheva

and reproducing the versions published by C.H. Stigand Alice Werner, M. Heepe and Alfred Voeltzkow, edited and partially translated by Marina Tolmacheva with the assisstance of Dagmar Weiler

Michigan State University Press
East Lansing
1993

All Michigan State University Press books are produced on paper which meets the requirements of American National Standard of Information Sciences—Permanence of paper for printed materials ANSI Z23.48-1984

Michigan State University Press
East Lansing, Michigan 48823-5202

Printed in the United States of America

01 00 99 98 97 96 95 94 93 1 2 3 4 5 6 7 8 9 10

The Pate Chronicle was published with the assisstance of the National Endowment of the Humanities and the Office of the Provost and Academic Vice President, Washington State University.

Library of Congress Cataloging-in-Publication Data.

The Pate Chronicle: edited and translated from MSS 177, 321, 344, and 358 of the Library of the University of Dar es Salaam / by Marina Tolmacheva: and reproducing the versions published by C.H. Stigand . . . [et al.], edited and partially translated by Marina Tolmacheva with the assistance of Dagmar Weiler.

p. cm.—(African historical sources: 4.)

Includes bibliographical references.

ISBN 0-87013-336-5 (alk. paper)

1. Pate (Kenya)—History —Sources. 2. Lamu (Kenya)—History—Sources. I. Tolmacheva, Marina. II Stigand, C.H. (Chauncy Hugh), 1877-1919. III. Weiler, Dagmar. IV. Series.

DT434.P38P38 1993

967.62'3—dc20

93-12769
CIP

African Historical Sources Series Editors:
Jay Spaulding and David Robinson

CONTENTS

TRANSCRIPTS AND TRANSLATIONS

ARABIC-SWAHILI TEXTS

ACKNOWLEDGEMENTS

This work began with a Social Science Research grant which enabled me in 1975 to spend three months at the University of Dar es Salaam copying Swahili historical manuscripts by hand. Before then came an introduction to Arabic-Swahili writing under the guidance of Viacheslav Mikhailovich Misiugin, late of the Department of African Studies of St.-Petersburg (then Leningrad) University. My work on Swahili chronicles received an important boost when a Research Grant-in-Aid from Washington State University afforded me the services of a Research Assistant for 1988-89. This was followed by a submission of a translation and editing proposal to the National Endowment for the Humanities on the initiative of the Association for Publication of African Historical Sources. The resulting grant, administered by David Robinson of Michigan State University, supported me and my Research Assistant Dagmar Weiler through the summer of 1990. Washington State University has supported my work through Initiation and Completion grants and a Faculty Summer Stipend in 1991. A Publication Subvention grant from WSU partially covered the publication costs.

Dagmar Weiler contributed organizational skills, word-processing services and translation from the German. Janice Morgan was instrumental in composing tables and preparing camera-ready copy. Imran Daudi did the initial word-processing of Arabic texts. Courtney Ingebritsen assisted in the production of computer-generated maps. From Michigan State University,

David Robinson and Andrew Clark, and later John Reid provided encouragement, friendly advice and firm deadlines. Carol M. Eastman of the University of Washington and Patricia Romero of Towson State University shared information and enthusiasm and gave generously of their advice. Jay Spaulding of Kean College and Michigan State University, the editor of the Series *African Historical Sources*, in which this volume is appearing, carefully read the translations and made sympathetic and useful suggestions. Julie Loehr and Fred Bohm, of Michigan State University Press, offered editorial guidance.

Marina Tolmacheva
Washington State University
Pullman, Washington

NOTE ON ORTHOGRAPHY

The transcription system adopted in my rendering of Arabic-script Swahili is a slightly revised version of the Library of Congress system. Its major distinctions from that used for Arabic words in the Encyclopedia of Islam are the use of *j* rather than *dj* for *jīm* and of *y* rather than *i* for *yā'* in diphtongs. On the other hand, *ḳ* was preferred to *q* to facilitate conformity with the current Swahili orthography. Swahili phonetics influenced other cases: for instance, *ghayn* was rendered with *gh* in Arabic loan-words but with *g* in Swahili words of Bantu origin. My transcription of the Arabic transliteration of Swahili consonants generally follows W.E. Taylor's system. The dental and explosive *t*'s and *d*'s are not marked. Those sounds appearing in parentheses (usually *n* and *w*) are inferred; transliteration enclosed in brackets offers the editor's emendation of the Arabic-script text, which is reproduced in Arabic version exactly as it was read at the time of copying.

Arabic words have been treated according to Swahili orthography: for example, *hata* or *ḥatā* rather than *ḥattā* unless a *tashdīd* was placed above the *tā'*. The one exception was Arabic personal names, often spelled without vowel marks or diacritical dots, which were rendered in Arabic rather than Swahili style. On the other hand, when phonetical marks normally absent in Arabic were present to indicate Swahili pronunciation, **bold** characters were used to distinguish ***p*** from *b* and ***v*** from *f*. Bold ***ch*** was used for the *ch* sound when rendered by a *kāf* with two dots rather than *tā'* an bold *ta' marbuta* when pronounced.

The Arabic titles such as *amīr, imām* or *sulṭān* were transcribed phonetically in the Swahili version but without diacritical marks in the English translation. Capitalization was followed when the title was used as part of a personal name. A few special terms, such as *mudabbir al-umūr*, were highlighted in italics and translated in parentheses ("director of affairs). The reverse practice was followed for some toponyms derived from common nouns (*Banadiri, Mrima*). The toponym *Sawaḥili* was rendered as "Sawahili (coast)."

The Arabic division pattern of many Swahili words differs from that accepted currently; this is especially noticeable in the orthography of verbal forms and particles. To the extent that it was possible to reconcile the manuscript versions with standard contemporary practice while preserving the original style of writing for historical-linguistic purposes, the dash was used to convey conjoint spelling of words which are now spelled separately, while the sign ‿ connects word parts scripted in the MSS separately which would today be spelled together. The varying separate or joint spelling of toponyms was followed in reproducing the Arabic-script original and in transcription, but abandoned in translation for the sake of uniformity.

Dates in the text appear without notation *AH* for the Muslim calendar; for the corresponding dates in the Western calendar notation *AD* has been added.

Map 1. The East African Coast

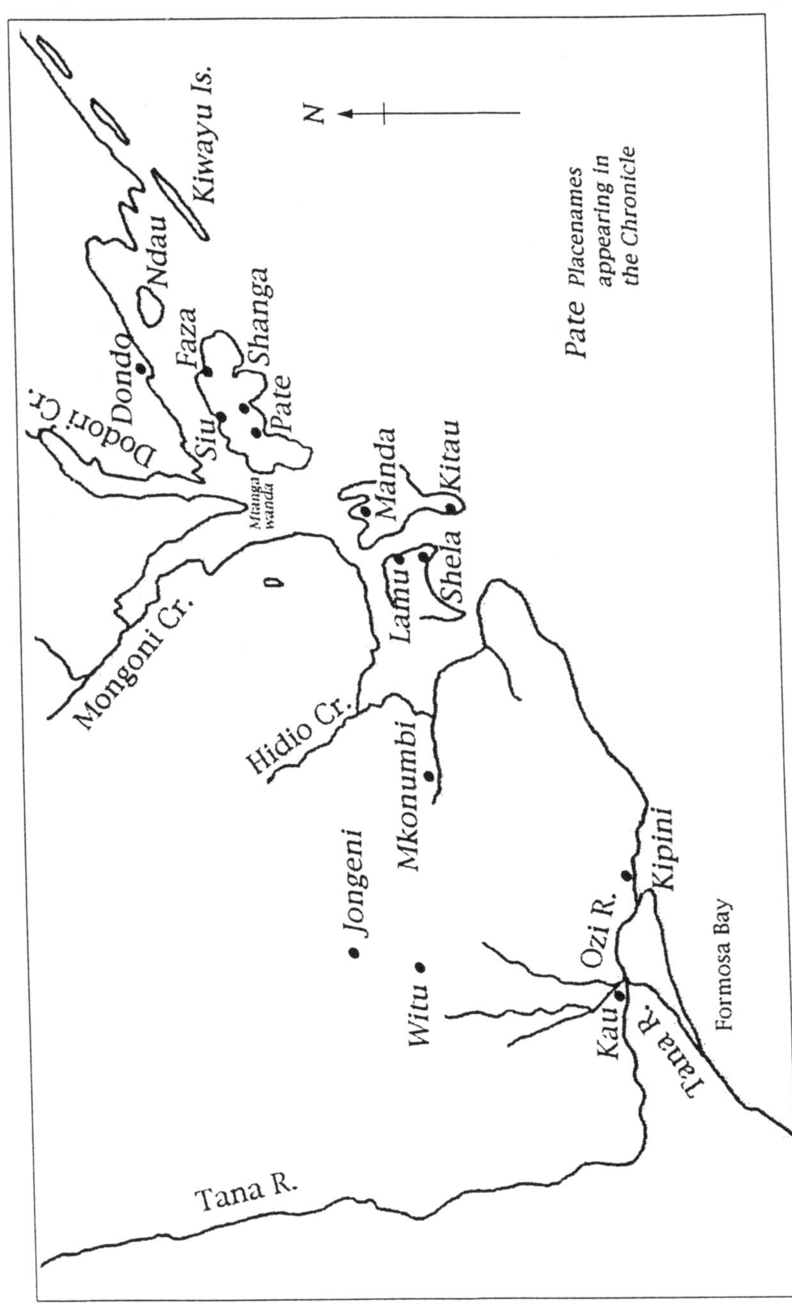

Map 2. Lamu Archipelago and Hinterland

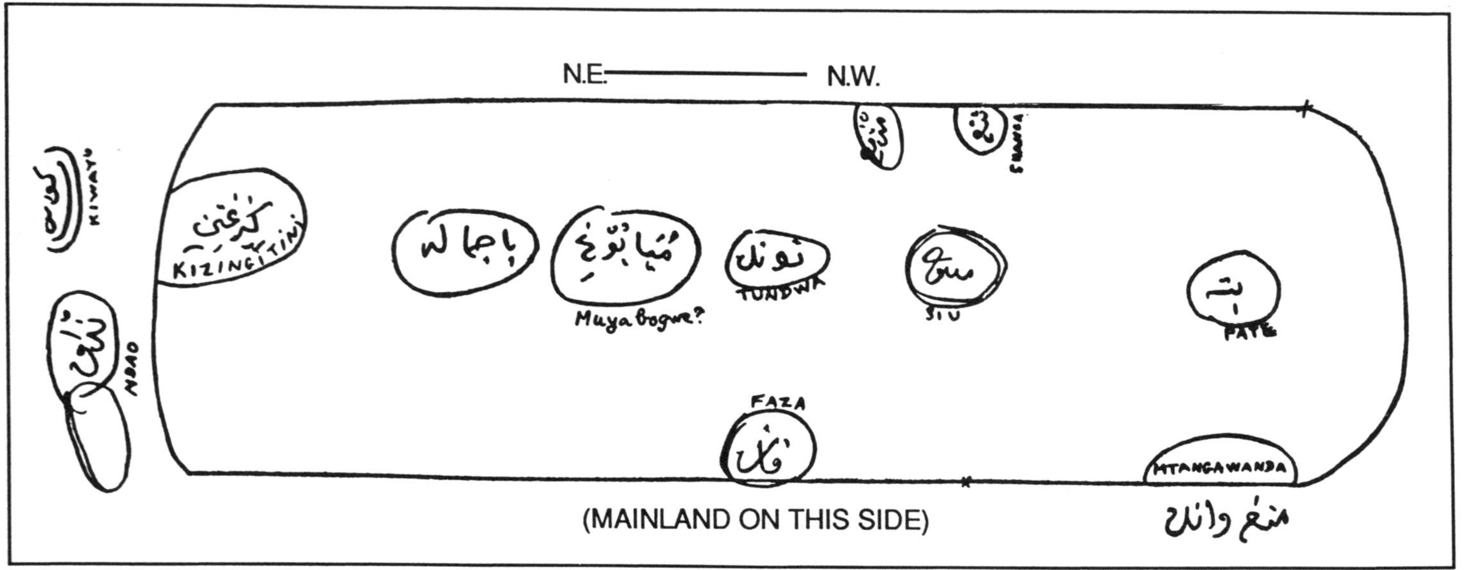

MAP 3. Map of the Island of Siu, drawn by Abdallah bin Muhammad, Wali of Faza.

Source: Alice Werner, "A Swahili History of Pate," *Journal of the African Society*, 1915, facing p. 280.

INTRODUCTION

On the morning of October 26, 1890 a British column of 950 men led by Admiral Fremantle advanced on the town of Witu, the last, mainland capital of the Nabahani rulers of Pate.

> A seven-pounder field gun failed to break down the gate, but explosives wrenched the tree trunks sufficiently to allow the attackers to enter. All the stone buildings, including the palace, and a great quantity of powder and ammunition were blown up. Every effort was "successfully used to utterly wreck and destroy the town and defences of Witu."[1]

The attack, which the British mounted in retaliation for murder of several German nationals, made an outlaw of the reigning Sultan Fumo Bakari. He never returned to Witu and was soon replaced on the throne by two younger brothers in quick succession. The second of these, Fumo 'Umari, tried to move his residence to Jongeni, where he had to face the double hostility of the British and the Bajun people of the coast.[2] Eventually, no amount of manoeuvering by Fumo 'Umari could prevent the 1895 British takeover of the Witu sultanate. The coast and the islands, in the words of the *Pate Chronicle*, "came under the Illustrious Administration of the British."

---

[1] Marguerite Ylvisaker, *Lamu in the Nineteenth Century: Land, trade, and Politics* (Boston: African Studies Center Boston University, 1979), 152-53.

[2] Ylvisaker, *Lamu*, 155.

When the Zanzibari protectorate was declared over Witu in 1891, its ruler, demoted from the office of *Sultan* to that of *Shaykh*, was given money by the Imperial British East Africa Company to rebuild his town. But irretrievably lost in the bombardment of Witu was the original manuscript history of Pate, *The Book of the Kings of Pate*. Gathered in this volume are later renditions of and extractions from this chronicle.

The chronicle, considered by many the single most important indigenous source for Swahili history, does not pretend to be a complete history of Pate (*PAH-teh*), formerly one of the most important trade centers on the northern Swahili coast in today's Kenya. Recent historical and anthropological writing has focused much more on Lamu, a city of a neighboring island in the Lamu (or Siu) archipelago, the area which, with the adjoining mainland, forms the historical *Swahilini*.[3] Along the length of the East African coast between Mogadishu and Mozambique, Pate and Kilwa (the latter now in Tanzania) represented two main termini of coast-oriented trade coming both from the sea and mainland. By the twelfth century a culture had emerged which thrived on long-distance trade, created city-states, and adopted Islam as its religion and found expression through various dialects of Swahili language.

While the flourishing of Kilwa in the fourteenth century has been documented, Pate's claims to greatness during roughly the same period are probably overstated.[4] Nevertheless, "abundant evidence was found in ruins

---

[3] *-ni* is used rather than *U-* because *Swahili* is a toponym. See Marina Tolmacheva, "The Origin of the Name Swahili," *Tanzania Notes and Records* 78 (1976): 27-37.

[4] G.S.P. Freeman-Grenville has speculated that a rise of Pate may have resulted from a change in Mamluk Egypt's trading policies. Roland Oliver and Gervase Mathew, eds., *History of East Africa*. Vol. I (Oxford, 1963), ch. 5 "The Coast to 1498."

all along the coast of a vibrant period of Swahili civilization in the fourteenth and fifteenth centuries, marked by extensive and elaborate building and large-scale imports of Islamic and Chinese pottery, that lasted until the Portuguese destroyed a number of towns during the sixteenth century in their attempt to monopolize Indian Ocean trade.[5]" Pate avoided destruction, briefly and reluctantly accepting Portuguese suzerainty; some of the intricacies of relations with the Portuguese are revealed in the *Chronicle*.

The rise of Pate's older rivals Mombasa and Lamu came probably during this period and at least in part at the expense of Kilwa for the former and Pate for the latter. The pressures of Portuguese dominance in the sixteenth and seventeenth centuries led to an alliance between coastal towns and the Mazru'i rulers of Oman. Especially after their establishment in Zanzibar, the Arabs exerted strong influences beyond the political sphere. It seems probable that this period, falling between the two eras of European dominance (Portuguese and British, briefly paralleled by German) was particularly instrumental in popularizing local claims to Arab or Persian antecedents which provide the core of legitimacy for the ruling houses and motivation for recording the dynastic past.

This chronicle is representative of the historical tradition developed in the coastal city-states as one of the important facets of their culture and society. The coastal people, formerly regarded as essentially alien to Africa, are in fact, demonstrably indigenous to the coast. This point has been argued successfully by J. de V. Allen, Randall L. Pouwels and Thomas T. Spear. In addition to

---

[5] Derek Nurse and Tomas Spear, *The Swahili: reconstructing the History and Language of an African Society, 800-1500.* (Philadelphia: University of Pennsylvania Press, 1985), 4.

the works already cited see R.L. Pouwels, *Horn and Crescent: Cultural Change and Traditional Islam on the East African Coast, 800-1900* (Cambridge: University Press, 1987). Forthcoming are J. de V. Allen, *Swahili Origins* (Athens, OH: Ohio University Press), and John Middleton, *The World of the Swahili: an African Mercantile Civilization* (New Haven: Yale University Press). However, "socially and traditionally [their] principal sources of identity lie elsewhere."[6]

According to the *Chronicle*, an Arabian ruler of the Nabahani house in Oman came to Pate in the year 600 A.H./1203-1204 A.D.[7] The record then focuses on the establishment and subsequent generations of the Nabahani dynasty, while the previous history of Pate is neglected. In oral traditions recorded at Pate and other sites along the coast, the foundation of the city of Pate, as well as many others, is projected back to the era of the Umayyad caliphate, when ʻAbd al-Malik bin Marwān (685-705) is said to have dispatched groups of Arabs who founded as many as thirty-two towns.[8] (Paradoxically, some of the same sites are later assigned dynasties of "Shirazi", i.e. Persian, descent). Regardless of veracity of such claims, current historiography of East Africa defines the Shirazi as "core Swahili" coastal, cosmopolitan Islamic speakers of Northeastern Banbie proto-language (Sabaki).

---

[6] Randall L. Pouwels, "Oral Historiography and the Problem of the Shirazi on the East African Coast," *History in Africa* 11 (1984): 237-67.

[7] Even according to the *Chronicle* which favors the Nabahani, they came to Pate *after* having been displaced in Oman by the Yaʻrubi *imāms*. The Nabahani dynasty in Oman reigned from 1154-1406.

[8] C.H. Stigand, *The Land of Zinj*. (London, 1913, reprint 1966), 29. On historical Arab migrations to the coast, see Bradford G. Martin, "Arab Migrations to East Africa in Medieval Times," *International Journal of African Historical Studies* 7/3 (1974): 367-90.

In regard to political system, J. de V. Allen speaks of a Shirazi "mode of dominance"[9] whose main institutions are terminology are Arabo-Islamic.

It is generally acknowledged that the coast, dotted as it is with archeological sites, had never been united. Various centers and regions rose, flourished, and competed in the Middle Ages. It is becoming apparent from recent archeological evidence that the northern Swahili coast may have played an earlier and more important role than previously thought, but the period between 700-1200 A.D. remains obscure in the records. Although recent archeological evidence suggests that Pate, as well as its neighbors Manda and Shanga, may have been prominent in the ninth or tenth centuries,[10] no external sources mention Pate until the late fifteenth century.[11] Pate is not prominent in the Portuguese records, either.

Arabic sources, aware of Mombasa and Malindi since at least mid-twelfth century, later focus on Kilwa and Mogadishu, and do not mention Lamu until the fourteenth century. While the presence of Islam on the coast was first noted by al-Mas'ūdī in the tenth century, the earliest evidence that Middle Eastern visitors to the coast were aware of the native (*Zanj*) claims to Arab descent does not come until the early thirteenth century, when Pemba is

---

[9] James de V. Allen, "The 'Shirazi' Problem in East African Coastal History," *Paideuma* 28 (1982): 21.

[10] Nurse and Spear, *Swahili*, 28. For the new interpretation based on recent archeological data see Mark Horton, "Asiatic Colonization of the East African Coast: Manda Evidence," *Journal of the Royal Asiatic Society* 2 (1986): 201-13; and "Early Muslim Trading Settlements on the East African Coast: New Evidence from Shanga," *Antiquaries Journal* 67 (1987): 290-323. I am grateful to Patricia Romero for these references.

[11] T.A. Shumovskii, *Tri neizvestnye lotsii Akhmada ibn Madzhida arabskogo lotsmana Vasko da-Gamy* (Three unknown sailing instructions of Ahmad ibn Majid, the Arab pilot of Vasco da Gama). (Moscow and Leningrad, 1957), ff. 87v, 88v.

first described by the Arabic geographer Yāḳūt:

> The Green Island (*al-Jazīrat al-Khaḍrā'*)... a large island off the Land of Zanj in the Sea of India... On it are two cities, one is called Mtambī and the other Mk.mb.lū. In each there is a sultan of their own who has no authority over the other. There are many hamlets and villages in it. Their sultan asserts that he is an Arab and descended from those who migrated to the island from Kufa. This was reported to me by the esteemed Shaykh 'Abd al-Malik al-Ḥallāwī al-Baṣrī; he saw it all and knew him (the sultan), and he (Shaykh 'Abd al-Malik) is a man worthy of trust.[12]

The bulk of the *Chronicle* is a chronological description of thirty-two reigns of Pate kings, beginning with Sulaymān bin Sulaymān bin Muẓaffar al-Nabahānī, whose claim to kingship rests on two foundations: for the patrilineal Arabs, the justification lies in his possession of the title and office of *sulṭān* prior to emigration from Arabia. For the matrilineal Bantu, the legitimacy is rooted in his marriage to the daughter of the Pate king of a previous dynasty, unrevealingly called *al-Batawiyyūn*, the Arabic for "Pate dwellers" or "those of Pate."

Subsequent rulers have the title of Sultan attached to their names, including even the one female ruler, Mwāna Khadīja. However, references to the office of the ruler most commonly speak of "kingship," the Bantu *ufalme (ufalume)*. Combinations of its derivative *fumo* with Arabic names (such as

---

[12] Ferdinand Wüstenfeld, ed. *Jacut's geographisches Wörterbuch* (Leipzig, 1866-1873), Vol. II: 75-6.

Fumomadi for *Fumo Ahmadi* or *Fumo Muhammadi* and *Fumomari* for *Fumo Omari*, commented on by the earlier editors of the *Chronicle*) have been mistaken in the past for an "Africanized" royal title or throne-name.[13] However, there is some real evidence of Bantuization of royal names, which goes beyond phonetical amalgamation. In one pattern, beginning with the twelfth ruler, the first use of a Bantu title or nickname occurs, later followed by a growing number of other personal names. Thus, *Bwana Mkuu* bin Muhammad (d. 973 A.H./1565-66 A.D.) is followed by *Bwana Bakari* bin Bwana Mkuu, an obviously "Swahilized" rendering of the Arabic for *Abū Bakr*. Two generations later occurs for the first time the use of a Swahili substitute for the Arabic patronymic: Bwana Mkuu *wa* Bwana Bakari *bin* Bwana Mkuu, etc.[14]

The frequency of meaningful names like *Bwana Mkuu* "Big Seigneur", Bwana Tamu *Mkuu* "Bwana Tamu Senior," Bwana Tamu *Mtoto* "Bwana Tamu Junior," and so on, including the use for personal names of such common nouns as *Shaykh (Shekhe,* for "Shehe," and *Sheye*) and *Sulṭān*, is a revealing sign of two processes: the assimilation of Arabic words into Swahili and the cultural Africanization of the royal office's most obvious symbol, the ruler's name. Together, they may serve as an example of what Pouwels has called the "historical predicament" of the "Shirazi."[15] If the first of these may be of greater interest to the historical linguists, the second demonstrates how

---

[13] G.S.P. Freeman-Grenville in Oliver and Mathew, *East Africa*, 116.

[14] As J. de V. Allen noted, parallel with the Arabo-Persian model, the "Shirazi" political mode had wholly Bantu vocabulary ("Shirazi," 20).

[15] Pouwels, "Historiography," 251.

significant historical information can be still elicited through a closer reading of the chronicles than heretofore. Admittedly, the chronology of these processes cannot be established solely from the text.[16]

The historiography of the *Pate Chronicle* has undergone its ups and downs. Largely neglected by African scholars in the inter-war years, it was subsequently used in together with chronicles and oral histories of other Swahili cities, to paint in broad strokes a history of the coast where no other indigenous documents existed, the Portuguese sources were limited geographically and chronologically, and archeological evidence was almost non-existent. The uncritical acceptance of the claims made by oral legends and chronicles to Arab origin of the cities' founders led some historians to present the East African coast as a historical arena for "Arab Vikings."[17] In the early 1960s the question was still being asked whether it is "possible to construct an exactly dated documentary history of the coast from the late seventh century. It is true that we now possess the documents. The problem is the extent to which they are historically reliable."[18]

In the first serious discussion of Swahili historiography, A.H.J. Prins characterized the *Pate Chronicle* as "the most complete" of the five then known written Swahili histories despite the fact that "it entirely omits the first five

---

[16] In addition to obvious conflict among the dates provided in the extant records, preliteral history has its own problems of chronology. See discussion of this in David Henige, *The Chronology of Oral Tradition: Quest for a Chimera* (Oxford: Clarendon Press, 1974).

[17] One unfortunate example is Richard Reusch, *History of East Africa* (Stuttgart, 1954). For a review by J.M. G[ray] see *Tanganyika Notes and Records* 38 (1955): 53-58.

[18] Roland Oliver and Gervase Mathew, *History of East Africa*. Vol. I (Oxford, 1963), 102.

centuries of Pate history (first dynasty of Pate)."[19] Since then, the study of the chronicles has followed three tracks: exploration of interrelatedness of written and oral history on the East African coast[20], the use of chronicles for the writing of Swahili history proper,[21] and historiography.[22]

---

[19] A.H.J. Prins, "On Swahili Historiography." *Swahili. Journal of the East African Swahili Committee*, No. 28 (1958), 26.

[20] Prins was probably the first among historians of East Africa to insist that "Swahili culture is a good case in point to show that this distinction [between literate and preliterate societies] as applied to whole societies is largely invalid, because here the recording of the past both orally and on record go hand in hand." (Prins, 1958: 26). More recently, the cause has been taken up by Randall L. Pouwels and Thomas Spear. See, for example, Pouwels, "Oral Historiography" 11 (1984), and "Swahili Literature and History in the Post-Structuralist Era: A Revisit and Riposte to Allen *et al*," forthcoming in *International Journal of African Historical Studies* 31; also Thomas Spear, "Oral Traditions: Whose History?" *History in Africa* 8 (1981): 163-79 and "The Shirazi in Swahili Traditions, Culture, and History," *History in Africa* 11 (1984): 291-305.

[21] See, for example, Neville Chittick, "A New Look at the History of Pate," *Journal of African History* 10 (1969): 375-91; for Chittick's discussion of other histories see his "Kilwa and the Arab Settlements on the East African Coast," *Journal of African History* 4 (1963): 179-190; "The 'Shirazi' Colonization of East Africa," *Journal of African History* 6 (1965): 275-94; and "The Book of the Zenj and the Mijikenda," *International Journal of African Historical Studies* 9 (1976): 68-73. For an early overview see G.S.P. Freeman-Grenville, "Swahili Literature and the History and Archaeology of the East African Coast," *Journal of the East African Swahili Committee* 28 (1958): 7-25. Both the Arabic and Portuguese versions of the *Kilwa Chronicle* were used by Freeman-Grenville in his *Medieval History of the Coast of Tanganyika* (London and Berlin, 1982). Typical of the later source-criticism efforts are B.G. Martin's "Arab Migrations to East Africa in Medieval Times," *International Journal of African Historical Studies* 7 (1974): 364-90 and Thomas T. Spear, "Traditional Myths and Historian's Myths: Variations on the Singwaya Theme of Mijikenda Origins," *History in Africa* 1 (1974): 85-100.

[22] See, for example, John de Vere Allen, "Traditional History and African Literature: the Swahili Case," *Journal of African History* 23 (1982): 227-36; John M. Gray, "Zanzibar Local Histories," *Swahili* 30 (1959): 24-50; 31 (1960): 111-39; Elias Saad, "Kilwa Dynastic Historiography," *History in Africa* 6 (1979): 177-209; L. Schaffer, "A Historiographic Appraisal of Kenyan Coastal History," *Ufahamu* 9 (1979): 61-77; Marina Tolmacheva, "The Arabic Influence on Swahili Literature: A Historian's View," *Journal of African Studies* 5 (1978): 223-43 and "'They Came from Damascus in Syria': A Note on

In the course of the 1960s and 1970s the *Pate Chronicle* and the *Kilwa Chronicle*, as the two most important ones on the coast, received some critical attention. The former, in particular, has been subject to doubts concerning usefulness as an historical source. It seems that a broad agreement existed in regard to its limitations. G.S.P. Freeman-Grenville wrote in 1963: "This may be treated, with caution, as an historic source from the time of the founding of the Nabhani dynasty in the thirteenth century; archaeology seems to be providing its fourteenth-century section with some curious corroborations."[23] After careful consideration of fragmentary oral tradition and early archeological evidence, Neville Chittick concluded in 1969: "Many or most of the events described in the early part have no historicity whatever; notably, Pate's conquest of the whole coast in the fourteenth century must be dismissed as without any historical foundation."[24] In 1982 Gill Shepherd formulated the general skepticism in the following way: "Such chronicles are less objective histories than annotated pedigrees of a single ruling lineage."[25]

Paradoxically, the publication of several chronicles in translation by G.S.P. Freeman-Grenville[26] seems to have slowed down the process of

---

Traditional Lamu Historiography," *International Journal of African Historical Studies* 12 (1979): 259-69.

[23] Oliver and Mathew, 104.

[24] Neville Chittick, "A New Look at the History of Pate." *Journal of African History*, Vol. X (1969), No. 3, 391.

[25] Gill M. Shepherd, "The Making of the Swahili. A View from the Southern End of the East African Coast." *Paideuma* 28 (1982), 143.

[26] G.S.P. Freeman-Grenville, *The East African Coast: Select Documents from the First Century to the Early Nineteenth Century* (Oxford, 1962).

historiographic inquiry by making the few selected versions of major coastal histories available in English.[27] Randall L. Pouwels, in addition to recording oral tradition, has successfully demonstrated a synthetic analysis of written and oral local histories focused on Lamu.[28] Nurse and Spear have concluded that "In highlighting the main periods and themes of Swahili history, the traditions accurately portray the historical development of Swahili society."[29]

The historicity of the chronicles needs to be evaluated in light of the total coastal historical tradition, in which written text may serve as *aide-mémoire* to the fuller oral narrative.[30] It is important to recognize that a most significant ingredient of historiography--the intent to record (and sometimes create) history--is amply demonstrated by the very survival of a manuscript tradition against heavy odds and by subsequent proliferation of copies of most prominent histories. In addition, it may be limiting to regard these texts as documents *sensu stricto* and to focus primarily on their data for political

---

[27] A welcome recent exception is A.Y. Omar and P.J.L. Frank, "The Mombasa Chronicle," *Afrika und Übersee* 73 (1990): 101-28. It may be hoped that the development of the East African Centre for Research in Oral Traditions and African National Languages in Zanzibar becomes a significant factor in reversing the trend.

[28] Randall L. Pouwels, *Horn and Crescent*, ch. 3. On general problems of oral historiography see David Henige, *Oral Historiography* (London, New York: Longman, 1982); Jan Vansina, *Oral Tradition: a Study in Historical Methodology* (Chicago: Aldine Publishing Co., 1965); Ronald Cohen, Jan Vansina, Aristide Folberg, *Oral History in Africa* (Evanston, IL: Northwestern University Press, 1965).

[29] Nurse and Spear, *Swahili*, 31.

[30] For general evaluation, see Jan Vansina, *Oral Tradition as History* (Madison, Wis.: University of Wisconsin Press, 1985). For specific arguments on the value and interpretation of African oral history see, e.g., Joseph Miller, ed., *The African Past Speaks* (Folkestone, 1980) and Thomas Spear, "The Interpretation of Evidence in African History," *African Studies Review* 30 (1987): 17-24.

history. While it is true that most available histories are dynastic chronicles of coastal city-states, and therefore narrowly focused and partisan, an argument can be made that their purpose goes beyond recording genealogy. Jack Rollins has suggested that

> the role of the Swahili chronicler was not what would be associated with a chronicler of history in any Western sense. They were in a broad sense preservers, archivists of traditions, stories, legends. . . They sought to include all the *mambo ni hakika* (true facts) but from their perspective. They were collectors of source material drawing form older chronicles, indigenous oral traditions, family genealogies and legends primarily to record their civilization . . .[31]

In their role as documents legitimizing the ruling status of one family over the city of a chronicle's origin, each history inevitably sheds light on that city's society and its interaction with the dynasty as well as the city's interaction with other cities of the region. The value of the *Pate Chronicle* as a source for social-political history was demonstrated in an innovative way when V.M. Misiugin elicited from what had seemed to be jumbled records of names and reigns of Pate sultans an apparently logical system of lateral succession[32], which may be applicable to other city-states as well. Chittick (1969) and Saad (1982) have shown that although the chronicles' limited concern results in the texts favoring one local dynasty--usually the most recent-

---

[31] Jack D. Rollins, *A History of Swahili Prose*, vol. I (Leiden: Brill, 1983), 45.

[32] V.M. Misiugin, "The Swahili Chronicle of the Medieval State of Pate" (in Russian), *Africana* 6 (Leningrad, 1966).

-it is possible to investigate their stories of preceding or competing dynasties as well.

In a different vein, the geographical range and vocabulary of the chronicles have been shown to reflect a broad range of local, regional and international outlooks and to throw some light on the extent to which the Swahili historians reflect an Islamic/Middle Eastern identity in terms of cultural geography.[33] It is well known, for example, that many of the chronicles begin with the assertion of the foreign (Arab or "Shirazi") origin of the rulers.[34] Because such assertions lie at the base of dynastic legitimacy, contacts with the Arab (specifically, Arabo-Muslim) world, especially in the sphere of government politics, loom large in the records.

This emphasis may be only partly explained by the historical reality of continuous interaction. For instance, episodic Turkish contacts with the coast during the Portuguese era are a historical fact,[35] but the Turkish cultural element, even though Muslim, was sufficiently remote from local concerns that the selective historiographic approach denied the Ottomans political significance. Consequently, the memory of Turkish presence found no place

---

[33] Marina Tolmacheva, "Arabic-Swahili Chronicles as a Source for Historical Geography of the Swahili Coast." Unpublished paper presented at the 1987 Annual Meeting of the American Historical Association (Washington, D.C.).

[34] In a comment on *Pate Chronicle* Stigand provides a list of thirty-two cities, all said to have been founded at the initiative of the Umayyad caliph ʻAbd al-Malik ibn Marwān (685-705 A.D.). See p. 24.

[35] Indeed, the Portuguese presence spurred Turkish advances: "In 1585 an Amir Ali Bey came in a single galley, and visited Mogadishu, Brava, Kisimayu, Faza, Pate, Lamu, and Kilifi, telling the people he had been sent by the Turkish sultan to free them from the Portuguese... Faza, at this time or shortly after, acquired a Turkish dynasty, which ruled until the end of the nineteenth century and whose descendants still survive." G.S.P. Freeman-Grenville in Oliver and Mathew, 138-9.

in the chronicles or may have been suppressed. Political interests of a dynasty may contrast with social aspirations of those coastal families who prize their Turkish pedigree to this day.[36] Conversely, the *Pate Chronicle's* claim of Pate's conquest of the coast from Pate to Kerimba islands (including Kilwa) in the fourteenth century is rejected by historians outright,[37] as is the record of a conquest of eight cities in the chronicle of Vumba Kuu.[38] On the other hand, the *Pate Chronicle* is silent on the subject of Shungwaya, a region north of the Tana R. which tradition presents as a motherland of northeastern Bantu-speakers.[39] Mentioned in passing and without comment is the town of Shungwaya, one of many "conquered" by the Pate ruler.

Moreover, against a background of Arab genealogical pretensions, the chronicles nevertheless provide striking evidence of tensions and resentments directed at more recent Arab arrivals.[40] Clearly, the largely negative passages mentioning the Arabs reflect attempts of Oman and Zanzibar rulers to control coastal trade and politics: they usually refer to governors, government ministers and troops, whose presence on the coast is seen as temporary and

---

[36] Personal communication by Patricia Romero. On general socio-cultural patterns of oral tradition see T.O. Beidelman, "Myth, Legend and Oral History," Anthropos 65 (1970): 74-97.

[37] Chittick, 1969: 391.

[38] Prins, 27.

[39] On Shungwaya see, for example, R.F. Morton, "The Shungwaya Myth of Miji Kenda Origins: A Problem of Late Nineteenth-Century Kenya Coastal History," *International Journal of African Historical Studies* 5 (1973): 397-423, and A.H.J. Prins, "Šungwaya, die Urheimat der Nordost Bantu," *Anthropos* 50 (1955): 273-82.

[40] Marina Tolmacheva, "Group Identity in the *Swahili Chronicles*," Paper presented at the 1991 Annual Meeting of the American Anthropological Association (Chicago).

often unwelcome.[41] Further, "Arabs" is only one of diverse examples of ethnonyms and socio-cultural terms, whose use in the chronicles allows for a retrospective exploration of group identities and interrelations as they existed (or were perceived) on the coast prior to European colonization.

In reconstructing the stemma of manuscripts and versions of the *Chronicle*, A.H.J. Prins chose to call the lost record of Pate history "State MS."[42] The existence of a prototype need hardly be doubted; a member of the ruling house, Bwana Kitini (Muhammad bin Fumo ‘Umar Nabahani) recited the oral version to Captain Stigand during his visit to the coast from a text Stigand was not allowed to consult but which his informant memorized and "made notes."[43] In 1903, on the order of the Lamu *liwali*, the same Bwana Kitini wrote the so-called Hollis manuscript, which was then transcribed from the Arabic and translated by Alice Werner.[44] About the same time a brief recapitulation of Pate history was recorded by the German explorer Alfred Voeltzkow who, with considerable delay (probably due to WWI), published only the German summary.[45] The accelerated exploration of the coast by Europeans witnessed a local effort to preserve Pate history in writing. In 1911

---

[41] On Swahili ("Shirazi")-Omani-Mazru‘i relations see, for example, Norman R. Bennett, *A History of the Arab State of Zanzibar* (London: Methuen & Co., 1978) and O.H. Al-Maamiry, *Oman and East Africa* (New Delhi: Lancers, 1979).

[42] A.H.J. Prins, *Historiography*, 31.

[43] C.H. Stigand, *The Land of Zinj* (London, 1913), p. 29.

[44] Alice Werner, "Swahili History of Pate," *Journal of the African Society* 14 (1914): 148-61, 278-97, 392-413.

[45] Alfred Voeltzkow, *Reise in Ostafrika in den Jahren 1903-1905* (Stuttgart, 1914-1923); Vol. 2, Part 2: *Witu-Inseln und Zanzibar-Archipel*.

two other copies were collected by the German Vice-Consul Wassmuss; these were published in reduced facsimile as well as transcribed and translated into German by M. Heepe.[46]

All versions of the *Chronicle* known to exist go back to Bwana Kitini. That Bwana Kitini was a narrator and not the author is evident both from contemporary comments and the references in some MSS to Bwana Kitini's reliance on his grandfather Muhammad bin Bwana Mkuu al-Nabahani, also known as Bwana Simba. Apparently, Bwana Simba, whom the version contained in MS 177 of the University Library, Dar es Salaam, calls "the senior elder of Pate," had a distinguished reputation as a keeper of the royal tradition[47] (Bwana Kitini, on the other hand, was rumored to be a story-teller). The form of the name, *Bwānah Kitīni*, of which Werner was not certain,[48] is borne out by the Wassmuss facsimile (MS M) as well as the MSS copies being published here for the first time.[49]

Importantly, the Wassmuss MSS were acquired in Mombasa, showing a diffusion of the written text beyond the immediate geographical area of the Nabahani Sultanate. Moreover, one of these (the incomplete MS M) was in the Swahili dialect of Mombasa (Ki-Mvita), rendered from the Lamu (Ki-Amu)

---

[46] M. Heepe, "Suaheli-Chronik von Pate., *Mitteilungen des Seminars für orientalische Sprachen*, 3. Abteilung; Afrikanische Studien 31 (1928): 145-92.

[47] Prins judges him to be an oral source. Prins, 1958: 29.

[48] Werner, p. 148.

[49] Bwana Kitini was still remembered by an informant of Chittick's named Jambeni Muhammad, who "spoke disparagingly of his reliability," Chittick, 1969: 376. B. Krumm called him a "history merchant" (*Words of Oriental Origin in Swahili*, [London: Sheldon Press, 1940], 9).

dialect of the other MSS by Muhammad bin Sa'īd bin Ahmad Tamāmī of Mombasa. The appearance of these geographically remote[50] but chronologically complete copies is an impressive evidence of a conscious effort to preserve the written history of the coast, whether or not related to legitimacy concerns of the Nabahan dynasty.

As a transmitter of the tradition, Bwana Kitini may be expected to abide by the interests of the royal house. As a member of the ruling family, who took part in court intrigue,[51] he may be expected to manipulate facts or attitudes. For example, the parts of the narrative dealing with the 19th century do not even mention European presence on the coast until the establishment of the German protectorate over Witu. On the other hand, the fawning use[52] of *dola tukufu* "Illustrious Administration" about the British sounds false from the mouth of an active participant in the Witu rebellion who kept the document of British pardon until his death.[53]

The existence of plural manuscript histories of Pate was first reported in 1905.[54] Bwana Kitini died in 1931, and manuscript postscripts show that

---

[50] It also appears that the Portuguese version of the *Kilwa Chronicle* was compiled at least in part on the basis of a text acquired by De Barros in Malindi (in addition to a Kilwa source). Oliver and Mathew, *East Africa*, 103. The author of the Arabic history of Kilwa, Shaykh Muhi al-Din (who figures prominently in the *Pate Chronicle*) served as *ḳāḍī* at Zanzibar.

[51] It was apparently this Bwana Kitini who poisoned Sultan Fumo Bakari in 1891. Ylvisaker suggests that this action was inspired by the British: Ylvisaker, 153.

[52] Pointed out to me by Patricia Romero.

[53] J.W. Cusack, *History of the Nabahan Sultans of Pate* (1931, Kenya National Archives, Introduction).

[54] Charles Eliot, *The East Africa Protectorate* (London, 1905), p. 40.

his autograph or the record of his dictation may have been repeatedly copied by at least one scribe (Sālih̩ bin Sālim) over the course of his life. In 1931 Salih bin Salim was still living but "too old to transcribe further."[55] Sadly, while more and different copies of Pate and other cities' histories may be confidently supposed to exist, the culture of the coast still prevents the owners of these documents from surrendering them to government repositories or even from revealing their existence.[56] In the instances where access to texts has been allowed, the originals were often photographed and then copies only deposited in libraries, such as the University Library of Dar es Salaam[57] (a microfilm set of MSS collected under the auspices of the Rockefeller Foundation in the 1960s was reportedly prepared for the London University School of Oriental and African Studies). On other occasions, judging from the obviously recent writing and the use of contemporary paper (including school notebooks), the owners may have been inclined to offer the outsiders copies made specially for surrender, with the originals retained as family treasures.

Included in the present volume are versions of the *Chronicle* contained in MSS 177, 321, 344 and 358, as well as the chronological list from MS 309 of the University Library, Dar es Salaam. All of these are in Ki-Amu, as also are the Hollis MS and the more complete of the two Wassmuss MSS, MS A.

---

[55] Cusack, *History*, "Introduction."

[56] For early comments on the difficulty of gaining access to manuscript documents see Stigand, p. 29, note. 1. Prins spoke directly: "more MSS could still be extant, hidden somewhere; treasured and protected against inquiry," (Prins, 29). Later collecting efforts are reported in J.W.T. Allen, "The Collection and Preservation of Manuscripts of the Swahili World," *Swahili* 38/2 (1966).

[57] J.W.T. Allen, *The Catalogue of the Swahili and Arabic Manuscripts of the University Library, Dar es Salaam*, (Leiden, 1970).

(Presumably, the Stigand version had been dictated also in Ki-Amu but only the English translation of it was published). All seven, including the Ki-Mvita Wassmuss MS (MS M), make reference to Bwana Kitini as the narrator, and all tell substantially the same story, although with variations in detail, specific terminology, vocabulary, and orthography. Despite their general proximity, these variations seem considerable enough to prefer the publication of each version separately to an attempt to consolidate them into one final, authoritative "proto-text." In fact, if G.S.P. Freeman-Grenville was correct in naming the Hollis version "a Swahili abstract,"[58] such an exercise may be counterproductive.

The Stigand version, dictated by the same Bwana Kitini, is considerably longer than any of the Arabic-Swahili records. It is distinguished by frequency of dialogue and stories missing in the other versions. In the narrative, these stories interrupt the flow of somewhat detached information focused on the reigns of Pate's thirty-two sultans. Punctuating the chronological arrangement, these gossipy passages[59] throw light on personal characters of the rulers, political choices made by citizens of Pate, as well as social tensions and regional rivalries.

At the other extreme, in their brevity, are the dynastic rolls of the Nabahani kings. The earliest of these king-lists was published in German in 1890.[60] The author of that list (the only one published before the original

---

[58] Oliver and Mathew, 104.

[59] According to Chittick, these parts of the Stigand version, distinguished by "appeal and literary merit," have now received circulation as children's tales. (Chittick, 1969: 391).

[60] "Die Rechte des Sultans von Witu," *Deutsche Kolonialzeitung*, 1890, No. 1, pp. 22/23.

manuscript was destroyed, if it ever existed) is unknown; the list may have been compiled from the chronicle. Another list was compiled by Reddie, the Provincial Commissioner of Lamu, from the oral information provided by a clerk named Mshamu (Mshahame) bin Kombo. This list was published by Alice Werner and may be found in Appendix 3. As first noted by Werner, there are considerable differences between this list's names and dates and those culled from the Stigand and Hollis versions (some differences in this respect may also be observed between the Stigand and Wassmuss-Heepe versions, while there is relative agreement between the Stigand and Voeltzkow data,[61] as demonstrated in Appendix 7). Although it did not seem possible at this stage to reconcile the discrepancies and restore the true order of the reigns (or at least the original order in the chronicle prototype), the originality of the brief lists seems to suggest a different source from that of the "Bwana Kitini" versions. Considering that Mshamu bin Kombo was Bwana Kitini's brother, the differences may present historiographical interest, as well as challenge.

On the other hand, what may at first glance seem to be a king-list of Pate rulers contained in MS 309 (no title), on a closer look appears to be a summary of a longer text, containing not only names and dates of rulers, but brief remarks on children and conquests of Pate kings. These names and comments are arranged in table-like format, with Arabic dates aligned at the end of the line on the left, names of children in the middle of the line, names of individuals active in a particular reign indented, and so on. This may be without the broader context provided by chronicle narratives the significance

[61] A.H.J. Prins (p. 30) considered Voeltzkow's edition to be based "entirely" on the Stigand version.

of such asides would have been occasionally obscured. In addition, the absence of narrative, in my view, diminishes the textological value of this part of MS 309. It is therefore reproduced only in translation into English in Appendix 2.

There exist other pieces which for various reasons remain outside the scope of the present edition. At least forty years before Stigand, pieces of a courtly oral tradition were recorded in French by Charles Gullain.[62] In 1931 a translation was made by J.W. Cusack of a copy made by Muhammad Kijuma from a 1925 facsimile of Bwana Kitini's 1901 record scripted by Sālih̩ bin Sālim. The typescript, formerly at the Lamu District Office, is preserved at the British Institute for Eastern Africa in Nairobi and a photocopy at Kenya National Archives. I was able to consult an imperfect photocopy of the latter after the work on this volume was completed. It is a fluent, slightly abbreviated translation of a text copied by Salih bin Salim, as in MSS 321, 344 and 358. The last two versions are especially close. Its title is "History of the Nabahan Sultans of Pate." The so-called Reddie MS is a five-page king list, with dates in A.D. reckoning, titled "An Account from Native Sources of the Rise and Fall of the Kingdom of Patte in the Lamu Archipelago, East Africa." Among the documents of the Lamu District Office now at the Kenya National Archives is a "History of the Lamu District" compiled for or by[63] J.W. Isaacs. It contains short comments on the origin of the Pate dynasty. At Zanzibar National Archives there is an English translation of a history dictated

---

[62] Charles Guillain, *Documents sur l'histoire, la géographie et le commerce de l'Afrique orientale*, Vol. 1 (Paris, 1856).

[63] Depending on whose judgment one follows. See Prins, 1958: 31 and Pouwels, 1987: 259.

by the German explorer Clemens Denhardt.[64] Prins reported the existence, without indicating the location, of an unedited MS compiled by Muhammad bin Famau, which may possibly be independent from the Bwana Kitini tradition. On the basis of historiographic analysis Prins composed a stemma of editions and published variants.[65] It is being reproduced at the end of Introduction.

Finally, the chronicles are a valuable resource for the history of the Swahili language, its dialects, and the writing tradition. Swahili writing in Arabic script has long been in decline, and of all the published chronicles only one version of the *Pate Chronicle* was accompanied by an Arabic text. (The *Kilwa Chronicle* was written and published in the Arabic language,[66] although a Swahili version apparently had existed.) On the basis of this one text, Misiugin explored the spelling variations of coastal toponyms and speculated on their significance to Swahili historical phonetics and geographical nomenclature of the coast.[67] The four additional Arabic-Swahili versions in this volume will add significantly to this pool of data which is of considerable import to historical linguistics. To this purpose all care has been taken to accurately read and Romanize the Arabic text, preserving the patterns of consonant and vowel use, whether arising from dialect or scribal variations,

---

[64] *April 14, 1890. Manda and Patta: Substance of a Statement made by Mr. C. Denhardt to the Acting German Counsel General, Zanzibar on the History of the Islands of Manda and Patta for some 40 years past.* I am grateful to Patricia Romero for the reference.

[65] Prins, 31.

[66] S.A. Strong, trans. and ed., "The History of Kilwa." *Journal of the Royal Asiatic Society* 27 (1895): 385-430.

[67] V.M. Misiugin, "Notes on the Swahili Place Names in the Pate Chronicle" (in Russian). *Africana* 9 (Leningrad, 1972).

and to clearly designate all the editorial conjectures.

The manuscripts being published here contain Swahili text written in Arabic characters. Although it has been suggested that the original *Book of the Kings of Pate* may have been in Arabic,[68] no copies of the Arabic text have been discovered. Arabic texts traditionally lack punctuation; in romanizing the Swahili transcription, punctuation has been added on a limited scale, so as to separate phrases and clarify syntax. The translation has been made as literal as possible, primarily for purposes of historical accuracy but also to clarify the lexical variants among the manuscripts. Inevitably, this has led to some awkwardness and repetitiveness, especially with the particle *na-*. I have also attempted to keep the wording and punctuation of the translations consistent; thus one and the same word in Swahili is normally translated by the same word in English, and in the same way in each of the four manuscripts introduced here for the first time. The rule has not been followed blindly, however. For example, *watu* is usually translated "people" when general population in concerned, but "men" has been used when the context pointed to selected individuals or the military.

In romanizing transcription from the Arabic, italics have been generally avoided. In translation, special terms (usually Arabic loan-words) are highlighted in italics. Titles such as "Sultan" are capitalized when used with personal names; ethnonyms consisting of two parts have double capitalization: *WaPate, WaNgereza*, etc. The Arabic reading has been preferred for personal names unless specifically voweled in the Arabic text according to Bantu pronunciation. The spoken-Arabic *bin* is preferred for Arabic patronymics

---

[68] Werner, p. 149.

(rather than *ibn*) because it agrees well with the Bantu spoken practice. The Swahili *wa-*, when used for a patronymic Possessive in Arabo-Swahili names, has not been translated, in order to avoid the cumbersome "[son] of" and to highlight the Africanization of Islamic names. The Arabic *bint* "daughter (of)" has also been left without translation in similar contexts. The Arabic *Abū* (as in *Abū Bakr*), which in the Arabic patronymic would be transformed in accordance with the Genitive case into *Abī*, is often left unchanged in Swahili, or contrariwise *Abī* may be used in the Nominative; in both instances the translation follows the original rather than correcting the mistake. The Swahili form *Nabahani* has been preferred to the Arabic *al-Nabhānī* except when so voweled and provided with the article *al-* in the original.

Place names have been transcribed phonetically in romanized Swahili; in the translation, current English forms are used for commonly known toponyms. Thus, both *Ungūja* and *Zinjibār(i)* are rendered as "Zanzibar." Some toponyms derived from common nouns (such as *Banadiri, Mrima*) have been transcribed without capitalization and then translated into English; the Swahili version has been added in parentheses in italics. The toponym *Sawaḥili* is rendered as "Swahili (coast)." No diacritical marks, with the exception of ʻ (for the Arabic *ʻayn*), have been used in translation.

The present author transcribed and translated texts from MSS 177, 309, 321, 344, and 358, and the genealogical chart reproduced in Appendix 1. She also translated the *"Swahili Chronicle of Pate"* into English from the Heepe transcript of the Wassmuss MSS M and A. *"History of the Witu Islands"* was translated from the German by Dagmar Weiler with an additional contribution by Tom Stewart. *"Ancient History from Swahili Sources"* reproduces the English version of the *Pate Chronicle* recorded and published by C.H. Stigand. Alice Werner's transcription and translation of the Hollis version of the chronicle is reproduced under the title originally given her publication: *"A Swahili History of Pate."* The Wassmuss versions, transcribed and published by M. Heepe under the title *"Suaheli-Chronik von Pate,"* are reproduced here in the Arabic and Romanized Swahili forms; the German translation has been omitted.

The Arabic texts of MSS 177, 321, 344 and 358 were transcribed by the present author from the originals and photocopies at the University Library, Dar es Salaam, Tanzania. The reader is offered computer-generated copy prepared by using the Al-Kaatib software. The source for the Arabic facsimile of MSS M and A is Heepe, *op. cit.* The tables contained in the *Appendices* have come from the following sources: *1.* MSS 309, 321, 358; *2.* MS 309; *3.* Werner, pp. 414-15; *4.* Voeltzkow, facing p. 65; *5.* Voeltzkow, p. 91; *6.* Heepe, pp. 148-49; *7.* Heepe, p. 181; *8.* G.P. Badger, *History of the Imâms and Seyyids of 'Omân by Salîl-ibn Razîk, from A.D. 661-1856* (London: Hakluyt Society, 1871); as edited by Werner, *op. cit.*, pp. 412-13. Map 3 is reproduced from Werner, plate facing p. 280

The sequence of documents adopted here follows the chronological emergence of the versions. All the published versions as well as those being introduced here are variations of Bwana Kitini's rendition of the *Chronicle.* With the exception of MS 177, the MSS versions all postdate the published ones. The Stigand version, in addition to appearing first in print, is the longest and may also be said to be the most original in some ways. Finally, the

Stigand version is frequently referred to by both Werner and Heepe in the commentaries that accompany their editions of the Hollis and Wassmuss versions. Although the Voeltzkow version was probably compiled by the time of the publication of his first volume, which preceded Werner's edition, it did not appear until much later (but in time to have been consulted by Heepe). Because the Voeltzkow version contains no Swahili text and is brief and redundant of Stigand, it is placed last among the four publications.

The German authors both ignore Werner for some reason. It is possible that WWI caused the journal issues where her work was published to be overlooked. They quote Stigand heavily, as also does Werner, and Heepe draws on both Stigand and Voeltzkow. The chains of cross-references among the three editions cannot avoid repetitiveness. Yet they are an evidence of a quarter century of research and faithfully reflect their authors' philological bias as well as lively, and on occasion informed, fascination with the history of the coast. The previously-published versions are followed by the manuscript transcripts arranged chronologically.

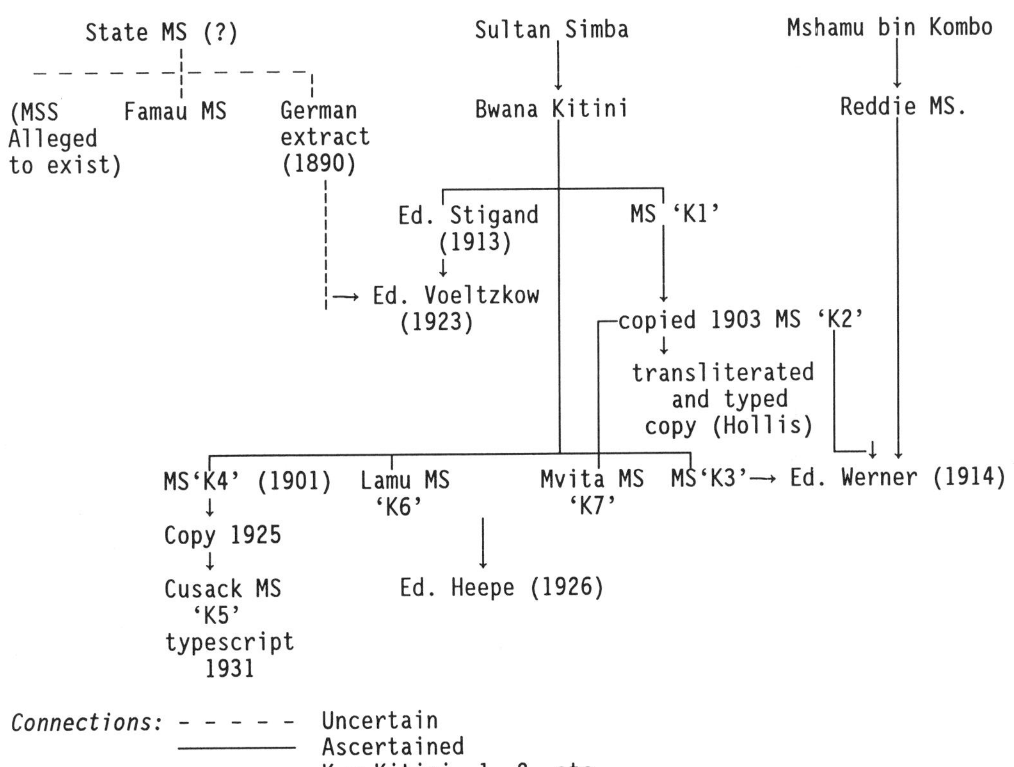
State MS (?)
(MSS Alleged to exist)
Famau MS
German extract (1890)
Sultan Simba
Bwana Kitini
Ed. Stigand (1913)
MS 'K1'
Ed. Voeltzkow (1923)
copied 1903 MS 'K2'
transliterated and typed copy (Hollis)
Mshamu bin Kombo
Reddie MS.
MS 'K4' (1901)
Copy 1925
Cusack MS 'K5' typescript 1931
Lamu MS 'K6'
Ed. Heepe (1926)
Mvita MS 'K7'
MS 'K3'
Ed. Werner (1914)
Connections: - - - - - Uncertain
———— Ascertained
K = Kitini, 1, 2, etc.

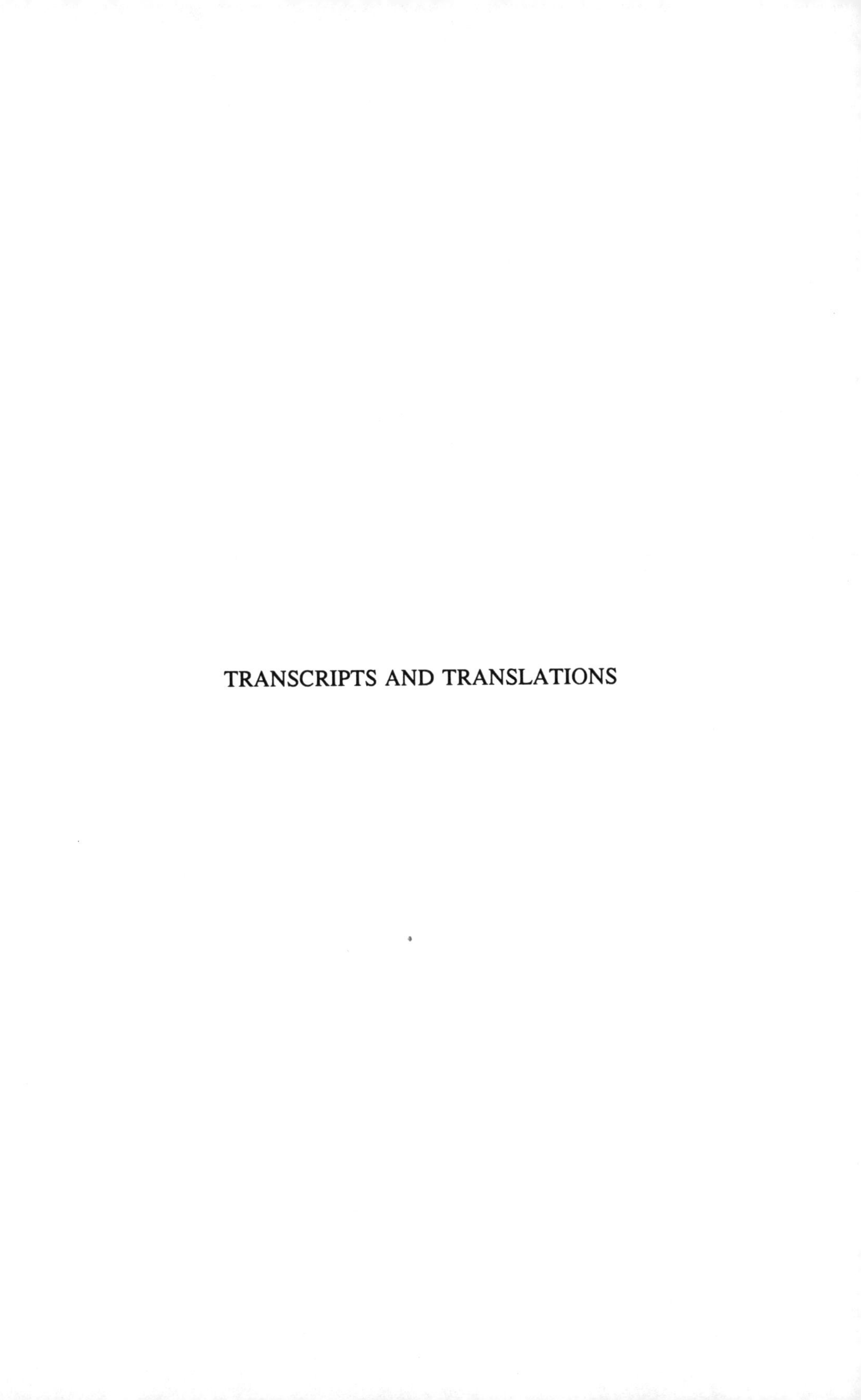

TRANSCRIPTS AND TRANSLATIONS

ANCIENT HISTORY FROM SWAHILI SOURCES

C. H. STIGAND

INTRODUCTION

The following text was published by Captain C.H. Stigand in chapters II, III and IV of his *Land of Zinj* (London, 1913). A reprint of that edition may be found in G.S.P. Freeman-Grenville's *The East African Coast* (Oxford, 1962) under the title "The History of Pate" (No. 47, pp. 241-299). Although the first to be published, it was recorded in 1908, which makes it later than the Hollis version, published by Alice Werner in 1914-5.

This is the longest version of the Pate Chronicle which exists only in English, and was personally communicated to Stigand, while an administrative officer, by Bwana Kitini. It is replete with stories attached to various episodes, including some events in Arabia. They are often told in the form of a dialogue and reveal much about local politics and social culture. Most of them are noticeably absent from other versions. This makes the Stigand version valuable in a unique way and also appears to lie at the root of the relative brevity of the other versions. It seems clear from the description of the circumstances surrounding the recording of the *Chronicle* that the orality of tradition comes into play here. As noted in the *Introduction*, all the versions transcribed directly from a written record conform to a pattern. Essentially the same set of reigns, dates and Pate-related events is listed without much variation. The stories in the Stigand version appear to be branches grafted onto the tree of the narrative in the process of recitation for Stigand's benefit. The notes which Bwana Kitini reportedly consulted served the narrator as an *aide-mémoire* and probably contained the bare skeleton of the whole story which could be expanded on while the memory lasted. While these stories need not have been invented, the verbal content of the dialogues needs to be approached with extreme caution. It is quite likely that the dialogue provided both structure and content, serving as a mnemonic device[1] at least as much as an oral record.

Because the following text is a translation of an oral narrative and comes unaccompanied by Swahili text or a transcript, Stigand's record is reproduced here without emendations whether in the text, orthography or punctuation. To modernize the transcription, Stigand's sign ' for the Arabic *'ayn* has been replaced with the correct '. However, none were added where he did not use one. Arabic terms, but not titles, have been highlighted in italics.
Introductory comments following the heading as well as footnotes are Stigand's. The present editor's notes have been added in brackets, not to interfere with Stigand's footnotes which have been assigned new sequential numbers. Later translators (A. Werner, M. Heepe and A. Voeltzkow) often refer to Stigand's text as well as comments, so to facilitate cross-reference the original pagination has been preserved here and indicated in parentheses. In his book, Stigand highlighted the dates occurring in the narrative by repeating them on margins with *AH* notation added. These have been omitted, but to assist the reader, A.D. dates were added in brackets. It will be noticed that many dates are uniquely cited here, often differing considerably from those offered in various other versions, although all claim the same source, Bwana Kitini. In the original, Chapter II (pp. 29-54) related the events to 1060 A.H./1650 A.D., Chapter III (pp. 55-77) went up to 1229 A.H./1813 A.D.,

---

[1] For a discussion of interdependence of oral contents and mnemonic gestures, etc., see Randall L. Pouwels, "Orality and Literacy: Culture and Cognitive Change as Reflected in Swahili Literature and Oral Tradition, 1500-1900." (Forthcoming)

and Chapter IV covered the rest of the nineteenth century. Chapter breaks are indicated by two vertical lines ‖.

ANCIENT HISTORY FROM SWAHILI SOURCES

The following histories are culled from old Pate records. They were communicated to me by Bwana Kitini who is a direct descendant of the Pate Sultans, and looked on locally as the authority on historical matters. For some reason or other I was not allowed access to the original documents, except one relating to recent Zanzibar history and evidently not much prized.[1]

My informant, who, like most Orientals, had a prodigious memory for learning by rote,[2] made notes and visited me daily for some months. I wrote the text down from his dictation and subsequently translated it as literally as possible.

The reader must please pardon the peculiar phrasing sometimes adopted so as to keep as near as possible to the Swahili.

The beginning of these coast towns,[3] he who first made them was a ruler called Abdul Malik bin Muriani [*Editor's note*: the Umayyad caliph 'Abd al-Malik ibn Marwān, 685-705]. The date was the seventy-seventh year of the Hejra [696-7]. He heard of this country, and his soul longed to found a new

---

[1] The Rev. W.E. Taylor, the greatest living authority on Swahili, told me that he had also heard of these documents but was unable to obtain access to them.

[2] Although learning is at a low ebb on the east coast, the retentive memory which enables a literate Arab to become a Hafiz is evident. A Hafiz is one who can repeat the Koran by heart from cover to cover.

[3] Ancient history only deals with the coast, as the interior was unknown.

kingdom. So he brought Syrians, and they built the cities of Pate, Malindi, Zanzibar, Mombasa, Lamu and Kilwa.[4]

(p. 30) After that Abdul Malik died, and his sons who reigned did not care for the work of founding towns, and so they left them.[5] Now Abdul Malik's tribe was the Bani Omaiya, and of these fourteen kings reigned. After this the Bani Omaiya dynasty went out, and there ruled the Bani Al Abbas. The third of this dynasty was Harun al Rashid,[6] who reigned in the year 170 [786-787. *Editor's note*: Hārūn al-Rashīd was the fifth 'Abbāsid caliph, 786-809.].

This Sultan heard that Abdul Malik had built in Africa, and he was pleased to call people and give them much wealth wherewith he sent them to build houses on the coast. The people he sent were Persians.

In the year 601 [1204-5] came the Nabahans to the coast coming forth from the Oman (Maskat). Now the origin of the Nabahans leaving the Oman is this. In the beginning at Maskat four tribes ruled. First reigned the tribe called the Kharusi. After that they were robbed of their kingdom by the Nabahans. A Nabahan Sultan called Imam[7] Muthafar took the kingdom and

---

[4] The following towns are said to have been built or commenced by Abdul Malik. In each town or group of towns he had a *Luwali* (Governor).

Mukadisho (*mui wa mwisho*=the end city), Marika, Barawa, Tula, Twavae, Koyama, Vumbi, Kismayu, Omwi, Ndao, Kiwayu, Pate, Paza, Shanga, Emezi (now Wangi), Magagoni (Tukutu), Amu (Lamu), Manda, Taka, Kitao, Komana, Uziwa, Shaka (said to be named from Persian *Shah*), Mea, Ozi, Malindi, Watamu, Mvita, Wasini, Kilwa, Tungi, Ngazija (the Comoro Islands).

[5] A legend on the coast says that his son Jafari ruled and died at Kiwayu.

[6] This was the Haroon al Rashid of the 'Arabian Nights', who ruled at Bagdad.

[7] '*Imam*, the hereditary title of the Maskat rulers.'

ruled over the whole of Oman. After him came his son Suleiman bin Muthafar, and the latter's son Suleiman bin Suleiman.

Then occurred a quarrel between the Arabs and the Nabahans amongst the two tribes of the Henawi and Ghafir. Then the Yorubi fought the Nabahans and they gained strength and defeated the ruling Nabahan. So he went forth and fled away and came to the Sawaheli[8] coast with some of his tribe, whilst others went to Jebel Riami; they are there at Riami until now. He who went to the Sawaheli coast was he who had been Sultan of Maskat.

He landed at Pate and the inhabitants of Pate were those people who had been sent by Khalif Abdul Malik bin Muriani.

So he remained in Pate with his people for he had arrived with many men and ships and much wealth. Presently they sent gifts to the chief of Pate and to every big man in Pate (p. 31) they made a present, and even to the small men of the town they gave goods. Then the people, both great and small, perceived the goodness of the Sultan who had come from Maskat.

After this he went to Is-hak, the chief of Pate, and asked for his daughter in marriage, and Is-hak gave him his daughter and he married her, and he rested with her the seven days of the honeymoon.[9]

On the seventh day he came forth and went to see his father-in-law.

When he came Is-hak said to him, "Your marriage portion is the kingdom of Pate."

So Suleiman ruled, and he had a son by that woman and he called him

---

[8] Swahili from Ar. *Sawahil*=coast.

[9] On marriage the bridal couple remain indoors for a period of seven days, called *Fungate*.

Muhammad.

Till in the year 625 [1227-8] Suleiman bin Suleiman died, and his son Muhammad bin Suleiman ruled and took possession of all his people, his wealth and his soldiers. It was he who first took the name of Sultan of Pate, and this by right, for his father came forth from their country bearing the title of Sultan.

The people of Pate loved him much for his own goodness, and because he was a child of the town, for his mother was of their kin.

Now Sultan Muhammad remained with them twenty-five years, and then he died leaving three sons, Ahmad, Suleiman, and Ali.

It was Ahmad who took his father's place. The townspeople, those people of Pate, wished to make trouble, and so they said to his brothers Suleiman and Ali, "Why does this one take the kingdom? Do not consent to it."

So rebellion was stirred up in the country and the townspeople then went to Sultan Ahmad and said, "These brothers of yours are makers of mischief."

So discord arose between them, Suleiman and Ali on one side, and Sultan Ahmad on the other, but Sultan Ahmad was together (p. 32) with those people whom his grandfather had brought from Arabia. Now these people of Pate purposely egged them on one against the other, so that they should waste their strength and then they might get back their country, for they regretted the arrangement made by their elders giving the kingdom to the Nabahans.

Sultan Ahmad's mother was a Pate woman, and she said to her son, "Understand that you must go and agree with your brothers. This is for your good, for my relations, the people of Pate, design to urge you on one against the other, until such time as you may expend your strength. Then they will turn you out and retake their country that its greatness may be restored to them.

"So you, my son, take my advice, and come to an agreement with your brothers here today."

Sultan Ahmad called Ali bin Othman bin Sef bin Muthafar, an old man who had been with his father, and sent him to his brothers according to the advice his mother had given him.

So Ali bin Othman went to Suleiman and Ali, they took his advice, and he brought them secretly by night to their brother, and the Pate people had no knowledge of this.

Till in the morning when day broke they perceived that there was no longer war in the town.

They knew then that their plan had failed, and so they went to Sultan Ahmad and said to him, "We rejoice exceedingly that you are acting as a guardian to your younger brothers—it is indeed good news."

Then they went to those brothers and said, "And for you to own allegiance to your elder brother is indeed proper."

In those days lived a man who strung some verses symbolical of the wiles of the Pate people which began,

"The Pate people weave discord, then it is unravelled and they ask, 'Who is it that began the quarrel?' "

So Sultan Ahmad lived in accord with his brothers, and placed many soldiers in the country, and enriched his subjects. The Pate people seeing this, gave allegiance to him, and peace came (p. 33) to the country and he made it prosper. He benefitted that country much, making plantations, digging wells, building stone houses, and sending expeditions by land and sea, till that country flourished exceedingly.

In the year 690 [1291. *Editor's note*: this date differs from that given in other versions.] Sultan Ahmad died, leaving two sons, Omar and Muhammad, and two daughters, Mwana Khadija, and Mwana Mimi.[10]

Muhammad bin Ahmad reigned, the third of the Nabahans[11] and this Sultan was the first who was called by the name of Bwana Fumomadi,[12] and he was given the name of "The Great".

This Sultan was a very fine man, both in appearance and disposition; he was moreover very generous. He still further established the country and conquered the whole island of Pate, and fought with the people of Shanga, a country near Pate on the side of the rising sun. This country,[13] which is even nearer to Siu, he conquered in war, plundering it and killing the males. The youths and the old women and maidens they made prisoners.

There was a maiden sitting on the ground grinding frankincense, and a soldier entered and seized her, intending to rob her of her goods and clothes and make her a captive.

This maiden said to the earth, "Open, that I may enter," and the earth opened and swallowed her up, leaving only the border of her upper robe above

---

[10] *Mwana*, meaning 'child' in present-day Swahili, also meant 'Queen' in old Swahili. When this child was born, it is said that the grandmother clasped it, saying, rather ungrammatically, '*Mwana mimi*'= my child.

[11] The first was Muhammad bin Suleimani. Suleimani bin Suleimani, who came from Maskat, is not counted in the dynasty.

[12] *Bwana* = master. *Fumo* = a chief (derived from old Swahili word meaning 'a spear'), *madi* = abbreviation of 'Muhammadi' (Swahili for 'Muhammad').

[13] The Swahili called every little town with a chief a 'country'.

ground. Now this is the truth, which has been obtained correctly from the people of those days who beheld the miracle, for this maiden was a God-fearing person.

That soldier, when he saw that, gave up the profession of arms, for he perceived that his calling did not lead to great things, saying, "I am a soldier and I am unable to say to the ground—'Open that I may be swallowed up.' Even my Sultan is (p. 34) unable to do this thing. This maiden is able to do this because she obeys her Master who created her. I also will obey him truly."

So this soldier led a devout life until he died.

Sultan Muhammad when he heard the news about this damsel went to the place and there saw the border of her garment. He tried to dig her up but was unable, so he built a shrine over the spot to honour her as a sign to posterity.

The soldier he put in the shrine to live there performing the services and to light the lamps at night, and pluck up the grass growing in the doorway.

When their father died, his sons tended the mausoleum, and their tribe was the Watui, but now there are no more of that tribe.

After Sultan Muhammad had conquered the country of Shanga, trouble arose between him and the people of the country originally called Rasini, but which is now called Faza.

So he made war against them and they fought together for many days. And it came to pass that the people of Pate were unable to go outside the town to draw water after the sun had risen for fear of those people of Rasini.[14]

---

[14] *'Rasini'*, meaning 'cape' or 'promotory'. Arabic *'Ras'*.

For it was the custom of those people to arrive daily as the sun commenced to mount in the heavens.[15] Till the women in their houses used to tell their slaves, "Go quickly and draw water before the sun mounts and those of the mounting sun have come."

So the people of Faza (or Paza) were called "those of the mounting sun". This is the origin of the word "Wapaza", for after a while the word "sun" was dropped out, and they were called "those of the mounting" (= "Wapatha" in Pate Swahili). After many days had passed the name of Wapaza stuck to them. [*Editor's note*: neither this story nor the late, folk etymology suggested to me by Professor Patricia Romero, which derives the toponym from the Turkish *feza* 'heavens,' explain its other form known from the Portuguese sources and early modern European maps: Ampaza.]

Later on when the country of Rasini had been taken by the Sultan of Pate, it remained uninhabited till the Watikuu came (p. 35) asking for a place in which to settle. The Sultan of that date told them that they could have the place of the Wapatha. That is why they are now called Paza (or Faza).

Now after the Sultan of Pate and the Sultan of Faza had warred together many days they made peace with each other and agreed each one to remain in his own country.

Then Bwana Shakwa, the Faza Sultan, married his daughter to Omar, the son of the Sultan of Pate, and they lived together at Faza for many days.

After that Omar took his wife and brought her to Pate secretly. When the girl's father heard in the morning he was very angry, and his son followed after his sister with a big expedition and came to Pate.

---

[15] Their town being four hours distant from Pate.

Omar said to his brother-in-law, "There is no need for you and me to quarrel, for your sister herself wished to accompany me her husband. So you go your way and she will rest here seven days and then I shall send her home."

The Sultan of Faza's son returned home to await the agreement made with Omar, but after seven days his sister had not come back and he was very angry and swore to conquer the country of Pate.

So he warred again against Pate going and returning daily for many days, and every day as the sun mounted the heavens at nine o'clock, the people of Faza had come, and the people of Pate were no longer able to leave the city to draw water.

So they fought for many days, the people of Faza coming to Pate, and at other times the people of Pate going to Rasini. Then the Sultan of Faza's son registered a vow not to shave his head[16] till he had entered the town of Pate. So he went many times to fight at Pate till one day fortune favoured him, and he entered the city of Pate, seizing a whole quarter of the town. Then he had a chair placed outside the mosque and there his head was shaved, and so he consummated his vow.

Meanwhile they were still fighting and the people of Pate (p. 36) held out in one side of the town, and they took counsel of a sage who said to them, "Do not go now into the fight, but wait till two o'clock has passed. If you fight then you will drive them out of your country, but you must follow them and kill of their number in the way, and retake your property which they have looted till they reach their home, when you will take their town also."

---

[16] Arabs and Swahilis do not cut their hair, but shave their heads when the hair is too long.

Now the Rasini people when they had captured part of the town were content to rest and loot, thinking that they would take the rest of the city when the sun had declined.

When two o'clock was past the people of Pate fought them and turned them out of the town, for they were carrying much loot and were unable to fight. So the Pate people followed them till they reached the town of Paza. The Rasini people entered the city and barricaded the gates while the Pate people besieged them closely, so that a man might not come out or enter in.

They besieged them for seven days, and each day they were losing strength by reason of lacking water to drink.[17] Now in the town of Faza was one of the captains of the troops called Haji Mwetha, and he said to the others, "My fellow captains, if I tell you my plan will you follow it?" They answered, "We will follow it."

Then Haji Mwetha said, "The reason that the Pate people drove us out of their town was that we found ourselves amongst their wealth, and they fell upon us when we were unable to fight because of the loot we had taken.

"Now my plan is to make a small breach in the wall and leave part of the town for them to loot. When they see our property there together with the things we have taken from them, they will leave off fighting and remain there.

"We shall remain with our women and children in the other part of the town, and when they withdraw with their loot we will fall upon them. The way out will be narrow so we shall kill and capture them and retake our property."

---

[17] The principal wells of these towns are generally outside the city.

(p. 37) So the people of the town took his advice and they broke part of the wall.

When the Pate people saw this the chiefs and ameers said to the captain and soldiers, "Do you perceive this matter? It is a ruse, so now everyone who enters the town must seize neither thing nor person. Everyone he meets he must smite whether it be man, woman, or child, and when we have finished conquering the town we will obtain all their property. Any people who are then left we will make our slaves."

So they acted on this advice and entered the town smiting all they met with.

When the people of Faza looked on the faces of those who had been killed, they ran away and wished to open the gates and fly, but the Pate men had surrounded the whole town so there was no way out.

They then desired quarter, but the people of Pate refused to give quarter except to those of them who had friends amongst the people of Faza; each man seized his friend and the remainder they killed or made slaves. The town and the houses they broke up leaving neither thing nor person.

For this reason the Swahilis say to anyone who gives advice which is not good, "Your advice is like the advice of Haji Mwetha."

From the day that the town of Faza was destroyed no man lived there till the coming of the Watikuu,[18] and the only inhabitants left alive were those who were made captive and men who were not present at the fight such as fishermen and those on a journey.

Even today there are descendants of these at Siu, Amu, the Mrima,

---

[18] When the Watikuu came to Faza they still found some of the houses inhabitable.

Zanzibar, and other places and they call their tribe the Mafazii.

Later on the Sultan Muhammad of Pate pardoned the captives and they were scattered abroad, every man living where he pleased.

Sultan Muhammad conquered the island of Pate from Yaya (p. 38) and Shanga as far as Mtangawanda—that is the length and breadth of the island. After that he sent expeditions to Kiwayu and Ndao, and the people of Kiwayu, when they saw the strength of Pate, did not fight with them but declared allegiance to them and paid tribute to them. Each chief man of his tribe had to give a slave and twenty dollars to every Sultan of Pate, and if there was any matter or case they sent written petitions to the Sultan who ordered their affairs for them.

When the people of Kiwayu made allegiance to Pate they became soldiers of the Sultan, and the Sultan fought and conquered all the countries beyond Kiwayu, viz. Kiunga, Tula, Koyama, Kismayu, Barawa, Marika and Mukadisho. He installed a governor at Mukadisho[19] for in those days this was an important place.

After conquering all these places Sultan Muhammad died in the year 740 [1339-40. *Editor's note*: this date differs from that given in other versions.], and his son Sultan Omar (Fumomari)[20] reigned. It was he who fought the towns of the coast, Manda, Uthiwa, Komwana, Malindi, and the Mrima and Kilwa till he came to Kirimba.[21]

---

[19] All these places are to the north of Pate in order.

[20] *Mari* abbreviation for Swahili Omari = Omar in the same way as (Fumo)madi is an abbreviation for Muhammadi.

[21] These are all to the south of Pate in succession.

Now the Sultan of Manda,[22] when he saw that the kingdom of Pate had become great, wished to place a governor over them, for before the coming of the Nabahans Pate used to be under his rule.

The people of Pate did not agree to this and so trouble arose between them.

Till during the north-east monsoon if a man was building a vessel in Pate harbour, when he hammered a nail to drive it into a plank, an order used to come from Manda, "The master is sleeping; do not make a noise."[23] It came about that a person was unable to work at boat-building save morning and evening.

(p. 39) To this the Pate people did not agree, so war arose between them and they fought together many days.

Till after a space of time had elapsed one day the elders of Manda were sitting in council, all the big men of the town, every tribe with its representative. However, one of their head men, Bakiumbe, was not present, for he had gone to sea fishing and they had not told him that there was to be a meeting.

So all the elders assembled except Bakiumbe and someone said, "Let us wait," but others said, "There is no necessity to wait for him; these words are not for fisher-folk but for elders."

So they transacted their business, and when Bakiumbe returned from the

---

[22] Manda was a much older city than Pate.

[23] Manda is south-west of Pate, but too far to hear any sound. The order was given presumably to impress the people with his importance. A very rare tense is used here in the original. *Ulele* meaning 'he is in the act of sleeping' as opposed to *analala* or *yualala* = 'he is sleeping'.

sea he was told of this matter by his relations, for he was the chief of the fisher-clan. Then he spoke and said to his clan, "These men have treated us fishermen as lowly folk like unto slaves, and we are all as well bred as they, save that everyone follows his calling. This one hoes, another is a smith, and another a palm-tapper. This is our town and everyone has his house, his property and his dependants. I will make a plan that I may pay back this insult that has been offered us till even those who come after us will not be able to scorn a man again."

Even today if there is an assembly people will speak together, and if one man is left out they say, "Do not leave out one man from amongst our people for he is our brother even though he is a lowly person. Did not Bakiumbe break up Manda for this reason, choosing to leave his property and his children without leaving even his name to the end of the world."[24]

Now this is the story of Bakiumbe and what he did. After having heard about the council he took his canoe and went over to Pate and demanded private audience of the Sultan. Then he said to him, "I want to give you the country of Manda without trouble or war and with but little expense. Will you follow my advice?" The Sultan said to him, "I will follow it; tell me what it is."

Bakiumbe said, "Whenever I ask for ambergris I want you (p. 40) to give me the amount I ask for. About the third or fourth time I will give you the town of Manda."

The Sultan of Pate said to him, "I have agreed, but you, for what reason

---

[24] Meaning that he did not leave his name through his descendants.

do you desire to break up your country in which are your children and your property? Tell me your reason that I may recognize for myself whether it be true or false."

Bakiumbe related to the Sultan the whole story of how he had been treated by the elders of Manda. At that time the Sultan knew truly that he would do as he said, for he was seized with anger, and if a man is seized with anger he loses all wisdom.

So he consented and gave him the ambergris that he required.

Bakiumbe set out and when he arrived at Manda it was late at night. He knocked at the gate, but the officer would not open it; because of the war with Pate all the gates of the city were closed at night. So he slept there outside, and the ambergris he put in his fish basket and poured water over it. In the morning he was permitted to enter and he went to the Sultan of Manda and gave him the ambergris.

The Sultan said, "Why did you leave the ambergris to get wet and why did you put it in your fish basket?"

Bakiumbe said, "I came last night and when I knocked at the gate your officer would not open it for me. This is my reason, for I slept on the shore and did not get a receptacle to put it in, so I poured out my fish and put this ambergris in my fish basket."

So the Sultan said to him, "If you get any more bring it to me and I will treat you very well."

Bakiumbe said, "I want permission to enter the gates at whatsoever time I shall come and you must tell your door-keeper to open to me. So if I get any at any time I will it to you, for you are my master and my Sultan, and at whatever you give me I will rejoice exceedingly."[25]

So the Sultan agreed, and Bakiumbe was glad in his heart, saying, "I have already attained my desires."

Then he remained for the space of one month and again he (p. 41) brought him ambergris bigger than the first. After that he remained more than a month and brought him some again.

Then he waited more than three months and again he brought him a piece.

After this he went to the Sultan of Pate and said to him, "Make ready—the work is finished. Tomorrow night at two o'clock I will come to fetch you. Have soldiers ready, a few I shall take myself and many must follow behind me."

They arranged after this manner till, when night had come and two o'clock was passed, Bakiumbe went to the Sultan of Pate and found soldiers ready as he had desired.

He took them and came with them to Manda and coming to the gate he knocked. The officer of the watch thought that this was Bakiumbe coming according to his custom with ambergris for the Sultan.

He unfastened the gate, and Bakiumbe entering with the soldiers seized the guard and killed them and straightway went to the Sultan's palace while other soldiers seized the gates of the city.

The Sultan, when he heard Bakiumbe's voice, descended from upstairs and said to the door-keeper, "Open quickly, for this is Bakiumbe," and his heart was exceeding glad.

---

[25] Ambergris has always been royal property wherever found.

When the door was opened Bakiumbe entered together with the Pate soldiers with naked swords held ready. When the Sultan saw the swords he wanted to run away, but there was no way in which he might run.

The soldiers struck him and killed him together with those of his people who were there in the house. The people of the town heard shouts so they came to the house of the ruler of the city. When they came, they met the people of Pate who had already seized the house.

Other people went to the gates, but the Pate men had already seized them.

So when dawn came, the townspeople had made no plan for assembling together or fighting because wherever they went they found Pate men already in possession. Thus it was that (p. 42) Pate conquered the country of Manda in one day, and when it dawned they seized as prisoners both the men and women, and all their property, silver and gold.

Now the Manda people had many gold ornaments, for which reason they were called "Wavaa ng'andu"[26] (the wearers of gold).

So Pate obtained much wealth, and they took both property and prisoners back with them to their city.[27] Half of the Pate troops went on to Taka and broke into the city.

The people of Kitao, when they heard that both Manda and Taka had fallen, sent their elders to Pate to sue for peace.

The ruler of Kitao was a woman called Mwana Inali. When she heard

---

[26] Old Swahili.

[27] Another story relates that Bakiumbe, the fisherman, came to the Sultan of Pate for a reward. The Sultan said that he was too clever to be allowed to live, for he might one day betray Pate as he had betrayed Manda, so he was executed.

that her elders, fearing war, had gone off to sue for peace with Pate, she said, "It will not do for me to live any longer. There is no cause that I should await the arrival of the Pate people, for they will kill me or make me captive, and treat me with every kind of abasement. Therefore it is better to die first."

So she arose and put on her gold ornaments, pearl buttons and ancient jewellery, and went out behind Cape Kitao, and threw herself into the sea.

When the people heard that their Queen was going down to the shore, they followed after her, but did not see her again; even a sign of her clothes or body they saw not.

This is the story of Kitao, Take, and Manda, and the people of Pate took prisoners of the two countries Manda and Taka, but the people of Kitao got peace because they made allegiance of Pate before the war reached their country.[28]

(p. 43) So they were left in their country, but everyone who cultivated land had to pay three loads of produce for every gang of slaves.

---

[28] Taka may have had its old power broken at this time, but, unlike Manda, it was still inhabited, and not finally abandoned till a much later date. There were people living at Taka as late as 1094 Hejra [1682-3]. Kitao was probably abandoned before this. Another story of the breaking up of Kitao attributed to the same date is that on a Friday a chicken came rushing into the congregational mosque at Kitao. A man rushed in after it and tried to seize it, saying that it was his. Another man rushed up and said it was his. They began fighting about it, and others joined in. It being a Friday, all the inhabitants of the town were coming to the mosque, so finally nearly everybody in the town was engaged in the fight.

After this the conflicting parties would not be reconciled, and so they split up; some went to Amu, some to Pate, and some to Ngoji (Bukini). Those that went to Amu and Pate afterwards came to Shela. Mwana Inali, the Queen of Kitao (said in above story to have drowned herself), went to Pate, and the Sultan of that place honoured her greatly, and gave her a house to live in. The ruins of this house are still pointed out at Pate, and called Nyumba ya Kitao (the house of Kitao).

Another legend says that Taka was not broken up by Pate, but that the Pate troops came to attack it and could not find it, as it had been made invisible by the Waanachuoni (Seers or Soothsayers).

Since that time the Sultan of the Nabahans taxed their subjects a *kikanda* (about 180 lbs.) for every gang of slaves,[29] and who first made this tax was Sultan Omar.

Now the captives of Manda were taken to Pate and put on the east side of the city, and a wall was built round making it one with the city of Pate.

This quarter was called "Weng'andu"[30] by reason of those people, "the wearers of gold," being there.

Now at the time of the building of the wall of this quarter the captives, both men and women, were made to carry the stones.

There was one woman of the people of Manda who refused to carry stones, so a soldier beat her and that woman wept.

There was a second Manda woman there and she said to her, "Friend, do not weep," and then she said the following couplet: -

"Tuli kwetu Manda twali tukitenda
Yeo tukitendwa twakataa kwani?
Hutupa ukuta wathipetapeta
Kutwa ni kuteta hatuna amani."

(When we were at our home in Manda it was we who were doing—today if we are done to, why should we refuse? They (p. 44) give us the wall to build winding hither and thither; all day it is quarrelling — we get no respite.)

So the people of Manda lived in the quarter of Weng'andu; this is the account of them till at last they were sent to Shela by Sultan Abubakr; its

---

[29] A curious word is used here in the original, "*cha*," meaning 'a group of slaves more than two in number'.

[30] The ruins of the Weng'andu quarter are still pointed out in the ruined city of Pate.

history will be related further on.

So Sultan Omar reigned on the coast, it was he who was the Sultan to conquer Manda, Taka, Kitao, and Emezi on the mainland and Tukutu. After this he fought Mea, Kiongwe, and Komwana and seven towns between Komwana and Shaka.[31]

The Sultan of these latter towns was called Liongo,[32] and he subdued the country from Mpokomoni to Malindi, and this district was called Ozi.

Now Sultan Omar fought with these towns for many days, and when he perceived the difficulty of taking them, he went to Magogoni, the harbour of Tukutu, and stayed there.

Every hour he sent out an expedition and he remained at Magogoni fifteen years till he got a son called Ahmad.

It was this son who finally overcame the towns of Ozi, and then sent the news to his father. So his father returned to Pate and then he went and fought Malindi.

When he and his troops reached Malindi there was a God-fearing man who invoked Allah against them so that the Pate soldiers became sick.

So they returned to Pate and Omar said to his son, "Now rest till we have seen about the sickness."

---

[31] This town is supposed to have been founded by Persians, and is called after Persian *Shah*.

[32] The famous Liongo, poet and bowman, of whom many tales are told. I have in my possession copies of some of his poems. [*Editor's note*: Already in Stigand's time a story of Liongo's as well as poetry ascribed to him were available in print. See Edward Steere, *Swahili Tales, as Told by Natives of Zanzibar* (London: Bell and Daldy, 1870). More poems are still to be found in manuscript collections, including that of the University Library, Dar es Salaam. For innovative interpretations of Liongo's historicity the reader is referred to works by James de Vere Allen and V.M. Misiugin, among others.]

So they rested, and after that the people of Malindi came to offer allegiance to the Sultan of Pate, and so they remained seven years without war.

Afterwards Sultan Omar collected many troops and made many ameers, and passed over to the mainland to go and fight against the towns there.

They passed on to Malindi and traversed the country in peace and then came to Mombasa.

(p. 45) The Mombasa people hid themselves in the interior and that is the origin of the place being called Mvita,[33] from "mfita" (one who hides).

Afterwards this place prospered exceedingly and became a very important place at the time the Portuguese came, for many tribes lived there.

Then the Pate people passed on overland and fought the whole of the Mrima coast from Wasini and Pangani to Saadani, Tanga, Kilwa, and Kilwa Island and the Mgao coast. They passed on, and in every place they took they put a chief.

That was the origin of the Jumbes of the Mrima coast, so called because they were slaves of the Yumbe[34] (the Sultan of Pate's palace).

So the Pate troops proceeded till they reached Kirimba; these were the ends of the Nabahan kingdom, Mukadisho and Kirimba, so Sultan Omar conquered the whole of the Swahili coast except only Zanzibar he did not get because at this time this town had no fame.

In the year seven hundred and ninety-five [1392-3. *Editor's note*: this date varies from that given in other versions.] Sultan Omar died and his son

---

[33] Mvita is the native name for Mombasa.

[34] A small chief is even now called *Jumbe* on the Mrima coast. The ruins of the Yumbe are still to be seen at Pate.

Muhammad bin Omar (Fumomadi the Great) reigned.

The sons left by Sultan Omar were this Muhammad and that Ahmad, who had been a soldier, and Abubakr. Sultan Muhammad lived in the country of Pate and made it prosper, making plantations and building vessels called *Gharabs* which are now called *Jahazis*.[35]

Now in those days Arab and Indian vessels used to come to Pate harbour.

Sultan Omar had a nephew who was very fond of travelling. On his first journey he set out for India, but was completely lost and his ship sank, and he himself, after meeting with great hardships and difficulties and losing everything, returned home. He remained at home for a year, but the next year he wished to (p. 46) travel abroad again. His mother said, "Ah, my son, do not travel again. You have been greatly afflicted, why do you want to travel? Money to spend is here; if you want anything or any matter, tell me."

He said to her, "I want neither thing nor matter. My soul longs to travel, and if I do not get leave from you, my father and my mother, I will travel away as best I can."

As they were unable to stop him they made up a fleet of seven ships for him, and he voyaged away and wrecked all his ships. He returned alone, and he had nothing and no one with him.

His father and mother said to him, "Now you will not be able to travel any more." So that youth stopped at home a year, and by the second year he had no more desire to travel by reason of the trials through which he had

---

[35] *Gharab* (from Arabic for 'raven') is a craft which appears in the Persian gulf. *Jahazi* from the Hindustani for a ship = *Jahaz*. [*Editor's note*: From the Arabic *jahaza* 'outfit', *jihāz* 'apparatus'.]

passed.

Till one day he went to the bathroom at night and saw a cockroach climbing the wall. When it had climbed a little it slipped down, then it rose up again, and again it slipped down. But it rose a third time and climbed up till it reached the top and passed out of sight.

That youth said, "I have been outdone by that cockroach, for it fell twice and tried a third time. I was not able to try a third time. God has sent it to teach me a lesson. I must set forth again."

In the morning he said to his parents, "I must set out again, and this time I want much wealth with me. If you do not give me a fleet according to my wishes you will not see me again."

His parents and relations and friends all besought him not to travel again, but he did not agree. When his parents found that they were unable to prevent him, they gave him a fleet according to his wishes.

So he set out and arrived in India where he traded and made much profit. During the return they were lost at sea for many days till from the vessel on board of which he was they saw an island near them.

So they disembarked as they were in need of water, and that (p. 47) youth wished to rest from the discomforts he had suffered. He lay under a tree and told his servants to cook his food and bring it him there.

They sat down to cook, and when the fire blazed up they saw the sand of that place melt and run away. When it had gone a little from the fire it cooled in separate little pieces.

The cooks told this to their master and he came to look at it and recognized what it was. However, he only said, "Cook food quickly," till after he had finished eating he called the captain and sailors and said to them, "Do you recognize here that our home is near?" They said, "We do not know this place, we have now come to this island for the first time, nor have we before even heard tell of it."

He answered, "I have made a plan; will you follow it?" They said to him, "Whatever you desire, that will we do." So he said, "I want to unload our food and everything we have on board leaving food and water for fifteen days only. Whatever is over and above this let us leave behind and let us load up our ship with this sand till she can carry no more, for this sand is silver ore, and we cannot help getting from it a return greater than from these other things we are carrying."

So they took his advice and unloaded all their goods and filled up with sand for three days till the ship could carry no more. They sailed away, and on the third day they met a bad storm and lost all hope of escape. The sailors jettisoned the sand till, when the boat was half empty, that youth stopped them, saying, "Have patience first."

Afterwards they got a safe and favourable wind and arrived home. When they arrived they found that those other vessels of his had arrived first, and on shore was a mourning for him.

He said to the captain and sailors, "I want you to hide the news about this sand till I know truly if it be silver ore, for if it is not so people will think me a fool, throwing away wheat and food and loading sand." They said to him, "Very good."

So the youth landed with great joy and his parents were overjoyed to see him.

(p. 48) He rested for three days, and then at dead of night he brought some of that sand and put it in a store in his house.

Then he called skilled workmen and showed them a little, and when they made an ornament out of it they found that it was very pure silver.

Now it was at this time that the Portuguese arrived in Pate, and first they came in friendship.

Afterwards he showed the ore to the Portuguese and they asked him where he got it. He told them the story from first to last because of his joy when he knew that it was real ore.

Those Portuguese wanted him to show them the spot, and they went together with the captain and searched for six months and returned again without finding it.

When he arrived back in Pate he found that Sultan Muhammad had died, and that his father Abubakr was now Sultan. The name of that youth was Mwana Mkuu.

So Sultan Abubakr reigned in the year 825 [1421-2. *Editor's note*: this date differs from that given in other versions. The date is obviously incompatible with the chronology of the Portuguese presence on the coast.].

The Portuguese came and they stayed at Pate and Dondo and they were in friendship with Sultan Abu Bakari (Swahili for "Abubakr"). Their influence grew great in the town of Pate, and they taught people how to excavate wells in the rocks by means of gunpowder.

The Portuguese built houses on the rock and made an underground passage to Pongwa rock.[36]

For a long time they lived together in friendship and traded with goods

---

[36] The Pate people believe that this underground way still exists, but they have been unable to find its entrance.

and every kind of thing.

The Portuguese said to Abubakr, "Your kingdom is very great, but there is no profit. Why do you not make taxes?"

So they made a customs house at a place in Pate harbour called Fandikani; in the language of the Portuguese it means "customs".[37]

Afterwards Sultan Abubakr died in the year 855 [1451. *Editor's note*: this date differs from that given in other versions.]. The Bwana (p. 49) Mkuu reigned and he had much wealth, and traded much till the whole country of Pate became very wealthy.

They made large houses and put in them brass lamps with chimneys, and they made ladders of silver to climb up into bed with, and silver neck chains. Into the pillars of the houses they beat silver studs and nails of gold on top of them.

The Portuguese lived on the coast and they set in order Dondo and Mombasa. Their governor lived at Mombasa, and they they built a fort which is there to this day.

So Bwana Mkuu reigned without falling out either with the Portuguese or with his own subjects.

In the year 903 of the Hejra [1497-8. *Editor's note*: this date differs from that given in other versions.] he died, leaving seven children, of whom Muhammad reigned, and he was called Bwana Fumomadi the Second.

There came about trouble between the people and his brother, a Nabahan called Bwani Mtiti, nephew of the Sultan Omar. They made war and defeated him, and so Sultan Muhammad reigned at peace with his subjects. He

[37] Portuguese *Alfandega*. In Swahili the *-ni* is only a locative postfix.

set the country of Siyu in order; this place was there before that time, but it had no power.

At that time was the beginning of the Wafamao coming to an agreement with the Portuguese governor; some accounts say that the Wafamao are Portuguese, and other that they are the Arabs originially sent by Abdul Malik.

That was the origin of the Siyu people.

Now they are called Swahilis and their clan is the Banu Sadi.

Afterwards trouble arose between the people of Siyu and Pate by reason of Portuguese intrigue. They fought together and Siyu was defeated, and the town broken into. Their chief went and complained to the Portuguese and they came and made peace and took the prisoners who had been made and returned them to Siyu. So they stayed in allegiance to Pate.

In the year 945 [1538-9. *Editor's note*: this date differs from that given in other versions.] Sultan Muhammad died, and Sultan Abubakr, son of Bwana Mkuu, reigned.

Now at this time the Portuguese conquered the whole Swahili (p. 50) coast. They instituted a tax, and afterwards their subjects would not agree to the tax.

Sultan Abubakr was of one accord with his people and strife arose between him and the Portuguese. The Portuguese came and fought with Pate, and the people of Pate were grievously afflicted.

Now at that time there was a Sherif[38] of Arabia in a country called Inati. So the Sultan of Pate sent a man to desire his supplications, for he was a very holy man, saying, "Pray to Allah on our behalf that he may deliver us

---

[38] *Sherif*, a descendant of the Prophet.

from our enemies." When he went to him, he gave him his two sons, and they were brought to Pate.

He said, "The Portuguese will not get your country again by the grace of Allah." So his sons came and settled at Pate and married there. It was after these Sherifs that the quarters of Sarambini, Inati and Shindoni were named, for these were the names of their houses.

Now at that time the ships of the Portuguese came round the Cape and they attacked Pate and afterwards there was a truce for six months.

The Portuguese always came during the season of the greater rains, and this time, after six months' truce, they came in great strength and stationed their ships in the neighbourhood of Pate. There is a small island near Pate which even today bears the name of Shaka Mzungu (the white man's Shaka) because of the Portuguese staying there.

They seized also the harbour of Mtangawanda and Shindakasi, and they blockaded the island of Pate, landing by way of Shindakasi. They fired cannons on the town and fought with the inhabitants.

The shots from their cannons passed overhead without damage by reason of the supplications of the holy man Sheikh Maulala Abubakr bin Salim.

When they saw that the shots did not hit they made channels in the ground of Shindakasi so that they might pump water into (p. 51) the town. When they had made these and brought water from the shore it would not rise. When they saw that they were not able to do this they made peace and came to an agreement with the Sultan of Pate.

Afterwards Sultan Abu Bakari died and his son Sultan Bwana Mkuu reigned in the year 995 [1586-7. *Editor's note*: this date differs from that given in other versions.].

At this time foreigners came into the country of Pate and they were called Wabarawa.

At one time they used to live at Barawa, but they were Arabs and their tribe is called Hatimii, a tribe renowned in Arabia, and their country was formerly called Andalusia.[39]

They arrived in Pate with much wealth, and they bought houses and even bought firewood and wells.

So the country of Pate prospered exceedingly till in the year 1010 [1601-2. *Editor's note*: this date differs from that given in other versions.] Sultan Bwana Mkuu died, and Sultan Ahmad, the son of his cousin, reigned. He was a very good man and loved his subjects much. He reigned seven years without rain falling, and then he abdicated of his own free will and gave the throne to Sultan Muhammad, the son of Sultan Abubakr.

Sultan Muhammad quarrelled with the Portuguese and they turned him out of the throne and gave it to a son of Bwana Mkuu called Abubakr, and he agreed with the Portuguese very well.

The Portuguese then had trouble with the people of Amu, and they fought and defeated them utterly, making many people prisoners.

Sultan Abubakr, by reason of his friendship for the Portuguese, desired them to give up these prisoners, and he returned them to Amu. From that date

---

[39] Some of the Arabs of the coast claim descent from Andalusians. See an Arabic book called *Fatuh al Baladin (The Opening up of the Countries)*, p. 239. [*Editor's note*: Rather, *Futūḥ al-buldān* (The Conquest of Countries) by al-Balādhurī (d. 892). Stigand's reference is apparently to the first printed edition: M.J. de Goeje (ed.), *Liber expugnationis regionum, auctore Imámo Ahmed ibn Jahja ibn Djábir al-Beládsori* (Leiden, 1866). For an English translation see P.K. Hitti, *The Origins of the Islamic State*, vol. I (New York: Columbia University Press, 1916; reprinted New York: AMS Press, 1968).]

the people of Amu made allegiance to Pate.

Sultan Abubakr loved to travel about and visit every place. Whilst he was on his travels, there behind him in Pate the people intrigued, and put Sultan Muhammad, the son of his brother on the throne in the year 1040 [1630-1. *Editor's note*: this date differs from that given in other versions.].

(p. 52) When Sultan Abubakr returned he landed at Amu; he was not able to get to Pate again. He and the Portuguese went together to fight Pate, but they were utterly defeated and so made peace, and Sultan Abubakr remained at Amu. He married at Amu, and later the people of Pate and Amu combined against the Portuguese who lived at Dondo, but they were not strong enough for them.

At Pate Sultan Muhammad married his son to the daughter of Abubakr. The name of the son was Bwana Mkuu.

Bwana Mkuu had not yet taken her to put her in his house when the people of Pate and Amu and the Portuguese intrigued together and brought back Sultan Abubakr, and Sultan Muhammad they locked up.

Sultan Abubakr then said to Bwana Mkuu, "Enter the house and take your wife. I am your father, do not be angry with me for locking up your father—it was the subjects and the Portuguese who wanted it."

So Bwana Mkuu took his wife and lived in peace with his father-in-law till Sultan Muhammad died.

The people of the town told Bwana Mkuu that his father had received poison and that presently he also would be poisoned. Bwana Mkuu did not listen to these tales, so the people went to the Sultan Abubakr and said, "Your son-in-law is about to kill you in revenge for his father's death, and the kingdom, he says, is his."

Sultan Abubakr believed their words and so made a plan with the Portuguese, saying, "When your governor comes from Mombasa I will pretend to be ill and will send my son-in-law Bwana Mkuu and forty great men in my stead.

Honour them greatly and feast them. Give them food of quality and strong drink. When they have finished getting drunk, hoist sail and carry them away that they return no more. For these are troublesome people; I am not able to reign while they are here."

The Portuguese took Sultan Abubakr's advice and did as he suggested.

(p. 53) When the Pate people came to know that these men had been taken away at Sultan Abubakr's instigation, they were at first silent and acted as if the matter had not reached their ears.

Sultan Abu Bakari[40] said to his daughter, "Your husband has gone to Goa—after six months he will return."

So she awaited her husband and meanwhile gave birth to a son. When her son had reached three years of age she knew that her father's words were false. Now at that time her father made a fête for the circumcision of his sons and told her that he would have her son circumcised at the same time.

She replied, "I do not want that, I will have him circumcised separately."

Sultan Abubakr replied, "You have joined in the intrigues of the other people; perish, both of you."

Now it was necessary that these festivities the royal horn should be blown and there was but one horn.

---

[40] Abu Bakari, Swahili pronounciation of Abu-bakr.

So his daughter came to borrow the horn of the Amu people secretly, but the Amu people would not give if for fear of the Sultan.

When she could not obtain the horn she called to her secretly a man in Pate called Mwenyi Baenyi, one well versed in skilled work.

She said to him, "I want you to make me a horn secretly that no man may know, and what you ask that will I give you." He said, "Very good," and so she put him in her house and gave him an elephant tusk[41] and everything he required, and he made a fine horn.

When he had finished she asked him what wages he required, and he replied, "My wages are the gifts given to the blower." She said, "Take them," and she gave out the horn and he sounded it through the town and people showered gifts on him.[42]

(p. 54) So she held the ceremony and rivalled her father.

After this the people of Pate made intrigue and rushed in on Sultan Abubakr, smiting him and his brother Bwana Madi—killing them both. ||

(p. 55) After the events described in the last chapter, another Sultan Abubakr was placed on the throne in the year 1060 [1650. *Editor's note*: this date differs from that given in other versions.]. His nickname was Bwana Tamu the Great.

---

[41] This horn is beautifully carved, and is now at Amu. It must have been made of two tusks. [*Editor's note*: See James de Vere Allen, "The *Siwas* of Pate and Lamu: Two Antique Sideblown Horns from the Swahili Coast," Art and Archaeology Research Papers G (1976): 38-47.]

[42] It was the custom of the people on hearing the horn to make presents to the blower. The old horn of Pate is said to have been lost at sea, while the old horn of Amu, which is of brass, and not ivory, is now in the possession of a descendant of the man whose office used to be to blow it on ceremonial occasions.

Then there arose strife between the Portuguese on one hand, and the whole Swahili coast together with the Yorubi Imam of Muskat on the other.

So they combined and fought the Portuguese on the whole coast, leaving Mombasa alone.

Afterwards the Imam sent word to the Sultan of Pate to drive the Portuguese out of the fort of Mombasa, and that he was to proceed about the matter with care and great guile.

So the people of Pate and Mombasa made plans together and the Pate men went to Mombasa in small parties of tens and twenties till many were gathered together at Mombasa. They waited for a Sunday[43] and then rushed in on them suddenly, killing them and gaining possession of their fort and their property.

Since that time the Portuguese have not had possession of any place on the coast.[44]

Afterwards Sultan Bwana Tamu sent a letter to the Yorubi Imam saying, "I have finished taking the fort and have turned out the Portuguese." So the Imam answered, "Give me the fort and I will send men to put in it, and you and I will combine that we may follow and drive out the Portuguese wherever we find them."

So the Imam sent a tribe called the Mazaru'i, and they came with their soldiers and chief and seized the fort. This was the (p. 56) beginning of the Mazaru'i coming to this coast. Later the Imam found himself in difficulties as

---

[43] Presumably on a Sunday so as to attack them when they were at church.

[44] The Portuguese have received but little attention in this history. The Pate historians appear to have magnified the part that they themselves played in east coast history, to the belittlement of the doings of others.

there were no receipts, only disbursements.

Then the Mazaru'i said to him, "This will not do—leave us to find our own expenses and the fort shall remain yours in name."

Later the Imam sent other people, seven men of the name of Sef, who were called the Seven Sefs. They rebelled against the Imam, so he came and fought them and the Mazaru'i commanded his troops. They took the fort, but in the taking many of the Mazaru'i were killed. After this the Imam gave the fort the Mazaru'i that they should govern the fort without reference to Maskat.

So the Mazaru'i stayed in the fort and conquered the country of Mombasa and its mainland.

There they stopped till they were ejected by Sa'id bin Sultan, but the account of this will come further on.

Now it was in the days of Bwana Tamu the Great that the Watikuu and Wakatwa came wanting a place in which to live, for formerly on the mainland there was war between the Mkilio and the Wakatwa.

So the Watikuu were given the country of Faza and they live there to this day.

Bwana Tamu lived at peace with his subjects and they loved him well till in the year 1100 [1688-9] he died, and Sultan Bwana Mkuu, the son of Sultan Abubakr, reigned.

Sultan Bwana Mkuu loved the country of Amu very much, and he sent to Amu and married a wife there, and he also built a mosque, and made Amu the harbour for the trading vessels brought in by the northeastern monsoon. His mother also was an Amu woman.

He lived at Amu and the Amu people loved him well. He was much given to trading and doing business. He made friends with the Mazaru'i and they divided together the taxes from the island of Pemba, each taking half.

They also made the Sabaki River frontier between them on the mainland.

(p. 57) Sultan Bwana Mkuu died in the year 1125,[45] [1713. *Editor's note*: this date differs from that given in other versions.] and Bwana Tamu the Younger reigned.

The Bwana Tamu was the son of that Bwana Mkuu who was carried away to Goa.

Now it was this Sultan who fought with the Yorubi Imam. The end of it was that he took the allegiance of the Imam and Maskat soldiers were put in Pate.[46]

Now this Sultan fought with the people of Amu twice, and the reason for war was that the Amu people unearthed some guns belonging to the Portuguese which had got buried on Hedabu Hill.[47] When the Pate Sultan heard this he wanted to get them from the Amu people.

The Amu people met together and took counsel together and they were all of one counsel, and answered him, "We will not give them to you, and we will no longer acknowledge you as our chief."

---

[45] These dates are probably only approximate. They are all multiples of five, which looks suspicious. They do not agree with those in Chapter I. [*Editor's note*: here, Stigand refers to the opening chapter of his book, "Ancient History from Arab, Portuguese and other Sources" (pp. 1-27), mostly culled from C. Guillain's Documents sur l'historie, la géographie et le commerce de l'Afrique orientale, vol. I (Paris, 1856). None of the dates cited in the chapter refer specifically to Pate.]

[46] Sef bin Sultan, a Yorubi bearing the ambitious title of Kaid al Ardh (lord of the earth), is said to have been the first man to bring Arabs to Amu.

[47] A sand hill between Shela and present-day Lamu. The ruins of old Lamu are supposed to lie under there.

When he received this letter he made war on them, coming by two routes.

He embarked soldiers in ships and sent them by way of Shela, and others in *dhows* and *mtepes* he sent by way of the Mkanda.[48]

When they came forth they fixed the guns on board their ships, but they were too heavy for the ships and sank them.

When the Amu saw that their ships were sinking, they pressed the Pate men hard and overcame them utterly, capturing some of their vessels.

Others fled away and returned to Pate.

When the Amu people had ensured their own safety they said, "We must certainly go to Pate and fight them even in like manner as they came to our town." The elders said, "This is (p. 58) not a good counsel. What we have accomplished here in holding our own country is no small matter."

However, the leaders of war would not profit by the advice of the elders and so they made a big expedition on their own account.

They went to Pate and landed their forces at a harbour called Ungwi.

The Pate people were very angry that the Amu people should try to capture their country and they came forth with all their might and fought them. A great battle was fought and the Amu people were defeated, many of them were killed, and they were spoiled of many vessels.

They were scattered in the mangrove swamps, while those who were left got vessels and retired to Amu.

When they arrived the elders said, "Did we not tell you after this manner? Now you will have to fight for your country, for the Pate chief will

[48] A narrow channel between Manda and the mainland.

not leave us alone; he will come to fight us again. It were better that we swear allegiance to him as heretofore."

The captains of war did not agree to this.

The Pate Sultan waited six months and then made war again. He made a *dhow* in the harbour of Magogoni and it was taken overland till they came with it to Kikoni.

This *dhow* carried soldiers across from the mainland whilst others came by way of the Mkanda.

When the Amu people saw these latter arriving on the shore they went down to fight them and did not leave a single man in the town, for they had not the tidings of the *dhow* at Kikoni.

They had no knowledge of this and so as they were fighting on the beach the Pate people entered the town and seized it.

At that time they were unable to make any dispositions, and so they were defeated and their country conquered.

The Pate people took forty of their chief men and brought them to Pate.

The elders who were left in Amu wrote to the Mazaru'i and (p. 59) asked them to intercede for them with the Sultan of Pate, saying that they were ready to return to his allegiance.

The Mazaru'i went to Pate and received those forty men whom they returned to Amu, and the Amu elders returned to the Pate allegiance saying, "Whilst we are alive there will be no more trouble between us."

After these events were finished trouble arose between Sultan Bwana Tamu and the Yorubi Imam. The latter made intrigue in Pate so that at his instigation the Sultan was stabbed with a dagger at a levée and was killed.

This was in the year 1135 [1722-3. *Editor's note*: this date differs from that given in other versions.], and Bwana Bakari his son reigned.

Now this time was the beginning of the Abusa'id dynasty of Maskat.

For the Yorubis had reigned many years in Maskat until there came to the throne one man who was very bad.

Now at this time there was a man of the Abusa'idi Arabs called Hamed bin Sa'id, who kept a shop in the village of the Oman called Adam.

The chief of the village one day entered his shop and ate some *Halwa*,[49] and took things out of the shop, refusing to pay for them.

Hamed bin Sa'id then killed the chief. He then asked his relations to support him, but they refused as the chief was a great man in that place, so Hamed fled to the chief of the Yorubi at Nazua in Maskat.

He told him, "I have quarrelled with a man and killed him."

When the relations of the dead man came to claim Hamed, the Sultan paid blood money for him and kept him at his court.

Hamed entered the service of the Sultan as a herdsman and afterwards became a soldier till he rose to be the head of the soldiers and then became the Sultan's Wazir.

Afterwards he sent him as governor of a province called Sahari.

Now that Sultan behaved very badly to his subjects, robbing (p. 60) them of their wives and becoming intoxicated with Indian hemp (*Bhang*).

When the subjects were much oppressed they sent to Hamed bin Sa'id saying, "We are unable to live with this Sultan any longer."

Hamed replied, "If you are able to kill him, do so." The people answered, "We will kill him, but you must consent to govern."

---

[49] An Arab sweetmeat.

He consented, and so they killed the Sultan and Hamed bin Sa'id ruled and was called Imam of Maskat. [*Editor's note*: the title of *Imām* here signifies the head of Ibāḍi, Khārijite Muslims of Oman. For the history of Ibāḍism in Oman see John C. Wilkinson, *The Imamate Tradition of Oman* (Cambridge: University Press, 1987).]

He lived at Nazua and was a very good man, and when he died he left two sons, Sa'id and Sultan. This was the beginning of the Busa'idi dynasty. [*Editor's note*: The Āl Bū Sa'id dynasty have controlled Oman since 1741. The *imamate* passed out of their family in the nineteenth century.]

Of these we will relate their history farther on.

Now when Bwana Bakari came to the throne of Pate the Mazaru'i had become very powerful, and they had entered Pate in friendship, but had become more powerful than the Nabahans.

Bwana Bakari stayed at Amu and the Pate people did not like him and made a plot to dethrone him.

In the middle of this strife Sultan Bwana Bakari died, and his brother, Sultan Ahmad, reigned in the year 1150 [1737-8. *Editor's note*: this date differs from that given in other versions.].

Intrigue arrived between the Mazaru'i and the people of Amu and of Pate, and both these people loved Sultan Ahmad.

Now at this time the Busa'idi Arabs used to come to the coast; they had got hold of Zanzibar through making friendship with the people, but had not yet taken it entirely.

The Mazaru'i went to Zanzibar and they fought together.

The Mazaru'i governor was intrigued against by his nephew till one day that nephew of his struck his uncle with a dagger and killed him. Those

Mazaru'i who were present fell on the youth and killed him. It thus happed that the Mazaru'i expedition to Zanzibar failed, and they returned to Pemba and then to Mombasa.

There they made another chief, but from that time they did not get to Zanzibar again.

Then they wanted to seize Pate and Amu and to take the (p. 61) kingdom of the Nabahans, but they were unable. So they lived with them in friendship and in guile, thinking, "If we get a chance we will take their kingdom."

In the year 1177 [1763-4] Sultan Ahmad died, and a Queen Mwana Khadija, sister of Bwana Tamu the Younger, reigned. She reigned seven years, and after that the Mazaru'i intrigued with the Pate people and they put Sultan Omari on the throne.

Then there were two rulers in one country and they fought together for five years inside the city. Afterwards Sultan Omari was defeated and he fled to the Bajuns at Faza.

Mwana Khadija sent her soldiers and *ameers* to fight him at Faza and he fled again and took a *dhow* and made for Barawa.

He fled secretly, but the soldiers of the Mwana Khadija followed him and came up with him in the way in their *dhows*.

When he saw that he would be seized he wrote on a piece of paper and threw it into the water, and at that place there sprang up behind his *dhow* a shoal of sand.

Even today it is there, and the Bajuns call it Sultan Omar's shoal.

The reason was that he was a great medicine man, but magic does not stay the decree of Allah and his luck was small. So he went to Barawa and stayed there one year till he gained strength to return to Pate of one accord with the people of Pate and the Mazaru'i.

He entered Pate and seized his house, called Diwani, and half the town. Then war returned to Pate, and after one year they broke into his house at Diwani and he was killed.

His brother's son, called Fumoluti, took his place and fought with Mwana Khadija.

In the year 1187 [1773-4] Mwana Khadija died.

So Sultan Fumoluti reigned, for the people of Pate saw that it was better to leave off strife because of the trials they had endured for many days. So he reigned over the whole town and all were of one accord, the people of Pate, the Mazaru'i, the people of Amu and Siu, and even the Bajuns.

The people of Pate said, "It were better that we leave off (p. 62) fighting and that he reign over the whole country, for our town has been laid waste."

For in the time of Sultan Omari and Mwana Khadija everybody cut down the cocoa-nut palms and fruit trees, everybody destroyed the property of his neighbour. For five years they were not able to cultivate or to trade or to do any work whatsoever. So a great famine raged till people ate oats and the skin seats of chairs. For this reason they were pleased that peace should reign and that their country might rest.

So they remained two and a half years, and after that time the great men who were of Mwana Khadija's faction made intrigues. These people said, "What sort of a Sultan is this? We do not want him, for he is of lowly origin."

For the mother of Sultan Fumoluti bin Sheikh was of humble birth, and her father's profession was that of a fisherman.

This fisherman had three daughters, one of whom was called Mwana Sukari binti Kae.

One night during Ramadhan her father was lying in his plantation and his daughter was fanning him, when the star of destiny[50] passed over them.

Her father pointed it out to his daughter and said to her, "My child, Allah will bless you so that you give birth to Sultans."

On the next evening the father of this Sultan Fumoluti passed the house of the fisherman and saw his daughter and loved her very much. He demanded her of her father and married her and took her to his home. She gave birth to this Sultan Fumoluti and one girl, who became Bwana Fumomadi's mother, and another boy, so she had three children.

Now from that time no other has reigned at Pate save descendants of that woman whose father prayed to Allah on her behalf.

So now by reason of the humble origin of his mother the Pate people refused to be governed by this Sultan Fumoluti, and the great men of Pate took counsel and made plans to destroy him.

(p. 63) Now the Sultan was a man of great strength and a brave warrior, so they said, "Who will confront him and smite him?"

They were in the midst of saying these words when a man called Fundi Suleimani, a craftsman, came forth. He drew near to the counsel of the free born.

They said to him, "What do you want here? You have no manners to

---

[50] This is a star called 'the star of the night of divine decree', or the night on which the Prophet ascended to heaven, a vision of which is, according to Arabs, vouchsafed only to very holy persons.

disturb our privacy." He replied, "The secret thing you desire I will do it for you." They said to him, "You are a lowly person, you will not dare do the thing we wish to do." He replied, "I will do what you want and more."

Now the reason was this: this artisan, Suleimani had had a very beautiful wife. Long ago, Sultan Fumoluti when a youth had taken her from him. Now that he had obtained the status of a free man he said to himself, "Now I will take my revenge that I may cure the old sore that is in my heart."

When the elders heard this, they knew that he would do truly as he had said. So they said to him, "If Allah will we will attend the levée and you must come and stand behind the Sultan. When the Mazaru'i governor enters the levée the Sultan will stand up for him, then strike him and we will be ready to seize his house."

Next day they went to the levée according to their agreement. When the Mazaru'i governor entered the Sultan rose, placing his hand on his sword. Suleimani struck him a sword cut, and the blow severed five fingers, and striking the regal chair cut off its arm.

Sultan Fumoluti's sword fell on the ground and he stooped and picked it up with his left hand.[51] Now Suleimani's sword was broken with the blow, and there remained only the stump, with which he struck the Sultan on the right arm.

When Fumoluti had seized his sword in his left hand he struck Suleimani, who ran away and fell, outside, split in two halves.

Then the Pate people attacked Sultan Fumoluti, and he drew (p. 64) nigh to them and smote them with his left hand and killed twenty-five men. So they

---

[51] The sword was worn, of course, on the right side, according to Arab custom.

fled away, and two of their number hid themselves under a cow.[52] Everybody fled, and his brother was killed there. When they had fled he went to the door and fastened it, and his own people and Bwana Sheikh his son were not present.

When they received tidings they came running and passed in by the back way, and Bwana Sheikh entered and found his father exhausted from loss of blood.

He said to his son, "Listen, my son, I give you my dying exhortation that you may act on it. I am finished and you after me they will kill you."

"Now if you want my counsel go and take Bwana Fumomadi and put him here in my place. It is he who is able avenge me, for the soldiers here belong to his father and his aunt. When these soldiers see him as ruler of the town they will come to their master. If you refuse to follow my advice you will die before me, for they will come again at once and come up into this house."

As they were in the midst of saying these words Bwana Fumomadi and his friends arrived. For when he had received the news he was not able to wait patiently because Fumoluti was his younger maternal uncle.

When Sultan Fumoluti and his son saw Bwana Fumomadi they said, "This is indeed Sultan Bwana Kombo."[53]

So Fumoluti spake and said to Bwana Kombo, "I gave this your brother

---

[52] It was usual to keep a few cows outside in the courtyard to give milk to the household, while the remainder were taken outside the city to graze.

[53] From *Kombo* = scraps, meaning that he was left over from the general slaughter. *Kombo ya Simba* = the lion's leavings, is a nickname often bestowed on a man who has been mauled by a lion.

just now my dying exhortation to obey you. Now I give you my dying request. Do not follow the counsels of the Pate people. Stand by yourself and avenge me, and Allah will give you a great kingdom, and you will defeat your enemies.

"Also follow the counsel of this your brother, Bwana Sheikh, for he is wise, moreover he is a valiant man and will be of (p. 65) service to you against your enemies. So you must love him and help him to a high place in your kingdom, and I will then be pleased with you, for he has nothing now."

When the Nabahans and the Pate people know that Bwana Kombo had been given the kingdom by his uncle, and that the uncle was still alive, they made an attack on the house.

So Bwana Sheikh and Bwana Kombo and their soldiers and relations fought well and resisted them.

Then the Pate people took Bwana Fumomadi's brother and made him Sultan in their quarter in place of Mwana Khadija his aunt.

They fought three days till on the fourth day, at night, Sultan Fumoluti died.

Some people said that he put his arm into burning oil, and others that he said, "There cannot be a Sultan with a stump for a right arm for how can his hand be kissed? Moreover, I will live to be called Sultan 'stump-arm'," and so he died.

So in the year 1190 [1776-7. *Editor's note*: this date differs from that given other versions.] Sultan Bwana Fumomadi reigned.

When Fumoluti was dead Sultan Bwana Fumomadi told a crier to beat the horn[54] in the town the same night and proclaim that the Sultan was dead, and that he had taken his place, and that this was the Sultan's dying bequest. Moreover, that he who wanted war must make war with the new Sultan, and he who wanted peace must come early in the morning to the burial.

So when the morning had dawned Bwana Fumomadi and his clan buried his uncle.

Those people of the other quarter did not come, so Bwana Fumomadi knew that they were still wanting to make war.

Now of those in that quarter there were two of Bwana Fumomadi's brothers; one was he whom they had set up as Sultan, and the other followed his brother.

Now this faction was the strongest, but half of the people (p. 66) and soldiers, when they saw how Bwana Fumomadi reigned, came over to him because they loved him most, and they were in the beginning soldiers of his father.

So Bwana Fumomadi, when he had gained strength, fought the other faction and took their town, leaving only forty houses in the whole town. After that he seized all these houses till there was left only forty people in one house, and these were very great men.

Then he wrote a letter and sent it to his two brothers who were there, saying, "I have pardoned you, come out from there and leave me to fight it out with the remainder. You will order his kingdom equally with me, but to me

---

[54] The criers in the old days used to issue proclamations of the Sultan and parade the city beating a horn with a stick. The Swahili expression *kupiga pembe* is ambiguous, as it is sometimes used for 'blowing a horn'. However, the ceremonial blowing has a separate word.

will be left the name of Sultan only." They answered him, "If you want us to come you must make peace with us together with these forty people of ours. We cannot leave them."

When their letters came, Bwana Fumomadi consulted with his cousin Bwana Sheikh, and the latter said, "If you leave these people they will make trouble again directly they have gained strength. It will not do to leave them."

"Now if your brothers have refused to come out it is best that you treat all these alike and eradicate this evil that our country may be saved, for it has suffered troubles for many days."

So he asked his brothers again to come out and they refused.

So Bwana Fumomadi did not hesitate, he sent soldiers to assault the house from back and front, and they killed everybody. Then he took either by stratagem or force every man who had been ringleader amongst the rebel soldiers of Pate, Amu, Siu or Ozi, and killed him.

For this reason he obtained a great kingdom and sat on the throne for thirty-three years without there being trouble anywhere in his kingdom.

The whole outlook became clear, so that even now women say when the sun comes out and there are no clouds, "Today the heavens are refulgent like the sovereignty of Bwana Fumomadi."

So the country of Pate flourished, and he turned out the (p. 67) Mazaru'i and they had no concern with it any more. Since they had come to Pate no one had been able to govern any more without their aid, but Sultan Fumomadi put an end to this state of affairs.

Now he was the last of the great Sultans of the Nabahans; after him there came not anyone who obtained a kingdom like his, for he restored the grandeur of the ancient kingdom with his own hands.

He loved his subjects and his soldiers and he spent much money. He was a clever man, powerful and brave, and he did not consent to have his subjects oppressed.

In his time towards the end of his reign there was a man of Amu called Abdallah bin Hafithi, a great man, who said, "This year I will not pay my tax of three loads of produce."

The Amu people said, "What will you do, then?" He replied, "This year I will not cultivate, and I will make all my slaves cut planks."

Bwana Fumomadi heard this and he waited till the time of the paying of the "kikanda" tax and then he held a levée and called his ameers and officers and the big men of his kingdom, and told them about Abdallah bin Hafithi. They asked him what was his wish, and he said, "I want a man to go at once to Abdallah bin Hafithi and bring me back one of three things. Either a thousand dollars as a fine or he himself or his head, but he must not excite the country of Lamu, and no one must know of it till one of these three things has been brought."

There was a captain among the Nabahans, a great warrior and also a friend of Abdallah bin Hafithi. This man said to the Sultan, "In the morning, if Allah wills and we are all alive, I will give you here at your levée one of these three things."

So that captain, Ahmad bin Othman was his name, went forth and took twelve good men from amongst his soldiers.

He then procured a canoe and twelve fisherman with oars and set out from Pate at sunset till when eleven o'clock had come he had arrived at Kitopemba in Lamu.

He landed and instructed the fishermen not to allow the canoe (p. 68) to beach itself with the ebbing tide. Then he entered the town and went, with his twelve soldiers, straight to the house of Abdallah bin Hafithi. The door was bolted, so he put four soldiers on either side and four at the door, telling them to let no one whatsoever pass in the way.

He knocked at the door and a slave girl opened it, and he entered in.

Abdallah when he saw his friend said, "Welcome, stranger. By what vessel have you arrived this time of night, and what is the news? For this is not your wont, for when you come you first send me a letter and today you have not sent me one."

He said, "Today I have not come on my own business—I have come by order of our Sultan, and I am to bring him one of three things."

He asked him, "What is the first?" He replied, "For you to give me a thousand dollars." "The second?" "That you go yourself to Pate." "And the third?" "If you refuse I must take your head."

Abdallah replied, "Very good, I hear and obey. Draw near, rest and go to the bathroom. Sleep here till morning and then I will give you a thousand dollars. There is no cause for me to quarrel with my Sultan over a thousand dollars."

He replied, "This will not do. You must not even leave here to go inside. Tell your wife to bring a thousand dollars to us here outside at once or you take my life or I will take yours."

Abdallah bin Hafithi said to him, "Gently, do not get angry. The money is ready. I shall give it to you. Take water and drink first."

He replied, "I have no need of water, nor have I leave from my Sultan to drink water or to delay." Then he said to Abdallah's wife, "Bring a thousand dollars quickly that you may save your husband's life and mine. It is indeed best that we obey the order of our Sultan or I will fight your husband now."

The slave girl who had opened the door told her mistress (p. 69) that there were soldiers outside, and when she heard this she took a a bag of a thousand dollars and gave it to the Pate captain.

He took charge of it and said to her, "You have behaved very wisely to save your husband's life and mine."

So he went forth with his soldiers and returned to Pate, arriving there before it had dawned.

He slept at his house, and next day he brought the bag of money to the levée, and many people were there. He gave it to the Sultan who thanked him and said, "I have no need of the money, keep it," and he also gave him as much again.

When the people of Lamu and all his subjects heard about this they were all very frightened and paid up the "kikanda" tax; even those who had hidden it gave it this year.

For this reason the women sing a song.

"Bwana Tauthe says to the Palace, 'There are not enough receptacles for the tax millet at Ndambwe.' "

Near the end of the reign of Bwana Fumomadi there was trouble with the people of Lamu and an elder called Bwana Zahidi Mgumi.

When Bwana Fumomadi heard about it he set out for Amu, and on reaching the Mkanda channel as the tide had ebbed he slept there the night.

Now Bwana Zahidi had a friend amongst the wazirs of the Sultan who told him of the approach of Fumomadi. When he heard that he was in the Mkanda he came to the Sultan and prostrated himself before him and said,

"The Amu people in their letters have told you that I am the cause of all the trouble, so now I have come to you; kill me or pardon me as you think fit."

Bwana Fumomadi said to him, "Since you have come to my feet alone I pardon you, be those words which have been said about you true or false."

He then gave him a thousand dollars, and he returned that same hour, and the Amu people had no knowledge of this.

When Bwana Fumomadi arrived at Lamu in the morning the elders and great ment went to meet him on the shore. He entered (p. 70) the town and after he had rested the chief elder of the town came to him and said, "Here much intrigue has been caused by Bwana Zahidi. You must kill him or there will be no peace."

He answered, "Bwana Zahidi has already come to me as far back as in the Mkanda, and I have already pardoned him. I cannot break my word to him." The elder said, "That man has deceived you as you will finally perceive. Now I will you another piece of advice. Do not go from here until you have put in here soldiers and a governor or you will lose the land of Lamu. For the people are resolved that they shall be governed no longer. I have now become an old man and they do not hearken to my words; they look upon me as if I have become foolish."

Now this was the origin of making the fort of Lamu which still stands.

Bwana Fumomadi began to dig the foundations. After that he was seized with illness there at Lamu, so he set out and went to Pate before he had yet built one tier of the fort. On the ninth day after setting out Bwana Fumomadi died.

After that, in the year 1224 [1809-10], his son-in-law, Sultan Ahmad bin

Sheikh, reigned by the testament of Bwana Fumomadi.[55]

Now Sultan Ahmad was a man of great strength and bravery, and he was able to cut through a coca-nut with his sword. He was a nephew of the Sultan Fumoluti who had had his arm cut off.

Now the youngest of Bwana Fumomadi's sons called Fumoluti made intrigue against the Sultan his brother-in-law. Now Fumomadi had begotten fifty children both male and female, but some had died before him.

Now Fumoluti said to his brothers, "Our father dies and we his sons are many grown-up men; why shall another reign?

"Why does not one of us reign? Another reigns with our (p. 71) soldiers under him and dispenses our property. This is a counsel of fools."

His brothers answered him, "Who did this was our father, and he told his wish to Bwana Mkuu who on his death took this Sultan Ahmad and put him on the throne saying, "This is the counsel of our father." Leave it thus and do not make trouble, for the Mazaru'i have already cast envious glances on your country and the allegiance of the people of Lamu is unsteady. If they see you fighting amongst yourselves they will find an opportunity, and the Mazaru'i will enter in and seize a quarter of Lamu."

Fumoluti Kipunga said to them, "I do not agree to this folly. I cannot relinquish the grandeur of my father. I am a full-grown man in health and strength."

So trouble arose between Sultan Ahmad and Fumoluti, and it was Sultan Ahmad who had brought up Fumoluti, for he had married his elder sister, and

---

[55] This was to restore the kingdom to the rightfdul line, viz. the heir of Fumoluti. It will be remembered that when Fumoluti was wounded he gave the kingdom to Bwana Kombo.

taken the place of his father.

Fumoluti Kipunga went to him and said, "I make it clear that I do not consent to you being my Sultan. Give up the title of Sultan and I consent to have you as my father as it was you who brought me up. You must arrange in three days, give up the throne and sit with Bwana Mkuu in the council of elders. Give the throne to Bwana Sheikh or another of Bwana Fumomadi's sons, and if they do not want it I want it myself.

"If after three days you have not made this arrangement I shall fight you. I am not able to let the kingdom go, for we are many children, and when people hear of this thing they will say that we are impotent and witless persons."

Afterwards Sultan Ahmad called Bwana Mkuu, Bwana Fumomadi's heir, and all his children and told them about Fumoluti Kipunga.

They answered him, "This is an irresponsible youth, foolish and without manners. It were better that you seize him and imprison him until he learns manners, or else he will make trouble for us with our enemies."

When Fumoluti heard of their advice to imprison him he (p. 72) collected his father's officers and fought against them, and there was war in the city for many days.

In the year 1227 [1812. *Editor's note*: this date recurs only in MS 177 and Heepe-Wassmuss MS M, see #33.] there began the trouble which led to the war called the battle of Shela.

When the position was serious the Mazaru'i came to Pate thinking that they had clearly obtained their desires.

Then the people of Pate went to Fumoluti Kipunga and told him to leave off fighting till the Lamu war was over, saying, "Wait, and presently you will become Sultan, for this Sultan Ahmad is like your father, he has become old and, moreover, he has a malady of the heart.

"Soon he will die and all your brothers have agreed to leave the kingdom to you after Sultan Ahmad, so do not make trouble till the Lamu war is over. If you do not do this you will destroy your own Sultanate. You say that you want the kingdom; when you have destroyed it how will you get it again?"

Fumoluti Kipunga followed the advice of the townspeople and went with them and made peace with Sultan Ahmad, and the plan of campagin against Lamu was left to him.

They made friends with the Mazaru'i governor and planned with him that the Mazaru'i should go to Lamu and pretend that they had quarrelled with Pate. Then they were to go on building the fort at Lamu, and when they had built two or three tiers[56] they were to put in their soldiers and send word to Pate. At that time Pate was to send soldiers to act in concert with the Mazaru'i and to seize the country of Lamu; having done which they were to divide the taxes as they did in Pemba, half to Pate and half to the Mazaru'i.

When the Lamu people heard that the Mazaru'i and the Sultan of Pate had agreed together they were afraid, thinking that they were not equal to either of them alone, still less when they were combined together. Therefore they made a plan to give their country to the Mazaru'i thinking that then they would (p. 73) quarrel with Pate, and that when the two fell out they would both lose strength.

---

[56] By a tier (*kiti*) is meant the height to which a man can build a wall while standing on the ground. The second tier is built from scaffolding the height of the first tier, and so on.

So they went to the Mazaru'i and said, "We want you to take our country and then we will be able to resist the strength of the Pate chief."

The Mazaru'i then thought that they had obtained their desires, so their governor said, "I am not able to keep the country of Lamu unless I build a fort and put my soldiers in it. Then shall I know that the country is mine, and I shall quarrel with the Pate chief to some purpose, for now he is my friend. I cannot fall out with him if you are to desert me afterwards."

So the Lamu people agreed, and the Mazaru'i came to Amu with their vessels and their soldiers, and the people of Lamu kept to their agreement and built their fort.

Now the Mazaru'i used to sleep at night on board their ships, and in the morning they used to land and build the fort in conjunction with the people of Lamu.

Now at that time there were at Lamu two factions; one was the party of Sudi and the other of Zena, and one party liked the Pate people which the other did not.

When the Mazaru'i landed each day they used to form together and march up together.

Now when they were marching up, a Lamu man said to them, "Now you have got a fine country."

There was one man amongst the Mazaru'i who answered, "What sort of country is this? A closet in Pate is better than your country."

When the Lamu people heard this they were silent and they went and told their elder Bwana Zahidi Mgumi,[57] saying, "We were praising up our country to those strangers of ours so as to please them and one man amongst them answered, 'Better is a Pate closet than your town.' "

The elder said, "Be silent, do not get angry with them, but continue to please and entertain them till our work is finished."

(p. 74) At that time, however, Bwana Zahidi Mgumi knew that they had not come in good faith, and that they had some stratagem with Pate or they would not have said these words.

So he called a fisherman and gave him a letter and told him to take it to the Mazaru'i governor at night and to pretend that he had been sent secretly by the Pate chief and that he was to wait for an answer.

In the letter he wrote, "Since going to Lamu till today we have not received an answer yet to our agreement. Answer me speedily that we may be ready. Greetings."

When night had come the fisherman took his canoe and went by way of the Mkanda and made as if he had come from Pate.

He came to the governor's ship, and said to the soldiers, quietly, "I want the master, for I have a letter." They said, "Give it to us."

He replied, "I am not able to give it to anyone else, I must give it into the master's own hand."

When they told the governor he was called, and the governor said to him, "What sort of a man are you?"

He answered, "I am a Pate man. I have been sent secretly with this

[57] The same man who had made trouble before but who now was the chief elder of Lamu.

letter from the Pate chief, and I want an answer quickly that I may return without meeting any of the Lamu fishermen."

The governor read the letter and answered it, saying, "Soon I will send you news. Wait, for there is first a little work to finish. When I am able to enter the fort I will send you word."

So he gave the fisherman this letter without recognizing that it was a ruse.

When this letter reached Bwana Zahidi, he collected his fellow elders that night and said to them, "Beat the horn in the morning so that every male comes to the shore when the Mazaru'i land. Every man must come with his weapons ready."

In the morning the Mazaru'i governor landed with but a few soldiers, and went to the fort having no fear because the Lamu people had wanted to give him their country.

When he had sat down, Bwana Zahidi, the Lamu chief, paid him respect according to custom.

(p. 75) After that he took out the letter and gave it him.

When he saw his letter he knew that a trick had been played on him and he was not able control his anger.

Then Bwana Zahidi said to him, "Is that how Arabs behave?"

The governor arose and went down quickly to the shore to enter his vessel. Lamu was then in an uproar with shouts and the blowing of warhorns, whilst many soldiers were on the shore and he knew that it meant war.

So he went to his boat, and Bwana Zahidi said to the people of Amu, "Do not fight him, for it would be a disgrace for us to commence, for did we not ask him to come here? Today we have learnt that he has deceived us—let him go his way. When he comes to fight us be ready, for then it will be war again."

So they made their dispositions for war and the Mazaru'i chief went to Pate in great dudgeon.

When he told Sultan Ahmad, the Pate chief said, "What is it you wish?"

He replied, "I want war now, at once."

Sultan Ahmad said, "The plan of campaign is not with me, it lies with your friend Fumoluti Kipunga and the elders of the country. Bwana Mkuu, Bwana Madi and Bwana Tamu, they have the final decision."

So the Pate people met together, some wanted war and others did not, but Sultan Ahmad was not able to dissuade the Mombasa[58] governor from his desires because of the friendship existing between him and the elders of Pate since the time of Fumoluti.

So they gave him troops, but Bwana Mkuu and Fumoluti did not like it because they feared the Mazaru'i who were at that time very powerful. For they thought that they would take Lamu for themselves and then turn round on Pate aided by the Lamu people and so obtain the rulership of the whole Swahili coast.

For at this time the people of Pate had no longer the power they had formerly because of the devastation of their country during the time of Mwana Khadija and Sultan Omari.

(p. 76) So in the year 1227 [1812. *Editor's note*: of the other versions only MS 177 and Heepe-Wassmuss MS M (#33) date the Battle of Shela.] the Mazaru'i together with Pate attacked Lamu.

---

[58] The Mazaru'i were then still holding Mombasa.

They came to Shela and landed, and seized Shela and came to the Hedabu Hill.

When the Lamu people saw that war had entered their country the two factions joined together, and they went forth and fought fiercely, but the troops of Pate and the Mazaru'i were pressing them grievously.

But there was a Lamu man called Mwenyi Shehi Ali who was versed in magic. He made a brass pot and a brass gong and buried them underground. When he had made this charm the Pate people and the Mazaru'i were driven back and utterly overcome.

So they ran away and came to the shore there at Shela, and they there found that their vessels had been stranded by the ebbing tide, so very many people were killed.[59]

So they went to Ntayu and made a *zeriba* there, and of those who were left some held out there and some in their stranded ships. So those who remained fought till their vessels floated and they returned to Pate.

Now those that were killed were very many people. It is narrated that it came to pass that forty men bearing one name[60] were killed.[61]

---

[59] Their bones may still be seen on Shela Hill.

[60] Meaning that among the dead there were forty Sa'ids or Muhammads or some other name.

[61] An old inhabitant of Shela, aged 104 (Muhammadan years), named Bwana Bakari, has given me the following details of the Shela war, which occurred when he was seven years old: -"The Mazaru'i, who were friends with the people of Siu and Pate and the Watikuu, sent word to Lamu that they were coming to attack them. They came in *dhows*, and passing by Lamu went to Siu and Pate to obtain people to help them. They then returned to attack Lamu, bringing with them witchcraft in the shape of one dog and one chicken. Directly they arrived some people came off the boats to sacrifice the dog and chicken on the beach, so as to make favourable medicine for their attack.

"The wise men of Amu made counter witchcraft, and dispatched two men, Bishale (p.77) So afterwards there was a great mourning at Pate, and the Mazaru'i returned to Mombasa and there held a mourning.

In the year 1229 [1813-4. *Editor's note*: this date differs from that given in other versions.] Sultan Ahmad died.

So Sultan Fumoluti Kipunga reigned, and the people of Pate rejoiced exceedingly to think that it was Bwana Fumomadi's son who reigned. They thought that he would be as fortunate as his father, and that their power would return to them as formerly. So they requested him to take vengeance on the Amu people for the Shela war.

So Sultan Fumoluti made ready on the mainland soldiers from the Watikuu from Siu and Ozi, and he made every warlike preparation.

Now after the Shela fight, although they were victorious, the Amu people mistrusted Pate because the island was near them, and they governed the same mainland, and moreover, Pate was an old kingdom.

Haji and Nyebuyu Faki, to kill the witchdoctors who had brought the dog and chicken ashore. They shot them with their matchlocks, which nullified their witchcraft, and also the Amu witchcraft paralysed the enemy so that they could not fight.

"All those who were on the shore were killed, and the remainder went off in their vessels. They were armed with spears, bows, matchlocks, and swords.

"After this they sailed round to the south, entering the creek behind Lamu by the Mlango wa kiungani, and landed on the west of the island. Here they cut down a number of cocoa-nut palms and built a *zeriba*."

My informant thought this a most heinous crime. They were surrounded in this *zeriba* by the islanders of Lamu and were not able to go outside it.

"After a few days here they re-embarked and returned home without further fighting. "The Mazaru'i then retaliated on the Amu people by catching any man they could find on the trading ships passing down the coast and executing him at Mombasa, each execution being celebrated by the firing of a cannon."

What is supposed to have really happened is that the invading forces landed in a muddy part of the shore, and that their progress was impeded by deep mud. Then they charged up the steep sand dunes of Shela, and what with the mud and the sand they arrived at the top scattered and blown, and were killed in detail, while the remainder fled and then found that some of their ships had stranded.

So because of this fear they sent to Maskat to get help from the Arabs of the Busa'idi dynasty.[62] ||

(p. 78) Now at that time there was at Maskat, Sa'id, son of Sultan,[63] and he was the first of the Busa'ids who reigned here on the Swahili coast.

Before this his father Sultan had already been to Zanzibar as far back as the time of Bwana Fumomadi. He who first came was Sa'id, Sultan's elder brother.

Now he had two nicknames; the first was Wadishah[64] and the second Hubub al Ghabshah.[65]

It was he who got a footing in Zanzibar by making friends with the people. He was the first governor of Zanzibar, and this was the beginning of the taking of the island after Sultan put in an officer there called Johar.

Now the people of Lamu, when they went to Maskat, said to Sa'id, "Come and take our country that you may resist for us the counsels of Pate and the Mazaru'i."

So he came and they gave him the country, and he put a governor there and soldiers in the fort.

When Hamed bin Sa'id died his eldest son Sa'id became Imam. Sa'id died, and the second son of Hamed, called Sultan, reigned. In the year 1200

---

[62] For origin of the Abusa'id dynasty (generally called Busa'idi on the coast), see p. 59.

[63] This was Sultan, brother of Sa'id, and son of Hamed bin Sa'id the first Busa'id Imam, referred to on p. 60.

[64] *Wadi shah* (or *Walad ishah*)= goat's son, because his mother died when he was a baby, and he was suckled by a goat.

[65] *Hubub al Ghabshah* = the tempest of dawn, so called as it was his practice in war to fall on his enemies before or at dawn.

(Hejra) [1785-6] Sultan's son Sa'id was born, and twelve years later Sultan died.

As Sa'id was too young to reign his uncle Badr bin Sef, was put in to act as regent. After two years' time Sa'id thought that his uncle wanted to get the throne himself. One day the boy (p. 79) Sa'id wept, and his uncle Badr seeing him called him a woman. This angered the young Sa'id and he killed his uncle with a sword. Another story says that he seized Badr's dagger from his waist and stabbed him with it. [*Editor's note*: for an eyewitness record of Sa'id's early years see Vincenzo Maurizi, *History of Seyd Said, Sultan of Oman*, with a new introduction by Robin Bidwell (New York: Oleander Press, 1984).]

This was the beginning of the Arabs taking Lamu and the reason that the Pate chief lost Lamu for ever.

When Pate and the Mazaru'i saw that Busa'idi had come to the coast they still further strengthened their union, for they thought, "This is a new power, and it were better that each of us take care not to lose his kingdom, and it will not do to make war again."

Now after this Sa'id said to the Arab of Mombasa, "This fort belongs to me. Take my soldiers and my flag and place them in the fort and you yourself remain there as my governor."

The Mazaru'i did not agree to this and Sa'id then said to him, "I have a document of your father's which he wrote for my father, Sultan bin al Imam proving that the fort was his."

Now the origin of this document was this: —

Those Mazaru'i, as has been narrated, first came to the fort by order of the Imam Sef of Maskat, a Yorubi Sultan. They then held the fort in the name of the Imam.

Then when the Yorubi Imam was killed by his subjects, because he was a bad man, Hamed, governor of Sahari, became the first Busa'id ruler of Maskat.

When he became ruler of Maskat he sent a letter to the Mazaru'i desiring them to come to Maskat and appear before him and give him their allegiance.

The Mazaru'i answered him, saying, "You were sent to govern the Sahari, and we were sent to govern here at Mombasa. Both of us were then governors under one ruler. Today you have seized Maskat and possessed yourself of its rulership. Leave us then here on the coast and do not worry us. We are both Arabs so we will be as friends, but do not ask us to become subject to you."

When the Imam received the answer of the Mazaru'i he had no leisure to deal with them, having the whole of the Oman to (p. 80) conquer, and so they remained having no one in authority over them.

Till in the time of Sultan bin al Imamu[66] when he came to Zanzibar he passed Mombasa, landed suddenly and walked straight into the fort.

Arriving there he found the gate open, and the doorkeeper seeing him and his men thought that they were trading Arabs who had come down with the monsoon.

So Sultan entered the fort without the knowledge of the governor till he suddenly appeared at his levée, and he had but few soldiers present.

---

[66] *Sultan bin al Imamu* = Sultan son of the Imam (*Imamu* = Swahili for Imam). He was Sultan bin Hamed, properly speaking.

Now the governor, called Ali, recongized Sultan bin al Imam when he saw him and rose from his seat and showed him great respect.

When Sultan had seated himself he asked the governor, "Whose is this fort?"

He replied, "It is yours."

Then Sultan said, "Give me a certificate to that effect."

So he gave him a document written with his own hand to the effect that he held the fort for Sultan.

Sultan then arose and took leave of him and returned to the shore accompanied by the governor. Then he took from his waist his gold-hilted dagger and presented it to the governor of Mombasa.

Soon after he had departed the Mazaru'i returned to the fort and when they heard what had happened, they blamed their relation, asking him why he had given to Sultan a document stating that the fort was his.

He replied, "I had no alternative, for he came in here suddenly with many soldiers and you were far away. I perceived that if I did not give him the document he was able to seize the fort for himself, barricade the door and prevent you from entering.

"For that reason I gave him a piece of paper so as to avoid the evil of that hour.

(p. 81) "If they come again wanting to take the fort, we are grown-up men and each man has his weapons."

Now when Sa'id bin Sultan claimed the fort from the governor who was at this time Ali's son, the governor replied, "The fort is not yours."

Sa'id answered him, "I have a document signed by your father which he gave to my father saying that the fort was his."

Now Sa'id left Maskat to go to fight with the Mazaru'i, and he stormed the fort three times and after much trouble took it. Then the Mazaru'i complained to the white man at Bombay, and the white man demanded of Sa'id why he had robbed them of their fort.

Then Sa'id produced the document and showed it to the white man, so the Mazaru'i did not win their case.

Now this is the story of the fort, and the remainder will be related, each matter in its place.

Now at that time Sa'id first sent a hundred Sudanese and a governor called Muhammad bin Nasir, and it came about that he took over the country of Lamu.

In the year 1233 [1817-8] the Lamu people seized one of the Nabahans called Fumoluti wa Bayae and wanted to make him their ruler. He was a youth of Amu, for his mother was a Lamu woman, but some of the Lamu people did not want him and the Pate people did not care to be governed by him because of his Lamu birth.

Subsequently the people of Lamu poisoned him.

When the news of this reached Pate, his aunt conducted the mourning and made the following little rhyme as a warning to the Pate people:

Old Swahili	*Modern Swahili*
Mwamu mwofu	Mwamu mnyofu
Thongo ni alifu	Matata ni alifu
Hoyo mpotofu	Mwamu mwovu
Uya kaa iye?	Ataketije?

"A good Lamu man has a thousand wiles,
So a bad Lamu man, what will he be like?"

For this reason people even now say if a man enter into any (p. 82) destiny with a Lamu man, "Do not be guided by a Lamu man, for has it not been said, 'A good Lamu man', etc."?

In the year 1230 [1814-5] the Mazaru'i governor had come to Pate because he had received tidings that Sultan Fumoluti Kipunga was very ill.

So he came to await an opportunity to seize the country, but the Pate people suspected his reasons for coming.

Fumoluti's brothers came to Lamu to Sa'id's governor to make friends with him. They agreed with him that they should keep Pate, but that they must turn the Mazaru'i out of Pate. After they had made a compact with him they returned to Pate asking him to follow them.

The people of Lamu sent to tell Sultan Fumoluti that his brothers Bwana Sheikh and Bwana Ahmad had made an agreement with the governor of Lamu.

Then they went to the governor and told him that Bwana Sheikh and his brother were deceiving him and that each in reality wanted the throne of Pate for himself. Therefore it was necessary to seize them by stratagem and to imprison them.

Now at this time had just arrived as Sa'id's governor in Lamu a certain one Hamad Maftaha. He sent a letter to Pate and invited Bwana Hamad, one of Fumoluti's brothers, over to Lamu. When Hamad had arrived the governor without telling him went over to Pate.

Now at that time the Sultan of Pate was very ill.

When he heard that Hamad Maftaha had arrived, he told his people to tie his turban for him and to give him his sword and put him on the throne.

Then he posted his brothers and *wazirs* and soldiers round him and said, "Let Hamad Maftaha come into the reception room."

So he came in and Sultan Fumoluti was not able to rise to him.

Hamad Maftaha, when he had looked upon Sultan Fumoluti, realized that he was very ill and would shortly die.

He did not stop long, but took leave, saying, "I will return to Lamu and come back again when you are better that we may make plans."

(p. 83) When Hamad Maftaha had gone out Sultan Fumoluti Kipunga said to his brothers, "Do not accompany him out of the town; stop at the gate, for this Arab's face shows the evil which is in his heart."

Hamad Maftaha, when he reached the gate, said to Bwana Sheikh, "I want a private word with you and Bwana Mkuu. Here is the gateway, there is no privacy. Let us go to my boat, and stop your soldiers from following."

Now at that time the tide was ebbing and his boat was on the water far away.

So they left their soldiers in the mangrove swamp, and they entered the boat.

When they had got in Hamad Maftaha ordered his solders and fishermen to row away quickly, and so he took them both to Lamu, saying that it was the command of Sa'id.

When he arrived at Lamu he took Bwana Hamad who was there and these two and imprisoned them all three.

There behind the soldiers of Pate saw their masters being taken away, and were unable to do anything, for the tide had ebbed.[67]

They returned to the town and told the tidings to Sultan Fumoluti, who said, "I told them not to accompany the Arab to the shore, but they did not follow my advice, so I have now no further advice to give."

Now at that time there was trouble on the Lamu mainland between Lamu and Pate, so that people were unable to cultivate because of fighting.

On account of this trouble the Lamu people went to Hamad Maftaha and asked him to release the prisoners to save further trouble, saying, "It were better that you ingratiate yourself slowly with the people of Pate until, when you have a hold on them, you will be able to get their country."

He replied, "They must each give me a thousand dollars ransom." The Lamu people informed Sultan Fumoluti, and he sent 3,000 dollars [*Editor's note*: these are Maria Theresa thalers.] as the ransom of the three. When (p. 84) the money arrived Bwana Hamad had already died in the prison, so he took the money and released the other two who were alive, Bwana Sheikh and Bwana Mkuu.

Now during all these events the Mazaru'i governor of Mombasa had been present at Pate with 500 soldiers.

In the year 1233 [1817-8. *Editor's note*: this date differs from that given in other versions.] Sultan Fumoluti Kipunga died. When he died all the people of Pate assembled to bury him.

After the burial they went to Bwana Mkuu to take counsel about the man to reign.

---

[67] When the tide ebbs it leaves an expanse of mud on which the boats are usually left stranded.

Now at that time the people of Pate had no power; they were unable to follow any counsels except those that the Mazaru'i wished.

When they went to Bwana Mkuu for advice, he said to them, "Go and call the Mazaru'i Liwali Hamed that we may arrange with him as to who should succeed." When Liwali Hamed arrived he said to them, "Whom do you yourselves want?" They said, "We want Bwana Sheikh, son of Bwana Fumomadi."

Liwali Hamed said, "He will not do do. Fumoluti bin Sheikh must reign."

The reason for this was that he was a friend of the Mazaru'i, and so the Liwali thought that by putting him on the throne he would be able to take over the country before Busa'id got it.

All the people of Pate who were present, the Nabahans and the great men, said, "We do not agree to Fumoluti reigning."

The Mazaru'i said, "And I do not want Bwana Sheikh to reign."

Now at that time Bwana Mkuu was the chief elder of Pate, and there was no man like him in any matter. He said, "Be silent, do not make a noise in my vestibule before people." When they were silent he said to them, "Follow the counsel of the Liwali Hamed, it is that with which I am in favour myself."

They answered him, "If you wish it we will have it so, for you are our father."

So at that time at nine o'clock they made Fumoluti bin Sheikh the Sultan.

When Fumoluti and the Liwali had gone Bwana Mkuu said (p. 85) to the people of Pate and the Nabahans, "I did not want us to fight just now here, for there is no use in coming to an agreement and commencing it by fighting.

"But now I am at one with you. I do not want Fumoluti; the Sultan is Bwana Sheikh. Take him and escort him to the palace and place over him many soldiers, seize the city gates and in every big house put soldiers. Munitions of war are ready here; take them. I will now write to Liwali Hamed and tell him that I will give him a respite of six hours from now, but before the six hours have passed he and Fumoluti must leave the country. Failing this that we shall fight them."

When he had received the letter Liwali Hamed said to Fumoluti bin Sheikh, "What shall we do now?"

He said, "My advice is that we go out, for we are not able to remain here; I have no munitions nor provisions and your country is Mombasa which is far away and Sa'id's Liwali is at Lamu.

"These Pate people, when they have defeated us, will call in the Arabs from Lamu who will seize you at once. It is best that we go forth to Siu to Bwana Mataka."

Now at that time Bwana Mataka was the Sheikh at Siu, and he was like a Sultan.

So in the evening they asked for leave to go out and the Siu gate was opened for them, and they went to Bwana Mataka at Siu.

Sheikh Mataka said to them, "What is your plan?"

The Liwali said, "I have come to you together with your Sultan Fumoluti. We have been turned out of Pate and have come to ask your advice."

He answered, "I have no advice; I am not able to keep you because the people of Pate have made an agreement with Busa'id.

"He will send Arabs from Lamu tomorrow with munitions of war and they will join forces with the people of Pate and the Bajuns.

"I am by myself and your country is far away.

"Here are no munitions, neither is there food for your soldiers. (p. 86) How can we fight them? My advice then is, stay and rest for three days, and after that I will ship you and Sultan Fumoluti and land you on the mainland and you must go overland to Mombasa. When you have arrived at Mombasa, if you get powerful enough come again that we may fight."

Now at that time at Pate and Siu there was a great famine; millet cost a dollar for three *kata*![68] For this reason the Mombasa Liwali went away overland and returned to Mombasa. After that the Pate people put Sultan Bwana Sheikh on the throne, and he made friends with the Maskat Arabs and Sa'id, who put 500 soldiers into Pate, Mazindigali and Beluchis. After that Sa'id went to Pemba and there fought the Mombasa Liwali Hamed together with Fumoluti bin Sheikh. At that time the chief Liwali of the Mazaru'i was Abdallah, Hamed's brother.

Hamed was at Pemba with Fumoluti's brother, called Bwana Madi wa Sheikh.

Sa'id's leader in war, Ameer Hamad, went and fought them at Pemba and overcame them completely and captured their food, water and fortifications while they were left in their strongholds only, and they were unable to get food and water.

Liwali Hamed, when he suffered these privations, asked for and was

---

[68] *Kata*, a measure of 4 old *vibaba*. One *kibaba* equals 1 1/2 lb. grain nowadays. The old *kibaba*, however, is said to equal 1 1/2 modern ones.

granted peace by the Ameer Hamad on condition that they should be shipped to Mombasa and that he should there entreat his brother Liwali Abdallah to enter Sa'id's allegiance.

They made an agreement after this manner: —

Bwana Madi wa Sheikh said to Hamed, "These Arabs, when they have embarked us on our vessels, will make us captive and send us to Sa'id at Maskat. Now we are great men and Sultans; to be made captive is a disgrace. It were better that we fight that we may once and for all die or conquer."

This was Bwana Madi's advice.

Liwali Hamed said, "How shall we fight when we have no food or water? We have no strength to hold our weapons; it will not do to fight. Wait till we obtain water and food. When (p. 87) they take us on their ships you and I must get on board the same boat.

"When we have quite recovered our strength we will fight on board the vessels, and we will get their property and their vessels and take them to Mombasa."

That was Liwali Hamed's advice and they agreed to do this. So Ameer Hamad embarked them on his ships, they and 700 men, after having given them food and water sufficient for them and over and above.

When they had embarked Bwana Madi wa Sheikh said to the Liwali, "Come on, we have eaten and we have had water. Now we have strength to fight. Let us carry out our agreement."

Liwali Hamed said, "It will not do; we are Arabs and we have given our promise to the ameer, to break it will be a great disgrace. Even to our children and grandchildren, its disgrace will reach them."

Bwana Madi wa Sheikh said to him, "There is no disgrace greater than that 700 able-bodied men with their arms should be captured. So if your need was first of all food and water because you lacked strength, now you have got both food and water. You are afraid, you are not able to die here, you would rather suffer the disgrace of being captured."

Liwali Hamed answered him, "A grown-up man is he who looks to today and tomorrow.[69] If we die here today what good have we done? We shall but please our enemies and Sa'id still remains at Maskat. These are his soldiers, and if these die he will send others. You are a fool. I am not afraid, but for what reason must we lose our lives?"

Bwana Madi answered, "You are afraid. For me there is no disgrace, for my home is not here. I am a stranger. The great disgrace is yours; for me it does not matter."

So they went with the ameer, they and their 700 men to Mombasa.

(p. 88) He landed them on the beach with their property intact, and he himself remained in his ship to await the answer of the agreement he had made with Hamed.

Now when Hamed went to see his elder brother he got no opportunity of persuading him to enter Sa'id's service, for he received from his brother very bad words because he had consented to become a captive.

Afterwards Ameer Hamad, when he heard that Hamed had got nothing out of his brother, knew that it was not his fault, and that he had not deceived him.

So he went off to Maskat.

---

[69] A Swahili proverb: 'today and tomorrow' are 'the present and the future', meaning that he looks far ahead and does not let the exigencies of the hour warp his judgment.

After that Liwali Abdallah died and his brother Hamed made a friendly peace with Sa'id.

Later, in the year 1236 [1820-1. *Editor's note*: this date differs from that given in other versions.], the Pate people made an agreement with Sa'id and they removed Bwana Sheikh from the throne.

At the instance of Sa'id they then put Sultan Bwana Wazir, son of Bwana Tamu, on the throne. He remained three years, after which the Pate people wanted Bwana Sheikh, and so they removed Bwana Wazir and Bwana Sheikh returned.

After this Bwana Wazir wanted Sa'id to send him soldiers, whose wages he was to pay himself, so that he might regain his kingdom.

So in the year 1240 [1824-5. *Editor's note*: this date does not appear in other versions.] Sa'id sent them, and Bwana Sheikh was ejected and Bwana Wazir returned.

While Bwana Wazir was reigning Liwali Hamed of Mombasa gave Sultan Fumoluti soldiers and money and he returned to Siu.

So he came to fight with Bwana Wazir who had a treaty with Sa'id while Fumoluti was in agreement with the Mazaru'i and Bwana Mataka of Siu.

So they fought together, and it was in this campaign that Ameer Hamad first came to fight on the Swahili coast.

Sultan Fumoluti was defeated, and he and Bwana Mataka left the town and went to Kang'ee and Deloo on the mainland.

They remained there while Bwana Wazir sent Arabs to Siu and they seized the town of Siu and broke the city wall.

(p. 89) Afterwards in the year 1242 [1826-7] Bwana Mataka and Fumoluti returned to Siu. Then they fought the Arabs and overcame them and they built another wall.

Now at that time a great famine arose at Pate, and Sultan Fumoluti said to Ali Koti, a great poet, "I want to send a load of millet to Pate and you must compose verses dividing this one load amongst all the people of Pate not leaving out one."

So Ali Koti composed the verses of "the load"[70] and one load of millet was left secretly by night outside the wall of Pate bearing these verses.

Sultan Fumoluti stayed at Siu and fought for three years, after which he died.

Bwana Wazir and Bwana Mataka then combined and submitted to Sa'id, but it was not true allegiance.

Later Bwana Wazir killed Bwana Mkuu. Then Bwana Mkuu's three heirs, Bwana Simba, his son, Bwana Fumobakari, son of Bwana Sheikh, and Bwana Kitini, son of Bwana Hamad, combined and killed Bwana Wazir.

Then Bwana Fumobakari bin Sheikh took the kingdom, helped by the other two heirs and the elders of Pate.

He became very powerful and turned the Arabs out of Pate, Siu and Faza, even as far as Tula.

The Arabs, however, remained at Amu.

Now in the year 1245 [1829-30] Sa'id took troops and fought with the Mazaru'i until he drove them out of Mombasa fort. He put his soldiers in the fort, while some of the Mazaru'i went to found Takaungu, and others with the Liwali lived in the town of Mombasa.

These Mazaru'i who stayed in Mombasa made a plan in conjunction

---

[70] I have this poem, which mocks at the starving people of Pate.

with the people of Mombasa and regained their fort, about which a little story is narrated. There was a Pate man of the Abdisalam, called Muhammad bin Nasir, who intended to go at this time to see Sa'id bin Sultan at Zanzibar.

(p. 90) He passed by way of Mombasa and there he went to the levée of the Mazaru'i Liwali, whom he found sitting in audience, he and all his kin.

When Muhammad bin Nasir had entered the audience chamber, the Liwali paid him respect, and then sat down. He then stood up his sword and rested his head on its hilt as he sat. Then he raised his head and sighed.

When he sighed all the Mazaru'i who were present drummed on their swords with their fingers.

Afterwards Muhammad bin Nasir went to Zanzibar and there saw Sa'id. Sa'id asked him, "Did you pass Mombasa?" He replied, "I passed it."

"What news have you from there?"

So he said to him, "The Mombasa news is that the Mazaru'i have retaken their fort."

Sa'id was very angry and said to him, "Why do you speak falsely, for there are no tidings of such an event?"

He replied, "When I passed Mombasa the fort was occupied by your soldiers and the Mazaru'i were in the town." Sa'id then said, "Why do you say that they have taken the fort?"

Muhammad answered, "I went to their levée and saw the Liwali put his head on his sword, then he raised it and sighed.

All his kin then drummed on their swords. It was for that reason that I told you that they had retaken their fort."

Sa'id asked, " What is the meaning of it?"

Muhammad answered, "The meaning is this. The Liwali rested his head on his sword and then sighed; that sigh was from the bitterness of thinking about the fort and as much as said to his kin, 'Oh! our fort has been lost to us.' They answered him and beat their swords, meaning, 'We will retake it with these swords we have here.' "

"When they all beat together I perceived them as if they were hammering on the fort and had already entered inside.

"It was then that I said to you that the Mazaru'i had retaken their fort."

(p. 91) Sa'id said to him, "Stay here; you have not permission to depart. If your words do not come to pass, I will know you for a mannerless person and will then teach you manners.

"If they come to pass, I will know that your counsel is that of a man of great perception."

After three days came the news that the Mazaru'i had retaken their fort, so Sa'id called Muhammad bin Nasir and gave him money and great honors.

He then sent him to Pate to Sultan Fumobakari to ask him to make a treaty with him to which he agreed.

From that time Sa'id blockaded the fort till after many years he captured it in the year 1252 [1836-7], and he has been in possession of the fort ever since.[71]

Some of the Mazaru'i ran away, but of the great men he seized twenty-five and sent them to Jaalani.

Now a little before this, trouble had arisen between Sa'id and the chief of Pate. Sa'id sent his son Khalid with an expedition, but he was unable to

---

[71] Mombasa and the coastline are leased by us from the Sultan of Zanzibar. [*Editor's note:* Stigand, writing in 1908, refers to the British Protectorate.]

take Pate, so he left.

Next year Sa'id came himself with his Liwali Muhammad bin Nasir,[72] who was the leader of his troops.

He went to Kiwakani in Rasini harbour and he landed troops there.

On the first day they were utterly defeated and Muhammad bin Nasir was driven away.

At that time the Bajuns strung a song:

> "Muhammad wa Nasir, disembark and fetch your
> Mother's dowry in a closed basket. Fumobakari
> Is not your brother, he was not born with you."[73]

After that Muhammad bin Nasir landed and he himself was killed and his troops utterly defeated.

Then Sa'id made peace with Sultan Fumobakari by the help of the great men of Lamu.

(p. 92) So peace was made, but Sa'id was not allowed to garrison Pate.

After that the Amu people arranged that Sa'id should pay some money to Fumobakari, and that he should then become Sa'id's vassal. He then quarrelled with his brother Bwana Kitini; each one wanted the kingdom by reason of Sa'id's intrigue and the plans of the Amu people.

Sultan Fumobakari lived at Pate and his brother lived at Siu, and they

---

[72] Not the man of this name in the story above.

[73] 'Closed basket', meaning that he did not know what fate was in store for him. The Bajuns were friendly to Fumobakari, Sultan of Pate.

fought together.

One year later Sultan Fumobakari seized his brother Bwana Kitini and killed him.

For this reason the people of Pate hated him, and so the Amu people said to Fumobakari, "It were better that you go to Sa'id at Zanzibar for people here have intrigued against you." So he went to Zanzibar.

The Amu people then said to Sa'id, "Seize him and then you will have got possession of the whole Swahili coast. So Sa'id seized and imprisoned him.

When the Pate people heard this they took Bwana Madi, son of Sheikh, and put him on the throne in the year 1259 [1843. *Editor's note*: the other versions do not date Bwana Madi's ascension.].

The Pate people were in agreement with Sheikh Mataka of Siu but the Bajuns were on Sa'id's side.

When Sa'id heard that Sultan Ahmad[74] was on the throne of Pate and was allied to Sheikh Mataka he released Sultan Fumobakari and gave him money.

Then Sa'id and Fumobakari, together with the Amu people, made war on Siu and Pate. Sa'id was defeated,[75] and he came again and was again defeated.

Again he came, and Sa'id himself disembarked at Rasini, he and Ameer

---

[74] Bwana Madi was called Sultan Ahmadi (Ahmad) when he came to the throne.

[75] During one of these expeditions, however, he built a fort at Siu, and Bwana Mataka bin Mbaruk fled to the mainland. Subsequently Mataka returned and ejected Sa'id's soldiers from the fort.

Hamad with all his wazirs and great men.

He went to a place called Kijangwa cha mpunga, and there he sat on his shield while he sent his troops to Siu. He instructed Ameer Hamad to build a *zeriba* at every hundred paces.

(p. 93) Ameer Hamad did not follow Sa'id's instructions for when he met the Siu people he defeated them and pursued them hotly. They entered the town and shut the gates, so Ameer Hamad seized *dhows*, turned them over and made them into forts, firing at the town so that they were not able to open the city gates again.

Then the people of Siu thought that their country would be captured.

At that time there was a Sherif at Siu called Mweniy Sa'id Mohothar. The people went to him to ask his advice as to whether they should abandon the country of Siu. He replied, "Wait, I will ask the advice of my namesake." So he called a man and told him to go to the sepulchre of his grandfather, who was also called Sherif Mwenyi Sa'id, and say, "Your namesake sends greetings, and asks must he go forth?"

So he asked after this manner, and a voice answered, "He must not go forth."

So the Sherif told the people of Siu not to leave the country.

When they heard this news they opened the rear gate and two captains went out; their names were Bwana Madi bin Omar and Bwana Madi, nicknamed Ngoma. Bwana Madi Ngoma inclined towards the side of the artillerymen, and the other captain went a different way and met Ameer Hamad in the way with only seventy men.

When he saw him he recognized him, fell upon him and killed him and all his soldiers.

The captain, Bwana Madi Ngoma, went and fought the artillerymen, and killed their chief and took the guns. All the soldiers who were left fled, and those in the *dhows* heard that Ameer Hamad had been killed, and so they ran into the mangroves and died in the mud.

The Siu women when they went for firewood saw them and struck them with axes.

When Sa'id heard of the death of the Ameer and defeat of his troops he arose and got into a boat and went off to his ship, and he spoke to no one till he reached Manda.

(p. 94) The Amu people came to see him, but he did not receive them until the next day.

Afterwards he returned to Maskat and did not come back till his last journey, when he died at sea and was landed at Zanzibar and was buried. He was then seventy-three years old, and had reigned for fifty-eight years. [*Editor's note*: Sayyid Sa'id's death occurred on 19 October 1856.]

His son Sayid Majid reigned on the coast, while at Maskat his son Sayid Thuen reigned.

Sayid Majid fought with his brother Sayid Barghash for Zanzibar, and Barghash was defeated and went to Bombay.

Sayid Thuen then prepared an expedition against his brother Majid, but when he reached Ras al Had the white man of Bombay made him return to Maskat. [*Editor's note*: reference to the British representative at Bombay.]

It was then agreed that Sayid Thuen should rule at Maskat and Sayid Majid should reign at Zanzibar and pay a yearly tribute of 60,000 dollars.

About that time Sheikh Mataka died, and his son Bakari bin Sheikh reigned.

He agreed with Majid who gave him troops with which to fight Sultan Ahmad of Pate.

The first time he fought was at Wangi, and he was defeated.

The second fight was at Siu, and Bakari was seized and taken to Pate and killed.

After he had been killed his brother Mwali Muhammad bin Sheikh seized the throne. He allied himself to Sayid Majid and Sultan Fumobakari, and fought with Sultan Ahmad.

When he heard that Fumobakari had come to Rasini with soldiers of Majid and with the Liwali Sefu Muru, Sultan Ahmad wanted to throw a garrison into Siu. So he set out from Pate to seize Siu before these soldiers had yet arrived.

He got to a palace called Mashimoni where he met Muhammad bin Sheikh of Siu, and in a fight a bullet hit him in the hip and a spear in the heel. He was taken back to Pate, and Sultan Fumobakari came to Siu with Sayid Majid's soldiers. They then went and seized Pate, but at midday they were turned out again.

(p. 95) After this Sultan Ahmad went to Ozi where he stayed till he died.

Then Sayid Majid placed soldiers in Siu and it remained subject to him.

After that trouble arose between the people of Siu and Pate and they fought together twice.

The people of Siu came with the intention of seizing the country of Pate and stealing all the women and children captive and killing the grown-up men.

The first time they came by way of the Siu gate and were defeated, and their leader Bwana Dumia was shot. They fled and came again a second time by the Shindakasi gate, and their leader Maulana, son of Ishakulu, was killed. So they were defeated and utterly routed, many being killed.

Even today their bones and heads are to be seen at Gomeni.

At that time there was no Sultan at Pate; Fumobakari was at Lamu.

The elders of the country were three in number. Bwana Simba, Bwana Rehema and Bwana Nasiri. These were those who conducted the war and Allah helped them.

When Sheikh Muhammad of Siu saw that his expedition was routed he made peace with Pate.

Then he said to Bwana Simba[76] (his name was Muhammad bin Bwana Mkuu), "I want you to reign at Pate," for Bwana Simba was at that time a great man in Pate, like a Sultan.

He answered, "I do not wish to reign."

Then Sheikh Muhammad said, "Give me another Sultan then from amongst your children."

So he said to him, "Go and take my namesake, Sultan Ahmad Simba."

Now at that time Sultan Ahmad had already died at Ozi, near Kao, and his brother's son had taken his place and was called Sultan Ahmad Simba.

(p. 96) In the year 1280 [1863-4. *Editor's note*: other versions do not date Simba's ascension.] Sheikh Muhammad sent for Sultan Simba and had him brought to Pate.

Now Muhammad, son of Bwana Mataka, broke up Sayid Majid's fort

---

[76] This was his nickname, meaning 'lion'. My informant says that this man made a speciality of ancient history, and used to narrate to him (Bwana Kitini) old stories of traditions for hours at a time. [*Editor's note*: Bwana Simba is formally acknowledged as Bwana Kitini's source for all the extant written versions.]

in Siu. So Sayid Majid came in force and fought Pate and Siu for many days both by sea and land.

He blocked the entrance to Siu harbour so that vessels could not pass in with food.

Afterwards he made peace, and Sheikh Muhammad sent his brother Omar to Sayid Majid's ship to present himself before him. Later Sheikh Muhammad went himself and received pardon.

Sayid Majid said to him in Arabic, "I pardon you for the great offence, *but* breaking the fort is before us a disgraceful thing."

Those who were present recognized that Sayid Majid had not wholly forgiven him or he would not have said "but."

Sultan Ahmad went to Kao and stayed there; afterwards Sheikh Muhammad sent his son Sheikh Mataka to Zanzibar.

Sayid gave him much wealth and sent a letter to his father, saying, "Do not you come to Zanzibar. It will suffice if you stay there at Siu as my vassal."

Sayid's Wazir Bwana Suleiman sent a letter to Sheikh Muhammad, saying, "Come, for the tree does not fall on him who is absent."[77]

So the next year Sheikh Muhammad went to Sayid at Zanzibar taking with him many great men.

Sayid wished to pardon him, but Wazir Suleiman did not agree, saying, "We must seize him and do away with the evil on the coast."

So they seized him together with upwards of thirty of his people and put

---

[77] This, like so many Swahili proverbs, bears a sense quite opposed to that which it would in English. The idea is that the falling tree rains fruit on those near.

them on a ship called the *Africa*, and imprisoned them at Mombasa in the fort.

There he remained till he died.

(p. 97) When his son heard of his capture he fled from Siu and went to live at Mongoni.

After this Sayid Majid sent an order to his Liwali at Lamu, Sa'id Sudi, to seize Sheikh Muhammad's brother Omar at Faza.

Sa'id Sudi was unable to seize Sultan Ahmad at Kao, so he made peace with him and took his cousin Fumobakari and his Wazir, Muhammad bin Hassan, and went with them to Zanzibar and they returned together to Lamu. Then Sayid sent an order to have these two imprisoned, and Sa'id Sudi shut them up.

The Wazir died in prison; some people say that Sa'id Sudi killed him. Fumobakari was afterwards released and lived with Sa'id Sudi and then ran off and went to Witu. For at that time Sultan Ahmad had already founded the town of Witu because of being harrassed by the Arabs.

Sa'id Sudi sent a man called Hamad Usi who made friendship with Sheikh Muhammad's son and had him murdered while he slept.

Then Sa'id Sudi went to fight Sultan Ahmad, going by way of Matomo, but he was defeated and returned to Lamu.

Next year he went by way of Kao and brought war against Sultan Ahmad and defeated him, killing his Wazir Baka Hassan, brother of Muhammad bin Hassan.

So Sultan Ahmad made peace and lived at Witu in allegiance to Sayid Majid.

Now by the year 1282 [1865-6] Sayid Majid had conquered the whole Swahili coast, islands and mainland.

Sa'id Sudi became his chief Liwali, and was as a Sultan ruling from Kismayu to Amu, doing as he pleased.

Now Sultan Ahmad remained in allegiance to Sayid Majid until he died, and then he swore allegiance to his successor Sayid Barghash.[78]

In the year 1297 [1879-80] trouble arose between the people and some bush-dwellers whose village was called Katawa.[79]

(p. 98) The Amu people went to fight them according to their instructions from Sa'id Sudi, but they were completely defeated and many were killed, including Sheikh Omar Wenyikae and Bwana Maka Bereki's son.

These two were the principal Sheikhs of Amu.

So they returned to Amu in abasement and bitterness.

Next year Sa'id Sudi was sent by Barghash to fight Sultan Ahmad at Witu, so as to remove that source of worry.

He was defeated by the Witu people, and he then made peace with Sultan Ahmad.

He then desired of Sultan Ahmad, his cousin, that he might take him with him to Zanzibar and so wipe the shame of defeat from his face.

When they arrived at Zanzibar Sayid Barghash was angry with him and did him no honour, and at first Sa'id Sudi had been a great man even as the Sayid himself.

Next year he put Sa'id Sudi out of office and sent Sa'id bin Hamed to Amu, and Abdallah bin Hamed he put at Malindi.

---

[78] Sayid Majid died in the year 1287 [1870], and Sayid Barghash reigned. The latter visited Makka and also Europe.

[79] This was a colony of Watoro, or runaway slaves. Many villages now found near Witu were founded by Watoro.

He behaved very badly to Sa'id Sudi taking away his property and sending him to Pemba. Afterwards he sent him to Sayid Turki at Maskat. Later Sayid Barghash was ashamed and brought him back and restored part of his property.

When Sayid Khalifa came he gave him back all his property.

The next year Sayid Barghash sent his Liwali, Sa'id bin Hamed, to Witu with a big expedition, saying to him, "Do not return, but break into Witu or die. I will send you more soldiers and munitions of war every day even if I have to sell the turban on my head."

When Sa'id bin Hamed had gone the Germans sent to Sayid Barghash saying, "If you fight Witu we will fight Zanzibar. Recall your troops, do not so much as break the leg of a chicken at Witu."

So the Sayid sent to his Liwali saying, "When you have read this letter return quickly and exercise great caution that you do not destroy anything of the Witu people's property."

(p. 99) Afterwards the Germans came in three ships and Sayid Barghash sent General Mathews and he divided the kingdom. The mainland from Kiwayu to Mkokoni he gave to Witu, while the islands and every place surrounded by creeks became Sayid Barghash's.

At last, in the year 1305, Sayid Barghash died [*Editor's note*: on 27 March, 1888.] and Sayid Khalifa reigned.

Now at this time the kingdom of the Nabahans was flourishing to such an extent that a person might think that it would return to its former greatness. Great disorders occurred in the towns; people were of two factions—one side were subjects of the Sayid and the other sought protection from Sultan Ahmad.

Till in the year 1306 [1888-9] Sultan Ahmad died, and he left his kingdom in the beginning of its aggrandisement. His cousin, Sultan Fumobakari, reigned.

In the year 1308 [1890-1] trouble arose between the Germans and the people of Witu.

There was a German called Küntzell who lived at Witu and taught the soldiers military exercises. There were about thirty who knew their drill, and the Sultan intended giving him many more to teach.

Küntzell went off to Europe and returned with ten Europeans and many tools and instruments for the purpose of clearing the forest and doing other work.

They had agreed with the Sultan to bring these things, but when he saw ten Europeans and many things he grew afraid and thought that eventually, when they had settled there, they would seize his country.

So he refused to let the forest be cut down, and Küntzell quarrelled with him and wanted to put his Europeans with their arms in the town.

Till one day the Sultan robbed them of all their arms by a stratagem!

When Küntzell went and found his comrades with no arms he was very angry and went to look for the Sultan without finding him.

(p. 100) He said to his comrades, "Let us go out." When they went to the gate[80] soldiers stopped them and Küntzell shot two men.

Then the soldiers, without an order from the Sultan, when they saw that two of their friends had fallen, fired on the Europeans.

They killed all the Europeans, but not before Küntzell had hit nine

---

[80] It is said that there was one entrance to the town through a narrow low gate. The Europeans came in one by one, and as each got inside he was robbed of his arms without the others outside being aware of it.

people.

This was the origin of the Witu expedition. Now at Mkunumbi and Ongoni there were white men.

These were killed at the instigation of Bwana Heri Makatwa and Bwana Ali Majesa, the Liwalis of Mkunumbi and Hidiyo.

When the British Government heard the news the consul and admiral came with fifteen ships, and they sent a letter to Sultan Fumobakari, saying, "Come to the ships at Shela; we will judge fairly between you and the Germans, and we will make an advocate for your side and you will be dealt with only according to law and equity."

The Sultan answered, "It is customary with us that if a man reigns he does not undergo judgment any more."

They answered, "Send us one man from amongst your brothers, and Bwana Heri and Bwana Ali Majesa that they may be tried for the white men who died at Witu; there is no case as they began the affray. The other two white men, however, who were killed did not shoot any one first, so it is necessary to judge those Liwalis. The Germans have left these things in our hands for judgment, so send them."

He did not send them, and that was the cause of the Witu expedition.

On the third day they stormed Hidiyo and Mkunumbi, on the tenth day of the sixth month after Ramadhan [*Editor's note*: Rabīʻ al-awwal, the third month of the Islamic year.]. On the eleventh at night the Witu people came to Kipini, so they fought them in the way at a place called Shaka la Simba at half-past twelve at night.

(p. 101) In the morning they went up to Witu and fought from two o'clock till five, and the Witu people slept in Witu and fastened the gates, and the white men slept at a place called Chakamba.

At seven in the morning they came to the town and fought together, and the Witu people were driven away, and the white men seized the town and set fire to it and broke the houses and set fire to the powder and percussion caps for the matchlocks which were stored there.

So the Witu people ran away and entered the bush and went to Jongeni and Pumuani and Katawa.

So the white men stopped in Witu, and in the evening returned to Kipini.

Afterwards they put 200 Sepoys and Sudanese soldiers in Kipini and two officers, one of whom was Mr. Rogers.

After that Sultan Fumobakari died, and after two months his brother Bwana Sheikh sat on the throne.

After three days they made him abdicate and his brother Fumomari sat. He fought with Mr. Rogers twice and made peace again.

After that he swore allegiance to the British Government.

He obtained powder and rifles on the plea that he lived in the same country as the Somalis. Afterwards he hid a supply in the bush, and Bwana Rogers heard of it from some Waboni[81] who took him to it. He then seized Fumobakari and bound him and sent him to the Consul General at Zanzibar. He stayed there till he died suddenly on the day of the bombardment of Zanzibar.

After that, at the advice of Bwana Rogers, the British Government put Omar Madi on the throne in the year 1312 [1894-5].

---

[81] These are a hunting tribe.

He had at one time been one of their soldiers, and he is Sultan of Witu to this day.

At Zanzibar Sayid Khalifa reigned till the year 1307 [1890], and he died, and his brother Sayid Ali reigned till he died in the year 1310 [1893].

(p. 102) Sayid Ali was the Sultan or Zanzibar who first came under British protection.

On his death Hamed bin Thuen reigned; he was the son of Sultan Thuen of Maskat.

In the year 1314 [1896] he died, and Sayid Khalid, son of Sayid Barghash, wanted to reign.

The English fought him and he fled to Dar as Salaam, and Sayid Hamud bin Muhammad reigned.

In the year 1319 [1902] he died, and Sayid Ali reigned, and it is he who is now Sultan of Zanzibar in the year 1326 of the Hejra and 1908 of the Europeans.

A SWAHILI HISTORY OF PATE

AKHBĀR PATE

ALICE WERNER

INTRODUCTION

The following text was transcribed by Alice Werner from a MS given to her in 1911 by A.C. Hollis, at that time Secretary for Native Affairs in the East Africa Protectorate and was published by her in three parts in the *Journal of the African Society*, vol. 14 (1914), pp. 148-61, and 15 (1915), pp. 278-97, 392-413. The publication of the transcript and translation was accompanied by a sketch-map of the Siu Island reproduced as Map 3 on p. xvi of the present book. The black-and-white photos accompanying the journal publication are not included.

Werner understood the Hollis MS to have the same originator as the Stigand version, Muhammad bin Fumo 'Umar al-Nabahani, commonly called Bwana Kitini. She comments: "At least this seems the most natural interpretation of the sentence, *'na hizi tumezonakili kwa Muhammad,'* etc. (The points over the name "Kitini" are somewhat indistinct, and it might be read "Kishini" or "Kisheni" -- in fact I am not sure but that one of the latter forms may have been intended by a careless copyist...)"[1] The copy was reportedly made in 1903 by order of the Lamu *Liwali* (governor) 'Ābid bin Ḥāmid from an autograph. This command is confirmed in some MSS; claims have been made to the effect that Bwana Kitini did the recording.[2] Werner was somewhat skeptical of the true authorship of the MS because it differs significantly from the Stigand version both in dates and the narrative; the discrepancies are carefully noted by her in the footnotes.

---

[1] Werner, *op. cit.*, p. 148.

[2] Jack D. Rollins, *A History of Swahili Prose* (Leiden, Brill, 1983), Part 1, p. 45.

Werner made an attempt to establish a chronological sequence of the rulers of Pate and tabulated three lists which accompany her edition of the *Chronicle*: one based on the Hollis MS (marked *A*), another derived from the Stigand version (marked *B*), and a third (marked *C*) based on a king list compiled by Mr. Reddie who had served as the Provincial Governor of Lamu; his informant was a clerk in the Provincial Commissioner's office named Mshamu bin Kombo. The three lists are not identical; lists *A* and *B* vary from each other slightly and both differ considerably from list *C*. The discrepancy is, in fact, more surprising than it may seem initially since Mshamu bin Kombo was Bwana Kitini's brother and therefore could be expected to provide more or less similar data. Werner' frustration is reflected in her remark: "I have given up the hopeless attempt to harmonize the dates, and have thought it best to present the three lists in a tabular form."[3] These lists appear in Appendix 3 without change. Following Werner's example, a list of the rulers of Maskat,[4] accompanying her translation, appears in Appendix 7.

A few minor corrections have been made to amend obvious typographical errors. Werner alerted the reader to the fact that while the Swahili version cites personal names exactly as they appear in Arabic script, the translation disregards the variations "for the sake of uniformity."[5] The journal edition had selected Muslim dates repeated on margins with notation *A.H.* and the

---

[3] *Ibid.*, p. 149.

[4] Originally from G.P. Badger, *History of the Imâms and Seyyids of Oman, by* Salîl-ibn-Razîk, *from* A.D. 661-1856 (London: Hakluyt Society, 1871). For a recent study of Imamate see J. C. Wilkinson, *The Imamate Tradition of Oman* (Cambridge: University Press, 1987).

[5] Werner, *op. cit.*, p. 150.

Christian equivalent underneath with notation *A.D.*, wherever supplied. The latter have been moved here into the body of the text in brackets. Page numbers are cited in parentheses. Two vertical lines ‖ mark the breaks between sections corresponding to the original journal issues. The text was accompanied by a sketch-map of the Siu (Pate) island, provided for Werner by the *wali* of Faza and Siu ʻAbdallah bin Muhammad, showing placenames in Arabic with English transcription added by Werner. It is reproduced as Map 3 (p. xvi). The footnotes both in the Swahili transcript and in the translation are by Alice Werner. The numbering of footnotes in the journal was inconsistent from issue to issue. New sequential numbers have been assigned.

This author's comments are placed in brackets. Where Werner used the abbreviation of *b.* for *bin*, "son," the full form has been used. Werner's inconsistent use of both *bin* and *son of* in translation has not been adjusted. Although I did not always agree with her rendition of the Swahili into English, no changes were made in the translation. The spelling follows Werner's based on the system of E.W. Taylor. The particulars of the language and Werner's methodology are explained by her in the following remarks quoted below in their entirety from the *Introduction* in the *Journal of the African Society*, 14 (1914), pp. 150-151.

In a few cases it has seemed impossible to make sense, no doubt owing to some corruption in the text; in one or two others obvious emendations have suggested themselves. In either case the doubtful or the substituted word has been enclosed in square brackets. Ordinary brackets indicate words introduced to complete the sense. The translation has been made as literal as possible, for the benefit of learners; but where a phrase is frequently repeated in the same words it has not been thought necessary to give it in full every time.

The MS. is written in the Lamu dialect (Kiamu), though not with invariable consistency. Apart from differences in the vocabulary (which are indicated where they occur), the chief peculiarities are:--

Change of initial l to y--*yeo* = *leo.*

Elision of intervocalic l (sometimes of other letters), carried to a greater extreme than at Mombasa and Zanzibar:--

Kitungu(w)e for *kitungule* = "hare"; *teua* for *chagua* = *chagula* = "choose."

z for *v*, *e.g.*, in the plural of the *ki*-class (*zisu* for *visu*), *zita* for *vita*, &c.

y for *j*: *yua*=*jua*, *kuya*=*kuja*, &c. Where j and i come together, the former is omitted: *mai* for *maji* = "water," *ina* for *jina* = "name."

s for *f*: *sita* = *fita*, *simbo* = *fimbo*,[6] *sikilia* (the simple form *sika* does not seem to be in use) = *fika*.

s for *sh*: *kisa* = *kwisha*, *pisa* = *pisha*.

The older form of the pronoun, *u*-, is often (though not invariably) used instead of *a*- with the third person singular of the verb. The reflexive pronoun is *-i-*, not *-ji-*, and the passive of *pa* = "give" is *powa*, not *pawa* or *pewa*. The old perfect in *-ene* for verbs in *-ana* (*e.g.*, *fuetene* from *fuatana*) occurs a few times in the text, but there is no example of the form with *-ile* suffixed. *Amkua* (elsewhere meaning "to salute") is used for "to call" (*amkuliwao* instead of *aitwae*), *zengea* for *tafuta* = "seek" and *angalia* for *tazama* = "look at."

---

6 *Cf.* Karanga ("Chizwina") *tsimbo*. This language shows some curious correspondence with Swahili, where different words are used in those geographically intermediate.

Akhbar Pate

(p. 152) Mtu[1] alokuya[2] kwanda katika Nabhanî ni Selemân bin Selemân bin Muthafar[3] en-Nabhani, na nduze[4] 'Ali bin Selemân wa[5] Athmân bin Selemân. Aliyokuwa Sultan ni Seleman 'l madhkûr naye alikuwa mfalme Arabuni, akatolewa na'l Ya'arubi, akaya Pate katika (sita mia)[6] sene 600 Hijra kuya kwake; (a)kaoa binti wa mfalme wa Pate, 'l Batawiuna ['l Batawîna]. Na dasturi ya Waswahili wote hata sasa—mtu (a)kikuolea[7] kijana chako, akisa siku

---

[1] In the original *mutu*, مُتُ. This may represent the older pronunciation, but I suspect it was found easier to write the "damma" than the *"sukûn"* which would otherwise have been necessary. Elsewhere, *mufalume*, *muke*, *humupa*, are written, with the vowel-points, for *mfalme*, *mke*, *humpa*. In the transliteration, it has been thought better to keep to the usual Swahili spelling, which represents the pronunciation of the present day.

[2] Kiamu relative: in Zanzibar Swahili aliyekuja. Note the substitution of *y* for *j*.

[3] Written in the MS. مظفر. The name is transliterated by Badger (*Imâms and Seyyids of Oman*) as "Muzhaffar," which is also the form I have noted down as given by Sherif Abdallah at Witu.

[4] Kiamu contraction for *ndugu zake*.

[5] This is not the Swahili possessive particle, but the Arabic conjunction "and." It is occasionally used by this writer instead of the Swahili *na*.

[6] It is quite common to write the date in words as well as figures.

[7] *Olea*, applied form of *oa*, "marry," governing as its direct object the pronoun *-ku-* of the second person singular. The meaning is "if he marries your daughter for" (or "away from") "you", *i.e.*, "takes your daughter away from you and marries her." "If he marries your daughter," would be *akimwoa kijana chako*. *Kijana* is generally used at Lamu instead of *mtoto*, which only occurs as an adjective = "small."

saba'a za arusi,[8] henda[9] kamwangalia babake mke wake, humpa kitu, ndiyo kaida[10] ya jamīī[11] ya Waswahili. Alipokwenda Selemân kumwangalia, kamupisa[12] yeye ufalme. Tangu hapo katawali Selemân bin Selemân 'l madhkur. Kwalina[13] na mui[14] katika matlai ya Pate, huitwa Kitaka; kwalina na mui wa pili (p.154) walikitwa[15] Shanga, katika matlai ya Pate[16], na Faza yaliko na wenyewe 'l Mafâziyûn.[17] Ukaketi ufalme wa Pate na mii hini,[18] Kitaka na Pate;[19] na Manda ina[20] mfalme wake, wa Manda mbali. Na

---

[8] Arabic عرس, usually pronounced and written by Swahilis *harusi*.

[9] For *hu-enda* "is wont to go."

[10] Ar. قاعدة.

[11] Ar. جَامِع.

[12] Causative of *pita* "pass." Mombasa and Zanzibar: *pisha*.

[13] Kiamu for *kulikuwa na*.

[14] Kiamu for *mji*, the full prefix *mu-* being retained and the *j* first changed into *y* and then dropped. In Pokomo and Giryama, the word is *mudzi*.

[15] It is difficult to account for the simultaneous presence of the particles *-li-* and *-ki-*; it may be due to clerical error.

[16] See map [*Editor's note*: Shanga is not shown on map published by Werner (see map 3)]. Shanga, about nine miles from Pate, must not be confused with Shaka, near Kipini.

[17] This looks like an Arab gentile name. At Witu, I was told that "there were Kings of Faza, their clan was called Mafazii." The present Sultan of Witu is descended from them. *Cf.* Stigand, p. 37.

[18] *Hini*, Kiamu for *hii*, as *hunu* for *huu*.

[19] Shanga seems to have been omitted by accident.

[20] Names of towns usually seem to be treated as belonging to the *n-* class.

Seleman (a)kazaa[21] zijana wawili,[22] Muhammad wa[23] Ahmad, kisa akata, sene 625.

Katawali Muhammad bin Seleman, na umri wake myaka ishrîn, na Ahmad mwana wa myaka khamst'ashar. Katawali Muhammad baada ya baba wake, [a]kapijana[24] na watu wa Shanga, [a]kawashinda, kavunda mui. Kisa watu wa Shanga wakaya Pate, na baadhi wakakimbia. Katika hao waliokuya Pate, kabila yao [Kibwana Ndanguu,] wakakimbia, wasiyuikane[25] wamezipokwenda, hata siku nyingi zikipita, ikaya khabari[26] kwa mfalme Muhammad bin Seleman na wawinda,[27] wakamwambia, "wale washindwao tumewaona katika mwitu." (A)kapeeka[25] watu kuwangalia, (wa)kawadirika[28] ndiani mwa mwitu, wamefanya zijumba, wameketi hapo. Wakawatukua, wakaya nao Pate; kisa mfalme kawarudisha papo mahala pao: ndiyo asili ya

---

[21] *Zaa*, as at Zanzibar: in Kimvita (Mombasa) *vyaa*. In this MS. the prefixes *a*-, *i*-, and sometimes *wa*- are usually omitted before *ka*- and *ki*- (no doubt for greater ease in writing). They have not been supplied in brackets after the first paragraph or two, except in cases where their absence is likely to create a difficulty.

[22] In this MS. *kijana* is sometimes treated as one of the *ki*- class, sometimes as of the person-class.

[23] Arabic conjunction.

[24] *Pija*, Kiamu for *piga*. I know no other instance of *j*=*g*.

[25] Kimvita, *wasijulikane*: *y*=*j*, and intervocalic *l* dropped, as in *peeka* (*peka*)=*peleka*. For the subjunctive construction, see Steere's *Handbook*, p. 148.

[26] So written throughout this MS., thought Swahilis usually say *habari*.

[27] The rule that verbal nouns in *a* must be followed by an object (as *mfanya biashara*—see Steere, *Handbook*, p. 230) is not invariable: *mwinda* (not *mwindi*), "hunter," *mgema* (not *mgemi*), "palm-tapper."

[28] Ar. درك, "follow, come up with," sometimes used in the sense of "meet," especially in the reciprocal form (*dirikana*).

Siu. Wakaya na watu wangine Waswahili, wakaketi Siu, kisa wakaya Wafamau, wakawa wakuu wa Siu, katika ta'a ya mfalme wa Pate, siku nyingi.

(p. 156) Sene 650 akafa Sultan Muhammad, katawali nduye, Sultan Ahmad bin Seleman, akaamirisha sana nti ya Pate kwa kutia mashamba na kuwaka majumba, asipije mahali, akafa sene 670. Katawali Ahmad bin Muhammad bin Seleman, akaketi kama siyara[29] ya 'ami[30] yake, katika imara ya mui wa Pate, naye (a)kazaa zijana wangi. Alipokufa katawali kijana chake, Muhammad bin Ahmad bin Muhammad bin Seleman, akaketi kafutahi[31] mii ya Sawahili, Faza[32] na Manda, kwa zita zingi, katika nti ya Paza. Wa amma Manda walingia kwa zita[33] za hila, wakaivunda kabisa, na watu wangine kawaeta[34] Pate, na baadhi wakakimbia, wakenda kulla mahali, wakaya Shela[35] na Malindi na mii mingine. Waliokwenda Shela wakangia katika

---

[29] Arabic, "conduct," "disposition"; *tabia* is more generally used in Swahili.

[30] Ar. عَم "paternal uncle," sometimes transliterated as *amu*. Usually, in Swahili, *baba mkubwa* (if the father's elder brother), or *baba mdogo* (if the younger.) The maternal uncle is *mjomba*.

[31] *Cf.* Ar. فتح "victory." [*Editor's note*: more properly, "conquest."]

[32] In this MS. this town is usually called "Faza," though we sometimes find "Paza," which, according to Captain Stigand (*op. cit.*, p. 34), is the original form. "Faza" would represent the Arab pronunciation, there being no *p* in Arabic. It is now, quite as often, called Rasini.

[33] *Zita*, Kiamu for *vita*.

[34] *Eta*, for *leta*.

[35] Shela, near Lamu. For its foundation, see *Stigand*, pp. 156-158. (The name is there said to be derived from the Portuguese "*Chela*," but there is no such word.)

himaya[36] ya watu wa Lamu. Mfalme kawataka kwa watu wa Lamu; wakaiza[37] katika maneno hayo.[38] Mfalme akafa, sene 732.

Kawata[39] kijana kimoja, Sultan ‘Omar[40] bin Muhammad (p. 158) bin Ahmad bin Muhammad bin Seleman. Akatawali baada ya baba wake, akarejea maneno ya baba wake kwa watu wa Lamu, kuwataka watu wa Manda; watu wa Lamu kawaiza kuwatoa, kawapija zita, wakataka amani watu wa Lamu, wakawa katika ta‘a ya Sultan ‘Omar bin Muhammad bin Ahmad bin Muhammad bin Seleman. Akapata nguvu sana, akapija jumla ya mii ya

---

[36] *Himaya*, Ar. (not in Krapf or Madan) "protection." [*Editor's note*: these are dictionaries of the Swahili language. J. L. Krapf, *A Dictionary of the Swahili Language* (London, 1882) and A. C. Madan, *Swahili-English Dictionary* (London, 1903).]

[37] *Iza*, Kiamu for *kataa*, "refuse."

[38] *Hayo*, the pronoun in *o* indicates something previously referred to, the *maneno* therefore are those implied in the king's demand. Apart from this, it is doubtful if *katika* could be used in a way which allow us to translate, "in these words" and suppose that the scribe had accidentally omitted the quotation intended to follow.

[39] As the object-pronoun *wa* is here out of the question, it seems that the و is only inserted for greater ease in writing.

[40] According to the document furnished by Mr. Reddie, this Sultan Omar reigned 1306-1344. Shaka, which is named among his conquests, is famous as the principality of Liongo, or rather of Liongo's brother, Shah Mringari. This town and another, called Wangwana wa Mashah (close to Kipini), were founded by some Persian immigrants during the reign of Harun er-Rashid (787-810). The story of Liongo is to a great extent mythical, but seems to have a substratum of historical fact.

Shaka is also called Mwanamtama, from a queen of that name, who, in her pride and ostentation,, had the millet (*mtama*) beaten out on the bare ground instead of spreading it on mats—to show they had so much that there was no need to guard against waste. Both Shaka and Wangwana wa Mashah were destroyed by Bwana Tamu. [*Editor's note*: for archeological evidence of the latter site see J. S. Kirkman, *Ungwana on the Tana* (The Hague, 1966).]

Sawahili: Ozi,[41] Malindi, Kiwayu,[42] Kitao,[43] Miya[43] na Imidhi[43] na Watamu,[43] hata kasikilia Kirimba;[43] mii yote katamalaki tangu Pate hata Kirimba; kula mui kaweka mtu wake kihukumu, ndiyo asili ya hawa majumba walioko mrima wote; maana majumbe watumwa wa yumbe. Hiyo yumbe ni ina la nyumba ya ufalme wa Pate.[44]

Na janibu ya matlai katamalaki hata Warsheikh kwa zita. Alikwanda kupija zita tangu Kiwayu na Tula na Shungwaya na bandari[45] zote—Barawa, Marika, Mukdishu. Hapo Makdishu kaweka luwali,[46] hukumu ya bandari zote zikawa Mukdishu. Akaishi na nti hizo zote zi katika ta 'a yake, isokuwa Unguja, hakutawali wakati hunu Unguja; haikuwa nti kuu ya mfalme. Na mfalme huyu alikipenda zita mno, nakupenda ra'iya, na ra'iya wakaona raha

[41] There have been several towns near the mouth of the Ozi. Probably Shaka and Wangwana wa Mashah are meant. Kau and Kipini seem to be of more recent date; Kau was founded by fugitives from Shaka, apparently in the seventeenth century.

[42] A small island off the northern end of Siu Island, near Kizingitini.

[43] Kitao was on Manda Island, opposite Lamu. Miya (called by Captain Stigand "mea") is possibly the same as Miyao, mentioned to me at Pate as a town of the Watikuu (Swahili of the mainland). Written "Emezi" by Captain Stigand: Mr. Reddie informs me that it is called Midhi and that its ruins are about a mile east of Wangi, on the mainland opposite Siu. Muhammadi Kijuma says it should be written Imezi; it is "an old town with large stone houses" and was built before the Arabs came to Africa. Watamu is south of Malindi.

[44] The palace of the Pate kings (also called Diwani) is still pointed out. See Stigand, pp. 45, 161, 163.

[45] Ar. بندر (bandar), plural (banādir), بَنَادِر , "seaport," is used in Swahili for a harbour, or even a landing-place for boats, such as that at the head of the Rabai Creek. The "Banadir" coast is that of the "Havens" enumerated in the text. "Marika"—so written in the text—usually called Marka or Merka—in Italian Somaliland. Tula and Shungwaya are in British territory: the latter is the traditional home of the "Nyika" tribes.

[46] Ar. ولي . In Swahili, usually *luwali* or *liwali*, by combination with the article (*il-wali*).

sana wakapata mali mangi. Ikasitawi mno nti ya Pate, akafa sene 749.

(p. 160) Akawata zijana wawili, Muhammad na Ahmad, akatawali Muhammad bin 'Omar bin Muhammad bin Ahmad bin Muhammad bin Seleman, wala hapakuwa na zita, katawali ufalme wa babake wote kwa amani. Naye alikipenda mali sana na biashara, akisafirisha watu na zombo, kapeeka 'l Hind, kafanya biashara; naye alina bakhti sana ya mali. Na mara moya kijana chake alisafiri kapata kisiwa baharini, kashuka, kapata ma'edini ya fedha, akapeaka watu wakafanya kazi, kappata mali mangi, yakazidi sana mali katika nti ya Pate, hata wakafanya zitara za fedha na ngazi za fedha na zombo zingi za kutumia za fedha. Kapata na zijana wane, Bwana Tamu Mkuu na Ahmad na 'Abubakar na 'Omar. [*Editor's note*: if Werner's notation is correct, the Arabic name Abū Bakr is misspelled, with *'ayn* replacing *alif*. While this mistake occurs occasionally in Arabic loanwords, it is unusual in a name.] Akafa sene 797.

Katawali nduye Ahmad bin 'Omar bin Muhammad bin Ahmad bin Muhammad bin Seleman, kaketi kwa amani nti zake zote, akafa sene 840.

Katawali Abubakar bin Muhammad bin 'Omar bin Muhammad bin Ahmad bin Muhammad bin Seleman, kaketi kwa siyara njema na mii yote katika ta'a yake pasina kuharibika yambo. Akafa sene 875. ||

(p. 278) Akawata zijana wawili, Muhammad na Ahmad. Akatawali Muhammad bin Abubakar bin Muhammad bin 'Omar bin Muhammad bin Ahmad bin Muhammad bin Seleman. Wakati wake wakaya wazungu Portugesi katika mii ya Sawahili[47] yote; wakaketi Mombasa wakafanya ngome. Na

[47] "Sawahili" here evidently has its original Arabic meaning of "the coast," but though plural in form (Sawahil, sing. Sahil) it is treated as a singular.

janibu ya Pate wakajenga Dondo[48] na watu wa bara wote wakawaafikiana[49] kwa kuwapa mali, wakangia katika ta 'a yao wakamu 'aridhi[50] na mufalme katika mui wa Pate. Wakamupija kwa janibu ya Shindakasi,[51] wakawaka tiati yakupija mui wa Pate, wasiwaweze. Kisa wakapatana kwa amani, wakafanya mukatab[52] wa sharuti zao, wakaketi Pate wazungu, wakafanya fordha kwa ina lao Wazungu, walitamukua "fundika."[53] Wakafanya mambo na mambo mangi katika kisiwa cha Pate. Baada ya hayo akafa mfalme, sene 900.

Kawata zijana, Bwana Mkuu na 'Abubakar. Akatawali Abubakar bin Muhammad bin Abubakar bin Muhammad bin 'Omar bin Muhammad bin Ahmad bin Muhammad bin (p. 280) Seleman; akaketi kwa amani na wazungu, wapetene[54] kama ka'ida ya baba wake. Akafa sene 945.

Kawata zijana wawili, Ahmad na Muhammad, katawali nduye, Bwana Mkuu bin Muhammad bin Abubakar bin Muhammad bin Omar bin Muhammad bin Ahmad. Wakawa na ikhtilafu na wazungu, lakini pasiwe na zita; akafa

---

[48] So written by Captain Stigand and confirmed by Muhamadi Kijuma. According to the MS. it might be either Dondo or Dundu.

[49] Krapf gives *afikana* "to make an agreement," as if from *afika*. The word in the text, if correct, would be the reciprocal of an applied form, *afikia*.

[50] *Aridhi* "to trouble, annoy" (عرض) not to be confused with *aridhi* (from *ridhi*, رضِيَ) "like," "be pleased."

[51] At the entrance to Pate Creek, Bwana Jambeni of Pate called it *Shindakazi* (possibly for *Kazi imetushinda* = "the work has been too much for us"), and said that it was originally "Shindanahás," a Portuguese word meaning "a bad place." This is probably a mistake—it seems impossible to trace any Portuguese etymology.

[52] More usually *khati*.

[53] Sometimes written *fandika*, from Port. *alfandega*.

[54] Old perfect of *kupatana*. *Umoya* = *mmoja* in N. dialect.

katika fitina za siku nyingi, sene 973. Akaata kijana umoya, Abubakar.

Katawali Muhammad Abubakar bin Muhammad bin Abubakar bin Muhammad bin Omar bin Muhammad bin Ahmad bin Muhammad bin Seleman. Akasilihiana[55] na Wazungu, nao wakatwaa baadhi ya mii; akafa sene 1002.

Kawata kijana Abubakar.[56] Akatawali Abubakar bin Mkuu bin Muhammad bin Abubakar bin Muhammad bin Omar bin Muhammad bin Ahmad bin Muhammad bin Seleman. Kaketi kwa siyara njema, kama babake; lakini ufalme wake wa asili umepungua. Akafa sene 1041, kawata zijana wawili, Bwana Mkuu wa Abubakar.

Katawali Abubakar bin Muhammad bin Abubakar bin Muhammad bin Abubakar. Akawa khitilafu na wazungu, kapeeka watu katika nti ya Pate wakapija wazungu. Zikaya zita za wazungu, wakapija mui kwa mizinga, wakaziwia[57] na ndia za baharini, wakapata mashaka sana watu wa Pate, wakafanya amani. Baada ya haya akafa mfalme, sene 1061.

Kawata zijana wawili, Bwana Mkuu na Ahmad. Akatawali Bwana Mkuu bin[58] Muhammad bin Abubakar bin Muhammad bin Omar. Akapatana na wazungu, naye akapenda kuketi Amu hata musimu[59] akauita Amu,[60]

---

[55] Applied reciprocal from Ar. صلح "reconcile, make peace." See Krapf, s.v. *sulukhi*.

[56] Another MS. which I have been able to consult adds here: *asitawali*.

[57] Or *zuia*.

[58] Two names seem to have been left out here: Abubakar and Bwana Mkuu.

[59] Properly the N.E. monsoon (Ar. موسم , from which our word is derived). Krapf defines it "the time when the ships come from the north, December to March." It is not very clear what is meant: possibly Bwana Mkuu used to stay at Lamu during the time of the N.E. monsoon, which would be favourable for the journey from Lamu to Pate, but not for the

akaoa kwa watu wa Lamu.

Na Wafamau wa Siu, muda hunu walitoka katika ta'a yake, akapijana nao akauvunda mui wa Siu; akatukua watu wa Siu kawaeta Pate. Mukuu wa Siu kakimbia, kenda Dondo kwa Portugali,[61] wakatwaa himaya. Mkuu wa wazungu Portugali (p. 282) kaya Pate, kataka watu wa Siu; akapowa[62] kawarejeza Siu, wakaketi kwa amani. Baada yake Portugali kafanya hila, akaya Pate kwa marikabu, kamutaka mfalme kenda marikabuni, asinende mfalme kamupeeka binami yake Bwana Mkuu, yeye na watu wa Pate. Wazungu wakawatukua katika marikabu kawapeeka kwao Uzunguni,[63] asirudi tena hatta mtu umoya. Baada ya hapo wakapija wazungu kula mahali waliopo, barani na zisiwani kawatoa, wakakimbia Mombasa. Baada ya hayo mfalme akafa, sene 1100. Akawata zijana wawili, Bwana Abubakar na Bwana Madi, na binti umoya, Mwana Khadija kuniya[64] lake Mwana Darini, binti Bwana

---

return. In that case one would have expected hatta *musimu umekwisha*, but the omission of the last word may be accidental.

[60] It seems impossible to make sense of this by reading *akaueta*, "and he brought it," and the reading adopted in the text is not much more intelligible, unless we are to suppose that he called the town "Amu," (or "Lamu") when it had previously had some other name.

[61] The forms "Portugali" and "Portugesi" seem to be used indifferently in this MS. Nowadays the Portuguese are usually spoken of as *Wareno* (from *reino* "kingdom") — but sometimes at Pate and Siu one hears "Portugéz," with the accent strongly marked on the last syllable; probably a traditional pronunciation derived from the invaders themselves. There is a current saying, "*Mwenye jauri* (or, *mwenye kiburi*) *kama Portugez*" — proud (or, violent) as a Portuguese."

[62] The passive of *pa*, "give," is in Kiamu *powa*, Kimvita *pawa*, Kiunguja *pewa*.

[63] Uzunguni, "the country of the Europeans"; later references show that Goa is meant.

[64] Ar. كني, "surname." Not in Krapf.

Mkuu bin Abubakar.[65]

Katawali kijana chake Abubakar bin Mkuu bin Abubakar bin Mkuu bin Muhammad bin Abubakar bin Muhammad bin Omar bin Ahmad bin Muhammad bin Seleman, kapijwa mufalume ghafula na Ahmad nduye Bwana Mkuu aliotukuliwa na Wazungu Portugali, katawali yeye, Ahmad 'l madhkûr, naye ni Ahmad bin Abubakar bin Muhammad bin Abubakar bin Muhammad bin Omar 'l madhkûr, sene 1103.

Kawandama Portugali kawatoa waliosalia, na wakati hunu Mwana Darini binti Bwana Mkuu bin Abubakar, muke wa Bwana Mkuu bin Abubakar mwenda[66] Goa katika zamani za Sultan Ahmad, akisa kuuawa nduze wawili, Abubakar na Bwana Madi, aliowaua ni Sultan Ahmad bin Abubakar, na (p. 284) mume wake alikuwa mepeekwa Goa sabiki,[67] akapata huzuni sana ya mume wake aliotangulia kwenda Goa, na kuuawa nduguze wawili. Hatta

---

[65] According to Captain Stigand, Mwana Darini was daughter of Abubakar bin Bwana Mkuu and wife of Bwana Mkuu bin Muhammad (this Muhammad was the son of Abubakar's brother). But the whole story is wrongly placed in one or other of the two accounts, for Captain Stigand says that, after the murder of Abubakar "another Sultan Abubakar was placed on the throne in the year 1060" (p. 55). The Bwana Mkuu bin Abubakar, who was so fond of visiting Lamu, is mentioned subsequently as having reigned rom A.H. 1100 to A.H. 1125: "Sultan Bwana Mkuu loved the country of Amu very much, and went to Amu and married a wife there, and he also built a mosque and made Amu the harbour for the trading vessels brought in by the N.E. monsoon." (p. 56). There is no mention of the Sultan Ahmad said in the text to have succeeded Abubakar bin Bwana Mkuu.

[66] A verbal noun formed from *enda*, used instead of *aliokwenda*. Elsewhere the term *mwendi* is used.

[67] Ar. سبق, "to go before"; *i.e.* the murder of her brothers was subsequent to his being carried away to Goa. Nothing is said about this murder in Captain Stigand's account, which, on the other hand, mentions a circumstance omitted in our text: the son whose cirumcision she wished to celebrate was born soon after the kidnapping of her husband. Her father assured her that he would return in six months, but she waited in vain, and "when her son had reached three years of age she knew that her father's words were false."

baadhi ya siku zikipita, kaazimu kufanya 'arusi[68] kumutahiri kijana chake, Bwana Tamu Mtoto, amkuliwao Sultan Abubakar Imâm Lihadi wa Bwana Mkuu mwendi Goa.

Mfalme Sultan Ahmad akapata khabari hini ya 'arusi, naye kaazimu 'arusi, ili kasidi kumukhini siwa.[69] Akisa kuyua Mwana Darini khabari ya kukhiniwa siwa, akamwita Mwenyi Bayayi[70] Mkuu, Sharifu katika jama'a 'l Lail, alikijua kazi ya ujume sana, akamwambia khabari yake yote, akataka kwake amfanyize siwa ishinde[71] ile, kakubali, akataka ijara yake reale mia wa 'ishrîn na pembe za ndovu atwae atakazo apate kuteua.[72] Mwana Darini kamutimizia kula sharuti iliotaka, akafanya siwa kwa siri, kaisita[73] hata

---

[68] *'Arusi* means, properly, "festivity," a "rejoicing," so can be used for other celebrations besides weddings. *Azimu* (عَزَم) "resolve," not to be confounded with *azima*, "borrow," which is pure Bantu.

[69] The horn or trumpet blown at weddings and other ceremonies. It seems to have been kept in the palace. There is a very ancient brass or copper one at Lamu, now in the custody of the Waziri family. (Muhamadi bin Abubakari Kijuma tells me that this originally came from Shiraz.) It is lent when required to any family entitled to use it — *i.e.* of unimpeachable descent. The Pate horn mentioned in the text was subsequently lost at sea, as will be related below, and the ivory horn which Mwana Darini caused to be made is now in the Provincial Commissioner's house at Lamu, and is lent to certain of the old families of Lamu for any marriage or any other family ceremony. [*Editor's note*: see J. de V. Allen, "The *Siwas* of Pate and Lamu: Two Antique Sideblown Horns from the Swahili Coast" *Art and Archaeology Research Papers* 9 (1976): pp. 38-47.]

[70] Captain Stigand reads this name Baenyi. In an account of the "Ivory Horn of Pate," which I owe to the kindness of Mr. Reddie, the Sharif is called Jamall Lail, but, as the text stands, it seems difficult to take it otherwise than I have done.

[71] A very common idiom to express the comparative.

[72] Kiamu for *chagua*, "choose."

[73] *Sita*, Kiamu for *ficha, fita*.

yalipokisa kaithihirisha[74] ghafula kaipeeka katika jami'i ya majumba ya nduze na masahibu zake, kwa matezo makuu, wakaituza[75] mali mangi. Kamwambia Mwenyi Bayayi alioifanya, "wataka ijara ama wataka tuzo?" Kamena [*Editor's note:* should be *Kanena*], "Nataka tuzo," kwa sababu yalikuwa mali mangi. Katakabadhi[76] siwa yake, kafanya 'arusi ya kijana chake.

(p. 286) Hatta zamani ya Bwana Tamu Mukuu, watu wa Lamu wakaya kazima siwa ya asili, mufalume kawapa, ikipata baharini, chombo kikafa mai, ikapotea siwa. Bwana Tamu Mukuu kaitaka siwa ya Mwana Darini, kamwambia, "Tupe sisi, tutumie katika mii," kamwambia, "Kulla kabaili alotuza siwa yangu natumie." Mwana Darini kawata mutumwa wake huri[77] ayuayo kuvuzia siwa, akanena, "Huyu ndiye mwenye kuvuzia siwa hini, yeye na nasila yake, na ada yake napowe reale tano na nguo yakutukulia siwa[78] na samli yakunwa[79] mwenye kuvuzia, na tunzo kulla mtu kwa kiasi yake

---

[74] Causative for *thihiri, thahiri* (Ar. ظهر) "be evident."

[75] *Tuza*, "to give a present, largesse, or reward." See Madan, *Swahili-English Dictionary*, s.v., and Krapf, s.v. *tussa*. Steere spells it *tunza*; توز might be read either way, but it must be distinguished from *tunza*, "take care of." Madan gives both *tuzo* and *tunzo* for the noun = "a present, especially a reward for success." I have heard *kutunza heshima* used for the practice of distributing lengths of cotton print (*leso*) at weddings — they are draped over the shoulders of the guests, and especially of the most successful performers in the dance.

[76] Derived from قبض, "receive," instead of the more usual *pokea*.

[77] More usually *huru* (but Krapf gives *huri*), from Ar. حر, "to be free."

[78] It is not clear whether the *siwa* was to be carried slung in a cloth, or merely wrapped in it. Doubtless a new one was provided on every occasion, and the horn wrapped in it before being put away, the previous cloth being the blower's perquisite.

[79] To lubricate his throat, apparently.

awezao." Wakaamkuliwa nasila[80] hiyo muyumbe[81] wa siwa, hatta yeo wako watuwe.[82] Basi, ikawa tangu wakati hunu, hutumia kabaili wa Pate wote na wa mii mingine, hazima[83] kwa sharuti hizo.[84]

Sultan Ahmad 'l madhkûr akaketi katika ufalume wake myaka sabaa, haikunya mvua; akai'uzulu[85] katika ufalume wake sene 1111, katawali Sultan Abubakar [bin] Bwana Tamu Mukuu wa Bwana Mutiti[86] bin Ahmad bin Abubakar bin Omar bin Ahmad bin Omar bin Muhammad bin Ahmad bin Muhammad bin Seleman. Akatuzanya na mfalme wa Maskati, Imam 'l Ya'arubi.[87] Huyu mufalume wa Pate akenda Arabuni, wakaagana na mfalume wa Arabuni, arudipo Pate awatoe Portugali Mombasa. Alipowasili, Sultani wa Pate kapeka zita Mombasa kawapija Wazungu siku ya Juma'a ya pili, kawaua katika ngome, ya Mombasa, akamuarifu 'l Imam 'l Ya'arubi. Akaita[88] 'l

---

[80] "Descendants," "family," from the Ar. نَسْل "produce" (not in Krapf or Madan).

[81] Kimvita and Kiunguja *mjumbe*, "messenger."

[82] For *watu wake*.

[83] For *hu-azima*, "they are in the habit of borrowing."

[84] Note *hizo*, not *hizi*, because it is "the conditions already stated."

[85] *a-ka-i-'uzulu*: *-i-* the reflexive pronoun in Kiamu. Ar., عَزَلَ, "deprive of office"; عُزِلَ, "be deprived, retire, abdicate." Krapf: *ku-ji-uzulu*, "to resign one's office."

[86] *-titi*, Kiamu for *-dogo-*.

[87] This was the Imam Seif bin Sultan I. (1688-1711), fourth of the Ya'arubi Imâms. (See Stigand, p. 54.)

[88] This may be read either *a-ka-ita*, "he called," or *a-ka-eta*, "he brought."

Wali katika [Mazru‘i][89] watu watatu, ndugu, Muhammad bin Athman na (p. 288) Ali bin Athman, wa tatu simuyui ina lake; nao walikuya na askari tarafu ya ’l Imam ’l-Ya‘arubi, ndiyo asili ya [Mazrui] ya Mombasa. Naye aliketi na ra‘ia kwa uzuri sana, akaishi sana katika ufalume, myaka arbaini, akafa sene 1152, naye aliwata zijana zingi.

Baada yake asitawali kijana chake, katawali Sultan Ahmad bin Abubakar bin Muhammad bin Abubakar bin ‘Omar bin Ahmad bin Muhammd bin ‘Omar bin Muhammad bin Ahmad bin Muhammad Seleman. Akaketi kwa neema nyingi sana, akapenda kuweka[90] ng’ombe wangi sana, akafa sene 1160. Akaata kijana, Bwana Gongo, baada yake akatawali Bwana Tamu Mtoto waamkuliwao Imam Lihadi wa bin Bwana Mkuu bin Abubakar bin Muhammad bin Abubakar bin Muhammad bin Abubakr bin Muhammad bin ‘Omar bin Muhammad bin Ahmad bin Muhammad bin Seleman. Akaeta zita Imamu ’l Ya‘arubi kupija Pate, wasiweze, wakafa Waarabu wangi, wakarudi wakafanya amani. Baada ya hapo watu wa Lamu [*Editor’s note*: MS 321 names Siu.] wakapija na mfalme wa Pate, walikhalifu wakapijana asiweze, na watu wa Lamu wakaya Pate kupija kwa janabu ya Kitaka, wakafukuzwa wakarejea Lamu. Baadaye mfalme wa Pate akafanya zita kwa bara na bahari, kawapija watu wa Lamu, kawatamalaki; kisa mufalume akauawa Pate na watu wa Pate pamoya na watu wa ’l Imam ’l Ya‘arubi, sene 1176. Akatawali nduye Sultani Mwana Khadija binti Bwana Mkuu bin Abubakar bin Muhammad bin

---

[89] This name is usually written Mazru‘i, but, as it stands in the text, it is مُزاريع, which is grammatically impossible. Burton writes Mazara’. [*Editor’s note*: *Mazrū‘ī* is the singular. Here a typical Omani plural (*Mazāri‘a*) was attempted but the voweling is incorrect.]

[90] Properly "to put aside"; here, apparently, "collect and keep in reserve."

Abubakar bin Muhammad bin Abubakar bin Muhammad bin 'Omar bin Muhammad bin Ahmad bin Muhammad bin Seleman. Akapata fitina nyingi katika nti ya Pate, ikawa katika mui wa Pate wafalume wawili, yeye Mwana Khadija na Sultan 'Omar, wakapijana katika mui [myaka][91] mitano, kakimbia Sultan 'Omar kenda Barawa kisa karejea Pate kwa nguvu kuu sana, akangiliwa[92] na watu wa Mwana Khadija usiku, akauawa. Baada yake kwa siku (p. 290) chache akafa Mwana Khadija, sene 1187. Akatawali Bwana Mkuu wa Bwana Sheikh wa Bwana Tamu Mukuu. Na ra'ia wakamuudhi sana kwa fitina, asipate raha, hatta sene 1191 wakangia watu wa mui wakamuua kwa tarikhi hini.

Katawali Bwana Fumo Madi, ina lake Sultan Muhammad bin Abubakar bin Bwana Mkuu bin Abubakar bin Muhammad bin Abubakar bin Muhammad bin Abubakar bin Muhammad bin 'Omar bin Muhammad bin Ahmad bin Muhammad bin Seleman. Akisa kutawali ra'ia wakataka kufanya fitina, kawapija kwa zita hatta kawashinda, akawashika na watu arbaini wakuu (na katika hao arbaini watu wawili ni nduze), akawatinda wote.[93] Kukawa amani, asipate mtu kumuudhi tena. Katawali kwa raha na amani na neema, na ra'ia

---

[91] In the MS. written *yake*, but it is clear from the context that *myaka* is meant.

[92] A good illustration of one use of the Bantu passive. Literally, "he was entered for," or "upon."

[93] The writer of the postscript adds, *kama kuku*, and this was the expression used by Bwana Jambeni at Pate—probably in reference to the same incident. His account was that Bwantauzi wa Hero "captured by guile forty nobles (*waungwana*) of Kau and had them killed like fowls on the *dari* (upper floor) of the Yumbe" — he pointed out the place — and the blood ran down like water." Another MS. which I have been enabled to consult (and which, though very faulty, occasionally gives fuller details), says that the forty (two of whom were Fumo Madi's brothers) were men of Kau, and that he slaughtered them "like goats" (*kawatinda kama mbuzi*).

wakaona raha sana hatta sene 1224, akafa. Baada yake hakutawali mufalume tena kama yeye, naye aliwata zijana zingi.

Katawali Sultan Ahmad bin Sheikh bin Fumo Luti bin Sheikh bin Bwana Tamu Mukuu; ikazidi fitina katika nti ya Lamu, akaya yeye kuwapija zita pamoya na watu wa Mombasa. Mazru'i wakaya Lamu, sene 1227, wakashuka Shela, jeshi nyingi sana, na watu wa Mombasa na watu wa Pate. Watu wa Lamu wakatoka wakapijana na watu wa Mombasa na watu wa Pate, wakavundika watu wa Mombasa na watu wa Pate, wakitaka kukimbia majahazi yamepwewa,[94] wakapijana tena zita zikuu, wakafa watu wangi sana sana wa Mombasa na watu wa Pate, watu maarufu, fulani bin fulani, 81 (wahid u themanin), watumwa na wasokuwa maarufu hawana 'idadi, kadhalika watu wa Mombasa hawana 'idadi.

Baada ya hapo, watu wa Lamu wakenda Arabuni (p. 292) wakamutaka Sayyid Sa'id bin Sultan bin Ahmad 'l Imam wakamupa nti sene 1228 ndipo Sayidi alipotawali Lamu; ufalume wa Pate ukawa katika kisiwa cha Pate na banadiri. Ikazidi fitina katika nti ya Pate, akatoka mtu wa pili Pate katika zijana wa Bwana Fumo Madi, hamkuliwa[95] Fumo Luti Kipunga, akapijana na Sultan Ahmad. Kisa Sultan Ahmad kapata maradhi, akafa, sene 1230. Katawali Sultan Fumo Luti wa Bwana Fumo Madi, naye alikuwa mtu hodar sana, shujaa, karimu.

---

[94] Passive of *pwea*, applied form of *ku pwa*, "ebb" (of the tide), whence *pwani*, "beach" — properly the beach below high-water mark.

[95] Contracted either from *a-ki-amkuliwa* or *hu-amkuliwa*. The "habitual" tense (*hu-*) is even more used at Lamu than elsewhere.

Na zamani hizo, Sheikh[96] Mataka bin Mbaraka ndipo alipotawali ushekhe wa Siu, kafanya[97] askari na bunduki, naye katika ta'a ya Sultan wa Pate, naye alipetene[98] sana na [Mazru'i]. Hatta sene 1236 ikazidi fitina bayina[99] yake na Sultan Zinjibar, Sayyid Sa'id[100] bin Sultan. Akafa Sultan Fumo Luti 'l madhkûr kwa tarikhi hini, katawali Fumo Luti bin Bwana Sheikh bin Fumo Luti bin Sheikh wa Bwana (Tamu) Mkuu, na huyu ndiye babake Sultan Ahmad, Sultan (wa) Witu, naye alitawali assubuhi hatta baada ya alasiri, watu wa mui wakamtoa, akenenda Siu pamoya na Mazru'i, kisa kenda Mombasa.

Akatawali baada yake Sultan Bwana Sheikh wa Bwana Fumo Madi, akapatana sana na Sayyidna Sa'id bin Sultan, akatia Waarabu Pate, wakaketi myaka mitatu. Baadaye watu wa mui wakamu 'uzulu pamoya na shauri la Sayyidna Sa'id bin Sultan.

Katawali Sultan Ahmad wa Bwana Waziri wa Bwana Tamu wa Bwana Sheikh wa Bwana Tamu Mukuu, sene 1237, kapatana na Sayyidna Sa'id bin Sultan, katawali myaka miwili, watu wa mui wakamu 'uzulu, wakamurejeza Bwana (p. 294) Sheikh wa Bwana Fumo Madi, akaketi katika 'ezi[101] kwa

---

[96] Written Arabic fashion in the MS., but usually pronounced *shehe* or *shee* in Swahili — or sometimes *shekh* (with short e) as in *Kwa Mashekh*, the popular name for a place near Mombasa containing many old tombs. *Shee* is not an uncommon name for a man.

[97] *Fanya* here evidently means "collect," or "obtain."

[98] Old perfect of *patana*. See Taylor's, *African Aphorisms*, Appendix, p. 166.

[99] Arabic بَيْنَ, "between."

[100] The title Sayyid (سيّد) must be distinguished from the proper name Sa'id (سعيد).

[101] Ar. عزّة from عزّ "to be powerful." The word is found in the common expression *Mwenyi-ezi Muungu*.

shauri la Sayyidna Sa'id bin Sultan miaka mitano, akafa sene 1239. Akarejea Bwana Waziri katika ufalme, akaya Fumo Luti bin Bwana Sheikh aliokwenda Mombasa, yeye na Mazru'i, wakashika Siu, wakapijana na Bwana Waziri wa Bwana Tamu Pate. Na Bwana Waziri ni shauri moya[102] na Sayyidna Sa'id bin Sultan, na Fumo Luto pamoya na Mazru'i, na Sheikh Mataka bin Mbarak, mtu wa Siyu, kwa shauri moya wakapijana, wakavundika[103] Fumo Luti na Mazru'i na watu Siu; ukavundwa na ukuta wa mui wa Siu, wakaushika na mui. Fumo Luti na Sheikh Mataka wakaimbia barani, wakaketi barani siku katiti,[104] wakarejea Siu kwa zita, wakashika mui wa Siu, wakawaka ukuta, wakapijana Pate kwa Siu.

Kisa Fumo Luti akafa Siu, akatanganya Bwana Waziri wa Bwana Tamu Pate na Siu katika ta'a yake pamoya na shauri la Sayyidina Sa'id bin Sultan. Baada ya mwaka akauawa Sultani Bwana Waziri wa Bwana Tamu, na Fumo Bakar bin Sheikh wa Bwana Fumo Madi katawali, yeye Sultan Fumo Bakar bin Sheikh bin Bwana Fumo Madi sene 1250. Kapatana sana na Sayyidina Sa'id bin Sultan muda wa kutawali, kisa kakhalifu yeye pamoya na Sheikh Mataka.

---

[102] A common expression to which *hali moya*, also sometimes used in this document, appears to be equivalent. For various uses of *shauri cf.* Madan's *Dictionary*, s.v.

[103] It might seem as if the passive were the more appropriate form here (*cf. ukavundwa ukuta*, below), but there may be an implication of a continuous *state* of defeat, whereas the wall was overthrown by a single definite *act*.

[104] Kiamu for *kidogo*. *Kititi* is given in Steere (*Handbook*, p. 314) as belonging to the Mombasa dialect, and meaning "a hare, a rabbit, a little thing." (*Cf.* also the Kimvita story, *Kititi na Fisi na Simba*, in Steere, *Swahili Tales*, p. 324). I have never heard it at Mombasa, in either sense ("hare," at Mombasa is *kitungule*, at Lamu *kitunguwe*). But the writer was probably connected with Lamu (see, Steere, *op. cit.*, Preface, p. ix), if his grandfather Sheikh Muhi'id-dîn was the same as the person whose name occurs in the latter part of this chronicle. [*Editor's note*: see Edward Steere *A Handbook of the Swahili Language* (London, 1884).]

Sayyidna Sa'id bin Sultan kamuita 'l Amir Hamad bin Hamad 'l Busaid 'l maîqab es-Samar, kapija Pate na Siu asiweze akafanya amani. Baada ya hapo, Sultan wa Pate, (p. 296) ikawa fitina baina yake[105] na binamu yake Muhammad bbin Ahmad wa Bwana Fumo Madi, akashika nyumba ya ufalme kwa zita. Kisa wakaya watu wa Lamu na mtu wa Sayyidna Sa'id bin Sultan wakawasilihisha Sultan Fumo Bakar na Muhammad bin Ahmad, kapeka Siu kuketi; Fumo Bakari kaketi Pate. Baadaye wakateta wakapijana myaka mitano, Pate na Siu; kisa Sayyidna Sa'id bin Sultan akaya Pate kuwapatanisha Sultan Fumo Bakari na Muhammad bin Ahmad, wakawa shauri moya yeye na binamu yake. Kisa Fumo Bakari kamushika ghafula kamuua kwa shauri la mtu wa Siu. Baadaye Sayyidna Sa'id bin Sultan kamwita Sultan Fumo Bakari kwenda Unguja, kaenenda, Sayyidna Sa'id bin Sultan kamufunga Fumo Bakari kwa shauri la watu wa Lamu, na sababu, kumuua binamu yake Muhammad bin Ahmad na kuata amani aliyofanya yeye Sayyidina Said bin Sultan. ||

Sene 1262 akashika Pate Sultan Ahmad bin Sheikh wa Fumo Luti bin Sheikh wa Bwana Tamu Mkuu kwa shauri la Sayyidina Sa'id bin Sultan, akakiti katika shauri la Sayyidina Sa'id bin Sultan, myaka miwili; baadaye akakhalifu, akaya Sayyidina Sa'id kumupija, akashuka 'l Amir Hamad bin

---

105 Literally, "After this — (as to) the Sultan of Pate, there was dissension between him and his uncle's son," etc. Observe *binamu* — elsewhere *binami*. The vowel-sounds in Arabic vary in a way which, to those unacquainted with the somewhat complex rules which govern them, seems accidental or capricious. Besides which, some of them are very indistinct, whereas Bantu vowels are nearly always clearly marked. It is therefore not surprising to find *suluhu* and *silihisha*, *Seleman*, *Suliman*, and *Silimani*, etc. used simultaneously.

Hamad Faza, kenda kupija zita Siu.[106] Na Sayyidina Sa'id kamufungua Sultan Fumo Bakar akamupa zita[107] pamoya na watu wa Lamu. Wakaketi Mtangawanda[108] katika zombo, yeye Sayyidina Sa'id bin Sultan na Amiri Hamad, wakenda Faza; Sayyidina Sa'id kaketi mahali huitwa Kijangwa cha Mpunga,[109] karibu na Faza. Amir Hamad akaya Siu kuwaka[110] maboma katika ndia baina ya Faza na Siu, kwa zita; akaya hatta Siu kashika mitepe

---

[106] Stigand, p. 92. "One year later, Sultan Fumobakari seized his brother Bwana Kitini and killed him. For this reason the people of Pate hated him, and so the Amu people said to Fumobakari, 'It were better that you go to Sa'id at Zanzibar, for people here have intrigued against you.' So he went to Zanzibar. The Amu people then said to Sa'id, 'Seize him, and then you will have got possession of the whole Swahili coast.' So Sa'id seized and imprisoned him. When the Pate people heard this, they took Bwana Madi [=Ahmad], son of Sheikh, and put him on the throne in the year 1259. The Pate people were in agreement with Sheikh Mataka of Siu, but the Bajuns were on Sa'id's side. When Sa'id heard the Sultan Ahmad was on the throne of Pate and was allied to Sheikh Mataka, he released Sultan Fumobakari and gave him money."

The discrepancy of date will be noticed: the figures are quite clear in our MS., but in careless handwriting it might be possible to mistake ١٢٦٢ for ١٢٥٩ or *vice versa*. Captain Stigand's account also implies that Sa'id acted at once, on hearing the news of Ahmad's accession, whereas the text distinctly states that Ahmad remained on good terms with him for two years.

[107] Evidently here equivalent to "forces." The next clause is ambiguous, but probably the words supplied in translation give the real meaning.

[108] Still the best landing-place for Pate. It is on the western side of the island, and Pate can be reached in about half an hour's walk.

[109] "The Little Marsh of the Rice." *Kijangwa*, diminutive of *wangwa* (pl. *nyanwga*), the name applied to the vast stretches of sand bordering the tidal creeks of East Africa. They abound in salsolaceous vegetation (sometimes shrubs of considerable size, growing in large patches), and might be described as salt-marshes, though in many cases so dry at low tide as scarcely to suggest a marsh. There may have been wild rice growing on the one in question. I do not know whether rice was ever actually cultivated on the island, as it is (and doubtless has been for centuries) on the Tana.

[110] *Waka* properly means "to build with stones" — hence *mwashi*, "mason" — and *jenga*, to erect a structure of poles or stakes, such as a *banda*, or the skeleton of a Nyika hut. But this writer does not always observe the distinction.

ilioko bandarini Siu, kaipindua kafanya maboma kaipija nti ya Siu.

Watu wa Siu wakaona taabu sana, na amiri Hamadi (p. 394) alipoona udhia, muda umekuwa mwingi,[111] karudi kenda kutwaa mzinga ulioko bomani, na watu. Akali kipita[112] ndiani, watu wa Siu wakamutokea[113] ghafula[114], amiri wa Sheikh Mataka, Bwana Hamad wa Omari, wakamupija Amiri Hamadi, wakapijana zita zikuu sana, akafa 'l Amir, yeye na watu wake. Na amiri wa pili wa Sheikh Mataka ni Bwana Hamad Ngoma; akenda bomani ghafula kawapija[115] katwaa mizinga. Khabari ikasikilia kwa Sayyidina Sa'id bin Sultan Faza, kangia markebuni, asinene na mtu, kenda Masikati. Mwaka wa pili karudi kamuweka Fumo Bakari Faza, kapija Siu na Pate.[116] Katika

---

[111] Literally, "the period has become long," as if in direct quotation.

[112] Compound tense = "he was passing." The MS. can be read either *kapita* or *kipata*, but unquestionably one of the vowel points is wrong, and *kipita* is the only justifiable reading.

[113] *Toka*, "come out"; *tokea*, "come out for, to, against," etc. It is the word used for the "appearing" of ghosts, etc. *Siku nitakayokufa nitakutokea*, "on the day when I die I will appear to you." But "appearing to anyone in a dream" is usually expressed by *otesha*, "cause to dream." Thus, in a popular song (Jomvu):

Baba aliniotesha:	"My father appeared to me (in a dream):
"Mwanangu nakutuma	My son, I send thee
Kitu (u)pawa ni Muungu	A thing (which) thou art given by God
Na malaika na mitume."	And the angels and apostles."

[114] The sense seems to require the insertion of *na* here.

[115] Probably *watu* should be understood.

[116] For the Siu expedition, *cf.* Badger, *Imâms and Seyyids of Oman*, Introduction, p. lxxxiii.:

"From 1829 to 1844 the Seyyid Sa'id was engaged in consolidating his territories on the east coast of Africa. His first visit to Zanzibar appears to have been towards the end of the former year, when he accompanied an expedition against Mombâsah, after the Indian wakati hunu akafa Sheikh Mataka (p. 396) kwa maradhi; ikawa ihtilafu kwa zijana zake kutaka ushekhe wa Siu, wakangia katika ta'a ya Sayyidina Sa'id bin Sultan Abubakar na Muhammad. Sayyid Sa'id kamupa Abubakar zita pamoya na Sultan Fumo Bakari; kenda kumupija Sultan Ahmad Pate. Akenenda Abubakar bin Sheikh Mataka pamoya na amiri wa Sultan Fumo Bakar, huitwa Bwana Mukuu bin Bwana Madi wa Baishi, wakangia Siu usiku wakapijana

---

authorities, at his strong remonstrances, had disallowed the convention which Captain Owen, of H.M. frigate *Leven*, had concluded five years previoulsy with the Arab settlers there, whereby they were placed under British protection. It was not, however, till after a third attack that H.H. succeeded in finally subjugating Mombâsah by the capture of the leading men of the Beni Mazrû'a, an 'Omâny tribe which had long been in possession of the locality, nominally subject to the sovereign of Oman, but virtually independent of his authority. These chiefs were transported to the island of Hormûz, in the Persian Gulf, 'where they subsequently died' — most probably of starvation."

Salîl-ibn-Razîk's account of the Siu expedition is as follows:

"Before returning to Zanzibar, the Seyyid appointed his son Thuwainy-bin Sa'id Wali over Maskat and made Hamâd bin Ahmad Wali over Nakhl; but in the meantime Hamâd accompanied him on his voyage, and he sent him to attack Sîwy while he himself went on to Zanzibar. Hamâd was successful at Sîwy, the people there agreeing to all the Seyyid's demands, so leaving some of his men in the place he went to Zanzibar, from whence, by the Seyyid's orders, he returned to Oman. From Maskat he went to take up his appointment at Nakhl. . . . The people of Sîwy having broken their engagements, the Seyyid wrote to Hamâd to undertake an expedition against them, sending him a large sum of money for that purpose. Hamâd was unsuccessful on this occasion, for the people resisted him, and he was obliged to flee to Zanzibar, after losing many of his followers."(p. 335).

". . . The Seyyid embarked for Zanzibar with a large force under the command of Hamâd bin Ahmad, Albû Saidy, and 'Abdallah bin Salim. On reaching Mombâsah, he dispatched these two commanders to attack Sîwy, while he proceeded to Zanzibar. The attack upon Sîwy failed, for the people engaged the assailants and drove them off, with the loss of Hamâd and 'Abdallah bin Salim, ezh-Zhâhiry, and a great many of their followers, who were killed on that occasion"(p. 360).

This expedition took place in 1844.

So little was known of the Swahili coast, even less than fifty years ago, that the editor speaks of "Sîwy near Brâwa" (Barawa), and adds the following note to the passage just quoted from p. 355:

"Colonel Rigby, who was for several years British Agent at Zanzibar, says that Sîwy is situated near Brâwa on the east coast of Africa, but I cannot find the name in any of our maps or charts."

hatta assubuhi; wakavundika Abubakar bin Sheikh Mataka na watu wake, akashikwa Abubakar akapekwa Pate kwa Sultan Ahmad, kauawa Abubakar. Baadaye akasimama Sheikh Muhammad bin Sheikh Mataka tarafu ya Sayyidina Sa'id bin Sultan pamoya na Fumo Bakar. Sayyidna Sa'id kawapa zita na askari na gharama,[117] wakamupija Sultan Ahmad bin Sheikh hatta wakamtoa Pate 1273, akenda Kau.[118]

Na nti ya Siyu akawa Sheikh Muhammad bin Sheikh Mataka, tarafu[119] ya Sayyidna Sa'id, akamupa na askari kuwaka gereza.[120] Baadaye wakateta na mtu wa Sayyidna Sa'id bin Sultan kwa sababu alivunda banda la mutepe alowaka Sheikh Muhammad mbee[121] ya gereza. Na Sheikh Muhammad naye kavunda gereza.

---

[117] غرم = "expenses," here, evidently, meaning supplies of all kinds. *Askari* and *gharama* are to be taken as defining *zita*, not as items in addition to it.

[118] A small town on the Ozi estuary, opposite the entrance of the Belezoni canal. I have the following note, made at Witu: "Both these towns (Shaka and Wangwana wa Mashah) were destroyed by Bwana Tamu; the people fled to Kau (*i.e.* the place where Kau was afterwards built) and hid there in the bush for seven years, so that people did not know what had become of them (*watu hawana habari myaka sabaa*); then they built Kau."

[119] Not in Krapf; and Madan's equivalents — "part, business, duty, work, task" — do not fit the present passage. The sense here required can be gathered from طرّف (second conjugation of طَرَف) "marcher sur les bords, côtoyer," طرف "partie, côté." (Belot, *Vocabulaire arabe français*, Beyrouth, 1899).

[120] Perhaps it is superfluous to observe that this word is derived from the Portuguese *igreja*, "church," churches being the first stone buildings erected by the Portuguese on the coast — or those which attracted most attention. The ruins of one such (known as *Kanisa ya ng'ombe*) were in existence at Mombasa in 1845, though even then in course of destruction (see Krapf, *Reisen*, I. 246 [*Editor's note*: for an English translation of this work see Johann Ludwig Krapf, *Travels, Researches and Missionary Labors* (Boston, 1860).]) — and the walls of the chapel of São José (afterwards turned into a fort by the Arabs) are still standing on Ras Serani.

[121] Kiamu for *mbele*.

Na wakati hunu akafa Sultan Ahmad Kau, babake Fumo Bakar Sultan wa Witu, akaketi mahala pake Kau Sultan Ahmad amukuliwao Simba, Sultani wa Witu.

Na kabla ya Sheikh Muhammad bin Sheikh Mataka asiyavunda gereza ya Siyu yalikuwa fitina yeye na Fumo Bakari bin Sheikh, kamutoa Pate, akaya Lamu Fumo Bakari. (p. 398) Katamalaki yeye Pate jinsi aliokuwa na nguvu, na udhaifu wa Pate wakati hunu wasikiri[122] wakuu wa Pate; akaya kuwapija wakubwa wa Pate wakasimamama[123] kuuana, wala hawana shauri la mtu wala mfalme, kwa shauri lao watu wa Pate: Muhammad Mkuu en-Nabhani na Bwana Rehema bin Ahmad en-Nabhani na Nasr bin Abdallah bin Abd-es-Salam ndiye aliokuwa *mudabiri 'l amûr*[124] ya mambo haya: wakataka zana na bunduku wakapijana na Sheikh Muhammad bin Mataka, wakamushinda, wakafa na watu wangi wa Sheikh Muhammad na maamiri wake watu wawili, bwana Damila na Maulana wa Sheyekulu. Akisa Sheikh Muhammad bin Mataka kaona mambo haya, akaya kutaka amani kwa Muhammad bin Bwana Mkuu[125] 'l madhkûr, kwani ndiye aliokuwa baba wao[126] katika hawa watu

---

[122] *Kiri* (Ar., قِرّ) "acknowledge, assent"; the rendering adopted seems to be the only one that will make sense in the context, and the subjunctive construction, I think, justifies taking it in connection with *udhaifu wa Pate* and supplying the words in brackets.

[123] *Simama* may mean either to cease (="stand still") or to remain *in statu quo*, persist in a course of action": the latter sense seems to be the only one which suits the context.

[124] Ar. مُدَبِّر "he who conducts an affair, administrator, director" — verbal noun from دبر, امُوْر pl. of اَمْر "thing, affair." *Ya mambo haya* seems like a tautology — it may be added as an explanation of the Arabic term.

[125] This is the man previously called Muhammad Mkuu en-Nabhani. He was also know as Bwana Simba.

[126] Meaning "the chief," or "senior."

watatu, wakapatana wakawa hali moya, kataka kumupa yeye Muhammad bin Bwana Mkuu ufalume wa Pate na Siu; kaiza Muhammad bin Bwana Mkuu, akamwambia, "Mimi ni mtu mzima,[127] kamutwae Sultani Ahmad mfalme wa Witu, Simba." Wakenda kumtwaa, kapeka watu wake Sheikh Muhammad bin Sheikh Mataka, na Pate akenenda Nasir bin Abdallah bin Abd-es-Salam, wakenenda Kau kumutwaa Sultan Ahmad Simba. Ikasikilia khabari Unguja, kwa Sultan Sayyidna Majid bin Sa'id, kwani, kabula ya hapo alikuwa (a)mekufa Sayyidna Sa'id;[128] akamweta waziri wake Sayyid Seleman bin Ahmad kwa marikabu, kushika Pate, kuvunda fitina. (p. 400) Akiwasili [Manda][129] Pate, ameziye[130] kushikwa[131] na mtu wa Sultan Ahmad Abubakar Nabhan iliokwenda naye, Nasr bin Abdallah bin Abd-es-Salam; akisa kupata khabari Sayyid Seleman bin Ahmad karejea Unguja, na Sheikh Muhammad bin Sheikh Mataka hapo ndipo alipovunda gereza ya Siu. Kisa kuwasili Sultan Ahmad Pate, akaba'iwa[132] na watu wa Pate, na Sheikh Muhammad bin Sheikh Mataka, na Watikuu; Sheikh Muzee bin Sefu na Sheikh

---

[127] At Lamu this usually means "old," — not merely "adult."

[128] Sa'id bin Sultan died at sea (on board his frigate the *Victoria*), October 19th, 1856.

[129] This is distinctly written ماند , with *nd*. Ordinarily the form of ر called *re kusuka* is used for this combination, so that مَارَ could be read either "mara" or "manda." If the latter is right, the meaning must be something like, "He arrived at Manda near Pate." But I cannot help thinking that it is a slip for *mara*, "at once" — or, in this context, "as soon as."

[130] Explained as equivalent to *amekwisha*.

[131] The *w* of the passive is seldom written, but seems to be required here. *Iliokwenda* in the next line is probably a mistake for *aliokwenda*.

[132] Bantu passive formed from Ar. باع , "to install in a position of authority." Krapf seems doubtful whether the word really occurs in Swahili. إِستَقَرَ, the tenth conjugation of قَرَ .

Sheku na Muhammad Mote, akasitakiri kwake Sultan Ahmad ufalme kwa jumla ya watu walioko katika kisiwa cha Pate.

Sayyidna Majid bin Sa'id kapeka watu wa Lamu [Pate][133] kwa nasaha, pamoya na Sheikh Muhî-ed-Dîn[134] kutaka atwae Sultan Ahmad baadhi ya askari wake waketi Pate, na Sheikh Muhî-ed-Dîn, huyu ndiye alowatoa askari wa Sayidna Majid katika gereza ya Siu, alipowapija Muhammad bin Sheikh

---

[133] The sense requires "Pate" here. [*Editor's note*: Werner's conjecture appears correct on the strength of MS 344.]

[134] This Sheikh Muhî-ed-Dîn was one of the two Kadhis of Zanzibar, and was still living when Burton was there in 1857 — "a Lamu doctor of the Sunni school" (*Zanzibar*, I., 263). Burton's account of these incidents is worth quoting, though it must be remembered that he obtained it at Zanzibar and seems to assume that Pate had always been subject to the Sayyid.

"Sayyid Sa'id was persuaded (January 6th, 1843) to attack that notorious plunderer, Bana M'takha [=Muhammad bin Sheikh Mataka], chief of Siwi, a small territory near Lamu, who had persuaded one Fumo Bakkari and afterwards his brother Muhammad bin Sheikh to delcare himself Lord of Patte [=Pate] and independent of the Arab power. . . . The second son [of Sayyid Sa'id], Sayyid Khalifa, then disembarked his 1,200 to 1,300 troops, Maskatis and Waswahili, 'cowardly as Maskatis,' who with the Suri are the proverbial dastards of the race. He served out, with Semitic economy, five cartridges per head, and he marched them inland without a day's rest, after a 'buggalow' — voyage from Arabia. Short of ammunition and worn out by fatigue, they soon yielded to the violent onslaught of the enemy. The Wagunya, or, as some write the word, Bajuni [=Watikuu], warriors described to be a fierce race of savages, descended from the Waswahili, the Somal and the Arab colonists, charged in firm line, brandishing spear-heads like those of the Wamasai, a cubit long, and shouting as they waved their standards, wooden hoops hung round with dried and stuffed spoils of men. The Arabs fled with such precipitation that some 300 were drowned, an indiscriminate massacre and mutilation took place, the *England* and the *Prince of Wales* (Sayyid Sa'id's warships) opened an effectual fire upon their own boats and friends; the guns which had been landed were captured, and the Sayyid Khalid saved himself only by the speed of his horse. The operation was repeated with equal unsuccess next year, Sayyid Sa'id himself embarking on board the *Victoria*; the general, Hammad bin Ahmad, fell into an ambuscade, and again the artillery were lost. After a blockade of the coast which lasted till 1866 [*sic*, query 1846], the Kazi of Zanzibar, Muhiyy el-Din, of Lamu, landing upon his native island, talked over the insurgents. Bana M'takha afterwards sent back the Arab cannon, saying that he could not afford to keep weapons which ate such vast meals of powder and acknowledging for a consideration the supremacy of Zanzibar, retaining his power and promising, but never intending, to pay an annual tribute of $5,000." *Zanzibar*, I., 298-300. [*Editor's note*: see Richard F. Burton *Zanzibar: City, Island, and Coast*. 2 vols. (London, 1872).]

Mataka; askari wa Sayyidna Majid wali[135] ndani gerezani,[136] akenda Sheikh Muhî-ed-Dîn kawatoa kwa amani, kwani ali mtu wa Sayyidna Majid. Alipokwenda nao kwa Sayyidna Majid kafanya hasira sana, akatwaa daraka[137] Sheikh Muhîdîn kurejeza askari, alipoona ghathabu ya Sayyidna Majid, kwani huyu Muhîdîn alina hila nyingi na ilimu nyingi; basi, akiya yeye na watu wa Lamu hatta Pate, na watu wa Lamu walokuya ni Sheikh Ahmad na nduye. Kanena na Sultan Ahmad, akatwaa askari kwa[138] baada ya shidda kwa sababu ya suhuba[139] ya Sheikh Ahmad na nduye. Akakhalifu shauri la waziri wake, Nasr bin Abdallah bin Abd-es-Seleman, kwani aliiza kutia Waarabu Pate hatta umoya. Wakisa kungia Waarabu Pate wakafanya shauri moya na Mwana Jahi binti Sultani Fumo Luti Kipunga wa Bwana Fumo Madi, mke wa Sultan Fumo Bakar bin Sheikh. Wakati hunu Sultani Fumo Bakar alikuweko Lamu tini ya shauri la Sayyidna Majid bin Sa'id tangu alipotolewa Pate.

Na kula siku wakitia askari na zana usiku usiku kwa siri, kisa alipojua Sultani Ahmad ikiwa fitina, na askari wamekuwa wangi Pate, wakamupija Sultan Ahmad ghafula, baada ya kisa hila kutaka kumushika wasiweze taratibu hiyo, kwani watu wote wa Pate walikuwa shauri moya na Sayyidna Majid bin Sa'id, illa waziri wake, Nasr bin Abdallah bin Abd-es-Salaam. Wakapijana

---

135 It is not very common to find the verb *li*, "to be," standing alone like this — *cf. ali* in the next line; more usually *walikuwa* etc.

136 *ndani gerezani*, not so usual as *ndani ya gereza*, unless *ndani* is to be taken as an adverb.

137 دَرَك in the text seems to be a mistake for دَرَق .

138 This *kwa* seems unnecessary to the consturction.

139 "Friendship," from Ar.صحب. Not in Krapf.

ndani ya mui wa Pate, wakamutoa Sultan Ahmad Pate, Sheikh Muhammad bin Sheikh Mataka kamutukulia Siu. Pate wakaketi Waarabu, na baharini wakatia marikabu. Zita zalipokuwa zikuu sana, akaya yeye Sayyidna Majid, waka [husuru][140] kisiwa cha Pate kwa bahari katia na salasili[141] katika kanwa ya mto wa Siu kuyo,[142] wakapijana miezi sita kwa bahari na kwa Pate[143] na janibu ya Tikuuni.[144] Mzee Sefu akakhalifu akawa mtu wa Sayyidna Majid bin Sa'id, kwa hila nyingi na maneno mangi, wakaona dhiki sana Sultan Ahmad na Sheikh Muhammad bin Sheikh Mataka.

Na nti ya Siu ikawa fitina, baadhi wapenda Sayidi kwa sababu ya mashaka wamezopata na watuwe ni Sharif Maulana bin Abubakar na 'Asi bin Ahmad es-Somali. Walipoona hiyao,[145] Sultan Ahmad na Sheikh Muhammad wakataka amani kwa Sayidi, kawapa. Katika maneno ya mani Sultan Ahmad kasafiri kwa siri usiku kenda zake barani, Kau. Na baada yake Sheikh Muhammad kenenda marikabuni kwa Sayyidi katika musamaha, na Sayyidi kamusamehe. Sayyidi kenda zake Unguja; kisa Sheikh Muhammad akenenda Unguja kumjisi.[146] Sayyidi kamfunga kamupeka Mombasa ngomeni, na watu

---

[140] The MS. has *hurusu*, but it should be *husuru*, "besiege" (Ar. حصر).

[141] Ar. سلسلة, "chain."

[142] This *kuyo* (or *kuyu*?) seems quite superfluous in the sentence, unless it is meant for *kwa yuu*, "above" (*ku yuu* is not used).

[143] Probably written by mistake for *nti*, "by land."

[144] The mainland east and north of the Lamu archipelago. For the settlement of Watikuu at Faza, see *Journal* for January 1915, p. 157.

[145] Kiamu for *haya* (sc. *mambo*).

[146] Ar. جس, "to spy out."

wangi. Akafa baada ya siku nyingi. Na zamani alipokwenda Unguja Sheikh Muhammad 'l madhkûr, alietewa na waraka S'ûd bin Hamad[147] kumushika Sultan Ahmad kwa hila, asiweze. Sultan Ahmad kenda zake Witu. Akenda na Paza S'ûd bin Hamad kamushika Omar wa Bwana Mataka, na zijana za Sheikh Muhammad wote wakashikwa Siu wakapekwa ngomeni Mombasa. Omari kamufunga Lamu.

Baada ya hapo, akatamalaki Sayidi Majidi Sawahili zote, pasiwe na mtu tena wakumuaridhi. Na Sultan Ahmad kaketi Witu katika ta'a ya Sayyid Majid bin Sa'id hatta wakati wa Sayyid Barghash, kataka kuweka askari Witu na bendera, asikiri Sultan Ahmad, kapeka zita kumpija, asiweze, kafanya amani.

Baada ya hapo, S'ûd bin Hamad asifurahi Sayyid Barghash, kwa sababu kufanya amani upesi, naye hakumupija sana; kapeka zita mara ya pili, zikuu, na Liwali S'ûd bin Hamad. Sultan Ahmad katwaa himaya kwa Jarman, wakamupa na baadhi ya bara ya Sawahili. Akafa Sultan Ahmad katika himaya ya Jarmani, sene 1306.

Akatawali Fumo Bakar bin Sultan Ahmad bin Sheikh, ikatokea fitina, yeye na Jarmani,[148] Küntzell alimpija bawabu wa lango rasasi kamuua; mabawabu wa lango la mui waliokuwapo nao wakampija Küntzell na wazungu waliofuetene,[149] wakawaua bighairi[150] ya kutaka amri kwa Sultan Fumo (p. 406) Bakar; kisa kuona meuawa mwendani wao nao wali[wa]ua. Na watu wa

---

[147] Sayyid Majid's Liwali. See Stigand, p. 97, where, however, nothing is said about the Sheikh's sons.

[148] For a fuller account of this affair, see Stigand, pp. 99-101.

[149] Old perfect of *fuatana*.

[150] Ar., "without."

Ndamuyu[151] na watu wa Mkonumbi wakisa kupata khabari nao waliwaua wazungu walokuweko. Baada ya hapo ikiya Dola tukufu ya Wangereza, wakataka watu wale wa Mkonumbi na wa Wandamuyu, kuwatia katika hukumu. Sultan Fumo Bakar asiridhiki kuwatoa.

Dola ya Wangereza ikamupija Sultan Fumo Bakar, lail 11 Rabbi 'l auwal,[152] sene 1308, hatta assubuhi yake saa ya pili, wakatamalaki mui, wakamutoa Witu kwa zita. Sultani kenda Jongeni, kaketi hatta tarikh 28 Jemad 'l Auwal,[153] sene 1308, akafa Sultan Fumo Bakar.

Baada yake kashika mahala pake nduye Bwana Sheikh bin Sultan Ahmad. Baada ya siku tatu akashikwa na nduye Fumo Omar na Bwana Afthul, wakamfunga Bwana Sheikh kashikwa yeye Fumo Omar bin Sultan Ahmad bin Sheikh, ikawa kama jinsi yalokuwa baina yake na Dola tukufu ya Wangereza. Wa ama ufalume, wakisa wakutamalaki Witu ni Sultan Fumo Bakar na wakisa kutamalaki Pate ni Sultan Ahmad Simba, Sultan wa Witu. Na Sultan wa kwanda ni Seleman bin Seleman bin Muthafar en-Nabhani Imâm 'l Ya'arubi.

Hii ndiyo khabari ya Nabhani kuya Sawahili, na khabari zao, wametawali wafalume 31, wahid wa thelathin,[154] na mwanamke umoya,

---

[151] I have been unable to identify this place, which, lower down, is called Wandamuyu (it might also be read Wandamunyu or Wandamoyo) [*Editor's note*: the latter name also spelt separately Wanda Muyu, recurs in other MSS.]. Stigand, p. 100. "Now at Mkunumbi and *Ongoni* there were white men. These were killed at the instigation of. . .the Liwalis of Mkunumbi and *Hidiyo*." [Editor's note: Yluisaker names Midiokoma and Midiojifa among the burned villages. Marguerite Yluisaker, *Lamu in the Nineteenth Century* (Boston: Boston University Press), p. 152.] Neither of these names can be made out of the text as it stands.

[152] October 25, 1890.

[153] January 9, 1891.

[154] Arabic numerals.

ndiye wa thenin wa thelathin. Na khabari zao ni hizi tumezonakili kwa Muhammad bin Fumo Omar en-Nabhani, amukuliwao Bwana Kitini, naye alipokea na bibye[155] Muhammad bin Bwana Mkuu en-Nabhani, amkuliwao Bwana Simba alodhibitiye[156] khabari za kae, na nasaba zao kama hizi tumezotangulia kuzitaya.

HAMAD SALEH MUHAMMAD

bi amri il Liwali Abed bin Hamad.[157]

21/4/03.

(p. 408) P.S.—Huyu Bwana Mkuu wa Sheikh zamani za ufalme wake alimpija kofi mtu wa Pate kabaili sana,[158] ukapita muda wa mwaka mmoja, ukisha, naye yuna wana thenini wa thalathini waume, wakafanya shauri na jama'a zao, wakatimia watu mia, wakamwendea usiku, akabisha lango la diwani, sauti ya mtu mmoja, yule bawabu alipojua kwamba ni mtu mmoja, bawabu akafungua lango. Kwanza wakamuua yule bawabu, tena kamuingilia mfalme ndani ghafula, hana selaha, wakampija dharuba ya mkono, wakamkata vipande viwili, kipande kimoja kiweko cha mkono kikaanguka tini. Pana kiti

---

[155] *Bibi* in the northern dialects is "grandfather," "grandmother" being *nana*.

[156] ضبت , not in Krapf.

[157] The MS. ends here, about the middle of the page. At the foot is written, in red ink, "T.P.O." (*sic*), and on the other side of the leaf is written (in a different, and inferior hand) the following passage, headed "P.S."

[158] The story is differently told in Stigand (p. 63 *et seq.*). Fumo Luti had taken away the wife of a craftsman named Fundi Suleiman, who plotted to be revenged on him, along with a party of malcontents, already disaffected towards the king because of his "lowly origin" — his mother having been a fisherman's daughter. Suleiman struck the blow, as described in the text, and the Sultan, with his left hand, clove him in two — "he ran away and fell, outside, split in two halves."!

cha ngovi, akakipija kwa ule mkono uliokatwa kigutu, akatoboa kiti, akfanya ngao, akamrukia mtu mmoja, akamnyang'anya upanga, na ngao ni kile kiti; akawapija watu thalatha wa arubaini, kwa mkono wa kushoto, ndio uliokuwa mzima. Na Diwani ni kubwa sana, ina nafasi, wangine wakaruka tangu juu hatta tini, wakavundika maguu.[159] Na mle Diwani wakaamka watu, wakawapija. Waliotoka salama ni watu saba'a. Tena yule mfalme Bwana Mkuu wa Sheikh akasema, "Mimi ni mfalme, watu ra'ia hunibusu,[160] na mkono wa kulia umekatwa; kubusu mkono wa kushoto haifai." Akatia mafuta ndani ya sifuria, yakawika[161] motoni, hatta yakawia[162] sana, akautia mkono ndani ya mafuta, akauzuia,[163] na mafuta yawia sana ndani ya sifuria akafa.—Akatawala mwana wa nduguye, Bwana Fumo Madi. Naye, alipoona Wapate wataka fanya fitina, akawashika watu arbaini, akawatinda kana kuku.

Bwana Fumo Madi, alipokufa, ndipo alipotawala mwanawe, Sultani Ahmadi bin Fumo Luti.

---

[159] Kimvita and Kiamu: sing. *guu*, instead of *mguu, miguu.*

[160] The usual salutation to one of high rank — paid nowadays, *e.g.*, to the Liwali of Mombasa. As a rule it consists of bowing the head over the hand and raising it towards the lips, without actually touching them, though no doubt this was formerly done. The left hand is considered unclean and never used in eating.

[161,162] The pure Bantu word, now replaced by Ar. *chemka*; — cf. Zulu *bila*, Chinyanja, *wira*, etc. *Wika*, neut. pass., perhaps denotes that it was in a state of growing hot, — *wia* the point when it actually came to the boil.

[163] The object-pronoun *u* evidently refers to *mknono*; "he hindered it"; we must supply "from bleeding" or some equivalent words.

HISTORY OF PATE

The first man who came (to Pate), among the Nabhans,[1] was Seleman, son of Seleman, son of Muthafar the Nabhan, with his brothers, Ali bin Seleman and Athman bin Seleman. He who was Sultan was this Seleman aforesaid, and he was king in Arabia and was driven out by the Ya'arubi[2] and came to Pate in the year 600 (six hundred) of the Hijra (was) his coming, and he married the daughter of the King of Pate, 'l Batawîna.[3] And the custom

---

[1] For the origin of the Nabhân (Nebhân) family, see Badger, *Imâms and Seyyids of Oman* (Introduction, p. viii). They reigned over Oman, with the title of *malik* ("king") from A.D. 1154 to A.D. 1406. Unfortunately, there is a gap in the records which form the material for the chronicle of Suleiman bin Sa'id (translated by Badger in the volume above referred to), and very few particulars of these kings are available. One of them was named Muzhaffar bin Suleimân, but he cannot be the same as the Muzhaffar (Muthafar) whose grandson became Sultan of Pate. The latter is not mentioned in the chronicle, though there is a reference to an earlier emigration to "the land of the Zanj," in the time of 'Abdu 'l Malik bin Marwan (A.D. 684-705). But *cf.* Stigand, p. 30.

[2] ". . . The el Ya'arubah, whose presence in Oman at a very early period is attested by concurrent tradition . . . supplied a succession of Imâms to the country from A.D. 1624-1741, when they were superseded by the existing dynasty of the Al-Bû-Sa'id" (Badger, p. vi). As the names of only four Nabhân kings are recorded during the interval between 1154 and 1406, it is probable that some names have dropped out, and also that one or more Ya'arubi chiefs reigned after the expulsion of Suleimân (Seleman) and his brothers, in or about 1204.

[3] This form of the name seems preferable. As the termination is feminine, the name would seem to be that of the King of Pate's daughter. [*Editor's note*: Werner's Arabic is inadequate here. The MS gives the correct Arabic plural of *nisba*, or family name, of the ruler. The reference is thus to the dynasty.] *Batawi* is the name of an Arab clan, some of whose representatives are still living at Mombasa. *Cf.* also Stigand, pp. 160, 161. This King of Pate is elsewhere called Ishak (Stigand, p. 31). The original foundation of Pate (not mentioned in the MS. before us) dates back to A.H. 69 (A.D. 689), and was no doubt due to the two brothers, Suleimân and Sa'id, who about that time were driven out of Oman by the invasion of El-Hajjâj (Badger, p. xii). [*Editor's note*: Werner is being overly trustful

of all the Swahili, to this day, is this: if a man carries your daughter, when the seven days of the wedding are finished, he goes to see his wife's father, (who) gives him something — this is the usage of all the Swahili. When Seleman went to see him, (his father-in-law) handed over the kingdom to him. From thenceforth he reigned, the aforesaid Seleman bin Seleman. And there was a town to the east of Pate, called Kitaka; there was also a second town called (p. 155) Shanga on the east of Pate; and Faza had its own rulers, the Mafâziyûn. The kingdom of Pate had these towns, Kitaka and Pate; and Manda had its own king — the (king) of Manda was separate.[4] And Seleman begat two sons, Muhammad and Ahmad, and afterwards he died, in the year 625 [A.D. 1228].

There reigned (in his stead) Muhammad bin Seleman, and his age was twenty years, and Ahmad was a boy of fifteen years. Muhammad reigned after his father and fought with the men of Shanga and conquered them and destroyed their town. Then the men of Shanga came to Pate, and some of them ran away. Among those who came to Pate (were some), their tribe (was that of) [Kibwana Ndanguu];[5] they escaped, and it was not known where they

---

of the legendary details. For archeological evidence of early settlement in the area see, for example, H.N. Chittick, "Discoveries in the Lamu Archipelago," *Azania* 2 (1967) pp. 37-68; Mark Horton, "Early Muslim Trading Settlements on the East African Coast: New Evidence from Shanga," *Antiquaries Journal*, 67/2 (1987), pp. 290-323; and his unpublished Ph.D. dissertation *The Early Settlement of the Northern Swahili Coast* (Cambridge University, 1984).

[4] Or: the (people) of Manda were separate. In the island of Pate, Shanga and Kitaka were subject to Pate, and Faza (Paza, or Rasin) was independent, and Siu, we learn from other sources, did not yet exist. (Its origin is referred to later on.)

[5] So in MS., but Muhammadi Kijuma informs me that it should be Kitakaungi, "a *shamba* in Pate where Seleman first landed and built (a town)."

had gone; (but) when many days had passed, news came to King Muhammad bin Seleman through some hunters. They told him: "Those who were conquered, we have seen them in the bush." He sent people to look for them, and they overtook them on the road to the bush; they had made (themselves) huts and lived there. They carried them off and came with them to Pate; and afterwards the king sent them back to their (own) place; this is the origin of Siu.[6]

There also came other Swahili people, and lived at Siu, and afterwards the Wafamau came and were chiefs of Siu, under the suzerainty of the King of Pate, for many days.

In the year 650 [A.D. 1252], Sultan Muhammad died, and his brother, (p. 157) Sultan Ahmad bin Seleman, ruled;[7] and he governed the land of Pate exceedingly well, by planting fields and building houses; he did not make war on any place. He died in 670 [A.D. 1271], and (there) reigned Ahmad bin Muhammad bin Seleman; and he followed his uncle's example in (securing) the prosperity of the town of Pate, and he begat many sons. When he died,[8] his

---

[6] This name is written, as Captain Stigand (p. 164) points out, both Siu (سِوُ) and Siyu (سِيُوْ). The former more nearly represents the usual pronunciation, but is liable, when written in the Arabic character, to be mistaken for *Si-wu*.

[7] According to Captain Stigand's version, it was Ahmad the son of Muhammad (not his brother, Ahmad bin Seleman) who succeeded him, A.H. 650 (Stigand, p. 31), and reigned till 690 (the year of Ahmad bin Muhammed's death is not given in the MS). Possibly the elder Ahmad only ruled as regent during his nephew's minority.

[8] The date of Ahmad bin Muhammad's death is not given by the chronicler. "C." puts it at A.D. 1291, thus giving him a reign of about 20 years, and also omits the reign of Ahmad bin Seleman. For the destruction of Faza, see Stigand, p. 37. The site was re-settled by the Watikuu (Swahili of the mainland) in the time of Bwanatamu (about A.D. 1700). Sherif Abdallah, of Witu, gave me the following information, in December, 1912: "There were ten clans of Watikuu and the Wakatwa (a tribe of Somali, who eat no fish to this day

son Muhammad bin Ahmad bin Muhammad bin Seleman reigned; and he kept on conquering the towns of the Coast — Faza and Manda, in many wars, in the land of Paza. And as to Manda, they entered it by a war of cunning,[9] and destroyed it utterly and carried off some of the people to Pate, and part (of them) ran away and went to every place: they came to Shela and Malindi and other towns. Those who came to Shela put themselves under the protection of the men of Lamu. The king demanded them of the men of Lamu, they refused, as regards those words [*i.e.*, they refused the demand]. The king died in the year 732 [A.D. 1331].

He left one son, Sultan Omar bin Muhammad bin Ahmad (p. 159) bin Muhammad bin Seleman. He reigned after his father and returned (to) his father's words to the men of Lamu, demanding from them the men of Manda; the men of Lamu refused to surrender them, and he made war on them; the men of Lamu sued for peace and were under the suzerainty of Sultan Omar bin Muhammad bin Ahmad bin Muhammad bin Seleman. He became very powerful and smote the whole of the Swahili towns: Ozi, Malindi, Kiwayu,

---

— and their distinctive mark, these Wakatwa, is that they wear neither *kanzu* nor *kofia* to this day). The Somalis drove them out — they lived at Miyao, at Kiunga, and higher up (the coast) at Burikao; and they escaped to Pate to Bwana Tamu, and he gave them Paza, which was then mere wilderness, and told them 'Stay here.' Miyao, Shungwaya and Burikao [Port Durnford], they were all towns of these Watikuu, (before) they were driven out by the Somalis."

Cf. Stigand, p. 56. The Somali were formerly called "wakatwa" by the Wapokomo; the word is said to mean "those who kill people." Old men are still living who remember the use of this name: the one now current is "Gavira." The Milky Way is sometimes called *njia ya Gavira*, as though, running as it does, more or less north and south, it indicated the track of the Somali raiders.

[9] The story is told in full by Captain Stigand, pp. 38-43. I heard the story of Bakiumbe at Faza, and noted down at Pate the song of the Manda captives, quoted by him on p. 43.

Kitao, and Miya and Imidhi and Watamu, till he came to Kirimba;[10] he gained possession of all the towns, from Pate to Kirimba, and in each town he placed a man of his own, as judge [*Editor's note*: rather, "to govern."]. This is the origin of those *majumbe* who are to be found on the whole coast; and the meaning of (the word) *majumbe* is "slaves of the Yumbe." This (word) *yumbe* is the name of the House of the Kingdom (= the royal Palace) of Pate.

On the eastern side, he extended his dominion as far as Warsheikh by war. He began to wage war from Kiwayu and Tula and Shungwaya and all the harbours: Barawa, Marka, Mukdishu. There at Mukdishu he placed a governor (to administer) justice in all the harbours which were (near) Mukdishu. And he lived, and all these lands were subject to him, except Zanzibar; he did not rule over Zanzibar at this time; it was not a country important (enough to have) a king. And this king was very fond of war; he also loved his subjects, and his subjects lived in great peace and obtained much wealth, and the land of Pate prospered greatly. He died in 749 [A.D. 1348].

---

[10] *Cf.* Stigand, p. 45, where it seems to be implied that Kirimba is as far south as Kilwa, if not farther: "Then the Pate people passed on overland and fought the whole of the Mrima coast from Wasini and Pangani to Saadani, Tanga, Kilwa and Kilwa Island and the Mgao coast. They passed on, and in every place that they took they put a chief . . . till they reached Kirimba; these were the ends of the Nabahan kingdom, Mukadisho and Kirimba." [*Editor's note*: indeed the Kirimba (Kerimba, Querimba) islands are south of Kilwa, off the Mazambique coast.] This important passage is omitted in our MS. The title of *Jumbe* for local headmen is still used in what is now German East Africa. I have not heard it in the neighbourhood of Mombasa, or further north. Muhammadi Kijuma says Kirimba was a town of the Portuguese, in the south. The King of Pate conquered it and carried off two carved wooden pillars, one of which is still preserved in the house of Mshaham Bin Kombo, at Lamu.

ERRATUM. — Miss Werner writes to say that it was erroneously stated in the January *Journal* (p. 149), that Mshamu bin Kombo (who, by the bye, is a brother of "Bwana Kitini") was a "clerk in the Provincial Commissioner's office," which is not the case.

She adds, "Mr. Reddie also informs me that Mshamu has presented the carved pillar mentioned on p. 159 (note) to the Nairobi Museum."

(p. 161) He left two sons, Muhammad and Ahmad; (the one who) reigned (was) Muhammad bin Omar bin Muhammad bin Ahmad bin Muhammad bin Seleman; and there was no war — he ruled the whole kingdom of his father by peaceable means. And he was extremely fond of money and of trade, and caused men to make voyages in ships and sent them to India and traded there, and he had great good luck as regards money. And on one occasion his son set out on a voyage and discovered an island in the sea, (where) he landed and found a silver-mine;[11] he sent people there, and they worked and obtained much wealth, (and) wealth increased greatly in the land of Pate, so that they even made swords of silver and ladders of silver and many vessels for (household) use of silver. And (the King) had four sons: Bwana Tamu, and Ahmad, and Abubakar and Omar. He died in 797.

(After him) reigned his brother, Ahmad bin Omar bin Muhammad bin Ahmad bin Muhammad bin Seleman, and he lived at peace in all his lands and died in the year 840.

(Then) reigned Abubakar bin Muhammad bin Omar bin Muhammad bin Ahmad bin Muhammad bin Seleman, and he remained in a good course of conduct, and (of) all the towns under his sway there was none destroyed for any reason whatever. He died in 875 [A.D. 1470].[12] ||

---

[11] This story of the silver-mine is told more fully in Captain Stigand's book, pp. 45-58. Its discoverer is there said to be Bwana Mkuu, son of Abubakar and nephew of Sultan Omar, not a son of Muhammad bin Omar. The "ladders of silver" mentioned a little lower down were, it here appears, meant "to climb up into bed with"; the best beds, in a wealthy house, being of considerable height.

[12] Abubakar's reign is given by Captain Stigand as A.H. 825-A.H. 855. The succession of sultans, too, is not the same. Omar is said to have been succeeded (in A.H. 795) by his son, Muhammad, and he in 825, by his brother Abubakar. Ahmad bin Omar is omitted. Muhammad bin Abubakar is evidently identical with the Bwana Mkuu bin Abubakar who

(p. 279) He left two sons, Muhammad and Ahmad, and (he who) reigned (was) Muhammad bin Abubakar bin Muhammad bin Omar bin Muhammad bin Ahmad bin Muhammad bin Seleman. In his time,[13] the Europeans, (viz), the Portuguese, came to all the Swahili towns; they stayed at Mombasa[14] and made a fort. And in the direction of Pate they built Dondo, and all the people of the mainland came to an agreement with them to give them money, and they entered into subjection to them, and they (the Portuguese) harassed the king in the city of Pate and defeated him on the side of Shindakasi and made a causeway,[15] in order to attack the town of Pate, but they could not do it. Afterwards they agreed as to peace and made a writing of the conditions, and the Europeans remained at Pate and made a customhouse

---

discovered the silver-mine, but the latter is stated to have reigned from A.H. 855 to A.H. 903.

[13] Either the dates in this document are wrong, or the chronicler has confused this Muhammad bin Abubakar with a later king of the same name, who invited the Portuguese into his dominions, on his accession in 1531 (C.). He was dethroned by Bwana Bakari, but returned in 1537 and reigned till 1570. B. places the coming of the Portuguese in the reign of Abubakar, A. H. 825-855 (= A.D. 1422-1452), which, of course, is impossible.

[14] This is the existing fort at Mombasa, built in 1595 and repaired (according to the inscription still legible over the gateway) by Francisco de Cabreira in 1635.

[15] *Kuwaka tiati*, "to build the ground" (*tiati* seems to be peculiar to the northern dialects) is a very curious expression, apparently referring to the construction of the paved causeway, of which traces were pointed out to me under the sand in Pate Creek. I was told the Portuguese had made it in order to drag their cannon from the landing-place at Shindakzai up to the town. [*Editor's note*: see, however, Heepe's version (#13), and Stigand's account of the underground passage (MS p. 48). MS 177 (f.5) also speaks of the Portuguese "building the ground of the beach" with military purposes. Other MSS have slightly varying wording.]

and called it, in their own language, *fundika*.[16] And they caused a very great deal of trouble in the island of Pate. After these things, the King died, in the year 900 [A.D. 1494], leaving two sons, Bwana Mkuu and Abubakar. (The one who) reigned (was) Abubakar bin Muhammad bin Abubakar bin Muhammad bin Omar bin Muhammad bin Ahmad bin Muhammad bin Seleman; he lived at peace with the Europeans, and they agreed, according to the custom of his father. He died in (p. 281) 945 [A.D. 1538] leaving two sons, Ahmad and Muhammad. He was succeeded by his brother, Bwana Mkuu bin Muhammad bin Abubakar bin Muhammad bin Omar bin Muhammad bin Ahmad. And they were at variance with the Europeans, but there was no war; he died (worn out) by the intrigues of many days, in 973 [A.D. 1565]. He left one son, Abubakar.

(Next) reigned Muhammad Abubakar bin Muhammad bin Abubakar, &c., who made a treaty with the Europeans and they took some of the towns; he died in 1002 [A.D. 1593].[17]

He left a son, Abubakar; and (there) reigned Abubakar bin Mkuu bin Muhammad bin Abubakar, &c. He remained in a good course, like his father, but his original kingdom had decreased (in extent). He died in 1041 [A.D. 1631], leaving two sons, Bwana Mkuu and Abubakar.

He was succeeded by Abubakar bin Muhammad bin Abubakar bin Muhammad bin Abubakar. He was at variance with the Europeans and sent

---

[16] Captain Stigand says that one of the gates of Pate is still called *Lango la Fandikani* (*Land of Zinj*, p. 162).

[17] It seems impossible to harmonise the dates and order of these kings with Captain Stigand's account, or the other document to which I have referred. The three lists drawn from these three sources are shown in a comparative table at the end of this paper. [*Editor's note*: the table is reproduced in Appendix 3.]

men into the land of Pate, and they smote the Europeans. There came war of the Europeans, and they attacked the city with cannon, and also cut off the roads to the sea, and the people of Pate met with great disasters, and they made peace. After these things, the King died, in 1061 [A.D. 1650].

He left two sons — Bwana Mkuu and Ahmad. He was succeeded by Bwana mkuu bin Muhammad bin Abubakar bin Omar, who made a treaty with the Europeans; and he liked to live at Lamu till the monsoon, and he called it "Amu" [*Editor's note*: this is the only use of "Amu" instead of "Lamu" in this version. It does not appear in the inedited MSS but occurs throughout the Heepe-Wassmuss versions of the *Chronicle*.] and took a wife from among the people of Lamu.

And the Wafamau of Siu at this time revolted from his sway, and he fought with them and destroyed the town of Siu and carried off the people of Siu and brought them to Pate. (p. 283) The headman of Siu escaped and went to Dondo to the Portuguese and claimed their protection. The chief of the Portuguese came to Pate and demanded the men of Siu; they were given up to him and he brought them back to Siu, and they remained at peace. After this the Portuguese used guile and came to Pate in a ship and desired the King to come aboard the ship, but he did not go; he sent his cousin, Bwana Mkuu, and with him (some of the) men of Pate. The Europeans carried them off in the ship and took them to their own country, and not one man ever returned.[18] After this, they defeated the Europeans in every place where they were and

[18] Captain Stigand gives a somewhat different account of this transaction. According to his version, the reigning Sultan at this time was Abubakar bin Bwana Mkuu, and he induced the Portuguese to kidnap his son-in-law Bwana Mkuu and send him to India. The number of men named — or nicknamed — Bwana Mkuu is very confusing.

drove them out, both from the mainland and the islands, and they retreated to Mombasa. After these things, the King died, in 1100 [A.D. 1688], leaving two sons, Bwana Abubakar and Bwana Madi, and one daughter, Mwana Khadija; her surname was Mwana Darini binti Bwana Mkuu bin Abubakar.

He was succeeded by his son, Abubakar bin Mkuu bin Abubakar bin Mkuu bin Muhammad bin Abubakar bin Muhammad bin Omar bin Ahmad bin Muhammad bin Seleman; and the king was smitten suddenly by Ahmad the brother Bwana Mkuu — of him who was carried off by the Europeans to Portugal. And he reigned (viz) the aforesaid Ahmad, the same is Ahmad bin Abubakar bin Muhammad bin Abubakar bin Muhammad bin Omar already mentioned — in the year 1103 [A.D. 1691].

He followed the Portuguese and drove out those who remained, and at that time, Mwana Darini, daughter of Bwana Mkuu bin Abubakar, and wife of Bwana Mkuu bin Abubakar who went to Goa in the time of Sultan Ahmad — when her two brothers had been killed, (namely) Abubakar and Bwana Madi (and he who killed them was Sultan Ahmad bin Abubakar), and her husband had been carried away to (p. 285) Goa previously; she grieved very greatly for her husband, who had been sent on before to Goa, and for the slaying of her two brothers. But after part of the days had passed, she resolved to make a feast for the circumcision of her son, Bwana Tamu the Younger, who was called Sultan Abubakar, Imâm 'l Hadi, son of Bwana Mkuu who went to Goa.

The King, Sultan Ahmad, heard this news of the feast, and he, too, resolved on a celebration (in his turn), on purpose to cheat her out of the horn. But when Mwana Darini became aware of this plan for doing her out of the Horn, she sent for Mwenyi Bayayi Mkuu, a Sharif of the clan of the Laili, who was highly skilled in carving, and told him the whole matter ("the whole of her news") and requested him to make (another) horn superior to that one; he agreed and asked as his wages 120 dollars, and tusks of ivory that he might take which he wanted so that he might be able to choose (the best). Mwana Darini fulfilled for him all the conditions that he wanted, and he made the horn, in secret, and hid it till it was finished and (then, Mwana Darini) produced it suddenly and brought it out into the whole (assembly) of the houses of her brothers and friends at a great dance, and they bestowed much largesse on it. And she said to Mwenyi Bayayi, who had made it: "Do you want your wages, or would you rather have the present?" He said, "I would like the present" — for it was much money. So she received her horn and celebrated her son's *fête*. (p. 287)

And in the time of Bwana Tamu Mukuu, the Lamu people came to borrow the original Horn; and the King gave it to them, and as it passed by sea, the vessel was wrecked and the horn was lost. Bwana Tamu Mukuu asked for the (other) horn from Mwana Darini, and said to her, "Give it to us, that we may use it in the towns," and she said, "Every clan who is willing to give largesse to my horn may use it." Mwana Darini freed a slave of hers who knew how to blow the horn, and said, "This is the (official) blower of the horn, he and his descendants, and for his fee let him be given five dollars and a cloth for carrying the horn and ghee for the blower to drink, and a present (from) every person who is able according to his means."

And that family was called (the house of) the Herald of the Horn, and to this day there are people belonging to it. So, from that time, it has been (the custom that) all the clans of Pate and of the other towns use (the Horn), borrowing it on the above conditions.

The aforesaid Sultan Ahmad remained in his kingship for seven years, and the rain did not fall, and he abdicated the kingdom in the year 1111.[19] He was succeeded by Sultan Abubakar [bin][20] Bwana Tamu Mukuu wa Bwana Mutiti bin Ahmad bin Abubakar bin Omar bin Ahmad bin Omar bin Muhammad bin Ahmad bin Muhammad bin Seleman. He came to an agreement with the King of Maskat, the Imâm 'l Ya'arubi. The King of Pate went to Arabia and came to an agreement with the King of Arabia, that, when he returned to Pate, he would expel the Portuguese from Mombasa. When he arrived, the Sultan of Pate led an expedition against Mombasa and attacked the Europeans on Sunday and slew them in the fort of Mombasa and informed the Imâm 'l Ya'arubi. And he summoned governors of the (house of the) Mazru'i, three men, brothers, Muhammad bin Athman (p. 289) and Ali bin Athman — the third, I do not know him (as to) his name; and they came with soldiers, on behalf of the Imâm 'l Ya'arubi, and that is the origin of the Mazru'i of Mombasa.

And he lived on the most excellent terms with his subjects, and continued long in the kingship (that is to say) forty years, and died in 1152 [A.D. 1739], leaving many children.

After him did not reign his son, (but) there reigned Sultan Ahmad bin Abubakar bin Muhammad bin Abubakar bin Omar bin Ahmad bin Muhammad bin Omar bin Muhammad bin Ahmad bin Muhammad Seleman. He dwelt in much prosperity, and was very fond of collecting great herds of cattle — he died in 1160 [A.D. 1747], and left a son named Bwana Gongo; (but) he was

---

[19] This Sultan is said in "C." to have reigned from 1570 to 1575.

[20] This *bin* must have slipped into the text by mistake. Clearly Abubakar was the same as "Bwana Tamu the Great," one of the most famous of the Pate kings, though the date of his reign (as already pointed out) differs considerably in A. and B.

succeeded by Bwana Tamu the younger who was called Imam 'l Hadi, (son) of Bwana Mkuu who was carried off by the Portuguese, and his (real) name was Abubakar bin Bwana Mkuu bin Abubakar bin Muhammad bin Abubakar bin Muhammad bin Abubakar bin Muhammad bin Omar bin Muhammad bin Ahmad bin Muhammad bin Seleman. And the Imâm 'l Ya'arubi brought an expedition to attack Pate, but they were not able (to subdue) it, and many Arabs were killed, so they returned and made peace. After this, the people of Lamu fought with the King of Pate; they revolted and fought against him, and he was not able (to subdue them) and the men of Lamu came to Pate to fight in the direction of Kitaka, (but) they were defeated and returned to Lamu. [*Editor's note*: MS 321 states that both Siu and Lamu revolted.] After this, the King of Pate waged war (both) by land and sea and attacked the men of Lamu and conquered them; afterwards the King was killed at Pate, by the Pate men, together with the people of the Imâm 'l Ya'arubi, in 1176 [A.D. 1762]. He was succeeded by his sister Sultani Mwana Khadija, daughter of Bwana Mkuu, son of Abubakar, son of Muhammad, son of Abubakar, son of Muhammad, son of Abubakar, son of Muhammad, son of Omar, son of Muhammad, son of Ahmad, son of Muhammad, son of Seleman. And she met with much intrigue in the land of Pate, and it was (so that there were) in the town of Pate two sovereigns, she, Mwana Khadija, and Sultan Omar, and they fought in the town for five years, and Sultan Omar ran away and went to Barawa; afterwards he returned to Pate with a powerful force, (but) he was attacked at night by Mwana Khadija's men and killed. A few days after this, Mwana Khadija died, (p. 291) in the year 1187 [A.D. 1773]. She was succeeded by Bwana Mkuu, son of Bwana Sheikh, son of Bwana Tamu Mkuu. And his subjects worried him greatly with intrigues, and he got no peace, till, in the year 1191 [A.D. 1777], some men of the town entered (his palace) and killed him, at that date.[21]

He was succeeded by Bwana Fumo Madi, whose (real) name was Sultan Muhammad, son of Abubakar, son of Bwana Mkuu, son of Abubakar, son of Muhammad, son of Abubakar, son of Muhammad, son of Abubakar, son of Muhammad, son of Omar, son of Muhammad, son of Ahmad, son of Muhammad, son of Seleman. After he had come to the throne, his subjects wished to make trouble, (but) he defeated them in battle till he had overcome them; and he seized forty men of high rank (and among these forty, two were his own brothers) and butchered them all. Then there was peace, and no man was able to annoy him again. He ruled in peace and no man was able to annoy him again. He ruled in peace and quiet and prosperity, and his subjects enjoyed much quiet till the year 1224 [A.D. 1809], (when) he died. After him there reigned no other king like him, and he left many sons.

He was succeeded by Sultan Ahmad, son of Sheikh, son of Fumo Luti, son of Sheikh, son of Bwana Tamu the Elder [*Editor's note*: the latter is the same person named above, Bwana Tamu Mkuu.]. And intrigues increased in the land of Lamu, (so that) he came to attack them together with the men of Mombasa. The Mazru'i came to Lamu in 1227 [A.D. 1812] and landed at Shela, with a great host, both Mombasa men and Pate men. The men of Lamu came out and fought with the Mombasa and Pate men, and the Mombasa and Pate men were utterly routed, and when they attempted to escape, (they found

---

[21] A detailed account of this event is given in the postscript to this chronicle. It appears that he was not killed on the spot. There is no mention of the murder in C. S[tigand] (pp. 63-65) says it was Fumo Luti who was killed, and his son, Bwana Sheikh, who succeeded him.

that) their ships had been left high and dry (by the ebb tide), and they fought again, a great battle,[22] and an exceeding great number of men were killed, both of Mombasa and Pate; of renowned men, "So-and-so, the son of So-and-so,"[23] eighty-one; but of slaves and those who were not well known there was no enumeration; and in like manner, of the Mombasa men there was no enumeration.

After that, (some) men of Lamu went to Arabia and asked (p. 293) for Sayyid Sa'id, son of Sultan, son of Ahmad the Imam (to be their king), and they handed over their country to him in 1228 [A.D. 1813], and that is when Sayyid Sa'id became the ruler of Lamu. And the kingdom of Pate was in the island of Pate and the harbours (only). [*Editor's note*: i.e., those of the Benadir coast.] And the intrigue increased in the land of Pate, and there arose a second man at Pate, among the sons of Bwana Fumo Madi, who was called Fumo Luti Kipunga, and he fought with Sultan Ahmad. Afterwards, Sultan Ahmad contracted a disease and died, in 1230 [A.D. 1814]. He was succeeded by Sultan Fumo Luti, son of Bwana Fumo Madi, who was a very strong man, and a brave warrior and generous.

And those were the times when Sheikh Mataka bin Mbaraka was Sheikh of Siu; and he acquired soldiers and guns, and he was a vassal of the Sultan of Pate, and he was on very good terms with the Mazru'i. At last, in 1236 [A.D. 1820], a violent quarrel broke out between him and the Sultan of Zanzibar, Sayyid Sa'id, son of Sultan. The aforesaid Sultan Fumo Luti died

---

[22] "The battle of Shela" lives in Lamu tradition to this day, and I believe that human bones are still occasionally found among the sand-hills.

[23] That is, to use the Scottish expression, "kent folk" — men of good family.

at this date and was succeeded by Fumo Luti, son of Bwana Sheikh, son of Fumo Luti, son of Sheikh, son of Bwana Mkuu, and this is he (who was) the father of Sultan Ahmad, Sultan of Witu; and he reigned from the morning till after the hour of afternoon prayers, (when) the men of the town drove him out, and he went to Siu together with the Mazru'i and afterwards to Mombasa.

He was succeeded by Sultan Bwana Sheikh, (son) of Bwana Fumo Madi; and he was on very good terms with our lord Sa'id bin Sultan, who placed (a garrison of) Arabs in Pate, and they remained (there) three years. After that, the people of the town induced him to abdicate, with the consent of our lord Sa'id bin Sultan.

He was succeeded by Sultan Ahmad, (son)[24] of Bwana Waziri, (son) of Bwana Tamu, (son) of Bwana Sheikh, (son) of Bwana Tamu the Elder, in 1237 [A.D. 1821], and he came to an agreement with our lord Sa'id bin Sultan and reigned for two years, (but) the people of the town forced him to abdicate and (p. 295) brought back Bwana Sheikh, son of Bwana Fumo Madi, and he remained in power with the consent of our lord Sa'id bin Sultan for five years and died in 1239 [A.D. 1823].

Bwana Waziri returned to power; and (there) came Fumo Luti bin Bwana Sheikh, who had gone to Mombasa, he and the Mazru'i, and they seized Siu and fought with Bwana Waziri, (son) of Bwana Tamu of Pate. And Bwana Waziri was of one mind with our lord Sa'id bin Sultan, and Fumo Luti likewise with the Mazru'i, and Sheikh Mataka bin Mbarak, a man of Siu; they made common cause and fought and were routed — that is, Fumo Luti and the

[24] The context shows that this is an error (though the *wa* is distinct in the MS.), and that Sultan Ahmad was the same man as Bwana Waziri (Stigand, p. 88). [*Editor's note*: this is also borne out by MSS 177, 321 and 344.] (C. gives "Bwana Wazir, died 1829.")

Mazru'i and the men of Siu; and the wall of the town of Siu was also broken (down), and they (*i.e.* Bwana Waziri's men) took the town. Fumo Luti and Sheikh Mataka escaped to the mainland and stayed on the mainland a few days; and (then) they returned to Siu by (way of) war, and seized the town of Siu and built a wall and fought Pate from Siu.

Afterwards Fumo Luti died at Siu, and Bwana Waziri, son of Bwana Tamu, united Pate and Siu under his sway, with the consent of our lord Sa'id bin Sultan. And after a year (had passed), the Sultan, Bwana Waziri, son of Bwana Tamu, was killed, and Fumo Bakar, son of Sheikh, son of Bwana Fumo Madi, reigned (in his stead), and he (was) Sultan, (that is to say), Fumo Bakar, son of Sheikh, son of Bwana Fumo Madi in the year 1250 [A.D. 1834]. He agreed very well with our lord Sa'id bin Sultan during the time of his reign;[25] but afterwards he revolted, together with Sheikh Mataka. Our lord Sa'id bin Sultan summoned the Amir Hamad bin Hamad 'l Busaid, surnamed es-Samar, and he attacked Pate and Siu, but was unable to take them and made peace. After this there was dissension between the Sultan of Pate and his uncle's son,[26] Muhammad, son of Ahmad, (son) of Bwana (p. 297) Fumo Madi, and (the latter) seized the palace by force. Then there came men from Lamu and also a man (sent by) our lord Sa'id bin Sultan, and they reconciled Sultan Fumo Bakar and Muhammad bin Ahmad and sent (Muhammad) to Siu to live; Fumo Bakar lived at Pate. Afterwards they quarrelled, and fought for five

---

[25] I do not know what to make of this expression. It is nonsense as it stands, whether we take *kutawali* as applying to Fumo Bakari or to Sayyid Sa'id.

[26] According to Captain Stigand (p. 92), it was "his brother, Bwana Kitini," but a first cousin is as often called *ndugu* as an actual brother, and "Bwana Kitini" was probably a nickname. Some cognomen is indispensable to discriminate between the countless Muhammads, Ahmads, Abubakars, etc. — especially as they often have the same patronymic.

years, (did) Pate and Siu; (but) at last our lord Sa'id bin Sultan came to Pate and made peace between Sultan Fumo Bakari and Muhammad bin Ahmad, so that they were of one mind (both) he and his cousin. (However), at last, Fumo Bakari seized him suddenly and killed him, by the advice of a man from Siu. After that, our lord Sa'id bin Sultan called Sultan Fumo Bakari to go to Zanzibar, and he went, and our lord Sa'id bin Sultan imprisoned Fumo Bakari by the advice of the men of Lamu, and the reason (was), his killing his cousin Muhammad bin Ahmad and breaking ("leaving") the peace which our lord Sa'id bin Sultan had made between them. || (p. 393)

In the year 1262 [A.D. 1846], Sultan Ahmad, son of Sheikh, (son) of Fumo Luti, son of Sheikh, (son) of Bwana Tamu the Elder, seized Pate, with the consent of our lord Sa'id bin Sultan, and he remained at one with [him] for two years, then he revolted, and our lord Sa'id bin Sultan attacked him, and the Amir Hamad bin Hamad landed at Faza and went to make war on Siu. And our lord Sa'id bin Sultan released Sultan Fumo Bakar and gave him a force (to act) together with the men of Lamu. They remained at Mtangawanda on board the ships — he, our lord Sa'id bin Sultan and the Amir Hamad, and went to Faza, (but) our lord Sa'id stayed at a place called Kijangwa cha Mpunga, near Faza. Amir Hamad came to Siu, to build forts on the road between Faza and Siu, for war; and he came to Siu and seized the dhows (*mitepe*) which were there in Siu harbour, and turned them over and made barricades of them, and attacked the land of Siu.

The people of Siu experienced much suffering, and Amir (p. 395) Hamad, when he found that his task was troublesome and likely to last a long time, returned and went to fetch a cannon which was in his fort, and men. As he was passing along the road, the men of Siu rushed out on him suddenly, and the Amir of Sheikh Mataka, Bwana Hamad wa Omari, routed Amir Hamadi, and they fought a great battle, and the Amir died, he and his men. And the second Amir of Sheikh Mataka was Bwana Hamad Ngoma; and he went suddenly to the fort and routed (the garrison) and took the cannon. And the news reached our lord Sa'id bin Sultan at Faza, and he went on board a ship without telling anyone, and went to Maskat. Next year he returned, and placed Fumo Bakari at Faza and attacked Siu and Pate. At this time, Sheikh (p. 397) Mataka died of disease, and there was variance between his sons, (each of whom) wanted the chieftainship of Siu, and they submitted to the suzerainty of our lord Sa'id bin Sultan, (both) Abubakar and Muhammad. Sayyid Sa'id gave Abubakar (some) troops together with Fumo Bakari, and went to attack Sultan Ahmad at Pate. Abubakar, son of Sheikh Mataka, went together with Sultan Fumo Bakar's amir, who was called Bwana Mkuu, son of Bwana Madi (son) of Baishi, and they entered Siu during the night and fought till morning, and Abubakar bin Sheikh Mataka and his people were utterly routed, and Abubakar was seized and taken to Pate, to Sultan Ahmad, and killed. After that, Sheikh Muhammad bin Sheikh Mataka remained on the side of our lord Sa'id bin Sultan, together with Fumo Bakar. Our lord Sa'id gave him both soldiers and supplies for war, and they attacked Sultan Ahmad bin Sheikh, till they drove him out of Pate in 1273 [A.D. 1856], and he went to Kau.

And Muhammad bin Sheikh Mataka was Sheikh in the land of Siu, (and was) on the side of our lord Sa'id, who gave him soldiers to build a fort. Afterwards he had a quarrel with a man of Sayyid Sa'id's because he had pulled down a shed for dhows which Sheikh Muhammad had built in front of the fort. And Sheikh Muhammad (in his turn) destroyed the fort.

At this time died Sultan Ahmad at Kau, father of Fumo Bakar [who was afterwards] Sultan of Witu, and there remained in his stead at Kau Sultan Ahmad who was called "the Lion" (*Simba*), Sultan of Witu.

Now, before Sheikh Muhammad bin Sheikh Mataka had pulled down the fort at Siu, there had been dissension between him and Fumo Bakari bin Sheikh, and he drove him out of Pate, and Fumo Bakari came to Lamu. And he--*i.e.* Sheikh (p. 399) Muhammad--ruled at Pate, because he was powerful, and the weakness of Pate at that time (was that) the chief men of Pate did not submit (to any authority). He came and attacked the chiefs of Pate (but) they kept on killing one another, and they took no counsel with any (outside) person, neither (had they) a king; to their deliberations (only) men of Pate were (admitted), viz., Muhammad bin Bwana Mkuu en-Nabhanî and Bwana Rehema[27] bin Ahmad en-Nabhanî and Nasr bin Abdallah bin Abd-es-Salam — he it is who was the director of affairs, as to these matters. So they demanded ammunition and matchlocks and fought with Sheikh Muhammad bin Mataka and defeated him, and many of Sheikh Muhammad's men died, also his two amirs, Bwana Damila and Maulana (son) of Sheyekulu.[28] When Sheikh Muhammad bin Mataka had seen these matters, he came to sue for peace from Muhammad bin Bwana Mkuu aforesaid.

For it was he who was their father [*Editor's note*: rather, "the senior elder."] among these three men; and they came to an agreement and were of one mind and wished to give to him, Muhammad bin Bwana Mkuu, the

---

[27] Rehema is usually a woman's name. In the original, being unpointed, it might be read "Rahim," but Captain Stigand's and another MS. to which I have had access both read "Rehema."

[28] See Stigand, p. 95, where these two men are called Bwana Dumia and Maulana, son of Ishakulu.

kingdom of Pate and Siu; but Muhammad bin Bwana Mkuu refused and said, "I am an old man, let them take Sultan Ahmad, king of Witu, (who is called) Simba." They went to fetch him, and Sheikh Muhammad bin Sheikh Mataka sent his men, and Nasir bin Abdallah bin Abd-es-Salam went from Pate, and they went to Kau to fetch Sultan Ahmad Simba. And the news came to Zanzibar, to the Sultan, our lord Majid bin Sa'id — for, before the above (events) had taken place, our lord Sa'id had died — and he sent his vizier, Sayyid Seleman bin Ahmad, in a ship, to seize Pate and put an end to the strife. As soon as he reached Pate, a man belonging to (p. 401) Sultan Ahmad Abubakar Nabhan who went with him, Nasr bin Abdallah bin Abd-es-Salam, was seized [*Editor's note*: rather, "By the time he reached Manda, Pate had been seized by Sultan Ahmad's man, Abubakar Nabhan, with whom came Nasr bin Abdallah bin Abd-es-Salam." For possible causes of misunderstanding, see Werner's note to p. 400 regarding MS reading.]; and when Sayyid Seleman bin Ahmad had received this information, he returned to Zanzibar — and that was when Sheikh Muhammad bin Sheikh Mataka pulled down the fort at Siu. Afterwards, Sultan Ahmad arrived at Pate and was acknowledged (as king) by the Pate people, and Sheikh Muhammad bin Sheikh Mataka, and the Watikuu, (*viz.*), Sheikh Mzee bin Sefu and Sheikh Sheku and Muhammad Mote; and Sultan Ahmad was quite at peace in his kingdom, as regards the whole of the people who were in the island of Pate.

(Then) our lord Majid bin Sa'id sent some Lamu men to Pate to give advice, together with Sheikh Muhî-ed-Dîn, to demand that Sultan Ahmad should take some of his soldiers, to stay at Pate. Now this Sheikh Muhî-ed-Dîn is he who turned out our lord Majid's soldiers from the fort at Siu, when Muhammad bin Sheikh Mataka defeated them. The soldiers of our lord Majid were inside the fort: — Sheikh Muhî-ed-Dîn went and took them out peaceably, for he was a man of Sayyid Majid's. And when they went to our lord Majid, he became very angry, and Sheikh Muhî-ed-Dîn made haste to take the soldiers back, when he saw the wrath of our (p. 403) lord Majid — for (you must know that) this Muhî-ed-Dîn had great cunning and great learning — well, he came with the men of Lamu as far as Pate, and the men of Lamu who came were Sheikh Ahmad and his brother. He spoke with Sultan Ahmad and took the soldiers, after much difficulty, because of his friendship with Sultan Ahmad [*Editor's note*: rather, Sheikh Ahmad.] and his brother. And [Sultan Ahmad] rejected the advice of his vizier, Nasr bin Abdallah bin Abd-es-Seleman [*Editor's note*: he is the same person named above (and elsewhere), Nasr bin Abdallah bin Abd-es-Salam.], for he refused to put Arabs into Pate — even one. And when the Arabs had made their entry into Pate, they made an agreement with Mwana Jahi, daughter of Sultan Fumo Luti Kipunga, (son) of Bwana Fumo Madi, and wife of Sultan Fumo Bakar bin Sheikh. At this time, Sultan Fumo Bakar was at Lamu, according to the agreement made with our lord Majid bin Sa'id from the time when he was driven out of Pate.

And every day they introduced soldiers and stores secretly by night, and at last, when Sultan Ahmad knew it, dissensions arose, and the soldiers were many at Pate, and they attacked Sultan Ahmad suddenly, and after they had finished (arranging) a stratagem, they wanted to seize him, but were not able (to carry out) that plan, for all the people of Pate were of one mind with our lord Majid bin Sa'id, except his vizier, Nasr bin Abdallah bin Abd-es-Salam. And they fought inside the town of Pate, and drove out Sultan Ahmad from Pate and carried off Sheikh Muhammad bin Sheikh Mataka to Siu. The Arabs stayed at Pate and placed their ships on the sea. And when the war became very fierce, he, our lord Majid, came (himself) and besieged the island of Pate by sea, and put a chain across the mouth of Siu Creek . . . and they fought for six months by sea and at Pate and in the direction of Tikuuni. Mzee Sefu revolted and became Sayyid Majid's man, by much cunning and many words, and Sultan Ahmad and Sheikh Muhammad bin Sheikh Mataka experienced great distress.

And (in) the land of Siu there was dissension: one faction loved the Sayyid, because of the troubles they had suffered; and his men were Sharif Maulana bin Abubakar and 'Asi [*Editor's note*: rather, 'Isa.] bin Ahmad the Somali. When they saw these (things), Sultan (p. 405) Ahmad and Sheikh Muhammad sued for peace from the Sayyid, and he granted it. And while the negotiations were going on, Sultan Ahmad set out secretly by night, and went away to the mainland — to Kau. And after that, Sheikh Muhammad went in a ship to the Sayyid, to ask for pardon, and the Sayyid pardoned him. The Sayyid went his ways to Zanzibar, and afterwards Sheikh Muhammad went to Zanzibar to sound him. The Sayyid threw him into chains and sent him to Mombasa, to the fort, along with many (other) people. He died after many days.[29] And at the time when the said Sheikh Muhammad went to Zanzibar, S'ûd bin Hamad had a letter brought to him (telling him) to seize Sultan Ahmad by treachery, but he was not able (to do) it. Sultan Ahmad went away to Witu. Then S'ûd bin Hamad went to Faza and seized Omar, (the son) of Bwana Mataka, and all the Sheikh's sons were seized at Siu and taken to the fort at Mombasa. Omar was imprisoned at Lamu. — After this, Sayyid Majid

[29] *Cf.* Stigand, p. 96.

was (undisputed) ruler of all the coast; there was not another man to trouble him.

And Sultan Ahmad remained at Witu under the suzerainty of Sayyid Majid bin Sa'îd, till the time of Sayyid Barghash (when the latter) wanted to place soldiers and a flag at Witu, and (when) Sultan Ahmad would not agree (to this), he brought an expedition to attack him, but could not (prevail) and (so) made peace. After this, Sayyid Barghash was not pleased with S'ûd bin Hamad, because of his making peace quickly and (because) he had not attacked (Ahmad) vigorously (enough); he sent a second and larger expedition with (=under the command of) the Liwali S'ûd bin Hamad. Sultan Ahmad put himself under the protection of the Germans, and they gave him also (*i.e.* in addition to Witu) part of the Swahili mainland. Sultan Ahmad died, under the protection of the Germans, in 1306 [A.D. 1888].

He was succeeded by Fumo Bakar bin Sultan bin Sheikh, and there arose trouble (between) him and the Germans. Küntzell shot the porter at the gate and killed him, and the porters of the town gate who were there — they (in their turn) fell upon Küntzell and the Europeans who had accompanied (p. 407) him and killed them, without asking for orders from sultan Fumo Bakar — (it was) after they had seen that their companions had been killed (that) they, too, killed them. And the people of Ndamuyu and the people of Mkonumbi, when they had received the news, they too killed the Europeans who were there. After that came the illustrious administration of the English, and they demanded those people of Mkonumbi and of Wandamuyu (in order) to bring them to trial. Sultan Fumo Bakar did not consent to deliver them up. The English Administration attacked Fumo Bakar, on the night of the 11th Rabi'l Auwal, 1308, and at eight o'clock in the morning they got possession of the town and drove him out of Witu by war. The Sultan went to Jongeni and lived there till the date of the 28th Jemad 'l Auwal, 1308 [A.D. 1891], (when) Sultan Bakar died.

After him, his brother, Bwana Sheikh bin Sultan Ahmad, took his place. And, after three days, he was seized by his brother, Fumo Omar, and Bwana Afthul, and they bound Bwana Sheikh. (But) he, Fumo Omar bin Sultan Ahmad bin Sheikh, was seized in his turn; it was just as it had been[30] between him and the illustrious Administration of the English. And, as to the kingship — the last who reigned in Witu was Sultan Fumo Bakar, and the last to reign in Pate was Sultan Ahmad Simba, (afterwards) Sultan of Witu. And the first Sultan was Seleman bin Seleman bin Mathfûr [*Editor's note*: rather, Muthafar.], of the (house of the) Nabhan, Imâm 'l Ya'arubi.

This is the account of the Nabhans coming to the Swahili Coast; and, as to their history, there reigned thirty-one kings, and one woman who was the thirty-second. And the account of them is this which we have copied from Muhammad bin Fumo Omar, the Nabhan, who is (usually) called Bwana Kitini, and he received it from his grandfather Muhammad bin Bwana Mkuu the Nabhan, who was called Bwana Simba, who was very exact as to the traditions of the old time and their pedigrees, (such) as those we have mentioned in the preceding (narrative).

HAMAD SALEH MUHAMMAD,

By order of the Liwali Abed bin Hamad.

April 21, 1903

---

[30] Or: "this is how matters stood."

POST-SCRIPT.

This Bwana Mkuu, son of Sheikh, in the time of his kingship, gave a slap (in the face) to a man of Pate, of very high rank; and after the space of a year had passed — now this man had thirty-two sons — they took counsel with their kinsmen and made up (a band of) a hundred men and went to (the King) at night. (One of them) knocked at the gate of the Palace, (and, hearing) the voice of one person (only), the porter, when he knew that it was (only) one person, opened the gate. First they slew the porter, then they rushed suddenly into the King's room; he was unarmed, and they struck him blow on the arm and cut it in two pieces, and the one piece — the wrist (with the hand) fell to the ground. There was a chair of hide — he struck it with the stump of the hand that had been cut off, and knocked a hole in the chair[31] and made a shield, and leapt upon one man and snatched his sword from him — and his shield was that chair; and he smote forty-three men with his left hand, which was sound. And the Palace is very large, it has (plenty of) space, and some jumped down from above (*i.e.* from the roof) to the ground, and broke their legs. And the people within the palace awoke and fell upon them, (so that) those who got out safe were seven men. Afterwards that King, Bwana Mkuu, son of Sheikh, said (to himself): "I am a king, the people (who are my) subjects are in the habit of kissing (my hand), and my right hand has been cut off, and it is not fitting to kiss the left hand." And he put oil into a metal pot, and it was boiling over the fire, till it boiled very much, and he put his arm into the oil and stopped (the bleeding), and the oil in the pot was boiling greatly, and he died.

---

[31] He passed his wrist through the opening, being unable to hold it otherwise.

And his brother's son, Bwana Fumo Madi, reigned. And he, when he saw that the Pate people wished to make trouble, seized of them forty men and cut their throats like fowls.

When Bwana Fumo Madi died, that is when his son, Sultan Ahmad bin Fumo Luti, reigned.

SWAHILI CHRONICLE OF PATE

Khabāri ya-awwali ya-Nabhānī

M. HEEPE

INTRODUCTION

The following synthetic text of two versions of the *Pate Chronicle* was published by M. Heepe under the title "Suaheli-Chronik von Pate" in the *Mitteilungen des Seminars für orientalische Sprachen.*[1] It was accompanied by a facsimile reproduction of two Arabic-script MSS reduced in size by 1/3. These are included at the end of the present volume as MS M and MS A (notation introduced by Heepe to correlate the MSS with the dialects: A for "Amu," M for "Mvita"). The original MSS were obtained by the German Vice-Consul at Mombasa Mr. Wassmuss in 1911. The sixteen-page long MS M contains the briefer text in the Ki-Mvita (Mombasa) dialect of Swahili, while MS A, on 39 pages, has the more complete text of the chronicle in Ki-Amu. To my knowledge, MS M is the only Ki-Mvita version of the chronicle discovered so far. This MS is also unique in consistently using the toponym *Amu* (isolated form without the locative particle *l-*) instead of the more common form *Lamu*). The Arabic text is reproduced here, as in the original German publication, in two columns on each page, numbered by Heepe from right to left according to Arabic style of writing. In addition, the plates (found at the end of the journal issue) carry Roman numerals. MS M is interrupted; the last one-and-a-half lines of MS A (the only text on page 39) were reproduced by Heepe in a note at the end of the romanized transcript. This pattern is followed in the present edition. The Arabic script reduced facsimile of MSS A and M will be found at the end of the volume.

Heepe was familiar with Stigand's version but not with Werner's, to

[1] 3. *Abteilung: Afrikanische Studien* 31 (1928): 145-92.

which his own text rather closely corresponds. He had also read Alfred Voeltzkow's paraphrase and made frequent references to both; these were marked with abbreviations **S** and **V** in his edition, fully cited in the present volume as "Stigand" and "Voeltzkow." In footnotes, but especially extensively in comments following the translation (pp. 172-191), Heepe often quotes the historical traditions and records published by Guillain[2] in matters relating especially to European and Omani dealings with the coast and to Zanzibar affairs. He also extensively used Justus Strandes' data[3] and extracted Portuguese information about Pate and Mombasa. Much of his effort aimed at pointing out discrepancies in the names of Pate rulers and in the chronology of their reigns as cited in his version of the *Chronicle* and those recorded by Stigand and Voeltzkow. Many of these comments are redundant in view of Heepe's footnotes already calling the reader's attention to relevant passages, or they focus on other documents. Here I have reproduced the footnotes but not the commentary.

For purposes of clarity, Heepe had divided his transcript into 67 paragraphs. These are assigned numbers in brackets; numbers in parentheses refer to pages of original MSS, *i.e.* to columns in the facsimile reproduction. Characters in brackets are conjectured by Heepe. Punctuation is absent in the MSS and sentence division often uncertain. Heepe used limited punctuation in transcription to reflect this lack of clear separation and often dropped

---

[2] M. Guillain, *Documents sur l'histoire, la géographie et le commerce de l'Afrique orientale*, 3 vols. (Paris, 1856).

[3] Justus Strandes. *Die Portugiesenzeit von Deutsch - und Englisch-Ostafrika* (Berlin, 1899). English translation by J.F. Wallwork, edited by J.S. Kirkman, "The Portuguese Period in East Africa," *Transactions of the Kenya History Society*, 2 (Nairobi, 1961).

capitalization after a period within the paragraph. He also treated the titles *Shaykh*, *Sultan*, *Iman*, and *Sayyid* as common nouns. Characters and words in parentheses occur alternately in versions A or M but not both.

The footnotes in transcription are those by Heepe and retain the original numbers. Halfway through the transcript Heepe started a series of notes with a supplementary notation. These have been placed as footnotes at the bottom of the paragraphs to which they refer. The present author's comments will be found in brackets appropriately marked. Following Heepe's practice, personal names are highlighted both in the transcript and in the translation. Bold Roman numerals in brackets mark the sequence of rulers as established by Heepe and refer to the genealogical table originally published by Heepe on pages 148-149 and reproduced in the present volume in Appendix 6. These reference numbers are used again in the chronological table (originally located on page 181), where on the left Heepe compiled his own list from the MSS, while presenting a coordinated list compiled from Stigand and Voeltzkow on the right. The dates of the Muslim calendar were provided by Heepe with European equivalents only in this last table which is reproduced in Appendix 7.

No attempt to change or adjust Heepe's transcription of the Arabic-script originals has been made. On the other hand, the German translation was found to be unsatisfactory, and the present author has made a new English translation directly from the Swahili. Those footnotes that have been retained are by Heepe; comments by Tolmacheva may be found in the endnotes. Heepe did not provide Christian equivalents to Muslim dates. These have been added in brackets in the translation. In the second half of Heepe's translation references to passages in Stigand's version appear also at the end of the paragraph. These have been moved to footnotes which have been assigned new numbers.

TRANSCRIPTION

[1] Habari ya auwali ya Nabhani kuja[9] Sawahili na habari zao zote. Wametawala wafalume wahidi wa salasini na mwanamke mmoja[1] ndiye wa sineni[2] wa salasini 32, na habari zao ni hizi zote. Tumenakili kwa Muhammadi bin Fumu 'Umari aitwaye[3] Bwana Kitini naye alipokea na bibye Muhammad bin Bwana Mkuuaitwaye[3] Bwana Simba an-Nabhani alizibiti[4] habari za kale[4a] na nasaba zao kama hizi nilizotaja.[5]

[2] Mtu wa kwanza[6] kuja[7] katika an-Nabhani Pate **Seliman Bin Seliman Bin Muzaffar** na nduuze wawili Ali bin Seliman na Asmani bin Seliman. Alokuwa sultani Seliman bin Seliman almazkur. ndiye aliyekuwa[8] mfalme 'Arabuni. Akatolewa nal [a]lya'rab(i) akaja[9] Pate katika ras sanati 600

---

[1] A. *umoya*

[2] A. *isnaini.*

[3] A. *amkuliwao.*

[4] A. *alizibitiye.* 4a= changed to *ka'e* with lead.

[5] A. *mezataya.*

[6] A. *kwanda.*

[7] A. *kuya.*

[8] A. *alokuwa.*

[9] A. *-ya.* [*Editor's note*: the reader will find this reading marked with the same number 9 throughout the length of MS A.]

hijriya akaoa katika[10] kabila ya Battawiyyuna binti wa mfalme wa Pate (p.2) na dasturi ya (wa)-Sawahili hatta sasa mtu [a]kikuoleya mtoto wako[11] akisha[12] (siku) saba'a huja[13] kukwangalia yule baba'ake[14] mke wako humpa kitu. Alipokwenda kumwangalia akampisha[15] yeye ufal(u)me. Tangu hapo katawala Seliman bin Seliman almazkur.

[3] Na Kitaka ualikuwa[16] muji katika matla'i ya Pate. [Na]wakati huu[17] ha[u]tasa kuweko muji[19] wa Siu kuwali[18] na muji[19] jina lake[20] Shanga katika matla'i ya Pate. Na Paza walikuwako[21] wenyewe wa Paza al-Mafaziyyuna. Aloketi ufal(u)me wa Pate na miji hii[22]: Kitaka na Pate na Mandra yali[kuwa]na mfal(u)me wake wa Mandra ni Seliman(i) bin Seliman(i)

---

[10] Beginning of page 2.

[11] A. *mwano*.

[12] A. *akisa*.

[13] A. *huya*.

[14] A. *uliye* or *ule babake*.

[15] A. *kampisa*.

[16] A. *walikuwa*.

[17] A. *hunu*.

[18] A. *kwalina*.

[19] A. *muyi*.

[20] A. *walitamkuliwa*.

[21] A. *walikuweko*.

[22] A. *miyi hini*.

almazkur. Akaza'a vijana[23] Muhammad na Ahmad, akafa sultan Seliman sanati 625.[24]

[4] Wakati huu[17] ulikuwa[25] um[u]ri wa Muhammad bin Seliman nyaka'ishrini na Ahmadi umri wake nyaka hamusta'ashara, katawala **Muhammad Bin Seliman** baada ya babake kapijana na watu wa Shanga [a]kawashinda [a]kauvunda (p.3) muji[19] akawatukua[26] watu wa Shanga wakaja[9] Pate na ba'zi wakakimbiya katika watu walokuja[9] Pate na ba'[a]zi yao kuna watu kabila ya Wakinandangu wakakimbiya wasijulikane[27] walipokwenda[28]. Hatta siku zikapita ikaja[9] habari kwa mfalme Muhammad bin Seliman na wawinda wakamwambiya: wale waliyokimbiya[29] tumewaona katika mwitu; [a]kape[le]ka watu kuwangalia wakawaona[30] ndani mwa mwitu. Wamefanya majumba[31] wameketi hapo wakawatukua wakaja[9] nawo Pate. Kisha[32]

---

[23] A. *zijana*. [*Editor's note*: the same reading in MS A is marked with the number 23 further on.]

[24] A. Beginning of page 3.

[25] A. *yalikuwa*.

[26] A. *kabisa*.

[27] A. *wasiyuwikane*.

[28] A. *wamezepo nenda*.

[29] A. *wa Shiu*.

[30] A. *wakawadirika*.

[31] A. *zijumba*.

[32] A. *kisa*.

[a]kawarudisha papo [alipo watukua] ndiyo[33] asli ya Siu[34]. Kisha[32] wakaja[9] na watu wangine wa Sawahili wakiketi Siu. Kisha[32] wakaja[9] Wafamau wakawa wakuu wa Siu katika ta'a ya mfal(u)me wa Pate siku nyingi[34a].

[5] Katika sanati 650 akafa sultani Muhammad bin Seliman akatawala nduye sultan **Ahmad Bin Seliman** aka'amirisha sana (p. 4) katika nti ya Pate. Akafanya[35] mashamba na kujenga[36] majumba asipije mahala. hatta sanati 670 akafa.

[6] Akatawala kijana wa sultan Muhammad bin Seliman jina lake Ahmad Bin Muhammad Bin Seliman. Akaketi kama siyara za 'ami yake katika 'imara ya muji[19] wa Pate. (Naye)akapata vijana[23] wangi.

[7] Alipokufa sanati 705 akatwaa ufal(u)me katika vijana[23] vyake[37] jina[3] lake **Muhammad Bin Ahmad Bin Muhammad Bin Seliman**. akaketi akafutahi miji[19] ya Sawahili Paza na Mandra kwa vita vingi[38] katika nti ya Paza.[39] Wa amma Mandra waliingia kwa vita vya[40] hila wakavunda kabisa. Na watu akawa[l]eta Pate. Na ba'zi wakakimbiya wakenda kulla mahala wakaja[9] Shela na Malindi na miji[19] mingine. [Na]wal[iy]okwenda Shela wakangia katika

---

[33] A. *ndipo*.

[34] A. Beginning of page 4. [34a] in A follows *hatta*, crossed out with lead.

[35] A. *kwa kutia*.

[36] A. *kuwaka*.

[37] A. *zake*.

[38] A. *zita zingi*.

[39] A. Beginning of page 5.

[40] A. *zita za*.

himaya ya watu wa Amu. Mfal(u)me akawataka kwa watu wa Amu akakata'a[41] kuwatoa. [walikuwa] katika maneno hayo mfal(u)me akafa sanati 732.

[8] Akwata kijana kimoja (p. 5) jina lake[42] sultani 'Umari. Akatawala ba'ada ya babake [a]karaji'i maneno ya babake kwa watu wa Amu kutaka watu wa Mandra; wakakata'a[41] watu wa Amu ku[wa]toa. [a]kawapija wakataka amani watu wa Amu, wakawa katika ta'a ya sultani **'Umari Bin Muhammad Bin Ahmad Bin Muhammad Bin Seliman**. Akapata nguvu sana akapija jumla ya miji[19] ya Sawahili[43]: Uziwa na Malindi na Kiwayu na Kitau na Miya na Imizi na Watamu hatta akafika[44] Kirimba. Miji[19] yote [a]kaitamalaki tangu Pate hatta Kirimba; ku[l]la muji[19] [a]kaweka mtu wake (ili) kuhukumu. ndiyo asli ya hao majumbe waliyo(ko) [katika] m[i]rima wote, ma'ana ni watumwa wa yumbe [na] hiyo yumbe ni [j]ina la nyumba ya ufalume wa Pate.

[9] Na janibu ya huku akatamalaki hatta Warshehi kwa vita[40] alikuwanza[6] kupija tangu Kiwayu na Tula na Tuwala na Shungaya na Banadiri zote Barawa Marka Mukdishu. Hapo Mukdishu (p. 6) [a]kaweka luwali hukmu ya Banadiri zote zikawa Mukdishu. aka'ishi na nti hizo zote zi katika ta'a yake illa[45] Unguja hakutawala. Wakati huu[17] Unguja haikuwa nti kuu.

---

[41] A. *wakaiza*.

[42] A. *hwamkuliwa*.

[43] A. Begiining of page 6.

[44] A. *kasikilya*.

[45] A. *isokuwa*.

Na mfalme huyu[46] ali [a]kipenda vita[40] za mno na kupenda ra'iya wakaona raha wakapata na mali mangi ikas(i)tawi mno nti ya Pate akafa sanati 749.

[10] Akawata watoto[23] wawili Muhammad na Ahmad. akatawala **Muhammad Bin 'Umari Bin Muhammad Bin Ahmad Bin Muhammad Bin Seliman** wala hapakuwa na vita[40] [a]katawala ufal(u)me wa baba['a]ke wote kwa amani naye [ali'a]kipenda mali sana na biyashara. akisafirisha na majahazi[47] akipeleka[48] al-Hindi kufanya biyashara. naye ali[kuwa] na bahti sana ya mali. na mara moja[9] mwan[aw]e alisafiri [a]kapata kisiwa bahrini [a]kashuka akaona[49] ma'deni ya feza akape[le]ka watu wakafanya kazi kapata mali mangi [sana] yakazidi[50] mno mali katika nti ya Pate hatta wakafanya vitanda vya[51] feza na ngazi za feza na vyombo vingi viya[47] feza [a]kapata na watoto[23] wane Bwana Mkuu na Ahmad na Abu Bakari[52] na 'Umari akafa (p. 7) umfal(u)me sanati 797:

[11] Akatawala ndu[gu] y[a]ke **Ahmad Bin 'Umari Bin Muhammad Bin Ahmad Bin Muhammad Bin Seliman** akaketi kwa amani katika nti zake (hatta) sanati 840 akafa.

[12] Akatawala **Abu Bakari Bin Muhammad Bin 'Umari Bin**

---

[46] A. Beginning of page 7.

[47] A. *zombo*.

[48] A. *kupeka*.

[49] A. *kapata*.

[50] A. *ikazidi*.

[51] A. *zitanda za*.

[52] A. Beginning of page 8.

Muhammad Bin Ahmad Bin Muhammad Bin Seliman [a]kaketi kwa siyara njema na miji[19] yote katika ta'a yake akai'amminisha[53] miji[19] yake [yote] akafa katika hali pasina kuharibikiwa (hatta) sanati 875. Akawata watoto[23] wawali Muhammad na Ahmad.

[13] **Akatwala Muhammad Bin Abi Bakari Bin Muhammad Bin 'Umari Bin Muhammad Bin ahmad Bin Muhammad Bin Seliman.** Wakati wake wakaja[9] wazungu Portugali miji[19] ya Sawahili yote wakaketi Mwambasa wakafanya ngome. na janibu ya Pate wakajenga Dondoo[54] na watu wa bara wakawafuwata kwa kuwapa mali wakangia katika ta'a yao. wakam[u]-warizi na mfal(u)me katika muji[19] wa Pate wakampija[55]. na[56] janibu ya Shindakasi wakajenga[57] na tiyati (p. 8) kasdi ya kupija bomba muji[19] wa Pate wasiweze. kisa wakapatana kwa amani wakafanya mkataba wa sharti zao. wakaketi Pate wazungu wakafanya foroza k[u]wa [j]ina lao wazungu waki'ita[58] [ili foroza] vyandika [*Editor's note*: rather, *fandīka*.]. wakafanya na mambo mangi katika kisiwa ta [*Editor's note*: rather, *cha*.] Pate. ba'ada ya hayo akafa mfal(u)me sanati 900 akawata watoto[23] Bwana Mkuu na Abu Bakari.

[14] Akatawala **Abu Bakari Bin Muhammad Bin Abi Bakari Bin Muhammad Bin 'Umari Bin Muhammad Bin Ahmad Bin Muhammad Bin**

---

[53] A. *na kuaminisha.*

[54] A. *Ndondo.*

[55] A. Beginning of page 9.

[56] A. *kwa.*

[57] A. *wakawaka.*

[58] A. *walitamkuwa.*

Seliman akaketi kwa amani na wazungu wakapatana[59] kama kaida ya babake. akafa sanati 945 kawata watoto[23] Ahmad na Muhammad.

[15] Akatawala ndu[gu] [y[ak]e **Bwana Mkuu Bin Muhammad Bin Abi Bakari Bin Muhammad Bin 'Umari Bin Muhammad Bin Ahmad Bin Muhammad Bin Seliman** wakawa na htilafu na wazungu lakin pasiwe na vita[40] akafa katika fitina[60] ya siku nyingi sanati 973 akawata kijana Bwana Bakari.

[16] Akatawala **Muhammad Bin Abi Bakari Bin Muhammad Bin Abi Bakari Bin Muhammad Bin 'Umari Bin Muhammad Bin Ahmad Bin Muhammad Bin Seliman** akasilihiyana[61] na wazungu nawo wakat[u]wa'a ba'[a]zi ya miji[19] akafa [a]kawata kijana Abu Bakari sanati 1002.

[17] Akatawala **Bwana Bakari Wa Bwana Mkuu Bin Muhammad Bin Abi Bakari Bin Muhammad Bin 'Umari** (p. 9) **Bin Muhammad Bin Ahmad Bin Muhammad Bin Seliman** kwa siyara kama za babake lakin ufal[u]me wawo wa as[i]li umepunguwa. akafa akawata Bwana Mkuu wa Bakari sanati 1041.

[18] Akatawala **Abu Bakari Bin Muhammad Bin Abi Bakari Bin Muhammad Bin Abu Bakari Bin Muhammad Bin 'Umari Bin Muhammad Bin Ahmad Bin Muhammad Bin Seliman** akahtalifiyana na wazungu [a]kape[le]ka watu kutaka[62] nti ya Pate wakawapija wazungu. vikaja vita

[59] A. *wapetene*.

[60] A. Beginning of page 10.

[61] A. *akasulihiyana*.

[62] A. *katika*.

vya[63] wazungu wakapija muji[19] k[u]wa mizinga wakaziwiya ndiya za bahari. wakapata mashaka watu wa Pate wakafanya amani. ba'ada ya hayo akafa mfal[u]me akawata vijana wasili[64] Bwana (Mkuu) na Ahmad sanati 1061.

[19] Akatawala **Bwana Mkuu Wa Bwana Bakari Wa Bwana Mkuu Bin Muhammad Bin Abi Bakari Bin Muhammad Bin 'Umari Bin Muhammad Bin Ahmad Bin Muhammad Bin Seliman** akapatana na wazungu naye akipenda kuketi Amu hatta musimu akau(y)eta Amu. aka'owa (p. 10) kwa watu wa Amu. na Wafamau wa Siu muda huu[17] walitoka katika ta'a yake. akapijana nawo akauvunda muji[19] wa Siu. akatukua na watu wote wa Siu akawa[l]eta Pate. Mkuu wa Siu [a]kakimbiya [a]k(a)enda Dondo k[u]wa (wa-)Portugali wakatwa'a himaya. Mkuu wa wazungu Portugali [a]kaja[9] Pate k[uw]ataka watu wa Siu. akapawa[65] [a]kawarejeza Siu wakaketi kwa amani.

[20] Ba'ada yake Portugali [a]kafanya hila akaja[9] Pate kwa marikabu akamtaka mfal(u)me ende[66] marikabuni. mfalme as(en)ende akampe[le]ka bin 'am[m]i yake Bwana Mkuu. yeye na watu wa Pate wazungu[67] wakawatukua katika marikabu [wa]kawape[le]ka kwao uzunguni asirudi (tena) hata (mtu) mmoja[1]. ba'ada ya hapo wakapijwa wazungu kula mahala wali(yo)po [watu]

---

[63] A. *zikaya zita za.*

[64] A. Beginning of page 11.

[65] A. *akapowa.*

[66] A. *kwenenda.*

[67] A. Beginning of page 12.

barani na visiwani[68] (p. 11) [wa]kawatoa wakakimbiya (wakenda) Mwambasa. ba'ada ya hayo mfal(u)me akafa sanati 1100 akwata vijana[23] wawili na binti [mmoja] Bwana Bakari na Bwana Madi na Mwana Darini.

[21] Akatawala mwan[aw]e **Bwana Bakari Bin Bwana Mkuu Bin Bwana Bakari Wa Bwana Mkuu Bin Muhammad (Bin Abi Bakari Bin Muhammad) Bin 'Umari Bin Muhammad Bin Ahmad Bin Muhammad Bin Seliman** akapijwa mfal(u)me ghafula na Ahmadi nduye Bwana Mkuu alotukuliwa na wazungu Portugal[i] akamu'ua kwa upanga.

[22] Akatawala yeye **Ahmad Bin Abi Bakari Bin Muhammad Bin Abi Bakari Bin Muhammad <Bin Abi Bakari Bin Muhammad>[68a]. Bin 'Umari Bin Muhammad Bin Ahmad Bin Muhammad Bin Seliman** sanati 1103. akawandama (wa-)Portugal kawatoa walosaliya. na wak(a)-ti huu Mwana Darini binti[69] Bwana Mkuu wa Bwana Bakari wa Bwana Mkuu bin Abi Bakari*[a]me[kwe]nda Goa, katika zamani ya sultani Ahmadi akisha[12] ku'uwawa ndu[gu]ze wawili Bwana Bakari bin Bwana Mkuu na Bwana Madi bin Bwana Mkuu alotukuliwa (mepekwa) Goa**, zamani[70] akapata huzuni sana ya mume wake nakuwaliwa ndu[gu] z[ak]e. Hatta ba'azi ya siku kupita[71] [a]ka'azimu kufanya 'arusi kumtahiri mwan[aw]e (p. 12) Bwana Tamu Mtoto

---

[68] A. *zi-*. 68[a] <....> is missing in both manuscripts.

[69] A. Beginning of page 13.
* Must read "Muhammad."
** Here, too, the addition "the one brought to Goa" is wrong. Because, as is shown by the following, it is obviously her husband that she yearns for and not her and her brothers' father.

[70] A. *sabiki*.

[71] A. *zikapita*.

aitwaye[3] sultan(i) Abu Bakari Imamu l-hudā wa Bwana (Mkuu) [a]me[kwe]nda Goa. mfal(u)me sultan(i) Ahmad(i) akapata habari naye ka'azimu 'arusi ili kasidi ya kumuhini siwa.

[23] Akisha[12] kujua[72] Mwana Darini habari ya kuhiniwa siwa akamwamkua Mwinyi Ba'iyi Mkuu Sharifu katika Jamali-llaili ali[kuwa a]kijua[72] kazi ya ujume sana akamwambiya habari yake akataka kwake amfanyiziye[73] siwa (ishinde yao). [y]ule akakubali akataka ijara yake akapawa[74] riyali mia wa ishrini na pembe za ndovu atakazo apate kutagua[75] zil[iz]o njema zifa[']azo. akatimiza shar(u)ti zake zote Mwana Darini akafanya siwa kwa miezi[76] sita. alipo kwisha[32] akaizihirisha ghafla kaipe[le]ka katika majumba ya ndu[gu] z[ak]e (na wende) kwa matezo makuu. wakaitoza mali mangi akamwambiya Mwinyi Ba'iyi alofanya siwa watake (p. 13) (i)jara yako ao utatwa'a tunzo? akatwa'a tunzo kwa sababu aliona ni mali mangi akatakabazi siwa yake ikafanyiziwa[77] 'arusi yake mwan[aw]e.

[24] Hatta zamani ya Bwana Tamu Mkuu watu wa Amu wakaja[9] kuazima siwa ya asli [a]kawapa wakipata[78] bahrini shombo[79] kikafa maji[80]

---

[72] A. *kiyua*.

[73] A. Beginning of page 14.

[74] A. *kupowa*.

[75] A. *kute'ua*.

[76] A. *nyezi*.

[77] A. *akafanyiliza* "she held the ceremony."

[78] A. *i-*.

[79] A. *tombo*.

ikapoteya siwa. Bwana Tamu Mkuu akaitaka[81] siwa ya Mwana Darini akamwambiya tupe sisi tutumiye katika miji[21]. akamwambiya kula kaba'ila aliye[82] toza siwa yangu natumiye.

[25] Basi Mwana Darini akawata mtumwa huri ajuwaye[83] kupija siwa hiyi[84] [ni] yeye na nasli yake na 'ada yake napawe[85] riyali tano na nguo ya kutuku(l)iya siwa na samli ya kunywa menye kuvuvia[86] siwa na tunzo kulla mtu kiyasi awezavyo[87]. wakaitwa[88] nasla hiyo majumbe[89] wa siwa. hatta leo[90] wako watu [wenyewe]. basi ikawa [tangu] wakati (p. 14) huu[17] hutumia kaba'ila wa Pate wote na wa miyi mingine hwenda ku'azima[90a] kwa shar(u)ti hizo.

Na m[u]falume akaketi muda wa miyaka[91] saba'a kaikuja[9] mvua aka[j]i 'uzulu katika ufal(u)me wake sanati 1111.

---

[80] A. *mayi.*

[81] A. Beginning of page 15.

[82] A. *alo.*

[83] A. *ayuwawo.*

[84] A. *hini.*

[85] A. *napowe.*

[86] A. *kuvuzia.*

[87] A. *-wo.*

[88] A. *wakaamkuliwa.*

[89] A. *muyumbe.*

[90] A. *yeo.* [90a] *kwazima.*

[91] A. *nyaka.*

[26] Akatawala sultani **Abi Bakari Bwana Tamu Mkuu Wa Bwana Mtiti Bin Ahmad**[92] **Bin Abi Bakari Bin 'Umari Bin Ahmad Bin 'Umari Bin Muhammad Bin Ahmad Bin Muhammad Bin Seliman** [w]akatunzanya na mfalme wa Mas(i)kati imamu l-ya'rab. huyu mfalume wa Pate k(en)enda 'Arabuni (mfalume wa 'Arabuni) wakaagana arudipo mfalume wa Pate awatowe Portugal(i) Mwambasa. alipo rudi mfalume wa Pate kapiga[93] vita[40] Mwambasa [a]kawapija wazungu Portugal(i) siku ya juma ya pili [a]kawauwa katika[93a] ngome ya Mwambasa.

[27] [A]kamu'arifu imamu l-ya'rab(i) aka[l]eta (l)wali katika Mazari'i watu watatu ndugu [moja] Muhammad bin 'Asman(i) na 'Ali bin 'Asman(i) na Kazibu bin 'Asman(i). nawo walikuja[9] pamoja[9] na 'askari tarafu (p. 15) ya imamu l-ya'rabi. ndiyo asli ya Mazari'i kuja[9] Mwambasa. naye huyu mfal(u)me wa Pate aliketi na ra'iya kwa uzuri sana aka'ishi akatimiza katika ufalme wake nyaka arba'ini akafa sanati 1152[94] akawata watoto[23] wangi[38] ba'ada yake asitawale mwan[aw]e.

[28] Akatawala sultani **Ahmad Bin Abi Bakari Bin Muhammad Bin Abi Bakari Bin 'Umari Bin Ahmad Bin 'Umari Bin Muhammad Bin Ahmad Bin Muhammad Bin Seliman** akaketi kwa ne'ma nyingi akipenda[95] kuweka nombe wangi sana akafa sanati 1160 akawata kijana Bwana Gogo.

[29] Ba'ada yake akatawala Bwana Tamu Mtoto aitwa'e[3] imamu l-hudā wa Bwana Mkuu alotukuliwa na Portugali na[j]ina lake **Abu Bakari Bin**

---

[92] A. Beginning of page 16.

[93] A. *kapeka*. [93a]A. *kashika* "and he captured"

[94] A. Beginning of page 17.

[95] A. *akapenda*.

Bwana Mkuu Bin Abi Bakari Bin Muhammad Bin Abi Bakari Bin Muhammad 'Umari Bin Muhammad Bin Ahmad Bin Muhammad Bin Seliman. aka[l]eta vita[40] imamu l-ya'rabi kupija Pate wasiweze wakafa wa'arabu (p. 16) wa(i)ngi wakarudi wakafanya amani. ba'ada ya hapo watu wa Amu wakapigwa[96] na mfal(u)me wa Pate walihalifu. wakapijana asiwaweze. na watu wa Amu wakaja[9] Pate kupija kwa janibu[97] ya Kitaka wakafukuzwa wakarejea Amu. ba'adaye mfal(u)me wa Pate akafa(nya) vita[40] kwa bara na bah(a)ri [a]kawapija watu wa Amu [a]-kawatamalaki. Kisha[32] akauwawa mfal(u)me wa Pate na watu wa Pate pamoja[9] na watu wa imamu l-ya'rabi sanati 1177.

[30] Akatawala ndu[gu] y[ak]e sultani **Mwana Hadija Binti Bwana Mkuu Bin Abi Bakari Bin Muhammad Bin Abi Bakari Bin Muhammad Bin Abi Bakari Bin Muhammad Bin 'Umari Bin Muhammad Bin Ahmad Bin Muhammad Bin Seliman** akapat[w]a [na] fitina nyingi katika nti ya Pate, ikawa katika muji[19] wa Pate wafalume wawili yeye Mwana Hadija almazkura na sultani 'Umari. wakapijana katika muji[19] miyaka[91] mitano. [a]kakimbiya sultani 'Umari [a]k(an)enda Barawa kisha[32] akarudi[98] kwa nguvu [nyingi a]kangiliwa usiku aka'uwawa na watu wa Mwana Hadija almazkura. ba'ada yake kwa siku kidogo[99] akafa Mwana[99a] Hadija (p. 19) sanati[100] 1187.

---

[96] A. wakapijwa.

[97] A. Beginning of page 18.

[98] A. *karejea*.

[99] A. *katiti*. [99a]A. End of the Mombasa manuscript.

[100] A. Beginning of page 19.

[31] Akatawala **Bwana Mkuu Wa Shi(i) Wa Bwana Tamu Mkuu** na ra'iya wakimuuzi ikangia fitina asipate raha hatta sanati 1191 wakangia watu wa muyi wakamu'ua.

[32] Kwa tarihi hini katawala Bwana Fumu Madi ina lake sultani **Muhammad Bin Abi Bakari Bin Bwana Mkuu Bin Abi Bakari Bin Muhammad Bin Abi Bakari Bin Muhammad Bin Abi Bakari Bin Muhammad Bin 'Umari Bin Muhammad Bin Ahmad Bin Muhammad Seliman**. kisa kutawala ra'iya wakataka kufanya fitina akawapija kwa zita kawashinda akawashika watu arba'ini 40 wakuu na katika hao watu arba'ini almazkuruna watu wawili ni nduze akawatinda watu kukawa amani asipate mtu wa kumu'uzi tena. katawala kwa raha na amani na ne'ma na ra'iya wakaona raha sana hatta sanati 1224 akafa. ba'ada yake hakutawala tena kama yeye (p. 20) naye aliwata zijana zingi.

[33] Akatawala sultani **Ahmad Bin Sheh Bin Fumu Luti Bin <Bwana>** [not in the MS] **Tamu Mkuu** ikazidi fitina katika nti ya Amu. akaya kawapija tarihi sanati 1227 yeye na watu wa Mwambasa Mazari'i. wakaeta watu wakashuka Shela jayish nyingi ya watu wa Pate na watu wa Mwambasa. watu wa Amu wakatoka wakapijana nao. wakavundwa watu wa Pate na wa Mwambasa. wakitaka kukimbiya majahazi waloelea zimepwewa. wakapijana zita zikuu waka'uwawa watu wangi wa Pate na wa Mwambasa hapana 'idadi. katika watu wa Pate walo ma'rufu isokuwa watumwa na wasoyuwikana ni watu wahidi wa samanini 'idadi 81 walo'uwawa na wa Mwambasa mbali.

[34] Ba'ada ya hapo watu wa Amu wakenda 'Arabuni wakamtaka sayyid Sa'idi (p. 21) babake sayyid Bargash wakampa nti sanati 1228. ndipo sayyid Sa'idi alipotawala Amu. ufalume wa Pate ukasaliya katika kisiwa ta

[*Editor's note*: this is an instance of the Arabic character, *tā'* used for the sound *ch*. See also ## 13, 43, 57.] Pate na Banadiri. ikazidi fitina katika nti ya Pate. akatoka mtu wa pili katika zijana wa Bwana Fumu Madi hwamkuliwa Fumu Luti Kipunga. akapijana na sultani Ahmadi. Kisa sultani Ahmadi akapata marazi akafa sanati 1220 [must read 1230].

[35] Akatawala sultani **Fumu Luti Wa Bwana Fumu Madi**. naye alikuwa mtu hodari sana shuja'a sahiy. na zamani hizo shehe Mataka bin Mbaraka ndipo alipotawala ushehe wa Siu akafanya 'askari na bunduki. naye katika ta'a ya sultani wa Pate naye alipatana sana na Mazari'i. hatta sanati 1236 ikazidi fitina baina yake na sultani Zenjibari (p. 22) sayyid Sa'idi. akafa sultan Fumu Luti sanata l-mazkura.

[36] Ba'ada yake akatawala **Fumu Luti Bin Shaihi Bin Fumu Luti Bin Shaih Wa Bwana Tamu Mkuu**, na huyu ndiye babake sultani Ahmad, sultani wa Witu, akatawala asubuhi hatta ba'da l'asri watu wa muyi wakamtoa akanenda Siu pamoya na Mazari'i; kisa wakanenda Mwambasa.

[37] Akatawala sultani **Bwana Shehe Wa Bwana Fumu Madi**. akapatana na sayyid Sa'idi akatia Wa'arabu Pate wakaketi nyaka mitatu. ba'adaye watu wa muyi wakamu'uzulu pamoya na shauri la sayyidi Sa'idi sultani Zenjibari kwa tarih sanati 1239.

[38] Wakamtawalisha sultani **Ahmad** amkuliwawo **Bwana Waziri Wa Bwana Tamu Wa Bwana Shaihi Wa Bwana Tamu Mkuu** (p. 23) akapatana na sayyid Sa'idi akatawala nyaka miwili.

[39] Ba'adaye watu wa muyi wakamu'uzulu wakamrejeza **Bwana Shaihi Wa Bwana Fumu Madi**. akaketi katika 'ezi kwa shauri la sayyidi Sa'idi nyaka mitano akafa sanati 1247.

[40] Akarejezwa **Bwana Waziri** katika ufalme. akaya **Fumu Luti Bin**

Shaihi alokwenda Mwambasa yeye na Mazari'i. wakashika Siu wakapijana na Bwana Waziri wa Bwana Tamu Pate. na Bwana Waziri pamoya na sayyidi Sa'idi na Fumu Luti pamoya na Mazari'i na sheh Mataka mtu wa Siu kwa shauri moya wakashinda Fumu Luti akashika muyi wa Siu. ukavunduwa ukuta wa muyi. Fumu Luti na shehe Mataka wakakimbiya barani wakaketi barani siku katiti wakarejea Siu kwa zita (p. 24) wakashika muyi wa Siu wakawaka ukuta wakapijana Pate kwa Siu, kisa Fumu Luti akafa Siu. akatanganya Bwana Waziri wa Bwana Tamu Siu na Pate, ikawa katiak ta'a yake pamoya na shauri la sayyidi Sa'id. ba'ada ya mwaka aka'uwawa sultani Bwana Waziri wa Bwana Tamu na Fumu Bakari wa Bwana Shehe wa Bwana Fumu Madi.

[41] Akatawala yeye sultani **Fumu Bakari Bin Sheh Wa Bwana Fumu Madi** sanati 1250. akapatana na sayyid Sa'idi mwando wa kutawala. Kisa kahalifu pamoya yeye na sheh Mataka. sayyidi Sa'idi kamweta amiri Hammadi kapija Pate na Siu asiweze akafanya amani. ba'ada ya hapo sultani wa Pate ikatokeya fitina baina yake na bin 'ami yake (p. 25) Muhammad bin Ahmad wa Bwana Fumu Madi akashika nyumba ya ufalume kwa zita. Kisa wakaya watu wa Amu pamoya na mtu wa sayyidi Sa'idi wakasilihisha. Muhammad bin Ahmad kapekwa Siu kuketi. Fumu Bakari kaketi Pate. ba'adaye wakateta wakapijana nyaka mitano Siu kwa Pate. Kisa wakapatanishwa na sayyid Sa'idi. akaya Pate Muhammad bin Ahmad wakawa shauri moya na bin 'ami yake fumu Bakari.

[42] Kisa kamshika ghafula kamu'ua kwa shauri la mtu wa Siu. kisa sayyid Sa'idi kamwamkua Fumu Bakari kenenda Unguja. sayyid Sa'idi kamfunga Fumu Bakari kwa shauri la watu wa Amu na kwa sababu ya kumu'ua bin 'ami yake na kuwata kufuwata amani alofanya sayyidi Sa'idi, katika sanati 1262.

[43] Akashika nti ya Pate sultani **Ahmad Bin Sheh Bin Fumu** (p. 26) **Luti Bin Shehe Wa Bwana Tamu Mkuu** kwa shauri la sayyidi Sa'idi akaketi katika shauri la sayyidi Sa'idi nyaka miwili wakateta akaya sayyidi Sa'idi kampija akashuka amiri Hammadi Paza kenenda kupija Siu. na sayyidi Sa'idi alimfungua sultani Fumu Bakari. akampa zita pamoya na watu wa Amu. wakaketi Mtangawanda katika zombo, yeye sayyid Sa'idid kaketi mahala hwamkuliwa Kijangwa ta [*Editor's note*: rather, *cha*.] Mpunga karibu ya Paza.

[44] Amiri Hammadi akaya Siu kuwaka maboma katika ndiya baina ya Paza na Siu. amiri Hammadi kanenda Siu kwa zita. hatta kashika mitepe iliyoko bandarini ya Siu kaipindua kafanya maboma kapija nti ya Siu. kaona uzia muda walipokuwa mwingi; karudi kenenda kutwa'a mizinga iliyoko bomani.(p. 27) kipata ndiyani watu wa Siu wakamtokeya ghafula. amiri wa shehe Mataka amkuliwawo Bwana Hammadi wa'Umari akampija kamu'uwa amiri Hammadi; na amiri wa pili wa shehe Mataka amkuliwawo Bwana Hamadi Ngoma kenenda bomani kawapija katwa'a mizinga. habari ikasikiliya kwa sayyidi Sa'idi Paza. kangia marikabuni asinene na mtu kenenda zake Masikati.

[45] Mwaka wa pili karudi kamuweka Fumu Bakari Paza akapija Siu na Pate. katika wakati hunu akafa shehe Mataka kwa marazi. ikawa hitilafu kwa zijana zake kutaka ushehe wa Siu. wakangia katika ta'a ya sayyidi Sa'idi, Abu Bankari na Muhammad.

[46] Sayyid Sa'idi kampa Abu Bakari zita pamoya na sultani Fumu Bakari kenenda kumpija sulutani (p. 28) Ahmad. akenenda Abu Bakar bin sheh Mataka pamoya na amiri wa sultani Fumu Bakari amkuliwawo Bwana Mkuu wa Bwana Madi wa Ba'ishi. wakangia Siu usiku wakapijana hatta asubuhi wakafukuzwa. Abu Bakari akashikwa ndiyani akapekwa Pate

aka'uwawa na sultani wa Pate.

[47] Ba'ada yake akasimama sheh Muhammad bin shehe Mataka tarafu ya sayyidi Sa'idi pamoya na Fumu Bakari. sayyidi kawapa zita 'asikari na gharama. wakampija sultani Ahmad bin Sheh, hatta wakamtoa Pate katika tarihi sanati 1273 akenda Kau.

[48] Siu ikawa shehe Muhammad bin shehe Mataka tarafu ya sayyidi kampa 'aksari kawaka gereza. ba'adaye wakateta na mtu wa sayyidi Sa'idi kwa sababu alivunda banda la mtepe (p. 29) alowaka shehe Muhammad mbey ya gereza. na shehe Muhammad naye kavunda gereza. na katika wakati hunu alikufa sultani Ahmad Kau babake Fumu Bakari sultani wa Witu.

[49] Akaketi mahala pake sultani Ahmadi amkuliwawo Simba sultani wa Witu. na kabla ya shehe Muhammad bin sheh Mataka asiyavunda gereza la Siu yalitokeya fitina yeye na Fumu Bakari bin Sheh kamtoa Pate. kaya zake Amu. kataka kutamalaki yeye Pate kwa sura aloona nguvu zake na udovu wa watu wa Pate. wakati hunu waku'u wa Pate wasikiri, akaya kawapija waku'u wa Pate.

[50] Wakasimama wala hawana mfalume kwa shauri la watu watatu wa Pate. Muhammad bin Bwana Mkuu an-Nabhani na Bwana Rehema (p. 30) bin Ahmad an-Nabhani na Nasiri bin 'Abdallah bin 'Abdissalami ndiye alokuwa mudabbiri l-umuri wa mambo hayo. wakataka zana na bunduki. wakapijana na shehe Muhammad bin shehe Mataka wakamshinda. walimwuliya watu wangi. na ma'rufu ni maamiri wake watu wawili Bwana Dumila na Maulana wa Shiy Kuulu.

[51] Akisha kuona shehe Muhammad bin sheh Mataka mambo haya akaya kutaka amani kwa Muhammadi bin Bwana Mkuu almazkur kwani ndiye alokuwa baba wao katika watu watatu kawo. wakapatana wakawa hali moya.

kataka kumpa yeye Muhammad bin Bwana Mkuu ufulamue wa Pate na Siu. ka'iza Muhammad bin Bwana Mkuu akamwambiya mimi ni mtu mzima kamtwaye sultani Ahmadi mufalume wa Witu (p. 31) Simba. wakenenda kumtwa'a. kapeka watu wake shehe Muhammad bin shehe Mataka. na Pate kenenda Nasiri bin Abdallah Kau kumtwa'a sulutani Ahmad Simba.

[52] Ikasikiliya habari kwa sultani wa Unguja sayyid Majid bin Sa'idi, kabla ya hapo sayyid Sa'idi alikuwa mekufa. akaeta waziri wake sayyid Majid, sayyid Selimani bin Hamad kwa marikabu ili ashike Pate kuvunda fitina hiyo. ikawasili Mandra. Pate imezeye kushikwa na mtu wa sultani Ahmad Abu Bakari bin Hasan. amekuya naye Nasiri bin 'Abdallah. akisa kupata habari sayyid Selimani bin Hamad karejeya Unguja. na Sheh Muhammad hapo ndipo alipovunda gereza la Siu.

[53] Kisa kawasili sultani Ahmad Pate akabaiwa na watu wa Pate na shehe (p. 32) Muhammad na Watikuu shehe Mze(e) bin Sefu na shehe Shakuwe na Muhammadi Muti ukastakiri kwake sultani Ahmad ufalume kwa jumla ya watu waliyoko katika kisiwa ta Pate.

[54] Sayyid Majidi akawapeka watu wa Amu Pate kwa nus-ha pamoya na sheh Muhiyy ad-dini kutaka atwaye sulutani Ahmad, ba'azi ya 'asikiri waketi Pate na shehe Muhiyy ad-dini huyu ndiye alowatoa 'asikari wa sayyid Majidi katika gereza la Siu alipowapija shehe Muhammad wali ndani. akenenda shehe Muhiyy ad-dini kawatoa kwa amani kwani ali mtu wa sayyid Majidi. alipo kwenenda nao kwa sayyid Majidi akafanya hasira sana akatwa'a daraka shehe Muhiyy ad-dini ya kurejeza 'askari alipoona ghazabu. (p. 33) kwani ali mtu na hila nyingi ya 'ilmu nyingi.

[55] Basi wakaya yeye na watu wa Amu hatta Pate. na watu wa Amu walokuya Pate ni shehe Ahmad na nduye. wakanena na sultani Ahmad,

akatwa'a 'askari kwa ba'da ya shida kwa sababu ya suhba yake na shehe Ahmad na nduye. akahalifu shauri la waziri wake Nasiri bin 'Abdallah, kwani aliiza kutiya 'askari hatta umoya.

[56] Wakisa kungia wa'arabu Pate wakafanya shauri moya na Mwana Jaha binti sultani Fumu Luti Kipunga wa Bwana Fumu Madi mke wa sultani Fumu Bakari bin Shehe. wakati hunu yeye Fumu Bakari aliko Amu tena kwa shauri la sayyid Majid tangu alipotolewa Pate. kulla siku wakitiya 'askari na zana usiku usiku kwa siri. kisa alipoyua sultani ahmad ikiwa fitina na 'askari wamekuwa wangi Pate (p. 34) wakampija ghafula ba'ada ya kwisa hila ya kumshika wasiweze kwani watu wote wa Pate walikuwa shauri moya na sayyid Majidid isokuwa waziri wake Nasiri bin 'Abdallah. wakapijana nao ndani mwa Pate wakamtoa shehe Muhammad kamtukuliya Siu.

[57] Pate wakaketi wa'arabu. na baharini wakatiya marikabu. zita zalipokuwa zikuu alikuya yeye sayyid Majid wakahurusu kisiwa ta [*Editor's note*: cha.] Pate kwa bahari. Katiya silsila katika kanwa la mto wa Siu Kuyyu wakapijana nyezi sitta kwa bahrini na kwa Pate. na janibu ya Tikuuni Mzee wa Sefu akahalifu akawa ni mtu wa sayyid kwa hila nyingi na maneno mangi. wakaona ziki sultani Ahmad na shehe Muhammad. na nti ya Siu ikawa na fitina. ba'zi wapenda kwa sayyid kwa sababu ya mashaka (p. 35) wamezopata. na watuwe ni sharifu Maulana bin Abi Bakari na 'Isa bin Ahmad.

[58] Walipoona hiyao sultani Ahmad na shehe Muhammad wakataka amani kwa sayyidi. kawapa katika maneno ya amani. sultani Ahmad kasafiri kwa siri usiku kanenda zake barani kenda Kau.

[59] Na ba'ada yake shehe Muhammad kenenda marikabuni kwa sayyidi kamsamehe. Na sayyid kenenda zake Unguja. kisa shehe Muhammad akanenda Unguja kumuwajihi sayyid. Kamfunga kampeka ngomeni Mwambasa

na watu wangi. akafa kwa ba'ada ya siku nyingi.

[60] Na sultani Ahmad alipokwenenda shehe Muhammad Unguja alipekewa Su'udi bin Hamad kumshika kwa hila asiweze kenenda zake Witu. Su'udi akaya Paza akamshika 'Umari wa Bwana Mataka, na zijana wa shehe (p. 36) Muhammad wote wakashikwa Siu wakapekwa ngomeni Mwambasa. 'Umari kafungwa Amu.

[61] Ba'ada ya hayo akatamalaki sayyid Majidi Sawahili zote pasiwe na mtu tena wa kumu'arizi[a]. [[a]MS: *kuma'arizi.*] na sultani Ahmadi kaketi Witu katika ta'a ya sayyid Majidi hatta wakati wa sayyid Baragashi.

[62] Akataka sayyid Bargash kuweka 'askari Witu na bendera asikiri sultani Ahmad. kapeka zita asiweze kufanya* [*better: *kafanya*] amani. ba'ada ya hapo Su'udi bin Hamad asifurahi sayyid Bargashi kwa sababu kufanya amani upesi naye hakumpija sana kapeka zita mara ya pili ziku(u) na luwali Sa'idi bin Hamad.

[63] Sultani Ahmad akatwa'a himaya kwa Jarmani wakati hunu zita zikarudi (p. 37) za sayyid Bargash. akaketi sultani Ahmad katika himaya ya Jarman. wakampa na ba'zi ya bara ya Sawahili. akafa sultani Ahmad katika hali hiyo sanati 1306.

[64] Akatawala **Fumu Bakari Bin Sultani Ahmad Bin Shehe**. ikatoya fitina yeye na Jarman. Kunsil Jarman akamu'ua bawabu wa lango la muyi. 'askari walokuwako wakampija Kunsil na wazungu walofuwetene wakawaua bighairi ya kutaka amri kwa sultani, 'askari kisa kuona ame'uwawa mwandani wao nawo wali'iuwa. na watu wa Wandamoyyo na wa Mkunumbi wakisa kupata habari nawo wakawauwa wazungu walokuwako.

[65] Ba'adaye ikaya dola tukufu ya Wangereza wakataka watu walo'uwa <wa>zungu, watu wa Mkunumbi na wa Wandamoyo asiriziki

kuwatoa. (p. 38) Sultani Fumu Bakari wakampija Wangereza bitarihi lailat 11 rabi'il awwal sanati 1308 hatta asubuhi ya tarihi 12 rabi'il awwal sanati 1308. wakamtoa Witu kwa zita Fumu Bakari kenenda Jongeni. Witu ikatamalikiwa na dola ya Wangereza. Fumu Bakari kaketi Jongeni hatta tarihi 28 jamad il awwal sanati 1308 akafa.

[66] Ba'ada yake akashika mahala pa nduye **Bwana Sheh Bin Sultani Ahmad**, ba'ada ya siku tatu akashikwa na nduye Fumu 'Umari na Bwana Avutula. wakamfunga Bwana Shehe ashike yeye **Fumu 'Umari Bin Sultani Ahmad**. ikawa jinsi yalokuwa baina yake yeye na dola tukufu ya Wangereza.

[67] Wa amma mfalme wakwisa wakutamalaki Witu ni sultani Fumu Bakari. wa amma wa Pate (p. 39) wakwisa ni sultani Simba sultani wa Witu wa amma sultani wa kwanda wa Pate ni Seliman bin Seliman bin Muzaffar an-Nabhani imamu l-'arab*.

* The text of p. 39 of MS A, which for reasons of space economy is not reproduced from the original reduced to two-thirds of its size, might find its place here; after the last two words of p. 38 follows (p. 39):

وكِيْسَ نِسُلْطَانِ وَ وِيتُوْ وَاَمّا سُلْطَانِ وَكَدَ وَيَاتِ نسِليمان بن سليمان بن مُظَفّر النّبْهَانِيْ اِمَامُ الْعَرَبْ

TRANSLATION

[1] Account of the first Nabhani who came to the Swahili (coast) and all accounts about them. There ruled thirty-one kings and one woman, she was the thirty-second, and the following are complete records of them. We have transmitted them from Muhammad bin Fumu 'Umari, who is called Bwana Kitini; and he received them from his grandfather[a] Muhammad bin Bwana Mkuu called Bwana Simba al-Nabhani; he knew the accounts exactly from earlier times and their genealogy, as I have told it here.

[2] The first of the Nabhani who came to Pate, (was) **[I] Sulayman bin Sulayman bin Muzaffar** and his two brothers 'Ali bin Sulayman and 'Uthman bin Sulayman. The aforementioned Sulayman bin Sulayman was the sultan. He was the one who had been king in Arabia (and) was expelled by al-Ya'rab (*i.e.*, al-Ya'rubi). He came to Pate at the beginning of the year 600 of the Hijra.[b] He married into the tribe of the Battawiyuna, the daughter of the king of Pate (p. 2). And the custom of the Swahili to this day (is the following): when somebody marries your[1] daughter, after seven days he will come to visit you (and) the father of your[1] wife will give him something. When (the former) went to greet him, (the latter) gave him the kingship; from then on reigned Sulayman bin Sulayman, the aforesaid.

[3] And Kitaka was a town east of Pate, and at this time there was not yet the town of Siu, (but) there was the town of Shanga, east of Pate. And

[1] Pronoun references here are uncertain.

at Paza the owners of Paza were the Mafaziyuna. He who reigned over Pate (also) ruled these towns: Kitaka, Pate and Mandra; the ruler of Mandra was (also) Sulayman bin Sulayman, the aforesaid.[c] He had [two] sons: Muhammad and Ahmad. Sultan Sulayman died in the year 625 [1227-8].

[4] At that time the age of Muhammad bin Sulayman was 20 years, and Ahmadi's age (was) 15 years. **[II] Muhammad bin Sulaymani** reigned after his father. He fought with the people of Shanga, won over them (and) destroyed (p. 3) the city. He led the people of Shanga away, (and) they came to Pate. And some of the people who had come to Pate ran away; and some of these were the people of the Wakinandangu tribe. They ran away, without it being known of them[d] where they had gone. After (some) days had passed, news came to the ruler Muhammad bin Sulayman from the hunters. They said to him, "Those who ran away, we have seen them in the forest." He sent people to look for them, (and) they saw them in the middle of the forest. They had built huts (and) had settled down there. They took them with them and brought them to Pate. Then he returned them to where he had (originally) fetched them from. This is the origin of Siu. Later came other people of the Swahili (coast), (and) settled in Siu. Then came the Famau; they became the chiefs of Siu under the suzerainty of the king of Pate, for a long time.

[5] About the year 650 [1252-3] Sultan Muhammad bin Sulayman died, (and) his brother Sultan **[III] Ahmad bin Sulayman** reigned. He governed (p. 4) the land of Pate very well. He started plantations and built houses, without making war anywhere, until he died in the year 670 [1271-2].[e]

[6] (Then) reigned the son of Sultan Muhammed bin Sulayman by the name of **[IV] Ahmad bin Muhammad bin Sulayman**. He carried forth according to the custom of his uncle, building up the city of Pate, and he had

many sons.

[7] When he died in the year 705 [1305-6],[f] the one of his sons with the name [V] **Muhammed bin Ahmad bin Muhammad bin Sulayman** ascended to the kingship. During his reign he conquered the cities of the Swahili (coast): Paza and Mandra, by conducting much war in the land of Paza. And as concerns Mandra, they invaded it by force through a stratagem and destroyed it totally. And the people he brought to Pate, and some of them ran away, (and) dispersed all over, coming to Shela and Malindi and other towns. And those who had gone to Shela put themselves under the protection of the people of Amu. The king demanded them (back) from the people of Amu, (but) they[2] refused to hand them over. While they were still in negotiations about this, the king died in the year 732 [1331-2].

[8] He had one son (p. 5) named Sultan 'Umar. He reigned after his father, (and) he returned to the demand of his father against the people of Amu demanding the people of Mandra; the people of Amu refused to surrender them. He made war on them; the people of Amu asked for peace (and) submitted to Sultan [VI] **'Umar bin Muhammad bin Ahmad bin Muhammad bin Sulayman**. He gained great power (and) conquered all towns of the Swahili (coast): Uziwa and Malindi and Kiwayu and Kitau and Miya and Imizi and Watamu, until he reached Kirimba. He gained possession over all the towns from Pate to Kirimba. In each city he installed one of his men to govern. This is the origin of the Jumbe[3] to be found on the whole coast. The

[2] In the Mombasa text it is "he."

[3] Compare Stigand, p. 45, note 2: "The ruins of the Yumbe (the Sultan of Pate's palace) are still to be seen in Pate."

(mrima) meaning [of the word] is "slaves of the Yumbe," and this *Yumbe* is the name of the royal palace of Pate.

[9] And on the other, [*i.e.*, northern] side he gained possession as far as Warsheikh by war which he first waged from Kiwayu and Tula and Tuwala and Shungwaya and all the harbors (*banadiri*): Brawa, Marka, Mogadisho. There in Mogadisho (p. 6) he installed a governor (*luwali*) in charge of all the harbors that were near Mogadisho. (As long) as he lived, all these lands stood under his overlordship, except Zanzibar, which he did not rule. At this time Zanzibar was not a great country.[4] And this king exceedingly loved war, (but) he (also) loved his subjects, and his subjects lived at ease (and) they gained much money, (and) the land Pate flourished. He died in the year 749 [1348-9].

[10] He had two children, Muhammad and Ahmad. (There) reigned **[VII] Muhammad bin 'Umar bin Muhammad bin Ahmad bin Muhammad bin Sulayman**. And there was no war, he ruled the whole kingdom of his father in peace. And he loved very much money and trade. He had sea voyages undertaken, that he sent to India to conduct trade. And he had much profit in money. And once his son travelled (and) came upon an island in the sea; he went ashore and found silver ore[5]. He brought people, and they worked, (and) he gained much money. The prosperity in the land of Pate increased exceedingly, so that they made silver bedsteads, and silver ladders

---

[4] Compare Stigand, p. 45: "Sultan Omar conquered the whole of Sawahili coast except only Zanzibar he did not get because at this time this town had no fame."

[5] Compare Stigand, p. 47: "for this sand is silver ore."

and many silver utensils.[6] He had four sons, Bwana Mkuu and Ahmad and Abu Bakari and 'Umari. The king died (p. 7) in the year 797 [1394-5].

[11] (Then) reigned his brother **[VIII] Ahmad bin 'Umar bin Muhammad bin Ahmad bin Muhammad bin Sulayman**. And he reigned over his land in peace (and) died in the year 840 [1436-7].

[12] (Then) reigned **[IX] Abu Bakr bin Muhammad bin 'Umar bin Muhammad bin Ahmad bin Muhammad bin Sulayman**. He ruled in a good manner toward all the towns that were subject to him, and he attended to all his towns in a way that, when he died in the year 875 [1470-1], none were damaged. He had two children, Muhammad and Ahmad.

[13] (Then) reigned **[X] Muhammad bin Abi Bakr bin Muhammad bin 'Umar bin Muhammad bin Ahmad bin Muhammad bin Sulayman**. During his time the Portuguese Europeans came to all the Swahili towns. They settled in Mombasa (and) made a fort. And near Pate they built Ndondo[7]. And the people of the mainland followed them for the reason of being given money, (and) subjected themselves to them. They required [the same] also from the king in regard to the city of Pate and they fought him. On the side of Shindakasi[8] they built (p. 8) underground,[9] in order to attack the town of Pate with pumps, but failed. Finally, they reconciled peacefully (and) made

---

[6] Compare Stigand, p. 49: "ladders of silver," "silver neck chains," "silver studs."

[7] Stigand, p. 48.

[8] Stigand, p. 50.

[9] Stigand, p. 48: "they taught people how to excavate wells in the rocks by means of gunpowder," "made an underground passage to Pongwa rock"; p. 50 f.: "they made channels in the ground of Shindakasi so that they might pump water into the town."

a written document with their conditions. The Europeans stayed at Pate (and) made a customshouse,[10] in the European language they called this customshouse "*Fandika.*" They introduced many more things to the Pate island. After this the ruler died in the year 900 [1494-5]. He left the sons, Bwana Mkuu and Abu Bakari.

[14] (Then) reigned **[XI] Abu Bakari bin Muhammad bin Abi Bakari bin Muhammad bin 'Umar bin Muhammad bin Ahmad bin Muhammad bin Sulayman**. He lived in peace with the Europeans, (and) they got along according to the practice of his father. He died in the year 945 [1538-9].[g] He left [two] sons, Ahmad and Muhammad.

[15] (Then) reigned his brother **[XII] Bwana Mkuu bin Muhammad bin Abi Bakari bin Muhammad bin 'Umar bin Muhammad bin Ahmad bin Muhammad bin Sulayman**. There arose disagreements with the Europeans, but there was no war. He died during long-lasting unrest in the year 973 [1565-6]. He left the son Bwana Bakari.

[16] (Then) reigned **[XIII] Muhammad bin Abi Bakari bin Muhammad bin Abi Bakari bin Muhammad bin 'Umar bin Muhammad bin Ahmad bin Muhammad bin Sulayman**. He came to an accommodation with the Europeans, and they occupied some of the towns. He died, leaving the son Abu Bakari in the year 1002 [1593-4].

[17] (Then) reigned **[XIV] Bwana Bakari bin Bwana Mkuu bin Muhammad bin Abi Bakari bin Muhammad bin 'Umar** (p. 9) **bin Muhammad bin Ahmad bin Muhammad bin Sulayman.** [He reigned] following the custom of his father, but the extent of their original realm

---

[10] Stigand, p. 48, 162: city gate *Fandikani* = Alfandega.

diminished. He died, leaving Bwana Mkuu wa Bakari, in the year 1041 [1631-2].

[18] (Then) reigned [XV] **Abu Bakari bin Muhammad bin Abi Bakari bin Muhammad bin Abu Bakari bin Muhammad bin 'Umar bin Muhammad bin Ahmad bin Muhammad bin Sulayman**. He quarrelled with the Europeans, (and) sent people to occupy the Pate land (and) they beat the Europeans. (Then) came troops of the Europeans; they shot at the town with cannons (and) blocked the entryways from the sea. The people of Pate suffered hardships (and) made peace. After this the king died, leaving two sons, Bwana Mkuu and Ahmad in the year 1061 [1650-1].

[19] (Then) reigned [XVI] **Bwana Mkuu wa Bwana Bakari bin Bwana Mkuu bin Muhammad bin Abi Bakari bin Muhammad bin 'Umar bin Muhammad bin Ahmad bin Muhammad bin Sulayman**. He got along with the Europeans. And he loved to live in Amu, even the monsoon season he spent at Amu.[h] He married (p. 10) amongst the people of Amu.[11] And the Famau of Siu at this time revolted against his authority. He fought with them (and) destroyed the town of Siu. He took all the people of Siu (and) brought them to Pate. The chief of Siu escaped (and) went to Ndondo, to the Portuguese, (and) they took (him) under protection. The superior of the Portuguese Europeans came to Pate to demand [the release of] the people of Siu. He regained them (and) returned them to Siu, (and) they remained (there) in peace.

---

[11] Compare [Stigand, p. 52: "Sultan Abubakr remained at Amu. He married at Amu..."] Stigand, p. 56: "Sultan Bwana Mkuu loved the country of Amu very much, and he went to Amu and married a wife there, and he also built a mosque, and made Amu the harbour for the trading vessels brought by the north-eastern monsoon. His mother also was an Amu woman. He lived at Amu and the Amu people loved him well."

[20] After this the Portuguese resorted to a ruse: they came to Pate in a ship (and) urged the king to come aboard. The king did not go, (but) sent the son of his (paternal) uncle, Bwana Mkuu. Him and (other) men of Pate the Europeans took with them on the ship and carried them away to [their] home in Europe,[12] not a single one of them ever coming back. After this the Europeans were fought at all places where there were people, on the mainland and on the islands (p. 11).[13] They drove them aw, (and) they escaped to Mombasa. After this the king died in the year 1100 [1688-9]. He had two sons and one daughter: Bwana Bakari and Bwana Madi and Mwana Darini.

[21] (Then) reigned his son **[XVII] Bwana Bakari wa Bwana Mkuu bin Bwana Bakari wa Bwana Mkuu bin Muhammad bin Abi Bakari bin Muhammad bin 'Umar bin Muhammad bin Ahmad bin Muhammad bin Sulayman**. The king was suddenly attacked by Ahmad, the brother of Bwana Mkuu who had been taken away by the Portuguese Europeans. He killed him with a sword.

[22] Then he reigned: **[XVIII] Ahmad bin Abi Bakari bin Muhammad bin Abi Bakari bin Muhammad <bin Abi Bakari bin Muhammad> bin 'Umar bin Muhammad bin Ahmad bin Muhammad bin Sulayman**, in the year 1103 [1691-2]. He pursued the Portuguese (and) chased away those that had remained. And at this time [lived] Mwana Darini, the daughter of Bwana Mkuu wa Bwana Bakari wa Bwana Mkuu bin Abi

---

[12] Later [22] it says "to Goa;" compare note 16 there. Compare Stigand, p. 52: "I will pretend to be ill and will send my son-in-law Bwana Mkuu and forty great men in my stead."

[13] Compare Stigand, p. 55: "the whole Swahili coast," "so they combined and fought the Portuguese on the whole coast, leaving Mombasa alone."

Bakari,[14] the one who had gone to Goa[i] - and afterwards, at the time of Sultan Ahmad, both her brothers Bwana Bakari bin Bwana Mkuu and Bwana Madi bin Bwana Mkuu were killed [the sons of the one] who had been carried off to Goa;[15] she had long grieved for her husband and because of the death of her brothers. Finally, after a while she decided to stage a celebration, to circumcise her son (p. 12) Bwana Tamu Mtoto, called Sultan Abu Bakari Imam al-Huda, son of Bwana Mkuu who had gone to Goa.[16] The king Sultan Ahmad received notice (of this), and he too decided on a celebration with the intention to withhold from her the [ceremonial] horn.[17]

[23] When Mwana Darini received news that the horn would be refused to her, she called Mwinyi Ba'iyi[18] Mkuu, the sherif of the *Jamali-l-laili*, who knew carving very well, and she told him her business (and) requested that he craft her a horn superior to those of the others. He agreed (and) demanded his wages, to be given 120 riyals and elephant tusks, as many as he demanded, so that he could choose those that were good (and) usable. Mwana Darini fulfilled all his conditions, (and) he crafted the horn in six months. When he had finished, she suddenly showed it (and) took it to her

---

[14] Should say "Muhammed."

[15] Here, too, the addition of "who had been brought to Goa" is wrong. For it is obviously, as the following shows, her husband for whom she yearns, and not her and her brothers' father.

[16] Compare Stigand, p. 53: "Sultan Abu Bakari said to his daughter, "Your husband has gone to Goa..."

[17] See illustrations in C. Eliot, *East Africa Protectorate* [London, 1905], p. 14 ; E.G. Ravenstein, *A Journal of the First Voyage of Vasco da Gama* [London: Hakluyt Society, 1898], p. 43.

[18] Compare Stigand, p. 53: "Mwenyi Baenyi."

kinsmen's houses for a big celebration play. They donated much money (for this), (so) she said to Mwinyi Ba'iyi who had made the horn,"Do you wish (p. 13) your wages or to take the donations?" He took the offerings for he saw that it was much money. She took her horn, and the celebration for her son was held.[19]

[24] Later, in the time of Bwana Tamu Mkuu the people of Amu came to borrow the original horn (and) he gave it to them. When they were out on the sea, the vessel sank in the water, (and) the horn was lost.[20] Bwana Tamu Mkuu demanded the horn of Mwana Darini, saying to her, "Give it to us that we may use it in the towns." She said to him, "Each clan who has donated for my horn may use it."

[25] Moreover, Mwana Darini set a slave free, who knew how to play this horn, him and his descendants. And it was his custom to receive five riyals and a cloth, to carry the horn, and butter as drink for the one who blows the horn,[j] and donations, from every man according to his means. This lineage were called "Chieftains of the Horn." To this day there are people belonging to it. And since that time (p. 14) the clans of all of Pate and of the other towns are in the habit of coming and borrowing [the horn] it under similar conditions.

And the king ruled for seven years while no rain fell, (so) he abdicated[21] his kingship in the year 1111 [1699-1700].

---

[19] Compare Stigand, p. 54: "So she held the ceremony."

[20] Compare Stigand, p. 54, note: "The old horn is said to have been lost at sea."

[21] Compare Stigand, p. 51: "Sultan Ahmad... reigned seven years without rain falling, and then he abdicated of his own free will."

[26] (Then) reigned Sultan **[XIX] Abi Bakari Bwana Tamu Mkuu wa Bwana Mtiti bin Ahmad bin Abi Bakari bin 'Umar bin Ahmad bin 'Umar bin Muhammad bin Ahmad bin Muhammad bin Sulayman**. They got together with the ruler of Maskat Imam al-Ya'rab. This king of Pate went to Arabia (*variant*: to the king of Arabia) (and) they arranged that when the ruler of Pate returns he should chase away the Portuguese from Mombasa. When the king of Pate came back, he started war against Mombasa; he attacked the Portuguese Europeans on a Sunday (and) killed them in[22] the fort of Mombasa.[23]

[27] He notified the Imam al-Ya'rab who placed a governor (*wali*) from the Mazru'i, three men (who were) brothers: Muhammad bin 'Uthman and 'Ali bin 'Uthman and Kadhibu bin 'Uthman.[k] And they came together with soldiers from the Imam al-Ya'rab. That is the origin of those Mazru'i who came to Mombasa.[24] And this king of Pate lived in harmony with the subjects; he completed forty years of his reign (and) died in the year 1152 [1739-40]. He had many children, (but) his sons did not reign after him.

[28] [Instead] reigned sultan **[XX] Ahmad bin Abi Bakari bin Muhammad bin Abi Bakari bin 'Umar bin Ahmad bin 'Umar bin Muhammad bin Ahmad bin Muhammad bin Sulayman**. He lived in great

---

[22] A. *kashika* "and he seized."

[23] Compare Stigand, p. 55: "They waited for a Sunday and then rushed in on them suddenly, killing them..." Strandes, p. 291 f., Guillain, I, p. 617.

[24] Compare Stigand, p. 55 f: "The Imam sent a tribe called the Mazaru'i..." "This was the beginning of the Mazaru'i coming to this coast."

comfort and loved to raise many herds of cattle.[25] He died in the year 1160 [1747], leaving the son Bwana Gogo.

[29] After him reigned Bwana Tamu Mtoto called Imam al-Huda, the son of Bwana Mkuu who had been taken away by the Portuguese.[26] And his (real) name was **[XXI] Abu Bakari bin Bwana Mkuu bin Abi Bakari bin Muhammad bin Abi Bakari bin Muhammad bin Abi Bakari bin Muhammad bin 'Umar bin Muhammad bin Ahmad bin Muhammad bin Sulayman.** The Imam al-Ya'rab sent an expedition to attack Pate (but) they failed. Many Arabs[27] died, (p. 16) so they turned back (and) made peace. After this the people of Amu were attacked by the king of Pate because they seceded.[27] They fought with each other, (and) he failed. And the people of Amu came to Pate to fight near Kitaka, (but) they were beaten back (and) returned to Amu. Afterwards the king of Pate conducted war on land and at sea (and) vanquished the people of Amu (and) established his authority over them. Finally the king of Pate was killed by the people of Pate together with the people of the Imam al-Ya'rab in the year 1177 [1736-4].[28]

[30] (Then) reigned his sister, Sultana[29] **[XXII] Mwana Khadija binti**

---

[25] Compare Gillain, I, p. 547: "Bouana M'kouhou, surnommé Mélani-Gniombé."

[26] Compare Stigand, p. 57: The Bwana Tamu was the son of that Bwana Mkuu who was carried away to Goa." "Now it was this Sultan who fought with the Yorubi Imam." "Maskat soldiers were put in Pate."

[27] Compare Stigand, p. 57 f.

[28] Compare Stigand, p. 58: "The Yorabi Imam made intrigue in Pate so that at his instigation the Sultan was stabbed with a dagger at a levee and was killed."

[29] Compare Stigand, p. 61: "In the year 1177... a Queen Mwana Khadija, sister of Bwana Tamu the Younger, reigned."

Bwana Mkuu bin Abi Bakari bin Muhammad bin Abi Bakari bin Muhammad bin Abi Bakari bin Muhammad bin 'Umar bin Muhammad bin Ahmad bin Muhammad bin Sulayman. She had to deal with much unrest in the Pate land. (Now) there were two rulers in the town of Pate - she, the aforesaid Mwana Khadija, and Sultan 'Umari. They fought with each other in the city for five years.[30] (Then) Sultan 'Umari fled, and went to Barawa. Afterwards he returned with a great force. (But) he was attacked in the night (and) killed by the people of the aforesaid Mwana Khadija. A few days after that Mwana Khadija died, (p. 19) in the year 1187 [1773-4].

[31] (Then) reigned **[XXIII] Bwana Mkuu wa Shii wa Bwana Tamu Mkuu**, and his subjects gave him trouble. Intrigue arose, so that he did not get rest, until in the year 1191 [1777] the people of the town invaded [his palace] (and) killed him.[31]

[32] About this date to power came Bwana Fumu Madi, by the name Sultan **[XXIV] Muhammad bin Abi Bakari bin Bwana Mkuu bin Abi Bakari bin Muhammad bin Abi Bakari bin Muhammad bin Abi Bakari bin Muhammad bin 'Umar bin Muhammad bin Ahmad bin Muhammad bin Sulayman.** After he came to power, (his) subjects desired to get rebellious, so he made war on them (and) won victory over them (and) took forty of the noblemen prisoner - and among these forty mentioned men, two were his brothers - and had them executed[32] to have peace. From then on

---

[30] Compare Stigand, p. 61: "Then there were two rulers in one country and they fought together for five years inside the city." "War returned to Pate, and after one year they broke into his house at Diwani and he was killed."

[31] Compare Stigand, p. 63 ff.: "Sultan Fumoluti 'stump-arm'."

[32] Compare Stigand, p. 66.

nobody dared to oppose him. He reigned in quiet and peace and wealth, and his subjects had great comfort. Then he died in the year 1224 [1809-10]. After him nobody ever reigned as he did[33] (p. 20). And he had many children.[34]

[33] (Then) reigned Sultan [XXV] **Ahmad bin Shaykh bin Fumu Luti bin <Bwana>[35] Tamu Mkuu**. Unrest increased in the Amu land. He went (and) made war on them in the year 1227 [1812], he and the people of Mombasa, the Mazru'i. They brought people (and) landed at Shela, a great army of men from Pate and men from Mombasa. The men of Amu came out and fought with them. The men of Pate and Mombasa were defeated. They wanted to escape, (but) ships in which they came were stranded. (Then) they fought a great battle, (and) many men from Pate and Mombasa were killed, without number. Out of the people from Pate alone, without slaves and the ones who remained unknown, the count was 81 dead, besides those from Mombasa.[36]

[34] Thereafter the people of Amu went to Arabia (and) asked [for help] from Sayyid Sa'id (p. 21), the father of Sayyid Barghash, (and) they gave him the country in the year 1228 [1813]. Thus Sayyid Sa'id came to reign

---

[33] Compare Stigand, p. 67: "Now he was the last of the great Sultans of the Nabahans; after him there came not anyone who obtained a kingdom like his."

[34] Compare Stigand, p. 70: "Now Fumomadi had begotten fifty children both male and female."

[35] <...> Not in MS.

[36] Stigand, p. 72 ff. 76.

over Amu[37]. (And) the sovereignty of Pate remained restricted to the Pate Island and the harbors *banadiri*. The unrest in the land of Pate increased. There rose a second among the sons of Bwana Fumu Madi, who was called Fumu Luti Kipunga. He fought with Sultan Ahmad. Finally Sultan Ahmad took sick (and) died in the year 1230[38] [1814-5].[39]

[35] (Then) reigned Sultan **[XXVI] Fumu Luti wa Bwana Fumu Madi**. And he was a very able, courageous (and) righteous man. And at this time Shaykh Mataka bin Mbaraka gained the office of *shaykh* of Siu;[40] (and) he gathered soldiers and guns. And he was under the suzerainty of the sultan of Pate, (but) he also got along very well with the Mazru'i. Later in the year 1236 [1820-1], hostilities arose between him and the sultan of Zanzibar (p. 22) Sayyid Sa'id. (And) Sultan Fumu Luti died in the above mentioned year.

[36] After him reigned **[XXVII] Fumu Luti bin Shaykh bin Fumu Luti bin Shaykh wa Bwana Tamu Mkuu**, and he was the father of Sultan Ahmad, the sultan of Witu. He came to power in the morning, and in the afternoon the people of the town expelled him; he went to Siu together with the Mazru'i; eventually they went to Mombasa.[41]

[37] (Then) reigned Sultan **[XXVIII] Bwana Shaykh wa Bwana**

[37] Compare Stigand, p. 81: "Now at this time Sa'id first sent... and it came about that he took over the country of Lamu."

[38] Instead of 1220 as in MS.

[39] Stigand, p. 77: 1229.

[40] Compare Stigand, p. 85 ff.: "Now at that time Bwana Mataka was the Sheikh at Siu, and he was like a Sultan."

[41] Stigand, p. 84 ff.

Fumu Madi. He made peace with Sayyid Sa'id (and) took Arabs into Pate, (and) they remained (there) three years. Afterwards the people of the town deposed him with the consent of Sayyid Sa'id, the sultan of Zanzibar, in the year 1239 [1823-4].[42]

[38] They put on the throne Sultan **[XXIX] Ahmad** who is called **Bwana Waziri wa Bwana Tamu wa Bwana Shaykh wa Bwana Tamu Mkuu**. (p. 23) He made peace with Sayyid Sa'id and ruled for two years.[43]

[39] Afterwards the people of the town deposed him (and) brought back **[XXVIII] Bwana Shaykh wa Bwana Fumu Madi**. He remained in power with the consent of Sayyid Sa'id for five years (and) died in the year 1247 [1831-2].

[40] (Then) **Bwana Waziri** was returned to power. (And) there came **[XXVII] Fumu Luti bin Shaykh**, who had gone to Mombasa together with the Mazru'i. They occupied Siu, (and) attacked Bwana Waziri wa Bwana Tamu at Pate. And Bwana Waziri together with Sayyid Sa'id, and Fumu Luti together with the Mazru'i and Shaykh Mataka, a man of Siu, were in consent [amongst themselves]. They defeated Fumu Luti, took the town of Siu, (and) the town wall was destroyed. Fumu Luti and Shaykh Mataka escaped to the mainland. They remained in the interior several days; (then) they returned to Siu fighting, (p. 24) occupied the town of Siu, built up the wall, and fought Pate from Siu. Finally, Fumu Luti died in Siu. Bwana Waziri wa Bwana Tamu united Siu with Pate, (and) it remained under his sovereignty with the consent of Sayyid Sa'id. After a year Sultan Bwana Waziri wa Bwana Tamu

---

[42] Stigand, pp. 86, 88.

[43] Stigand, p. 88.

was killed by Fumu Bakari wa Bwana Shaykh wa Bwana Fumu Madi.[44]

[41] (Then) reigned this very Sultan **[XXX] Fumu Bakari bin Shaykh wa Bwana Fumu Madi** in the year 1250 [1834-5]. He came to an agreement with Sayyid Sa'id in the beginning of his reign. But soon he seceded with Shaykh Mataka. Sayyid Sa'id sent Amir Hammadi; he attched Pate and Siu (but) failed (and) made peace. After this hostilities erupted between the sultan of Pate and the son of his (paternal) uncle (p. 25) Muhammad bin Ahmad wa Bwana Fumu Madi, (who) occupied the royal palace by force. Finally, came the people of Amu together with a man of Sayyid Sa'id, (and) they brought about peace.[45] Muhammad bin Ahmad was taken to Siu, to remain there. (And) Fumu Bakari stayed in Pate. Afterwards they fought (and) quarrelled for five years, Siu against Pate. Finally they were reconciled with each other by Sayyid Sa'id. Muhammad bin Ahmad came to Pate, (and) they were of one mind, he and his cousin Fumu Bakari.

[42] Later, he [Fumo Bakari] suddenly attacked him (and) killed him at the instigation of a man from Siu. Then Sayyid Sa'id called Fumu Bakari to him, (and) he went to Zanzibar. Sayyid Sa'id imprisoned Fumu Bakari on the advice of the people of Amu, and because he had killed his cousin, and because he had strayed away from the peace that Sayyid Sa'id had established. [This was] in the year 1262 [1845-6].[46]

[43] Sultan **[XXXI] Ahmad bin Shaykh bin Fumu** (p. 26) **Luti bin**

---

[44] Stigand, p. 88 f.

[45] Compare Stigand, p. 91: "Then Sa'id made peace with Sultan Fumobakari by the help of the great men of Lamu."

[46] Stigand, p. 92.

Shaykh wa Bwana Tamu Mkuu took over the land of Pate on the advice of Sayyid Sa'id. He lived in agreement with Sayyid Sa'id for two years. (Then) they quarrelled; Sayyid Sa'id came (and) fought with him, and Amir Hammadi landed at Paza (and) went to occupy Siu. And Sayyid Sa'id released Sultan Fumu Bakari (from imprisonment). He gave him troops together with the people of Amu. They remained at Mtangawanda in ships, (and) he, Sayyid Sa'id, remained at a place called Kijangwa cha Mpunga, nearby Paza.[47]

[44] Amir Hammadi came to Siu to build fortifications on the road between Paza and Siu. Amir Hammadi marched towards Siu with his army, then he seized the *mtepe* boats that were in the harbor of Siu, turned them upside down, built fortifications, (and) attacked the land of Siu. As time grew long he came into trouble; (then) he returned (and) went to fetch cannon that were in the fort (p. 27). (And) while he was on his way, the people of Siu attacked him unexpectedly. The *amir* of Shaykh Mataka called Bwana Hamadi wa Umari,[1] fought and killed Amir Hammadi; and the second *amir* of Shaykh Mataka, called Bwana Hamadi Ngoma, went to the fort, attacked them (and) took the cannon. The news (about) this reached Sayyid Sa'id at Paza; he went to the ship without speaking to anyone, (and) went away to Maskat.[48]

[45] The next year he came back (and) installed Fumu Bakari in Paza, (and) he (Fumu Bakari) fought against Siu and Pate. During this time Shaykh Mataka died of an illness. There arose differences amongst his sons because of they desired the shaykhdom of Siu. They submitted to the suzerainty of Sayyid Sa'id: Abu Bakari and Muhammad.

---

[47] Stigand, p. 92.

[48] Stigand, p. 93.

[46] Sayyid Sa'id gave Abu Bakari troops, together with Sultan Fumu Bakari, (and) he went to war against Sultan (p. 28) Ahmad. Abu Bakari bin Shaykh Mataka went together with the *amir* of Sultan Fumu Bakari, called Bwana Mkuu wa Bwana Madi wa Ba'ishi. They invaded Siu by night (and) fought until the morning (but) were driven back. Abu Bakari was captured on his way, brought to Pate (and) killed by the sultan of Pate.

[47] After this Shaykh Muhammad bin Shaykh Mataka (remained) on the side of Sayyid Sa'id, together with Fumu Bakari. The Sayyid gave them troops, soldiers and money funds. They fought against Sultan Ahmad bin Shaykh until they expelled him from Pate at the date of the year 1273 [1856-7]. He went to Kau.

[48] At Siu, Shaykh Muhammad bin Shaykh Mataka, was an ally of the Sayyid; he gave him soldiers, (and) he (Shaykh Muhammad) built a fort. Then they had a quarrel with one of Sayyid Sa'id's men, because he had destroyed a boat shack (p. 29) that Shaykh Muhammad had built in front of the fort. And Shaykh Muhammad, for his part, destroyed the fort. And about this time Sultan Ahmad died in Kau, the father of Fumu Bakari, the sultan of Witu.

[49] In his place came Sultan **[XXXII] Ahmad**, who is called **Simba** ["Lion"], the sultan of Witu. And before Shaykh Muhammad bin Shaykh Mataka destroyed the fort of Siu, there arose a quarrel between him and Fumu Bakari bin Shaykh, (and) he drove him out of Pate, and he [Fumo Bakari] came away to Amu. And he [Shaykh Muhammad] demanded to rule Pate, seeking to match his power with the grandeur of the people of Pate. (But) at this time the noblemen of Pate refused; (then) he came (and) made war against the noblemen of Pate.

[50] They were obstructive and had no king following the advice of

three men of Pate, (namely) Muhammad bin Bwana Mkuu al-Nabhani and Bwana Rehema (p. 30) bin Ahmad al-Nabhani and Nasiri bin ‘Abdallah bin ‘Abd al-Salam, the one who was director of affairs *(mudabbir al-umur)* in these things. They demanded weapons and guns, fought with Shaykh Muhammad bin Shaykh Mataka (and) defeated him. They killed many of his people, and of prominent men, his two *amirs*, Bwana Dumila and Maulana wa Shii Kuulu.

[51] When Shaykh Muhammad bin Shaykh Mataka saw these matters, he came to ask for peace from Muhammad bin Bwana Mkuu the aforesaid, because it was he who was the oldest amongst them, that is amongst those three men. They negotiated (and) came to an understanding. He wished to give him, this Muhammad bin Bwana Mkuu, the reign over Pate and Siu but Muhammad bin Bwana Mkuu refused (and) said to him, "I am an old man, take (instead) Sultan Ahmad, the ruler of Witu (p. 31), the Lion (*Simba*)." They went to fetch him; Shaykh Muhammad bin Shaykh Mataka sent his men, and from Pate went Nasiri bin ‘Abdallah, to Kau, to fetch Sultan Ahmad Simba.

[52] This news reached the sultan of Zanzibar, Sayyid Majid bin Sa‘id; prior to this Sayyid Sa‘id had died. Sayyid Majid sent his *wazir* Sayyid Sulayman bin Hamad by ship, that he occupy Pate, to crush this conspiracy. When he arrived at Mandra, Pate had been taken in possession by a man of Sultan Ahmad, Abu Bakari bin Hasan, (and) with him had come Nasiri bin ‘Abdallah. When Sayyid Sulayman bin Hamad received this news, he returned to Zanzibar. And that was when Shaykh Muhammad destroyed the fort of Siu.

[53] Finally Sultan Ahmad came to Pate. He was given an oath by the people of Pate and Shaykh (p. 32) Muhammad and the *shaykh* of the WaTikuu

Mzee bin Sefu[49] and Shaykh Shakuwe and Muhammad Muti. Sultan Ahmad, for his part, formally accepted the reign over the whole of the people who were on the island of Pate.

[54] (Then) Sayyid Majid sent men of Amu to Pate with the charge to try, together with Shaykh Muhi al-Din, to capture Sultan Ahmad. Part of the soldiers settled down in Pate. And it was Shaykh Muhi al-Din who freed the soldiers of Sayyid Majid from the fort of Siu when Shaykh Muhammad attacked those who were in it. Shaykh Muhi al-Din[50] went (and) led them out in peace, for he was a man of Sayyid Majid. When he went with them to Sayyid Majid, (the latter) became very angry, (so) Shaykh Muhi al-Din took the responsibility to lead the soldiers back when he saw the wrath. (p. 33) For he was a man of much cunning and much knowledge.

[55] (So) they came, he and the people of Amu, up to Pate. And the men of Amu who had come to Pate were Shaykh Ahmad and his brother. They talked with Sultan Ahmad, (and) he took the soldiers after resisting, for reasons of friendship between him and Shaykh Ahmad and his brother.[m] Acting against the advice of his *wazir* Nasiri bin 'Abdallah, because that one advised against taking in even one soldier.

[56] When the Arabs arrived at Pate, they acted together with Mwana Jaha, the daughter of Sultan Fumu Luti Kipunga wa Bwana Fumu Madi, the wife of Sultan Fumu Bakari bin Shaykh. At this time he, Fumu Bakari, was again in Amu with the consent of Sayyid Majid, since he had been brought away from Pate. Each day they brought in soldiers and war materiel, night

---

[49] Compare *Deutsche Kolonialzeitung*, 1889, p. 219.

[50] Compare Guillan, II_2, p. 102.

after night, in secret. When finally Sultan Ahmad came to know that a conspiracy existed and that soldiers in great numbers had come to Pate, (p. 34) then they suddenly attacked him, after the ruse to seize him had been discovered. They failed, for all the people of Pate stood on the side of Sayyid Majid with the exception of his *wazir* Nasiri bin ‘Abdallah. They fought with them inside Pate, expelled Shaykh Muhammad (and) brought him to Siu.

[57] The Arabs remained at Pate. And on the sea side they posted (war) ships. When the fighting was at its strongest, Sayyid Majid himself came, (and) they blockaded the Pate Island from the sea. He laid a chain across mouth of the Siu creek Kuyyu,[51] (and) they fought for six months from the sea and at Pate. And on the side of Tikuuni Mzee wa Sefu[52] changed his mind (and) became a man of the Sayyid, through much cunning and many words. Sultan Ahmad and Shaykh Muhammad experienced distress, and the land of Siu was in turmoil. Some of them inclined toward the Sayyid because of the misery (p. 35) they had come to. And his people were Sharif Maulana bin Abi Bakari and ‘Isa bin Ahmad.

[58] When Sultan Ahmad and Shaykh Muhammad saw this, they sued for peace from the Sayyid, (and) he granted it. During peace Sultan Ahmad secretly sailed during the night, went away to the mainland (and) went to Kau.

[59] And after him Shaykh Muhammad went to the ship (to see the) Sayyid, (and) he pardoned him. And the Sayyid went away to Zanzibar. Later Shaykh Muhammad went to Zanzibar, to submit to the Sayyid. (The latter) took him prisoner (and) brought him to the Mombasa fort with many others,

---

[51] "River mouth"(?). Compare Fitzgerald, Travels, 1898, p. 386: "Koyo."

[52] See note 41.

(and) he died (there) after a long time.

[60] And to Sultan Ahmad, when Shaykh Muhammad had gone to Zanzibar, was sent Su'udi bin Hamad to catch him with a ruse, (but) he failed and the former went away to Witu. Su'udi came to Paza (and) seized 'Umar wa Bwana Mataka prisoner. The sons of Shaykh (p. 36) Muhammad were all seized at Siu (and) brought to the Mombasa fort. 'Umar was imprisoned in Amu.

[61] From this time on Sayyid Majid reigned over the whole Swahili (coast), without anyone else opposing him. And Sultan Ahmad remained in Witu under the sovereignty of Sayyid Majid until the time of Sayyid Barghash.

[62] (Then) Sayyid Barghash wished to put soldiers in Witu with a flag, (but) Sultan Ahmad did not agree. (Then) he sent troops, (but) failed (and) made[53] peace. After this Sayyid Barghash was displeased that Su'udi bin Hamad had made peace so quickly (and) not fought him more, (so) he sent a second, stronger expedition under the *luwali* Sa'idi bin Hamad.

[63] (Then) Sultan Ahmad sought the protection of the Germans. At this time returned the troops (p. 37) of Sayyid Barghash, (and) Sultan Ahmad remained under the protection of the Germans. They gave him a part of the Swahili mainland. Sultan Ahmad died under such circumstances in the year 1306 [1888-9].

[64] (Then) reigned **Fumu Bakari bin Sultan Ahmad bin Shaykh**. He got into trouble with the Germans. The German Küntzel shot the porter of the town gate. The soldiers who were there shot Küntzel and shot the Europeans who had accompanied him. They killed them without waiting for

[53] Instead of *kufanya* in the text we should probably read *kafanya*.

a command from the sultan. When the soldiers had seen that their comrade had been killed, they killed too in turn. And the people of Wandamuyyu and Mkunumbi, when they received news of this, killed the Europeans who were there.

[65] Afterwards came the Exalted Administration of the English. They sought the people who had killed the Europeans, the people of Wandamuyyu and Mkunumbi. Sultan Fumu Bakari (p. 38) did not consent to surrender them. The English attacked him on the 11th night of Rabi‘ al-awwal of the year 1308 until the morning of 12 Rabi‘ al-awwal of the year 1308. They drove him out from Witu by force of arms. Fumu Bakari went to Jongeni. Witu came under the administration of the English. Fumu Bakari remained in Jongeni until the date of 28 Jumad al-awwal of the year 1308, (when) he died.

[66] After him **Bwana Shaykh bin Sultan Ahmad** took over his brother's position. After three days he was seized by his brother Fumu ‘Umari and Bwana Avutula. They imprisoned him, Bwana Shaykh, so that he, **Fumu ‘Umari bin Sultan Ahmad**, could seize the power. Thus it was between him and the Exalted Administration of the English.

[67] And as to the last king who reigned over Witu, it was sultan Fumu Bakari. And as for Pate, (p. 39) the last [ruler] was Sultan Simba, the sultan of Witu; but as for the first sultan of Pate, that was Sulayman bin Sulayman bin Muzaffar al-Nabhani, Imam of the Arabs.

ENDNOTES

a. Heepe translated the Swahili *bibi* "grandmother," (p. 147) but according to Werner, in the northern dialects the word means "grandfather." This makes Bwana Simba, Bwana Kitini's grandfather and not his contemporary whose grandmother told the story. The other MSS use the Arabic loan *jadd* 'grandfather' which leaves no room for ambiguity.

b. Heepe translated "came to Ras," that is, Rasini (Faza). *Ras* (from the Arabic *ra's*) means "head," thus both "cape" and "start (of the year)."

c. This statement varies significantly and emphatically with the stories of Mandra's early independence in the Werner-Hollis version and other MSS. It also contraicts this MS #7.

d. This passage, especially in its Ki-Amu version, explains the Swahili etymology of the name of the town of Siu based on the verb *jua* "to know" in the passive voice and negation *si-*; *wasijulikane* (Ki-Mvita) and *wasiyulikane* (Ki-Amu) mean "it was not known to them."

e. This date recurs only in MS 177. Other versions give 660 A.H.

f. This date does not recur in any other version.

g. This date does not recur in any other version.

h. Heepe translated "even the marketfair (annual festival?) he transferred to Amu." (p. 155)

i. This passage confuses Mwana Darini's father Bwana Mkuu with her husband, also called Bwana Mkuu and the former's cousin, as indicated in #20. The confusion makes her brothers into sons of her husband, who is mentioned in the next sentence. The next passage #22 correctly indentifies her kidnapped husband as the father of her son.

j. Two verbs are used here for "blowing the horn": *kupija*, "beat," "play," and *kuvuzia* (*kuvuvia*) "to blow" proper. The first is more common in context relating to *siwa* horns. While the root *piga* primarily means "strike," in relation to music it has both the general meaning "play" and the narrower sense of beat. Apparently the ceremonial horn was both blown and beaten with a stick during processions.

k. This is the only version naming the third brother.

l. Although the Arab name *'Umar* is meant, the MS gives *Umārī*, without the *'ayn* and with Swahilisized long vowels.

m. This brother is named 'Abd al-Rahman in MSS 177, 321, 344 and 358.

HISTORY OF THE WITU ISLANDS

The following text is abstracted from the section entitled "Geschichte der Witu-Inseln" of Alfred Voeltzkow's *Reise in Ostafrika 1903-1905*.[1] The full section (pp. 48-91) is a compilation of oral tradition, previous records (including the texts published by Stigand and Gullain, cited earlier in this volume), reports by explorers and colonial servants, and Voeltzkow's own observations from his 1903-4 stay in the northern part of the East African coast. Data referring to Mombasa and Zanzibar are also to be found in the chapter "Geschichte von Zanzibar und Pemba" (pp. 305-328). In the years elapsed between Voeltzkow's expedition and the completed publication of his book, Germany lost its African possessions, but the very name the explorer uses for the archipelago, "Witu islands," is a reminder of a turbulent and politically charged period when the Pate monarchy was fast becoming an inland principality before being extinguished.

Although the bulk of Voeltzkow's study is a survey of geography and economy of the coast, he treated local history as part of his charge and offered a serviceable summary of major political developments, especially valuable for its late nineteenth century information. Dynastic and external affairs loom large in this narrative. In discussing Portuguese activities in the archipelago,

---

[1] Alfred Voeltzkow. *Reise in Ostafrika*, in den Jahren *1903-1905*. *Wissenschaftliche Ergebnisse*. vol. 2 (Stuttgart, 1923).

Voeltzkow largely relies on Strandes;[2] for the eighteenth and nineteenth centuries he offers more original observations on Pate's relations with the mainland, the Mazru'i of Mombasa and the Zanzibar Sultanate. On the European side, the German interests in the area and the Küntzell affair (1890) receive considerable attention.

The narrative is obviously synthetic but its parts cannot be easily separated in Voeltzkow's paraphrase. The passages below were somewhat arbitrarily selected from pp. 65-74 on the basis of their content and likely origin of information; in most instances they were also relatively easily identified through their use of Islamic dates. Voeltzkow indicates both starting and ending dates of reigns, but their origin is unclear. Voeltzkow was familiar with the Stigand version, but not that published by Werner. The period covered in the following selections runs from 601 A.H. to 1240 A.H. (1204-1824 A.D.). Although it may appear, both from the contents and a comment by Voeltzkow (*Reise*, p. 64), that the narrative is abstracted from Stigand, the dates of some reigns, and, on occasion, generational and family connections of rulers differ in Voeltzkow. Voeltzkow never indicated the nature of his source; he speaks of "this chronicle" without informing the reader whether in addition to Stigand and the chronology in the *Deutsche Kolonialzeitung* (1890 he consulted a manuscript or had oral informants, as may appear from hi considerable familiarity with 19th-century events. Voeltzkow's data were late used by Heepe, who frequently refers to them in the footnotes and also in hi chronological table (Appendix 7).

---

[2] Justus Strandes. *Die Portugiesenzeit von Deutsch- und Englisch-Ostafrika* (Berlin 1899). *The Portuguese Period in East Africa* (Nairobi: Kenya History Society, 1961).

The present translation into English was made by Dagmar Weiler from the German. Tom Stewart provided the translation of p. 73. The numbers in parentheses, highlighted in bold font, refer to the sequence of rulers and coordinate with the genealogical table, originally placed facing p. 65 and reproduced in the present volume in Appendix 4. A chronology cross-referenced with these numbers and provided with Christian dates for the eighteenth and nineteenth centuries, was included by Voeltzkow on p. 91. It is reproduced below in Appendix 5. The present author provided Christian equivalents to Islamic dates in the narrative and notes placed in brackets, and modernized the spelling. The footnotes are Voeltzkow's. Those of Voeltzkow's comments, interspersed with the text, which throw important light on the content were not excised but are reproduced in a smaller font. Page numbers of the 1923 edition are indicated in parentheses.

History of the Witu Islands

(p. 65) According to this chronicle, the Nabahanids had ruled in Oman until they were toppled and expelled; following this, they migrated: some to the Swahili coast, others to Jebel Riami [area west of Maskat], where their descendants are still living [*Editor's note*: Randall Pouwels indicates that the Nabahani arrived in East Africa from Hadramawt. See: Pouwels, *Horn and Crescent*, p. 222.].

In the year 601 of the Hijra [1204-5], Sulayman bin Sulayman, the expelled Sultan of Maskat, landed with his people and goods in many ships at Pate. Pate, along with many other cities, had been founded in 77 A.H. [696] with the help of Syrian settlers, by Abdul Malik bin Muriani who reigned in 65-86 A.H. [685-705] and who moved far away to form a new reign for himself [*Editor's note*: the base of Umayyad authority was Syria, centered on Damascus. 'Abd al-Malik ibn Marwan made an attempt to transform Jerusalem into a major Islamic center.]. These settlements, though, remained without support for a long time, until in 170 A.H. [786] Harun al-Rashid heard about them and sent Persians [*Editor's note*: an echo of the spurious Persian pedigree claimed by East Africa's coastal, urban elite, the "Shirazi."] there for support. Sulayman found the descendants of these immigrants in Pate, and since he liked it there, he decided to stay. He immediately sent gifts to the chief of Pate and to every member of the aristocracy. He also gave to the lesser people, so that he gained recognition from rich and poor. Later, he married the daughter of prince Is-hak and received the sovereignty.

His son (**1**)Muhammad (625-650 A.H. [1227-1253]) succeeded him as ruler, and was the first to take the name of Sultan of Pate. This was appropriate, since his father in his native country had already used this title. He was well liked by the people, because he was a son of the city, and his mother was of their blood. He ruled for 25 years and left behind three sons: (**2**)Ahmad, Sulayman, and 'Ali. Of those Ahmad succeeded him as ruler, 650-690 A.H. [1253-1291. *Editor's note*: this date does not recur in other versions.]. Incited by some Pate people, who would have liked to see a decline of the newcomers' power through mutual trouble amongst them, his brothers rose up against him, until their mother finally succeeded in effecting a reconciliation.

Ahmad left behind two daughters, Mwana Khadija and Mwana Mimi, and two sons, 'Umar and Muhammad, the latter becoming his successor. (**3**)Muhammad the First, who had the nickname Fumo Madi[1] and the surname Mkuu the Great, ruled from 690-740 A.H. [1291-1339. *Editor's note*: the date 740 A.H. does not recur in other versions.] He conducted war with Shanga near Siu and fought with [the town of] Rasini, today called Faza. The dispute lasted many years, but finally the city was conquered and destroyed completely and left deserted until, after many years, the WaTikuu were resettled there [*Editor's note*: Tikuu, or Tikuuni, is the name of the mainland to the north and east of the Lamu archipelago. The WaTikuu are also called Bajun. Werner (*Translation*, note 8) dates their resettlement at Faza about 1700.].

---

[1] *Fumo* = "chief" (abbreviation from an old Swahili word which means 'spear', *Madi* = abbreviated *Muhammadi* (Swahili for *Muhammad*), *Mari* = abbreviated *Omari* (Swahili for *Omar*).

Later, he not only conquered the whole island but also made Kiwayu and Ndao tributaries and extended his reign up to Mukadishu at the northern coast.

His son Sultan 'Umar, called (**4**)Fumo Mari (740-795), [1339-1383. *Editor's note*: the date 795 A.H. does not recur in other versions.] fought all the cities on the coast, up to Malindi and Kilwa, even up to Kerimba, with the only exception of Zanzibar, which at this time was of no importance. In addition, a dispute arose with the much older Manda on the neighboring island; Manda's sultans, in former times, had exercised a kind of sovereignty over Pate. The city was conquered without a big fight, though, and all goods and prisoners were brought to Pate, where the latter were resettled in the Weng'andu quarter. Taka on the island Manda, too, was afflicted but remained inhabited and was deserted by its inhabitants only much later, because up until 1094 A.H. [1683] there were still people living there. Finally, Kitao escaped the same fate because its inhabitants asked for peace. Nevertheless, it was probably deserted before 1094 A.H. [1683]. Sultan 'Umar installed overseers, *jumbe*, everywhere and even came to Mombasa, but its inhabitants fled. Therefore, they were called *"Mfita"* (one who flees) by the Pate people; later this developed into *"Mvita"*, which means war and sounded better to the inhabitants.

His son Muhammad bin 'Umar, called (**5**)Fumo Madi Mkuu (795-825 A.H. [1383-1422. *Editor's note*: the date 825 A.H. does not recur in other versions.]), started plantations and built ships, because at that time Arab and Indian ships used to frequent the Pate harbor, and brought the country to great prosperity. He had a nephew [*Editor's note*: the other versions speak of a son of Sultan Muhammad's. The son is not named.], called Bwana Mkuu, who was a passionate traveller, who suffered various shipwrecks, reached India and acquired many goods. On the journey home, his ship was tossed by the storm to an island where he stopped to get water and to rest. While boiling the water, he noticed with surprise that the heated sand began to melt in the fire and, after cooling off, clotted into pieces. He recognized the sand as silver ore, took his goods off the ship and loaded it [with as much sand] as it could take. During the journey, though, he was caught by a storm; as a result, he had to throw half of his load overboard. Upon his arrival home, the rest of the sand turned out to be pure silver ore that could be used to make jewelry. Right about this time, the Portuguese had come to Pate; they immediately inquired where the silver sand came from. They convinced Bwana Mkuu to show them the place; after six months of fruitless search, though, the expedition returned without having found the place.

At the time of the return, it turned out that Sultan Muhammad had died and Abu Bakr, the traveller's father, was now the ruler.

Under Sultan (**6**)Abu Bakari (Swahili for *Abu Bakr)*, 825-855 A.H. [1425-1451. *Editor's note*: the date 855 does not recur in other versions.], the Portuguese firmly established themselves at Pate and Dondo, on the opposite mainland at the entrance to the Creek of Dondori. They gained great influence in the city, (p. 66) taught the people to build wells in the rocks with the help of powder, built houses of stone, and built an underground walkway to Pongwa Rock. Today, the Pate people still firmly believe in its existence, although they have not been able to discover it again. In addition, they convinced Abu Bakari to erect a customs station at Fandikani and to levy taxes.

He was succeeded by his son (**7**)Bwana Mkuu (855-903 A.H. [1451-1497. *Editor's note*: the date 903 A.H. does not recur in other versions.]), the one who travelled much. As a result of extended trade, the country flourished under him. Large houses were built with metal lamps, silver ladders were used to climb into the beds, silver chains adorned necks, and silver nails were driven into doors. Thus Bwana Mkuu lived in peace with his subjects and with the Portuguese who had strongholds in Dondo and Mombasa, where their governor resided and where they built a fort. In 903 A.H. [1497-8] he died, leaving seven children.

Of those, he was succeeded by Muhammad, with the surname (**8**)Fumo Madi II (903-945 A.H. [1497-1538. *Editor's note*: the date 945 A.H. recurs only in the Heepe version.]). Under him, stirred by the Portuguese, trouble arose between Pate and Siyu. The latter, formerly unimportant, had gained in power. Siyu was destroyed, but as a result of Portuguese efforts the captives were released.

He was succeeded by his brother (**9**)Abu Bakr (945-995 A.H. [1538-1587. *Editor's note*: the date 995 A.H. does not recur in other versions.]), during whose reign the Portuguese conquered the whole coast and built customs stations, but when they collected taxes they met with resistance. Pate, too, resisted, so the Portuguese attacked the island. They anchored close to the small island that still bears the name *Shaka Mzungu*, "Island of the Foreigners." They conquered the harbors of Mtangawanda and Shindakasi and blockaded the city. After many fruitless attempts, though, the dispute was settled through negotiations.

His son (**10**)Bwana Mkuu ruled from 995-1010 A.H. [1587-1601. *Editor's note*: the date 1010 A.H. does not recur in other versions.]. During his reign, strangers, called WaBarawa came into the country from Barawa. They were Arabs of the Hatimii tribe who carried many goods with them and bought houses and wells, so the land flourished. He was followed by Sultan

(**11**)Ahmad II, his cousin's son (1010-1017 A.H. [1601-1608. *Editor's note*: the date 1017 A.H. does not recur in other versions.]). However, the latter resigned after seven years of no rain. He left the throne to Sultan (**12**)Muhammad (1017-1018 A.H. [1608-9]), the son of Sultan Abu Bakr. The latter was constantly fighting the Portuguese, who relieved him of his office after a year and installed (**13**)Abu Bakr (1018-1060 A.H. [1609-1650. *Editor's note*: these dates do not recur in other versions.]), the son of Bwana Mkuu, who got along very well with the Portuguese. The Portuguese, though, had many troubles with Lamu, which was finally conquered. As a result, many prisoners fell into the victors' hands; following the request of Abu Bakr these were released. Since that time Lamu and Pate have been allies.

Abu Bakr loved to travel and visit every place of his realm. However, during his absence in 1040 A.H. [1630-1. *Editor's note*: this date does not recur in other versions.] unrest broke out in Pate, and his brother's son was installed as a counter-ruler, named Sultan Muhammad. Despite Portuguese support, Abu Bakr was unable to regain Pate and thus, for the time, remained in Lamu where he married, until he was finally reinstated by the Portuguese. Previously, he had already married his daughter to his rival Muhammad's son, Bwana Mkuu, who lived peacefully with his dethroned father. At the death of the latter, some troublemakers spread the rumor that he had been poisoned by Abu Bakr. Abu Bakr, fearing that Bwana Mkuu would believe this and would try to take his life out of revenge, convinced the Portuguese to lure Bwana Mkuu with 40 noblemen on board a ship and to take him to Goa. This caused a gradual development of unrest which finally led to the Sultan's murder. The occasion presented itself as a result of the custom to blow the royal horn during high festivities. During the circumcision of her son, Abu Bakr refused his daughter, the wife of the deported Bwana Mkuu, the use of the horn. The woman had a skilled artisan make a new, ornately decorated horn out of a tusk. Shortly afterward, the people rose and killed Sultan Abu Bakr and his brother Bwana Madi [*Editor's note*: This version sheds a very different light on the intricacies of Pate relations with the Portuguese and court intrigue. The number 40 here is reminiscent of the 40 slaughtered victims of Sultan Muhammad bin Abu Bakr (Bwana Fumo Madi), whose reign is dated 1191-1224 in MS 177. According to the same MS, the Portuguese kidnapping occurred in the reign of Bwana Mkuu bin Abu Bakr (1061-1100), while the *siwa* episode came in the reign of Sultan Ahmad (1103-1111) who had previously killed Mwana Darini's brothers, Bwana Madi and Abu Bakr, their father's namesake.].

This horn, which supposedly had come from Siyu, is now in the sub-commissioner's house in Lamu and was pictured in Elliot (p. 14).[2] It is ornately carved and must have been put together from two tusks. The old horn of Pate is said to have been lost at sea. The horn of Lamu, on the other hand, which is made of metal and of ivory, is now in the possession of the descendants of the man whose duty it was to blow the horn at festive occasions. The travel report of Vasco da Gama, too, repeatedly mentions such a horn. In Mozambique, for example, where the travelers were received amicably, the ruler appeared on board of the flagship accompanied by ten people, including musicians who were blowing on tusk horns and other instruments. He wore a long, white dress that touched his ankles and a velvet vest adorned with braids. A multi-colored, satin turban interwoven with gold complemented the outfit. In his satin belt he wore a richly embellished dagger and in his hand was a silver-studded sword. Even today, this would probably be the outfit of a wealthy East African Arab (*Roteiro*, p.25). In greater detail such a horn is also mentioned during a meeting with the shaykh of Malindi: "The king was wearing a robe of damask trimmed with green silk and an expensive turban; an old, dignified Negro carried his sword with the silver scabbard.

---

[2] Elliot, Charles, *The East Africa Protectorate* (London: Edward Arnold, 1905).

The chair he was sitting on was adorned with beautiful brass work, covered with silk cushions and shaded with a red satin umbrella on a golden stick. With the king came two well-dressed courtiers and musicians. The musicians produced a concert on trumpets and two man-high elephant tusks that had their hole in the middle, which sounded as if coming from different instruments than those of these barbarians."

On his journey back, Vasco da Gama asked the natives for one of these big elephant tusks made into a horn, an instrument called *siwa* in East Africa today. His wish was willingly fulfilled (*Roteiro*, p. 103). Compare the picture of a *siwa* in Ravenstein [3] *l.c.*, p. 43, based on a photograph by John Kirk, according to whom (p. 67) the royal trumpet was peculiar to the coastal towns ruled by the descendants of Persians from Shiraz. They were made of ivory, copper and wood, and consisted of three parts; the ivory or copper was often intricately carved and bore Arabic texts. [*Editor's note*: the present *siwa* of Lamu is of brass. A photograph of the horn by C. S. Reddie is reproduced in the *Journal of African Society* edition of the Werner version (plate facing p. 289). On the Lamu horns see, in addition to J. de V. Allen's article cited above, Mamo Sassoon, *The Siwa of Lamu: Two Historic Trumpets in Brass and Ivory*, (Nairobi, 19-159).]

The heralds, by the way, used to announce the king's edicts with the beating of the horn with a stick. So the Swahili expression *kupiga pembe* ["to beat the horn"] has a double meaning since it also describes the blowing of the horn. Thus, for example, when Fumo Luti died, his successor Bwana Fumo Madi ordered a herald to blow the horn in town during that same night to announce the Sultan's death (Stigand, p. 165).

After him [(**13**) Abu Bakr], another Sultan (**14**)Abu Bakr (1060-1100 A.H. [1650-1689]), with the surname Bwana Tamu Mkuu ascended the throne. He was identical with the ruler Bwana Tamu Mkuu who in 1717 concluded the treaty with the Portuguese mentioned on p. 64. [*Editor's note*: on p. 64 Voeltzkow discusses Pate's involvement in Omani-Portuguese relations and the tradition of origin of the Nabahani dynasty.] But the chronicle only mentions the fights with the Portuguese that finally led to the taking of Mombasa, about which we will hear later. In this treaty he called himself Buanatamu Bubacar Bin Muhameth, and so was probably a son of Bwana Madi who was killed during the uprising against his brother Abu Bakr III together with him.

---

[3] Ravenstein, E.G.A., *A Journal of the First Voyage of Vasco da Gama*. London: Hakluyt Society, 1898.

(p. 71) In Pate, Bwana Tamu Mkuu who had died in 1733 was succeeded by his son (**15**)Bwana Mkuu (1100-1125 A.H. [1689-1713]). About him, the chronicle only says that he had very much loved Lamu, his mother's town, taken a wife there, erected a mosque, and had expanded Lamu into a harbor for the ships coming in with the northeast monsoon.

He was followed by (**16**)Bwana Tamu Ndogo, or the Younger (1125-1135 A.H.), the son of that Bwana Mkuu who had been taken to Goa. He is said to have fought with the people of Lamu over some Portuguese canons found there, which had been excavated on the Hedabu hills and which he claimed. Although a settlement was reached, he was soon afterwards murdered at the instigation of the Ya'rubi Imam.

Under his successor and son (**17**)Bwana Bakari (1135-1150 A.H. [1722-1737]), the country flourished and was strengthened until he expanded his power not only over Lamu and Manda, but also over Pemba and the whole coast line between the mouth of the Kilifi in 3° 40' southern latitude and the Juba River. Because he feared the influence of the Arabs residing on the island, he had a number of them killed and expelled the others. As a result of this disciplinary action he managed to maintain his independence for a while; but he had a dangerous neighbor in Mombasa and conflicts with it, mainly over Pemba often caused entanglements.

According to the chronicle, he was followed by his brother (**18**)Ahmad (1150-1177 A.H. [1737-1763]), who was followed by (**19**)Mwana Khadija (1177-1187 A.H. [1763-1773]), a sister of Bwana Tamu Ndogo, with the surname Mwana Mimi [*Editor's note*: notice the coincidence with the names above. Sultan Ahmad who died in 690 A.H. reportedly had two daughters, named Mwana Khadija *and* Mwana Mimi. These daughters are mentioned only in Stigand's version.], or rather 'Umar, a son of Bwana Tamu Mkuu. Under the title of *wazīr* he claimed the reign and he upheld Pate's independence against the Imam of Maskat. The trouble began when the inhabitants of Pemba, which at the time was ruled by Pate, dissatisfied with 'Umar's administration, offered the governor of Mombasa to come under his protection. 'Ali bin 'Uthman, who in the meantime had taken his murdered brother's position at Mombasa [*Editor's note*: i.e., 'Ali became the second Omani (Mazru'i) governor of Mombasa.], took the occasion to send an expedition to Pemba. In agreement with the inhabitants, the expedition expelled Fumo 'Umar's agent and soldiers and installed his uncle on his mother's side, Khamis bin 'Ali, as governor. A later campaign for revenge against Mombasa that took the Pate people to the gates of Mombasa, remained without result for reasons which are not clear. The fleet returned to home without any further fights (*Guillain* I, p. 549).

After the death of 'Ali bin 'Uthman of Mombasa, who was murdered in 1755, the old trouble started anew under his successor and cousin Mas'ud bin Nasir. Differences arose between Mwana Mimi and Fumo 'Umar],[4] who urged her to legitimize her reign through marriage to him. Notwithstanding, to remove him, Mwana Mimi succeeded in convincing him to start a campaign against Barawa to settle disputes over [Pate's] sovereignty over the Juba area.

---

[4] *Fumo*, High Sovereign, Master, is the title accorded by the inhabitants of Sofala to their leaders. As it appears, this title was also customary in other places, far removed from Sofala. So it also was until recently in Pate, where this title preceded the ruler's name and then was contracted with his name into one word. *Fumo Aluti* became *Fumoluti*, *Fumo Amadi* - *Fumomadi*; the separate spelling is still used now and again.

In his absence his brother's son snatched the reins of government. When 'Umar returned, the fight over the sovereignty flared up between the two rivals, who both called for the intervention of Mas'ud bin Nasir. The governor of Mombasa sent troops to Pate and finally decided in favor of Fumo Luti; however, he was not able to see him triumph over his opponent. At the end of the five-year-long struggle, they finally succeeded to lure 'Umar to Mombasa and to imprison him there. But 'Umar managed to escape the trap and to return to Pate. He might have triumphed over his opponent had he not been murdered[5]. (p. 72) Since Mwana Mimi, too, soon died, Fumo Luti was named ruler under the condition that he acknowledge the sovereignty of Mombasa. A representative of the Shaykh of Mombasa was installed at Pate.

For a short time there was peace in the country, which had suffered much after the civil war between Mwana Khadija and Sultan 'Umar. For, in the attempt to harm each other, the parties had cut down coconut palm trees, fruit trees, and destroyed the fields, so it was not possible to work in the fields for years, engage in trade or assume any other orderly work. The famine was so bad that the people ate grass and leather seats of chairs. Thus, the people were relieved when order finally returned although it lasted only a few years.

(**20**)Fumo Luti bin Shaykh (1187-1190 A.H.[1773-1776]) did not find approval with some of the aristocracy, especially the supporters of the late ruler Mwana Khadija. They reproached him for his mother's low birth, because his father had married a poor fisher-woman. They conspired against

[5] The Chronicle subsequently has 'Umar, after a lengthy war, vanquished by Mwana Khadija, flee first to Faza and then to Barawa, from where he, after a year's sojourn, reasserted his power and came back, but after a lapse of one year was murdered. In his place his brother's son, Fumo Madi, now fought against Mwana Khadija. When the latter died in 1187 A.H., he was acknowledged as ruler.

him and finally decided to murder him under the leadership of one Fundi Sulayman, who wanted to take revenge because years earlier the Sultan had forced the latter's wife into his harem.

Upon the entrance of the conspirators for the morning greeting, Sultan Fumo Luti, out of respect to the Mazru'i governor, rose from his chair carved out of ebony, his right hand resting on his sword. A sword blow by Sulayman cut off the five fingers of his right hand and also a part of the chair's back. The sword broke apart but Sulayman, with the remaining stump, struck a second blow on the sultan's right arm. Fumo Luti, a man of great strength and a courageous warrior, quickly bent over, with his left hand grasped his sword that had fallen on the floor and struck down Sulayman who had attempted to flee. Then the conspirators wanted to encircle him but he threw them back and is said to have struck down twenty of them. His brother, too, fell during this occurrence, whereupon the others escaped. As a result of a great loss of blood, though, he died three days later from his injury [*Editor's note*: Werner's version (p. 408-9) calls this ruler Bwana Mkuu bin Shaykh and provides different motivation for the conspiracy.]. The chair with the broken back still stands in the Pate palace and, during my visit there, I was given the chair as an honorary seat.

Following the advice of the dying ruler, his son Bwana Shaykh, who had also been there during the attack, left the reign to (**21**)Fumo Madi (1190-1224 A.H. [1776-1809, but later Voeltzkow gives 1774-1807.]), also called Bwana Kombo. The latter was a son of Bwana Tamu Ndogo and cousin of Bwana Shaykh, because his [Fumo Madi's] mother and that of his [Bwana Shaykh's] sisters were daughters of the fisher-woman that Fumo Luti's father had married. Fumo Madi took drastic action, killed almost all conspirators, including two of his brothers, and, in 1774, with the help of the Bajuni, the inhabitants of Faza, declared himself independent from Mombasa whose emissary lost his life during the unrest.

The sultan of Mombasa passed up the occasion to take immediate revenge for the murder of his agent but had Pate's governor on Pemba, Budi Sulayman, killed. Further war was prevented by the death of Mas'ud a few months later. But even his successor 'Abdallah bin Muhammad saw no reason for intervention.Fumo Madi was the last great ruler of the Nabahan and during his long reign (1774-1807), the country was a peace.

Nevertheless, already in 1776-7, he was peacefully persuaded by a certain Na'san bin Muhammad, an envoy and relative of the ruler of Oman, to recognize the sovereignty (p. 73) of the Imam of Maskat. Then in 1785, when Sa'id bin Muhammad prevailed over the Mazru'i, the Arabs effectively became the undisputed rulers of the entire coast from Somaliland to as far down the coast as Cape Delgado.

In 1806, Sa'id bin Sultan, the actual founder of Arab control on the East African coast, came to power in Oman. During this time, Fumo Madi, who was still in possession of the sultanate of Pate, thought it best for the Mazru'i of Mombasa to recognize his supreme sovereignty as well. In this way the calm of the island of Pate was ensured, if for only a brief time, because already in the next year (January 28, 1807) Fumo Madi died and, according to the chronicle, his adolescent son-in-law (**22**)Ahmad bin Shaykh, nephew of Fumo Luti with the amputated hand, assumed power at the expressed wish of the deceased, an act which was intended to return the throne to the old line of succession and which was supported by the governor of Mombasa. He is supposed to have been a man of great strength and courage, capable of splitting a coconut with a sword. For the execution of this performance, an old coconut with dry bast is hung on a string. One must strike it horizontally so that the one half remains hanging on the string and the other falls to the ground. Not only exceptional strength is required, but one also needs a sure eye, because the nut must be struck at exactly that point of the sword which at rest is located some two thirds of the way from the handle and one third of the way from the end point. Unfortunately, I have never had the opportunity to witness a demonstration of this type, yet Curt Toeppen told me by chance of this gallant feat, which still serves as the culminating point during the competitions. [*Editor's note*: In 1887 Toeppen became chief representative of the Witu Company, trading in ivory and making attempts at plantation farming.]

In February 1811, Captain Smee visited the city of Pate and paid a call to Sultan Ahmad, whom he portrayed as being of medium build, almost corpulent, having a pleasant outward appearance and being approximately 35 years of age.

Lamu, which did not acknowledge the new ruler, became the stage for intense battles, in which the Governor of Mombasa personally took part. Only reluctantly did Sultan Ahmad grant the assistance which was requested, because at this time the Mazru'i were very strong and he feared, not without reason, that they would hold Lamu for themselves and then, with the help of the population of the city, they would expand their rule over the entire Swahili Coast.

Joined by the people of Pate, the Mazru'i landed near Shela, advanced toward Lamu and, after failing to seize the city during their initial assault, began to lay siege to it. Their second attack seemed at first to be more encouraging. The soldiers reached the base of the wall through which an opening had already been smashed, when the inhabitants launched a strong thrust which forced the attackers to retreat. They were pursued the entire way back to their landing area in Shela, where, owing to the tide, their ships could not immediately depart and they were killed in great numbers. Those who survived set off once they could get a ship out, whereupon Ahmad bin

Muhammad returned to Mombasa, and the people of Pate went back to their home land. The bones of the soldiers killed are occasionally exposed by the movement of the blowing sand dunes on the hills of Shela and the battle is still vivid in the memory of the people as the Battle of Shela.

The short reign of Sultan Ahmad was disputed by his brother-in-law Fumo Luti Kipunga, Fumo Madi's youngest son, whose older sister he [Sultan Ahmad] had married and for whom he had acted as a father. Later, they reached a settlement and after the death of Ahmad (1229 A.H. [1814]), Fumo Luti Kipunga took over the reign and decided to take revenge on Lamu for the defeat of Shela. He conscripted soldiers from the WaTikuu on the continent, from Siu and from Ozi, and started other war preparations. To protect themselves against new attacks, the unfortunate people of Lamu turned to Maskat for protection. The clever Sayyid Sa'id used the situation for his own purpose, (p. 74) offered the requested support and sent as emissary, a governor named Khalif bin Nasir. Following his master's demand, and to better defend the town, the latter immediately started to build a fort, which is still standing. It was completed under his successor Muhammad bin Nasir, whereupon Sa'id transferred there a garrison of 100 Sudanese. According to the chronicle, Fumo Madi had already started with its construction and built it up to 1 1/2 meters above ground before his death. Then the Mazru'i, in agreement with the inhabitants of Lamu, are said to have raised the existing walls further, to at least twice the height, and also installed a contingent there. Thereafter, they were driven out by the hostile party of the enemies of Sultan of Pate (an ally of the Mazru'i),[6] who feared for the independence of their city. This event was the cause for the battle of Shela described above.

Without having fulfilled his plans, Fumo Luti Kipunga died in 1233 A.H. [1817-8]. The Mazru'i who kept a small garrison in Pate headed by Liwali Hamad, the brother of Mombasa's governor, to prevent the intervention of Sayyid Sa'id wanted as successor Fumo Luti bin Shaykh who had shown a friendly disposition towards them. But they encountered strong opposition from the population, who chose Bwana Shaykh, a son of Fumo Madi, as ruler. The latter had gone to Maskat after the installation of Sultan Ahmad to call for the Imam's intervention against him, but returned to the island about this time with some soldiers under the command of 'Abd al-'Adi. Under these circumstances, especially since the inhabitants were showing a threatening demeanor, the pretender Fumo Luti and the Liwali of Mombasa considered it wise to leave the city. First they went to Siu, where at that time Bwana Mataka was Shaykh and was almost regarded as sultan, and following his advice they went to Mombasa. At Siu, which had suffered under the oppression by the mighty Pate for a long time, the inhabitants had, since distant past turned to the Somali, who lived on the opposite coast, for help and offered them a voice, seat, and reign in the city in return for their protection. In consequence, a peculiar double administration was erected. It consisted of a chief (a Famau), a descendant of the first Asian colonists and of a Somali shaykh. This system lasted from the 17th century until 1812 when the Famau shaykh Mataka consolidated the whole power in his hands.

After a short period of reign, there arose unrest incited by Bwana Wazir bin Bwana Tamu, a nephew of Bwana Shaykh. The young ruler was able to withstand pressure only by approaching Mombasa whose superiority he was

[6] Rivalry between the Omani Arabs of Zanzibar and the Mazru'i is explained in part by affiliation with different clans who were antagonists in Oman.

forced to acknowledge. In 1236 A.H. [1820-1] he was dethroned; in agreement with Sayyid Sa'id, whose help he had requested, Bwana Wazir was installed as sultan. But after only three years, the people expelled him and recalled Bwana Shaykh to the throne. As a result, Wazir once more turned towards Sayyid Sa'id, who installed him again as sultan in 1240 A.H. [1824-5].

Bwana Shaykh died soon thereafter; at this point, Fumo Luti bin Shaykh, the former pretender, considered it the right moment to raise his old claims on Pate. [*Editor's note*: no Islamic dates occur hereafter. While the events described by Voeltzkow may be cross-referenced to the chronicle, too much European influence is evident in the text to consider it a traditional narrative.]

Voeltzkow's comment (p. 91): The periods of government listed in the chronology of the ruler of Witu, which is based on the Pate chronicle, naturally are only of approximate value. Although rather dependable for recent periods, the old dates are regularly dated too early. Thus, the appearance of the Portuguese on Pate under Sultan Abu Bakr has been dated at least 60 years too early. For a better understanding of the succession of rulers, though, I have kept the information listed in the chronology (based on the Islamic chronology), not only in the chronology but also in the text. [*Editor's note*: see the Chronology in Appendix 5.]

MS 177

This is the only original MS among the copies of the *Pate Chronicle* in the Library of the University of Dar es Salaam. The paper is old, of European manufacture. The sheets appear to have been formerly sewn together at the top in the middle. The text is written on one side only. Attached to the pink-yellow folios is a smaller, newer sheet with English notation in black ink, in an old-fashioned hand: "History of Pate. For another MS of this history see volume 10." According to the late Neville Chittick, a translation of MS 177 was made by G. S. P. Freeman-Grenville and circulated in typescript. This was never published and this author has not seen it.

The text is in Ki-Amu. In general outline, it follows the narrative of the Hollis-Werner MS. There are two postscripts, each naming Muhammad bin Fumo 'Umar al-Nabahani as the source; only the first postscript cites his nickname "Bwana Kitini." In turn, Bwana Kitini's source is said to be his grandfather Muhammad bin Bwana Mkuu al-Nabahani. The first postscript cites the latter's nickname "Bwana Simba," the second names him "the senior elder of Pate," *mukūp(w)a wa-wazee wa-Pate.* The MS names as its copyist Salih bin Salim bin Ahmad bin 'Abd Allah bin Muhammad bin 'Abd Allah Ba Sharahil. There is no date but the absence of other names as well as references to Salih bin Salim in other MSS make this the earliest of the four inedited versions being offered here. Moreover, MS 321 dates Salih bin Salim's copy 1318/1900, which makes MS 177 or its prototype the earliest extant version, if not the earliest copy. This would correspond to MS "K1" in A. M. J. Prins'

Stemma (see *General Introduction*), from which MS "K2" was produced in 1903 (the Hollis-Werner MS).

Some of the readings offered by MS 177 are an improvement over the Hollis MS (as on ff. 5, 11, 15). Alice Werner mentions that she consulted a MS which, though faulty, on occasion provided better readings than the Hollis MS which she published. There is great likelihood that MS 177 is the one, as both it and the unnamed MS Werner saw mention "forty men of Kau" seized by Bwana Fumo Madi about 1191/1777. (The detail does not occur elsewhere). Especially important seem passages on ff. 16 and 17 concerning the government of Pate during the transition period from 1273/1856 to the accession of sultan Ahmad Simba. This version also contains a unique wording of the passage on f. 19 regarding negotiations between Shaykh Muhammad Mataka and Sayyid Majid (cf. MS 321, p. 24). F. 21 uniquely names the village of Ndapi as a target of the British punitive expedition of 1891 (other names, in addition to those in the Hollis MS above, are Kilimani and Nyando-za-Pwani). A relatively rare use of ethnonyms *Wa-Pate* and *Wa-Mombasa* (instead of the more usual *watu wa-Pate, watu wa-Mombasa*) occurs in the description of the Battle of Shela on f. 11. Also in a unique reading, MS 177 reports the nickname of Sultan Ahmad, the father of Fumo Bakari, to be Bwana Madushi (f. 16).

On the other hand, the passage on f. 10 regarding a war between Lamu and Pate seems corrupt; the mention of Siu in the Hollis MS and MS 321 makes better sense. On f. 18 one presumably should read "Pate" for "Lamu" in the description of Shaykh Muhi al-Din's negotiations (as in MS 321). Names of rulers occasionally differ from those in Hollis MS and in the following MS 321 (ff. 7, 11, 19); some of the differences may be due to scribal error. In fact, the copyist occasionally had to insert skipped passages on the right margin. The narrator exhibits a somewhat irregular familiarity with Arabic grammar, to the extent of using the form *Abī* in the name *Abū Bakr*, but sometimes incorrectly placing it also at the start of the name (as the first *kunyā*), where the nominative *Abū* is appropriate rather than the genitive of the status constructus following *bin*. The founding Nabahani is assigned the title *Imām al-'Arab* (f. 21; *cf.* the incorrect *Imām al-'Arabī* in MS 321). This is not historically correct since the Nabahani rulers in Arabia were not considered *imāms*.

As a point of Swahili-Arabic orthography, MS 177 was *tā'* rather than dotted *kāf* for *ch*. It is not clear whether the scribe on occasion wrote *sīn* like *hā'* or the switch reflects dialect variation. Dots are sometimes omitted in Arabic loanwords: *sīn* appears for *shīn* and *ḥā'* for *khā'*. One-dot *fā'* is used for *v*. Three-dot *pā'* sometimes replaces *bā* for *b*. Occasional ligatures in Arabic names and titles were transcribed in full. No changes were made in the Arabic-script text reproduced in typed form at the end of the volume. The transcript follows MS line for line and page for page. Where occasionally a computer-generated line could not be accommodated in length, the sign < < marks its end. Pages are separated with the double slash //. The Arabic ligature of *nūn* and *dāl*, scripted as a curved *rā'* is noted with an asterisk *. The asterisk is also used for *sic* following obvious mistakes in Arabic as misspellings. Because of the priority of this version and to avoid duplicate references in sections dealing with MSS 321, 344 and 358, the translator's notes have been concentrated in this part. The reader is referred to earlier sections for more complete substantive comments on the text. The Swahili transcript contains corrections and editorial conjectures in brackets. The translation has conjectured words in brackets; those added to ease the flow of the narrative are placed in parentheses. Christian dates are given in the footnotes.

AKHBĀR PATEH

(f. 1) Mutu wa-k(w)ānda kuya Pate katika Nabahāni Sulaymān bin Sulaymān bin Muẓaffar al-Nabahanī na-(n)duze watu wawili, ‘Alī bin Sula[y]mān na-‘Uthmān bin Sulaymān. Na-hūyu Sula[y]mān bin Sulaymān al-madhkūr (n)diye aliyo‿kuwa sulṭāni ‘Arabūni, alipo‿tawali al-Ya‘rubī akaya Pate, sanati 600 sitamia hijriyah akaya **P**ate. Kataka ‘arūsī k(w)a-mufalume wa-**P**ate katika ha-Wa-al-Bata‿wīn, nā-ye ni-ma‘arūfu Sulṭān Sulaymān, mufalume wa-Pate kamuuza binti kiki. Na-dastūri ya-jamī‘i ya-Wa˘Sawāḥili ḥatā sāsa mutu kikuoleya binti yake, siku ilī ya-saba‘a ‘arūsī he(n)da kum(w)a(n)galia mukewe baba wa-muke wāke humupa kitu, kula mutu k(w)a-ḳadiri yake. Sulaymān bin Sulaymāni alipo‿ke(n)da kum(w)a(n)galia ba‘ada [si]ku saba‘a ulī mufalume wa-**P**ate kawapea wātu, hiyo Sulaymān bin Sulaymān, (n)diye mufalume mahala pa(n)gu akamupa ufalume wāke. Tan (n)gu ha**p**o katawali Sulaymān bin Sulaymān.

K(w)alina na-muji katika iyo jazīrah ya-Pate hit(w)a K[ita]ka katika maṭila‘a ya-**P**ate, na-Sīu hatasa‿kuwa mji. Waliko na-muji mu(n)gine katika iyo jazīrah ya-**P**ate hit(w)a Shā(n)ga. Nā-yo miji hiyo yalikuwa katika ṭā‘a ya-mufalume wa-**P**ate. Na-Fāzah waliko muji we(n)yewe wa **P**āzah al-Mafāziyūna. Ukaketi ufalume hunu na-miji hi[z]i, **P**ate na-Shā(n)ga na-Kitaka, katika ṭā‘a ya-mufalume wa-**P**ate. Na-Mā(nd)ra alīko mufalume wāke (m)bāli, nā-ye alina (n)guvu sana.

Na-hūyu (f. 2) Sulṭān Sulaymān akapata zijana wawili, Muḥammad wa Aḥmad. Akafa Sulṭāni Sulaymāni sanati 625. Na-Muḥammad ‘umuri wāke (n)yaka ‘ishirīn, Aḥmad ‘umri wāke (n)yaka [k]hamsata ‘ashara.

Katawali Muḥammad bin Sulaymān ba‘ada ya-babāke. Wātu wa-Shā(n)ga wakakhalifu kapijāna nao kawa‿shi(n)da na-muji kau‿vu(n)da kao(n)dowa, aṣili ba‘aḍa ya-watu wakaja Pate. Na-ba‘aḍi ya-watu ḳabila yao Kina(n)dā(n)gu wakaki(m)bia wasijuwekāne wamezi‿**po**‿ke(n)da, ḥattā siku zika**p**ita ikaja khabari k(w)a-Sulṭān Muḥammad bin Sulaymān na-wātu wi(n)dā’o kue(n)da wakam(w)ab(m)bia, "Walē wa [S]īu tumewaona katika m(w)itu." Kapeka watu kuwa‿(n)galia wakawadirika, wamefā(n)ya zijū**mp**a ndāni ya-m(w)itu, wakawa‿tukua wakaja nao **P**ate. Sulṭān Muḥammad kawa‿sāmeḥe kawaru‿disha mahala **p**ao. (N)diyo aṣili ya-muji wa-Sīu.

Na-WaSawaḥili wa(n)gine wakaketi wote wakaja na-Wa‿Famāu waka‿keti wote wakawa (n)dio wakū**p**(w)a wa-Sīu katika ṭā‘a ya-mufalume wa-**P**ate. Akafa Sulṭān Muḥammad bin Sulaymān.

Katawali (n)duye Aḥmad bin Sulaymān aka‘amirisha sana nti ya-**P**ate katia na-mashā**mp**a na-kuwaka maju(m)**p**a na-nti hizi zote katika ṭā‘a asipiji mahala, akafa sanati 670.

Katawali kijana wa-(n)duye jina lake Aḥmad bin Muḥammad bin Sulaymān. Kaketi siyāra ya-‘ami-yake katika ‘imāra ya-muji wa-Pate k(w)a-muju(m)ba na-mashān**p**ah. Na-ye kapata zijana wa(n)gi.

Akat(w)ā’a ufalume katika (f. 3) zijana zāke Muḥammad bin Aḥmad bin Muḥammad bin Sulaymān. Akaketi na-watu sana. Watu wa-Fāzah wakakhalifu, kawapija kawatia katika ṭā‘a yake ba‘ada ya-zita zi(n)gi sana ḥattā ali**po**‿washi(n)da. Kafutaḥi na-Mānda kaitamalaki, ama Mā(n)drā aliitamalaki k(w)a-zita na-ḥīla (n)yi(n)gi sana k(w)āni [a]lina (n)guvu sāna sulṭāni wa-Mā(n)ra ya-watu na-māli ma(n)gi, kaivūnda kabisa na-watu wa(n)gine kawāeta **P**ate.

Na-ba'aḍi wakaki(m)bia wake(n)da kula mahala, wa(n)gine wakaja Shēla waka(n)gia katika ḥimāya ya-watu wa-Lāmūh, mufalume kawa‿taka k(w)a-watu wa-Lāmūh, watu wa-Lāmūh wakaiza kuwa‿toa. Na-wa(n)gine wake(n)da Malindī na-ba'aḍi ya-buludāni. Mufalume wa-Pate kawa'a(n)dama sana hawa waliyo‿kuja Shēla, watu wa-Lāmūh wakaiza kuwa‿toa ḳaṭa'an. Maneno haisa mufalume akafa sanati 732. Kamuwata kijāna umōja hit(w)a 'Umari.

Katawali usulṭāni 'Umar ba'ada ya-babāke, karāje'i maneno ya-babāke k(w)a-watu wa-Lāmūh kutaka wātu wa-Māndah, wakaiza wātu wa-Lamūh kuwa‿toa. Kawa‿pija zita wakataka amāni wātu wa-Lāmūh, wakawa katika ṭā'a yake.

Na-Sulṭān 'Umar bin Muḥammad bin Aḥmad bin Muḥammad bin Sulaymān akapata (n)guvu sana kapija na-miji ya-Sawāḥīli, Uzī Malindī Kiwāyū Kitāo Miya nā-'Imīdhi na-Watāmu ḥatā akasikilia Kirīm**p**ā. Miji yote katamalaki ta(n)gu **P**ate ḥatā Kirīm**p**ā, kula muji kaweka wātu wāke weye kuḥukumu. (N)diyo aṣili ya-hawa maju(m)be waliyoko (f. 4) mirīma yote. Ma'ana ni-wa˘tūm(w)a wa-yūm**p**e na-hiyo yūm**p**e ni-(n)yūm**p**a ya-ufalume wa-**P**ate.

Na-jānibu ya-maṭla'i katamalaki ḥatā Warshēkh k(w)a-zita zi(n)gi, alika(n)da kupija zita ta(n)gu Kiwayū na-Ṭūla na-Ṭuwāla na-Shu(n)g(w)āya na-banādiri zote, Barāwah Marika Muḳudishu. Kaweka al-wālī jamī'i aḥkām za banādiri zote zikawa Muḳudisho.

Ka'īshi na-nti zote hizi katika ḥukumu yake na-ṭā'a yake illā U(n)gūja hakutawali waḳati hunu na-U(n)guja haikuwa nti kū**p**(w)a. Na-mfalume huyu Sulṭāni 'Umar alikipe(n)da zita na-kupe(n)da ra'iya, na-ra'iya wakimupe(n)da sana, ikat(w)ā'a (n)guvu sana **P**ate. Akafa sanati 749. Kawata zijana wawili Muḥammad na-Aḥmad.

Akatwali Muḥammad bin ʻUmar bin Muḥammad bin Aḥmad bin Muḥammad bin Sulaymān. Walā hapakuwa na-zita, akashika ufalume wa babāke k(w)a-amāni. Nā-ye alikipe(n)da māli sana, akisafirisha na-zo(m)bo kipeka Hind kufā(n)ya biʻashara nā-ye alino bakhati sana ya-māli. Na-mara mōja alisafiri kijāna chake kapata maʻadini ya-feḍa kaya nayo **P**ate kafā(n)ya watu kuyofā(n)ya kazi kapata māli ma(n)gi sana wakafā(n)ya zitara za fīḍa na-(n)gāzi za fīḍa na-zo(m)**p**o zi(n)gi za kutumie feḍa. Nā-ye ka**p**ata zijana wā(n)ne, B(w)ānah Mkuu na-Aḥmad na-Abū Bakr na-ʻUmar. Nā-ye mufalume akafa sanati 797.

Katawali (n)duye Aḥmad bin ʻUmar bin Muḥammad bin Aḥmad bin Muḥammad bin Sulaymān. Kaketi na-watu k(w)a-amāni na-sayra (n)jema sana, akafa sanati 840 kusitaḥaraki ya(m)bo.

Katawali muluku (f. 5) Abū Bakr bin Muḥammad bin ʻUmar bin Muḥammad bin Aḥmad bin Muḥammad bin Sulaymān. Kaketi k(w)a-siyāra (n)jema na-miji yote katika ṭāʻa yake, akafa sanati 875. Nā-ye kakhalifu zijana wawili Muḥammad na-Aḥmad.

Katawali Muḥammad bin Abū Bakr bin Muḥammad al-madhkūr. Waḳati wāke wakaya WaZu(n)gu Portugīsi katika miji ya-Sawāḥili yote, wakaketi Mombāsah wakafā(n)ya ngōme, na-janibu ya-**P**ate wakaje(n)ga Indōndo. Na-wātu wa-bara wakawa‿fuāta wak[a]wa**p**a māli wakawa katika ṭāʻa yao. Wakamuʻariḍi mufalume wa-**P**ate katika nti ya-**P**ate wakamupija mufalume zita k(w)a-jānibu ya-Shi(n)dakāsi, wakawaka na-nti ya-p(w)ani k(w)a-maʻana ya-chochoto, ilā al-āna mawāshi ya(m)**p**o, ḳaṣidi ya-kupija (n)yūm**p**a za muji wa-**P**ate wasiweze. Kisa wakapatāna k(w)ā-'amāni wakafā(n)ya mikātaba ya-shurṭi zāo.

Wakaketi **P**ate WaZu(n)gu wakafā(n)ya furuḍa k(w)a-jina la-WaZu(n)gu walichamkuwa "fandika." Wakafā(n)ya na-ma(m)**p**o ma(n)gi katika kisiwa cha-Pate. Akafa mufalume sanati 900. Kakhālifu zijana wawili, B(w)ānah Mkuu na-'Abu Bakari.

Katawali Abū Bakr bin Muḥammad bin Abū Bakr bin Muḥammad bin 'Umar bin Muḥammad bin Aḥmad bin Muḥammad bin Sulaymān. Kaketi na-WaZu(n)gu k(w)a-amāni kama ḳa'ida ya-babāke, akafa sanati 940 kusitaḥaraki ya(m)**p**o nā-ye kakhalifu zijāna wawīli Aḥmad wa Muḥammad.

Katawali (n)duye B(w)ānah Mkuu bin Muḥammad al-madhkūr. Wakawa na-khitilāfu yeye na-WaZu(n)gu lākini pasiwe n-zita, ni-fitina siku (n)yi(n)gi walā hawa‿ku'ariḍiyana. Akafa sanati 973. Kakhālifu kijāna umōya hit(w)a Abū Bakr.

Katawali Muḥammad bin Abu Bakr bin Muḥammad bin Abū Bakr bin Muḥammad bin 'Umar bin Muḥammad bin Aḥmad bin Muḥammad bin Sulaymān. (f. 6) Akaṣiliḥiyana na-WaZu(n)gu wakat(w)ā'a ba'aḍi ya-miji. Akafa sanati 1002. Kawata kijāna jina lake Abū Bakr asitawali.

Katawali Abū Bakr bin B(w)ānah Mkuu bin Muḥammad bin Abū Bakr bin Muḥammad bin 'Umar bin Muḥammad bin Aḥmad bin Muḥammad bin Sulaymān. Kaketi na-WaZu(n)gu kama siyāra ya-waliyo‿ta(n)gulia wazee wāke, lākini **P**ate i**p**u(n)guzia (n)guvu. Akafa sanati 1041. Kawata zijana wawili, Abū Bakr na-B(w)āna Mkuu.

Katawali Abū Bakr bin Muḥammad bin Abū Bakr bin Muḥammad bin Abū Bakr bin Muḥammad bin 'Umar bin Muḥammad bin Aḥmad bin Muḥammad bin Sulaymān. Ikawa ikhitilāfu na-WaZu(n)gu **P**orutugīs, kapijāna nao kawavu(n)da WaZu(n)gu ba'ada ya-zita zi(n)gi sana. Ba'adāye zikaja tena zita za-WaZu(n)gu, wakapija muji wa-**P**ate k(w)a-mizi(n)ga wakaziweya na-(n)dia baḥarini kusipiti chō(m)**p**o. Wātu wakaona mashaka sana wakafā(n)ya amāni. Akafa mufalume sanati 1061. Kawata zijana wawili B(w)ānah Mkuu na-Aḥmad.

Katawali B(w)ānah Mkuu bin Abū Bakr bin [B](w)ānah Mkuu bin Muḥammad bin Abū Bakr bin Muḥammad bin ‘Umar bin Muḥammad bin Aḥmad bin Muḥammad bin Sulaymān. Akapata‿na na-WaZu(n)gu sana nā-ye ali**p**e(n)da sana kuketi Lāmūh ḥatā mūsimu kuwaeta Lāmūh, kafā(n)ya arūsi k(w)a-watu wa-Lāmūh.

Na-katika waḳati hunu WaFamāu watu wa-Sīu walitoka katika ṭā‘a yake, akawa‿pija kavūndā na-muji wa-Sīu kauvu(n)da ba‘aḍi kashika na-wātu wa(n)gine katika watu wa-Sīu kawaeta Pate. Mukūb(w)a wa-Sīu ka‿ki(m)bia ake(n)da Ndōndo k(w)a-**P**ortugāli katāka (f. 7) ḥimāyah. Mukū**p**(w)a wa-**P**orutugāli akaja katika wātu wa- Sīu k(w)a-mufalume kawasāmeḥe aka**p**owa kawarejeza mahali **p**[ao] Sīu katika amāni.

Ba‘adāye **P**ortugāli kafā(n)ya ḥila, akaja **P**ate k(w)a-marikabu akamutaka mufalume ke(n)da marikabuni, asi[n]e(n)da kamupeka ibn ‘ami-yake B(w)ānah Mkuu, yeye na-wātu wa-**P**ate. WaZu(n)gu wakawa‿tukua katika marikabu kawapeka k(w)ā-’UZu(n)guni asiridi ḥatā mutu umōja.

Ba‘ada ya-ha**p**o mufalume kawapija WaZu(n)gu k(w)a-jānibu zote k(w)a-barāni zisiwāni kawa‿toa jānibu za huku, wakakimbilia Mombāsah. Ba‘ada ya-hapo akafa mufalume sanati 1100. Kawata zijana wawili Bū Bakr na-B(w)ānah Madi na-binti umōja hit(w)a M(w)āna Darini.

Katawali B(w)ānah Abū Bakr bin B(w)ānah Mkuu bin Abū Bakr bin Mkuu bin Muḥammad bin Abī Bakr bin Muḥammad bin ‘Umar bin Muḥammad bin Aḥmad bin Sulayman. Aka**p**ijuwa ghafula na-Aḥmad (n)duye B(w)ānah Mkuu aliyo‿tukuliwa na-WaZu(n)gu, nā-ye alimpija upa(n)ga. Akafa sanati 1103.

Katawali yeye Aḥmad bin Abū Bakr bin Muḥammad bin Abū Bakr bin ‘Umar bin Muḥammad bin Aḥmad bin Muḥammad bin Sulaymān. Na-kisa kutawali akamu’ua na-B(w)āna Madi (n)duye. Mufalume kawaa(n)dāma Porutugāli kawa‿toa katika nti zāke zote.

Na-waḳati hunu M(w)ana Darini binti B(w)ānah Mkuu bin Abū Bakr, muke wa B(w)ānah Mukuu bin Abī Bakr aliyo‿ke(n)da Goa katika zamani za Sulṭāni Aḥmad, akisa ku’uwaliwa (n)duze wawili Bū Bakr na-B(w)āna Madī, na-mūme wāke ke(n)da Goa, kapata ḥuzu‿ni sana. Hatā zikapita siku (n)yi(n)gi kataka kumutahiri kijāna chake B(w)āna Tāmu Mutoto aliyo amukuliwa Sulṭān Abū Bakr Imām al-Hudā, kijāna wa-B(w)ānah Mukuū aliyo ke(n)da Goa.

Mufalume alī**po**‿**pa**ta khabari ya-ḥāpa M(w)ana Darini (f. 8) mi‘azimu kufā(n)ya ‘arūsi kumutahiri kijāna chake, nā-ye mufalume ka‘azimu ‘arūsī kuwatahiri zijana zake ma‘ana kumukhini M(w)āna Darini sīwa .

Akisa kuyuwa khabari M(w)āna Darini kam(w)eta M(w)e(n)yi Bayāyi bin Mkuu Jamāl al-Layl alikuwa hudari sana kazi ya-ujume, kataka amufa(n)yizi siwa ishi(n)de siwa ya-Pate. Kariḍika ijara riyāli mia ‘ishrīn, akamu**pa** **pe**(m)**pe** za-(n)dovu kati’uwa moja. Akafā(n)ya siwa k(w)a-siri ḥatā siku yali**po**‿kisa kaiẓihirisha ghafula kapeka katika maju(m)ba ya-jama‘a zāke, kula mutu kitūza ḥatā fūndī kasema "Mimi sitaki ujira nataka tuzo." Ka**po**wa, kapata māli ma(n)gi k(w)a-tūzo kafā(n)ya ‘arūsī ya-kijāna chake.

Ḥatā zamani ya-B(w)āna Tāmu Mukuu wakaja wātu wa-Lāmūh kazima siwa ya-Pate ya-aṣili, kawa**pa**, cho(m)**po** kikafa māi baḥarini, siwa ikafutu. B(w)āna Tāmu kaitaka sīwa ya-M(w)ana Darini, kam(w)a(m)bia "Tupe tutumiye katika mūi." M(w)āna Darini kam(w)a(m)bia "Siwa hini za kula ḳabāili aliyo‿tuza natumiye."

Kawata na-mutūm(w)a ḥuri ayowā'u kuvuzia siwa, akasema "Huyu (n)diye m(w)e(n)yi kupija siwa hini, yeye na-nasili yake. Na-'ada yake niriyāli tano na-(n)guo yakutukulia siwa na-kupowa samuli ya-kūn(w)a m(w)e(n)yi kuvuzia na-tūzo kula mutu k(w)a-ḳadiri yake aweză'o." Wakīt(w)a nasila yao "muyu(m)**p**e wa siwa," ḥatā yeo wāko watuwe ikawa. Ta(n)gu (f. 9) waḳati hunu hutumiwa na-ḳabāili za-**P**ate na-watu wa-mii mi(n)gine he(n)da kazima k(w)a-sharuṭi hizo kupowa muyu(m)**p**e wa-siwa ilā al-āna.

Zikazidi fitina (n)dāni ya-muji na-katika ufalume wake (n)yaka saba'a mikavu hapana mivua, akai'uzulu sanati 1111.

Katawali Sulṭān Abī Bakr B(w)ānah Tāmu Mkuu wa-B(w)āna Mutiti bin Aḥmad bin Abī Bakr bin 'Umar bin Aḥmad bin 'Umar bin Muḥammad bin Aḥmad bin Muḥammad bin Sulaymān. Akapatana sana na-mufalume wa-Maskati al-Imām Sayf bin Nabahān al-Ya'rubī. Na-hūyu mufalume wa-**P**ate ake(n)da 'Arabūni wakawa‿(n)gana mufalume wa-'Arabūni na-mufalume wa-**P**ate kuwa‿toa **P**orutugāli Mombāsah ali**po**‿rudi 'Arabūni. Mufalume wa **P**ate kapeka zita Mombāsah kawapija **P**orutugāli siku ya-jūma ya-pili, wakafa Porutugāli wātu wa(n)gi sana, katamalaki (n)gōme ya-Mombāsah.

Kamu'arifu al-Imām Sayf bin Nabahān al-Ya'rubī, aka'ēta al-wālī katika Mazārī', wātu watatu Muḥammad bin 'Uthmān na-'Alī bin 'Uthmān, watatu nisimuyahao jina nāo, walikuwa (n)dugu mōya. Wakaja na-'askari ṭarafu al-Imām Sayf bin Nabahān al-Ya'rubī. (N)diyo aṣili ya-Mazārī' kuja Mombāsah.

Na-mfalume wa-**P**ate aliketi na-ra'iya sana, katimiza (n)yaka arba'īn katika ufalume. Akafa sanati 1152. Kawata zijana wa(n)gi, ba'ada yake wasitawali zijana zake.

Katawali Aḥmad Abū Bakr bin Muḥammad bin Abī Bakr bin 'Umar bin Aḥmad bin 'Umar bin Muḥammad bin Aḥmad bin Sulaymān. Akaketi sana na-watu, nā-ye aki**pe**(n)da sana (n)go(m)be kaweka (n)go(m)**pe** wa(n)gi. Akafa sanati 1160. Kawata kijana kam(w)ita B(w)āna Gō(n)go asitawali.

Akatawali B(w)āna Tāmu Mutoto (f. 10) amkuliwā'o Sulṭān Abū Bakr Imām al-Hudā, kijāna wa-B(w)ānah Mukuu aliyo‿tukuliwa na-**P**ortugāli. Akaeta zita Imāmi al-'Arab Sayf bin Nabahān al-Ya'rubī kupija Pate wasiweze, wakafa Wa'Arabu wa(n)gi wakafā(n)ya amāni.

Ba'ada ya-ha**po** watu wa-Lāmūh wakakhālifu, kawapija zita mufalume wa-Pate asiweze wātu wa-Lāmūh. Na-wātu wa-Lāmūh wakafu(n)ga zita kupija Pate wakaya na-jaishi jānibu ya-Kitaka, wakapijāna na-watu wa-**P**ate zita zikū**p**(w)a sana, wakavu(n)dika k(w)a-watu wa-Lāmūh wakarejea Lāmūh. Mufalume wa-**P**ate kafā(n)ya zita k(w)a-baḥari kaya kuwapija watu wa-Lāmūh kawa‿tamalaki. Ba'ada ya-ha**po** wakawa ḥāli mōja watu wa-**P**ate na-wātu wa-Lā[mūh. I]mām al-Ya'rubī wakafā(n)ya shauri [mōja]. Wakamu'ua mufalume sanati 1177.

Katawali (n)duye m(w)anamuke Sulṭān M(w)ānah Khadījah binti B(w)ānah Mkuu bin Abī Bakr bin Muḥammad bin Abī Bakr bin Muḥammad bin Abī Bakr bin Muḥammad bin 'Umar bin Muḥammad bin Aḥmad bin Muḥammad bin Sula[y]māni. Akapata fitina (n)yi(n)gi katika nti ya-Pate, ikawa katika nti ya-Pate wafalume wawili, M(w)ānah Khadījah al-madhkūrah [na-]Sulṭān 'Umar. Wakapijāna katika muji wa-Pate, kaki(m)bia Sulṭān 'Umar ake(n)da Barāwah karejea **P**ate k(w)a-(n)guvu kū**p**(w)a sana. Wakapijāna na-wātu wa-M(w)ana Khadījah zita zikū**p**(w)a sana, kila mtu kaketi mahala **p**ake.

Ba'ada ya-hāyo M(w)ana Khadījah akafa sanati 1187 k(w)a-maraḍi. Katawali B(w)ānah Mkuu wa-Shee wa-B(w)ānah Tāmu Mukuu. Ra'iya wakamufa(n)yiza udhia sana, asitapati rāḥa ḥatā sanati 1191 wakamu(n)gilia wātu wa-mūi wakamu'u‿a k(w)a-tārīkhi hiyo.

Katawali B(w)āna Fūmo Madi ina lake Sulṭān Muḥammad bin Abī Bakr (f. 11) bin Muḥammad bin Abī Bakr bin Muḥammad bin Abī Bakr bin Muḥammad bin ʻUmar bin Muḥammad bin Aḥmad bin Muḥammad bin Sulaymān. Kisa kutawali raʻiya wakataka kufā(n)ya fitina, kawapija k(w)a-zita kawashi(n)da akashika wātu arbaʻīna wa-kāu. Na-katika arbaʻīna hao wawili ni-(n)duze yeye mufalume khaṣa, kawati(n)da kama (m)būzi juu ya-sakafu damu. Ikishuka katika maku**p**[(w)a], ikawa amāni, asitoki mutu tena kutaka kufā(n)ya fitina. Katawali k(w)a-amāni na-raḥa, na-raʻiya wakaona rāḥa sana ḥatā sanati 1224 akafa. Baʻada yake hakutawali tena mufalume k(w)a-rāḥa kama yeye. Akakhalifu zijana wā(n)gi.

Katawali Sulṭān Aḥmad bin Shaykh bin Fūmo Lūṭi bin B(w)ānah Tāmu Mukuu. Ikazidi fitina katika muji wa-Lāmūh, akaya kawapija zita sanati 1228 yeye na-wātu wa-Mombāsah Muzārīʻ. Wakaeta na-wātu wakashuka Shēla jaishi (n)yi(n)gi sana ya-watu wa-**P**ate na-wātu wa-Mombāsah. Watu wa-Lāmūh wakatoka wakaja Shēla wakapijāna nao zita zikū**p**(w)a sana, zita za-wātu wa-Lāmūh zikawa na-(n)guvu sana, jaishi ya-Mombāsah na-**P**ate zali**po**‿fu(n)dika zita wak[ā]ja majahazini yao ma(n)gine yamejahabu, wakasimāma ha**p**o wakapijāna zita zikūb(w)a sana. Wakafa watu wa(n)gi wa-Mombāsah na-wa **P**ate hapana ʻidadi, katika watu wa-**P**ate waliyo maʻarūfu isukua watūm(w)a na-watu ḍaʻīfu wāḥidi wa-thamānīn fulān bin fulān we(n)ye wake yake(n)da maʻida hayo, na-watu wa-Mombāsah (m)bāli.

Baʻada ya-ha**p**o wātu wa-Lāmūh wake(n)da ʻArabūni wakamutoka Sayyid Saʻīd bin Sulṭān, (f. 12) wakamupa nti sanati 1228. (N)dipo Sayyid Saʻīd bin Sulṭān bin al-Imām ali**po**‿tawali Lāmūh na-ufalume wa-**P**ate ukasilia katika jazīrah ya-Pate.

Katoka na-mutu wa-pīli katika zijana za-B(w)ana Fūmo Madi, Fūmo

Lūṭi Kipu(n)ga, kapijāna na-Sulṭāni Aḥmad. Akafa Sulṭān Aḥmad k(w)a-maraḍi sanati 1230.

Katawali Fūmo Lūṭi wa-B(w)ānah Fūmo Madi, nā-ye alikuwa mutu hudari sana shujā'a karīmu. Na-zamani hizo (n)dipo alipo‿tawali ushēḥe Sha[yk]h Matākā bin Shaykh Mubārak kutawali Sīwi. Kafā(n)ya bu(n)duki na-'askari nā-ye ni-katika ṭā'a ya-sulṭāni wa-**P**ate, na-ye alipata‿na sana na-Muzārī'i, wātu wa-Mombāsah. Ḥatā sanati 1236 ikazidi fitina baina yake [na-]sulṭāni Zinjibār Sayyid Sa'īd bin Sulṭān. Akafa Sulṭān Fūmo Lūṭi, akafa m(w)aka hunu.

Ba'ada yake katawali Fūmo Lūṭi bin Shaykh bin Fūmo Luṭi bin Shaykh wa-B(w)ānah Tāmu Mukuu. Na-hūyu (n)diye **pa**pāke Sulṭān Aḥmad, sulṭāni Witu. Katawali aṣubuḥi ḥatā ba'ada ṣalāti al-'aṣiri, wātu wa-mūi wakamutoa, ke(n)da Sīu pamōja na-Muzarī'i, kisa ake(n)da Mombāsah.

Katawali Sulṭān B(w)ānah Shaykh wa-B(w)ānah Fūmo Madi, kapatana na-Sayyidi Sa'īd bin Sulṭāni, katia Wa'Arabu Pate, wakaketi (n)yaka mitatu. Ba'ada-ye wātu wa-muji wakamu'uzulu pamōya na-shauri la-Sayyid Sa'īd bin Sulṭān k(w)a-tārīkhi sanati 1239. Wakamutawalisha Sulṭān Aḥmad amukuliwā'o B(w)ānah Wazīri wa-B(w)ānah Tāmu wa-B(w)ānah Shaykh wa-B(w)ānah Tāmu Mukuu. Akapatana sana [na-]Sayyid Sa'īd, katawali (n)yaka miwili, wātu wa-muji wakamu'uzulu wakamurejēza B(w)ānah Shaykh wa B(w)ānah Fūmo Madi. Kaketi katika 'izi k(w)a-shauri Sayyid Sa'īd bin Sulṭāni (n)yaka mitāno, akafa sanati 1247.

Akarejea B(w)ānah Wazīri katika ufalume. Akaja Fūmo Lūṭi bin Shaykh aliyo‿k(w)e(n)da Mombāsah, yeye na-Muzārī'i wakashika Sīu wakapijāna na-B(w)āna Wazīri wa-B(w)ānah Tāmu Pate. Na-B(w)āna Wazīri pamōja na-Sayyid Sa'īd bin Sulṭān na-Fūmo Lūṭi al-madhkūr pamōja na-

Muzārī'i (f. 13) [na] Shaykh Matākā bin Shaykh Mubārak, shaykh wa-Sīu. Wakaja Pate k(w)a-zita wakapijāna watu wa-**P**ate wakashika nti ya-Sīu wakavūndā na-ukuta wa-muji wa-Sīu.

Na-Shaykh Matāka bin Shaykh Mubārak na-Fūmo Luṭi wakatoka Sīu wakaki(m)bilia barāni, ba'ada ya-siku tati wakarejea Sīu k(w)a-zita zikū**p**(w)a sana wakauashika mji wa-Sīu wakaje(n)ga ukuta wakapijāna Pate na-Siu. Ba'ada-ye akafu Fūmo Lūṭi, kata(n)gā(n)ya B(w)āna Wazīri Siu na-**P**ate ikawa katika ṭā'a yāke pamōja na-shauri Sayyid Sa'īd bin Sulṭān bin al-Imām. Ba'ada ya-m(w)aka umōja aka'uwā'a Sulṭāni B(w)ānah Waziri wa B(w)āna Tāmu wa-B(w)ānah Shaykh wa-B(w)ānah Tāmu Mukuu na-Sulṭāni Fūmo Bakr wa-B(w)ānah Shaykh wa B(w)ānah Fūmo Madī al-Nabahānī.

Katawali yeye ufalume wa-**P**ate sanati 1250 alf wa-miatayn wa-khamsīn hijriyah, akapatana sana yeye na-Sayyid Sa'īd bin Sulṭān bin al-Imām sulṭāni Zinjibār muda ulī wakutawali. Kīsa (f. 14) kakhalifu pamōya na-Shaykh Matākā. Sayyid Sa'īd kaeta zita nā-'amīr al-jaysh ni-'Amīr Ḥamād bin Ḥamad al-Samār, kazipija **P**ate na-Sīu asiweze kafā(n)ya amāni.

Ba'ada ya-hapo ikawa fitina baina ya-sulṭāni wa-Pate na-'ami-yake Muḥammad bin Aḥmad wa-B(w)ānah Fūmo Madī. Akashika (n)yū(m)ba ya-ufalume k(w)a-zīta. Kīsa wakaja watu wa-Lāmūh pamōya na-mutu wa-Sayyid Sa'īd bin Sulṭāni wakawa‿ṣiliḥisha Sulṭān Fūmo Bakr na-Muḥammad bin Aḥmad, kapek(w)a Sīu kuketi, Fūmo Bakari kaketi **P**ate.

Ba'ada-ye wakateta wakapijāna (n)yaka mitano Siu na-**P**ate, kisa kawa‿patanisha Sayyid bin Sa'īd bin Sulṭān, akaja **P**ate Muḥammad bin Aḥmad, wakawa shauri moja na-Fūmo Bakari. Kisa Fūmo Bakari kamushika ghafula kamu'ua k(w)a-shauri mōja yeye na-mutu wa-Sīu.

Kisa Sa'īd bin Sulṭān kam(w)ita Sulṭān Fumo Bakr, ake(n)da U(n)gūja, sayyid kamufū(n)ga Fumo Bakari k(w)a-shauri la-wātu wa-Lāmūh na-k(w)a-sababu ya-kumu'ua ibn 'ami-yake Muḥammad bin Aḥmad na-kuwata kufuāta ṣuluḥu yake aliyo‿fā(n)ya yeye Sayyid Sa'īd katika tārīkh sanati 1262.

Akashika **P**ate Sulṭān Aḥmad bin Shaykh bin Fūmo Lūṭi bin Shaykh wa-B(w)ānah Tāmu Mukuu k(w)a-shauri Sayyid Sa'īd bin Sulṭan. Akaketi katika shauri la-Sayyid Sa'īd (n)yaka miwili, wakat[o]ka na-Sayyid. Akaja Sayyid Sa'īd kamupija, akashuka Amīr Ḥamād bin Ḥamad Fāzah, kapija Sīu. Na-sayyid kamufu(n)gua Sulṭān Fūmo Bakr akamu**p**a na-zita pamōya na-wātu wa-Lāmūh, wakaketi Muta(n)ga‿wāndā.

Katika (n)dipo (f. 15) yeye Sayyid Sa'īd na-Amīr Ḥamād wake(n)da **P**aza. Sayyid Sa'īd bin Sulṭān kaketi mahala hit(w)a Kijā(n)ga cha-Mupū(n)ga ḳaribu ya-Fāzah. Amīr Ḥamādi akaja Sīu kaweka mabōma katika (n)dia ya-Fāzah na-Sīwī. Amīr Ḥamād ake(n)da Sīu k(w)a-zita ḥatā kashika mite**p**e iliyoko ba(n)darini Sīu, kapi(n)dua kafā(n)ya mabōma kapija Siu, kaona udhia sana muda wali**p**o‿kuwa mi(n)gi sana wa-zita. Karudi Amīr Ḥamād na-ba'aḍi ya-wātu ke(n)da bomāni kut(w)ā'a mzi(n)ga, kipata (n)diani watu wa-Sīu wakamutokea ghafula. Amīr wa-Shaykh Matāka Ḥamad 'Umar nā-'amīr wa-pīli Ḥamad (N)gōma wakapijāna (n)diani wakamu'ua Amīri Ḥamādi wake(n)da na-mabomāni wakawapija na-Wa'Arābu waliyoko bomāni wakat(w)ā'a mizi(n)ga na-zāna, na-jaishi aliyoko Siu hupijāna.

Wali**p**o‿**p**ata khabari ya-'Amiri Ḥamādi ku'a jaishi ya-sayyidi ikavu(n)dika nāo walikuwa wame[s]otamalaki Siu, Sayyid Sa'īd kisa kupata khabari ya-mauti ya-Ḥamād bin Ḥamad ka(n)gia marikabūni asinene nēno ke(n)da zāke Masikati.

M(w)aka waili karudi kamuweka Fūmo Bakari Fāzah akapija Sīu na-**P**ate. Katika waḳati hunu akafa Shaykh Matāka k(w)a-maraḍi. Ikawa khitilāfu k(w)a-zijana zāke k[u]t[a]ka ushēkhe, waka(n)gia katika ṭā'a ya-sayyidi Muḥammad na-Abū Bakr zijana za Shaykh Matāka. Sayyid kamu**p**a Abū Bakr bin Shaykh Matāka zita pamōya na-Sulṭān Fūmo Bakr, ke(n)da kumupija Sulṭāni Aḥmad. Ake(n)da Abū Bakr bin Shaykh Matāka pamōya na-'amīri (f. 16) wa-Fūmo Bakr, B(w)ānah Mkuu wa-Ḥamad bin Baishi al-Nabahānī, waka(n)gia Siu usiku wakapijāna ḥatā wakavu(n)dika Abū Bakr na-wātu wāke. Wātu wa-Siu wakawa(n)dama yūma wakamushika Abū Bakr bin Shaykh Matāka wakamu**p**eka k(w)a-Sulṭān Aḥmad Pate, kauwaw(awa)a na-Sulṭān Aḥmad.

Ba'adā-ye kasimāma Shaykh Muḥammad bin Shaykh Matāka ṭarafu ya-Sayyid Sa'īd bin Sulṭān Yeye na-Fūmo Bakari Sayyid Sa'īd kawa**p**a zita na-'askari na-gharāma, wakamupija Sulṭān Aḥmad bin Shaykh ḥatā wakamutoa **P**ate sanati 1273, ake(n)da Kāu. Sīu ikawa na-Shaykh Muḥammad bin Matāka ṭarafu ya-Sayyidi, kamu**p**a na-'askari kawaka gereza. Wakateta na-mutu wa Sayyid Sa'īd k(w)a-sababu mutu wa-sayyidi alivūndā bāndā la-mute**p**e alowaka Shaykh Muḥammad bin Shaykh Matāka (m)bee ya-gereza, na-Shaykh Muḥammad kavūndah gerēzah.

Na-katika waḳati hūnu alikufa Sulṭān Aḥmad al-mulaḳab B(w)ānah Madūshī, babake Fuumo Bakari sulṭāni Wītūh. Akaketi mahala **p**ake Sulṭāni Aḥmad al-mulaḳab Sīm**p**ā, sulṭāni Wītūh.

Na-ḳabula ya-Shaykh Muḥammad Matāka asiyavu(n)da gereza la-Siu yalitoka fitina yeye na-Fuumo Bakr bin Shaykh, kamutoa Fuumo Bakar bin Shaykh **P**ate, akaja Lāmūh k[u]tamalaki **P**ate. Wali**p**o‿'ona (n)guvu zāke wakū**p**(w)a wa-Pate na-kite(n)do mizofā(n)ya Shaykh Muḥammad Matāka na-miso‿ataka kuwa‿tawali wasikiri, kawapija zita, wakasimāma wakū**p**(w)a wa-**P**ate. Wa-lā hawana mufalume k(w)a-shauri la-wātu watatu, Muḥammad bin

B(w)ānah Mkuu al-Nabahānī na-B(w)ānah Reḥema bin Aḥmad al-Nabahānī na-Nāṣir bin ‘Abd Allāh bin ‘Abd al-Salām, (n)diye aliyo‿kuwa mudabir al-umūr. Wakakusāya zana wakapijāna na-Shaykh Muḥammad Matākā wakamushi(n)da sana, wakafa wātu ma‘arūfu katika (f. 17) mā’amiri wa-Shaykh Muḥammad Matākā, B(w)ānah Damīla na-Mawlānā wa-Shee Kūli.

Shaykh Muḥammad Matāka akaya kutaka amāni k(w)a-Muḥammad bin B(w)ānah Mkuu k(w)āni (n)diye aliyo‿kuwa mukū**p**(w)a wā’o katika hawa watu watatu tumezo‿watāya. Wakapatana kumu**p**a yeye Muḥammad bin B(w)ānah Mkuu [u]falume wa-Sīu na-**P**ate, akaiza kasema "Mimi ni-mtu mzima." Wake(n)da kumut(w)ā’a Sulṭāni Aḥmad al-mulaḳab Sīm**p**ā aliko Kāu.

Khabari ikafika k(w)a-suluṭāni wa-U(n)guja Sayyid Mājid bin Sa‘īd, kamueta wazīri wake Sayyid Sulaymān bin Ḥamad k(w)a-marikabu, akaja ili‿aji **P**ate uvūndi fitina. Na-marikabu ikiwa‿ṣili Mā[nd]ra **P**ate mek(w)isa kushika mutu wa Sulṭāni Aḥmad, Abū Bakr bin Ḥasan al-Būrī alikūja nā-ye ni-Nāṣir bin ‘Abd Allāh bin ‘Abd al-Salām. Akisa kupata khabari Sayyid Sulaymāni bin Ḥamad karejea U(n)gūja, na-Shaykh Muḥammad Matāka waḳati hunu (n)di**p**o ali**p**o‿vu(n)da gereza la-Siu.

Akisa kuwaṣili Sulṭān Aḥmad **P**ate jamī‘i ya-wātu wakamubā‘i kuwa (n)diye mufalume, ni-Shaykh Muḥammd Matākā na-Muzee wa Sēfu na-Shaykh Shikuuh na-Muḥammad Mōte, ukasitaḳiri kuwa-Sulṭān Aḥmad kuwā (n)diye mufal[u]me, wakamubā‘i wātu hawa wote.

Sayyid Mājid kapeka wātu wa-Lāmūh **P**ate k(w)a-nuṣḥa pamōja na-Shaykh Muḥī al-Dīn kutaka Sulṭāni Aḥmad aweke ‘askari **P**ate. Na-hūyu Shaykh Muḥī al-Dīn (n)diye aliyo‿watoa ‘askar[i] wa-sayyid Sīu ali**p**o‿wapija zita Shaykh Muḥammad Matākā; ‘asikari wali-(n)dāni ya-gereza ya-Sīu, Shaykh Muḥī al-Dīn kawa‿toa ‘askari k(w)a-amāni, k(w)āni huyu Shaykh Muḥī al-Dīn alikuwa mutu wa-Sayyid Mājid bin Sa'īd.

(f. 18) Zamani alipo na-'askari U(n)gūja Sayidi Mājidi kafā(n)ya hasira sana kuwa‿toa 'askari Sīu, kat(w)ā'a daraka Shaykh Muḥī al-Dīn alipo‿muona Sayidi Mājidi mefā(n)ya ghaḍabu. Na-hūyu Shaykh Muḥī al-Dīn alina ḥīla sana na-'ilimu (n)yi(n)gi, akaja Lāmūh katukua na-khiyāri ya-wātu wa-Lāmūh na-Shaykh Aḥmad na-Shaykh 'Abd al-Raḥmān, awlād shaykh Pateh, kumunāṣiḥi Sulṭān Aḥmad k(w)a-ṣuḥuba yaliyo‿kuwa baina yao. Kariḍika kuweka 'askari ba'ada ya-shiddah sana, akakhālifu shauri la-wazīri wāke Nāṣir bin 'Abd Allāh k(w)āni aliiza kutia Wa'Arabu ḥatā mutu umōja.

Kīsa wātu wa-**P**ate wakafā(n)ya shauri na-M(w)āna Jāha bint al-Sulṭān Fūmo Lūṭi Kipu(n)ga wa-B(w)āna Fūmo Madi, muke wa-Sulṭāni Fūumo Bakr bin Shaykh. Na-wakati hunu Fūmo Bakari oko Lāmūh tini ya-shauri la-Sayidi Mājid bin Sa'īd ta(n)gu alipo‿tolewa **P**ate.

Basi kula siku wakatia 'askari na-zāna usiku k(w)a-siri, ḥatā alipo‿jua khabari Sulṭāni Aḥmad 'asikari wamekuwa wa(n)gi **P**ate, ikawa fitina, wakamupija Sulṭān Aḥmad ghafula ba'ada ya-kutaka kumushika k(w)a-ḥīla wasiweze k(w)āni watu wote walikuwa shauri moja na-Sayyid Mājid bin Sa'īd iso‿kuwa waziri wāke Nāṣir bin 'Abd Allāh [bin] 'Abd al-Salām. Wakapijāna (n)dāni ya-muji wa-**P**ate zita zikū**p**(w)a sana, katoka Sulṭān Aḥmad yeye na-Shaykh Muḥammad bin Matāka wake(n)da Sīu.

Pate wakaketi Wa'Arabu ṭarafu ya-Sayyid Mājid na-baḥarini katia marikabu, zita zalipo‿kuwa zikuu sana akaja yeye Sayyid Mājid bin Sa'īd. (f. 19) Wakaḥu[ṣ]u[r]u kisiwa cha-**P**ate k(w)a-baḥāri kusipiti cho(m)**p**o, katia silisila katika kan(w)a la-muto wa Sīu Kūyo. Wakapijāna (n)yezi sitah k(w)a-baḥari na-k(w)a-jānibu ya-**P**ate. Na-janibu [ya-Fāzah] Muzee wa-Sēfu kakhālifu akawa mutu wa-Sayidi Mājidi k(w)a-ḥīla (n)yi(n)gi na-manēno ma(n)gi. Kaona ḍiḳi Sulṭān Aḥmad na-Shaykh Muḥammad Matāka.

Na-nti ya-Siu ikawa fitina, ba'aḍi ya-watu wape(n)da Sayyid Mājidi k(w)a-sababu ya-mashaka wamezo‿pata, na-watuwe ni-Sharif Mawlānā bin Abū Bakr na-'Isā bin Aḥmad al-Somālī. Walipo‿ona hāya Sulṭān Aḥmad na-Shaykh Matākā wakataka amāni k(w)a-Sayyid Mājidi, kawapa amāni. Katika maneno yā-'amāni Sultān Aḥmad kasafiri k(w)a-siri u‿siku ake(n)da barāni karajea Kāu.

Na-Shaykh Muḥammad Matākā akamupeka kijāna chake marikabūni Shaykh bin Muḥammad, na-sayyid kamusāmeḥe kamupa na-ḥeshima sana. Sayyid kasafiri ake(n)da zāke U(n)gūja. Ba'adā-ye Muḥammad bin Matāka ake(n)da U(n)gūja kumuwājihi Sayyid Mājidi. Sayidi kamufū(n)ga kamupeka (n)gomeni Mombāsah na-watu wā(n)gi. Akafa ba'ada ya-siku tati.

Sulṭāni Aḥmad alikọ Kāu. Kapekwa al-Wālī Sa'ūd bin Ḥamad kumushika k(w)a-ḥīla asiweze, katoka ke(n)da Witu. Al-Wālī Sa'ūd bin Ḥamad karejea Lāmūh ake(n)da Fāzah kafā(n)ya taratibu kamushika 'Umar Matāk[a] na-zijana wa-Shaykh Muḥammad Matākā wote, wakashikuwa Sīu wakaja Lāmūh. 'Umar Matākā kamufu(n)ga Lāmūh, zijana wote kawapeka (n)gomēni Mombāsah.

Ba'ada ya-hapo katamalaki Sayyid Mājid Sawāḥili zote, pasiwe na-mutu wakumu'ariḍi. Na-Sulṭān Aḥmad kaketi Witu katika ṭā'a ya-Sayidi Mājidi ḥatā waḳati wa-Sayyid Baraghashi bin Sa'īd. Akataka kuweka 'askari Witu na-be(n)dera, Sulṭān Aḥmad (f. 20) asiriḍiki, kapeka zita Sayyid Barghash kamupija Sulṭān Aḥmad, asiweze kafā(n)ya amāni al-wālī Sa'ūd bin Ḥamad.

Sayyid Barghash hakumufuraḥiya tena al-Wālī Sa'ūd bin Ḥamad k(w)a-sababu kufā(n)ya amāni upesi nā-ye hakumupija sana zita. Sayyid Barghash kapeka tena zita zamani na-al-Wālī Sa'ūd bin Ḥamad. Sulṭān Aḥmad kat(w)ā'a ḥimāyah k(w)a-Jarmani. Waḳati hunu zikarudi zita za Sayidi Barghash. Kaketi Sulṭān Aḥmad katika ḥimāyah ya-Jarmani, wakamu**pa** na-ba'aḍi ya-bara ya-Sawāḥili. Akafa Sulṭān Aḥmad ḥāli hiyo katika ḥimāyah sanati 1306.

Katawali Fūmo Bakr bin Sulṭān Aḥmad bin Shaykh katika ḥāli hiyo. Akatoka fitina baina yake na-Jarmani. Mutu umōja hit(w)a Kinsili kamupija bawabu wa-lā(n)go la-mūi k(w)a-raṣāṣi, walikuweko ni-'asikari chāo wakamupija Kinsili na-WaZu(n)gu waliyo‿fuetene, nā-ye wakawau wa-wote min ghayri amri ya-Sulṭān Fūmo Bakr. 'Askari wali**po**‿muona jama'a yao mekufa hawa‿ku(n)guja amri. Na-watu wa-Mukunū(m)bi na-Wa(n)da‿mūyu wali**po**‿pata khabari ya-kā(m)**pa** WaZu(n)gu wamepijāna w[o]t[e] nao wakawa‿ua WaZu(n)gu waliyo‿kuweka.

Ba'adā-ye akaja dōlah tukufu ya-Wa(N)gereza, wakataka kufā(n)ya inṣāfi wakataka wātu wa-Mukunū(m)bi na-wātu wa-Wa(n)da‿mūyu ma'ana awatiye katika ḥukumu. Asiriḍiki Sulṭān Fūmo Bakr kuwa‿toa, kwakamupija zita zikaya mashua ḥatā Mukunū(m)bi na-Wa(n)da‿mūyu na-Kilimāni (f. 21) na-(N)da**pi** na-(N)ya(n)do‿za-p(w)ani, wakazipija k(w)a-mizinga wakazi‿tia mōto. Ḥatā laylah 11 Rabī' al-Awwal sanati 130[8] wakapijāna wātu wa-Witu katika ndia ya-Kipīni, na-watu wa-dolah tukufu, wātu wa-Witu wakavu(n)dika. Ḥatā aṣubuḥi m(w)ezi 12 Rabī' al-Awwal sanati 1308 wakamupija Sulṭāni Fūmo Bakari Wītu wakamutoa k(w)a-zita. Sulṭān Fūmo Bakr ake(n)da Jo(n)gēni.

Wītūh ikatamalakiwa na-dōla tukufu. Fūmo Bakar kaketi Jo(n)gēni ḥatā m(w)ezi 28 Jumād al-Awwal sanati 1308 akafa. Akashika mahali **pa**ke (n)duye B(w)ānah Shaykh bin Sulṭān Aḥmad. Ba'ada ya-siku tati ikawa fitina, akashikuwah na-(n)dūye Fūmo 'Umar nā-'Avuṭūla wa-Bakhīru. Wakamufu(n)ga B(w)āna Shaykh ya-Sulṭān Aḥmad.

Katawali Fūmo 'Umar bin Sulṭān Aḥmad bin Shaykh. Ikawa kama jinsi yalo‿kuwa baina yake na-dōlah tukufu.

Ama mufalume wa-k(w)isa kutamalaki Witu ni-Sulṭān Fūmo ‘Umar al-madhkūr na-wa-k(w)isa kutamalaki Pate ni-Sulṭān Aḥmad, sulṭāni Witu al-mulaḳab Sīmpā. Na-aliyo‿tamalaki k(w)ā(n)da ni-Sulaymān bin Sulaymān bin al-Muẓaffar al-Nabahānī Imām al-‘Arab.

Hini (n)diyo khabari ya-Nabahāni kuja Sawāḥili na-khabari zāo. Wametawali wafalume wāḥid wa thalāthīn na-m(w)anamuke umōja kama tumezo‿ta(n)gulia kutāja mpili.

Nasi‿talinaḳili hāya k(w)a-Muḥammad bin Fūmo ‘Umar al-Nabahānī al-mulaḳab B(w)ānah Kitīnī, nā-ye alipo‿kea na-jadi yake Muḥammad bin B(w)ānah Mkuu al-Nabahānī al-mulaḳab B(w)ānah Sīmpā k(w)āni (n)diye aloḍibitiye sana khabari za kāe na-nasaba zāo kama tumezo‿ta(n)gulia kutāya.

Katabah Sāliḥ bin Sālim bin Aḥmad bin ‘Abd Allāh bin Muḥammad [B]ā- Sharāḥīl bi-yadih.

(f. 22) Hizi ya-’akhbāri za-Pate na-zita zāo nasaba za Nabahāni, nasi‿tali‿naḳili hāya sābiḳan k(w)a-Muḥammad bin Fūmo ‘Umar nā-ye alinaḳili k(w)a-jadi yake Muḥammad bin B(w)ānah Mkuu al-Nabahānī, mukūp(w)a wa-wazee wa-Pate.

Li-ya‘lam [faḳr al-faḳīr(?)] li-llāh ta‘ā[lā] Sāliḥ bin Sālim bin Aḥmad bin ‘Abd Allāh bin Muḥammad bin ‘Abd Allāh [B]ā-Sharāḥīl bi-yadih.

HISTORY OF PATE

The first man to come to Pate of the Nabahani was Sulayman bin Sulayman Muzaffar al-Nabahani and his siblings, two men: ‘Ali bin Sulayman and ‘Uthman bin Sulayman. And this Sulayman bin Sulayman the aforesaid, it was he who had been sultan in Arabia. Then reigned al-Ya‘rubi (and so) he came to Pate, in the year 600 six hundred of Hijra[1] he came to Pate.

He asked for marriage from the king of Pate, from among the al-Batawin. And he was an important man, (this) Sultan Sulayman, (so) the king of Pate married him to his daughter. And the custom of all the WaSwahili till now (is that) a man takes your daughter (in marriage), (then after) seven days pass since the wedding, he goes to see the father-in-law, the father of his wife, [and he] gives him something, each man according to his means. Sulayman bin Sulayman, when he went after these seven days to see the king of Pate to be given (gifts) from the people, this Sulayman bin Sulayman — that king instead (of a gift) gave him his kingdom. From then on reigned Sulayman bin Sulayman.

There was a town on the same island of Pate, called Kitaka, east of Pate; and Siu was not yet a town. There was another town, on the same island of Pate, called Shanga.[2] And this town, it was under the overlordship of the

---

[1] 1203-4.

[2] For archeological evidence on Shanga, see Mark Horton, *Shanga 1980: An Interim Report* (Nairobi: National Museums of Kenya, 1981). For Horton's interpretation of Shanga's place in coastal history, see his "Early Muslim Trading Settlements on the East

king of Pate. And Faza was a town (by itself), the lords of Paza (were) al-Mafaziyun.[3] And these towns, Pate and Shanga and Kitaka (were) under the overlordship of the king of Pate. And Mandra[4] had a separate king, and he had great power.

And this (f. 2) Sultan Sulayman begat two sons, Muhammad and Ahmad. In the year 625[5] Sultan Sulaymani died. Muhammad's age (was) twenty years, Ahmad's age fifteen years. Muhammad bin Sulayman reigned after his father. The people of Shanga seceded, he made war on them, conquered the town, destroyed it (and) took away (the residents). [This is] the origin of some of the people who came to Pate. And some of the people, of the tribe of WaKinandangu, ran away, and it was not known where they had gone. Until some days passed and the news came to Sultan Muhammad bin Sulayman from the hunters. They said to him, "Those unknown, we have seen them in the forest." He sent people to look for them, they caught up with them; they had made huts inside the forest. They carried them off and came to Pate. Sultan Muhammad forgave them (and) returned them to their (own) place. This is the origin of the town of Siu.[6]

African Coast: New Evidence from Shanga," *The Antiquaries Journal* 67 (1987): 290-323.

[3] The Arabic plural of the Swahili plural, approximately conforming to the Arabic participial adjective signifying "Faza-dwellers." The presence of the Swahili plural prefix *ma-* may explain the form *Ampaza*, known from the Portuguese sources.

[4] *Māndra*, rather than *Mānda*, is marked both by the ligature of *nūn* and *dāl*, which looks like a hooked *rā'*, and the *tashdīd*. It occurs infrequently.

[5] 1227-8.

[6] This passage explains the folk etymology of the name "Siu": *wasijuwekane*, "it was not known about them," from the verb *jua* "to know."

(Later) also all the other WaSwahili settled (and then) came the WaFamau, they all settled; the latter were the chiefs of Siu under the overlordship of the king of Pate.[7]

(Then) Sultan Muhammad bin Sulayman died, (and) his brother Ahmad bin Sulayman reigned. He governed the land of Pate very well, planting fields and building houses, and all this country was under his authority. He did not make war anywhere (and) died in the year 670.[8]

(Next) reigned the son of his brother, by the name of Ahmad bin Muhammad bin Sulayman. He followed the example of his (paternal) uncle in regard to building up the town of Pate, the houses and the farms, and he had many children.

Of his sons ascended to kingship (f. 3) Muhammad bin Ahmad bin Muhammad bin Sulayman. He governed the people well. (Then) the people of Faza seceded; he fought them (and) brought them under his authority after very many battles, until he overcame them. He conquered Manda (and) gained possession of it. As to Mandra, he acquired it through numerous military ruses because the sultan of Manra[9] had great power (in terms) of numerous men and money. He destroyed it utterly, and carried off some people to Pate.[10]

---

[7] The Famau, whom Pouwels regards as "clearly 'Arabs,'" claim Portuguese, Chinese and Persian descent. See Randall L. Pouwels, *Horn and Crescent*, 49.

[8] 1271-2. This is the only new MS to contain 670 rather than 660. See also Heepe #5.

[9] Yet another variation of the name Manda.

[10] For archeological evidence on Manda see: H. Neville Chittick, *Manda: Excavations at an Island Port on the Coast of Kenya* (Nairobi: British Institute in Eastern Africa, 1984. For a more contemporary contrasting interpretation, consult Mark Horton, "Asiatic

And some (of them) ran away (and) went to all places; some came to Shela (and) put themselves under the protection of the men of Lamu. The king demanded them from the men of Lamu. The men of Lamu refused to surrender them. And some went to Malindi and other towns. The king of Pate pursued vigorously (the case of) those who came to Shela. The men of Lamu refused to surrender them decisively. In the course of this dispute the king died in the year 732.[11] He had one son named 'Umar.

'Umar ascended to sultanship after his father. He returned to his father's case against the men of Lamu, demanding the people of Manda. The men of Lamu refused to surrender them. He made war on them, the men of Lamu sued for peace (and) submitted to his overlordship.

And Sultan 'Umar bin Muhammad bin Ahmad bin Muhammad bin Sulayman gained great power (and) conquered the towns of the Swahili (coast) - Ozi, Malindi, Kiwayu, Kitao, Miya and Imidhi and Watamu - until he reached Kirimba. He gained possession of all the towns from Pate to Kirimba. In each town he placed his own men to govern. This is the origin of those *Majumbe* who are to be found (f. 4) on the whole coast (*mrima*). The meaning [of the word] is "slaves of the Yumbe", and this *yumbe* is the royal palace of Pate.

And on the east side he gained possession as far as Warsheikh by many wars. He began to wage war, beginning with Kiwayu and (then against) Tula and Tuwala and Shungwaya and all the harbors (*banadiri*): Brawa, Marka,

---

Colonization of the East Coast of Africa: The Manda Evidence," *Journal of the Royal Asiatic Society* no. 2 (1986): 201-13.

[11] 1331-2.

Mogadisho. He placed a governor (*al-wali*) in charge of all administration for all the harbors near Mogadisho.[12]

(As long as) he lived, all these countries were under his administration and his overlordship, except Zanzibar he did not rule at that time, and Zanzibar was not a great country (then). And this king Sultan ‘Umar loved war and loved (his) subjects, and the subjects loved him very much. Pate gained great power. He died in the year 749.[13] He had two sons, Muhammad and Ahmad.

(Next) reigned Muhammad bin ‘Umar bin Muhammad bin Ahmad bin Muhammad bin Sulayman. And there was no war, he ruled the kingdom of his father in peace. And he loved money a great deal; he sent voyages in ships to go to India to conduct trade; and he had great profit in money.

And one time his son set out on a voyage (and) came upon a silver mine. He brought (the ore) to Pate (and) made people do the work. He obtained very great wealth, (so that) they made swords of silver and ladders of silver and many household vessels of silver. And he had four sons: Bwana Mkuu and Ahmad and Abu Bakr and ‘Umar. And this king died in the year 797.[14]

His brother Ahmad bin ‘Umar bin Muhammad bin Ahmad bin Muhammad bin Sulayman reigned. He ruled over the people in peace and

---

[12] For the system of government at Pate and related terminology see C. S. Nicholls, *The Swahili Coast*, 62-64.

[13] 1348-9.

[14] 1394-5.

(observed) very good custom. He died in the year 840,[15] with affairs in order.

To kingship ascended (f. 5) Abu Bakr bin Muhammad bin ‘Umar bin Muhammad bin Ahmad bin Muhammad bin Sulayman. He ruled in a good manner toward all the towns under his authority. He died in the year 875.[16] And he left two sons, Muhammad and Ahmad.

Muhammad bin Abu Bakr bin ‘Umar the aforesaid reigned. In his time the Portuguese Europeans came to all the Swahili towns. They stayed at Mombasa (and) made a fort. And near Pate they built Ndondo. And the people of the mainland obeyed them (and) paid them money, (and) accepted their authority.

They (the Portuguese) harassed the king of Pate throughout the Pate land (and) fought a war against the king on the side of Shindakasi. They built the ground of the beach by means of drilling and firing--that masonry (is there) until now--in order to attack the Palace of the town of Pate, (but) failed. Then they sued for peace (and) made a (written) document stating their conditions. The Europeans remained at Pate (and) made a customs-house; in the European language they called it "*Fandika*." They made many things around the island of Pate. The king died in the year 900.[17] He left two sons, Bwana Mkuu and Abu Bakari.

(Then) reigned Abu Bakr bin Muhammad bin Abu Bakr bin Muhammad

---

[15] 1436-7.

[16] 1470-1.

[17] 1494-5. Clearly, this date precedes the arrival of the Portuguese by sea and must be treated with caution.

bin 'Umar bin Muhammad bin Ahmad bin Muhammad bin Sulayman. He maintained peace with the Europeans, as was the practice of his father. He died in the year 940,[18] with affairs in order. And he left two sons, Ahmad and Muhammad.

His brother Bwana Mkuu bin Muhammad the aforesaid reigned. (There) arose hostility (between) him and the Europeans, but there was no war. The trouble lasted many days but they did not obstruct each other. He died in the year 973,[19] leaving one son called Abu Bakr.

(Next) reigned Muhammad bin Abu Bakr bin Muhammad bin Abu Bakr bin Muhammad bin 'Umar bin Muhammad bin Ahmad bin Muhammad bin Sulayman. (f. 6) He made peace with the Europeans, (and) they took some of the towns. He died in the year 1002.[20] He had a son named Abu Bakr who did not reign.

(Next) reigned Abu Bakr bin Bwana Mkuu bin Muhammad bin Abu Bakr bin Muhammad bin 'Umar bin Muhammad bin Ahmad bin Muhammad bin Sulayman. He treated the Europeans according the manner of his ancestors who preceded him. However, Pate diminished in strength. He died in the year 1041.[21] He had two sons, Abu Bakr and Bwana Mkuu.

(Next) reigned Abu Bakr bin Muhammad bin Abu Bakr bin Muhammad bin Abu Bakr bin Muhammad bin 'Umar bin Muhammad bin Ahmad bin

---

[18] 1533-4.

[19] 1565-6. This ruler is not found in MSS 321 and 344. Elsewhere, an uncle is stated to succeed.

[20] 1593-4.

[21] 1631-2.

Muhammad bin Sulayman. (There) arose discord with the Portuguese Europeans. He fought them, (and) defeated the Europeans after many extensive battles. After that came in turn an expedition of the Europeans. They attacked the town of Pate with cannons, cut off the roads from the sea to block the ships. The people saw grave hardships (and) made peace. The king died in the year 1061.[22] He had two sons, Bwana Mkuu and Ahmad.

(Next) reigned Bwana Mkuu bin Abu Bakr bin [B]wana Mkuu bin Muhammad bin Abu Bakr bin Muhammad bin 'Umar bin Muhammad bin Ahmad bin Muhammad bin Sulayman. He got along with the Europeans very well. And he loved very much to stay at Lamu, even the monsoon (season) he spent at Lamu. He contracted a marriage among the people of Lamu.

And at this time the WaFamau, the men of Siu, revolted against his authority. He fought them, destroyed the town of Siu, captured some (people), seized many men of the people of Siu (and) carried them off to Pate. The chief of Siu escaped, went to Ndondo, to the Portuguese (and) requested (f. 7) protection. The chief of the Portuguese came on behalf of the people of Siu to the king; he allowed them to be released to him (and) had them returned to their (former) place at Siu under safe conduct.

Afterwards the Portuguese devised a stratagem. They came to Pate in a ship (and) invited the king to come aboard. He did not go (but) sent the son of his (paternal) uncle Bwana Mkuu, him and (some) men of Pate. The Europeans carried them off in the ship, sent them to Europe, (and) not even one man (ever) returned. After this the king attacked the Europeans from all directions, on the mainland and on the islands, (and) drove them away

[22] 1650-1.

everywhere. They fled to Mombasa. After this the king died in the year 1100.[23] He had two sons, Bu Bakr and Bwana Madi, and one daughter named Mwana Darini.

(Then) reigned Bwana Abu Bakr bin Bwana Mkuu bin Abu Bakr bin [Bwana] Mkuu bin Muhammad bin Abi Bakr bin Muhammad bin 'Umar bin Muhammad bin Ahmad [bin Muhammad] bin Sulayman.[24] He was suddenly attacked by Ahmad, the brother of the Bwana Mkuu who had been taken away by the Europeans. And he (Ahmad) struck him with a sword. He died in the year 1103.[25]

This (very) Ahmad bin Abu Bakr bin Muhammad bin Abu Bakr bin Muhammad bin 'Umar bin Muhammad bin Ahmad bin Muhammad bin Sulayman reigned. And after he ascended to power, he killed Bwana Madi, his (the former king's) brother. He pursued the Portuguese (and) drove them out of his whole country.

And at this time Mwana Darini, the daughter of Bwana Mkuu bin Abu Bakr, wife of the Bwana Mkuu bin Abi Bakr who had gone away to Goa before the time of Sultan Ahmad, (who) later killed her two brothers Bu Bakr and Bwana Madi, — and (as) her husband went to Goa, she grieved greatly. After many days passed she wished to circumsize her son Bwana Tamu Mtoto ("Junior") who was called Sultan Abu Bakr Imam al-Huda, the son of Bwana Mkuu who went to Goa.

(When) the king received the news of this, (that) Mwana Darini (f. 8)

---

[23] 1688-9.

[24] Compare the name in MS 321.

[25] 1691-2.

had decided to make the celebration of circumcision for her son, this king resolved on a celebration of circumcision for his (own) sons, in order to deny Mwana Darini the [ceremonial] horn. When the news arrived, Mwana Darini sent for Mwenye Bayayi bin Mkuu of the *Jamal al-Layl*[26] who had great skill in carving, (and) requested that he make a horn superior to the horn of Pate.[27] He accepted a wage of one hundred twenty riyals.[28] She gave him elephant tusks to select [the best] one. He made the horn in secret, and then some days later she showed it suddenly (and) took it around the houses of her kin. Every man gave an offering, (so that) the master said, "I do not want the wage, (but) want the offerings." He was given (them); she got much wealth from the gifts, (and) made the celebration for her son.[29]

Later, at the time of Bwana Tamu Mkuu ("Senior") the people of Lamu came to borrow the original horn of Pate. He gave it to them (but) the ship sank in the water at sea, (and) the horn perished. Bwana Tamu asked for the horn of Mwana Darini, saying to her, "Give it for us to use in the town." Mwana Darini said to him, "This horn (is) for every clan who makes an offering, they may use it."

She set a slave free who knew how to blow the horn. She said, "This

---

[26] The *Jamal al-Layl* were a Sharifian clan from Hadramawt who came to East Africa on their continued migrations. See Randall L. Pouwels, *Horn and Crescent*, 138-9.

[27] This is the best articulation of the *siwa* episode in the new MSS.

[28] These are normally taken to mean Marina Theresa thalers, but since the episode occurred in the late seventeenth century this obviously would be anachronistic. We do not know if Portuguese currency is meant; Portuguese coin did not circulate on the coast.

[29] The role of ceremony and regalia in royal claims is discussed by Christine S. Nicholls, *The Swahili Coast*, 63-4.

one is the official beater of this horn, he and his descendants. And his fee is to be five riyals and a cloth for carrying the horn; and let ghee be given for the blower to drink and a present from every man according to his means." Their family was called "the Heralds of the Horn," (and) to this day there are to be found people (belonging) to it. From that time the custom of all the clans of Pate and of the other towns has been to come (and) borrow it under such circumstances, (and) the Heralds of the Horn are paid until now.

Mischief increased within the city, and during his reign for seven years there was drought, there was no rain, (and so) he abdicated in the year 1111.[30]

(Next) reigned Sultan Abi Bakr [bin] Bwana Tamu Mkuu wa Bwana Mutiti bin Ahmad bin Abi Bakr bin ‘Umar bin Ahmad bin ‘Umar bin Muhammad bin Ahmad bin Muhammad bin Sulayman. He made a strong alliance with the king of Maskat, al-Imam Sayf bin Nabahan al-Ya‘rubi. And this king of Pate went to Arabia, (and) they agreed, the king of Arabia and the king of Pate, to drive out the Portuguese from Mombasa. When he returned from Arabia, the king of Pate sent an expedition to Mombasa (and) attacked the Portuguese on Sunday. Numerous Portuguese men died, (and) he gained possession of the fort of Mombasa.

He informed al-Imam Sayf bin Nabahan al-Ya‘rubi. (The latter) brought governors (*al-wali*) of the Mazru‘i (family), three men: Muhammad bin ‘Uthman and ‘Ali bin ‘Uthman, (as to) the third, I do not know him (as to) his name, they were all brothers. They came with soldiers from al-Imam Sayf bin

---

[30] 1699-1700. This date does not recur elsewhere.

Nabahan al-Ya'rubi. This is the origin of the Mazru'i who came to Mombasa.[31]

And the king of Pate remained on good terms with his subjects (and) continued in his kingship for forty years. He died in the year 1152.[32] He had many children (but) his sons did not reign after him.

(Instead) reigned Ahmad [bin] Abu Bakr bin Muhammad bin Abi Bakr bin 'Umar bin Ahmad bin 'Umar bin Muhammad bin Ahmad bin Muhammad bin Sulayman.[33] He was benevolent toward the people, and he was very fond of cattle (and) collected numerous herds. He died in the year 1160.[34] He had one son named Bwana Gongo who did not reign.

Bwana Tamu Mtoto ("the Younger") reigned, (f. 10) who was called Sultan Abu Bakr Imam al-Huda, the son of Bwana Mkuu carried away by the Portuguese. The Imam of the Arabs Sayf bin Nabahan al-Ya'rubi brought an expedition to attack Pate (but) they failed (and) many Arabs died, (so) they made peace. After this the people of Lamu revolted. The king of Pate waged war on them, (and) the people of Lamu failed.[35] (Then) the people of Lamu equipped an army to fight Pate. They came with the troops on the side of

---

[31] The date of the appeal to the Ya'rubi's of Oman is 1698. According to Hawley, however, the request at the time came from the Mazru'i already at Mobasa. Donald Hawley, *Oman & Its Renaissance* (London: Stacey Intl., 1987): 31. The Oman takeover of Mombasa gave Pate short-lived control over Pemba, formerly ruled out of Mombasa. This lasted until 'Ali bin 'Uthman's governorate and was then reduced to a share. Only the Stigand version (p. 56) refers to the arrangement, which lasted until 1776 (Nicholls, *The Swahili Coast*, 58).

[32] 1739-40. This date does not recur elsewhere.

[33] Compare the name in MS 344.

[34] 1747.

[35] MS 321 has Siu'.

Kitaka. They fought against the people of Pate in a very great battle. The men of Lamu were deafeated (and) returned to Lamu.

The king of Pate made war from the sea, he came to attack the people of Lamu (and) conquered them. After this they were united, the people of Pate and the people of [Lamu]. Al-Imam al-Ya'rubi established single administration. The king was killed in the year 1177.[36]

(Then) reigned his sibling, a woman, Sultana Mwana Khadija binti Bwana Mkuu bin Abi Bakr bin Muhammad bin Abi Bakr bin Muhammad bin Abi Bakr bin Muhammad bin 'Umar bin Muhammad bin Ahmad bin Muhammad bin Sulayman. (There) arose much intrigue in the land of Pate. It was so that in the land of Pate there were two kings: Mwana Khadija the aforesaid (and) Sultan 'Umar. They fought in the town of Pate, Sultan 'Umar fled (and) went to Barawa,[37] (then) returned to Pate with a very powerful force. They were killed by the men of Mwana Khadija in a big battle, each man remained (dead) where he was. After this Mwana Khadija died, in the year 1187,[38] of disease.

(Then) reigned Bwana Mkuu wa Sheye wa Bwana Tamu Mkuu. The subjects made for him much trouble, he had no peace until, in the year 1191,[39] the men of the town invaded [his palace] (and) killed him at this date.

(Then) reigned Bwana Fumo Madi, whose (real) name was Sultan

---

[36] 1763-4.

[37] MS 321 has *barāni* "to the mainland." The Bajun and mainland troops were regularly sought out by rival leaders, since few regular soldiers were kept.

[38] 1773-4.

[39] 1777.

Muhammad bin Abi Bakr (f. 11) [bin Bwana Mkuu bin Abi Bakr] bin Muhammad bin Abi Bakr bin Muhammad bin Abi Bakr bin Muhammad bin 'Umar bin Muhammad bin Ahmad bin Muhammad bin Sulayman. After he came to power the subjects wished to make intrigue. He fought them in battle, overcame them, seized forty men of Kau. And among these forty,[40] two were this king's own brothers. He slaughtered them like goats, (so) blood (ran down from) the roof. In this way he suppressed the great men. (Then) there was peace, no other man rose to make trouble, he reigned in peace and quiet, and the subjects experienced great calm until he died in the year 1224.[41] After him no other king reigned in peace like him.[42] He left many children.

(Then) reigned Sultan Ahmad bin Shaykh bin Fumo Luti bin Bwana Tamu Mkuu.[43] Trouble increased in the town of Lamu. He came and attacked them in the year 1227,[44] he and the people of Mombasa, the Mazru'i. They brought men (and) landed at Shela a very large army of men of Pate and men of Mombasa. The men of Lamu came out, came to Shela (and) fought with them in a great battle. The army of the men of Lamu had great force. The army of Mombasa and Pate was defeated in battle. (When)

---

[40] Pouwels discusses a tradition which refers to the killing of forty Africans (rather than forty Shirazis). See Randall L. Pouwels, *Horn and Crescent*, 49.

[41] 1809-10. At this time Pate was the strongest town in the Lamu archipelago (Nicholls, p. 61).

[42] This is the best articulation of the passage in the MSS. The emphasis on tranquility is significant because of the picture of constant political instability reflected in the passages above. In Nicholls' words, "no ruler of the last half of the eighteenth century avoided agitation by a rival claimant or other rebellious forces" (Nicholls, *The Swahili Coast*, p. 62).

[43] Cf. MS 321.

[44] 1812. This date recurs only in the Stigand and Heepe versions.

they came to the ships, some were stranded (by the tide). Then they stopped (and) fought (another) great batttle. Many men died, men of Mombasa and men of Pate, without counting. Out of the men of Pate, the important ones, without slaves and lowly people, (there were) eighty-one of "So-and-so, the son of So-and-so;" and (as to) the men of Mombasa, (those were) in addition.[45]

After that, the men of Lamu went to Arabia (and) asked for Sayyid Sa'id bin Sultan, (f. 12) (and) they gave him the land in the year 1228.[46] Thereafter Sayyid Sa'id bin Sultan bin al-Imam ruled over Lamu. And the kingdom of Pate extended (only) over the island of Pate.

(There) arose a second man from among the sons of Bwana Fumo Madi, Fumo Luti Kipunga. He fought Sultan Ahmad. (Later) Sultan Ahmad died of disease in the year 1230.[47]

(Then) reigned Fumo Luti wa Bwana Fumo Madi. And he was a man of great strength, brave and generous. It was during this time that the office of *shaykh* was held by Shaykh Mataka bin Shaykh Mubarak who reigned over Siu. He obtained guns and soldiers, and he was under the suzerainty of the sultan of Pate and on very good terms with the Mazru'i, the men of Mombasa,

---

[45] The dates offered for the battle of Shela vary from 1808-9 to 1812. For a brief overview of the events, see Marquerite Ylvisaker, *Lamu in the Nineteenth Century* (Boston: Boston University, 1979), 70-71. A more detailed study based on written sources and oral tradition by Patricia Romero is forthcoming. For the historical significance of the battle see Randall L. Pouwels, "The Battle of Shela: The Climax of an Era and a Point of Departure in the Modern History of the Kenya Coast," *Cahiers d'Études africaines*, 123, XXXI-3 (1991): 363-389.

[46] 1813.

[47] 1814-5.

until the year 1236.[48] (Then) trouble increased between him (and) the sultan of Zanzibar Sayyid Sa'id bin Sultan. Sultan Fumo Luti died, he died that year.

After him reigned Fumo Luti bin Shaykh bin Fumo Luti bin Shaykh wa Bwana Tamu Mkuu. And this is the one who was the father of Sultan Ahmad, the sultan of Witu. He reigned from dawn till after the mid-afternoon prayer.[49] The men of the town drove him out. He went to Siu together with the Mazru'i (and) afterwards he went to Mombasa.

(Then) reigned Sultan Bwana Shaykh wa Bwana Fumo Madi. He negotiated with Sayyid Sa'id bin Sultan, took Arabs into Pate, (and) they remained (there) three years. Afterwards the people of the town deposed him with the consent of Sayyid Sa'id bin Sultan at the date of the year 1239.[50] They installed Sultan Ahmad called Bwana Waziri wa Bwana Tamu wa Bwana Shaykh wa Bwana Tamu Mkuu. He was on very good terms with Sayyid Sa'id (and) reigned for two years. (Then) the men of the town deposed him (and) returned Bwana Shaykh wa Bwana Fumo Madi. He remained in power with the consent of Sayyid Sa'id bin Sultan for five years (and) died in the year 1247.[51]

Bwana Waziri returned to kingship. (Then) came Fumo Luti bin Shaykh who had gone to Mombasa, he and the Mazru'i; they captured Siu (and) attacked Bwana Waziri wa Bwana Tamu at Pate. And Bwana Waziri was at

---

[48] 1820-1. Cf. MS 321. This date occurs only in the two MSS.

[49] This is the best articulation of the passage in the new MSS. Stigand (p. 85) has the time span from 9 a.m. to 6 p.m.

[50] 1823-4.

[51] 1831-2.

one with Sayyid Sa'id bin Sultan, and Fumo Luti the aforesaid (was) at one with the Mazru'i (f. 13) [and] Shaykh Mataka bin Shaykh Mubarak, the *shaykh* of Siu.[52] They came to Pate with troops (and) attacked. The men of Pate seized the country of Siu (and) destroyed the city wall of Siu.

And Shaykh Mataka bin Shaykh Mubarak and Fumo Luti left Siu (and) fled to the mainland. After three days they returned to Siu with a strong force, captured the town of Siu (and) rebuilt the wall. Pate and Siu fought each other. Afterwards Fumo Luti died. Bwana Waziri united Siu and Pate, they came under his authority with the consent of Sayyid Sa'id bin Sultan bin al-Imam. After one year Sultan Bwana Waziri wa Bwana Tamu wa Bwana Shaykh wa Bwana Tamu Mkuu was killed by Sultan Fumo Bakr wa Bwana Shaykh wa Bwana Fumo Madi al-Nabahani.

He gained the kingship of Pate in the year 1250, one thousand two hundred fifty of the Hijra.[53] They were on very good terms with Sayyid Sa'id bin Sultan bin al-Imam, the sultan of Zanzibar, during (the latter's) reign.[54] (But) later (f. 14) he revolted, together with Shaykh Mataka. Sayyid Sa'id sent an expedition under the *amir al-jaysh*[55] who was Amir Hamad bin

---

[52] Shaykh Mataka, also known as Bwana Mataka, was a member of the Famau family who had men and weapons and managed to fight off Omani advances, sometimes with the help of their rivals the Mazru'i. See Marguerite Ylvisaker, *Lamu in the Nineteenth Century*, 76. Bwana Mataka's wife composed the well-known orally-transmitted poem *The Advice of Mwana Kupona upon the Wifely Duty* (Utenzi wa Mwana Kupona), ed. and trans. Alice Werner and William Hichens (Medstead, 1934).

[53] 1834-5.

[54] For the Arab role during this period of coastal history, consult Norman R. Bennett, *A History of the Arab State of Zanzibar* (London: Methuen & Co., 1978) and Reginald Coupland, *East Africa and Its Invaders* (Oxford: Clarendon Press, 1956).

[55] The Arabic term for "commander-in-chief."

Hamad al-Samar; he attacked Pate and Siu (but) failed (and) made peace.

After this arose trouble between the sultan of Pate and his (paternal) uncle Muhammad bin Ahmad wa Bwana Fumo Madi who seized the royal palace by force. Later came the men of Lamu together with a man of Sayyid Sa'id bin Sultan. They made a peace treaty between Sultan Fumo Bakr and Muhammad bin Ahmad; (the latter) was sent to stay at Siu, (and) Fumo Bakari remained at Pate.

Afterwards they quarrelled (and) fought for five years, Siu and Pate. After they were reconciled by Sayyid Sa'id bin Sultan, Muhammad bin Ahmad came to Pate; they came under the single administration of Fumo Bakari. Later Fumo Bakari seized him suddenly (and) killed him, in concert with a man of Siu.

Later Sa'id bin Sultan summoned Sultan Fumo Bakr. He went to Zanzibar. The Sayyid imprisoned Fumo Bakari on the advice of the men of Lamu for the reason of (his) killing his (paternal) cousin Muhammad bin Ahmad and for failing to obey the peace which was made between them by Sayyid Sa'id. At the date of the year 1262.[56]

Sultan Ahmad bin Shaykh bin Fumo Luti bin Shaykh wa Bwana Tamu Mkuu seized Pate with the consent of Sayyid Sa'id bin Sultan. He ruled with the consent of Sayyid Sa'id for two years. (Then) they fell out with the Sayyid. Sayyid Sa'id came to attack him. Amir Hamad bin Hamad landed at Faza (and) attacked Siu, and the Sayyid released Sultan Fumo Bakr (and) gave him an army together with the men of Lamu. They stayed at Mtanga Wanda.[57]

---

[56] 1845-6.

[57] Ras Mtangawanda provided the deep-water anchorage for Pate.

About then (f. 15) Sayyid Sa'id himself and Amir Hamad went to Faza; Sayyid Sa'id bin Sultan stayed at a place called Kijanga cha Mpunga, near Faza. Amir Hamadi came to Siu (and) built forts along the road between Faza and Siu. Amir Hamad went to Siu with troops, seized the *mtepe* boats which were in the harbor of Siu, turned them over, made barricades (and) attacked Siu. He saw much hardship while they were at war for a long time, (so) Amir Hamadi with some men went back to the forts to fetch a cannon. While he was on his way, the men of Siu rushed out on him suddenly, an *amir* of Shaykh Mataka, Hamad 'Umar, and the second *amir*, Hamad Ngoma. They fought on the road (and) killed Amir Hamadi, (then) went to the fort, attacked the Arabs who were in the fort (and) took the cannons and ammunition. And the troops that were at Siu did not fight.[58]

When the news came that Amir Hamadi was killed (and that) the army of the Sayyid was defeated and failed to take possession of Siu, Sayyid Sa'id, when he got the news of the death of Hamad bin Hamad, went to the ship without saying a word (and) went away to Maskat.

Next year he returned (and) placed Fumo Bakari at Faza, (and the latter) attacked Siu and Pate. At this time Shaykh Mataka died of disease.[59] There was discord among his sons, (each) wanted the shaykhdom; they submitted to the overlordship of the Sayyid: Muhammad and Abu Bakr, the sons of Shaykh Mataka.

The Sayyid gave Abu Bakr bin Shaykh Mataka troops together with

---

[58] Ylvisaker (p. 80) ascribes Mataka's success to a large number of Oromo fighters in his forces.

[59] The date of Mataka's death varies from 1848 to 1856. Ylvisaker, *Lamu in the Nineteenth Century*, p. 81 and note 71.

Sultan Fumo Bakari, (and) he went to attack Sultan Ahmad. Abu Bakr bin Shaykh Mataka went together with the *amir* of Fumo Bakari, Bwana Mkuu wa Hamad bin Baishi al-Nabahani. They entered Siu by night (and) fought until Abu Bakr and his men were defeated. The men of Siu chased them, captured Abu Bakr bin Shaykh Mataka (and) took him to Sultan Ahmad at Pate; he was killed by Sultan Ahmad.

Afterwards Shaykh Muhammad bin Shaykh Mataka took a stand on the side of Sayyid Sa'id bin Sultan. To him and Fumo Bakari Sayyid Sa'id gave a troop of soldiers and supplies. They fought Sultan Ahmad bin Shaykh till they drove him out of Pate in the year 1273.[60] He went to Kau.[61]

Siu, under Shaykh Muhammad bin Mataka, was on the side of the Sayyid. He (Sayyid Sa'id) gave him soldiers to build a fort. (Later) they quarrelled with a man of Sayyid Sa'id because the man of Sayyid Sa'id destroyed a boat shed which Shaykh Muhammad bin Shaykh Mataka had built in front of the fort. And Shaykh Muhammad destroyed the fort.

And about this time died Sultan Ahmad nicknamed Bwana Madushi, the father of Fumo Bakari, (later) the sultan of Witu. In his place ruled Sultan Ahmad nicknamed *Simba* ("the Lion"), sultan of Witu.

And before Shaykh Muhammad bin Mataka destroyed the fort of Siu, there had been trouble between him and Fumo Bakr bin Shaykh; Fumo Bakar drove him out of Pate, (and) he came to Lamu to [re]gain possession of Pate;

---

[60] 1856-7. For a relevant outline of politics following this date see Ylvisaker's chapter 6 "The Establishment of the Witu State and Other Activities 1856-1876," largely based on archival sources and interviews.

[61] Kau was situated so that the trade from the Pokomo and Oromo met on Ozi River with dhows ascending at the high tide (Ylvisaker, *Lamu in the Nineteenth Century*, p. 84).

when the great men of Pate saw his power and the acts committed by Shaykh Muhammad Mataka, they did not wish him to reign (and) they did not accept (him). (Then) he made war on them (but) the great men of Pate persisted. And they had no king, due to the advice of three men: Muhammad bin Bwana Mkuu al-Nabahani and Bwana Rehema bin Ahmad al-Nabahani and Nasir bin 'Abd Allah bin 'Abd al-Salam, the one who was director of affairs (*mudabbir al-umur*). They collected munitions, fought Shaykh Muhammad Mataka, (and) defeated him soundly; prominent men died, out of the *amirs* of Shaykh Mataka - Bwana Damila and Mawlana wa Sheye Kuli.

Shaykh Muhammad Mataka came to seek peace from Muhammad bin Bwana Mkuu because it was he who was the chief (elder) of the three men whom we named. They wished to offer him, Muhammad bin Bwana Mkuu, the kingship of Siu and Pate. He refused, saying: "I am an old man." They went to fetch Sultan Ahmad nicknamed *Simba* who was (then) at Kau.

The news reached the sultan of Zanzibar, Sayyid Majid bin Sa'id, (and) he sent his *wazir* Sayyid Sulayman bin Hamid by ship, [to] come urgently to Pate (and) crush the conspiracy. But by the time the ship arrived at Mandra, Pate had been seized by a man of Sultan Ahmad, Abu Bakr bin Hasan al-Buri who had come with this Nasir bin 'Abd Allah bin 'Abd al-Salam. When he received the news, Sayyid Sulayman bin Hamid returned to Zanzibar, and that was the time when Shaykh Muhammad Mataka destroyed the fort at Siu.

Later, (when) Sultan Ahmad arrived at Pate, all the people acknowledged him as king (including) Shaykh Muhammad Mataka and Mzee wa Sefu and Shaykh Shekuh and Muhammad Mote. In order to confirm Sultan Ahmad in regard to this kingship, all these people (formally) acknowledged him.

Sayyid Majid sent men of Lamu to Pate, to give counsel, together with Shaykh Muhi al-Din,[62] to request that Sultan Ahmad put soldiers at Pate. And this Shaykh Muhi al-Din, he was the one who had turned out the soldiers of the Sayyid from Siu, when they were defeated by Shaykh Muhammad Mataka. The soldiers were inside the fort of Siu; Shaykh Muhi al-Din took them out in peace, because this Shaykh Muhi al-Din was a man of Sayyid Majid bin Sa'id.

(f. 18) At the time he [went] with the soldiers to Zanzibar, Sayyid Majid became very angry that he had withdrawn soldiers from Siu; Shaykh Muhi al-Din took the blame when he saw Sayyid Majid fall into wrath. And this Shaykh Muhi al-Din had great cunning and much learning. He came to [Pate] with the best men of Lamu and Shaykh Ahmad and Shaykh 'Abd al-Rahman, sons of the shaykh of Pate, to persuade Sultan Ahmad on account of the friendship that was among them. He (Sultan Ahmad) agreed to place the soldiers after reluctance, rejecting the advice of his *wazir* Nasir bin 'Abd Allah, for (the latter) refused to take in the Arabs, even one man.

Later the people of Pate made an agreement with Mwana Jaha, the daughter of Sultan Fumo Luti Kipunga wa Bwana Fumo Madi (and) wife of Sultan Fumo Bakari bin Shaykh. At this time Fumo Bakari was in Lamu, with the consent of Sayyid Majid bin Sa'id, since the time he was driven out of Pate.

But every day they brought in soldiers and munitions, at night in secret. (When) at last Sultan Ahmad knew (that) the soldiers were many at Pate (and)

---

[62] The *Ḳāḍī* (judge) of Zanzibar who had previously lived at Lamu and Mombasa and had written the Arabic *Kilwa Chronicle*.

there was a plot, they attacked Sultan Ahmad suddenly, since they wished to seize him by a ruse. They failed because the people were of one mind with Sayyid Majid bin Sa'id except his *wazir* Nasir bin 'Abd Allah [bin] 'Abd al-Salam. They fought within the town of Pate a fierce war. Sultan Ahmad got away, he and Shaykh Muhammad bin Mataka went to Siu.

At Pate stayed the Arabs (who were) on the side of Sayyid Majid. They placed (their) ships on the sea. When the war became very fierce, Sayyid Majid bin Sa'id came himself. (f. 19) They besieged the island of Pate from the sea to block the ships. He placed a chain across the mouth of the Siu creek, the Kuyo. They fought for six months at sea and next to Pate. And on the side of Faza Mzee Sefu seceded (and) became a man of Sayyid Majid, through much cunning and many words.[63] Sultan Ahmad and Shaykh Muhammad Mataka experienced great distress.

And in the land of Siu arose dissent: some of the people loved Sayyid Majid because of the troubles they had suffered, and his men were *Sharif* Mawlana bin Abu Bakr and 'Isa bin Ahmad al-Somali. (When) they saw these (things), Sultan Ahmad and [Shaykh Muhammad bin] Shaykh Mataka sued for peace from Sayyid Majid, and he granted them peace. During peace negotiations Sultan Ahmad sailed secretly by night, went to the mainland (and) returned to Kau.

Shaykh Muhammad Mataka sent his son to the ship, Shaykh Bin Muhammad, and the Sayyid pardoned him (and) gave him great respect. (Then) the Sayyid sailed (and) went home to Zanzibar. Afterwards,

---

[63] Ylvisaker (p. 85) calls this leader of the Bajun "one of the most influential leaders in the Lamu area during the latter half of the nineteenth-century."

Muhammad bin Mataka went to Zanzibar to appear before Sayyid Majid. The Sayyid imprisoned him (and) sent him to the fort of Mombasa along with many (other) people. He died after three days.[64]

Sultan Ahmad was at Kau. The governor (*al-wali*) Sa'ud bin Hamad[65] was sent to seize him by a ruse (but) he failed. He (Sultan Ahmad) got away (and) went to Witu.[66] The *wali* Sa'ud bin Hamad returned to Lamu. He went to Faza (and) made arrangements to seize 'Umar Mataka and all the children of Shaykh Muhammad Mataka, they were seized at Siu (and) came to Lamu. 'Umar Mataka he imprisoned at Lamu. All the children he sent to the fort of Mombasa.

Afterwards Sayyid Majid ruled over all the Swahili (coast), no one could challenge him there. And Sultan Ahmad stayed at Witu under the suzerainty of Sayyid Majid, until the time of Sayyid Barghash bin Sa'id.[67] He wished to place soldiers at Witu with a flag (but) Sultan Ahmad (f.20) did not agree. Sayyid Barghash sent an expedition, it attacked Sultan Ahmad (but) failed; the *wali* Sa'ud bin Hamad made peace.

Sayyid Barghash returned the *wali* Sa'ud bin Hamad for the reason that he had made peace quickly and had not atacked him vigorously enough. Sayyid Barghash sent the expedition again under the *wali* Sa'ud bin Hamad. Sultan Ahmad took the protection of the Germans. At this time returned the

---

64 For a contemporary report see Guillain, *Documents*, 3:444-5.

65 Member of an influential Busa'idi family who provided several governors of Lamu. Sa'ud served as *liwali* until late 1884 (Ylvisaker, p. 128).

66 Ahmad was in his forties at this point (Ylvisaker, p. 86).

67 1870-1888.

expedition of Sayyid Barghash. Sultan Ahmad remained under the protection of the Germans who gave him some of the Swahili mainland. Sultan Ahmad died under this condition of protection in the year 1306.[68]

(Then) reigned Fumo Bakr bin Sultan Ahmad bin Shaykh, under the same condition, (but) there arose a conflict between him and the Germans. One man, called Küntzell, shot the porter of the city gate. There were soldiers (present), they attacked Küntzell[69] and the Europeans who had accompanied him, and killed them all without Sultan Fumo Bakari's order. When the soldiers saw their company dead, they did not wait for orders. And the people of Mkonumbi and of Wanda Muyu, when they received the news of the attack on the Europeans at Witu, they all attacked (and) killed all the Europeans who were there.[70]

Afterwards came the Illustrious Administration of the English. They wished to make justice (and) demanded the people of Mkonumbi and the people of Wanda Muyu, in order to bring them to trial. Sultan Fumo Bakari did not consent to surrender them. They attacked him, sending an expedition in boats to Mkonumbi and Wanda Muyu and Kilimani (f. 21) and Ndapi and Nyando za Pwani. They shot from cannons (and) set [houses] on fire.

---

[68] 1888-9. Sultan Ahmad died in early 1889. He was then about seventy years old (Ylvisaker, p. 142).

[69] Andreas Küntzel, also spelt Künzel, a German planter and entrepreneur. On the Küntzel affair see Voeltzkow, *Reise in Ostafrika* I/2, pp. 83-84, and Ylvisaker, pp. 149-151. The case became the subject of a Reichstaf investigation.

[70] Only one man (Menschel) escaped the massacre and later guided the punitive expedition, Voeltzkow, p. 84.

Then on the night of 11 Rabi' al-Awwal of the year 130[8][71] the men of Witu fought on the Kipini road with the men of the Illustrious Administration; the men of Witu suffered defeat. Then on the morning of 12 of the month Rabi' al-Awwal of the year 1308[72] they attacked Sultan Fumo Bakari at Witu (and) drove him out by force. Sultan Fumo Bakari went to Jongeni.[73]

Witu was taken over by the Illustrious Administration.[74] Fumo Bakari remained at Jongeni until 28 of the month Jumad al-Awwal of the year 1308[75] (when) he died.[76] His brother Bwana Shaykh bin Sultan Ahmad occupied his place. After three days a conspiracy arose, he was seized by his brother Fumo 'Umar[77] and Avutula wa Bakhiru.[78] Bwana Shaykh ya-Sultan Ahmad was imprisoned.

---

[71] 25 October 1890. The MS mistakenly has 1309 here but 1308 later.

[72] 27 October 1890. Ironically, 12 Rabi'al-Awwal is a Muslim holiday (birthday of the Prophet Muhammad, celebrated in *mawlidi* ceremonies).

[73] Ylvisaker (p. 154) states that Jongeni had existed in 1889 but apparently was a newer settlement.

[74] Apparently, the narrator means the Imperial British East Africa Company which took over Witu in March 1891.

[75] 9 January 1891.

[76] He was reportedly poisoned by the chronicle's narrator Bwana Kitini, his nephew (Ylvisaker, 153).

[77] Bwana Kiniti's father, whose title was reduced to *Shaykh* and authority largely limited to Jongeni; it ended in 1895 with the establishment of British Protectorate.

[78] Voeltzkow calls Avutula (Avatula, Futula) a Boni (p. 85), but Ylvisaker (p. 88) states that he was a Bajun of part-Somali ancestry. He rose to prominence in the 1860s through command of hundreds of Waboni and *watoro* warriors. Avatula wa Bahero died in late 1892 or early 1893 (Ylvisaker, p. 155).

(Then) reigned Fumo ‘Umar bin Sultan Ahmad bin Shaykh. (Things) became the way they were between him and the Illustrious Administration.

As to the last king to rule Witu, it was Sultan Fumo ‘Umar the aforesaid, and the last to rule Pate was Sultan Ahmad, the sultan of Witu, nicknamed *Simba*. And the one who ruled first was Sulayman bin Sulayman bin al-Muzaffar al-Nabahani, Imam al-‘Arab.

This is the account of the Nabahans who came to the Swahili (coast) and their history. (There) reigned thirty-one kings and one woman, as we have mentioned above twice.

We have transmitted this from Muhammad bin Fumo ‘Umar al-Nabahani, nicknamed Bwana Kitini, and he received it from his grandfather Muhammad bin Bwana Mkuu al-Nabahani, nicknamed Bwana Simba, who was very reliable in regard to the accounts of the past and their pedigrees, such as we have mentioned above. Salih bin Salim bin Ahmad bin ‘Abd Allah bin Muhammad bin ‘Abd Allah Ba Sharahil wrote this in his own hand.

(f. 22) These are the accounts of Pate and its wars and the pedigree of the Nabahans. We have transmitted this previously from Muhammad bin Fumo ‘Umar, and he transmitted it from his grandfather Muhammad bin Bwana Mkuu al-Nabahani, the chief of the elders of Pate.

For the information of the humblest beggar of Allah the Most High, Salih bin Salim bin Ahmad bin ‘Abd Allah bin Muhammad bin ‘Abd Allah Ba Sharahil in his own hand.

MS 321

This MS was transcribed from a photocopy; its original was written in a lined school notebook. The text is contained on pp. 37-24 (the reverse pagination is due to a discrepancy between European and Arabic styles of writing). On page 23 of the same MS a genealogical chart, by a different scribe, is contained, identical to that sketched on f. 17 (21) of MS 309 and on p. 29 of MS 358. It is reconstructed in Appendix 1 of the present volume. The photograph reproduces what claims to be a copy made by Salih bin Salim bin Ahmad and is dated 3 February 1925 (because of the paper used it is more likely that this was a copy of a copy). That, in turn, claims to be a copy of another version, scripted by Salih bin Salim bin ʻAbd Allah Sharahil (apparently the same person as in MS 177) on 6 Safar 1318/1900 for the Illustrious Infant (*al-walad al'azīz*), a possible mistake for "Illustrious Liwali" (cf. MS 344, but the same reading is found also in MS 358, p. 26). The patron is identified as a member of the Nabahani family, Muhammad bin Ahmad bin Sultan bin Fumo Bakr bin Shaykh bin Bwana Fumo Madi wa-Simba or Sultan Muhammad bin Abu Bakr bin Bwana Mkuu bin Abu Bakr bin Ahmad bin Muhammad bin Abu Bakr bin Muhammad bin ʻUmar bin Muhammad bin Ahmad bin Sulayman bin Sulayman bin Muzaffar Nabahani.

Almost as closely related to the Hollis-Werner text as MS 177, this MS seems to be highly reliable. However, the sequence of rulers between 900 A.H. and 973 A.H. (p. 35) differs from that in MS 177; on p. 34 the names of the rulers ascending in 1100 A.H. and 1103 A.H. differ from those in MS

177 but are identical to the forms in MS 344. Some readings on p. 32 differ from both MS 344 and MS 358. The identification of the Pate delegates in the negotiations conducted by Shaykh Muhi al-Din (p. 26), absent in the Werner and Heepe versions, differs from that given in MS 177, f. 18. A passage on p. 30 concerning an Omani attack on Pate offers the clearest reading among the accounts of the episode, but the whole of page 29 was missing in 1975. Among its other special features is the use of the ethnonym *Wa-Pate* on p. 26, naming the *liwali* of Sayyid Barghash sent against Sulṭān Ahmad "Sa'id bin Hamad bin Sa'ud" (also p. 26; cf. "S'ud bin Hamad" in the Hollis MS[1]), and attaching the title *Imām al-'Arabī* to the name of the Nabahani founder (p. 24). The town called elsewhere Kitaka is named Kitoki, and the pronunciation is confirmed by the use of a long vowel on p. 32 (see also MSS 344 and 358).

The text is in Ki-Amu. Among the orthographic distinction of this MS is the use of *kāf* with two dots above the top strike for *ch*, more commonly rendered with *tā'*. On the other hand, the scribe rarely uses *pā'* with three dots for *p*, commonly resorting to *bā'* for both *p* and *b* sounds. In another respect, the MS reads more easily than MSS 177 because the *n* sound is more consistently recorded with *nūn*. Occasionally, words were missed in copying; in other instances the final words of a line were repeated at the beginning of the new line and on p. 26 almost a whole line was repeated before the scribe realized his mistake. The writer's Arabic imperfections show up especially in the name of the Islamic month *Rabī' al-Awwal* (see p. 25). Also noticeable is the substitution of *hā'* for *ḥā'* in Arabic words, and (more extraordinarily) of *'ayn* for *hamza* in *amīr*. The Arabic text is reproduced without changes.

---

[1] Werner, *op. cit.*, pp. 404/405.

Obvious mistakes, ligatures, missing words and repetitions are marked with an asterisk *. The length of MS pages made it impossible to accommodate each page of the Arabic transcript on the computer-generated page. Page breaks are indicated with two slashes //. Corrections and editorial conjectures are placed in brackets in the transcript. The translation has conjectured words in brackets; those added to ease the flow of the text are placed in parentheses.

Awali al-mubdī al-wāṣil bandari Pateh

al-Hijra 600.

AKHBĀR PATEH.

(p. 37) Hāhunā Sulaymān bin Sulaymān [bin] Muẓaffar al-Nabāhānī. M(w)andu wa-k(w)anda kuja Pateh Nabahānī ni-Selemāni bin Sulaymān bin Muẓaffar Nabahānī na-(n)duze wawīli ʻAlī bin Sulaymān nā ʻUthmān bin Sulaymān. Nā huyu Sulaymān bin Sulaymān al-madhkūr (n)diye alo‿kuwa sulṭāni, na-ye alikuwa sulṭāni akisa kutawali bara yā li-ʻArābu al-ʻArabī, akayā Pate sulṭān al-madhkūr k(w)a-tārīkhi sanati 600 min ʼl-Hijr kuyā k(w)ake Pate. Kataka ʻarūsi k(w)a-mfalume wa-Pateh katika hao-ali‿Batawī, na-ye Sulṭān Sulaymān bin Sulaymān ni-mtu maʻrūfu, mfalume wa-Pate akamu‿uza binti yāke. Na-dasituri yōte yā Sawaḥīli hata sa‿sa mtu akuoleyāye kijāna **ch**ako, akisa siku sabʻa za harūsi hē(n)da kum(w)a‿(n)galia mkēwe (n)yūmbanih mk(w)e babā wa-mke wake, kawā‿mpea watu. Huyu Sulaymān bin Sulaymān (n)diye mfalume wēno aka‿mpa ufalume wake alo‿kuwa nao, aka‿tawali Sulaymān.

K(w)alinā mūyi hīt(w)a Kitoki i(n)yo yā jazira yā Pateh katika maṭilaʻi yā-Pate na-Siu hata‿kuwa mji. Waliko mji mgini hīt(w)a Sha(n)ga katika maṭilaʻi yā-Pate nā Fāza waliko mji we(n)yewe wa-**P**aza al-Mafāzī. Ikaketi miji hiyo yōte ika‿keti yōte taḥati yā Sulṭān Sulaymān bin Sulaymān, nā Mānda k(w)alinā mfalume mbali na-ye ona (n)guvu sāna. Akafa Sulṭān Sulaymān bin Sulaymān sanati 625 al-Hijr. Akakhalifu zijāna wawīli

Muḥammad nā Aḥmad, Muḥammad ‘umri wake (n)yaka ‘ishirīni nā Aḥmad ‘umri wake (n)yaka khams[a]t[u] ‘ashara.

Akatawali Muḥammad bin Sulaymān bin Sulaymān ba‘ada yā babake. Ikawa khitilafu yeye na-watu wa Sha(n)ga, kapijana na-miji kiyā‿vunda kabisa. Nā ba‘aḍi yao wakayā Pate na-wa‿(n)ginewe ḳabila yao Kinā‿(n)da(n)gu wakakimbiā wasiyuwe‿kane mahāla walo kimbilia. Hata siku zikipita ikayā khabāri k(w)ā Sulṭān Muḥammad bin Sulaymān nā hao watu we(n)dao kuwenda wakam(w)a(m)bia wale washiwo tume‿waona katika m(w)ītu. Sulṭāni kapeka watu kawa‿a(n)galia kawa‿dirika wame‿fa(n)ya zijūmba (n)dani yā m(w)ītu. Sulṭān Muḥammad bin Sulaymān kawa‿sameḥe kawarudisha mahāli pao. (N)diyo aṣili yā mūi wa-Siu. Wakayā na-Wa‿Sawaḥīli wa(n)gine wakaketi wote wakayā na-Wa‿Famau wakaketi wote wakawa WaFamau (n)dio waku[u] wa-Siu katika ṭa‘a yā Sulṭān Muḥammad bin Sulaymān. Akafa sanati 650.

Akatawali (n)duye Sulṭān Aḥmad bin Sulaymān. (p. 36) Aka‿amirisha sāna arḍi yā Pate akaje(n)ga majumba kafanya na-mashāmbah asipiji mahāli kafa sanati 660.

Katawali kijāna **ch**a-nduye ina lake Aḥmad bin Muḥammad bin Sulaymān akaketi na-watu k(w)a-uzuri sāna kama sīra za ‘ami zāke ku‘amirisha mji wa-Pate nā-mashāmbah hata sanati 700 akafa. Akakhalifu zijāna wangi.

Katawali kijāna **ch**ake Sulṭān Muḥammad bin Aḥmad bin Muḥammad bin Sulaymān. Akaketi na-watu k(w)a-wēma sāna. Watu wa-Fāzah wakakhalifu akawa‿pija kawatia katika ṭā‘a ba‘ada ya-zita zingi hata alipo‿washi(n)da. Akayā futaḥi na-Ma(n)dra kai‿tamalaki k(w)a-zita na-ḥīla k(w)āni alina (n)guvu sāna sulṭāni wa Māndra ya-māli na-watu. Aka‿ivunda kabisa na-watu wa(n)gine kawaeta Pate na-ba‘ḍi wa‿kat‿oa nyika wakakimbilia kūla mahāli wa(n)gine wakaja Shēlah waka(n)giā katika ḥimāya ya-watu wa-

Lāmūh. Sulṭān Muḥammad bin Aḥmad al-madhkūr kawataka watu wa-Lāmūh wakaiza kuwa‿toa. Na-wa(n)gine wakē(n)da Malī(n)dī na-ba'aḍi ya-buldani. Sulṭān Muḥammad bin Aḥmad akawa‿andama sāna hao waliyo‿kūja Shēlah, watu wa-Lāmūh wakaiza kuwatoa ḳaṭa'an. Maneno hiyo ya-shi‿isa Sulṭān Muḥammad akafa sanati 732.

Katawali kijāna **ch**ake ufalume Sulṭān 'Umar bin Muḥammad bin Aḥmad bin Muḥammad bin Sulaymān. Akai‿rejea maneno ya-baba-wake k(w)a-watu wa-Lāmūh kawataka watu wa-Māndra, watu wa-Lāmūh wakaiza kuwatoa kawa‿pija zita, wakataka amāni watu wa-Lāmūh wakawa katika ṭa'a Sulṭān 'Umar bin Muḥammad. Zikazidi (n)guvu akapija jumla ya-miji yā Sawaḥīli: Ozi, Malī(n)dī, Kiwayū, Kitao, Miya, Imīdhī, Watāmu kasiki‿liyā Kirīmbā. Miji yōte kai‿tamalāki ta(n)gu Pate ḥata Kirīmbā, kula mji kaweka mtu akiḥukumu. (N)diyo aṣili ya-hao majūmbe liyo‿ko-mirīma wote. Ma'ana yāke ni-wa‿tūm(w)a wa Yūmbē na-hiyo "yūmbe" ma'a‿na ni-yūmba ya-mfalume wa-Pate.

Na-janibu ya-maṭila'i katama‿laki ḥata Warshaykh. Akenda kupija zita ta(n)gu Kiwayū nā Ṭūla nā Ṭuwala nā Shu(n)g(w)aya na-banadīri zote Bārawa nā Marika nā Muḳudishū. Hapo Muḳudishū kaweka al-wālī jami'i yā ḥukumu za banadiri zikao Muḳudishū. Aka‿'ishi nā nti zote hizi katika ṭa'a yāke ila U(n)guja haku‿tawali, na-waḳati huu U(n)guja haikuwa nti kuub(w)a zamani hizo. Nā huyu Sulṭān 'Umar alik[ip]e(n)da zita na-ku‿penda ra'iya nā ra'iya wakimpe(n)da, ikat(w)ā'a (n)guvu sāna nti yā Pate. Akafa Sulṭān 'Umar sanati 749. Kakhalifu zijāna wawīli Muḥammad nā Aḥmad.

Katawali kijāna mkuuh Sulṭān (p. 35) Muḥammad bin 'Umar bin Muḥammad bin Aḥmad bin Muḥammad bin Sulaymān. Wala hapakuwa na-zita [katawali] ufalume wa-babāke k(w)ā-amani, na-ye alikipenda sāna māli yā biyashara akisafirisha nā-zombo zake Hindī kufa(n)ya biyashara na-ye alina bahti sāna yā māli. Na-mara mōya alimsafiri‿sha kijāna **ch**ake kapata kisiwa katika bāhari kapata ma'adini yā feḍa kayā nayo Pate kafa(n)ya watu kuyā fa(n)ya kazi ma'adini kapata māli ma(n)gi sāna yākazidi māli katika nti yā Pate hata wakafa(n)ya zitara za feḍa nā (n)gazi za feḍa na-zombo zi(n)gi za feḍa. Na-ye mfalume akafa sanati 797. Akakhalifu zijāna wa(n)ne B(w)ānah Mkuuh nā Aḥmad nā Abū Bakr nā 'Umar.

Akatawali (n)duye Sulṭān Aḥmad bin 'Umar bin Muḥammad bin Aḥmad bin Muḥammad bin Sulaymān. Akaketi na-watu k(w)ā amāni na-siyara njema nā jami'i ya-watu. Akafa.

Akatawali Abū Bakr bin Muḥammad bin 'Umar bin Muḥammad bin Aḥmad bin Muḥammad bin Sulaymān. Kaketi sāna nā jami'i ya-watu nā-miji yōte katika ṭa'a yāke bilā khilafu. [Akafa] sanati 875 na-ye ali‿khalifu zijāna ziwīli Muḥammad nā Aḥmad.

Akatawali ba'ada babāke Muḥammad bin Abū Bakr bin Muḥammad bin 'Umar bin Muḥammad bin Aḥmad bin Muḥammad bin Sulaymān. Wakati wake wakaja WaZu(n)gu Portuka‿li katika m[i]ji ya-Sawaḥili yōte kaketi Mombāsah wakafa(n)ya (n)gome, nā janibu yā Pate wakaje(n)ga Ndōndo. Watu wa-barāni wakawa‿fūta wakawapa māli wakawa katika ṭa'a yao. Wakamua‿riḍi nā mfalume katika nti yā Pate waka‿mpija zita mfalume k(w)a-janibu yā Shi(n)dakasi wakawaka nti yā Pate p(w)āni k(w)a-ma'ana yā tūpe k(w)a-hīli yā kupija mūi wa-Pate wasiweze wakapa‿tana k(w)ā amāni wakafa(n)ya mkitabu wa-sharuti zao. Wakaketi Pate WaZu(n)gu wa‿kafa(n)ya furuḍa k(w)a-jina lao WaZu(n)gu wale **ch**amkuwa "fandika." Wakafa(n)ya na-ma(m)bo ma(n)gi katika kisiwa **ch**a-Pate. Akafa sulṭāni sanati 900. Akakhalifu zijāna wawīli B(w)ānah Mkuuh nā Abū Bakr.

Akatawali ufalume Sulṭān Abū Bakr bin Muḥammad bin Abū Bakr bin Muḥammad bin Aḥmad bin Muḥammad bin Sulaymān ba'ada yā babāke al-madhkūr. Akaketi na-watu sāna akatuza(n)ya k(w)ā amāni kama ḳa'di-yā babāke. Akafa sanati 940, kusipadi‿liki ya(m)bo na-ye kakhalifu zijāna wawīli Aḥmad wa-Muḥammad.

Katawali 'ami yao ufalume B(w)ānah Mkuuh bin Muḥammad bin Abū Bakr bin Muḥammad bin 'Umar bin Muḥammad bin Aḥmad bin Muḥammad bin Sulaymān. Ikawa khitilafu na-WaZu(n)gu lakini pasiwe nā zita. Ikawa fitina siku (n)yi(n)gi, akafa sanati 973. (p. 34) Akakhalifu kijāna mmōya hīt(w)a Abū Bakr.

Akatawali Muḥammad bin Abū Bakr bin Muḥammad bin 'Umar bin Muḥammad bin Aḥmad bin Muḥammad bin Sulaymān. Akaṣilihīna na-WaZu(n)gu wakat(w)ā'a ba'ḍi yā miji. Akafa sanati 1002. Akakhalifu kijāna mmōya hīt(w)a Abū Bakr asitawali.

Katawali Abū Bakr bin B(w)ānah Mkuuh bin Muḥammad bin Abū Bakr bin Muḥammad bin 'Umar bin Muḥammad bin Aḥmad bin Muḥammad bin Sulaymān. Akaketi na-WaZu(n)gu kama siyara yā-wazee wake walota(n)gulia, na-ufalume wakupu(n)gua (n)guvu. Akafa sanati 1041. Akakhalifu B(w)ānah Mkuuh nā Abū Bakr k(w)a-[j]īna la-babake.

Akatawali Abū Bakr bin Muḥammad bin Abū Bakr bin Muḥammad bin Abū Bakr bin Muḥammad bin 'Umar bin Aḥmad bin Muḥammad bin Sulaymān. Ikawa khitilafu na-WaZu(n)gu wakapijana kawa‿vunda WaZu(n)gu k(w)a-zita zikuu sāna. Ba'daye zikayā tena zita za-WaZu(n)gu wakapijana mūi wa-Pate k(w)a-mizi(n)ga wakaziweya nā ndia k(w)ā bāharini kusipiti **ch**ombo. Watu wakaona mashaka wakafa(n)ya amāni. Akafa mfalume sanati 1061. Akakhalifu zijāna wawīli B(w)ānah Mkuuh nā Aḥmad.

Akatawali B(w)ānah Mkuuh wa-B(w)ānah Bakr wa-B(w)ānah Mkuuh bin Muḥammad bin Abū Bakr bin Muḥammad bin ʻUmar bin Muḥammad bin Aḥmad bin Muḥammad bin Sulaymān. Akapatana na-WaZu(n)gu sāna na-ye alikipe(n)da sāna kuketi Lāmūh hata musimu kupita Lāmūh akafa(n)yā nā harūsi k(w)a-watu wa-Lāmūh.

Na-katika waḳati hunu WaFamāu wa-Siu wali‿toka katika ṭaʻa yāke, akawa‿pija akau‿vunda na-mji wa Siu kashika na-watu wa(n)gine kawatia Pate. Mkūb(w)a wa-Siu aka‿kambia ake(n)da (N)dō(n)do k(w)a-Portugāl kat(w)a'a himāya. Mkūb(w)a wa-WaZu(n)gu akaja Pate k(w)ā mfalume, awa‿sameḥe watu wa Siu. Mfalume kawa‿sameḥe kawa‿rejeza mahāli yao Siu katika amāni.

Baʻada yāke Portugāl akafa(n)ya ḥīla akaja Pate k(w)a-marikabu akamtaka mfalume ke(n)da marikabuni. Asine(n)da akampeka bin ʻami yāke B(w)ānah Mkuuh yeye na-watu wa-Pate. WaZu(n)gu wakawa‿tukua katika marikabu asirudi mtu hata mmōya. Baʻada-yā hayo mfalume kawapija WaZu(n)gu k(w)a-janibu zote, k(w)a-barāni na-zisiwani kawa‿toa janibu za-huko zote wakaki‿mbilia Mombāsah. Akafa mfalume sanati 1100. Akawata zijāna B(w)ānah Bakr nā B(w)ānah Mādī nā binti mmōya hīt(w)a M(w)ānah Darīni.

Akatawali Abū Bakr bin B(w)ānah Mkuuh bin Abū Bakr bin Muḥammad bin Abū Bakr bin Muḥammad bin ʻUmar bin Muḥammad bin Aḥmad bin Muḥammad bin Sulaymān. Akapija mfalume ghafu‿la nā Aḥmad (n)duye B(w)ānah Mkuuh aliyo‿tukū‿liwa na-WaZu(n)gu Portugāl k(w)a-upa(n)ga. Akafa mfalume sanati 1103.

Katawali yeye Aḥmad bin Abū Bakr bin Muḥammad bin Muḥammad bin Abū Bakr bin Muḥammad bin ʻUmar bin Muḥammad bin Aḥmad bin

Muḥammad bin Sulaymān. (p. 33) Alipo‿tawali kawandama Portugāl ikawa‿toa katika nti zake. Na-waḳati hunu M(w)ānah Darīni binti B(w)ānah Mkuuh wa-B(w)ānah Bakr, mkeh wa-B(w)ānah Mkuuh bin Abū Bakr aliyo‿tukūliwa na-Portugāl katika zamāni yā Sulṭān Aḥmad kuuwa (n)duze wawīli Abū Bakr nā B(w)ānah Mādī Sulṭān Ahmad, n[a]-mume wake aliyo‿tukūliwa kafa(n)ya huzuni sāna, zikipita siku nyi(n)gi kat[a]ka kuu‿ṭahiri kijāna **ch**ake B(w)ānah Tamu Mtoto aliyo‿mtukuwa Sulṭān Abū Bakr Imamu Huda kijāna wa-B(w)ānah Mkuuh aliyo‿te(n)da Goa.

Mfalume alipo‿pata khabāri aka'azimu yeye kufa(n)ya harūsi yā zijāna zake sababu kumu‿khini siwa-yā-sha(m)ba. Akapata khabāri M(w)ānah Darīni akam(w)eta m(w)e(n)yi Bayayi bin Mku, sharīfu katika Jamali Leyli alikuwa hudari sāna kazi yā u‿jume. Akataka amfa(n)yizi siwa ishi(n)de siwa yā Pate. Aka‿riḍīka ijāra riyali mia wa 'ishirīni. Kamupa pembe za ndovu akatauva mōja. Akafa(n)yā siwa k(w)a-sīri hata yalipo‿kuwa ṭayari kaiẓihirisha ghafula kai‿peka katika majūmba ya-jama'a zake. Kula mtu ikatuuza ya-kuu māli mi(n)gi sāna, fūndi kā‿iza ijāra akataka tuuzo. Akampa tuuzo akafa(n)ya 'arūsi yā kijāna **ch**ake.

Hata zamāni ya-B(w)ānah Tamu Mkuuh wakaja watu wa-Lamūh waka‿azimu siwa, akawapa waka‿itukua siwa yā aṣili hata baḥarīni, **ch**ombo kikafa mai akaghību. B(w)ānah Tamu Mkuuh akataka siwa yā M(w)ānah Darīni kam(w)ambiā, "Tupe sī‿si tutumiye katika mji yote." Akamjibu, "Kila ḳabīla aliyo‿tuza natumiye siwa ya(n)gu."

Nā M(w)ānah Darīni kawat[a] mtum(w)a ḥuri ayowao kuvuzia, akasema, "Huyu (n)diye m(w)e(n)yi kupija siwa hini, yeye na-nasila yāke, na-'ada yāke napowe riyāli tano na-(n)guo -yā kutuku‿lia siwa tena apowa sāmlī na-tuzo, kūla mtu awezao." Wakamku‿liwa nasla hiyo "Muyūmbe wa siwa."

Hata yeo wako watuwē ta(n)gu waḳati hunu ila li-ana hutu‿miwa nā jami'i yā ḳabāili yā Pate na-ma‿ḳabāili wa-mii mi(n)gine he(n)da kazima k(w)a-sharuti hizo kupowa muyū(m)be wa siwa.

Zikazidi fitina (n)dani yā mji na-katika ufalume wake nyaka saba'a ikawa mii mikavu, hakuna mvua, mfalume kai‿yūzulu. Katawali Sulṭān Abū Bakr bin B(w)ānah Tamu Mku wa-B(w)ānah Mtiti bin Aḥmad bin Abū Bakr bin 'Umar bin Aḥmad bin 'Umar bin Muḥammad bin Aḥmad bin Muḥammad bin Sulaymān. Akapatana sāna (p. 32) nā sulṭāni wa Masikati [al] Imamu Sayf bin Nabahāni al-Ya'rubī. Huyu sulṭāni wa-Pate ake(n)da 'Arabūni waka‿a(n)gana na-mfalume wa 'Arabūni, nā huyu mfalume wa-Pate kawa‿toa Portugāl siku yā jūma pīli kuu‿wa-watu katamalaki (n)gome yā Mombāsah.

Akamu'arifu [al-Imām] al-Ya'rubī, aka‿eta al-wālī katika Mazari', watu watatu Muḥammad bin 'Uthmān nā 'Alī bin 'Uthmān, (n)dūgu watatu siku‿muyuwa jina lake. Wakaya pamōya nā 'asikari [al] Imamu Sayf Nabahānī al-Ya'rubī. (N)diyo aṣili yā Mazari'.

Nā mfalume wa-Pate alinā siyara njema nā jami'i yā watu, aka‿'ishi nyaka aruba'īni katika ufalume wake, akafa sanati 1154. Akawata zijāna wa(n)gi, ba'ada yāke wasita‿wali zijāna zake.

Akatawali Aḥmad bin Abū Bakr bin Muḥammad bin Abū Bakr bin Aḥmad bin 'Umar bin Muḥammad bin Aḥmad bin Muḥammad bin Sulaymān. Akaketi k(w)ā wema nā-ra'iya, na-ye ali‿kipe(n)da kuweka (n)gombe wa(n)gi sāna. Akafa sanati 1160. Akakhalifu kijāna mmōya kam(w)eta B(w)ānah Gō(n)go asita‿wali.

Katawali B(w)ānah Tamu Mtoto amku‿liwao Imamu li‿Hudā wa-B(w)ānah Mkuuh alo‿tukuu‿liwa nā-Portugāl, na ina lake Abū Bakr bin B(w)ānah Mkuuh bin Abū Bakr bin Muhammad bin Abū Bakr bin Muhammad bin Abū Bakr bin Muḥammad bin ʻUmar bin Muḥammad bin Sulaymān. Katika waḳati hunu Imamu al-Yaʻrubī akae‿ta zita kupija Pate wasiweze, wakafa Waʻ Arabu wa(n)gi sāna, wakafa(n)ya amāni.

Baʻada yā hayo watu wa-Siu waka‿khalifu. Mfalume kawapija zita asiwa‿weze, watu wa Siu na-watu wa-Lāmūh wakafu(n)ga zita, wakayā Pate k(w)a-janibu yā-Kitōki, wakapijana watu wa-Pate zita zikuu sāna wakavundika watu wa-Lāmūh. Baʻada-ye mfalume wa-Pate akafu(n)ga zita k(w)a-bara nā baḥari, kawapija watu wa-Lāmūh kawatama‿laki. Baʻada yā hayo ali‿kuwa ḥali mōya mfalume wa-Patte na-watu wa-Lāmūh. Imamu al-Yaʻrubī akafa(n)ya shauri mōya. Waka‿muua mfalume sanati 1177.

Akatawali (n)duye m(w)āna‿mkeh Sulṭān M(w)ānah Khadījah binti B(w)ānah Mkuuh bin Abū Bakr bin Muḥammad bin Abū Bakr bin Muḥammad bin Abū Bakr bin Muḥammad bin ʻUmar bin Muḥammad bin Aḥmad bin Muḥammad bin Sulaymān. Ikawa fitina (n)yi(n)gi (p. 31) katika nti yā Pate. Ikawa wafalume wawīli, M(w)ānah Khadījah al-madhkūrah [na-]Sulṭān ʻUmar. Waka‿pijana katika mūi wa-Pate nyaka mitatu, Sulṭān ʻUmar ake(n)da barāni wakarejea Pate k(w)ā (n)guvu kuu sāna. Usiku wakapijana na-watu wa-M(w)ānah Khadījah kūla mtu mahāli pake. Akafa M(w)ānah Khadījah sanati 1187.

Akatawali B(w)ānah Mmkuuh wa-Shee. Raʻiya wakafa(n)yā udhia sāna asipate raḥa katika ufalume wake, hata sanati 1191 waka‿mu(n)gilia watu wa-mūi wakamuua k(w)a-tārīkhi hiyo.

Katawali B(w)ānah Fūmo Mādī ina lake Sulṭān Muḥammad bin Abū Bakr bin B(w)ānah Mkuuh bin Abū Bakr bin Muḥammad bin Abū Bakr bin Muḥammad bin Abū Bakr bin Muḥammad bin ʻUmar bin Muḥammad bin Aḥmad bin Muḥammad bin Sulaymān. Baʻada yā kutawali raʻiya wakataka kufa(n)ya fitina. Kawapija zita kawa‿shi(n)da kawa‿shika watu āruba'īni wawīli ni-(n)duze khaṣa, kawatinda kama mbūzi yuu na-sakafu damu. Ikashuka ndiani katika makūb(w)a, ikawa amāni, asitoki mtu tena kufa(n)ya fitina. Akatawali k(w)a-raḥa sāna hata akafa sanati 1224. Wala haku‿tawali mfalume kama yeye. Akakhalifu zijāna wa(n)gi sāna.

Akatawali Sulṭān Aḥmad bin Shaykh Fūmo Luṭi bin Shaykh bin B(w)ānah Mkuuh. Ikazidi fitina katika mji wa-Lāmūh, akawa‿pija zita yeye na-watu wa-Mombāsah Mazarī'i hali mōja, waka‿shuka Shēlah jeyshi kuu sāna wa-watu wa-Pate na-watu wa-Mombāsah. Watu wa-Lāmūh waka‿toka wakaja Shēlah wakapijana na-watu wa-Pate na-watu wa-Mombāsah zita za-watu wa-Lāmūh zikuu na-(n)guvu sāna. Jeyishi yā Pate na-ya Mombāsah wakavundika wakaki(m)bia majāhazini [n]ao, majāhazi ma(n)gi‿ne yaka‿jahabu **p**(w)āni wakasimama hapo wakapijana zita zikuuh sāna. Wakafa watu wa(n)gi sāna watu wa-Mombāsah na-watu wa-Pate hapana idadi, katika watu wa-Pate walo ma'arufu isu‿kuwa watūm(w)a na-watu [ḍ]a'ifu, watu waḥidi wa-thamānīni 81 fulāni bin fulāni we(n)ye wake yake(n)da māidha hayo Pate, na-watu wa-Mombāsah hawana idādi.

Ba'ada yā hapo watu wa-Lāmūh wake(n)da 'Arabūni wakamtaka Sa'īd bin Sulṭān bin 'l-Imām wakampa nti yā Lāmūh sanati 1228 alipo‿tawali Lāmūh. Ufalume wa-Pate wakasili‿ya katika **ch**a-Pāte nā banadiri. (p. 30)

[Ikazidi] fitina akatoka mtu wa-pīli katika zijāna wa-B(w)ānah Fūmo Mādī hīt(w)a Fūmo Lūṭi Ki**p**u(n)ga, akapijana Sulṭān Aḥmad kisa Sulṭān Aḥmad akafa k(w)a-maraḍi sanati 1230.

Akatawali Fūmo Lūṭi wa-B(w)ānah Fūmo Mādī na-ye alikuwa hudari sāna shuja'a karīmu. Na-zamani hizo Shaykh Matāka bin Shaykh Mubārak (n)dipo alipo‿tawali ushēkhe wa Siu akafa(n)ya 'asikari nā būnduki na-ye ni-katika ṭa'a yā sulṭāni wa-Pate na-ye alipata‿na sāna na-Mazuru'ī hata sanati 1236. Hata ikazidi fitina baina yāke Sulṭān Sa'īd bin Sulṭān Zinjibār. Akafa Sulṭān Fūmo Lūṭi al-madhkūr sanati 1270.

Ba'ada yāke akatawali Fūmo Lūṭi bin Shaykh bin Fūmo Lūṭi wa-B(w)ānah Tamu Mkuuh, na-huyu (n)diyo babāke Sulṭān Aḥmad[1] sulṭāni Wītūh. Akatawali aṣubuḥi hata ba'ada li-'aṣirī, watu wa-mūi wakamtoa, ake(n)da Siu pamōja nā-Mazuru'ī ake(n)da wote Mombāsah.

Akatawali Sulṭān B(w)ānah Shaykh bin B(w)ānah Fūmo Mādī. Akapatana Sayyid Sa'īd bin Sulṭān, akatia Wa'Arabu Pate, wakaketi nyaka mitatu. Ba'adaye watu wa-mūi waka‿muuzulu pamōya nā-shauri lā Sayyid Sa'īd bin Sulṭān bi-tārīkhi sanati 1239. Wakamtawa‿lisha Sulṭān Aḥmad amku[l]iwao B(w)ānah Wazīri wa-B(w)ānah Tamu wa-B(w)ānah Shaykh wa-B(w)ānah Tamu Mkuuh. Kapatana Sayyid Sa'īd bin Sulṭān katawali nyaka miwīli, watu waka‿muuzulu wakamrejea B(w)ānah Shaykh wa-B(w)ānah Fūmo Mādī. Akaketi katika 'ezi k(w)a-shauri yā Sayyid Sa'id bin Sulṭān nyaka mitano, akafa sanati 1247.

Akarejea B(w)ānah Wazīri katika u‿sulṭāni wake kayā B(w)ānah Fūmo Lūṭi bin Shaykh aliyo‿ke(n)da Mombāsah pamōya nā-Mazuru'ī, waka‿[sh]ika Siu wakapijana nā B(w)ānah Wazīri wa-B(w)ānah Tamu Pate. B(w)ānah Wazīri ni-shauri mōja nā Sayyid Sa'īd bin Sulṭān nā-Fūmo Lūṭi pamōya na-Mazuru'ī nā Shaykh Matāka mtu wa-Siu. Waka‿ja Pate k(w)a-zita wakapijana jeyishi ya-Siu ikavundika B(w)ānah Wazīri aka‿ishika nti ya-Siu akavunda na-ukuta wa-mūi. Shaykh Matāka bin Shaykh Mbāraka nā Fūmo Lūṭi wakaki‿mbilia barāni pamōya na-b‿ā'aḍi yā watu. Ba'ada yā siku kitete

[1] In MS incorrectly *bin sulṭāni*. This mistake is repeated in MS 358.

akarejea Siu k(w)a-zita ku[u] sāna, akawa‿toa watu wa-B(w)ānah Wazīri k(w)ā zita waka‿u‿shika wao mūi wa-Sīu waka‿je(n)ga ukutā wa-mūi, waka‿pijana Pate na-Siu, ikawa katika ṭa'a pamōya nā-shauri yā Sayyid Sa'īd bin Sulṭān.

[p. 29 of MS missing]

(p. 28)...ndiani watu wa-Siu wakamtokea ghafu‿la 'āmiri wa-Shee Matāka hītuuh Bin Mbāraka, Aḥmad 'Umar nā 'āmiri wa-pīli hītuuh Ḥamad (N)goma. Wakapijana wakamuua 'āmiri Ḥamādi, wake(n)da nā-bomani waka‿wapija Wa'Arabu wali‿yōko bomani waka‿t(w)ā'a nā mizi(n)ga. Nā-jeyishi ili‿yōko Siu hupijana.

Walipo‿pata khabāri yā kumba 'āmiri Ḥamādi miuao jeyishi yā Sayyid Sa'īd bin Sulṭān ikavundikam nao wali‿kuwa katika kuta‿malaki Siu, Sayyid Sa'īd bin Sulṭān kisa kupata khabāri ya-mūti yā 'āmir Ḥumād kao‿(n)doka ka(n)gia marikabūni asinene neno, ake(n)da zake Masikati.

M(w)aka wa-pīh akamuweka Sulṭān Fūmo Bakari Fāzah, akapija Siu na-Pate. Katika waḳati hunu akafa Shaykh Matāka k(w)a-maraḍi, ikawa khilafu k(w)a-zijāna zake, kūla mtu ataka ushēkhe, waka(n)gia katika ṭa'a yā Sayyid Sa'īd, Abū Bakr nā Aḥmad zijāna za Shaykh Matāka. Sayyid akampa Abū Bakr zit[a] pamōya Sulṭān Fūmo Bakari kumpija Sulṭān Aḥmad Siu. Ake(n)da Abū Bakr bin Shaykh Matāka pamōya nā amiri wa Sulṭān Fūmo Bakari amkuliwao Ḥamad wa-Bāishi Nabahānī ka(n)gia Siu u‿siku, wakapijana hata wakavu‿ndika watu wa Sulṭān Fūmo Bakari waka‿anda‿miwa ndi‿ani, waka‿mshika Abū Bakr bin Shaykh Matāka wakampeka Pate kau‿uwa na-Sulṭān Aḥmad.

Ba'adaye akasimāma (n)duye Shaykh Muḥammad bin Shaykh Matāka ṭarafu ya-Sayyid Sa'īd bin Sulṭān. Yēye Sulṭān Fūmo Bakari Sayyid Sa'īd bin Sulṭān kawapa zita na-'asikari na-gharāma wakampija Sulṭān Aḥmad hata wakamtoa Pate sanati 1273. Ake(n)da Kau. Siu ikawa Shaykh Muḥammad bin Shaykh Matāka ṭarafu yā Sayyid Sa'īd bin Sulṭān, aka‿mpa 'asikari kuwaka nā gereza. Wakateta na-mtu wa Sayyid Sa'īd bin Sulṭān k(w)a-sababu ali‿vunda pānda la-mtepe alo‿waka Shaykh Muḥammad Matāka iliwaka mbee yā gereza, na-Shaykh Muḥammad Matāka kavunda gereza.

Na-katika waḳati hunu alikufa Sulṭāni Aḥmad bin Shaykh Kau, babake Fūmo Bakari sulṭāni Wītūh. Akaketi mahāla pake Aḥmad amkuliwao "Simbah," sulṭāni Wītūh.

Na-ḳabula ya-Shaykh Muḥammad asiya‿vunda gereza lā Siu yalitoka fitina. Sulṭān Fūmo Bakari bin Shaykh akamtoa Pate k(w)a-zita, akayā Lāmūh akataka kuitamalaki Pate alipo‿ona (n)guvu zake na-ukuu wa Pate. Alipo‿ona kite(n)do mizo‿fa(n)ya Shaykh Muḥammad bin Shaykh Matāka misowe‿ataka kuwa‿tawali wasikiri, kawa‿pija zita wakasimāma wakūbuu wa-Pate. Walā hapana mfalume k(w)a-shauri lā watu watatu, Muḥammad bin Mkuuh Nabahānī nā-B(w)ānah Reḥema bin Aḥmad Nabahānī na-Nāṣiri bin 'Abd Allāh bin 'Abd Salām, (n)diye alo‿kuwa "mdabiri ali-umūri."

(p.27) Akaku‿sa(n)ya zana wakapijana Shaykh Muḥammad bin Shaykh Matāka waka‿mshi(n)da, wakafa watu mā‿'arūfu mā‿amiri makūuh, watu wawīli B(w)ānah Damīla nā Maulanā wa-Shee Kūli. Shaykh Muḥammad bin Shaykh Matāka kisa koona ma(m)bo hayā akaya kutāka amāni k(w)ā Muḥammad bin B(w)ānah Mkuuh Nabahānī k(w)ani-(n)diye aliye‿kuwa mkūb(w)a wao katika hao watu watatu tume‿zo‿ta(n)gulia kutaya. Akataka kumpa yeye Muḥammad bin Mkuuh sulṭāni wa Siu nā Pate, aka‿iza akajibu, "Mimi ni-mtu mzima." Wake(n)da kumt(w)a Sulṭān Aḥmad wa-Wītūh.

Kapeka watu Shaykh Muḥammad bin Shaykh Matāka na-watu wa Pate, wa‿kampeka Shaykh Nāṣiri bin ʻAbd Allāh bin ʻAbd Salām. Ke(n)da Kāu kamt(w)a Sulṭān Aḥmad al-mulaḳabu "Simbah" kaya na-ye Pate.

Khabāri ikasiki‿lia U(n)gūja Sulṭān Sayyid Mājidi bin Saʻīd bin Sulṭān k(w)ani Sayyid Saʻīd uta‿(n)guliye kufa sanati 1273. Kabula yā-hayo Sayyid kam[we]ta wazīri wake Sayyid Sulaymān bin Ḥamad k(w)a-marikabu ili kushika Pate ku[v]u(n)disha fitina. Marikabu akiwaṣili Ma(nd)ra Pate ime‿k(w)isa kushikuu mtu wa Sulṭān Aḥmad, Abū Bakr bin Ḥasani ʼl-Būrī, amekuya na-ye Nāṣiri bin ʻAbd Allāh bin ʻAbd Salām.

Akisa kupata khabāri hiyo Sayyid Sulaymān Ḥamad akarejeyā U(n)gūja, nā Shaykh Muḥammad bin Shaykh Matāka waḳati hunu (n)dipo alipo‿vunda gereza lā Siu. Akisa kuwaṣili Sulaymān bin Ḥamad Pate watu wakampa kuwa (n)diye sulṭāni Shaykh Muḥammad bin Shaykh Matāka kuna Mzee Sēfu nā Shaykh Shikuweh nā Muḥammad Mōte, akasitakiri k(w)ā Sulṭān Aḥmad ufalume wake.

Sayyid Mājidi bin Sayyid Saʻīd bin Sulṭān akapeka watu wa-Lāmūh Pate k(w)a-na‿ṣaḥa pamōya nā Shaykh Muḥui Dīni, kamtaka Sulṭān Aḥmad iweka ʻasikari wa Sayyid Pate. Nā huyu Shaykh Muḥui Dīni (n)diye alo‿toa ʻasikari wa sayyid katika gereza lā Siu alipo‿wapija Shaykh Muḥammad bin Shaykh Matāka; ʻasikari wali (n)dani yā gereza, ake(n)da Shaykh Muḥui Dīni kawa‿toa k(w)ā amāni k(w)ani ali‿kuwa mtu wa Sayyid Mājidi bin Sayyid Saʻīd katika mawazīri. Alipo‿ke(n)da U(n)gūja nā ʻasikari sayyid kafa(n)ya hasira sāna yuu lā Shaykh Muḥui Dīni, nā Shaykh Muḥui Dīni kat(w)āʼa daraka (p. 26) alipo‿muona Sayyid Mājid nā ghaḍabu (n)dipo ali‿po‿ke(n)deyā na-watu wa Lāmūh. Na-ye Shaykh Muḥui Dīni alinā ḥīla sāna na-ʻilimu nyi(n)gi, ake(n)da Pate nā -khiyāri ya-watu wa-Lāmū pamōya nā Shaykh Aḥmad nā Shaykh ʻAbd al-Raḥmān aye na-ye shaykh Pate. Wakanena nā Sulṭān Aḥmad akariḍīka ba'ada yā shida k(w)a-sababu yā ṣuḥuba yā shaykh Pate nā Shaykh 'Abd al-Raḥmān, aka‿khalifu shauri la-wazīri wake Nāṣiri bin 'Abd Allāh bin 'Abd Salām k(w)ani wali‿iza kutia Wa'Arabu hata mtu mmōya.

Watu wa-Pate wakafa(n)ya shauri mōya M(w)ānah Jāha binti Fūmo Lūṭi Kipu(n)ga wa-B(w)ānah Fūmo Mādī, mke wa Sulṭān Fūmo Bakr bin Shaykh. Waḳati hunu Sulṭān Fūmo Bakr woko Lāmūh tini yā shauri la Sayyid Mājidi bin Sa'īd ta(n)gu alipo‿tuuliwa Pate. Bāsi kula siku wakitia 'asikari k(w)a-siri na-zana usiku usiku. Alipowa khabāri Sulṭān Aḥmad ikawa fitina na-'asikari wame‿kuwa wa(n)gi Pate, wakampija Sulṭān Aḥmad ghufu‿la ba'ada yā-kisa ḥila kutaka kumshika wasi‿weze k(w)ani WaPate wote wali‿kuwa shauri mōya nā Sayyid Mājidi bin Sa'īd il[l]a wazīri wake Nāṣiri bin 'Abd Allāh bin 'Abd Salām. Wakapijana (n)dani yā mūi wa Pate akatoka Sulṭān Aḥmad yeye nā Shaykh Muḥammad bin Shaykh Matāka, wake(n)da Siu.

Pate waka‿shika Wa'Arabu nā baharini wakatia marikabu, zita zalipo‿kuwa zikuu sāna alipo‿kuya Sayyid Mājidi bin Sa'īd, kai‿ḥu[ṣuru] Siu na-Pate. Na-bahari kusipiti **ch**ombo **ch**o**ch**ote mā‿dau mitepe, wakapijana baharini wa**ch**enda barāni kut(w)a'a **ch**akūla na-ma‿jira yā-kurudi huwāna ḥai maiti. Sayyid Mājidi akatia silisili katika kān(w)a la-mto wa Siu Kūyo, kusipiti **ch**ombo, tena nao waliwa[o]na nyezi sita k(w)a-bahari na-k(w)a Pate. Na-jānibu yā Fāzah mzee Sēfu akakhalifu mtu wa Sayyid Mājidi bin Sa'īd k(w)ā ḥīla nyi(n)gi na-ma‿neno ma(n)gi. Akaona ẓīki sāna Sulṭān Aḥmad nā Shaykh Muḥammad bin Shaykh Matāka. Na-nti ya-Siu ikawa fitina, ba'aḍi ya-watu wampe(n)da Sayyid Mājidi k(w)a-sababu yā mashaka walo‿pata na-watuwe ni-hao Sharīf Mawlanā bin Abū Bakr nā 'Isa bin Aḥmad al-Somālī.

Alipo‿ona Sulṭān Aḥmad [nā] Shaykh Muḥammad bin Shaykh [Matāka] kama haya wakat[a]ka amāni k(w)a-Saydi Mājidi. Akawapa amāni, katika maneno yā amāni Sulṭān Aḥmad akasafiri usiku ake(n)da barāni akarejea Kāu. Ba'ada-ye Shaykh Muḥammad bin Shaykh Matāka akampeka kijāna **ch**ake, Shaykh Muḥammad bin Shaykh Matāka, ake(n)da marikabūni k(w)ā Sayyid Mājidi, nā Sayyid Mājidi kam‿sameḥe akampa na-'aṭayā (n)yi(n)gi. Sayyid Mājidi kasafiri karejea U(n)gūja, kisa Shaykh Muḥammad bin Shaykh Matāka ake(n)da U(n)gūja kumu‿wajihi Sayyid Mājidi. Sayyid akamshika kamfu(n)ga katika (n)gōme yā-Mombāsah na-watu, akafa Shaykh Muḥammad.

(p. 25) Na-ba'ada ya-siku Sayyid Mājidi akampeka al-wālī Sa'ūd bin Ḥamad kumshika Sulṭān Aḥmad Kau k(w)ā ḥīla nyi(n)gi, asiweze, kutoka Kau k(w)ā siri ake(n)da Wītūh. Al-wālī Sa'ūd bin Ḥamad akayā Fāza kumshika 'Umar Matāka Fāzah na-zijāna za Shaykh Muḥammad bin Shaykh Matāka kawashika Siu kawapeka (n)gomeni Mombāsah, 'Umar Matāka aka‿mfu(n)ga Lāmūh.

Ba'ada-ye Sayyid Mājidi akatamālaki Sawaḥīli zote, hakuna mtu wakumu‿'ariḍi, na-Suluṭāni Aḥmad kaketi Wītūh katika ṭa'a yā Sayyid Mājidi hata alipo‿tawali Sayyid Barghash bin Sa'īd bin Sulṭān. Akataka Sayyid Barghash kuweka 'asikari Wītūh nā bendera, Sulṭān Aḥmad asi‿riḍiki, kapeka zita kumupija asiweze akafa(n)ya amāni.

Na-ye al-wālī Sa'ūd bin Ḥamad haku‿mpija sāna zita, Sayyid Barghash kapeka zita zamāni za liwāli Sa'īd bin Ḥamad bin Sa'īd. Sulṭān Aḥmad akat(w)a'a ḥimaya k(w)ā Jaru‿mani, akampa na-ba'adhi yā bara ya-Sawaḥīli. Akafa Sulṭān Aḥmad katika ḥali hiyo yā ḥimaya sanati 1306.

Akatawali Sulṭān Fūmo Bakr bin Sulṭān Aḥmad bin Shaykh Nabahānī. Akaketi katika ḥali hiyo yā ḥimaya. Ikatokea fitina yeye nā Jarumani, mtu mōja hīt(w)a Kisili akampija bawabu wa-lā(n)go, kampija ghafu‿la ra‿ṣāṣi, wali‿kuweko ‘asikari kawa‿pija k(w)ā ra‿ṣāṣi nā ‘asikari wakampija Kisili nā WaZu(n)gu walo‿fuetene, nao waka‿ua WaZu(n)gu mi(n)-ghiri amri yā Sulṭān Fūmo Bakr. ‘Asikari walipo‿waona jami‘i zao wame‿kufa hawaku(n)gūja amri-yā sulṭāni, waka‿wapija WaZu(n)gu. Na-watu wa-Mkonūmbih na-Wanda‿mūyu walipo‿pata khabāri WaZu(n)gu wame-pijana wakau‿a-WaZu(n)gu waliyo‿kuweko.

Ba‘ada-ye ikaya dūla ya-Wa(N)gereza, wakataka kufa(n)ya inṣafi akawataka watu wa-Mkonūmbah na-Wanda‿mūyu, ma‘ana awatie katika ḥukumu. Fūmo Bakr asi‿riḍīki kuwa‿toa, wakampija zita Sulṭān Fūmo Bakr zikaya ma[sh]ua hata Mkonūmbih na-Wanda‿mūyu na-Ki‿limani [na-](N)yando‿za‿p(w)āni, wazipiji k(w)a-mizi(n)ga wakatia nā mōto hata leila 11 Rabi‘ [al-]awalā sanati 1308. Wakapijana watu wa- Wītūh katika ndia yā Kipīni, na-watu wa-dōla tukufu wakavu(n)dika watu wa-Wītūh hata aṣubuḥi siku yā jūma tatu m(w)ezi 12 Rabi‘ al-Awalā sanati 1308. Wakampija Sulṭān Fūmo Bakr wakamtoa Wītūh k(w)a-zita che(n)da Jo(n)geni.

Wītūh ikatamalaki‿wa nā dōla tukufu. Sulṭān Fūmo Bakari kaketi Jo(n)geni hata Jumāda Ulā sanati 1308 akafa. Akashika mahāla pāke (n)duye B(w)ānah Shaykh bin Sulṭān Aḥmad bin Shaykh Nabahānī. Ba‘ada siku chache ikawa fitina na-(n)duye Fūmo ‘Umar Nabahānī nā Avu‿tūla wa-Bāhiru, waka‿mfu(n)ga B(w)ānah Shaykh bin Sulṭān bin Ḥamad. (p. 24) Akatawali Sulṭān Fūmo ‘Umar na-wak(w)isa kutamalaki Pate Sulṭān Aḥmad wa-Wītūh.

Nā alo‿tamalaki k(w)anda Sulaymān bin Sulaymān bin Mu[ẓ]affar Nabahānī Imāmu li-‘Arabī. Hini (n)diyo khabāri yā Nabahānī kuya Sawaḥīli nā khabāri zao kama tume‿zo‿ta(n)gulia kutaya. Wamezotawali wa‿falume waḥidi wa-thalāthīni nā m(w)ānah mkeh mmōja, jumla ithinīni wa-thalāthīni min ghairi walo‿kitā‿wali wake‿uzuliwa wakarejea kuw[a]‿tawali.

Tume‿naḳīli haya k(w)ā Muḥammad bin Fūmo ‘Umar Nabahānī al-mulaḳab B(w)ānah Kitīni, na-ye ali‿naḳīli k(w)ā jādi yāke Muḥammad bin B(w)ānah Mkuuh Nabahānī amkuliwao B(w)ānah Simbah ali‿dhibi‿tishi‿ye sāna khabāri yā nasaba zao kama tume‿zo‿taja.

Katabah Sāliḥ bin Sālim bin ‘Abd Allāh Sharaḥīl bi-yadih 6 fī Safar sanati 1318. Nuḳilat hadhā li-l-walad al-‘azīz Muḥammad bin Aḥmad bin Sulṭān bin Fūmo Bakr bin Shaykh bin B(w)ānah Fūmo Mādī wa-Simbah Sulṭān Muḥammad bin Abū Bakr bin B(w)ānah Mkuuh bin Abū Bakr bin Aḥmad bin Abū Bakr bin Muḥammad bin Abū Bakr bin Muḥammad bin ‘Umar bin Muḥammad bin Aḥmad bin Sulaymān bin Sulaymān bin Mu[ẓ]affar Nabahānī.

Nuḳilat fī 1 Rajab sanati 1343. Katabah al-aḳal[l] Sāliḥ bin Sālim bin Aḥmad bi-yadih fī 3 Februūrī sanati 1925.

HISTORY OF PATE

The first beginning arrival at Pate harbor.
[The year] 600 of al-Hijra.

(p. 37) There (was) Sulayman bin Sulayman bin Muzaffar al-Nabahani. The first man to come to Pate of the Nabahani was Sulayman bin Sulayman bin Muzaffar Nabahani and his two brothers, 'Ali bin Sulayman and 'Uthman bin Sulayman. And this Sulayman bin Sulayman the aforementioned had been sultan; then al-Ya'rubi ruled the land of the Arabs. The aforementioned sultan came to Pate, on the date of the year 600 from the Hijra[1] was his coming to Pate.

He asked for marriage from the king of Pate among those al-Batawi.[2] And he, Sultan Sulayman bin Sulayman, (was) an important man, (so) the king of Pate married him to his daughter. And the custom of all the Swahili to this day (is that) a man takes your daughter (in marriage), (then) seven days after the wedding he goes to the house of his wife's father to see the father-in-law, to be given (gifts) by the people. This Sulayman bin Sulayman, that king gave him his kingship that had been theirs. (Thereafter) reigned Sulayman.

There was a town called Kitoki on the same island of Pate, east of Pate;

---

[1] 1203-4.

[2] The Swahili plural pronoun is followed here by the Arabic singular *Batawī* "Pate dweller," the name of the ruling clan.

and Siu was not yet a town. There was another city called Shanga, east of Pate. And Faza was a town by itself; the rulers of Paza (were) al-Mafazi. He reigned over all these towns, all these were under Sultan Sulayman bin Sulayman. And Manda had a separate king, and he had great power.

Sultan Sulayman bin Sulayman died in the year 625 of the Hijra.[3] He left two sons, Muhammad and Ahmad. Muhammad's age (was) twenty years, and Ahmad's age fifteen years. Muhammad bin Sulayman bin Sulayman reigned after his father. A conflict arose between him and the people of Shanga; he made war on the city (and) destroyed it completely. And some of these (people) came to Pate, and a separate (group) whose tribe (was) Kinandangu, fled (and) the place where they fled was not known. Then some days passed, and the news came to Sultan Muhammad bin Sulayman from the hunters (who) came and said to him: "Those unknown,[4] we have seen them in the forest." The sultan sent people to look for them, (and) they caught up with them; they had made huts inside the forest. Sultan Muhammad bin Sulayman forgave them (and) returned them to their (own) place. This is the origin of the town of Siu.

(Later) came other WaSwahili (and) they all settled. (Then) came the WaFamau (and) they all settled, (and) the WaFamau were the chiefs of Siu under the overlordship of Sultan Muhammad bin Sulayman.

He died in the year 650.[5] His brother Sultan Ahmad bin Sulayman[6]

---

[3] 1227-8.

[4] The form *shiwo* in the MS obscures the folk etymology of the toponym *Siu* being explained here. It is well shown above by the plural *wasiyuwekane* (*siyu*= "not know").

[5] 1252-3.

(p. 36) reigned. He governed the land of Pate very well, building houses (and) planting fields. He did not make war anywhere (and) died in the year 660.[7]

(Next) reigned the son of his brother, by the name Ahmad bin Muhammad bin Sulayman. He treated the people very well, following the example of his (paternal) uncle, building up the town of Pate and the farms, until he died in the year 700.[8] He left many children.

(Then) reigned his son Sultan Muhammad bin Ahmad bin Muhammad bin Sulayman. He governed the people in an excellent manner. (Then) the people of Faza seceded; he fought them (and) brought them under his authority after many battles, until he overcame them. He conquered Mandra (and) captured it through a military ruse, because the sultan of Mandra had great power (in terms) of money and men. He destroyed it utterly and carried off some people to Pate.

And a few fled into the wilderness (*nyika*) (and) ran away to all places; some came to Shela (and) put themselves under the protection of the men of Lamu. Sultan Muhammad bin Ahmad the aforesaid demanded them of the men of Lamu; they refused to surrender them. And some went to Malindi and other towns. Sultan Muhammad bin Ahmad pursued vigorously (the matter of) those who came to Shela. The men of Lamu refused to surrender them decisively. While this matter still lasted, Sultan Muhammad died in the year 732.[9]

---

[6] Properly, Ahmad bin Muhammad bin Sulayman.

[7] 1261-2. MSS 177 has 670.

[8] 1300-1.

[9] 1331-2.

His son ascended to kingship, Sultan 'Umar bin Muhammad bin Ahmad bin Sulayman. He returned to his father's case against the men of Lamu demanding the people of Mandra. The men of Lamu refused to surrender them. He made war on them; the men of Lamu sued for peace (and) submitted to the overlordship of Sultan 'Umar bin Muhammad.

He gained great power (and) conquered all the towns of the Swahili (coast)--Ozi, Malindi, Kiwayu, Kitao, Miya, Imidhi, Watamu--until he reached Kirimba. He gained possession of all the towns from Pate to Kirimba. In each town he placed (his own) man to govern. This is the origin of those *Majumbe* who are to be found on the whole coast (*mrima*). The meaning of this (word) is "slaves of the Yumbe," and this *yumbe* means the palace of the king of Pate.

And on the east side he gained possession as far as Warsheikh. He went to wage war, beginning with Kiwayu and (then against) Tula and Tuwala and all the harbors (*banadiri*): Brawa and Marka and Mogadisho. There at Mogadisho he placed a governor (*al-wali*), to govern all the harbors that were (near) Mogadisho. (As long as) he lived all these lands were under his authority, only Zanzibar he did not rule, and at the time Zanzibar was not a great country in this period. And this Sultan 'Umar was fond of war (and) he also loved his subjects, and the subjects loved him. The land of Pate held great power. Sultan 'Umar died in the year 749.[10] He left two sons, Muhammad and Ahmad.

The elder son reigned, Sultan (p. 35) Muhammad bin 'Umar bin Muhammad bin Ahmad bin Muhammad bin Sulayman. And there was no war, [he ruled] the kingdom of his father in peace, and he loved very much money

---

[10] 1348-9.

from trade. He sent voyages in ships to India to conduct trade, and he had great profit in money.

And one time he sent his son on a voyage; he came upon an island at sea, found a silver mine, came with (the ore) to Pate (and) made people come to work the mine. He obtained very great wealth; wealth (so) increased in the land of Pate that they made swords of silver and ladders of silver and many silver vessels. And this king died in the year 797.[11] He left four sons, Bwana Mkuu and Ahmad and Abu Bakr and 'Umar.

His brother Sultan Ahmad bin 'Umar bin Muhammad bin Ahmad bin Muhammad bin Sulayman reigned. He ruled over the people in peace and (observed) good custom toward all the people. (Then) he died.

(Next) reigned Abu Bakr bin Muhammad bin 'Umar bin Muhammad bin Ahmad bin Muhammad bin Sulayman. He ruled well over all the people and all the towns under his authority without discord. [He died] the year 875,[12] leaving two sons, Muhammad and Ahmad.

After his father reigned Muhammad bin Abu Bakr bin Muhammad bin 'Umar bin Muhammad bin Ahmad bin Muhammad bin Sulayman. In his time the Portuguese Europeans came to all the Swahili towns. They stayed at Mombasa (and) made a fort. And near Pate they built Ndondo. The people of the mainland obeyed them, paid them money, (and) accepted their authority. They harassed the king throughout the land of Pate (and) fought a war against the king on the side of Shindakasi. They built the ground of Pate from the beach by means of making hollows in order to attack the town of Pate. They

---

[11] 1394-5.

[12] 1470-1.

failed (and) agreed to peace (and) made a (written) document stating their conditions. The Europeans remained at Pate (and) made a customs-house; in their European language they called it "*Fandika*". They made many things around the island of Pate. The sultan died in the year 900.[13] He left two sons, Bwana Mkuu and Abu Bakr.

After his father, the aforementioned Sultan Abu Bakr bin Muhammad bin Abu Bakr bin Muhammad bin Ahmad bin Muhammad bin Sulayman ascended to kingship.[14] He ruled over the people well, prospering in peace, as (was) the practice of his father. He died in the year 940,[15] with affairs in order. And he left two sons, Ahmad and Muhammad.

Their (paternal) uncle[16] ascended to kingship, Bwana Mkuu bin Muhammad bin Abu Bakr bin Muhammad bin ‘Umar bin Muhammad bin Ahmad bin Muhammad bin Sulayman. There arose hostilities with the Europeans, but there was no war. The trouble lasted many days. He died in the year 973,[17] (p. 34) leaving one son called Abu Bakr.

(Next) reigned Muhammad bin Abu Bakr bin Muhammad bin ‘Umar bin Muhammmad bin Ahmad bin Muhammad bin Sulayman. He made peace with the Europeans, (and) they took some of the towns. He died in the year

[13] 1494-5.

[14] This order of succession differs from that described in MS 177.

[15] 1533-4.

[16] MS 177 calls him a "sibling" *ndugu*.

[17] 1565-6.

1002.[18] He left one son named Abu Bakr who did not reign.

(Next) reigned Abu Bakr bin Bwana Mkuu bin Muhammad bin Abu Bakr bin Muhammad bin 'Umar bin Muhammad bin Ahmad bin Muhammad bin Sulayman. He treated the Europeans according to the manner of his ancestors who had preceded (him), (but) the kingdom diminished [in strength]. He died in the year 1041.[19] He left Bwana Mkuu and Abu Bakr, named after his father.

(Next) reigned Abu Bakr bin Muhammad bin Abu Bakr bin Muhammad bin Abu Bakr bin Muhammad bin 'Umar bin Ahmad bin Muhammad bin Sulayman. There arose discord with the Europeans; they fought (and) he defeated the Europeans in a very powerful battle. After that came in turn an expedition of the Europeans. They attacked the town of Pate with cannon (and) cut off the roads from the sea to block the ships. The people saw hardships (and) made peace. The king died in the year 1061.[20] He left two sons, Bwana Mkuu and Ahmad.

(Next) reigned Bwana Mkuu wa Bwana Bakr wa Bwana Mkuu bin Muhammad bin Abu Bakr bin Muhammad bin 'Umar bin Muhammad bin Ahmad bin Muhammad bin Sulayman. He got along very well with the Europeans. And he loved very much to stay at Lamu, even the monsoon (season) he spent at Lamu. He contracted a marriage among the people of Lamu.

And about this time the WaFamau of Siu revolted against his authority.

---

[18] 1593-4.

[19] 1631-2.

[20] 1650-1.

He fought the town of Siu, seized some people (and) brought them to Pate. The chief of Siu escaped, went to Dondo, to the Portuguese (and) claimed protection. The chief of the Europeans came to Pate, to the king, to ask that he release the people of Siu. The king released them (and) returned them to their (former) place at Siu under safe conduct.

After that the Portuguese devised a stratagem. They came to Pate in a ship (and) invited the king to come aboard ship. He did not go (but) sent the son of his (paternal) uncle Bwana Mkuu, him and (some) men of Pate. The Europeans carried them off in the ship, (and) not even one man (ever) returned. After that the king attacked the Europeans from all directions, on the mainland and on the islands, (and) drove them away from these locations. They fled to Mombasa. The king died in the year 1100.[21] He had two sons, Bwana Bakr and Bwana Madi, and one daughter named Mwana Darini.

(Then) reigned Abu Bakr bin Bwana Mkuu bin Abu Bakr bin Muhammad bin Abu Bakr bin Muhammad bin ‘Umar bin Muhammad bin Ahmad bin Muhammad bin Sulayman.[22] The king was suddenly attacked with a sword by Ahmad, the brother of the Bwana Mkuu who had been taken away by the Portuguese Europeans. The king died in the year 1103.[23]

This (very) Ahmad bin Abu Bakr bin Muhammad bin Muhammad bin Abu Bakr bin Muhammad bin ‘Umar bin Muhammad bin Ahmad bin Muhammad bin Sulayman[24] reigned. (p.33) After he ascended, he pursued

[21] 1688-9.

[22] This name coincides with the one given in MS 344 but differs from that in MS 177.

[23] 1691-2.

[24] This pedigree is abbreviated in MS 177 but repeated in full in MS 344.

the Portuguese (and) drove them out from throughout his country.

And at this time Mwana Darini, the daughter of Bwana Mkuu wa Bwana Bakr, wife of the Bwana Mkuu bin Abu Bakr who had been taken away by the Portuguese before the time of Sultan Ahmad, whose two brothers Abu Bakr and Bwana Madi had been killed by Sultan Ahmad,—so (as) her husband had been carried away she grieved greatly. (Then, after) many days passed, she wished to circumcise her son Bwana Tamu Mtoto ("Junior") who was called Sultan Abu Bakr Imamu Huda, the son of Bwana Mkuu who went to Goa.

(When) the king received the news, he decided to make a celebration himself, for his own sons, in order to deny her the ceremonial horn. (When) the news came to Mwana Darini, she sent for Mwenyi Bayayi bin Mkuu, *Sharif* of the *Jamali Layli*, who had great skill in carving, (and) she requested that he make a horn superior to the horn of Pate. He accepted the wage of one hundred and twenty riyals, (and) she gave him elephant tusks to choose [the best] one. He made the horn in secret, (and) then she showed it suddenly (and) took it around the houses of her kin. Every man gave large offerings of much money, (so that) the master declined the wage (and) asked for the offerings; she gave him the offerings (and) made the celebration for her son.

Later, at the time of Bwana Tamu Mkuu ("Senior"), the people of Lamu came to borrow the horn; he gave it to them, (and) they carried the original horn to the sea. The ship sank in water (and) perished. Bwana Tamu Mkuu asked for the horn from Mwana Darini, saying to her, "Give it to us, so that we may use it in all the towns." She answered him, "Every clan who makes an offering may use my horn." And Mwana Darini set free a slave who knew how to blow (the horn). She said, "This is the chief beater of this horn, he and his descendants. And for his fee let him be given five riyals and a cloth to carry the horn, (and) besides give ghee and a present, from every man according to his means." And that family was called "the Heralds of the Horn," (and) to this day there are people (belonging) to it. From that time until now the custom of all the clans of Pate and the clans of other towns (has been) to come (and) to borrow [the horn] under such circumstances; the Heralds of the Horn are paid.

Mischief increased within the city, and during his reign for seven years there was drought in the city, there was no rain, (and so) the king abdicated. (Next) reigned Sultan Abu Bakr bin Bwana Tamu Mkuu wa Bwana Mtiti bin Ahmad bin Abu Bakr bin 'Umar bin Ahmad bin 'Umar bin Muhammad bin Ahmad bin Muhammad bin Sulayman. He made a strong alliance (p. 32) with the sultan of Muscat, with Imam Sayf bin Nabahani al-Ya'rubi. This sultan of Pate went to Arabia, (and) they agreed with the king of Arabia. And this king of Pate drove out the Portuguese on Sunday, killed the men (and) gained possession of the fort of Mombasa.

He informed [al-Imam] al-Ya'rubi. (The latter) brought governors (*al-wali*) of the Mazru'i (family), three men: Muhammad bin 'Uthman and 'Ali bin 'Uthman, the third brother's name is unknown. They came with soldiers of the Imam Sayf Nabahani al-Ya'rubi. This is the origin of the Mazru'i.

And the king of Pate conducted (himself) in an excellent manner toward all the people. He lived forty years in his kingship (and) died in the year 1154.[25] He left many children (but) his sons did not reign after him.

(Instead) there reigned Ahmad bin Abu Bakr bin Muhammad bin Abu Bakr bin Ahmad bin 'Umar bin Muhammad bin Ahmad bin Muhammad bin

---

[25] 1741-2.

Sulayman. He was benevolent toward (his) subjects, and he was very fond of collecting great herds of cattle. He died in the year 1160[26] (and) left one son called Bwana Gongo who did not reign.

Bwana Tamu Mtoto ("the Younger") reigned, who was called Imam al-Huda, the son of Bwana Mkuu carried away by the Portuguese. And his (real) name was Abu Bakr bin Bwana Mkuu bin Abu Bakr bin Muhammad bin Abu Bakr bin Muhammad bin Abu Bakr bin Muhammad bin ʻUmar bin Muhammad bin Sulayman.

At this time the Imam al-Yaʻrubi brought an expedition to attack Pate (but) they failed, (and) very many Arabs died, (so) they made peace. After that the people of Siu revolted. The king waged war (but) failed. The people of Siu and the people of Lamu equipped an army (and) came to Pate on the side of Kitoki.[27] They fought the men of Pate in a great battle. The men of Lamu were defeated. After this the king of Pate waged war by land and by sea; he attacked the people of Lamu and conquered them. After this the king of Pate and the people of Lamu became united, and the Imam al-Yaʻrubi established single administration. The king was killed in the year 1177.[28]

(Then) reigned his sibling, a woman, Sulṭān Mwana Khadija binti Bwana Mkuu bin Abu Bakr bin Muhammad bin Abu Bakr bin Muhammad bin Abu Bakr bin Muhammad bin ʻUmar bin Muhammad bin Ahmad bin Muhammad bin Sulayman. There was much intrigue (p. 31) in the land of Pate (because)

---

[26] 1747. Compare the name of this ruler in MSS 344 and 358.

[27] This passage differs from MSS 177, 344 and 358 in naming both Siu and Lamu as rebel towns.

[28] 1763-4.

Pate (because) there were two kings, Mwana Khadija the aforesaid and Sultan 'Umar. They fought in the town of Pate for three years;[29] Sultan 'Umar went to the mainland[30] (and) returned to Pate with a powerful force. One night they were killed by the men of Mwana Khadija, each man where he was. Mwana Khadija died in the year 1187.[31]

(Then) reigned Bwana Mkuu wa Sheye. The subjects made much trouble; he got no peace during his reign until, in the year 1191,[32] the men of the town invaded [his palace] (and) killed him at this date.

(Then) reigned Bwana Fumo Madi, whose (real) name was Sultan Muhammad bin Abu Bakr bin Bwana Mkuu bin Abu Bakr bin Muhammad bin Abu Bakr bin Muhammad bin Abu Bakr bin Muhammad bin 'Umar bin Muhammad bin Ahmad bin Muhammad bin Sulayman. After he came to power the subjects wished to make intrigue; he fought them in battle, overcame them, seized forty men--and two were his own brothers--(and) slaughtered them like goats, so that blood (ran off) the roof. In this way he suppressed the great men (of the city). (Then) there was peace, (and) no other man made trouble; he reigned in great quiet until he died in the year 1224.[33] And (there) reigned no (other) king like him. He left many children.

(Then) reigned Sultan Ahmad bin Shaykh Fumo Luti bin Shaykh bin

[29] Werner's version has "five years."

[30] MSS 177 and 344 have "to Barawa."

[31] 1773-4.

[32] 1774.

[33] 1809-10.

Bwana Mkuu.[34] Trouble increased in the town of Lamu, he attacked them--he and the men of Mombasa, the Mazru'i, (being) on the same side. They landed a great army of men of Pate and men of Mombasa at Shela. The men of Lamu came out, came to Shela (and) fought with the men of Pate and the men of Mombasa. The army of men of Lamu had great force; the army of Pate and of Mombasa was defeated. They ran to their ships, (but) some ships were stranded on the beach. Then they stopped (and) fought (another) great battle. Very many men died, men of Mombasa and men of Pate, without counting. Out of the men of Pate, the important ones, without slaves and lowly men, (there were) eighty-one 81 of "So-and-so, the son of So-and-so,"[35] persons of Pate who went to the next life;[36] and as to the men of Mombasa, there was no counting.

After that the men of Lamu went to Arabia (and) asked for Sa'id bin Sultan bin al-Imam, and they gave him the land of Lamu in the year 1228;[37] thereafter he ruled Lamu. The kingdom of Pate included Pate (itself) and the harbors (*banadiri*). (p.30)

(Then) unrest [increased], (and there) arose a second man from among the sons of Bwana Fumo Madi, called Fumo Luti Kipunga. He fought Sultan

---

[34] This name is different in MS 177 but the same in MSS 344 and 358.

[35] Steere suggests that *fulani bin fulani* means "unimportant person" but the context seems to bear out Werner's assertion to the contrary. (See Edward Steere, *A Handbook of the Swahili Language*, London: Society for Promoting Christian Knowledge, 1917).

[36] Cusack translates: "having wives to go into mourning there in Pate."

[37] 1813.

Ahmad. (Later) Sultan Ahmad died of disease in the year 1230.[38]

(Then) reigned Fumo Luti wa Bwana Fumo Madi. And he was very strong, brave (and) generous. It was during this time that Shaykh Mataka bin Shaykh Mubarak held the office of *shaykh* of Siu. He obtained soldiers and guns, and he was under the suzerainty of the sulṭān of Pate and on very good terms with the Mazru'i until the year 1236.[39] (Then) trouble increased between him (and) Sultan Sa'id bin Sultan of Zanzibar. Sultan Fumo Luti the aforesaid died in the year 1270.[40]

After him reigned Fumo Luti bin Shaykh bin Fumo Luti wa Bwana Tamu Mkuu. He was the father of Sultan Ahmad, (later) sultan of Witu. He reigned from dawn till after the mid-afternoon [prayer]. The men of the town drove him out. He went to Siu together with the Mazru'i; (then) they all went to Mombasa.

(Then) reigned Sultan Bwana Shaykh bin Bwana Fumo Madi. He negotiated with Sayyid Sa'id bin Sultan, took Arabs into Pate, (and) they remained (there) three years. Afterwards the people of the town deposed him with the consent of Sayyid Sa'id bin Sultan at the date of the year 1239.[41] They installed Sultan Ahmad called Bwana Waziri wa Bwana Tamu wa Bwana Shaykh wa Bwana Tamu Mkuu. He was on good terms with Sayyid Sa'id bin Sultan (and) reigned for two years. (Then) the people deposed him (and) returned Bwana Shaykh wa Bwana Fumo Madi. He remained in power with

---

[38] 1814-5.

[39] 1820-1.

[40] 1852-3. MS 177 dates Fumo Luti's death 1236.

[41] 1823-4.

the consent of Sayyid Sa'id bin Sultan for five years (and) died in the year 1247.[42]

Bwana Waziri returned to the sultanship. (Then) came Bwana Fumo Luti bin Shaykh who had gone to Mombasa together with the Mazru'i; they captured Siu and attacked Bwana Waziri wa Bwana Tamu at Pate. Bwana Waziri was at one with Sayyid Sa'id bin Sultan, and Fumo Luti (was) at one with the Mazru'i and Shaykh Mataka, a man of Siu. They came to Pate with troops (and) fought. The Siu army was defeated, (and) Bwana Waziri captured the land of Siu (and) destroyed the city wall.

Shaykh Mataka bin Shaykh Mubarak and Fumo Luti fled to the mainland together with some of the men; after a few days he returned to Siu with a strong force, drove out the people of Bwana Waziri by attack, captured from them the town of Siu (and) rebuilt the city wall. Pate and Siu fought each other (and) came under one authority with the consent of Sayyid Sa'id bin Sultan. [*Page 29 missing in MS.*]

(p. 28)... on the way, the men of Siu rushed out on him suddenly, an *amir* of Shaykh Mataka called Bin Mbaraka, Ahmad 'Umar, and the second *amir*, called Hamad Ngoma. They fought and killed Amir Hamadi, (then) went to the fort (and) attacked the Arabs who were in the fort, and took cannons. And the troops that were at Siu did not fight.

(When) the news came of the attack on Amir Hamadi, the killing of the army of Sayyid Sa'id bin Sultan (and) the defeat of those who were to capture Siu, when Sayyid Sa'id bin Sultan got the news of the death of Amir Hamad, he went to the ship without saying a word (and) went away to Maskat.

---

[42] 1831-2.

Next year he placed Sultan Fumo Bakari at Faza, (and the latter) attacked Siu and Pate. At this time Shaykh Mataka died of disease. There was discord among his sons, (for) each man wanted the shaykhdom; they submitted to the overlordship of Sayyid Sa'id: Abu Bakr and Ahmad,[43] sons of Shaykh Mataka.

The Sayyid gave Abu Bakr troops together with Sulṭān Fumo Bakari to attack Sultan Ahmad at Siu. Abu Bakr bin Shaykh Mataka went together with the *amir* of Sulṭān Fumo Bakari called Hamad wa Baishi Nabahani. He entered Siu by night; they fought until the men of Sultan Fumo Bakari were defeated and chased away. They captured Abu Bakr bin Shaykh Mataka (and) took him to Pate; he was killed by Sultan Ahmad.

Afterwards his brother Shaykh Muhammad bin Shaykh Mataka took a stand on the side of Sayyid Sa'id bin Sultan. To him and Sultan Fumo Bakari Sayyid Sa'id bin Sultan gave a troop of soldiers and supplies. They fought Sultan Ahmad till they drove him out of Pate in the year 1273.[44] He went to Kau.

Siu, under Shaykh Muhammad bin Shaykh Mataka, was on the side of Sayyid Sa'id bin Sultan. He (Sayyid Sa'id) gave him soldiers to buid a fort. (Later) they quarrelled with a man of Sayyid Sa'id bin Sultan because he destroyed a boat shed which Shaykh Muhammad Mataka had built in front of the fort. And Shaykh Muhammad Mataka destroyed the fort.

And about this time Sultan Ahmad bin Shaykh died at Kau, the father

---

[43] In the account below, Muhammad bin Shaykh Mataka figures prominently. MS 177 names Muhammad in this passage.

[44] 1856-7.

of Fumo Bakari, (later) sultan of Witu. In his place ruled Ahmad who was called *Simba* ("the Lion"), sultan of Witu.

And before Shaykh Muhammad destroyed the fort of Siu there had been trouble. Sultan Fumo Bakari bin Shaykh drove him out of Pate by force, (and) he came to Lamu. He (Shaykh Muhammad) wished to gain possession of Pate because he saw his (own) strength. And when the great men of Pate saw the acts committed by Shaykh Muhammad bin Shaykh Mataka, they did not wish him to rule, (and) they did not accept (him). (Then) he made war on them, (but) the great men of Pate persisted. And there was no king due to the advice of three men: Muhammad bin Mkuu Nabahani and Bwana Rehema bin Ahmad Nabahani and Nasiri bin ‘Abd Allah bin ‘Abd Salam, the one who was director of affairs (*mudabbir al-umur*). (p. 27) He collected munitions, they fought Shaykh Muhammad bin Shaykh Mataka (and) defeated him; prominent men died, (including) great *amirs*, two men - Bwana Damil and Mawlana wa Sheye Kuli.

When Shaykh Muhammad bin Shaykh Mataka saw these matters, he came to seek peace from Muhammad bin Bwana Mkuu Nabahani, because it was he who was the chief (elder) of the three men named above. They wished to offer him, Muhammad bin Mkuu, the sultanship of Siu and Pate. He refused, answering: "I am an old man." They went to fetch Sultan Ahmad of Witu. Shaykh Muhammad bin Shaykh Mataka sent some men, and men of Pate sent Shaykh Nasiri bin ‘Abd Allah bin ‘Abd Salam. [They] went to Kau, to fetch Sultan Ahmad nicknamed *Simba*, (and) came with him to Pate.

The news reached Zanzibar, Sultan Sayyid Majid bin Sa‘id bin Sultan, for Sayyid Sa'id had died previously in the year 1273.[45] Prior to this the Sayyid had sent his *wazir* Sayyid Sulayman bin Hamad by ship to seize Pate, to crush the conspiracy. By the time the ship reached Mandra, Pate had been seized by a man of Sultan Ahmad, Abu Bakr bin Hasan al-Buri, who had come with this Nasiri bin 'Abd Allah bin 'Abd Salam. When he received this news, Sayyid Sulayman Hamad returned to Zanzibar, and that was when Shaykh Muhammad bin Shaykh Mataka destroyed the fort at Siu.

When Sulayman bin [Hamad] arrived at Pate, the people gave an oath on behalf of that sultan to Shaykh Muhammad bin Shaykh Mataka, among them Mzee Sefu and Shaykh Shikuwe and Muhammad Mote, to affirm Sultan Ahmad's kingship.

Sayyid Majid bin Sayyid Sa'id bin Sultan sent men of Lamu to Pate, to give counsel together with Shaykh Muhi al-Din, to request that Sultan Ahmad put soldiers of the Sayyid at Pate. And this Shaykh Muhi al-Din, he was the one who had turned out the soldiers of the Sayyid from the fort at Siu when they were defeated by Shaykh Muhammad bin Shaykh Mataka. The soldiers were inside the fort; Shaykh Muhi al-Din took them out in peace, because he was a man of Sayyid Majidi bin Sayyid Sa'id, (one) of the *wazirs*.

When he went to Zanzibar with the soldiers, the Sayyid became very angry at Shaykh Muhi al-Din; and Shaykh Muhi al-Din took it upon himself, (p.26) when he saw Sayyid Majid and (his) wrath, to go (back) right then with the men of Lamu. And this Shaykh Muhi al-Din had great cunning and much learning; he went to Pate with the best men of Lamu, together with Shaykh Ahmad and Shaykh 'Abd al-Rahman, and that one was the *shaykh* of Pate.

---

[45] 1856-57.

They spoke with Sultan Ahmad, and he accepted, with much reluctance, because of his friendship with the *shaykh* of Pate[46] and Shaykh 'Abd al-Rahman. He rejected the advice of his *wazir* Nasir bin 'Abd Allah bin 'Abd Salam, for he refused to take in the Arabs, even one man.

The men of Pate made an agreement with Mwana Jaha binti Fumo Luti Kipunga wa Bwana Fumo Madi, wife of Sultan Fumo Bakr bin Shaykh. At this time Sultan Fumo Bakr was in Lamu, with the consent of Sayyid Majid bin Sa'id, since the time he was driven out of Pate.

But every day they brought in soldiers in secret, and munitions, night after night. (When) news reached Sultan Ahmad (that) there was a plot and the soldiers were many at Pate, they suddenly attacked Sultan Ahmad after the ruse was arranged, wishing to seize him. (However), they failed because all the Pate people were of one mind with Sayyid Majid bin Sa'id, except his *wazir* Nasir bin 'Abd Allah bin 'Abd Salam. They fought within the town of Pate, Sultan Ahmad got away, he and Shaykh Muhammad bin Shaykh Mataka went to Siu.

The Arabs at Pate held fast (and) placed their ships on the sea. (When) the war became very fierce, Sayyid Majid bin Sa'id came (himself) to lay siege to Siu and Pate, and to block ships at sea (and) to sink *dhows* (and) *mtepes*; they fought at sea (and) went to the mainland to obtain food (but) could not pass back. (It was a matter of) life and death. Sayyid Majid placed a chain across the mouth of the Siu creek, the Kuyo, to block the ships. Consequently

---

[46] This seemed to make Shaykh Ahmad the *shaykh* of Pate. The Werner version calls the two visitors brothers. Elsewhere they are said to be the sons of the *shaykh* of Pate.

they suffered six months [of blockade] from the sea and at Pate.[47] On the side of Faza Mzee Sefu seceded (to become) a man of Sayyid Majid bin Sa'id, through much cunning and many words. Sultan Ahmad and Shaykh Muhammad bin Shaykh Mataka experienced great distress.

Dissent arose in the land of Siu. Some of the people loved Sayyid Majid because of the troubles that they had suffered, and (his) men were *sharif* Maulana bin Abu Bakr and 'Isa bin Ahmad al-Somali. (When) they saw (these things), Sultan Ahmad (and) Shaykh Muhammad bin Shaykh [Mataka] sued for peace from Sayyid Majid, and he granted them peace. During peace negotiations Sultan Ahmad sailed by night, went to the mainland (and) returned to Kau.

After this Shaykh Muhammad bin Shaykh Mataka sent his son, Shaykh Muhammad bin Shaykh Mataka[48] to the ship to Sayyid Majid, and Sayyid Majid pardoned him (and) gave him many presents. (Then) Sayyid Majid sailed (and) returned to Zanzibar. Later Shaykh Muhammad bin Shaykh Mataka went to Zanzibar to appear before Sayyid Majid. The Sayyid seized him (and) imprisoned him in the fort of Mombasa, along with (other) people. (Then) Shaykh Muhammad died.

(p. 25) And after (some) days Sayyid Majid sent the governor (*al-wali*) Sa'ud bin Hamad to seize Sultan Ahmad at Kau by many ruses, (but) he failed. He (Sultan Ahmad) left Kau secretly (and) went to Witu. The *wali* Sa'ud bin Hamad came to Faza, to seize 'Umar Mataka at Faza, and the sons of Shaykh

---

[47] MS 344 provides a better account of this episode.

[48] The name of the son appears confused here. See also MS 177, f. 19 and MS 358, p.23.

Muhammad bin Shaykh Mataka he captured at Siu (and) sent (them) to the fort of Mombasa. 'Umar Mataka he imprisoned at Lamu.

Afterwards Sayyid Majid ruled over all the Swahili (coast), there was no one to challenge him. And Sultan Ahmad remained at Witu under the suzerainty of Sayyid Majid until Sayyid Barghash bin Sa'id bin Sultan came to reign. Sayyid Barghash wished to place soldiers at Witu with a flag, (but) Sultan Ahmad did not agree. He (Sayyid Barghash) sent an expedition to fight him (but) failed (and) made peace. And this *wali* Sa'ud bin Hamad did not fight vigorously enough, (so) Sayyid Barghash sent an expedition again under the *liwali* Sa'id bin Hamad bin Sa'id.[49] Sultan Ahmad took the protection of the Germans who gave him some of the Swahili mainland. Sultan Ahmad died, under this condition of protection, in 1306.[50]

(Then) reigned Sultan Fumo Bakari bin Sultan Ahmad bin Shaykh Nabahani. He remained under this condition of protection, (but) there arose conflict between him and the Germans. One man, called Küntzell, killed the porter of the gate; he suddenly shot him. The soldiers who were there shot, and the soldiers killed Küntzell and the Europeans who had accompanied him. And they killed the Europeans without Sultan Fumo Bakar's order. When the soldiers saw all their company dead, they did not wait for an order from the sultan (and) attacked the Europeans. And when the people of Mkonumbi and of Wandamuyu received the news of the Europeans, they attacked (and) killed those Europeans who were there.

After that came the Administration of the English. They wished to

---

[49] Werner's version (pp. 404/405) has the same *walī* returning.

[50] 1888-9.

make justice (and) demanded (those) people of Mkonumbi and Wandamuyu, in order to bring them to trial. Fumo Bakr did not consent to surrender them. They sent an expedition against Sultan Fumo Bakr, the boats came to Mkonumbi and Wandamuyu and Kilimani and Nyando za-Pwani. They shot from cannons (and) set [houses] on fire.

Then on the night of 11 Rabi‘ al-Awwal of the year 1308,[51] the men of Witu fought on the Kitini road with the men of the Illustrious Administration; the men of Witu suffered defeat. Then on the morning of Monday, 12 of the month Rabi‘ al-Awwal of the year 1308,[52] they attacked Sultan Fumo Bakari (and) drove him out of Witu by force. He went to Jongeni.

Witu was taken over by the Glorious Administration. Sultan Fumo Bakari remained at Jongeni until Jumad al-Awwal of the year 1308[53] (when) he died. His brother Bwana Shaykh bin Sultan Ahmad bin Shaykh Nabahani occupied his place. After a few days a conspiracy arose between his brother Fumo ‘Umar Nabahani and Avutula wa Bahiru. They imprisoned Bwana Shaykh bin Sultan bin Hamad. (p. 24) (Then) reigned Sultan Fumo ‘Umar.

And the last to reign at Pate (was) Sultan Ahmad of Witu, and the one who ruled first (was) Sulayman bin Sulayman bin Muzaffar Nabahani, Imam al-‘Arabi.

---

[51] 25 October 1890.

[52] According to the Christian calendar, 26 October 1890, Sunday. However, according to Muslim time reckoning, the new day begins after sunset, so the narrator probably means the morning of Monday 27 October 1890.

[53] 13 December 1890 - 11 January 1891.

This is the account of the Nabahani who came to the Swahili (coast), and their history as we have mentioned above. (There) reigned thirty-one kings and one woman, to the total of thirty-two, without (counting) those who reigned, were deposed (and) returned to rule.

We have transmitted this from Muhammad bin Fumo 'Umar Nabahani, nicknamed Bwana Kitini, and he transmitted it from his grandfather Muhammad bin Bwana Mkuu Nabahani called Bwana Simba, who was very reliable in regard to the accounts of their pedigree such as we have mentioned.

Salih bin Salim bin 'Abd Allah[54] Sharahil wrote this in his own hand on the 6th Safar of the year 1318.[55] This was copied for the Honorable Infant Muhammad bin Ahmad bin Shaykh bin Bwana Fumo Madi wa Simba, Sultan Muhammad bin Abu Bakr bin Bwana Mkuu bin Abu Bakr bin Ahmad bin Abu Bakr bin Muhammad bin Abu Bakr bin Muhammad bin 'Umar bin Muhammad bin Ahmad bin Muhammad bin Sulayman bin Sulayman bin Muzaffar Nabahani.

Copied on the 1 Rajab of the year 1343.[56] The humble Salih bin Salim bin Ahmad wrote this in his own hand on the 3 February of the year 1925.[57]

---

[54] MSS 177 and 344 name the scribe Salih bin Salim bin Ahmad bin 'Abd Allah.

[55] 5 June 1900.

[56] 26 January 1925.

[57] In 1925, 1 Rajab fell on 26 January. For a possible reason for confusion, see dates of copies listed in MS 344.

MS 344

This MS contains the text of the Chronicle on pp. 92-76 (the pagination running in reverse of Arabic writing right-to-left). The copyist names himself ‘Abd Allah bin ‘Ali bin Muhammad al-Ma‘awi. This appears to be a fourth copy, undated, of three earlier copies, all crediting Bwana Kitini as narrator. The first copy is ascribed to Salih bin Salim bin Ahmad bin ‘Abd Allah Sharahil, dated 1318/1900. That copy was commissioned by the Nabahani *liwali* Muhammad bin Ahmad bin Sulṭān bin Fumo Bakr, etc. (see however, MS 321). A second copy, by Salih bin Salim bin Hamad (same person as above?), is dated 1343/1925 and a third, by ‘Ali Muhammad, possibly the father of the fourth scribe, 1363/1944.[1] At the top of p. 92 are inserted the date (*tārīkh al-hijra 600*) and an elaborately contemporary title: *Riwāyah ya-tawārīkh za Pāte nā ba‘aḍi sihīmi yā Ifrīḳah sharīḳiyah*. The text which follows is of the common "Hollis" pattern. Apparently the copyist could not decipher parts of the original: a lacuna is marked on p. 90, and omissions of text are evident on pp. 92, 85 and 80. By contrast, other parts seem to be repeated twice (sometimes jumbled), e.g. on pp. 85, 81, 80.

The text is in Ki-Amu. In an intresting variation, the sound *ch* often becomes *sh* (*shake* for *chake*). The orthography of this copy is distinguished

[1] This date or its translation by the scribe to the Christian calendar may be wrong: the text cites the Muslim month of Dhu 'l-Ka‘da but then gives the date 3 February (as in MS 321). However, in 1363 A.H. Dhu '-Ka‘da began on 18 October and ended on 17 November. See also note 61 to *Translation* below.

by a consistent notation of nasal *n* with *nūn*, a relatively unusual notation of the sound *w* after consonants, frequent use of *bā'* with *p* notation of three dots underneath, *fā'* with three dots above for *v*, and of dotted *kāf* for *ch*. Among irregularities are the substitution of *sīn* for *ṣād* and of *kāf* for *ḳāf* in Arabic loanwords. The diacritical marks are not always accurately placed or written, with the curved *ḍamma* (for *u*) occasionally being confused with the straight *fatḥa* (for *a*) or round *sukūn* (for no vowel). The passive voice of verbs, rarely shown in Swahili-Arabic writing, is clearly voweled here. The name *Pate* is given an unusually varied rendition including one in which *tā marbūṭa* ṭ is pronounced (these are shown in the transcript in bold font). A modern innovation is the use of punctuation (colon, applied extremely irregularly to separate passages). The dynastic *nisba* of Pate rulers is voweled in the Arabic way *Nabhānī* and the earlier dynasty of Pate is referred to in correct Arabic as *(wa)al-Batawiyīn*. Infrequently, the names Aḥmad and Ḥamad are used interchangeably.

As regards contents, on p. 90, under the year 749 A.H., an important variation is found in the statement of trading interests of Sultan Muhammad bin 'Umar. While other MSS assert his initiative in trading with India (*Hind, Hindi*), MS 344 merely has him "traveling to make commerce" (*henda kufānyā bi'ashara*). On p. 89 occurs the term *wātu wa-barāni*, "people of the mainland." The full name of Sultan Ahmad bin Abu Bakr (d. 1160/1747) differs from that given in MSS 177 and 321. Only a little bit further the passage about a Pate-Lamu conflict probably wrongly substitutes *wātu wa-Lāmū* for *wātu wa-Sīu* on at least one occasion (cf. introductory remarks to MS 177).

RIWĀYAH YA-TAWĀRĪKH ZA PĀTE

nā ba'aḍi sihīmu yā Ifrīḳah sharīḳiyah

Tārīkh al-Hijra 600

(p. 92) Hāhunā Sulaymān bin Sulaymān Mu[ẓ]affar al-Nabhānī. Alawal al-mubdī Nabhānī muwandu wa-kūya **P**ateh Nabhānī ni-Selēmāni bin Sulaymān bin Muẓaffar Nabhānī nā-nduze wawīli: 'Alī bin Sulaymān nā 'Uthmān bin Sulaymān. Na-hūyu Sulaymān bin Sulaymān al-madhkūr ndiye alikuwa sulṭān nā-ye akisa kutawālī bāra li-'Arābu akāya **P**atteh sulṭān al-madhkūr katika tārīkh sanati 600 (sitami'ah) min al-Hijra kūya kuwake **P**āte. Akata͜ka 'arūsi kuwa mfalme wa-**P**ateh katika hā Wa-al-Batāwīyīn. Sulṭān Sulaymān bin Sulaymān ni-mtu mu'arufu: mfalme wa-**P**āte akamuuza binti yake. Na-dastūri ya-wātu yā WaSawāḥili ḥatā sāsa mtu aku'uliyao kijāna shako, akisa siku saba'a za-harūsi henda kumu'angāliyā mkuwe wei (n)yumbāni, make bābā wa-mke wake kawampia watu. Hūy[ū] Sulaymān bin Sulaymān ndiye mfalme weno akampa ufalume wake alokuwa nao. Akatawali Sulaymān bin Sulaymān.

Kuwa͜lina mūi hā'itwa Kitaka iyo jazīrah ya-**P**āte katika maṭla'i ya-**P**āte, nā Siu ḥasā͜kuwa mji. Waliko mji mūngine hītuwā Shānga katika maṭla'i yā Patteh, na-Fāza wayiko mji wenyewe wa-**P**āzah al-Mafāzī. Ikakēti miji hiyo yōte [t]aḥti yā Sulṭān Sulaymān bin Sulaymān. Nā-Manda kuwa͜līna mfalme mbālī nā-ye ona nguvu sāna. Akafa Sulṭān Sulaymān bin Sulaymān tārīkh 625 Hijrah. Akā͜khalifu zijāna wawīli Muḥammad na-'Aḥmad, Muḥammad 'umri wake miyāka 'ishrīn na-'Aḥmad 'umri wāke nyāka khamsata 'ashara.

Akatawali Muḥammad bin Sulaymān bin Sulaymān ba'ada ya-ba‿bake. Ikawa khitlāfu (p. 91) yeye na-wātu wa Shānga, kapijāna nā-miji kā'ivunda kābisa, na-ba'ḍi yao wakāya Pateh nā-wanginīwe ḳabila yao Kinda(n)gu wakakimbiya wasiyu‿wikāne mahā[la] wamezo‿kimbilia ḥatā siku zikāpita akāya khabāri kwa Sulṭān Muḥammad bin Sulaymān naḥāwa wātu windāo kuwenda wakamuwambia, "Wāle wa-Siu tumewaona katika muwitu." Sulṭān kapeka wātu kuwa‿ngāliyā kawa‿dirika, wamefānyā zijūmbā ndāni yā-muwītu. Sulṭān Muḥammad bin Sulaymān kawa‿sameḥe kawarudisha mahāla yao, ndiyo aṣli yā-mūi wa-Sīyū. Wakāya na-Wa‿Sawāḥīli wangine wakāketi wote. Wakāya na-wa‿Wafamāu wakā‿keti wakāwa ndio wakuu wa-Siyū katika ṭā'a yā Sulṭān Muḥammad bin Sulaymān. Sulṭān Muḥammad al-madhkūr akafa sanati 650.

Akatawali nduye Aḥmad bin Sulaymān. Aka'amirisha sāna arḍi ya-Pate kā‿jenga maju(m)ba kafā‿nya mashānbah asipiji mahāli na-'akafa sanati 660.

Kātawali kijāna shā-nduye ina lake Aḥmad bin Muḥammad bin Sulaymān. Akāketi na-watu uzuri sāna kama sira za 'ami zake, ku'amirisha mji wa-Pateh na-mashānbah ḥatā sanati 700 akāfa. Akakhalifu zijāna wangi.

Katawali kijāna shake Sulṭān Muḥammad bin Aḥmad bin Muḥammad bin Sulaymān. Akaketi na-wātu kuwa wēma sāna. Wātu wa-Fāzah wakakhalifu, akawa‿pija kawa‿tia katika ṭā'ah ba'da ya-zita zingi ḥatā alipō‿washinda. Aka'i‿futaḥi na-Ma(n)da kawa-ka'i‿tamalaki kuwa-zi‿ītah nā ḥilah kuwe k(w)ani alikuwa nā-nguvu sāna mfalme wa-Ma(n)da kuwa ya-māli na-watu, akā‿ivunda kābisah. Na-watu wungīne kawaeta Pateh na-ba'ḍi wakātawa nyika wakā‿kimbilia kila mahāla, wangīne wakājah Shēlah wakāngiyā katika ḥimāyah ya-wātu wa-Lāmwwu.

Sulṭān Muḥammad bin Aḥmad al-madhkūr kawataka kwa wātu wa-Lāmū wakā'iza kuwa‿toa, nā wangīne wakenda Malindiyy na-ba'ḍi yā bildāni. Sulṭān Muḥammad bin Aḥmad al-madhkūr kawa‿ndāma sāna hāwa waliyo‿kūjah Shēlah, wātu wa-Lāmūh waka'iza kuwa‿toa ḳaṭ'an. Kisa Sulṭān Muḥammad akafa 732.

Akatawāli kijāna shāke ufalume Sulṭān 'Umari bin Muḥammad bin Aḥmad bin Muḥammad bin Sulayman. Akai‿rejeyā maneno (p. 90) ya-bāba wāke kuwa wātu wa-Lāmmū, kawa‿taka wātu wa-Mānda. Watu wa-Lāmūh waka'iza kuwa‿toa, kawa‿pija zita, wakātaka amāni watu wa-Lāmūh wakuwa katika ṭā'ā yā sulṭani.

Sulṭān 'Umar bin Muḥammad zikazidi nguvu akāpija jumla yā miji yā-Sawaḥili: Ozi, Malindi, Kiwayū, Kitā... [*lacuna in MS*] Miji yōte ka'itamalāki tōka Pateh ḥatā Kirīmbā. Kila -mji kaweka mtu wake ki-ḥukumu, ndiyo aṣli ya-hāwa majūmbē iliyoko mrīma. Ma'ana ni-wa‿tūmuwa wa-yu'mbē, na-hiyo "yu'mbē" ma'anā ni-nyūmupā ya-mfalme wa-**P**ateh.

Na-jānibu ya-maṭula'i akatamalaki ḥatā Wārsh-ikh, alikuwenda kapija zita [t]angu Kiwayū na-Tūlah nā Tuwāla nā Shu[n]gawāya nā bana‿diri zōte Barāwa Marika nā Maḳdishū. Aka'ishi nā-nti zōte hizo katika ṭā'ah yake ilā Ungūjah hakutawāli, na-waḳati huu Ungūjah hā'ikuwa nti ku'‿buwa. Hūyu Sulṭān 'Umar al-madhkūr alishinda zita na-kupenda ra'iyah, nā ra'iyah wakimpenda, ikatwā'a nguvu sāna nti ya-**P**a**t**eh. Akafa Sulṭān 'Umar sanati 749. Kākhalifu zijāna wawīli Muḥammad na-Aḥmad.

Katawāli kijāna mkuu, Sulṭān Muḥammad bin 'Umar bin Muḥammad bin Aḥmad bin Muḥammad bin [Sulaymān] ufalme wa-babāke kuwa amāni hapa‿kuwa na-zita. Nā-ye alikipenda māli sāna na-bi'ashara, akisafirisha na-zombo zake, henda kufānyā bi'ashara nā-ye alīna bakhti sāna ya-māli. Nā-mara mōya alimsafirisha kijāna shake ka[p]a‿ta kisiwa kati‿ka baḥri, akapāta ma'adini ya-fiḍah, kāya nāyo Pate kafa‿nya wātu wakuyafānya kāzi mu'dini hāyo. Kapāta māli sāna mangi yākāzidi māli katika nti ya-Pateh ḥatā wakāfa(n)ya zitāra za fiḍah na-ngāzi za fiḍah na-zombo zingi za fiḍah. Nā-mfalme akāfa sanati 797. Akākhalifu zijāna nne: Buwāna Mukuu na Aḥmad nā Abū Bakr nā 'Umar.

Aka‿tawali nduye Sulṭāni Aḥmad bin 'Umar bin Muḥammad bin Aḥmad bin Muḥammad bin Sulaymān bin Sulaymān. Akaketi na-wātu sāna kuwa amāni (p. 89) nā sira njema kuwa jamī'i ya-wātu. Akāfa.

Akātawali Abū Bakr bin Muḥammad bin 'Umar bin Muḥammad bin Aḥmad bin Muḥammad bin Sulaymān. Kāketi sāna nā-jami'i ya-wātu nā-miji yōte katika ṭā'a yake bilā khilāfu, nā-ye akafa sanati 785. Akā‿khalifu zijāna ziwīli Muḥammad na-Aḥmad.

Akatawali mahāli baba yake mtoto wake Muḥammad bin Abū Bakr bin Muḥammad bin Muḥammad bin 'Umar bin Muḥammad bin Aḥmad bin Muḥammad bin Sulaymān. Waḳati wake wakājah WaZungu **P**ortukil katika miji ya-Sawāḥili wote, wakāketi Mombāsah wakāfānya ngome nā-janibu yā-**P**ateh kajenga Ndōndō. Wātu wa-barāni wakāwafu'āta wakāwa**p**a māli wakāwa katika ṭā'ah yao. Wakam'ariḍi mfalme katika nti yake ya-**P**ateh wakampija zita mfalme kwa jānibu yā-Shi(n)da‿kāsi, wakawaka nti yā-**P**ate pwāni k(w)a-ma'ana ya-tūpe kaṣidi-yā kupija mūi wa-**P**ateh, wasiweze, wakā**p**atāna kuwa amāni wakafa‿nya mkatabuh sharuti zao. Wakāketi **P**ate WaZung[u] wakafānya farḍa kuwa jina lao WaZungu wāli‿shamkuwa "fandika." Wakāfānya na-māmbo māngi katika kisiwa shā **P**ateh. Akafa sulṭāni sanati 900. Akā‿khalifu zijāna wawīli Buwāna Mkuu na-Abū Bakr.

Akatawāli ufalme Sulṭān Abū Bakr bin Muḥammad bin Abū Bakr bin

Muḥammad bin Aḥmad bin Muḥammad bin Sulaymān ba'ada ya-baba‿ke al-madhkūr. Akāketi na-wātu sāna kuwa amāni kamā ḳā'idah ya-babāke, akafa sanati 940. Kusipadi‿liki yāmbō, nā akakhalifu zijana ziwīli Aḥmad wa Muḥammad.

Akatawali 'ami yao ufalme, Buwāna Mkuu bin Muḥammad bin Abū Bakr bin Muḥammad bin 'Umar bin Muḥammad bin Aḥmad bin Muḥammad bin Sulaymān. Ikawa khitilāfu na-WaZungu lakin pasiwe na-zita. Ikawa fitnah siku nyingi, akafa sanati 973. Akākhalifu kijāna mmōya Abū Bakr.

Akatawali Muḥammad bin Abū Bakr bin Muḥammad bin 'Umar bin Muḥammad bin Aḥmad bin Muḥammad bin Sulaymān. Akā‿ṣiliḥiyāna na-WaZungu 'akatuwā'a ba'ḍi ya-miji akafa sanati 1002. Akakhalifu kijāna mmōja hituwa Abū Bakr asitawali.

Alitawali Abū Bakr bin Buwāna Mkuu bin Muḥammad bin Abū Bakr bin Muḥammad bin 'Umar bin Muḥammad bin Aḥmad bin Muḥammad bin Sulaymān. Akaketi na[o] kama siyara ya-wazee zake walota‿nngulia na-[u]falme, ukapū‿ngua nguvu. (p. 88) Akafa sanati 1041, akakhalifu Buwāna Mkuu na-Abū Bakr kuwa jina la-babake.

Akatawali Abū Bakr bin Muḥammad bin Abū Bakr bin Muḥammad bin Abū Bakr bin Muḥammad bin 'Umar bin Aḥmad bin Muḥammad bin Sulaymānu. Ikawa khitilāfu na-WaZungu wakapijāna kawavunda WaZungu k[u]w[a]-zītah zikuu sāna. Ba'ada-ye zikāya zita tenā za WaZungu, wakapijāna mūi wa-Pateh kuwa mizingah wakaziweya nā-ndia kuwa baḥarīni kusipiti shōmpo. Wātu wakāona mashaḳah wakafānya amāni. Akāfa mfalme sanati 1061. Akakhālifu zijāna wawīli Buwāna Mkuu na-Aḥmad.

Akatawali Buwāna Mkuu wa-Buwāna Bakr wa-Buwāna Mkuu bin Muḥammad bin Abū Bakr bin Muḥammad bin 'Umar bin Muḥammad bin

Aḥmad bin Muḥammad bin Sulaymān. Akapatāna na-WaZungu nā-ye alikipenda sāna kuketi Lāmūh ḥatā mūsimu kupīta Lāmwuh, akafā‿nya 'arūsi kuwa wātu wa-Lāmūh.

Na-katika waḳti hūnu WaFamāu wa Siyū walitoka katika ṭā'ah yāke, ak[a]wa‿pija na-mji wa-Siu kashika na-wātu wangīne kawatia **P**ateh. Mkūbwa wa-Siyū akā‿kimbia akenda (N)dō(n)do kuwa Portugāli katwā'a ḥimāyah. Mkūbwa wa-WaZungu akāja **P**ate kuwa mfalme awasameḥe wātu wa-Siyū, mfalme kawa‿sāmeḥe kawarejeza mahāli yao Siyū katika amāni.

Ba'ada yake Portugāli akafa‿nya ḥila, akāja **P**ateh kuwa markab akamtāka mfalme kuwenda markabūni, asine(n)da akamupeka ibn 'ami yake Buwāna Mkuu, yeye na-wātu wa-**P**ateh. WaZungu wakakawa‿tukua katika markab, asirudi ḥatā mtu mmōya. Ba'ada ya-hāyo mfalume kawapija WaZungu kuwa jānibu zōte, kuwa barāni na-zisiwāni, kawa‿toa jānibu za-hūku zote, kākimbilia Mombāsah. Akāfa mfalme sanati 1100. Akawata zijāna Buwāna Bakar na-Buwāna Madi na-binti mmōya hu'ituwa Muwāna Darīni.

Akatawāli Abū Bakr bin Buwāna Mkuu bin Abū Bakr bin Muḥammad bin Abū Bakr bin Muḥammad bin 'Umar bin Muḥammad bin Aḥmad bin Muḥammad bin Sulaymān. Akā‿pijwa mfalme ghafulah na-Aḥmad nduye Buwāna Mkuu alotukū‿liwa WaZungu (p. 87) Portugāli kuwa upānga. Akāfa mfalme sanati 1103.

Katawali yeye Aḥmad bin Abū Bakr bin Muḥammad bin Muhammad bin Abū Bakr bin Muḥammad bin 'Umar bin Muḥammad bin Aḥmad bin Muḥammad bin Sulaymān.

Alipō‿tawāli kawandāma Portugāli akiwatoa katika nti zake. Na-waḳti hūna Muwāna Darīni binti Buwāna Mkuu wa-Buwāna Bakr, mke wa-Buwāna Mkuu bin Abū Bakr aliyō‿tukulīwa na-Portugāl katika zamāni yā Sulṭān

Aḥmad, kaua (n)duze wawīli Abū Bakr nā-Buwāna Madī nā Suluṭāni Aḥmad, ni-mume wake akiyotukūlīwa kafānya ḥazni sāna zikapīta nyingi siku nyingi, akatāka ku‿ṭahira kijāna shake Buwāna Tamu Mtoto aliyō‿mtukua Sulṭān Abū Bakr Im[a]mu Hudā, kijāna wa-Buwāna Mkuu aliyō‿tenda n-Gōa.

Mfalme alipō‿**p**ata khabāri aka'izīmu yeye kufa‿(n)ya 'arūsi ya-zijāna zake sabābu kumkhini siwa ya-shā(m)ba. Akawāta kh[a]bāri Muwāna Darīni akamuweta Muwenyi Bayāyi bin Mkuu, sharīfu katika Jamāli al-Layl, alikuwa hudāri sāna kaziya-ujume. Akata‿ka amfānyizi[ya] siwa ishi(n)de siwa ya-**P**āte, akariḍika ijāra riyāli mi'a wa 'ishrīn, kam**p**a **p**embe za ndovu akā‿tiwua mōya. Akafa‿nya siwā kuwa siri ḥatā yālipōkuwa ṭayāri kā‿aẓihirisha ghafulah kā'ipe‿ka katika majūmbah yā-jamā'a zake. Mutu akitūza ya-kwa māli māngi sāna, fundi kā'iza ijārah akata‿ka tuzo, akam**p**a tūzo akafa‿nya 'arūsi.

Ḥatā zamāni ya-Buwāna Tamu Mkuu wakājah wātu wa-Lāmū wakāazima siwa, akawa wakā'etu‿kuwa siwa-ya-aṣli ḥatā baḥarini shō‿m**p**o-kikafa māi akighību. Buwāna Tāmu Mkuu akata‿ka siwa ya-Muwāna Darīni kamuwambia, "Tūpe sisi tutumie katika m[i]ji wote." Akamjibu, "Kila ḳabīlah yālituuza natumiye siwa yangu."

Nā-Muwāna Darīni kawāta mtūmwa ḥurri ayowao kuvuzia akasema, "Hūyu ndiye muwenyi kupija siwa hini, yeye nā-nasla yake. Nā 'ada yake na**p**owe riyāli tāno nā-nguo yā kutukulia siwa tena a**p**owe nā-samli nā tuzo kila mtu awezao." Wakamkū‿līwa naslah hiyo "muyūm**p**e wa-siwa," ḥatā yeo wako watuwe tangu waḳti (p. 86) ilā 'l-āna. Hutumīwa nā-jamī'i yā-ḳabā'ili wa-Pateh na-maḳaba'ili wa-mii mingīne huwenda kuazima kuwa sharṭi hizo kubuwa muyūmbē wa-siw[a].

Izi‿kazidi fitnah ndāni ya-mji. Na-katika ufalme wake nyāka saba'a ikawa miji mikāvu hakūna mvua, mfalme akā‿i'uzulu.

Katawāli Sulṭān Abū Bakr bin Buwāna Tamu Mkuu wa-Buwāna Mtiti bin Aḥmad bin Abū Bakr bin 'Umar bin Aḥmad bin 'Umar bin Muḥammad bin Aḥmad bin Muḥammad bin Sulaymān. Akapata‿na sāna nā sulṭani wa-Ma[skat] al-Imām Sayf bin Nabhānī al-Ya'rubī. Hūyu sulṭāni wa-**P**ateh ikawa 'Arabūni, wakawajāna mfalme wa-'Arabūni na-hūyu mfalme wa-Pate kuwatua **P**ortugāli siku yā juma'ah pili kuuwa wātu kutamalaki ngōme, akatamalaki ngōme ya-Mombāsah. Akamwa[ri]fu al-Imām al-Ya'rubī, akā'eta liwalī katika Mazāri', wātu watātu Muḥammad bin 'Uthmān nā 'Alī bin 'Uthmān, ndugu watatu sikumyawa ina lake. Wakāya pamōya na-'askari wa-al-Imām Sayf Nabhānī al-Ya'rubī. Ndiyo aṣli ya-Mazāri'.

Nā mufalme wa-Pateh alina sira njema nā jamī'i ya-wātu, akā'ishi nyāka arba'īn katika ufalme wake. Akafa sanati 1154, akawāta zijāna wangi, ba'ada yake wasitawāli zijāna zake.

Akatawāli Aḥmad bin Abū Bakr bin Muḥammad bin Abū Bakr bin Muḥammad bin 'Umar bin Aḥmad bin 'Umar bin Muḥammad bin Aḥmad bin Muḥammad bin Sulaymān. Akaketi kuwa wēmā, akafa sanati 1160. Akakhalifu kijāna kam(w)ēta Buwāna Gō(n)go, asitawāli.

Akatawāli Buwāna Tāmu Mtoto amkū‿liwāo Imāmu 'l-Hudā wa-Buwāna Mkuu alotukuwa‿līwa na-**P**ortugāl, na-'ina lake Abū Bakr bin Buwāna Mkuu bin Abū Bakr bin Muḥammad bin Abū Bakr bin Muḥammad bin Abū Bakr bin Muḥammad bin 'Umar bin Muḥammad bin Sulaymān. Katika waḳti hūnu Imām al-Ya'rubī aka'eta zīta kupija **P**ateh, wasiweze wakāfa Wa'Arābu wāngi sāna wakafānya amāni.

Ba'ada ya-hāyo wātu wa-Lāmū wakakhālifu, mfalme kawapija zita, asiwa‿wēze wātu wa-Lāmū. Na-wātu wa-Lāmūh wakafūnga zītah wakāya

Pateh kuwa jānibu yā-Kitoki wakapijāna na-wātu wa-Patteh zītah zikuu (p. 85) wa[k]avundika wātu wa-Lāmū. Ba'ada-ye mfalume wa-Pāte akafūnga zītah kuwa bāra nā-baḥri, kāpija wātu wa-Lāmū kawa‿tamalaki. Ba'ada ya-hāya waliko ḥāli mōya mfalme wa-Pāte na-wātu wa-Lāmū, Imām al-Ya'rubī akafa‿nya shauri mōya. Wakamu'uwa mfalme sanati 1177.

Akatawāli nduye muwāna mke Sulṭān Muwāna Khadījah binti Buwāna Mkuu bin Abū Bakr bin Muḥammad bin Abū Bakr bin Muḥammad bin Abū Bakr bin Muḥammad bin 'Umar bin Muḥammad bin Aḥmad bin Muḥammad bin Sulaymān. Ikawa fitunah nyingi katika nti yā Pāte, ikawa wafalme wawīli, Muwāna Khadījah al-madhkūrah nā Sulṭān 'Umar. Wakapijāna katika mūi wa-Pāte nyāka mitātu, Sulṭān 'Umar akenda Barāwa karajeyā Pāte kwa nguvu kuu sāna. Usiku [...] na-wātu wa-Muwāna Khadījah kula mtu mahāli pake. Akafa Muwāna [K]hadījah sanati 1187.

Alitawāli Buwāna Mkuu w[a]-Shee wa-Buwāna Tāmu Mkuu. Ra'iya wakafānyā udhia sāna asipate rāḥa katika ufalme wake ḥatā sanati 1191 wakam(w)angalia wātu wa-mūi wakamu'uwa tārīkhi hiyo.

Katawāli Buwāna Fūmo Mādi ina yake Sulṭān Muḥammad bin Abū Bakr bin Bwāna Mkuu bin Abū Bakr bin Muḥammad bin Abū Bakr bin Muḥammad bin Abū Bakr bin Muḥammad bin 'Umar bin Muḥammad bin Aḥmad bin Muḥammad bin Sulaymān. Ba'ada ya-kutawāli ra'iyah wakatāka kufānyā fitnah, kāwapija zītah kawashinda kawashīka wātu arba'īni, na-wawīli ni-nduze khāṣa, akawatinda kama mbūzi yuu, na-saḳafu dāmu. Ikashuka ndiāni katika makūpu, ikawa amāni asitōki tena mtu kufa‿nyā fitnah, akatawāli kuwa rāḥa sāna, 1224 kāfa. Wa-lā hakutawāli mfalme tenā kama yeye. Akakhālifu zijāna wāngi.

Akatawāli Sulṭān Aḥmad bin Shaykh Fūmo Lūṭi bin Shaykh bin Buwāna

Mkuu. Ikazidi fitnah katika mji wa-Lāmū, akawapija zīta yeye na-wātu wa-Mombāsah Māzarī'i ḥāli mōja. Wakashūka Shēlah jayshi kuwā sāna ya-wātu wa-Pāte na-wātu wa-Mombasah. Wātu wa-Lāmū wakatoka wakājah Shēlah wakapijāna na-wātu wa-Pateh na-wātu wa-Mombāsah, zita za-wātu wa-Lāmū zikāwa ngu'vu sāna, jaishi ya-**P**āte nā Mombāsah wakāvundika wakākimbilia majahazini muwāwo, majahazi mangīne yākajahābu **p**uwāni. Wakasimama hāpo wakapijāna zita zikuu sāna wakua wātu wangi sāna wa-**P**āte na-wa Mombāsah (p. 84) hapāna 'idadi. Katika wātu wa-Pāte wālo ma'arufu ishikuwa watumwa na-waḍa'ifu, wātu wāḥidwa-thamānīn fulān bin fulān, wenye wake yakenda ma'ida hāyo Pāte, na-wātu wa-Mombāsah hawāna 'idadi.

Ba'ada ya-hāyo wātu wa-Lāmū' wakenda 'Arabūni wakumutāka Sa'īd bin Sulṭān ibn[1] al-Imam, wakampa nti yā-Lāmūh sanati 1228, alipō‿tawāli Lāmū.

Ufalme wa-**P**āte akasilia katika Pāte nā-Banādiri. Ikazidi fitunah, akatōka mtu wa pili katika zijāna wa-Buwāna Fūmo Mādī hūituwa Fūmo Lūṭi Kip**ū**‿ngah, akapijāna Suluṭān Aḥmad. Kisa Sulṭān Aḥmad akafa kuwa maraḍi 1230.

Akatawāli Fūmo Lūṭi wa-Buwāna Fūmo Mādī nā-ye alikuwa hudāri sāna shujā'a karīmu. Na-zamāni hizo Shaykh Matāka bin Shaykh Mubārak ndi**p**o alipō‿tawāli ushēkhe wa-Siu, akafānya 'askari na-bunduki na-ye ni-katika ṭā'ah sulṭāni wa-Pāte, nā-ye alipatāna sāna na-Muzāri'i. Ḥatā sanati 1236 ikazidi fitnah bayna yake nā Sulṭān Sa'īd bin Sulṭāni Zinjibāri. Akafa Sulṭān Fūmo Lūṭi al-madhkūr sanati 1270.

Ba'ada yake akatawāli Fūmo Lūṭi bin Shaykh bin Fūmo Lūṭi wa-Buwāna

---

[1] A rare use of the Arabic *ibn* "son" with the *alif*, incorrect in a patronymic formula.

Tamu Mkuu. Na-hu'yu ndiyo ba[b]āke Sulṭān Aḥmad, sulṭāni wa-Wītu. Akatawāli aṣubḥi ḥatā ba'da al-'aṣri, wātu wa-mūi wakamtoa, akenda Siu pamōya na-Muzāri'ī wakenda wōte Mombāsah.

Akatawāli Sulṭān Buwāna Shaykh bin Fūmo Mādī akapa‿tana nā Sayyid Sa'īd bin Sulṭān, akatia Wa'Arabu Pateh, wakāketi nyāka mitātu. Ba'ada-ye watu wa-mūi wakamu'uzulu nā shauri [lā] Sayyid Sa'īd bin Sulṭān sanati 1259,[2] wakamtawa‿alīsha Sulṭān Aḥmad a[m]ku'‿[l]iwāo Bwāna Wazīri wa-Buwāna Tamu wa-Buwāna Shaykh wa-Buwāna Tamu Mku'u. Kapatana nā Sayyid Sa'īd bin Sulṭān. (p. 83) Akatawāli nyāka miwīli, wātu wakamu'uzulu wakamrejea Buwāna Shaykh wa-Buwāna Fūmo Mādī. Akākēti katika 'ezi kuwa shau[ri] yā Sayyid Sa'īd bin Sulṭān nyāka mitātu, akafa sanati 1247.

Akarejea Buwāna Waziri katika usuluṭāni wake. Kaya Buwāna Fūmo Lūṭi bin Shaykh aliyo‿tuwenda Mombāsah [p]amōjah na-Muzāri'i, wakashuka Siyū wakapijāna na-Buwāna Wazīri wa-Buwāna Tamu Pateh. Na-Buwāna Waziri ni-shauri mōja nā Sayyid Sa'īd bin Sulṭān, nā Fūmo Lūṭi pamōja na-Mazāri'ī nā Shaykh Matāka mutu wa-Siu. Wakaja Pāte kuwa zītah kapijāna nā-jeyshi yā-Siu, ikavundika Buwāna Waziri ikā‿ishika nti ya-Siyū, akavunda na-ukuta wa-mui.

Shaykh Matāka nā Fūmo Lūṭi wakākimbilia barāni pamōja na-ba'ḍi ya-wātu, ba'da ya-siku kashēti karejeyā Siu kuwa zita zikuu sāna. Wakawatoa wātu wa-Buwāna Waziri kuwa zīta wakā‿washika wao mūi wa-Siu wakajengah ukuta wa-mūi, wakapijāna Pāte nā Siyū, ikawa katika ṭā'ah nā shauri yā Sayyid bin Sa'īd bin Sulṭān. Ba'ada ya-muwāka mmōjah akā'uwāwa Sulṭān Buwāna Wazīri nā Fūmo Bakr wa-Buwāna Shaykh wa-Buwāna Fūmo Mādī.

---

[2] This date is obviously incorrect. Probably 1239 is meant.

Akā‿tawāli yeye Sulṭān Fūmo Bakr bin Shaykh bin Buwāna Fūmo Mādī sanati 1250. Akapatana sāna Sayyid Sa'īd bin Sulṭān mudda wa-kutawāli. Kisa akakhalifu pamōjah nā Shaykh Mataka bin Shaykh Mubārak. Sayyid Sa'īd bin Sulṭān akapeka zītah na-amīr Ḥamād al-Samār al-Bū‿sa'īdī, akapija Pāte nā Siu asiw[a]weze akafa‿nyā amāni. Ba'ada ya-hāyo akitōka fitnah bayna yā sulṭāni wa-Pāte Fūmo Bakr nā-'ami yake Muḥammad bin Aḥmad wa-Buwāna Fūmo Mādī, akashika nyūmbā yā ufalme yā Sulṭān Fūmo Bakar ghaflah kuwa zītah, wātu wa-Lāmū pamōya na-mtu wa Sayyid Sa'īd bin Sulṭān wakuwa‿ṣiliḥisha, Muḥammad bin Aḥmad akampeka Siu kuketi nā-Fūmo Bakar akāyi Pateh. Ba'ada-ye wakatēta wakapijāna tena nyāka mitātu, na-Fūmo Bakari Siu na-Pāte. (p. 82)

Kisa Sayyid Sa'īd bin Sulṭān akawa‿siliḥisha, akāya Pāte Muḥammad bin Aḥmad kuwa shauri mōya yeye nā bin 'ammi yake. Fūm[o] Bakar akamshika Muḥammad bin Aḥmad ghafulah akāmu'uwa kuwa shauri mōya yeye na-mtu wa-Siu.

Sayyid Sa'īd bin Sulṭān akamuwīta Fūmo Bakr akenda U(n)gūjah. Sayyid Sa'īd bin Sulṭān akamfūnga kuwa shauri yā-wātu wa-Lāmū na-sababu ya-kumu'uwa Muḥammad bin Aḥmad ni-kutufuwāta amāni aliyūfānya Sayyid Sa'īd bin Sulṭān Katika sanati 1262.

Akashika Pāte Sulṭān Aḥmad bin Shaykh Fūmo Lūṭi bin Shaykh wa-Buwāna Tāmu Mkuu kuwa shauri yā Sayyid Sa'īd bin Sulṭān. Akaketi nyāka miwīli, ba'ada-ye akakhalifu. Akāya Sayyid Sa'īd bin Sulṭān akamfū‿ngua Sulṭān Fūmo Bakr, akampa zītah pamōja nā watu wa-Lāmū. Wakāketi Mtānga‿wanda katika majahāzi yā Sayyid Sa'īd. Alipō‿kuwa‿nda Fāzah akākēti mahāla hituwa Kijāngah shā-Mpūngah karibu na-Fāzah. Amīr Ḥamād akaya Siu kuwaka mabōma katika ndia ya-Pāte na-yā Fāzah na-yā Siu. Amīr

Ḥamād akenda Siu kuwa zītah zikuu sāna ḥatā akashika michōmbē iliyōko katika bandari yā Siu kapindua kafānyā mābōma kapija nti ya-Siu, kaona udhia sāna mudda wa-zzītā kuwa zingi sāna wa-zita. Akar[u]di amīr Ḥamād na-ba'ḍi yā 'askari akenda bommāni kutuwaa mzingah, akipītā ndiani wātu wa-Siu wakamtokea ghafulah, amīri wa-Shee Matāka hituwāye Bin Mubārak, Ḥamad 'Umar nā amīri wa-pīli hitwawo Ḥamād Ngoma. Wakapijāna wakamu'uwa amīri Ḥamād wakenda nā bomāni wakawapija Wa'Arabu waliyōko bomāni wakutwā'a na-mizingah. Nā jeyshi aliyōko Siu hupijāna.

Walipo‿pāta khabāri kuumpā amīri Ḥamādi miuwāwo jeyshi yā Sayyid Sa'īd bin Sulṭān ikavundika nao walik[u]wa katika (p. 81) kutamal[a]ki Siu. Sayyid Sa'īd bin Sulṭān akisa kuwāta khabāri ya-mūti yā amīri Ḥamād kawondoka kangia markabūni asinene nēna akenda zake Masḳaṭ.

Muwāka wa-pīli akamuweka Sulṭān Fūmo Bakr Fāzah akapija Siu na-**P**āte. Katika waḳti hūnū akafa Shaykh Matāka kuwa maraḍi. Ikawa khitilāfu kuwa zijāna zake, kula mtu ataka ushēkhe, wakā'ingia katika ṭā'ah ya-Sayyid Sa'īd bin Sulṭān, Abū Bakr nā Muḥammad zijāna za Shaykh Matāka. Sayyid akampa Bū Bakr zītā pamōja nā Sulṭān Fūmo Bakr, kumpija Sulṭān Aḥmad Siu.

Akenda Abū Bakr bin Shaykh Matāka pamōya nā amīri wa Sulṭān Fūmo Bakr amukuliwāo Ḥamādi wa-Bā'ishi Nabhānī kāngia Siu usiku, wakapijāna ḥatā wakavundika wātu wa Sulṭān Fūmo Bakr waka'anda‿miwa ndiāni wakamshika Abū Bakr bin Shaykh Matāka, wakampeka **P**āte ku'uwāwa nā Sulṭān Aḥmad.

Ba'ada-ye akasimāma nduye Shaykh Muḥammad bin Shaykh Matāka ṭarafu yā Sayyid Sa'īd bin Sulṭan, yeye nā Sulṭān Fūmo Bakr. Sayyid Sa'īd bin Sulṭān kawā**p**a zītah nā 'askari nā-gharāmah, wakampija Sulṭān Aḥmad ḥatā wakamutoa **P**āte sanati 1273, akenda Kwau. Siu ikawa n[a]-Shaykh

Muḥammad bin Shaykh Matāka ṭarafu yā Sayyid Sa'īd bin Sulṭān, akamupa nā 'askari kawaka nā gereza. Wakateta na-mtu wa Sayyid Sa'īd bin Sulṭān kuwa sabābu alivunda bānda la-mutēpe alowaka Shaykh Muḥammad Matāka aliwaka mpee yā-gerēzah, nā Shaykh Muḥammad Matāka kavunda gereza.

Na-katika waḳti hūnu alikufa Sulṭān Aḥmad bin Shaykh Kāu, babāke Fūmo Bakar sulṭāni wa-Wītū. Akakēti mahāla pake Sulṭān Aḥmad amkū‿liwao Simbā, sulṭāni wa-Wītū.

Na-ḳabla yā Shaykh Muḥammad asiyāvunda gerēza la-Siu yalitoka fitnah. Sulṭān Fūmo Bakr bin Shaykh akamutoa Pāte kwa zītah, akāya Lāmū akatāka ku'i‿tamalāki Pateh alipoona nguvu zake. Na-wakuu wa-Pāte alipoona kitendo mizofānya Shaykh Muḥammad bin Shaykh Matāka mawisowe‿atāka kuwa‿tawāli wasikiri. Kawapija zītā wakasimāma (p. 80) wakuu wa-Pāte walā hapāna mufalme kuwa shauri la-wātu watatu, Muḥammad bin Mkuu Nabhānī na Buwāna Reḥema bin Aḥmad Nabhānī na-Nāṣir bin 'Abd Allāh bin 'Abd al-Salām, ndi walokuwa mudabir al-umūr. Akākū‿sānyā zānah wakapijāna Shaykh Muḥammad bin Shaykh Matāka wakamshinda wakāfa wātu ma'rufu nā mā‿amiri makuu, wātu wawīli Buwāna Dumīlī nā-Mawlanā wa-Shee Kūlī.

Shaykh Muḥammad bin Shaykh Matāka kisa kuona māmbō hāya akayā kutāka amāni kuwa Muḥammad bin Buwāna Mkuu al-Nabhānī kuwani ndiye aliekuwa mkūbwa wāo katika hāwa wātu watatu tumezo‿tāngulia kutaya. Akatāka kumpa yeye Muḥammad bin Mukuu usulṭāni wa-Siu wa-nā Pate, aka'iza kajibu "Mimi ni-mtu mzima." Wakenda kumtuwā'a Sulṭān Aḥmad wa-Wītū, kapeka wātu Shaykh Muḥammad bin Shaykh Matāka na-wātu wa-Pāte wakampeka nā Shaykh Nāṣir bin 'Abd Allāh bin 'Abd al-Salām Kāu kumtuwā'a Sulṭān Aḥmad al-mulaḳab Simbā, kāya na-ye Pāte.

Khabāri ikasililia Ungūjah, Sulṭān Sayyid Mājid bin Sa'īd bin Sulṭān kuwani Sayyid Sa'īd bin Sulṭān utānuguli[a] kufa sanati 1273. Kabla ya-hāyo Sayyid kām'ēta wazīri wake Sayyid Sulaymān bin Ḥamad kuwa markab īlī kushika **P**āte kur[undi]sha fitnah, markab aliwa‿waṣili Mā(nd)ra **P**ate imekuwisa kushika mtu wa-Sulṭān Aḥmad, Abū Bakr bin Ḥasan al-Bū[r]ī, amekūya Nāṣir bin 'Abd Allāh bin 'Abd al-Salām. Akisa kupāta khabāri hiyo Sayyid Sulaymān bin Aḥmad akarejea Ungūjah, nā-Shaykh Muḥammad bin Shaykh Matāka waḳti hūnu ndi**p**o alipō‿vunda gereza wa Siu.

Akisa kuwaṣili Sulṭān Aḥmad **P**āte wātu waakampa kuwa ndiye sulṭān. Shaykh Muḥammad bin Shaykh Matāka kunā Mzee Sēfu nā Shaykh Shikuwe nā Muḥammad Mōte akāsitākiri k(w)ā Sulṭān Aḥmad ufalme wake.

Sayyid Mājid bin Sa'īd bin Sulṭān akā‿**p**eka wātu wa-Lāmū Pāte kuwa nāṣaḥa pamōya nā Shaykh Muḥī al-Dīn kamtaka (p. 79) Sulṭān Aḥmad aweke 'askari wa-sayyid Pāte. Na-hūyu Shaykh Muḥī al-Dīn ndiye alotuwa 'askari wa-sayyid katika gerēza lā Sīu wa**p**ija Sha[yk]h Muḥammad bin Shaykh Matāka, 'askari wālī akenda Shaykh Muḥī al-Dīn kuwa‿toa kuwa amāni kuwā alikuwa mtu wa-Sayyid Mājid bin Sa'īd katika mawazīri.

Alipōkuwenda Ungūja nā 'askari sayyid kafa‿nya hasira sāna yu' la-Shaykh Muḥī al-Dīn, nā Shaykh Muḥi al-Dīn akata‿daraki alipō‿mu'ona Sayyid Mājid na-ghaḍab. Ndipo kenda yeye na-wātu wa-Lāmū, nā-ye Shaykh Muḥī al-Dīn alina ḥila sāna nā 'ilmu nyīngi. Akenda **P**āte na-khiyāri ya-wātu wa-Lāmū pamōjah nā Shaykh Aḥmad nā Shaykh 'Abd al-Raḥmān, aye na-ye shaykh **P**ate. Wakanēna nā Sulṭān Aḥmad akariḍika ba'uda yā shida kuwa sababu yā ṣaḥabah yā Shaykh Aḥmad nā Shaykh 'Abd al-Raḥmān, akakhālifu shauri la-wazīri wake Nāṣir bin 'Abd Allāh bin 'Abd al-Salām kuwāni wali'iza kutia Wa'Arābu ḥatā mtu mmōya.

Wātu wa **P**āte wakafānyā shauri mōjah Muwāna Jāha binti Fūmo Lūṭi

Kipu(n)ga wa-Buwāna Fūmo Mādī, mke wa-Sulṭān Fūmo Bakr bin Shaykh. Waḳti hūnu Sulṭān Fūmo Bakar uweko Lāmūh tini yā shauri lā Sayyid Mājid bin Sa'īd tāngu akipō‿tuliwa **P**āte.

Bāsi kila siku wakitia 'askari kwa siri na-zāna usiku usiku. Alipō khabāri Sulṭān Aḥmad ikawa fitunah na-'askari wamekuwa wāngi **P**ate, wakampija Sulṭān Aḥmad ghafulah ba'ada-ye kisa ḥ[il]a kutaka kumshika wasiweze kuwani Wa**P**ate wote walikuwa shauri mōjah nā Sayyid Mājid bin Sa'īd ili wazīri wake Nāṣir bin 'Abd Allāh bin 'Abd al-Salām. Wakapijāna ndāni ya-mūi wa-Pāte, akatoka Sulṭān Aḥmad yeye nā Shaykh Muḥammad bin Shaykh Matāka wakenda Siu.

Pāte wakashika Wa'Arābu na-baḥrini wakatiye markab, zīta zalipo‿kuwa zikuu sāna alipokūya Sayyid Mājid bin Sa'īd ku'i‿ḥuṣuri Siu na-**P**āte, na-baḥri kusi**p**ita (p. 78) kusipindiye **ch**ōmbo **ch**o**ch**ōte madau na-mitē**p**e. Wakapijāna na-baḥrīni waken‿da barāni kutwaa shakūlah na-majira yā kurudi huwana ḥali ḥayy mayti. Sayyid Mājid akatia silsila kutika kānnwa lā-mto wa-Siu Ku'yu kusi**p**iti **ch**ōmbo, tena naouliwaona nyezi sita kwa baḥri nā-kwa **p**uwāni. Nā jānibu ya-Fāzah Mzee Sēfu aka[kh]ālifu wa-Sayyid Mājid bin Sa'id kuwa ḥila nyī(n)gi na-māneno māngi, akaoni ḍiḳi sāna Sulṭān Aḥmad nā Shaykh Muḥammad bin Shaykh Matāka.

Nā-nti yā Sīu ikawa fitnah ikawa ba'ḍi ya-wātu wampenda Sayyid Mājid kuwa sabābu ya-mashaka walopāta, na-wa‿tuwe ni-hāwa Sharīf Mawlāna bin Abū Bakr nā 'Isā bin Aḥmad al-Sōmālī. Alipoona Sulṭān Aḥmad nā Shaykh Muḥammad bin Shaykh [Matāka] kama hāya, wakatāka amāni kwa Sayyid Mājid, akawāpa. Katika maneno ya-amāni Sulṭān Aḥmad akasifiri kuwa siri usiku akenda barāni akarejea Kāu.

Ba'ada-ye Shaykh Muḥammad bin Shaykh Matāka akampeka kijāna

shake, Shaykh Muḥammad bin Shaykh Matāka akenda markabuni kuwa Sayyid Mājid bin Sa'īd nā Sayyid Mājid akamsameḥe akampā nā 'aṭāyā nyingi. Sayyid Mājid kasafiri akarejea Ungūjah, kisa Shaykh Muḥammad bin Shaykh Matā[ka] akenda Ungūjah kumuwajihi Sayyid Mājid akamushika akamfu'ngah katika ngōme ya-Mambāsah na-wātu. Akafa Shaykh Muḥammad.

Na-ba'di ya-siku akampeka liwālī Sa'ūd bin Ḥamad kumshika Sulṭān Aḥmad kuwa ḥilla nyingi asiweze, katoka Kāu kuwa siri akenda Wītū. Al-wālī Sa'ūd bin Ḥamad akāya Fāzah kumshika 'Umar Matāka Fāzah nā zijāna za Shaykh Muḥammad bin Shaykh Matāka kuwashika Siu kawa‿**p**eka ngomeni Mombāsah. 'Umar Matāka akamfūnga (p. 77) Lāmūh.

Ba'ada-ye Sayyid Mājid akatamalaki Sawāḥili zote hakūna mtu wakum'ariḍi. Nā Sulṭān Aḥmad kāketi Wītū kat[i]ka ṭā'ah Sayyid Mājid ḥatā alipō‿tawāli Sayyid Barghash bin Sa'īd bin Sulṭān. Akataka Sayyid Barghash kuweka 'askari Wītū nā bendera, sulṭāni asiriḍiki kapeka zita kumpījah asiweze akafa‿nyā amāni. Nā-ye Sa'ūd bin Ḥamad hakumpija sāna zītā, Sayyid Barghash kapeka zītā zamāni za al-wālī Sa'īd bin Ḥamad bin Sa'īd. Sulṭān Aḥmad katāka ḥimāyah kuwa Jaramāni, wakam**p**a na-ba'ḍi ya-bāra ya-Sawāḥili. Akafa Sulṭān Aḥmad katika ḥāli hiyo yā ḥimāya sanati 1306.

Akatawāli Sulṭān Fūmo Bakari bin Sulṭān Aḥmad bin Shaykh al-Nabhāni. Akakēti katika hiyo yā ḥimāya, ikutokea fitna yeye na-Jarmani. Mtu mmōja hu'tuwa Kunshil akampija bawābu wa-lāngo kampija ghafulah kuwa raṣāṣi, walikuweko 'askari kawapijah kuwa raṣāṣi na-'askari wakampija Kinsil na-watu wangi walofūetene lao waka'wāwa WaZungu min ghayri amri yā Sulṭān Fūmo Bakr. 'Askari waliyō'aona jamā'a zao wamekufa hāwakungūjah amri yā sulṭāni wakawāpija WaZūngu, na-wātu wa-Mkonūmbī na-Wanda‿mūnyu walipo‿**p**āta khabāri na-kuumpa lā WaZūngu wamepijāna wakāwa‿ūwa WaZungu waliyō‿kuweko.

Ba'ada-ye akāya dōlah ya-WaNgereza wakatāka kufānyā inṣāfu akawa‿taka watu wa Mukunūmbī na-Wanda‿mūnyu ma'ana awatia katika ḥukmu. Fūmo Bakar asiriḍiki kuwatoa, wakampija zītah Sulṭān Fūmo Bakr, zikayā mashua ḥatā Mkonūmbī na-Wana‿mūnyu nā Kilimāni Nya(n)do‿za‿**p**uwāni, wazipiji kuwa mizingah wakatia na-mōto. Ḥatā layla 11 Rabī' al-Awwal sanati 1308 wakapijāna watu wa-Wītū katika ndia yā-Kipini na-wātu wa-dolah tukufu, wakāvundika wātu wa-Wītū. Ḥatā aṣubuḥi (p. 76) siku yā jum'a tātu muwezi 12 Rabī' al-Awwal sanati 1308 wakampija Sulṭān Fūmo Bakar wakamtoa Wītū akenda Jō‿nge[n]i ḥatā 28 Jumādā al-Awwal sanati 1308 akafa.

Kashika mahāla yake nduye Buwāna Shaykh bin Sulṭān Aḥmad Nabhānī. Ba'ada ya-siku **ch**ā**ch**i ikawa fitnah akashika ndūye Fumo 'Umar Nabhānī na-'Avu‿tūla wa Bāhiru wakamfūnga Buwāna Shaykh bin Sulṭān Aḥmad. Akatawāli Sulṭān Fūmo 'Umar.

Nawākuwisa kutamalaki **P**āte Sulṭān 'Aḥmad, suluṭāni wa-Wītū, a[ka]tamalaki kuwanda Sulaymān bin Sulaymān al-Muẓaffar Nabhānī Imam al-Ya'rubī. Hidhi ndiyo khabāri yā Nabhānī kuwa Sawāḥili na-khabāri zao k[a]ma tumezo‿tangulia kutayā. Wamezo‿tawāli wafalume wāḥid wa thalāthīn na-muwāna‿mke mmōjah, jumulah ithnāni wa thalāthīn min ghayri alikatawālah wakiuzuliwa wakarejeyā kutawālī'.

Tume‿nāḳili hāya kuwa Muḥammad bin Fūmo 'Umar al-Nabhānī al-mulaḳab Buwāna Kitīni, nā-ye alinā‿ḳili kuwa jadi yake Muḥammad bin Buwāna Mkuu al-Nabhānī amkuliwāo Buwāna S[ī]m[b]ā, aloḍibiti sāna khabāri yā nasab yao kama tumezo‿tājah.

Naḳalah yā awwali al-aḳall Sāliḥ bin Sālim bin Aḥmad bin 'Abd Allāh Sharāḥīl 6 fī Safar sanati 1318. Naḳalat hadhā al-liwālī al-'azīz Muḥammad bin Aḥmad bin Sulṭān bin Fūmo Bakr bin Shaykh bin Buwāna Fūmo Mādī wa-Simbā Sulṭān Muḥammad bin Abū Bakr bin Buwāna Mkuu bin Abū Bakr bin Ḥamad bin Abū Bakr bin Muḥammad bin Abū Bakr bin Muḥammad bin 'Umar bin Muḥammad bin Aḥmad bin Muḥammad bin Sulaymān bin Sulaymān al-Muẓaffar al-Nabhānī.

Naḳalah al-thānī 1 fī Rajab sanati 1343 wa-katabah al-aḳall Sāliḥ bin Sālim bin Ḥamad.

Naḳalat al-thālith fī Dhī al-Ka'da 1363 fī 3 Febrūrī wa-katabah 'Alī Muḥammad.

Naḳalat dhālika naḳalā ḥarfan bi-ḥarfi anā l-haḳīr li-Llāh ta'ālā, 'Abd Allāh bin 'Ali bin Muḥammad al-Ma'āwī.

TALE OF THE HISTORY OF PATE
AND THOSE OF IMPORTANCE TO EAST AFRICA[1]

Date of Hijra 600

(p. 92) There was Sulayman bin Sulayman Muzaffar al-Nabhani. The first beginner of the Nabahani, the first to come to Pate of the Nabhani, was Sulayman bin Sulayman bin Muzaffar Nabhani and his two brothers: 'Ali bin Sulayman and 'Uthman bin Sulayman. And this Sulayman bin Sulayman the aforesaid, it was he who had been sultan, and he formerly ruled the land of the Arabs. The aforesaid sultan came to Pate at the date of the year 600—six hundred—from the Hijra,[2] (was) his coming to settle at Pate.

He asked for marriage from the king of Pate, from among the Wa-al-Batawiyin. Sultan Sulayman bin Sulayman was an important man, (so) the king of Pate married him to his daughter. And the custom of all the WaSwahili till now (is that) a man takes your daughter (in marriage), (then) seven days after the wedding he goes to see the father-in-law at his house, the father of his wife, to be given gifts from the people. This Sulayman bin Sulayman, that king gave him his kingship that had been theirs. (Thereafter) reigned Sulayman bin Sulayman.

---

[1] This is not the original title, which is absent. The text begins directly with the narrative. If the prototype had a title, it was probably *Akhbār Pateh*.

[2] 1203-4.

There was a town called Kitaka on the same island of Pate, east of Pate; and Siu was not yet a town. On the side of the water there was a city called Shanga, east of Pate. And Faza had its own rulers, WaPaza, (or) al-Mafazi. All these towns were under Sultan Sulayman bin Sulayman. And Manda had a separate king, and he had great power.

Sultan Sulayman bin Sulayman died at the date of 625 of the Hijra.[3] He left two sons, Muhammad and Ahmad. Muhammad's age (was) twenty years, and Ahmad's fifteen years. Muhammad bin Sulayman bin Sulayman reigned after his father. A conflict arose (p. 91) between him and the people of Shanga; he made war on the city (and) destroyed it completely. And some of those (people) came to Pate, and a separate (group, whose) tribe (was) Kinandangu, fled, (and) the place where they ran away was not known. After some days passed the news came to Sultan Muhammad bin Sulayman from the hunters (who) came (and) said to him: "Those unknown,[4] we have seen them in the forest." The sultan sent people to look for them, (and) they caught up with them; they had made huts inside the forest. Sultan Muhammad bin Sulayman forgave them (and) returned them to their (own) place. This is the origin of the town of Siu.

(Later) came other WaSwahili, (and) they all settled. (Then) also came the WaFamau (and) settled; and they were the chiefs of Siu under the overlordship of Sultan Muhammad bin Sulayman.

---

[3] 1227-8.

[4] The best clarification of Siu etymology: *wa-siu* may mean either "those of Siu" or "those unknown."

Sultan Muhammad the aforesaid died in the year 650.[5] His brother Ahmad bin Sulayman reigned. He governed the land of Pate very well, constructing houses (and) planting fields. He did not make war anywhere (and) died in the year 660.[6]

(Next) reigned the son of his brother, by the name Ahmad bin Muhammad bin Sulayman. He treated the people very well, following the example of his (paternal) uncle, building up the town of Pate and the farms, until he died in the year 700.[7] He left many children.

(Then) reigned his son Muhammad bin Ahmad bin Muhammad bin Sulayman. He governed the people in an excellent manner. (Then) the people of Faza seceded. He fought them (and) brought them under his authority after many battles, until he overcame them. He conquered Manda (and) gained possession of it through a military ruse, because the king of Manda had great power in terms of money and men. He destroyed it utterly and carried off some people to Pate.

And some (of those) fled into the wilderness (*nyika*), and they ran away to all places; some came to Shela (and) put themselves under the protection of the men of Lamu. Sultan Muhammad bin Ahmad the aforesaid demanded them of the people of Lamu (but) they refused to surrender them. And some went to Malindi and other towns. Sultan Muhammad bin Ahmad the aforesaid pursued vigorously (the matter of) those who came to Shela. The men of Lamu refused to surrender them decisively. Finally, Sultan Muhammad died

---

[5] 1252-3.

[6] 1261-2.

[7] 1300-1.

in the year 732.[8]

His son ascended to kingship, Sultan ‘Umar bin Muhammad bin Ahmad bin Muhammad bin Sulayman. He returned to his father's case (p. 90) against the men of Lamu, demanding the people of Manda. The men of Lamu refused to surrender them. He made war on them; the men of Lamu sued for peace, (and) submitted to the overlordship of the sulṭān.

Sultan ‘Umar bin Muhammad gained great power (and) conquered all the towns of the Swahili (coast): Ozi, Malindi, Kiwayu, Kita...[*lacuna in MS*]. He gained possession of all the towns from Pate to Kirimba. In each town he placed (his own) man to govern. This is the origin of those *Majumbe* who are to be found on the whole coast (*mrima*). The meaning (of this word) is "slaves of the Yumbe," and this *yumbe* means the palace of the king of Pate.

And in the east he gained possession as far as Warsheikh. He went to wage war, beginning with Kiwayu (and then against) Tula and Tuwala and Shungwaya and all the harbors (*banadiri*): Brawa, Marka and Mogadisho.

(As long as) he lived, all these lands were under his authority, only Zanzibar he did not rule, for at that time Zanzibar was not a great country. This Sultan ‘Umari the aforesaid excelled in war and loved (his) subjects, and the subjects loved him. The land of Pate gained great power. Sultan ‘Umar died in the year 749.[9] He left two sons, Muhammad and Ahmad.

The elder son, Sultan Muhammad bin ‘Umar bin Muhammad bin Ahmad bin Muhammad bin Sulayman reigned over the kingdom of his father. There was peace, there was no war. And he loved very much money and

---

[8] 1331-2.

[9] 1348-9.

trade; he sent voyages in his ships to go (and) conduct trade, and he had much profit in money.

And one time he sent his son on a voyage; he came upon an island at sea, found a silver mine, returned to Pate (and) made people to work the mine. He obtained great wealth; money (so) increased in the Pate land that they made swords of silver and ladders of silver and many silver vessels. And the king died in the year 797.[10] He left four sons: Bwana Mkuu and Ahmad and Abu Bakr and 'Umar.

His brother, Sultan Ahmad bin 'Umar bin Muhammad bin Ahmad bin Muhammad bin Sulayman bin Sulayman reigned. He ruled over the people well, in peace (p. 89) (and) in an excellent manner toward all the people. He died.

(Next) reigned Abu Bakr bin Muhammad bin 'Umar bin Muhammad bin Ahmad bin Muhammad bin Sulayman. He ruled well over all the people and all the towns under his authority without discord. And he died in the year 875,[11] leaving two sons, Muhammad and Ahmad.

His son reigned in place of his father, Muhammad bin Abu Bakr bin Muhammad bin Muhammad bin 'Umar bin Muhammad bin Ahmad bin Muhammad bin Sulayman. In his time the Portuguese Europeans came to all the Swahili towns. They stayed at Mombasa (and) made a fort. And near Pate they built Ndondo. The people of the mainland obeyed them, paid them money (and) accepted their authority. They harassed the king throughout his land of Pate (and) fought a war against the king on the side of Shindakasi.

---

[10] 1394-5.

[11] 1470-1.

They built the ground of Pate on the beach by means of (making) hollows with the goal of attacking the town of Pate, (but) failed. They sued for peace (and) made a (written) document (stating) their conditions. The Europeans remained at Pate (and) made a customs-house; in their European language they called it "*Fandika.*" They made many things around the island of Pate. The sultan died in the year 900.[12] He left two sons, Bwana Mkuu and Abu Bakr.

After his father the aforementioned, Sultan Abu Bakr bin Muhammad bin Abu Bakr bin Muhammad bin Ahmad bin Muhammad bin Sulayman ascended to kingship. He ruled over the people well, in peace, as was the practice of his father. He died in the year 940,[13] with affairs in order. And he left two sons, Ahmad and Muhammad.

Their (paternal) uncle Bwana Mkuu bin Muhammad bin Abu Bakr bin Muhammad bin ‘Umar bin Muhammad bin Ahmad bin Muhammad bin Sulayman ascended to kingship. (There) arose hostilities with the Europeans, but there was no war. The trouble lasted many days. He died in the year 973,[14] leaving one son, Abu Bakr.

(Next) reigned Muhammad bin Abu Bakr bin Muhammad bin ‘Umar bin Muhammad bin Ahmad bin Muhammad bin Sulayman. He made peace with the Europeans, (and) they took some of the towns. He died in the year 1002.[15] He left one son named Abu Bakr who did not reign.

(Next) ruled Abu Bakr bin Bwana Mkuu bin Muhammad bin Abu Bakr

---

[12] 1494-5.

[13] 1533-4.

[14] 1565-6.

[15] 1593-4.

bin Muhammad bin 'Umar bin Muhammad bin Ahmad bin Muhammad bin Sulayman. He ruled the people according to the manner of his ancestors who had preceded (him), but the kingdom diminished in strength. (p. 88) He died in the year 1041.[16] He left Bwana Mkuu and Abu Bakr, named for his father.

(Next) reigned Abu Bakr bin Muhammad bin Abu Bakr bin Muhammad bin Abu Bakr bin Muhammad bin 'Umar bin Ahmad bin Muhammad bin Sulayman. (There) arose discord with the Europeans; they fought, (and) he defeated the Europeans in a very powerful battle. After this came in turn an expedition of the Europeans. They attacked the town of Pate with cannons (and) cut off the roads from the sea to block the ships. The people saw hardships (and) made peace. The king died in the year 1061.[17] He left two sons, Bwana Mkuu and Ahmad.

(Next) reigned Bwana Mkuu wa Bwana Bakr wa Bwana Mkuu bin Muhammad bin Abu Bakr bin Muhammad bin 'Umar bin Muhammad bin Ahmad bin Muhammad bin Sulayman. He got along with the Europeans. And he loved to stay at Lamu; even the monsoon (season) he spent at Lamu. He contracted a marriage among the people of Lamu.

And about this time the WaFamau of Siu revolted against his authority. He fought the town of Siu, seized some people (and) carried them off to Pate. The chief of Siu escaped, went to Dondo, to the Portuguese, (and) claimed protection. The chief of the Europeans came to Pate, to the king, (to ask that he) release the people of Siu. The king released them (and) returned them to

---

[16] 1631-2.

[17] 1650-1.

their (former) place at Siu under safe conduct.

After that the Portuguese devised a stratagem. They came to Pate in a ship (and) invited the king to come aboard ship. He did not go, (but) sent the son of his (paternal) uncle Bwana Mkuu, him and (some) men of Pate. The Europeans carried them off in the ship, (and) not even one man (ever) returned. After that the king attacked the Europeans from all directions, on the mainland and on the islands, (and) drove them away from all these locations. They fled to Mombasa. The king died in the year 1100.[18] He had sons, Bwana Bakr and Bwana Madi, and one daughter named Mwana Darini.

(Then) reigned Abu Bakr bin Bwana Mkuu bin Abu Bakr bin Muhammad[19] bin Abu Bakr bin Muhammad bin 'Umar bin Muhammad bin Ahmad bin Muhamamd bin Sulayman. The king was suddenly attacked with a sword by Ahmad, the brother of the Bwana Mkuu who had been taken away by the Europeans, (p. 87) the Portuguese. The king died in the year 1103.[20]

(Then) reigned this Ahmad bin Abu Bakr bin Muhammad bin Muhammad bin Abu Bakr bin Muhammad bin 'Umar bin Muhammad bin Ahmad bin Muhammad bin Sulayman. After he ascended, he pursued the Portuguese (and) drove them out from throughout his country.

And at this time Mwana Darini, the daughter of Bwana Mkuu wa Bwana Bakr, wife of the Bwana Mkuu bin Abu Bakr who had been taken away by the Portuguese before the time of Sultan Ahmad, whose two brothers, Abu Bakr and Bwana Madi, had been killed by Sultan Ahmad,—and (as) her husband had

---

[18] 1688-9.

[19] This form of the name is the same as in MS 321 but not MS 177.

[20] 1691-2.

been carried away, she grieved greatly. (So after) many days passed, she wished to circumcise her son Bwana Tamu Mtoto ("Junior"), who was called Sultan Abu Bakr Imamu Huda, the son of Bwana Mkuu who went to Goa.

(When) the king received the news, he decided to make a celebration himself, for his own children, in order to deny her the ceremonial horn. (When) the news came to Mwana Darini, she sent for Mwenyi Bayayi bin Mkuu, *Sharif* of the *Jamal al-Layl*, who had great skill in carving, (and) she requested that he make a horn superior to the horn of Pate. He accepted the wage of one hundred and twenty riyals, (and) she gave him elephant tusks to choose [the best] one. He made the horn in secret, till it was finished (and then) she showed it suddenly (and) took it around the houses of her kin. Every man gave an offering of very much money, (so that) the master declined the wage (and) asked for the offerings. She gave him the offerings (and) made the celebration.

Later, at the time of Bwana Tamu Mkuu ("Senior"), the people of Lamu came (and) borrowed the horn; he gave it to them, (and) they carried the original horn to the sea. The ship sank in the water (and) perished. Bwana Tamu Mkuu asked for the horn of Mwana Darini, saying to her, "Give it to us, so that we may use in all the towns." She answered him, "Every clan who makes an offering may use my horn."

And Mwana Darini set free a slave who knew how to blow (the horn). She said, "This is the chief beater of the horn, he and his descendants. And for his fee let him be given five riyals[21] and a cloth to carry the horn, (and)

---

[21] In the text, *riyāli (reale)*. The currency used is unknown: the value of this unit, usually translated "dollar," changed according to variety. Regarding the *siwa* ritual, see comments by Stigand and Werner in the present volume.

let him be given ghee and a present, from every man according to his means." And that family was called "the Heralds of the Horn," (and) to this day there are people (belonging) to it. (p. 86) From that time until now the custom of all the clans of Pate and the clans of other towns (has been) to go (and) borrow [the horn] under such circumstances, (and) the Heralds of the Horn are paid.

Mischief increased within the city, and during his reign for seven years there was drought; there was no rain, (and so) the king abdicated. (Next) reigned Sultan Abu Bakr bin Bwana Tamu Mkuu wa Bwana Mtiti bin Ahmad bin Abu Bakr bin ‘Umar bin Ahmad bin ‘Umar bin Muhammad bin Ahmad bin Muhammad bin Sulayman.

He made a strong alliance with the sultan of Maskat, al-Imam Sayf bin Nabhani al-Ya‘rubi. This sultan of Pate went to Arabia, (and) they came to an agreement with the king of Arabia. And this king of Pate drove out the Portuguese on Sunday, he killed (many) men to gain possession of the fort of Mombasa.

He informed the Imam al-Ya‘rubi. (The latter) brought governors (*liwali*) of the Mazru‘i (family), three men: Muhammad bin ‘Uthman and ‘Ali bin ‘Uthman, the third brother's name is unknown. They came with soldiers of the Imam Sayf Nabhani al-Ya‘rubi. This is the origin of the Mazru‘i.

And the king of Pate conducted (himself) in an excellent manner toward all the people. He lived forty years in his kingship (and) died in the year 1154.[22] He had many children (but) his sons did not reign after him.

(Instead) reigned Ahmad bin Abu Bakr bin Muhammad bin Abu Bakr bin Muhammad bin ‘Umar bin Ahmad bin ‘Umar bin Muhammad bin Ahmad

---

[22] 1741-2.

bin Muhammad bin Sulayman.[23] He was benevolent[24] (and) died in the year 1160.[25] He left one son named Bwana Gongo (who) did not rule.

(Instead) ruled Bwana Tamu Mtoto ("the Younger") who was called Imam al-Huda,[26] the son of Bwana Mkuu who was carried away by the Portuguese. And his (real) name was Abu Bakr bin Bwana Mkuu bin Abu Bakr bin Muhammad bin Abu Bakr bin Muhammad bin Abu Bakr bin Muhammad bin ʻUmar bin Muhammad bin Sulayman.

At this time the Imam al-Yaʻrubi brought an expedition to attack Pate, (but) they failed, (and) very many Arabs died, (so) they made peace. After this the people of Lamu revolted. The king waged war on them (and) failed against the people of Lamu.[27] And the people of Lamu equipped an army (and) they came to Pate on the side of Kitoki. They fought the men of Pate in a great battle. (p. 85) The men of Lamu were defeated. After this the king of Pate waged war by land and by sea; he attacked the people of Lamu (and) conquered them. After this the king of Pate and the people of Lamu became united, the Imam al-Yaʻrubi established single administration. They killed the king in the year 1177.[28]

(Then) reigned his sibling, a woman, Sultana Mwana Khadija binti

---

[23] Compare this name in MS 321.

[24] Or "prosperous," since MS 177 talks of numerous herds of cattle.

[25] 1747.

[26] The use of a religious term ("the Rightly-Guided Imam") is unusual. The repetitious addition of the phrase about his father's kidnapping makes it look like a patronymic formula.

[27] MS 321 has "the people of Siu" in this passage.

[28] 1763-4.

Bwana Mkuu bin Abu Bakr bin Muhammad bin Abu Bakr bin Muhammad bin Abu Bakr bin Muhammad bin 'Umar bin Muhammad bin Ahmad bin Muhammad bin Sulayman. There was much intrigue in the land of Pate (because) there were two kings - the aforesaid Mwana Khadija and Sultan 'Umar. They fought in the town of Pate for three years. Sultan 'Umar went to Barawa (and) returned to Pate with a very powerful force. One night [*lacuna in MS*[29]] by the men of Mwana Khadija, each man where he was. Mwana Khadija died in the year 1187.[30]

(Then) reigned Bwana Mkuu wa Sheye wa Bwana Tamu Mkuu. The subjects made much trouble; he got no peace during his reign until, in the year 1191,[31] the men of the town invaded [his palace] (and) killed him on that date.

(Then) reigned Bwana Fumo Madi, whose (real) name was Sultan Muhammad bin Abu Bakr bin Bwana Mkuu bin Abu Bakr bin Muhammad bin Abu Bakr bin Muhammad bin Abu Bakr bin Muhammad bin 'Umar bin Muhammad bin Ahmad bin Muhammad bin Sulayman. After he came to power, the subjects wished to make intrigue; he fought them in battle, overcame them, seized forty men--and two were his own brothers--(and) slaughtered them like goats so blood (ran off) the roof. In this way he suppressed the great men (of the city). (Then) there was peace, (for) no other man rose to make trouble; he reigned in great calm (and) died in 1224.[32]

---

[29] A word or passage missing in the copy refers to an attack on Sultan 'Umar's forces.

[30] 1773-4.

[31] 1777.

[32] 1809-10.

And (there) reigned no other king like him. He left many children.

(Then) reigned Sultan Ahmad bin Shaykh Fumo Luti bin Shaykh bin Bwana Mkuu.[33] Trouble increased in the town of Lamu, he attacked them - he and the men of Mombasa, the Mazru'i, (being) on the same side. They landed at Shela a great army of men of Pate and men of Mombasa. The men of Lamu came out, came to Shela (and) fought with the men of Pate and men of Mombasa, (and) they were defeated. The army of the men of Lamu had great force; the army of Pate and of Mombasa was defeated. They ran to their ships, (but) some ships were stranded on the beach. (Then) they stopped (and) fought (another) great battle. Very many men were killed, men of Pate and men of Mombasa, (p. 84) without counting. Out of the men of Pate, the important ones, who were not slaves or lowly people, (there were) eighty-one of "So-and-So, the son of So-and-so," the persons of Pate who went to the next life;[34] and as to the men of Mombasa, there was no counting.

After that the men of Lamu went to Arabia (and) asked for Sa'id bin Sultan, son of Imam, and they gave him the land of Lamu in the year 1228;[35] thereafter he ruled Lamu. The kingdom of Pate included Pate (itself) and the harbors (*banadiri*).

(Then) unrest increased, (there) arose a second man from among the sons of Bwana Fumo Madi, called Fumo Luti Kipunga. He fought Sultan Ahmad. Later Sultan Ahmad died of disease in 1230.[36]

---

[33] This name is the same as in MS 321 but not in MS 177.

[34] Cusack translates: "having wives to go into mourning there in Pate."

[35] 1813.

[36] 1814-15.

(Then) reigned Fumo Luti wa Bwana Fumo Madi. And he was very strong, brave and generous. And those were the times when Shaykh Mataka bin Shaykh Mubarak held the office of *shaykh* of Siu. He obtained soldiers and guns, and he was under the suzerainty of the sulṭān of Pate and on very good terms with the Mazru'i until the year 1236.[37] (Then) trouble arose between him and Sultan Sa'id bin Sultan of Zanzibar. Sultan Fumo Luti the aforesaid died in the year 1270.[38]

After him reigned Fumo Luti bin Shaykh bin Fumo Luti wa Bwana Tamu Mkuu. He was the one who was the father of Sultan Ahmad, the sultan of Witu. He reigned from dawn until after the mid-afternoon [prayer[39]]. The men of the town drove him out. He went to Siu together with the Mazru'i; (then) they all went to Mombasa.

(Then) reigned Sultan Bwana Shaykh bin Fumo Madi. He negotiated with Sayyid Sa'id bin Sultan, took Arabs into Pate, (and) they remained (there) three years. Afterwards the people of the town deposed him with the consent [of] Sayyid Sa'id bin Sultan in the year 12[3]9.[40] They installed Sultan Ahmad called Bwana Waziri wa Bwana Tamu wa Bwana Shaykh wa Bwana Tamu Mkuu. He was on good terms with Sayyid Sa'id bin Sultan (p. 83) (and) reigned for two years. (Then) the people deposed him and returned Bwana Shaykh wa Bwana Fumo Madi. He remained in power with the consent

[37] 1820-1.

[38] 1852-3. This date is probably incorrect. MS 177 gives 1236.

[39] The precise time is indicated in MS 177.

[40] 1823-4.

of Sayyid Sa'id bin Sultan for three years[41] (and) died in the year 1247.[42]

Bwana Waziri returned to his sultanship. (Then) came Fumo Luti bin Shaykh who had gone to Mombasa together with the Mazru'i; they captured Siu and attacked Bwana Waziri wa Bwana Tamu at Pate. Bwana Waziri was at one with Sayyid Sa'id bin Sultan, and Fumo Luti was at one with the Mazru'i and Shaykh Mataka, a man of Siu. They came to Pate with troops (and) fought. The army of Siu was defeated; Bwana Waziri captured the land of Siu (and) destroyed the city wall.

Shaykh Mataka and Fumo Luti fled to the mainland together with some of the men; after a few days he returned to Siu with a very strong force, drove out the men of Bwana Waziri by attack, captured from them the town of Siu (and) rebuilt the city wall. Pate and Siu fought each other (and) came under the authority and administration of Sayyid Sa'id bin Sultan. After one year Sultan Bwana Waziri was killed by Fumo Bakr wa Bwana Shaykh wa Bwana Fumo Madi.

This Sultan Fumo Bakr bin Shaykh bin Bwana Fumo Madi ascended in the year 1250.[43] He was on very good terms with Sayyid Sa'id bin Sultan during (the latter's) reign. (But) later he revolted, together with Shaykh Mataka bin Shaykh Mubarak. Sayyid Sa'id bin Sultan sent an expedition under Amir Hamad al-Samar al-Busa'idi; he attacked Pate and Siu (but) failed (and) made peace.

After this arose trouble between the sultan of Pate Fumo Bakr and his

---

[41] MS 177 has "five years" but the same date of death.

[42] 1831-2.

[43] 1834-5.

(paternal) uncle Muhammad bin Ahmad wa Bwana Fumo Madi, who seized the royal palace of Sultan Fumo Bakr suddenly by force. (Later) came the men of Lamu together with a man of Sayyid Sa'id bin Sultan to make peace between them; Muhammad bin Ahmad was sent to stay at Siu, (and) Fumo Bakari came to Pate. Afterwards they quarrelled and fought another five years, and Fumo Bakari [came to rule both] Siu and Pate. (p. 82) After Sayyid Sa'id bin Sultan made peace between them, Muhammad bin Ahmad came to Pate to be under single administration with the son of his (paternal) uncle. (Then) Fumo Bakari seized Muhammad bin Ahmad suddenly (and) killed him, in concert with a man of Siu.

Sayyid Sa'id bin Sultan summoned Fumo Bakari. He went to Zanzibar. Sayyid Sa'id bin Sultan imprisoned him on the advice of the men of Lamu, and for the reason of his killing Muhammad bin Ahmad and for failing to obey the peace which Sayyid Sa'id bin Sultan had made in the year 1262.[44]

Sultan Ahmad bin Shaykh Fumo Luti bin Shaykh wa Bwana Tamu Mkuu seized Pate with the consent of Sayyid Sa'id bin Sultan. He ruled for two years; afterwards he revolted. Sayyid Sa'id bin Sultan came, released Sultan Fumo Bakr (and) gave him an army together with the men of Lamu. They stayed at Mtanga Wanda aboard the ships of Sayyid Sa'id.

When (the latter) landed at Faza, he stayed at a place called Kijanga sha Mpunga, near Faza. Amir Hamad came to Siu to build forts on the road between Pate and Faza and Siu. Amir Hamad went to Siu with a very strong force, so that he seized the vessels which were in the harbor of Siu, turned [them] over, made barricades (and) attacked the Siu land. He saw much

---

[44] 1845-6.

hardship in the course of the war going strong, (so) Amir Hamadi returned with some of the soldiers (and) went to the fort to fetch the cannon. As he was on the way, the men of Siu rushed out on him suddenly, an *amir* of Shaykh Mataka called bin Mubarak, Hamad 'Umar and the second *amir*, called Hamadi Ngoma. They attacked and killed Amir Hamad, (then) went to the fort (and) attacked the Arabs who were at the fort and took the cannons. And the troops that were at Siu did not fight.

When the news came of the attack on Amir Hamadi, the killing of the army of Sayyid Sa'id bin Sultan (and) the defeat of those who were (p. 81) to take possession of Siu, when Sayyid Sa'id bin Sultan received the news of the death of Amir Hamad, he went fleeing to the ship without saying a word (and) went away to Maskat.

Next year he placed Sultan Fumo Bakr at Faza, (and the latter) attacked Siu and Pate. About this time Shaykh Mataka died of disease. There was discord among his sons, each man wanted the shaykhdom; they came under the overlordship of Sayyid Sa'id bin Sultan: Abu Bakr and Muhammad, the sons of Shaykh Mataka.

The Sayyid gave Bu Bakr troops together with Sultan Fumo Bakr, to attack Sultan Ahmad at Siu. Abu Bakr bin Shaykh Mataka went together with the *amir* of Sultan Fumo Bakr called Hamadi wa Ba'ishi Nabhani,[45] entered Siu by night (and) fought until the men of Sultan Fumo Bakr were defeated and chased away. They captured Abu Bakr bin Shaykh Mataka (and) sent him to Pate; he was killed by Sultan Ahmad.

Afterwards his brother Shaykh Muhammad bin Shaykh Mataka took a

---

[45] MS 177 calls this *amīr* not Ḥamādi but Ḥamad, i.e. Aḥmad.

stand on the side of Sayyid Sa'id bin Sultan. To him and Sultan Fumo Bakr Sayyid Sa'id bin Sultan gave a troop of soldiers and supplies. They fought Sultan Ahmad till they drove him out of Pate in the year 1273.[46] He went to Kau.

Siu, under Shaykh Muhammad bin Shaykh Mataka, was on the side of Sayyid Sa'id bin Sultan. He (Sayyid Sa'id) gave him soldiers to build a fort. (Later) he quarrelled with a man of Sayyid Sa'id bin Sultan because he destroyed a boat shed built by Shaykh Muhammad Mataka, built in front of the fort. And Shaykh Muhammad Mataka destroyed the fort.

And about this time Sultan Ahmad bin Shaykh died in Kau. (He was) the father of Fumo Bakar, (later) sultan of Witu. In his place ruled Sultan Ahmad who was called *Simba* ("the Lion"), the sultan of Witu.

And before Shaykh Muhammad destroyed the fort of Siu, there had been trouble. Sultan Fumo Bakr bin Shaykh drove him out of Pate by force, and he came to Lamu. He (Shaykh Muhammad) wished to gain possession of Pate, because he saw his (own) power. But when the great men of Pate saw the acts committed by Shaykh Muhammad bin Shaykh Mataka, they did not want him to rule, (and) they did not accept (him). (Then) he made war on them, (but) the great men of Pate (p. 80) persisted. And there was no king due to the advice of three men: Muhammad bin Mkuu Nabhani and Bwana Rehema bin Ahmad Nabhani and Nasir bin 'Abd Allah bin 'Abd Salam, the one who was director of affairs (*mudabbir al-umur*). He collected ammunition; they fought Shaykh Muhammad bin Shaykh Mataka, (and) defeated him. Prominent men died, (and) out of the great *amirs* two men--Bwana Dumili and Mawlana wa

[46] 1856-7.

Sheye Kuli.

When Shaykh Muhammad bin Shaykh Mataka saw these matters, he came to seek peace from Muhammad bin Bwana Mkuu al-Nabhani, because it was he who was the chief (elder) of the three men named above. He wished to give him, Muhammad bin Mkuu, the sultanship of Siu and of Pate. He refused, answering, "I am an old man." They went to fetch Sultan Ahmad of Witu. Shaykh Muhammad bin Shaykh Mataka sent (some) men, and the men of Pate sent Shaykh Nasir bin ‘Abd Allah bin ‘Abd Salam to Kau to fetch Sultan Ahmad nicknamed *Simba* and came with him to Pate.

The news (of this) reached Zanzibar, Sultan Sayyid Majid bin Sa‘id bin Sultan, for Sayyid Sa‘id bin Sultan had died previously in the year 1273.[47] Prior to this the Sayyid had sent his *wazir* Sayyid Sulayman bin Hamad by ship to seize Pate, to crush the conspiracy. By the time the ship arrived at Manda, Pate had been seized by a man of Sultan Ahmad, Abu Bakr bin Hasan al-Buri who had come with Nasir bin ‘Abd Allah bin ‘Abd al-Salam. When Sayyid Sulayman bin Ahmad received this news, he returned to Zanzibar, and that was the time when Shaykh Muhammad bin Shaykh Mataka destroyed the fort at Siu.

Later, (when) Sultan Ahmad arrived at Pate,[48] the people acknowledged him as sultan: Shaykh Muhammad bin Shaykh Mataka with Mzee Sayf and Shaykh Shikuu and Muhammad Mote (formally) acknowledged

---

[47] 1856-7.

[48] This MS dates the ceremony at Sultan Ahmad's arrival, while MSS 177 and 344 place it earlier. Apparently it was designed to prevent Zanzibari takeover.

Sultan Ahmad's kingship.[49]

Sayyid Majid bin Sa'id bin Sultan sent men of Lamu to Pate, to give counsel together with Shaykh Muhi al-Din, to request (p.79) that Sultan Ahmad put soldiers of the Sayyid at Pate. And this Shaykh Muhi al-Din, he was the one who turned out the soldiers of the Sayyid from the fort at Siu when Shaykh Muhammad bin Shaykh Mataka defeated them. The soldiers had gone (there), and Shaykh Muhi al-Din took them out in peace, because he was a man of Sayyid Majid bin Sa'id, one of the *wazirs*.

When he went to Zanzibar with the soldiers, the Sayyid became very angry at Shaykh Muhi al-Din, and Shaykh Muhi al-Din took [this undertaking] upon himself, when he saw Sayyid Majid and (his) wrath. That was when he went with the men of Lamu. And this Shaykh Muhi al-Din had great cunning and much learning; he went to Pate with the best men of Lamu, together with Shaykh Ahmad and Shaykh 'Abd al-Rahman, (and) that one[50] was the *shaykh* of Pate. They spoke with Sultan Ahmad, (and) he accepted after reluctance because of (his) friendship with Shaykh Ahmad and Shaykh 'Abd al-Rahman, rejecting the advice of his *wazir* Nasir bin 'Abd Allah bin 'Abd al-Salam, for he refused to take in the Arabs, even one man.

The men of Pate made an agreement with Mwana Jaha binti Fumo Luti Kipunga wa Buwana Fumo Madi, the wife of Sultan Fumo Bakr bin Shaykh. At this time Sultan Fumo Bakar was in Lamu, according to the decree of Sayyid Majid bin Sa'id, since the time he was driven out of Pate.

---

[49] Cusack translates: "Sultan Ahmad behaved properly in his princeship."

[50] Pronouns are uncertain: *aye na-ye* may also mean "the one with him." Cusack has "children of Shaykh of Pate."

But every day they brought in soldiers in secret, and munitions, night after night. (When) Sultan Ahmad was informed (that) there was a plot and the soldiers were many at Pate, they suddenly attacked Sultan Ahmad, after the ruse was arranged, wishing to seize him. They failed because all the Pate people were of one mind with Sayyid Majid bin Sa'id, except his *wazir* Nasir bin 'Abd Allah bin 'Abd al-Salam. They fought inside the town of Pate, (but) Sultan Ahmad got away; he and Shaykh Muhammad bin Shaykh Mataka went to Siu.

The Arabs stayed at Pate (and) placed the ships on the sea. (When) the war became very fierce, Sayyid Majid bin Sa'id came (himself) to (lay) siege to Siu and Pate, and at sea to stop shipping (p. 78) (and) to sink the *dhows* and *mtepes*. They fought on the sea and went to the mainland to obtain food but the return route was unavailable, (it became a matter) of life (and) death. Sayyid Majid placed a chain across the mouth of the creek of Siu, the Ku'yo, to block the ships. Consequently they suffered six months [of blockade], from the sea and from the beach. On the side of Faza, Mzee Sayf seceded [to become a man] of Sayyid Majid bin Sa'id, through much cunning and many words. Sultan Ahmad and Shaykh Muhammad bin Shaykh Mataka experienced great distress.

Dissent arose in the land of Siu: some of the people loved Sayyid Majid because of the troubles they had suffered, and his men were *Sharif* Maulana bin Abu Bakr and 'Isa bin Ahmad al-Somali. (When) Sultan Ahmad and Shaykh Muhammad bin Shaykh Mataka saw how things were, they sued for peace from Sayyid Majid, and he granted it to them. During peace negotiations Sultan Ahmad sailed secretly by night, went to the mainland (and) returned to Kau.

After Shaykh Muhammad bin Shaykh Mataka sent his son, Shaykh Muhammad bin Shaykh Mataka.[51] He went to the ship, to Sayyid Majid bin Sa'id, and Sayyid Majid pardoned him, (and) gave him many presents. (Then) Sayyid Majid sailed (and) returned to Zanzibar. Later Shaykh Muhammad bin Shaykh Mataka went to Zanzibar to appear before Sayyid Majid. He seized him (and) imprisoned him in the fort of Mombasa, along with (other) people. (Then) Shaykh Muhammad died.

And after some days he (Sayyid Majid) sent the *liwali* Sa'ud bin Hamad to seize Sultan Ahmad by many ruses (but) he failed. He (Sultan Ahmad) left Kau secretly (and) went to Witu. The *wālī* Sa'ud bin Hamad came to Faza, to seize 'Umar Mataka at Faza, and the sons of Shaykh Muhammad bin Shaykh Mataka he seized at Siu (and) sent them to the fort of Mombasa. 'Umar Mataka he imprisoned (p.77) at Lamu.

Afterwards Sayyid Majid ruled over all the Swahili (coast), there was no one to challenge him. And Sultan Ahmad remained at Witu under the suzerainty of Sayyid Majid, until the reign of Sayyid Barghash bin Sa'id bin Sultan. Sayyid Barghash wished to place soldiers at Witu with a flag, (but) the sultan did not agree. He (Sayyid Barghash) sent an expedition to fight him (but) failed and made peace.

And this Sa'ud bin Hamad did not fight very vigorously, (so) Sayyid Barghash sent an expedition again, under *al-wali* Sa'id bin Hamad bin Sa'id.[52] Sultan Ahmad asked for protection from the Germans, who gave him some of the Swahili mainland. Sultan Ahmad died, under this condition of protection,

---

[51] The scribe probably confused the names of father and son.

[52] This is the brother of the preceding *wālī*.

in the year 1306.[53]

(Then) reigned Sultan Fumo Bakari bin Sulṭān bin Ahmad bin Shaykh al-Nabhani. He remained under this [condition of] protection, (but) there arose conflict between him and the Germans. One man, called Küntzell, killed the porter of the gate; he suddenly shot him. There were soldiers (present); they shot at them, and the soldiers killed Küntzell and the people who had accompanied him. They killed the Europeans without Sultan Fumo Bakr's order. When the soldiers saw their company dead, they did not wait for an order from the sultan (and) attacked the Europeans. And the people of Mkonumbi and Wanda Munyu, when they received the news of the attack on the Europeans, they attacked (and) killed the Europeans who were there.

Afterwards came the Administration of the English. They wished to make justice (and) demanded the people of Mkonumbi and Wanda Munyu, in order to bring them to trial. Fumo Bakar did not consent to surrender them. They attacked Sultan Fumo Bakr, sending boats to Mkonumbi and Wanda Munyu and Kilimane [and] Nyando za Pwani. They shot from cannons (and) set (houses) on fire.

Then on the night of 11 Rabi' al-Awwal of the year 1308[54] the people of Witu fought on the Kipini road the men of the Illustrious Administration; the men of Witu suffered defeat. Then on the morning (p. 76) of Monday, 12 of the month of Rabi' al-Awwal of the year 1308,[55] they attacked Sultan Fumo Bakar (and) drove him out of Witu. He went to Jongeni.

---

[53] 1888-9.

[54] 25 October 1890.

[55] 26 October 1890.

Witu was taken over by the Illustrious Administration. Sultan Fumo Bakar remained at Jongeni until 28 Jumada al-Awwal of the year 1308[56] (when) he died. His brother Bwana Shaykh bin Sultan Ahmad Nabhani occupied his place. After three days a conspiracy arose, he was seized by his brother Fumo ʻUmar Nabhani and Avutula wa Bahiru. They imprisoned Bwana Shaykh bin Sultan Ahmad. (Then) reigned Sultan Fumo ʻUmar.

And the last to rule Pate (was) Sultan Ahmad, the sultan of Witu. The one to rule first (was) Sulayman bin Sulayman al-Muzaffar Nabhani, Imam al-Yaʻrubi.[57]

This is the account of the Nabhani who were on the Swahili (coast) and their history, as we have mentioned (above). (There) reigned thirty-one kings and one woman, the total of thirty-two, without counting those who reigned, were deposed and returned to rule.

We have transmitted this from Muhammad bin Fumo ʻUmar al-Nabhani nicknamed Bwana Kitini, and he transmitted it from his grandfather Muhammad bin Bwana Mkuu al-Nabhani, called Bwana Simba, who was very reliable in regard to the accounts of their pedigree, such as we have named.

The first copy was by the humble Salih bin Salim bin Ahmad bin ʻAbd Allah Sharahil on 6 Safar in the year 1318.[58] This copy was made [for] the Honorable *al-Liwali* Muhammad bin Ahmad bin Sultan bin Fumo Bakar bin

---

[56] 9 January 1891.

[57] This title is incorrect: the Nabhani and the Yaʻrubi are different families. It is a likely corruption of *Imām al-ʻArab* (as in MS 177) via *Imām al-ʻArabī* (as in MS 321).

[58] 5 June 1900.

Shaykh bin Bwana Fumo Madi wa Simba, Sultan Muhammad bin Abu Bakr bin Bwana Mkuu bin Abu Bakr bin Hamad bin Abu Bakr bin Muhammad bin Abu Bakr bin Muhammad bin 'Umar bin Muhammad bin Ahmad bin Muhammad bin Sulayman bin Sulayman bin al-Muzaffar al-Nabhani.

The second copy, 1 Rajab of the year 1343,[59] wrote the humble Salih bin Salim bin Hamad.[60]

The third copy [no day] Dhu 'l-Ka'da 1363,[61] on 3 February, wrote 'Ali Muhammad.

This copy I, 'Abd Allah bin 'Ali bin Muhammad al-Ma'awi,[62] the beggar for the goodness of Allah the Most High, copied letter for letter.

---

[59] 26 January 1925.

[60] An example of substituting the name Hamad for Ahmad. Another may be found the genealogy of the *liwali* immediately above.

[61] 18 October - 16 November 1944; the date of 3 February fell within the month of Dhu'l-Ka'da during the years A.H. 1354 and 1355, corresponding to 1936-7. Conceivably, A. H. 1353 was meant, when Dhu'l-Ka'da began on February 5.

[62] The Ma'awi are an important Lamu clan.

MS 358

This is a photocopy of a MS copied in a check-lined copy-book. Uniquely among the known MSS, in the upper left margin of p. 2 (the pages are not numbered) is inscribed the name of the owner: Ahmad bin Hasan bin Hamad Ba Husayn al-Murshidi of Lamu. The postscript states the usual provenance from Bwana Kitini and his grandfather Bwana Simba. The original is again indicated to have been commissioned by Muhammad bin Ahmad bin Sultan bin Fumo Bakr, etc., whose title here again is awkwardly scripted with an extra *lām* so it resembles more *al-walad al-'azīz* (as in MS 321) rather than *al-wālī al-'azīz*, 'the Illustrious *liwali*', as in MS 344. A second copy dated 1343 by Salih bin Salem bin Hamad is also mentioned, the mention of a third is missing, and the fourth and fifth copies are dated 1365/1946 as made by 'Ali Khalifa. On p. 29 is sketched the same genealogical chart as in MSS 309 and 321, reproduced in Appendix 1 below.

The text is in Ki-Amu. The use of the particle *na-* is frequent (as in *akavunda na-mui wa-Siu*). For *ch* the dotted *kāf* is used. Occasionally, words or phrases with the predicate were missed in copying, which are sometimes restored by the scribe. These are placed in brackets in the Arabic-script transcript. A whole reign is skipped on p. 7. Apparently the paper had several holes which on occasion make the reading uncertain. In the early passages the MS mistakenly names Marika (Marka, Merca) for Manda (Mandra). On p. 6 the passage about trade has the voweled verb *henda* (as in MS 344) rather than *Hindi* of the other versions ("He sent ships to go and conduct trade," rather than "he sent ships to India"). Importantly, on p. 22 the wording makes it clearer than in Hollis MS that Shaykh Ahmad or Pate was a key participant in negotiations between Zanzibar and Pate, and on p. 24 Sayyid Barghash is reported to have wished to place soldiers at Witu and the harbor (*kuweka ʻaskari Wītu na k(w)a-bandari*), rather than ʻsoldiers and a flag' (*bendera*), as elsewhere.

The writer exhibits some flexibilty in the use of Arabic loanwords (e.g., replacing *ḳabīla* with *nasila*). Orthographic peculiarties include the use of two *alifs* next to each other, raising the tails of final consonants (e.g., so that *fā* looks like a *fā'-alif* ligature, and occasional substitution of *ṣād* for *sīn* and *kāf* for *ḳāf* in Arabic loanwords. The Arabic original is reproduced in the transcript without changes; location of slips and lacunae is marked with the asterisk *. The romanized transcript offers corrections and editorial conjectures in brackets. The translation has conjectured readings in brackets; the words added to ease the flow of the text are placed in parentheses.

AKHBĀR PATEH

al-Hijra sanati 600

Hāhunā Sulaymān bin Sulaymān Muẓaffar al-Nabahānī, alawal al-mubdī Nabahānī, m(w)andu wa-k(w)anda kuya Pate ni-Sulaymān bin Sulaymān bin Muẓaffar Nabahānī na-(n)duze wawīli, 'Alī bin Sulaymān nā 'Uthmān bin Sulaymān. Na-huyu Sulaymān bin Sulaymān al-madhkūrii alokuwa sulṭān, na-ye akisa kutawalī bara li-'Arabu. Akaya Pate sulṭān al-madhkūr katika tārīkh sanati 600 al-Hijra kuya k(w)akē Pate. Akataka 'arūsi k(w)a-mfalume wa-Pate katika al-Batawīyīn. Sulṭān Sulaymān bin Sulaymān ni-mtu ma'rufu; mfalume wa-Pate aka‿muuza binti yāke. Na-dasituri ya-wote yā wa-Sawaḥili ḥatā sasa mtu aku‿waliyaye kijāna **ch**ako, akisa sīku saba'a za-harūsi henda kum(w)a(n)galia mkewe nyu(m)bāni mak(w)e, baba wa-mke wake, kūmpia watu. Huyu Sulaymān bin Sulaymān (n)diye mfalume wēno aka‿mpa ufalume wake alo‿kuwa nao. (p. 3) Akatawali Sulaymān bin [Sulaymān] (n)diye mfalume.

K(w)ālina mūi hīt(w)a Kitoki iyo jizira yā-Pate, katika maṭila'i yā Pate, na-Sīu hatasa‿kuwa mūi. Waliko mūi mgine hīt(w)a Sha(n)ga katika maṭila'i yā Pate na-Fāzah waliko mūi, we(n)yewe wa-**P**āza al-Mafāzī. Ikaketi mii hiyo yote, ikaketi yōte taḥati yā Sulṭān Sulaymān bin Sulaymān. Nā Ma(n)dra k(w)alinā mfalume mbali naiona (n)guvu sana. Akafa Sulṭān Sulaymān bin Sulaymān sanati 625 Hijra.

Aka‿khalifu zijāna wawīli Muḥammad nā Aḥmad, Muḥammad 'umri

yake ‘ishīrīn, Aḥmad ‘umri wake nyaka khamsata ‘ashara. Akatawali Muḥammad bin Sulaymān bin Sulaymān ba‘ada yā babake. Ikawa khitilafu yeye na-wātu wa-Sha(n)ga. Kapijana na-mii kaivu(n)da kabisa. Na-ba‘aḍi yao wakayā Pate, na-wa(n)gine wa-ḳabila yao Kina(n)da(n)gu wakakimbiā, wasiyūwe‿kane mahāla wamezo‿kimbilia, ḥatttā sīku zikipita ikaya khabari k(w)ā Sulṭān Muḥammad bin Sulaymān naḥua wātu wi(n)do kuwenda wakimbiā "Wale wa-Siu, tumewaonā katika m(w)ītu." Sulṭāni kapeka wātu kuwa(n)galia kawadirika, wamefanya zijūmba (n)dāni yā m(w)itu. Sulṭān Muḥammad bin Sulaymān (p. 4) kawa‿ṣameḥe kawa‿rudisha mahāla pao. (N)diyo aṣili yā mūi wa-Sīu.

Wakayā na-Wasawaḥili wa(n)gīne wakaketi wote, wakayā na-WaFamau wakaketi, wakawa Wafamau (n)di wakuu wa-Siu katika ṭa‘a yā Sulṭān Muḥammad bin Sulaymān. Akafa sanati 650.

Akatawali (n)duye Sulṭān Aḥmad bin Sulaymān, aka‿amirisha sana arḍi yā Pate kaje(n)ga majumba nā mashāmba āsipiji mahāli, akafa sanati 660.

Katawali kijāna **ch**a-nduye, ina lake Aḥmad bin Muḥammad bin Sulaymān. Akaketi na-wātu k(w)a-uzu‿ri sana kama sīra za ‘ami zāke, ku‘amirisha mui wa-Pate na-mashā‿mba ḥatā sanati 700 akafa. Akakhalifu zijāna wangi.

Katawali kijāna **ch**ake Sulṭān Muḥammad bin Aḥmad bin Muḥammad bin Sulaymān. Akaketi na-wātu k(w)a-wema sana. Wātu wa-Fāzah wakakhalifu, akawapija kawatia katika ṭa‘a ba‘ada ya-zita zingi ḥatā alipo‿washi(n)dā. Ika‿ifutaḥi na-M[andra] kai‿tamalaki k(w)a-zita na-khīla k(w)āni alina (n)guvu sana sulṭān wa-M[andra] ya-māli na-wātu, aka’ivunda kabisa. Na-wātu wa(n)gine kawaeta Pate, na-ba‘aḍi wakatoa (n)yika wakakimbilia kula mahāla, wa(n)gine wakaya Shēlah waka(n)gia katika himayā ya-wātu wa-Lāmūh. Sulṭān (p. 5) Muḥammad bin Aḥmad al-madhkūr kawataka wātu [wa] Lāmūh, wakaiza kuwa‿toa. Na-wa(n)gine wakē(n)da Malindī na-ba'aḍi ya-buldani. Sulṭān Muḥammad bin Aḥmad akawa‿ andama sana hao waliyo‿kūya Shēlah, wātu wa-Lāmūh wakaiza kuwa‿toa ḳaṭa'an. Maneno hiyo kisa Sulṭān Muḥammad akafa sanati 732.

Akatawali kijāna **ch**ake ufalume Sulṭān 'Umar bin Muḥammad bin Aḥmad bin Muḥammad bin Sulaymān. Akairejea maneno yā baba-wake k(w)a-wātu wa-Lāmūh, kawataka wātu wa-Mān(d)ra. Wātu [wa] Lāmūh wakaiza kuwa‿toa, kawapija zīta, wakataka amāni wātu wa-Lāmū, wakawa kati‿ka ṭa'a Sulṭān 'Umar bin Muḥammad.

Zikazidi (n)guvu, akapija jumla yā mī'i yā Sawaḥīli: Ozi, Malindī, Kiwayū, Kitā‿o, Miyah, Imīzii, Watāmu kasikilia Kirimbā. Mii yōte kai‿tamalaki ta(n)gu Pate ḥatā Kirīmbā, kula mui kaweka mtu wāke kuḥukumu. (N)diyo aṣili ya-hao majūmbe waliyoko mirīma, ma'ana ni-yūmba yā-mfalume wa-Pate, ma'ana yāle ni-watum(w)a wa-yūmbē, ni-hiyo yūmbe.

N[a]-jānibu ya-maṭila'i katamalaki ḥatā Warshīkhi. Alik(w)enda kipija zita ta(n)gu Kiwa‿yū na-Tūla nā Tuwala nā Shu(n)g(w)aya na banadiri zōte: Barawa, Marika nā Muḳudishū. Kaweka al-wālī jami'i yā ḥukumu (p. 6) za bandari zikao Muḳudishū. Aka'ishi na-nti zote hizi katika ṭa'a yāke ilā U(n)guja hakutawali, na-waḳati huu U(n)guja hai‿kuwa nti kūu zamani hizo. Nā huyu Sulṭān 'Umar alike(n)da zita na-kupenda ra'iya, nā ra'īya wakimpe(n)da, ikat(w)ā'a (n)guvu sana nti yā Pate. Akafa Sulṭān 'Umar sanati 749. Kakhalifu zijāna wawīli Muḥammad nā Aḥmad.

Katawali zijāna mkuu Sulṭān Muḥammad bin 'Umar bin Muḥammad bin Aḥmad bin Muḥammad bin Sulaymān, walā ha**p**akuwa na-zita, [kaketi] ufalume wa-babake k(w)ā amāni. Na-ye alikipe(n)da sana māli yā bi'ashara, akisafirisha na-zombo zake, h(w)enda kufa(n)ya bi‘ashara na-ye alina bakhti sana yā māli. Na-mara mōya alimsafirisha kijāna **ch**ake kapata kisiwa katika baḥari kapata ma‘adini yā fiḍah kaya-nayo Pate kafa(n)yā wātu kuifa(n)ya kazi ma‘adini kapata māli mi(n)gi sana. Yakazidi māli katika nti-yā Pate, ḥattā wakafa(n)ya zitara za fiḍah nā (n)gazi za fiḍah. Naye mfalume akafa sanati 797. Akakhalifu zijāna wanne, Bwānah Mkuu nā Aḥmad nā Abū Bakr nā ‘Umar.

Akatawali (n)duye Sulṭān Aḥmad bin ‘Umar bin Muḥammad bin Aḥmad bin Muḥammad bin Sulaymān. Akaketi na-wātu k(w)a amāni na-sīra njema nā jami‘i yā wātu. Akafa.

Akatawali Abū Bakr (p. 7) bin Muḥammad bin ‘Umar bin Muḥammad bin Aḥmad bin Muḥammad bin Sulaymān. Kaketi sana nā jami‘i yā wātu nā mii yōte katika ṭa‘a yāke bila khilafu. [Akafa] sanati 875. Na-ye alikhalifu zijāna ziwīli, Muḥammad nā Aḥmad.

Akatawali ba‘ada yā babake Muḥammad bin Abū Bakr bin Muḥammad bin ‘Umar bin Aḥmad bin Muḥammad bin Sulaymān. Waḳati wake wakaya WaZu(n)gu Portukāli katika mii yā Sawaḥīli wote, wakaketi Mombāsah wakafa(n)ya (n)gome, nā janibu yā Pate kaje(n)ga Ndōndo. Wātu wa-barāni wakawafuata wakawa[pa] māli wakawa katika ṭa‘a yao. Wakamu‘ariḍi mfalume katika nti yā Pate. Wakampija (z)ita mfalume k(w)a-janibu yā Shi[nda]kasi, wakawaka nti yā Pate pwāni k(w)a-ma‘ana ya-tūpe ḳaṣidi yā kupija mūi wa-Pate, wasiweze wakapatana k(w)ā amāni wakafanya mkitabu wa sharuti zao. Wakaketi Pate WaZu(n)gu wakafa(n)ya furḍa k(w)ā ina lao WaZu(n)gu wali**ch**amkuwa "fandiki." Wakafa(n)ya na-ma(m)bo ma(n)gi katika kisiwa **ch**a-Pate. Akafa sulṭāni sanati 900. Akakhalifu zijāna wawīli, B(w)ānah Mkū nā Abū Bakr.

Akatawali ufalume Sulṭān Abū Bakr bin Muḥammad bin Abū Bakr bin Abū Bakr bin Muḥammad bin Aḥmad bin Muḥammad bin Sulaymān ba'ada yā babake al-madhkūr. Akaketi (p. 8) na-wātu sana akatuzae k(w)ā-amāni kama ḳawa'ida yā babake. Akafa sanati 940 kusipadi‿liki ya(m)bo. Na-ye kakhalifu zijāna wawi[li], Aḥmad wa Muḥammad.

Akatawali 'ami yao ufalume B(w)ānah Mkū bin Muḥammad bin Abū Bakr bin Muḥammad bin 'Umar bin Muḥammad bin Aḥmad bin Muḥammad bin Sulaymān. Ikawa khitilafu na-WaZu(n)gu lakin pasiwe na-zita. Ikawa fitina sīku (n)yi(n)gi, akafa sanati 973. Akakhalifu kijāna mmōya hitawā Abū Bakr.

Akatawali Muḥammad bin Abū Bakr bin Muḥammad bin 'Umar bin Muḥammad bin Aḥmad bin Muḥammad bin Sulaymān. Akaṣiliḥiina na-WaZungu, wakat(w)ā'a ba'aḍi mii; akafa sanati 1002. Akakhalifu kijāna mmōya hīt(w)a Abū Bakr, asitawali. Katawali Abū Bakr bin B(w)ānah Mkū bin Muḥammad bin Abū Bakr bin Muḥammad bin 'Umar bin Muḥammad bin Aḥmad bin Muḥammad bin Sulaymān. Akaketi na-WaZungu kama sīra ya-waze wake walota(n)gulia, na-ufalume ukapu(n)gua (n)guvu. Akafa sanati 1041. Akakhalifu B(w)ānah Mkū nā Abū Bakr, k[wa-ji]na la-babake.

Akatawali Abū Bakr bin Muḥammad bin Abū Bakr bin Muḥammad bin Abū Bakr bin Muḥammad bin 'Umar bin Aḥmad bin Muḥammad bin Sulaymān. Ikawa khitilafu na-WaZu(n)gu, wakapijana kau‿vunda WaZu(n)gu k(w)a-zita zikuu sana. Ba'ada-ye zikaya tena zita za-WaZu(n)gu, wakapijana mui wa-Pate k(w)a-mizi(n)ga wakaziweya nā ndia k(w)a-baḥarini, kusipiti **ch**ombo. Wātu wakaona (p. 9) mashaka, wakafa(n)ya amāni. Akafa mfalume sanati 1061. Akakhalifu zijāna wawīli, Bwānah Mkū nā Aḥmad.

Akatawali B(w)ānah Mkū wa-B(w)ānah Bakr wa-B(w)ānah Mkū bin

Muḥammad bin Abū Bakr bin Muḥammad bin 'Umar bin Muḥammad bin Aḥmad bin Muḥammad bin Sulaymān. Akapatana na-WaZu(n)gu sana, na-ye alikipe(n)da sana kuketi Lāmūh ḥattā msimu kupita Lāmūh, akafa(n)ya nā harūsi k(w)a-wātu wa-Lāmūh.

Na katika waḳati hunu WaFamau wa-Siu walitoka katika ṭa'a yāke, akawapija akawavunda na-mui wa-Siu, kashika na-wātu wa(n)gine kawatia Pate. Mkuu wa-Siu akakimbia, ake(n)da (N)dō(n)do k(w)a-Portugāli, kat(w)ā'a ḥimaya. Mkuu wa-WaZungu akaya Pate k(w)ā-mfalume, awaṣameḥe wātu wa Siu. Mfalume kawaṣameḥe kawarejeza mahāla pao Siu katika amāni.

Ba'ada yāke Portugāli akafa(n)ya khīli, akaya Pate k(w)a-marikabu, akamtaka mfalume ke(n)da marikabuni, asi[ne]nda akampeka bin‿'ami yake B(w)ānah Mkū, yeye na-wātu wa-Pate. WaZu(n)gu wakawatukua katika marikabu, asirudi mtu ḥatā mmoya. Ba'ada yā-hayo mfalume kawapija WaZu(n)gu k(w)ā janibu zote, k(w)a-barāni na-zisiwāni, kawatoa janibu za-huku zote, kakimbilia Mombāsah. Akafa mfalume sanati 1100. Akawata zijāna B(w)ānah Bakar nā-B(w)ānah Mādī, nā binti mmōya hīt(w)a M(w)ānah Darīni.

Akatawali Abū Bakr bin B(w)ānah Mkū bin Abū Bakr bin Muḥammad bin Abū Bakr bin Muḥammad bin 'Umar (p. 10) bin Muḥammad bin Aḥmad bin Muḥammad bin Sulaymān. Akapija mfalume ghafla nā Aḥmad, (n)duye B(w)ānah Mkū ali[o]‿tukuliwa na-WaZungu Portugāli, k(w)a-u‿pa(n)ga. Akafa mfalume sanati 1103.

Akatawali yeye Aḥmad bin Abū Bakr bin Muḥammad bin Muḥammad bin Abū Bakr bin Muḥammad bin 'Umar bin Muḥammad bin Aḥmad bin Muḥammad bin Sulaymān. Alipo‿tawali kawandama Portugāli akiwa‿toa katika nti zake. Na-waḳati hunu M(w)ānah Darīni binti B(w)ānah Mkū wa

B(w)ānah Bakr, mke wa-B(w)ānah Mkū bin Abū Bakr alio‿tukuliwa na-Portugāli katika zamāni yā Sulṭān Aḥmad, kuua (n)duze wawīli Abū Bakr nā B(w)ānah Madī nā Sulṭān Aḥmad, n[a]-mume wāke alio‿tukuliwa kafa(n)ya huzuni sana, zikipita sīku nyi(n)gi, akataka kuṭahiri kijāna **ch**ake B(w)ānah Tamu Mtoto, alio‿mtukuwa Sulṭān Abū Bakr Imāmu Huda kijāna wa-B(w)ānah Mkū alī‿te(n)da Goa.

Mfalume alipo‿pata khabāri aka'azimu yeye kufa(n)ya harūsi ya-zijāna zake sababu kumukhini siwa ya sha(m)ba. Akapata khabāri M(w)ānah Darīni, akam(w)ita M(w)e(n)ye Bayayi bin Mku, sharīfu katika Jamali Layl, alikuwa hudari sana kazi ya-ujume, akataka amfanyiziye [siwa ishinde] siwa yā Pate, aka‿riḍīka ijāra riyali mia wa 'ishīrīn, kampa pembe za ndovu akiteu umōya. Akafa(n)ya siwa k(w)a-sīri ḥatā yalipo‿kuwa ṭayari kaiẓihirisha ghafula kaipeka katika majumba ya-jami'i zake, kula mtu akitūza ya-kuu mali mangi sana. (p. 11) Fundi ka'iza ijāra akataka tūzo. Akampa tūzo, akafa(n)ya 'arūsi ya-kijāna **ch**ake.

Ḥatā zamāni yā B(w)ānah Tamu Mkū wakaya wātu wa-Lāmūh waku'azima siwa, akawapa, wakaītukuwa siwa yā aṣili ḥatā baḥarini, **ch**ombo kikafa mā'i, ikaghibu. B(w)ānah Tamu Mkū akataka siwa yā M(w)ānah Darīni kambia "Tupe sīsi, tutumie katika mii yote." Akamijibu "Kula ḳabīla ilio‿tuza natumie siwa yangu." Nā M(w)ānah Darīni kawata mtum(w)a ḥuru ayowao kuvuzia akasema "Huyu (n)diye m(w)e(n)ye kupija siwa hini, yeye nā nasila yāke, na-'ada yāke napowe riyāli tāno na-(n)guo ya-kutukulia siwa teno apowa nā samli nā tuzo kula mtu awezao." Wakamkuliwa nasila hiyo "muyū(m)be wa siwa," ḥatā yeo wako watuwe, ta(n)gu waḳati huuna ilā l-āna hutumiwa nā jami'i yā maḳabā'ili yā Pate nā maḳabāili wa-nti nyi(n)gine he(n)da kazima k(w)ā sharti hizo kupowa muyū(m)be wa siwa.

Zikazidi fitina (n)dani yā-mūi, na-katika ufalume wake nyaka saba'a ikawa mīi mikavu hakuna mvua, mfalume kaiizulu.

Katawali Sulṭān Abū Bakr bin B(w)ānah Tamu Mkū wa-B(w)ānah Mtiti bin Aḥmad bin Abū Bakr bin 'Umar bin Aḥmad bin 'Umar bin Muḥammad bin Aḥmad bin Muḥammad bin Sulaymān. Akapatana sana nā sultāni wa Maskati al-Imam Sayf bin Nabahānī li-'Arabī. Huyu (p. 12) [mfalume] wa-Pate ake(n)da 'Arabūni, wakawa(n)gana mfalume wa-'Arabūni nā huyu mfalume wa-Pate kuwatoa Portugāli sīku jum'ah pili kuu‿a wātu kutamalaki (n)gōme yā Mombāsah.

Akamu'arifu al-Imām al-Ya'rubī, aka'eta al-wālī katika Mazari'i, wātu watatu, Muḥammad bin 'Uthmān nā 'Alī bin 'Uthmān, wa-tatu sikumuyua inalake. Wakaya pamōya nā 'askari wa-al-Imām Sayf Nabahānī al-Ya'rubī. (N)diyo aṣili yā Mazru'i.

Nā mfalume wa-Pate alina sīra-(n)jema nā jami'i yā wātu. Aka'ishi nyaka arba'īnī katika ufalume wake, akafa sanati 1154. Akawata zijāna wa(n)gi ba'ada yāke wasi‿tawali zijāna zake.

Akatawali Aḥmad bin Abū Bakr bin Muḥammad bin Abū Bakr bin'Umar bin Aḥmad bin 'Umar bin Muḥammad bin Aḥmad bin Muḥammad bin Sulaymān. Akaketi k(w)a-wema, akafa sanati 1160. Akakhalifu kijāna kam(w)ita B(w)ānah Gō(n)go, asitawali.

Katawali B(w)ānah Tamu Mtoto, amkuliwao Imām l-Hūdā wa-B(w)ānah Mkū alotokuliwa nā Portugāli, nā-ina lake Abū Bakr bin B(w)ānah Mkū bin Abū Bakr bin Muḥammad bin Abū Bakr bin Muḥammad bin Abū Bakr bin Muḥammad bin'Umar bin Muḥammad [bin Aḥmad bin Muḥammad] bin Sulaymān. Waḳati hunu Imām l-Ya'rubī aka'eta zita kupija Pate, wasiweze wakafā Wa'Arabu wa(n)gi sana, wakafa(n)ya amāni.

Ba'ada yā hayo wātu wa-Lāmū wa[ka]khalifu, (p. 13) mfalume kawapija zita, asiwaweze wātu wa-Lāmūh, na-wātu [wa] Lāmūh wakafu(n)ga zita wakaya Pate k(w)a-janibu ya-Kitoki, wakapijana na-wātu wa-Pate zita zikuu sana, wakavundika wātu wa-Lāmūh. Ba'ada-ye mfalume wa-Pate akafu(n)ga zita k(w)a-bara na-baḥari, kawapija wātu wa-Lāmūh kawatamalaki. [Ba'ada] ya hayo alikuwa ḥali mōya mfalume wa-Pate na-wātu wa-Lāmūh. Imām l-Ya'rubī akafa(n)ya shauri muuya, kamuuwa mfalume sanati 1177.

Akatawali (n)duye m(w)ānah mke Sulṭān M(w)ānah Khadījah binti B(w)ānah Mkū bin Abū Bakr bin Muḥammad bin Abū Bakr bin Muḥammad bin Abū Bakr bin Muḥammad bin 'Umar bin Muḥammad bin Aḥmad bin Muḥammad bin Sulaymān. Ikawa fitina nyi(n)gi katika nti yā Pate. Ikawa wafalume wawīli, M(w)ānah Khadījah al-madhkūr nā Sulṭān 'Umar. Wakapijana katika mui wa-Pate nyaka mitatu, Sulṭān 'Umar ake(n)da Barawa, karejea Pate k(w)a-(n)guvu kuu sana, usīku wakapijana na-wātu wa M(w)ānah Khadījah, kula mtu mahāli pake. Akafa M(w)ānah (K)hadījah sanati 1187.

Akatawali B(w)ānah Mkuu wa-Shee wa-B(w)ānah Tamu Mkū. Ra'iya wakafa(n)ya udhia sana, asipate raḥa katika ufalume wake ḥatta kai(n)gia sanati 1191, wakamgilia wātu wa-mui wakamuua k(w)a-tārīkhi hiyo.

Katawali B(w)ānah Fūmo Mādī ina lake Sulṭān Muḥammad bin Abū Bakr bin B(w)ānah Mkū bin Abū Bakr bin Muḥammad bin Abū Bakr bin Muḥammad bin Abu Bakr bin Muhammad bin 'Umar bin Muḥammad bin Aḥmad bin Muḥammad bin Sulaymān. Ba'ada ya-kutawali (p. 14) ra'iya wakataka kufa(n)ya fitina, kawapija zita kawashi(n)da kawashika wātu arba'īni, wawīli ni-(n)duze khaṣa, akawatinda kama mbūzi yuu, na-sakafu dāmu. Ikashuka ndiani katika makūbu, ikawa amāni, asitoki mtu tena kufa(n)ya fitina, akatawali k(w)a-raḥa sana ḥatā sanati 1224 kafa. Wa lā hakutawali mfalume tena kama yeye, akakhalifu zijāna wa(n)gi sana.

Akatawali Sulṭān Aḥmad bin Shaykh Fūmo Lūṭi bin Shaykh bin B(w)ānah Mkū. Ikazidi fitina katika mui wa-Lāmūh. Akawapija zita na-wātu wa-Mombāsah Ma[za]rī'i ḥali mōya, wakashuka Shēlah jeyshi kuu sana yā wātu wa Pate nā wātu wa-Mombāsah. Wātu wa-Lāmūh wakatoka wakaya Shēlah, wakapijana nā wātu wa Pate nā wātu wa-Mombāsah, zita za-wātu wa-Lāmūh zikuu na-(n)guvu sana. Jeyshi yā Pate nā Mombāsah wakavu(n)dika wakakimbilia majahazini māo, majahazi ma(n)gine yakajahabu pwāni, wakasimama hapo wakapijana zita zikuu sana. Wakafa wātu wa(n)gi sana, wātu wa-Mombāsah nā wātu wa-Pate, hapana 'idadi. Katika wātu wa-Pate walo ma'arufu asikuwa watum(w)a nā wātu ḍa'ifu, wātu waḥidi wa-thamanīni 81 "Fulān bin Fulān," we(n)ye wake ya-ke(n)da ma'īdi hiyo Pate, nā-wātu wa Mombāsah hawana 'idadi.

Ba'ada yā hayo wātu wa-Lāmūh wake(n)da 'Arabūni (p. 15) wakamtaka Sa'īd bin Sulṭan bin l-Imam wakampa nti Lāmūh sanati 1228. Alipo‿tawali Lāmūh Ufalume wa-Pate ukasilia Pate nā banādiri. Ikazidi fitina, akatoka mtu wa-pili katika zijāna wa-B(w)ānah Fūmo Mādī, hu'itawā Fūmo Lūṭi Kipu(n)ga, akapijana nā Sulṭān Aḥmad. Kisa Sulṭān Aḥmad akafa K(w)a-māraḍi sanati 1230.

Akatawali Fūmo Lūṭi wa B(w)āna Fūmo Mādī, na-ye alikuwa hudari sana, shuja'a, karīmu. Na-zamani hizo Shaykh Mātāka bin Shaykh Mbārak ndipo alipo‿tawali u‿shēkhe wa-Siu, akafa(n)ya 'askari nā būnduki, na-ye ni-katika ṭa'a yā sulṭāni wa-Pate, na-ye alipatana sana na-Mzari'ī ḥatā sanati 1232. Ikazidi fitina bayna yāke nā Sulṭān Sa'īd bin Sulṭān Zanjibar. Akafa Sulṭān Fūmo Lūṭi al-madhkūr.

Ba'ada yāke akatawali Fūmo Lūṭi bin Shaykh bin Fūmo Lūṭi wa-

B(w)ānah Tamu Mkū, nā huyu (n)diye babāke Sulṭān Aḥmad bin sulṭān Wītu. Akatawali aṣubḥi ḥatā ba'ada li-'asrī, wātu wa-mui wa‿kamtoa ake(n)da Siu pamōya na-Mzari'ī wake(n)da wote Mombāsah.

Akatawali Sulṭān B(w)ānah Shaykh bin Fumo Mādī. Akapatana nā Sayyid Sa'īd bin Sulṭān akatia Wa‿'Arabu Pate, wakaketi nyaka mitatu. Ba'adaye wātu wa-mui wakamuuzulu nā (p. 16) shauri Sayyid Sa'īd bin Sulṭān tārikh sanati 12[42]. Wakamtawalisha Sulṭān Aḥmad amkuliwao B(w)ānah Wazīri wa-B(w)ānah Tamu wa-B(w)ānah Shaykh [wa B(w)ānah] Tamu Mkū. Kapatana nā Sayyid Sa'īd bin Sultān. Akatawali nyaka miwīli, wātu wakamu'uzulu wakamrejea B(w)ānah [Shaykh] wa B(w)ānah Fūmo Madī. Akaketi katika 'ezi k(w)a-shauri yā Sayyid Sa'īd bin Sulṭan nyaka mitatu. Akafa sanati 1247.

Akarejea B(w)ānah Wazīri katika u‿sulṭāni wake, kaya B(w)ānah Fūmo Lūṭi bin Shaykh aliyo‿k(w)e(n)da Mombāsah pamōya na-Mazari'ī, wakashuka Siu wakapijana nā B(w)ānah Wazīri wa B(w)ānah Tamu Pate. Na B(w)ānah Wazīri ni-shauri mōya nā Sayyid Sa'īd bin Sulṭan nā Fūmo Lūṭi pamōya na-Mzari'ī nā Shaykh Matāka mtu wa-Siu. Wakaya Pate k(w)a-zita wakapijana jeyshi yā Siu, ikavundika B(w)ānah Wazīri, aḳaishika nti yā Siu, aḳavu(n)da na-ukuta wa-mui.

Shaykh Matāka bin Shaykh M(u)bārak nā Fūmo Lūṭi wakakimbilia barāni pamōya na-ba'aḍhi ya-wātu, ba'ada yā sīku katete karejea Sīu k(w)a-zita zikuu sana wakawatoa wātu wa-B(w)ānah Wazīri k(w)a-zita, wakau‿shika wāo mui wa-Siu wakaje(n)ga ukuta wa-mui, wakapijana Pate nā Siu. Ikawa katika ṭa'a [yāke] nā shauri yā Sayyid Sa'īd bin Sulṭān. Ba'ada yā m(w)aka mmōya akauawa Sulṭān (p. 17) B(w)ānah Wazīri nā Fūmo Bakr wa-B(w)ānah Shaykh wa B(w)ānah Fūmo Mādī.

Akatawali yeye Sulṭān Fūm[o] Bakr bin Shaykh bin B(w)ānah Fūmo Madī sanati 1250. Akapatana sana nā Sayyid Sa‘īd bin Sulṭān mūda wa kutawali, kisa akakhalifu pamōya nā Shaykh Matāka bin Shaykh Mubārak. Sayyid Sa‘īd bin Sulṭān akapata zita nā Amiri Ḥamād al-Samār al-Bū‿sa‘īdī, akapija Pate nā Siu asiweze kafa(n)ya amāni.

Ba‘ada yā hayo ikatōka fitina bayna yā sulṭāni wa-Pate Fūmo Bakr nā ‘ami yāke ghafula, Muḥammad bin Aḥmad wa-B(w)ānah Fūmo Madī akashika nyumba ya-u‿falume yā Sulṭān Fūmo Bakr ghafula k(w)a-zita. Wātu wa-Lāmūh pamōya na-mtu wa-Sayyid Sa‘īd bin Sulṭān wakawaṣiliḥisha Muḥammad bin Aḥmad, akampeka Siu kuketi; nā Fūmo Bakr aketi Pate.

Ba‘ada-ye wakateta wakapijana tena nyaka mitatu nā Fūmo Bakr Siu nā Pate; kisa Sayyid Sa‘īd bin Sulṭān akawaṣiliḥishi, akaya Pate Muḥammad bin Aḥmad kwa shauri mōya yeye nā bin ‘ami yāke Fūmo Bakr. Akamshika Muḥammad bin Aḥmad ghafula akamuua k(w)a-shauri mōya yeye nā-mtu wa Siu. Sayyid Sa‘īd bin Sulṭān akam(w)ita Fūmo Bakr, ake(n)da U(n)guja. Sayyid Sa‘īd bin Sulṭān akamfu(n)ga k(w)a-shauri yā wātu wa-Lāmūh na-sababu ya-kumuua Muḥammad bin Aḥmad na-kufu‿uwata amāni aliyo‿fanyā Sayyid Sa‘īd bin Sulṭān katika sanati 1262. Akashika Pate Sulṭān Aḥmad bin (p. 18) Shaykh Fūmo Lūṭi bin Shaykh wa-B(w)ānah Tamu Mkū k[w]a shauri yā Sayyid Sa‘īd bin Sulṭān, akaketi nyaka miwīli.

Ba‘adaye akakhalifu, akaya Sayyid Sa‘īd bin Sulṭān na-zita zikuu sana nā Amiri Ḥamād Fāzah, akapija Siu. Nā Sayyid Sa‘īd bin Sulṭān akamfu(n)gua Sulṭān Fūmo Bakar akampa zita pamōya nā wātu wa-Lāmūh. Wakaketi Mta(n)ga‿wanda katika majahazi nā Sayyid Sa‘īd alipo‿k(w)enda Fāzah akaketi mahali hīt(w)a Kija[ng]a **ch**ā-Mpu(n)ga, karibu nā Fāzah. Amiri Ḥamād akaya Siu kuwaka mabōma katika ndia yā Pate nā Fāzah nā Siu. Amiri Ḥamād ake(n)da Siu k(w)a-zita zikuu sana ḥatā akashika mitepe iliōko katika bandari yā Siu kapi(n)dua kafa(n)ya mabōma kapija nti yā Siu. Kaona udhia sana muuda wa-zita kua zi(n)gi sana. Akarudi Amiri Ḥamād na-ba'aḍi yā 'askari akenda bōmani kut(w)ā'a mzi(n)ga. Akipita ndiani wātu wa Siu wakamtokea ghafula, amiri wa-Shee Matāka hitawā Bin Mubārak, Ḥamād 'Umar nā amiri wā pīli hītawā Ḥamad (N)goma; wakapijana wakamuua Amiri Ḥamād. Wake(n)da nā bōmani wakawapija Wa'Arabu waliyoko bōmani wakat(w)ā'a nā-mizi(n)ga, nā jeyshi iliyoko Siu hupijana.

Walipo‿pata khabāri ya-kamba Amiri Ḥamād miu‿ua jeyshi yā Sayyid Sa'īd bin Sulṭān, ikavu(n)dika nao walikuwa katika kutamalaki Siu. Sayyid Sa'īd bin Sulṭān kisa kupata khabāri ya-mauti (p. 19) yā Amiri Ḥamād kao(n)doka ka(n)gia markabūni asinēne neno ake(n)da zake Masḳaṭi.

M(w)aka wā pīli akamuweka Sulṭān Fūmo Bakr Fāzah, akapija Siu nā Pate. Katika waḳati hunu akafa Shaykh Matāka k(w)a-maraḍi. Ikawa khilafu k(w)a-zijāna zake, kula mtu ataka ushēkhe, waka(n)gia katika ṭa'a yā Sayyid Sa'īd bin Sulṭān, Abū Bakr nā Muḥammad zijāna za Shaykh Matāka. Sayyid akampa Abū Bakr zita pamōya nā Sulṭān Fūmo Bakar; kumpija Sulṭān Aḥmad Siu. Ake(n)da Abū Bakr bin Shaykh Matāka pamōya nā amiri wa Sulṭān Fūmo Bakr amkuliwa‿o Ḥamad wa Bāishi Nabahāni ka(n)gia Siu usīku, wakapijana ḥatā wakavundika watu wa Sulṭān Fūmo Bakr waka‿anda‿miwa ndiani wakumshika Abū Bakr bin Shaykh Matāka wakampeka Pate, kuuawa Sulṭān Aḥmad.

Ba'ada-ye akasimāma (n)dūye Shaykh Muḥammad bin Shaykh Matāka ṭarafu yā Sayyid Sa'īd bin Sulṭān, yēye [na] Sulṭān Fūmo Bakr. Sayyid Sa'īd bin Sulṭān kawapa zita na 'asikari na-gharamā, wakampija Sulṭān Aḥmad ḥatā wakamtoa Pate sanati 1273, ake(n)da Kau. Siu ikawa na-Shaykh Muḥammad bin Shaykh Matāka, ṭarafu yā Sayyid Sa'īd bin Sulṭān, akampa na-'asikari kuwaka na-gereza. Wakateta na-mtu wa-Sayyid Sa'īd bin Sulṭān k(w)a-sababu alivu(n)da bānda la-mtepe alowaka Shaykh (p. 20) Muhammad Mataka aliwaka mbee ya-gereza. Nā Shaykh Muḥammad Matāka kavu(n)da gereza.

Na-katika waḳati hunu alikufa Sulṭān Aḥmad bin Shaykh Kāu, babake Fūmo Bakr sulṭāni Wītu. Akaketi mahāla pake Sulṭān Aḥmad amkuliwao Simba, sulṭāni Witu.

Nā ḳabula yā Shaykh Muḥammad asiyavu(n)da gereza la-Siu yalitoka fitina, Sulṭān Fūmo Bakr bin Shaykh akamtoa Pate k(w)a-zita, akaya Lāmūh akataka kuitamalaki Pate alipo‿ona (n)guvu zāke. Na-wakuu wa Pate alipo‿ona kite(n)do mizofa(n)ya Shaykh Muḥammad bin Shaykh Matāka misowe‿ataka kuwa‿tawali wasikiri, kawapija zita, wakasimāma wakuu wa-Pate. Walā-hapana mfalume k(w)a-shauri la-wātu watatu, Muḥammad bin Mkū Nabahānī nā B(w)ānah Reḥema bin Aḥmad Nabahānī nā Nāṣir bin 'Abd al-Salām, ndiye alokuwa mdabiri l-umūri.

Akakusanya zanā wakapijana Shaykh Muḥammad bin Shaykh Matāka, wākamshi(n)da, wakafa wātu ma'rūfu nā ma'amiri makuu wātu wawīli, B(w)ānah Damīl nā Maulanā wa Sheye Kūli. Shaykh Muḥammad bin Shaykh Matāka akisa kuona mambo haya akaya kutaka amāni k(w)ā Muḥammad bin B(w)ānah Mkū al-Nabahānī k(w)āni (n)diye aliyokuwa mkū wāo katika hawa-watu watatu tumezota(n)gulia kutayā. Akataka kumpa yeye Muḥammad bin Mkū usulṭāni wā Siu nā-Pate, akaiza ka‿jibu "mimi ni-mtu mzima." Wake(n)da **ch**a-mt(w)ā Sulṭān Aḥmad wa-Wītu. Kapeka wātu Shaykh Muḥammad bin Shaykh (p. 21) Matāka na-wātu wa-Pate wakampeka nā Shaykh Nāṣir bin 'Abd al-Salām. Kumt(w)āa Sulṭān Aḥmad al-mulaḳabu Simba kaya na-ye Pate.

Khabāri ikasikilia U(n)guja Sulṭān Mājid bin Sa'īd bin Sulṭān k(w)āni Sayyid Sa'īd uta(n)gulia kufa sanati 1273. Kabula yā-hayo Sayyid kumu(w)eta wazīri wāke Sayyid Sulaymān bin Ḥamad k(w)a-marikabu ili kushika Pate kuu(n)disha fitina. Marikabu ikiwaṣili Ma[nd]ra Pate imek(w)isa kushika mtu wa-Sulta[n] Aḥmad Abū Bakr bin Ḥasan al-Būrī amekuya nai Nāṣir bin 'Abd al-Salām.

Akisa kupata khabāri hiyo Sayyid Sulaymān bin Ḥamad akarejea U(n)guja nā Shaykh Muḥammad bin Shaykh Matāka waḳāti hunu (n)dipo alipo‿vunda gereza la Siu. Akisa kuwaṣili Aḥmad Pate wātu wakampā kuwa (n)diye sulṭāni, Shaykh Muḥammad bin Shaykh Matāka kuna Mze Sēfu nā Shaykh Shikuwe nā Muḥammad Mōteh, akasita‿kiri k(w)ā Sulṭān Aḥmad ufalume wake.

Sayyid Mājid bin Sa'īd bin Sulṭān akapeka wātu wa-Lāmūh Pate k(w)a-naṣaḥa pamōya nā Shaykh Muḥī al-Din kamtaka Sulṭān Aḥmad aweke 'askari wa-Sayyid Pate. Nā-huyu Shaykh Muḥui al-Dīn (n)diye alotoa 'askari wa sayyid katika gereza la-Siu alipo‿wapija Shaykh Muḥammad bin Shaykh Matāka. 'Askari wili ndāni yā gereza, ake(n)da Shaykh Muḥui al-Dīn kuwatoa k(w)ā amāni (p. 22) k(w)āni alikuwa mtu wa Sayyid Mājid bin Sa'īd katika mawaziri.

Alipo‿k(w)ē(n)da U(n)guja nā 'askari Sayyid kafa(n)ya hasira sana yuu la-Shaykh Muḥī al-Dīn, nā Shaykh Muḥī al-Dīn akat(w)a'a daraka alipo‿moona Sayyid Mājid na-ghaḍabu, (n)dipo ke(n)da yeye na-wātu wa-Lāmūh. Na-ye Shaykh Muḥī al-Dīn alina khīla sana na-'ilimu nyi(n)gi. Ake(n)da Pate nā kheyri ya-wātu wa-Lāmūh pamōya nā Shaykh Aḥmad nā Shaykh 'Abd al-Raḥmān, aye nai Shaykh Pate. Kanena nā Sulṭān Aḥmad, akariḍīka ba'a da-yā shida k(w)a-sababu ya-'uṣuḥuba wa-Shaykh Aḥmad nā Shaykh 'Abd al-

Raḥmān, akakhalifu shauri la-waziri wake Nāṣir bin 'Abd Salām k(w)āni wali'iza kutia Wa'Arabu ḥatā mtu mmōya.

Wātu wa-Pate wakafa(n)ya shauri mōya M(w)ānah Jāha binti Fūmo Lūṭi Kipu(n)ga wa-B(w)ānah Fūmo Madī [mke] wa-Sulṭān Fūmo Bakr bin Shaykh. Waḳati hunu Sulṭān Fūmo Bakr woko Lāmūh tini yā shauri la-Sayyid Mājid bin Sa'īd ta(n)gu alipo‿tolewa Pate.

Basi kula sīku wakitia 'askari k(w)a-siri na-zana usīku usīku. Alipoa khabāri Sulṭān Aḥmad ikawa fitina nā 'askari wamo‿kuwa wa(n)gi Pate, wakampija Sulṭān Aḥmad ghafula, ba'ada-ye kisa ḥila katoka kumshika, waziweze k(w)āni WaPate wote walikuwa shauri mōya nā Sayyid (p. 23) Mājid bin Sa'īd, ili waziri wāke Nāṣir bin 'Abd Salām. Wakapijana ndāni yā mui wa-Pate akatoka Sulṭān Aḥmad, yeye nā Shaykh Muḥammad bin Shaykh Matāka, wake(n)da Siu.

Pate wakashika Wa'Arabu na-baḥarini wakatia marikabu. Zita zalipo‿kuwa zikuu sana alipokuya Sayyid Mājid bin Sa'īd kai‿[h]uṣuru Siu nā Pate. Nā baḥari kusipiti **ch**ombo **ch**o**ch**ote madau nā-mitepe, wakapijana baḥarini wa**ch**e(n)da barāni kut(w)a'a **ch**akula na-majiri ya-kurudi huwāna ḥai‿ḥai maiti.

Sayyid Mājidi akatia silisili katika kān(w)a la-mtō wa-Siu Kawāya, kusipiti **ch**ombo, tena nao waliona nyezi sita k(w)a-baḥarini nā-k(w)a-barāni. Na-janibu yā Fāzah Mze Sēfu akakhalifu akawa mtu wa Sayyid Mājid bin Sa'īd k(w)a-khīla nyingi na-manēno ma(n)gi. Akaona ẓīki sana Sulṭān Aḥmad nā Shaykh Muḥammad bin Shaykh Matāka.

Nā-nti yā Siu ikawa fitina, ba'aḍi yā wātu wampe(n)da Sayyid Mājid k(w)a-sababu ya-mashaka walopata na-wa‿tuwe ni-hawa Sharīf Mawlanā bin Abū Bakr nā 'Īsā bin Aḥmad al-Sōmalī. Alipoona Sulṭān Aḥmad nā Shaykh

Muḥammad bin Shaykh [Matāka] kama hayo wakataka amāni k(w)ā Sayyid Mājid, akawapa amāni. Katika manēno yā amāni Sulṭān Aḥmad akasaifiri k(w)ā siri usīku ake(n)da barāni akarejea Kau.

Ba'ada-ye Shaykh Muḥammad bin Shaykh Matāka akampeka kijāna chake, Shaykh Muḥammad bin Shaykh Matāka (p. 24) uk(w)ē(n)da marikabuni k(w)a-Sayyid Mājid bin Sa'īd na Sayyid Mājid kamṣameḥe akampa na-'aṭayā nyi(n)gi. Sayyid Mājid kasafiri karejea U(n)guja; kisa Shaykh Muḥammad bin Shaykh Matāka ake(n)da U(n)guja ku‿muwajihi Sayyid Mājid akamshika kamfu(n)ga katika (n)gome ya-Mombasah na-watu, akafa Shaykh Muhammad.

Na ba'ada-ya sīku Sayyid Mājid akampeka al-wali Sa'ūd bin Ḥamad kumshika Sulṭān Aḥmad k(w)ā khīla nyi(n)gi, asiweze, kutoka Kau k(w)a-siri ake(n)da Witu. Al-wālī Sa'ūd bin Ḥamad akaya Fāzah nā zijāna za Shaykh Muḥammad Matāka kawashika Siu kawapeka (n)gomeni Mombāsah,'Umar Matāka akamfu(n)ga Lamuh.

Ba'ada-ye Sayyid Mājid akatamalaki Sawaḥili zote, hakuna mtu wakumu'ariḍi. Na Sulṭān Aḥmad kaketi Wītu katika ṭa'a yā Sayyid Mājid. Alipo‿tawali Sayyid Barghash bin Sa'īd bin Sulṭān akataka Sayyid Barghash kuweka 'askari Wītu na k(w)a-bandari. Sulṭān Ahmad asiriḍīki, kapeka zita kumpijia, asiweze akafa(n)ya amani.

Na-ye Sa'ūd bin Ḥamad hakumpija sana zita, Sayyid Barghash kapeka zita zamāni zā al-wālī Sa'īd bin Ḥamad bin Sa'īd. Sulṭān Aḥmad akat(w)āa ḥimaya k(w)ā Jarmani, kawapa na-ba'aḍi ya bara ya Sawaḥīli. Akafa Sulṭān Aḥmad katika ḥali hiyo yā ḥimaya sanati 1306.

Akatawali Sulṭān Fūmo Bakr bin Sulṭān (p. 25) Ahmad bin Shaykh al-Nabahānī. Na-ye akaketi katika hiyo ḥimaya. Ikatokea fitina yeye nā Jarmani, mtu mmōya hīt(w)a Kisīli akampija bawabu wa-la(n)go, kampija ghafula k(w)a-ra‿ṣāṣi, wali kuweko ʻaskari kawapija k(w)ā raṣāṣi nā ʻaskari wakampija Kisīli na-WaZungu walofuetene. Nao wakauwa WaZu(n)gu min ghayri amri yā Sulṭān Fūmo Bakr. ʻAskari walipo‿waona jamiʻ zao wamekufa hawa‿ku(n)gūja amri ya sulṭāni wakawapija WaZu(n)gu na-wāna. Nā wātu wa-Mkonū(m)bi na-Wanda‿munyu walipo‿pata khabāri ya-kampa WaZu(n)gu wamepijana wakawaua WaZu(n)gu waliyo‿kuweko.

Baʻda-ye ikayā d‿ōlah yā Wa(N)gereza, wakataka kufa(n)ya inṣafu akawataka wātu wa-Mkonū(m)bi na-Wanda‿munyu maʻana awatiye katika ḥukumu. Fūmo Bakr asiriḍīki kuwatoa, wakampija zita Sulṭān Fūmo Bakr zikayā mashua ḥatā Mkonū(m)bi na-Wanda‿munyu na-Kilimani nā Nya(n)dō za-Pwāni, wazipiji k(w)ā mizi(n)ga wakatia na-moto ḥatā layla Rabīʻ al-Awwal sanati 1308. Wakapijana wātu wa-Wītu katika ndia ya Kipīni na-wātu wa-dōlah tukufu wakavundika wātu wa-Wītu, ḥata aṣubuḥi sīku ya juma tatu m(w)ezi 12 Rabīʻ al-Awwal sanati 1308 wakampija Sulṭān (p. 26) Fūmo Bakr wakamtoa Wītu k(w)a-zita, ake(n)da Jongeni.

Wītu akitamalakiwa na-dōla tukufu. Sulṭān Fūmo Bakr kaketi Jongeni ḥatā 28 Jumād al-Awwal sanati 1308 akafa. Akashika mahala pake (n)duye B(w)ānah Shaykh bin Aḥmad Nabahānī. Baʻada-ya sīku **chache** ikawa fitina, akashikwa na-(n)duye Fūmo ʻUmar Nabahānī nā Avu‿tūla wa-Bāhiru, wakamfu(n)ga B(w)anah Shaykh bin Sulṭān Aḥmad. Akatawali Sulṭān Fūmo ʻUmar. Na-wak(w)isa kuta‿m[a]llaki Pate Sulṭān Aḥmad, sulṭāni Wītu. Aku‿tamalaki k(w)anda Sulaymān bin Sulaymān al-Muẓaffar Nabahānī Imām al-ʻArabi.

Hini (n)diyo khabāri yā Nabahānī kuya Sawaḥīli na-khabāri zao kama tumezo‿ta(n)gulia kutayā. Wamezo‿tawali wafalume waḥidi wa-thalāthīni nā m(w)ānah mke mmōya, jumla thi[n]ēni wa thalāthīn min ghayri wa‿likatawali wakiuzu‿liwa wakarejea kutawali.

Tume‿naḳīli hiyo k(w)ā Muḥammad bin Fūmo ʻUmar Nabahānī al-mulaḳab B(w)ānah Kitīni, na-ye alinaḳīli k(w)ā jadi yāke Muḥammad bin B(w)ānah Mkū Nabahānī amkuliwao B(w)ānah Simba aliḍibitiye sana khabāri ya nasaba zao kama tumezo‿taya. Naḳ[a]la yā awali Sāliḥ bin Sālim bin Aḥmad bin ʻAbd Allāh Sharāḥīl 7 fī Safar sanati 1318. Naḳalat hadha li-l-walad al-ʻazīz Muḥammad bin Aḥmad bin Sulṭān (p. 27) bin Fūmo Bakr bin Shaykh bin B(w)ānah Fūmo Madī wa Simba Sulṭan Muḥammad bin Abū Bakr bin B(w)ānah Mkū bin Abū Bakr bin Aḥmad bin Abū Bakr bin Muḥammad bin Abū Bakr bin Muḥammad bin ʻUmar bin Muḥammad bin Aḥmad bin Muḥammad bin Sulaymān bin Sulaymān bin Mu[ẓ]affar Nabahānī. Naḳalat al-thānī 1 fī Rajab sanati 1343 li-aḳall Sāliḥ bin Sālim bin Ḥamad. Naḳalat l-rabīʻ wa-khamsa 23 Shaʻbān sanati 1365. [...] ʻAlī Khalīfa.

HISTORY OF PATE

Year 600 of the Hijra

(p. 2) There was Sulayman bin Sulayman Muzaffar al-Nabahani. The first in sequence to come to Pate was Sulayman bin Sulayman bin Muzaffar Nabahani and his two brothers, 'Ali bin Sulayman and 'Uthman bin Sulayman. And this Sulayman bin Sulayman the aforesaid had been sultan, and previously he reigned in the land of the Arabs. The aforesaid sultan came to Pate, about the date of the year 600 of al-Hijra[1] was his coming to Pate.

He asked for marriage from the king of Pate, from among the al-Batawiyin. Sultan Sulayman bin Sulayman was a prominent man, the king of Pate married him to his daughter. And the custom of all the WaSwahili till now (is that) a man takes your daughter (in marriage), (then) seven days after the wedding he goes to see his father-in-law at the house of his wife, the father of his wife, to be given (gifts) from the people. This Sulayman bin Sulayman, that king gave him his kingship that had been theirs. (p. 3) (Thereafter) reigned Sulayman bin [Sulayman], this king.

There was a town called Kitoki, on the same island of Pate, east of Pate; and Siu was not yet a town. There was another town called Shanga, east of Pate. And Faza was a town, the rulers of Faza were al-Mafazi. He ruled all these towns, all were under Sultan Sulayman bin Sulayman. And Mandra had

---

[1] 1203-4.

a separate king, [and he had] great power.

Sultan Sulayman bin Sulayman died in the year 625 of the Hijra.[2] He left two sons, Muhammad and Ahmad. Muhammad's age (was) twenty, (and) Ahmad's age (was) fifteen. Muhammad bin Sulayman bin Sulayman reigned after his father. A conflict arose between him and the people of Shanga, he made war on the city (and) destroyed it completely. And some of those (people) came to Pate, and a separate (group, whose) tribe (was) WaKinandangu, fled, (and) the place where they ran away was not known, until some days passed (and) the news came to Sultan Muhammad bin Sulayman from the hunters (who) came and said to him, "Those unknown,[3] we have seen them in the forest." The sultan sent people to look for them, (and) they caught up with them; they had made huts inside the forest. Sultan Muhammad bin Sulayman (p. 4) forgave them (and) returned them to their (own) place. This is the origin of the town of Siu.

(Later) came other WaSwahili (and) they all settled. (Then) came the WaFamau (and) settled; they were the chiefs of Siu under the overlordship of Sultan Muhammad bin Sulayman.

He died in the year 650.[4] His brother Sultan Ahmad bin Sulayman reigned. He governed the land of Pate very well, building houses (and) farms; he did not make war anywhere, (and) died in the year 660.[5]

---

[2] 1227-8.

[3] This phrasing is similar to MS 344. *Wale wa-Siu* "those unknown" is here taken to explain the etymology of the toponym *Siu*.

[4] 1252-3.

[5] 1261-2.

(Next) reigned the son of his brother, by the name Ahmad bin Muhammad bin Sulayman. He treated the people very well, following the example of his (paternal) uncle, building up the town of Pate and the farms, until he died in the year 700.[6] He left many children.

(Then) reigned his son Sultan Muhammad bin Ahmad bin Muhammad bin Sulayman. He governed the people in an excellent manner. (Then) the people of Faza seceded; he fought them (and) brought them under control after many battles, until he overcame them. He captured Mandra through a military ruse, because the sultan of Mandra had great power (in terms of) money and men. He destroyed it utterly, and carried off some people to Pate.

And a few fled (and) ran away to all places; some came to Shela (and) put themselves under the protection of the men of Lamu. Sultan (p. 5) Muhammad bin Ahmad the aforesaid demanded (them) of the men of Lamu; they refused to surrender them. And some went to Malindi and other towns. Sultan Muhammad bin Ahmad pursued vigorously (the matter of) those who came to Shela. The men of Lamu refused to surrended them decisively. While this matter still lasted, Sultan Muhammad died in the year 732.[7]

His son ascended to kingship, Sultan ‘Umar bin Muhammad bin Ahmad bin Muhammad bin Sulayman. He returned to his father’s case against the men of Lamu, demanding the people of Mandra. The men of Lamu refused to surrender them. He made war on them; the men of Lamu sued for peace (and) came under the overlordship of Sultan ‘Umar bin Muhammad.

He gained power (and) conquered all the towns of the Swahili (coast):

---

[6] 1300-1.

[7] 1331-2.

Ozi, Malindi, Kiwayu, Kitao, Miya, Imizi, Watamu, [until] he reached Kirimba. He gained possession of all these towns from Pate to Kirimba. In each town he placed his own man to govern. This is the origin of those *Majumbe* who are to be found on the coast (*mrima*). The meaning (of the root) is "the Palace of the king of Pate", and the meaning of (the expression) is "the slaves of the Yumbe," and the former is the *yumbe*.

And in the east he gained possession as far as Warsheikh. He went to wage war, beginning with Kiwayu and (then against) Tula and Tuwala and Shungwaya and all the harbors (*banadiri*): Brawa, Marka and Mogadisho. He placed a governor (*al-wali*) in charge of all adminsitration for the harbors near Mogadisho.

(As long as) he lived, all these lands were under his authority, only Zanzibar he did not rule, for at that time Zanzibar was not a great country. And this Sultan 'Umar loved war and loved his subjects, and the subjects loved him. The land of Pate gained great power. Sultan 'Umar died in the year 749.[8] He left two sons, Muhammad and Ahmad.

The elder son reigned, Sultan Muhammad bin 'Umar bin Muhammad bin Ahmad bin Muhammad bin Sulayman. And there was no war. [He ruled] the kingdom of his father in peace. And he loved very much money from trade; he sent voyages in his ships to go (and) conduct trade, and he had much profit in money.

And one time he sent his son on a voyage; he came upon an island at sea, found a silver mine, returned to Pate (and) made people to work the mine. He obtained very great wealth; money (so) increased in the land of Pate that

---

[8] 1348-9.

they made swords of silver and ladders of silver. And this king died in the year 797.[9] He left four sons, Bwana Mkuu and Ahmad and Abu Bakr and 'Umar.

His brother, Sultan Ahmad bin 'Umar bin Muhammad bin Ahmad bin Muhammad bin Sulayman reigned. He ruled over the people in peace and in an excellent manner toward all the people. (Then) he died.

(Next) reigned Abu Bakr (p. 7) bin Muhammad bin 'Umar bin Muhammad bin Ahmad bin Muhammad bin Sulayman. He ruled well over all the people and all the towns under his authority without discord. [He died] in the year 875.[10] And he left two sons, Muhammad and Ahmad.

After his father reigned Muhammad bin Abu Bakr bin Muhammad bin 'Umar bin Ahmad bin Muhammad bin Sulayman. In his time the Portuguese Europeans came to all the Swahili towns. They stayed at Mombasa (and) made a fort, and near Pate they built Ndondo. The people of the mainland obeyed them, payed them money (and) accepted their authority. They harrassed the king throughout the land of Pate (and) fought a war against the king on the side of Shindakasi.

They built the land of Pate on the beach by means of (making) hollows with the goal of attacking the town of Pate, (but) failed. They sued for peace (and) made a (written) document (stating) their conditions. The Europeans remained at Pate (and) made a customs-house; in their European language they called it '*Fandika*.' They made many things around the island of Pate. The

---

[9] 1394-5.

[10] 1470-1. It appears that a reign is skipped here.

sultan died in the year 900.[11] He left two sons, Bwana Mkuu and Abu Bakr.

After his father the aforesaid, Sultan Abu Bakr bin Muhammad bin Abu Bakr bin Abu Bakr bin Muhammad bin Ahmad bin Muhammad bin Sulayman[12] ascended to kingship. He ruled over the people well, prospering in peace, as was the practice of his father. He died in the year 940[13] with affairs in order. And he left two sons, Ahmad and Muhammad.

His (paternal) uncle ascended to kingship, Bwana Mkuu bin Muhammad bin Abu Bakr bin Muhammad bin 'Umar bin Muhammad bin Ahmad bin Muhammad bin Sulayman. There arose hostilities with the Europeans, but there was no war. The trouble lasted many days. He died in the year 973,[14] leaving one son called Abu Bakr.

(Next) reigned Muhammad bin Abu Bakr bin Muhammad bin 'Umar [bin] Muhammad bin Ahmad bin Muhammad bin Sulayman. He made peace with the Europeans, (and) they took some of the towns. He died in the year 1002.[15] He left one son called Abu Bakr who did not reign.

(Next) reigned Abu Bakr bin Bwana Mkuu bin Muhammad bin Abu Bakr bin Muhammad bin 'Umar bin Muhammad bin Ahmad bin Muhammad bin Sulayman. He treated the Europeans according to the manner of his ancestors who had preceded (him), (but) the kingdom diminished in strength.

---

[11] 1494-5.

[12] This name appears incomplete.

[13] 1533-4.

[14] 1565-6.

[15] 1593-4.

He died in the year 1041.[16] He left Bwana Mkuu and Abu Bakr, [named after] his father.

(Next) reigned Abu Bakr bin Muhammad bin Abu Bakr bin Muhammad bin Abu Bakr bin Muhammad bin 'Umar bin Ahmad bin Muhammad bin Sulayman. (There) arose discord with the Europeans; they fought (and) he defeated the Europeans in a very powerful battle. After that came in turn an expedition of the Europeans. They attacked the town of Pate with cannons (and) cut off the roads from the sea to block the ships. The people saw (p. 9) hardships (and) made peace. The king died in the year 1061.[17] He left two sons, Bwana Mkuu and Ahmad.

(Next) reigned Bwana Mkuu bin Bwana Bakr wa Bwana Mkuu bin Muhammad bin Abu Bakr bin Muhammad bin 'Umar bin Muhammad bin Ahmad bin Muhammad bin Sulayman. He got along very well with the Europeans. And he loved very much to stay in Lamu, even the monsoon (season) he spent at Lamu. He contracted a marriage among the people of Lamu.

And about this time the WaFamau of Siu revolted against his authority. He fought them, destroyed the town of Siu, seized some people (and) brought them to Pate. The chief of Siu escaped, went to Dondo, to the Portuguese, (and) claimed protection. The chief of the Europeans came to Pate to the king, to ask that he release the people of Siu. The king released them (and) had them returned to their (former) place at Siu under safe conduct.

---

[16] 1631-2.

[17] 1650-1.

After that the Portuguese devised[18] a stratagem. They came to Pate in a ship (and) invited the king to come aboard ship. He did not go (but) sent the son of his (paternal) uncle Bwana Mkuu, him and (some) men of Pate. The Europeans carried them off in the ship, (and) not even one man ever returned. After this the king attacked the Europeans from all directions, on the mainland and the islands, (and) drove them away from all these locations. They fled to Mombasa. The king died in the year 1100.[19] He had sons, Bwana Bakar and Bwana Madi, and one daughter called Mwana Darini.

(Then) reigned Abu Bakr bin Bwana Mkuu bin Abu Bakr bin Muhammad bin Abu Bakr bin Muhammad bin 'Umar (p. 10) bin Muhammad bin Ahmad bin Muhammad bin Sulayman. The king was suddenly attacked by Ahmad, the brother of the Bwana Mkuu who had been taken away by the Portuguese Europeans, with a sword. The king died in the year 1103.[20]

This very Ahmad bin Abu Bakr bin Muhammad bin Muhammad bin Abu Bakr bin Muhammad bin 'Umar bin Muhammad bin Ahmad bin Muhammad bin Sulayman reigned. After he ascended, he pursued the Portuguese (and) drove them out from throughout his country.

And at this time Mwana Darini, the daughter of Bwana Mkuu wa Bwana Bakr, wife of the Bwana Mkuu bin Abu Bakr who had been taken away by the Portuguese before the time of Sultan Ahmad, whose two brothers, Abu Bakr and Bwana Madi, had been killed by Sultan Ahmad,—and (as) her husband had been carried away she grieved greatly. After many days passed, she wished

---

[18] In MS *akafanya*, 3rd person singular.

[19] 1688-9.

[20] 1691-2.

to circumcise her son Bwana Tamu Mtoto ("Junior"), (the one) who was called Sultan Abu Bakr Imam Huda, the son of Bwana Mkuu who went to Goa.

When the king received the news, he decided to make a celebration himself, for his own sons, in order to deny her the ceremonial horn.[21] (When) the news came to Mwana Darini, she summoned Mwenyi Bayeyi bin Mkuu, *Sharif* of (the) *Jamal Layl*, who had great skill in carving, (and) she requested that he make [a horn superior] to the horn of Pate. He accepted a wage of one hundred and twenty riyals, (and) she gave him elephant tusks to choose [the best] one. He made the horn in secret till it was finished (and then) she showed it suddenly (and) took it around the houses of her kin. Every man gave offerings of much money, (p. 11) (so that) the master declined the wage (and) asked for the offerings; she gave him the offerings and made the celebration for her son.

Later, at the time of Bwana Tamu Mkuu ("Senior"), the people of Lamu came to borrow the horn; he gave it to them, (and) they carried the original horn to the sea. The ship sank in the water (and) perished. Bwana Tamu Mkuu asked for the horn from Mwana Darini, saying to her, "Give it to us, so that we may use it in all the towns." She answered him, "Every clan who makes an offering may use my horn."

And Mwana Darini set free a slave who knew how to blow the horn. She said, "This is the chief beater of the horn, he and his descendants. And for his fee let him be given five riyals and a cloth for carrying the horn, and

---

[21] A rare and meaningful wording, *siwa ya-shamba*, lit. "horn of proclamation." From the verb *amba* "to say," *cf. mgambo* "public proclamation." Johnson mentions *mbiu ya mgambo* "formerly a buffalo horn blown to call people together to hear a proclamation or announcement." See Frederick Johnson, *A Standard Swahili-English Dictionary* (Oxford: University Press, 1959).

let him be given besides ghee and a present, from every man according to his means."

That family was called "the Heralds of the Horn," (and) to this day there are people (belonging) to it. From that time until now the custom of all the clans of Pate and of the clans of other countries has been to go (and) borrow under such circumstances; (and) the Heralds of the Horn are paid.

Mischief increased within the city, and during his reign for seven years there was drought in the city, there was no rain, (and so) the king abdicated.

(Next) reigned Sultan Abu Bakr bin Bwana Tamu Mkuu wa Bwana Mtiti bin Ahmad bin Abu Bakr bin 'Umar bin Ahmad bin 'Umar bin Muhammad bin Ahmad bin Muhammad bin Sulayman. He made a strong alliance with the sultan of Maskat, al-Imam Sayf bin Nabahani al-'Arabi. This [king] (p. 12) of Pate went to Arabia, (and) they made an agreement between the king of Arabia and this king of Pate to drive out the Portuguese on Sunday, to kill the men (and) to gain possession of the fort of Mombasa.

He informed[22] al-Imam al-Ya'rubi. (The latter) brought governors (*al-wali*) of the Mazru'i (family), three men: Muhammad bin 'Uthman and 'Ali bin 'Uthman and the third's name is unknown. They came with soldiers of the Imam Sayf Nabahani al-Ya'rubi. This is the origin of the Mazru'i.

And the king of Pate conducted (himself) in an excellent manner toward all the people. He lived for forty years in his kingship (and) died in the year 1154.[23] He had many children (but) his sons did not reign after him.

(Instead) reigned Ahmad bin Abu Bakr bin Muhammad bin Abu Bakr

---

[22] The use of the verb *'arifu* here specifically implies notification in writing.

[23] 1741-2.

bin ‘Umar bin Ahmad bin ‘Umar bin Muhammad bin Ahmad bin Muhammad bin Sulayman.[24] He was benevolent (and) died in the year 1160.[25] He left a son called Bwana Gongo who did not reign.

Bwana Tamu Mtoto ("the Younger") reigned, who was called Imam al-Huda, (the son) of Bwana Mkuu carried away by the Portuguese. And his (real) name was Abu Bakr bin Bwana Mkuu bin Abu Bakr bin Muhammad bin Abu Bakr bin Muhammad bin Abu Bakr bin Muhammad bin ‘Umar bin Muhammad bin Sulayman.

At this time the Imam al-Ya‘rubi brought an expedition to attack Pate (but) they failed, (and) very many Arabs died, (so) they made peace. After this the people of Lamu revolted. (p. 13) The king waged war on them (but) failed against the people of Lamu. And the people of Lamu equipped an army (and) came to Pate on the side of Kitoki. They fought the men of Pate in a great battle. The men of Lamu were defeated. After this the king of Pate waged war by land and sea; he attacked the people of Lamu (and) conquered them. [After] this the king of Pate and the men of Lamu became united (and), the Imam al-Ya‘rubi established single administration. The king was killed in the year 1177.[26]

(Then) reigned his sibling, a woman, Sultana Mwana Khadija binti Bwana Mkuu bin Abu Bakr bin Muhammad bin Abu Bakr bin Muhammad bin Abu Bakr bin Muhammad bin ‘Umar bin Muhammad bin Ahmad bin Muhammad bin Sulayman. There was much intrigue in the land of Pate,

---

[24] Compare the name of this ruler in MS 321.

[25] 1747.

[26] 1763-4.

(because) there were two kings, Mwana Khadija the aforesaid[27] and Sultan 'Umar. They fought in the town of Pate for three years; Sultan 'Umar went to the mainland (and) returned to Pate with a very powerful force. One night they were killed by the men of Mwana Khadija, each man where he was. Mwana Khadija died in the year 1187.[28]

(Then) reigned Bwana Mkuu wa Sheye wa Bwana Tamu Mkuu. The subjects made much trouble; he got no peace during his reign, until, in the year 1191,[29] [his palace] was invaded: the men of the town invaded and killed him on this date.

(Then) reigned Bwana Fumo Madi, whose (real) name was Sultan Muhammad bin Abu Bakr bin Bwana Mkuu bin Abu Bakr bin Muhammad bin Abu Bakr bin Muhammad bin Abu Bakr bin Muhammad bin 'Umar bin Muhammad bin Ahmad bin Muhammad bin Sulayman. After he came to power, (p. 14) the subjects wished to make intrigue; he fought them in battle, overcame them, seized forty men (of whom) two were his own brothers, (and) slaughtered them like goats, (so) blood (ran off) the roof. In this way he suppressed the great men (of the kingdom). (Then) there was peace; no other man rose to make trouble. He reigned in great quiet until he died in the year 1224.[30] And (there) reigned no other king like him. He left very many children.

---

[27] Unlike MS 177, this MS uses the Arabic masculine form *al-madhkūr* for Mwana Khadīja. The use of *sulṭān* is gender-neutral.

[28] 1773-4.

[29] 1777.

[30] 1809-10.

(Then) reigned Sultan Ahmad bin Shaykh Fumo Luti bin Shaykh bin Bwana Mkuu. Trouble increased in the town of Lamu; he attacked them, with the men of Mombasa, the Mazru'i, (being) on the same side. They landed at Shela a great army of men of Pate and men of Mombasa. The men of Lamu came out, came to Shela (and) fought with the men of Pate and men of Mombasa. The army of the men of Lamu had great force, (and) the army of Pate and Mombasa was defeated. They ran to their ships, (but) some ships were stranded on the beach. Then they stopped (and) fought (another) great battle. Very many men died, men of Mombasa and men of Pate, without counting. Out of the men of Pate, the important ones, without slaves and lowly people, (there were) eighty-one 81 men of "So-and-so, the son of So-and-so," persons of Pate who went to the next life;[31] and (as to) the men of Mombasa, there was no counting.

After that the men of Lamu went to Arabia (p. 15) (and) asked for Sa'id bin Sultan bin al-Imam, and they gave him the land of Lamu in the year 1228;[32] thereafter he ruled Lamu. The kingdom of Pate included Pate (itself) and the harbors (*banadiri*).

(Then) unrest increased. (There) arose a second man from among the sons of Bwana Fumo Madi, called Fumo Luti Kipunga. He fought Sultan Ahmad. Later Sultan Ahmad died of disease in the year 1230.[33]

(Then) reigned Fumo Luti wa Bwana Fumo Madi. And he was very strong, brave (and) generous. And it was during this time (that) Shaykh

---

[31] Cusack translates: "having wives to go into mourning there in Pate."

[32] 1813.

[33] 1814-5.

Mataka bin Shaykh Mubarak held the office of *shaykh* of Siu. He obtained soldiers and guns, and he was under the suzerainty of the sultan of Pate and on very good terms with the Mazru'i until the year 1232.[34] (Then) trouble increased between him and Sulṭān Sa'id bin Sultan of Zanzibar. Sultan Fumo Luti the aforesaid died.

After him reigned Fumo Luti bin Shaykh bin Fumo Luti wa Bwana Tamu Mkuu. And he was the one who was father of Sultan Ahmad, (later) sultan[35] of Witu. He reigned from dawn till after the mid-afternoon [prayer]. The men of the town drove him out. He went to Siu together with the Mazru'i; (then) they all went to Mombasa.

(Then) reigned Sultan Bwana Shaykh bin Fumo Madi. He negotiated with Sayyid Sa'id bin Sultan, took Arabs into Pate, (and) they remained (there) for three years. Afterwards the people of the town deposed him with (p. 16) the consent of Sayyid Sa'id bin Sultan at the date of the year 12[42].[36] They installed Sultan Ahmad called Bwana Waziri wa Bwana Tamu wa Bwana Shaykh [wa Bwana] Tamu Mkuu. He was on good terms with Sayyid Sa'id bin Sultan (and) reigned for two years. (Then) the people deposed him (and) returned Bwana [Shaykh] wa Bwana Fumo Madi. He remained in power with the consent of Sayyid Sa'id bin Sultan for three years (and) died in the year 1247.[37]

Bwana Waziri returned to the sultanship. (Then) came Bwana Fumo

[34] 1816-7. Other new MSS have 1236.

[35] In MS incorrectly "son of the sultan of Witu." See below, p. 20 and MS 344.

[36] 1826-7. In MS incorrectly 1224. This date does not occur in MS 344.

[37] 1831-2.

Luti bin Shaykh who had gone to Mombasa to gether with the Mazru'i; they captured Siu (and) attacked Bwana Waziri wa Bwana Tamu at Pate. And Bwana Waziri was at one with Sayyid Sa'id bin Sultan, and Fumo Luti was at one with the Mazru'i and Shaykh Mataka, a man of Siu. They came to Pate with troops (and) fought. The army of Siu was defeated, Bwana Waziri captured the land of Siu (and) destroyed the city wall.

Shaykh Mataka bin Shaykh Mubarak and Fumo Luti fled to the mainland together with some of the men; after a few days he returned to Siu with a very strong force, drove out the men of Bwana Waziri by attack, captured from them the town of Siu, (and) rebuilt the town wall.

Pate and Siu fought each other (and) came under the authority and administration of Sayyid Sa'id bin Sultan. After one year Sultan (p. 17) Bwana Waziri was killed by Fumo Bakr wa Bwana Shaykh wa Bwana Fumo Madi.

This Sultan Fumo Bakr bin Shaykh bin Fumo Madi ascended in the year 1250.[38] He was on very good terms with Sayyid Sa'id bin Sultan during the latter's reign. (But) later he revolted, together with Shaykh Mataka bin Shaykh Mubarak. Sayyid Sa'id bin Sultan sent an expedition under Amir Hamad al-Samar al-Busa'idi; he attacked Pate and Siu but failed (and) made peace.

After this suddenly arose trouble between the sultan of Pate Fumo Bakr and his (paternal) uncle. Muhammad bin Ahmad wa Bwana Fumo Madi seized the royal palace of Sultan Fumo Bakr suddenly by force. The men of Lamu together with a man of Sayyid Sa'id bin Sultan made a peace treaty with Muhammad bin Ahmad; he was sent to stay at Siu, and Fumo Bakari remained at Pate.

---

[38] 1834-5.

Afterwards they quarrelled and fought for three years,[39] and Fumo Bakr [came to rule both] Siu and Pate. After Sayyid Sa'id bin Sultan made them reconcile, Muhammad bin Ahmad came to Pate, [to be] under the single administration with the son of his (paternal) uncle Fumo Bakr. (Then) he seized Muhammad bin Ahmad suddenly (and) killed him, in concert with a man of Siu.

Sayyid Sa'id bin Sultan summoned Fumo Bakr. He went to Zanzibar. Sayyid Sa'id bin Sultan imprisoned him on the advice of the men of Lamu, for the reason of his killing Muhammad bin Ahmad and for breaking the peace which Sayyid Sa'id bin Sultan had made.

In the year 1262[40] Sultan Ahmad bin (p. 18) Shaykh [bin] Fumo Luti bin Shaykh wa Bwana Tamu Mkuu seized Pate with the consent of Sayyid Sa'id bin Sultan. He ruled for two years; afterwards he revolted. Sayyid Sa'id bin Sultan came with a very powerful army under Amir Hamad to Faza, (and the latter) attacked Siu, and Sayyid Sa'id bin Sultan released Sultan Fumo Bakr (and) gave him an army together with the men of Lamu. They stayed at Mtanga Wanda aboard the ships.

And when Sayyid Sa'id went to Faza, he stayed at a place called Kijanga cha-Mpunga, near Faza. Amir Hamad came to Siu, to build forts along the road between Pate and Faza and Siu. Amir Hamad went to Siu with a very strong force, seized the *mtepe* boats which were in the harbor of Siu, turned them over, made barricades (and) attacked the land of Siu. He saw much hardship in the course of the war going strong, (so) Amir Hamadi with

[39] Elsewhere "five years."

[40] 1845-6.

some soldiers went back to the forts to fetch a cannon. While he was on his way, the men of Siu rushed out on him suddenly, an *amir* of Shaykh Mataka called Bin Mubarak, Hamad ‘Umar, and the second *amir*, called Hamad Ngoma. They fought (and) killed Amir Hamad, went to the fort, attacked the Arabs who were in the fort (and) took the cannons. And the troops that were at Siu did not fight.

When news came of the attack on Amir Hamad, the killing of the army of Sayyid Sa‘id bin Sultan (and) the defeat of those who were to take possession of Siu, when Sayyid Sa‘id bin Sultan received the news of the death (p. 19) of Amir Hamad, he went fleeing to the ship without saying a word (and) went away to Maskat.

Next year he placed Sultan Fumo Bakari at Faza, (and the latter) attacked Siu and Pate. At this time Shaykh Mataka died of disease. There was discord among his sons, each man wanted the shaykhdom; they submitted to the overlordship of Sayyid Sa‘id bin Sultan: Abu Bakr and Muhammad, the sons of Shaykh Mataka.

The Sayyid gave Abu Bakr troops together with Sultan Fumo Bakar, to attack Sultan Ahmad at Siu. Abu Bakr bin Shaykh Mataka went to Siu together with an *amir* of Sultan Fumo Bakr called Hamad wa Baishi Nabahani. He entered Siu by night; they fought until the men of Sultan Fumo Bakr were defeated (and) chased away. They captured Abu Bakr bin Shaykh Mataka (and) took him to Pate; he was killed by Sultan Ahmad.

Afterwards his brother Shaykh Muhammad bin Shaykh Mataka took a stand on the side of Sayyid Sa‘id bin Sultan. To him and Sultan Fumo Bakr Sayyid Sa‘id bin Sultan gave a troop of soldiers and supplies. They fought

Sultan Ahmad till they drove him out of Pate in the year 1273.[41] He went to Kau.

Siu, under Muhammad bin Shaykh Mataka, was on the side of Sayyid Sa'id bin Sultan. He gave him soldiers to build a fort. (Later) they quarreled with a man of Sayyid Sa'id bin Sultan because he destroyed a boat shed which Shaykh (p. 20) Muhammad Mataka had built in front of the fort. And Shaykh Muhammad Mataka destroyed the fort.

And about this time at Kau died Sultan Ahmad bin Shaykh at Kau, died the father of Fumo Bakr, (later) sultan of Witu. In his place ruled Sultan Ahmad called *Simba* ('the Lion'), sultan of Witu.

And before Shaykh Muhammad destroyed the fort of Siu, there had been trouble. Sultan Fumo Bakr bin Shaykh drove him out of Pate by force, (and) he came to Lamu. He (Shaykh Muhammad) wished to gain possession of Pate because he saw his (own) strength. And when the great men of Pate saw the acts committed by Shaykh Muhammad Mataka, they did not wish him to rule, (and) they did not accept (him). (Then) he made war on them, (but) the great men of Pate persisted. And there was no king due to the advice of three men: Muhammad bin Mkuu Nabahani and Bwana Rehema bin Ahmad Nabahani and Nasir bin 'Abd Allah bin 'Abd Salam, the one who was the *mudabbir al-umur*. He collected munitions, they fought Shaykh Muhammad bin Shaykh Mataka (and) defeated him; many promiment men died, and of great *amirs* two men - Bwana Damila and Mawlana wa Sheye Kuli.

(When) Shaykh Muhammad bin Shaykh Mataka saw these matters he came to seek peace from Muhammad bin Bwana Mkuu al-Nabahani, because

[41] 1856-7.

it was he who was the chief (elder) of the three men we named above. He wished to give him, Muhammad bin Mkuu, the sultanship of Siu and Pate. He refused, answering: "I am an old man." They went to fetch Sultan Ahmad of Witu. Shaykh Muhammad bin Shaykh (p. 21) Mataka sent (some) men, and the men of Pate sent Shaykh Nasir bin 'Abd Salam, to fetch Sultan Ahmad nicknamed Simba, (and) came with him to Pate.

The news reached Zanzibar, Sultan Sayyid Majid bin Sa'id bin Sultan, for Sayyid Sa'id had died previously in the year 1273.[42] Prior to this the Sayyid sent his *wazīr* Sayyid Sulayman bin Hamad by ship to seize Pate (and) crush the conspiracy. By the time the ship arrived at Manda, Pate had been seized by a man of Sultan Ahmad, Abu Bakr bin Hasan al-Buri who had come with Nasir bin 'Abd Salam. When Sayyid Sulayman bin Hamad received this news, he returned to Zanzibar, and this was when Shaykh Muhammad bin Shaykh Mataka destroyed the fort at Siu.

When [Sultan] Ahmad arrived at Pate, the people acknowledged him as sulṭān: Shaykh Muhammad bin Shaykh Mataka as well as Mzee Sefu and Shaykh Shikuwe and Muhammad Mote, to affirm Sultan Ahmad's kingship.

Sayyid Majid bin Sa'id bin Sultan sent men of Lamu to Pate, to give counsel together with Shaykh Muhi al-Din, (and) to request that Sultan Ahmad put soldiers of the Sayyid at Pate. And this Shaykh Muhi al-Din was the one who turned out the soldiers of the Sayyid from the fort at Siu when they were defeated by Shaykh Muhammad bin Shaykh Mataka. The soldiers were inside the fort; Shaykh Muhi al-Din went to take them out in peace (p. 22) because he was a man of Sayyid Majid bin Sa'id, one of the *wazirs*.

---

[42] 1856-7.

When he went to Zanzibar with the soldiers, the Sayyid became very angry at Shaykh Muhi al-Din, and Shaykh Muhi al-Din took the blame when he saw Sayyid Majid and his wrath. That was when he went back with the men of Lamu. And this Shaykh Muhi al-Din had great cunning and much learning; he went to Pate with the best men of Lamu, together with Shaykh Ahmad and Shaykh 'Abd al-Rahman, the *shaykh* of Pate himself.[43] He spoke with Sultan Ahmad, and he accepted, after much reluctance, because of (his) friendship with Shaykh Ahmad and Shaykh 'Abd al-Rahman, rejecting the advice of his *wazīr* Nasir bin 'Abd Salam, for he refused to put up the Arabs, even one man.

The men of Pate made an agreement with Mwana Jaha binti Fumo Luti Kipunga wa Bwana Fumo Madi, [wife] of Sultan Fumo Bakr bin Shaykh. At this time Sultan Fumo Bakr was in Lamu, according to the decree of Sayyid Majid bin Sa'id, since the time when he was driven out of Pate.

But every day they brought in soldiers secretly, and munitions, night after night. (When) Sultan Ahmad was informed (that) there was a plot and the soldiers were many at Pate, they suddenly attacked Sultan Ahmad, after the ruse was arranged, aiming to seize him suddenly. They failed because all the Pate people were of one mind with Sayyid (p. 23) Majid bin Sa'id, except his *wazir* Nasir bin 'Abd Salam. They fought within the town of Pate, Sultan Ahmad got away, he and Shaykh Muhammad bin Shaykh Mataka went to Siu.

The Arabs seized Pate and placed (their) ships on the sea. (When) the war became very fierce, Sayyid Majid bin Sa'id came (himself) to lay siege to

---

[43] According to Werner, these men are brothers. Cusack calls them "children of Shaykh of Pate."

Siu and Pate, and to stop shipping at sea (and) to sink *dhows* and *mtepes*. They fought at sea (and) went to the mainland to obtain food (but) the return route was unavailable; (it became a matter of) life and death. Sayyid Majid placed a chain across the mouth of the Siu creek, the Kawaya, to block the ships. Consequently they suffered six months [of blockade] on the sea and on dry land. And on the side of Faza, Mzee Sefu seceded (and) became a man of Sayyid Majid bin Sa'id, through much cunning and many words. Sultan Ahmad and Shaykh Muhammad bin Shaykh Mataka experienced great distress.

Dissent arose in the land of Siu: some of the people loved Sayyid Majid because of the troubles they had suffered, and his men (there) were *Sharif* Mawlana bin Abu Bakr and 'Isa bin Ahmad al-Somali. (When) they saw how things were, Sultan Ahmad and Shaykh Muhammad bin Shaykh Mataka suedfor peace from Sayyid Majid, (and) he granted them peace. During peace negotiations Sultan Ahmad sailed secretly by night, went to the mainland (and) returned to Kau.

Afterwards Shaykh Muhammad bin Shaykh Mataka sent his son, Shaykh Muhammad bin Shaykh Mataka,[44] (p. 24) to go to the ship, to Sayyid Majid, and Sayyid Majid pardoned him (and) gave him many presents. (Then) Sayyid Majid sailed (and) returned to Zanzibar. Later Shaykh Muhammad bin Shaykh Mataka went to Zanzibar to appear before Sayyid Majid. He seized him (and) imprisoned him in the fort of Mombasa, along with (other) men. (Then) Shaykh Muhammad died.

---

[44] The name of the father is repeated here, as also in MS 321, p. 26. Voeltzkow (*Reise*, p. 78) talks of a brother bringing about a reconciliation: that may have been 'Umar Mataka mentioned below. But Voeltzkow also mentions a son of Muhammad's named Mataka (*Reise*, p. 79). It is possible that scribes of MSS 344 and 358 reversed the first name and patronymic (Shaykh Mataka bin Shaykh Muhammad).

And after (some) days Sayyid Majid sent the governor (*al-wālī*) Sa'ud bin Hamad to seize Sultan Ahmad by many ruses, (but) he failed. He (Sultan Ahmad) left Kau secretly (and) went to Witu. The *wālī* Sa'ud bin Hamad came to Faza; he seized the children of Shaykh Muhammad Mataka at Siu (and) sent them to the fort of Mombasa. 'Umar Mataka he imprisoned at Lamu.[45]

Afterwards Sayyid Majid ruled over all the Swahili (coast), (for) there was no man to challenge him. And Sultan Ahmad remained at Witu under the suzerainty of Sayyid Majid. When Sayyid Barghash bin Sa'id bin Sultan came to the throne, Sayyid Barghash wished to place soldiers at Witu and at the harbor. Sultan Ahmad did not agree; he (Sayyid Barghash) sent an expedition to fight him (but) failed, (and) made peace. And this Sa'ud bin Hamad did not fight vigorously enough, (so) Sayyid Barghash sent an expedition again, under the *wālī* Sa'id bin Hamad bin Sa'id. Sultan Ahmad took the protection of the Germans (and) gave them some of the Swahili mainland.[46] Sultan Ahmad died, under this condition of protection, in the year 1306.[47]

(Then) reigned Sultan Fumo Bakr bin Sultan (p. 25) Ahmad bin Shaykh al-Nabahani. And he remained under this protection, (but) there arose conflict (between) him and the Germans. One man, called Küntzell, killed the porter of the gate; he shot him suddenly. The soldiers who were there shot, and the soldiers killed Küntzell and the Europeans who had accompanied him. And

---

[45] According to Voeltzkow (*Reise*, p. 79), 'Umar was captured by Mzee bin Sef (the arabized form of *Mzee wa Sefu*) at the instigation of the *Liwali* of Lamu.

[46] In MS *kawapa* "he gave them." This differs from the other versions stating the reverse: *wakampa* "they gave him."

[47] 1888-9. This date does not occur in MS 344.

they killed the Europeans without Sultan Fumo Bakr's order. (When) the soldiers saw all those dead,[48] they did not wait for an order from the sultan, (and) attacked the Europeans who were there. And when the people of Mkonumbi and Wanda Munyu they received the news of the attack on the Europeans they attacked (and) killed the Europeans who were there.

Afterwards came the Administration of the English. They wished to make justice (and) demanded the people of Mkonumbi and of Wanda Munyu in order to bring them to trial. Fumo Bakr did not consent to surrender them. They attacked Sultan Fumo Bakr, sending boats to Mkonumbi and Wanda Munyu and Kilimani and Nyando za Pwani. They shot from cannons (and) set [houses] on fire.

Then on the night of 11 Rabi' al-Awwal of the year 1308[49] the men of Witu fought on the Kipini road with the men of the Illustrious Administration; the men of Witu suffered defeat. Then on the morning of Monday, 12 of the month Rabi' al-Awwal of the year 1308,[50] they attacked Sultan (p. 26) Fumo Bakr (and) drove him out of Witu by force. He went to Jongeni.

Witu was taken over by the Illustrious Administration. Sultan Fumo Bakr remained at Jongeni until 28 Jumad al-Awwal of the year 1308[51] (when) he died. His brother Bwana Shaykh bin Ahmad Nabahani occupied his place. After three days a conspiracy arose, he was seized by his brother Fumo 'Umar

---

[48] Two men had been shot.

[49] 25 October 1890.

[50] 26 October 1890.

[51] 9 January 1891.

Nabahani and Avutula wa Bahiru.[52] They imprisoned Bwana Shaykh bin Sultan Ahmad. (Then) reigned Sultan Fumo 'Umar.

And the last to rule Pate was Sultan Ahmad, the sultan of Witu. The one to rule first was Sulayman bin Sulayman al-Muzaffar Nabahani, Imam al-'Arabi.

This is the account of the Nabahani who came to the Swahili (coast), and their history, as we have mentioned above. (There) reigned thirty-one kings and one woman, to the total of thirty-two, without (counting) those who reigned, were deposed (and) returned to rule.

We have transmitted this from Muhammad bin Fumo 'Umar Nabahani, nicknamed Bwana Kitini, and he transmitted it from his grandfather Muhammad bin Bwana Mkuu Nabahani called Bwana Simba, who was very reliable in regard to the accounts of their pedigree, such as we have named.

The first copy is by Salih bin Salim bin Ahmad bin 'Abd Allah Sharahil, 7 Safar of the year 1318.[53] This copy made for the Honorable Infant Muhammad bin Ahmad bin Sultan (p. 27) bin Fumo Bakr bin Shaykh bin Bwana Fumo Madi wa Simba, Sultan Muhammad bin Abu Bakr bin Bwana Mkuu bin Abu Bakr bin Ahmad bin Abu Bakr bin Muhammad bin Abu Bakr bin Muhammad bin 'Umar bin Muhammad bin Ahmad bin Muhammad bin Sulayman bin Sulayman bin Muzaffar Nabahani. The second copy, 1 Rajab

[52] At the time, Avutula had considerable influence and attracted international attention. See Adolf von Tiedemann, "Ein Besuch beim Suaheli-Hauptling Futula," *Deutsche Kolonialzeitung* (1889): 271-3.

[53] 6 June 1900. MSS 321 and 344 have 6 Safar.

of the year 1343,[54] is by the humble Salih bin Salim bin Hamad. Copies four and five, 23 Sha'ban of the year 1365,[55] are by 'Ali Khalifa.

[54] 26 January 1925.

[55] 23 July 1946.

APPENDICES

APPENDIX 1 -	Genealogical chart found, with minute variations, in MSS 309, 321 and 358, University Library, Dar es Salaam.
APPENDIX 2 -	Translation of the abstract of Pate history found on folios 5-20 of MS 309, University Library, Dar es Salaam.
APPENDIX 3 -	"Sultans of Pate." Table compiled by Alice Werner from the data found in the Stigand version (Bwana Kitini B), Mollis-Werner version (Bwana Kitini A) and the Reddie MS (Mshahame bin Kombo). Reproduced from the *Journal of the African Society* 15 (1915): 410-11.
APPENDIX 4 -	Genealogical table of the Rulers of Witu compiled by Alfred Voeltzkow. From *Reise in Ostafrika*, facing p. 65.
APPENDIX 5 -	Chronology of the rulers of Witu compiled by Alfred Voeltzkow. From *Reise in Ostafrika*, p. 91.
APPENDIX 6 -	Genealogy of the Nabhani rulers of Pate compiled by M. Heepe. From *Mitteilungen des Seminars für orientalische Sprachen* 31 (1928): 148-9.
APPENDIX 7 -	Chronology of the Nabhani rulers of Pate compiled by M. Heepe from the data of the Wassmuss-Heepe version (Chronicle) and the Voeltzkow abstract of the Stigand version (Stigand and Voeltzkow). From *Mitteilungen des Seminars für orientalische Sprachen* 31 (1928): 181.
APPENDIX 8 -	Imams and Seyyids of Oman, edited by Alice Werner from G. P. Badger's translation of Salil ibn Raziq. From the *Journal of the African Society* 15 (1915): 412-3.

GENEALOGICAL CHART OF BWANA KITINI

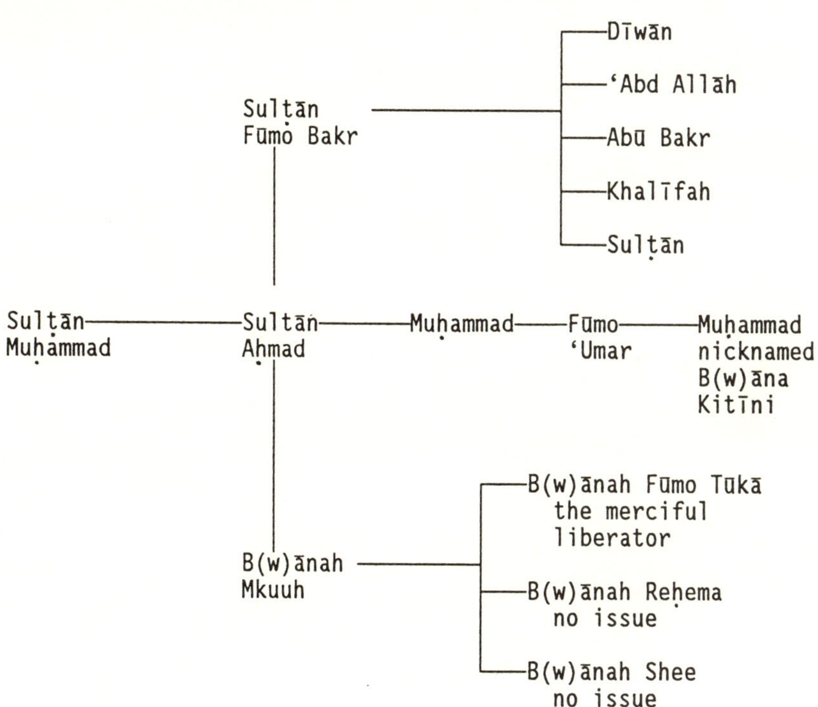

MS 309

ABSTRACT OF PATE HISTORY

(f.5) The first person to come to Pate from the Nabahānī is Sulaymān bin Seleman bin Muẓaffar Nabahānī [year 600 A.H.]

601-†625 Sulaymān bin Sulaymān

(f.6) Muḥammad bin Sulaymān -
†650 - Pate, Siu, WaSawahīli

†660 Aḥmad bin Sulaymān -
- Lamūh, Mān(d)ra

†700 Aḥmad bin Aḥmad bin Sulaymān
- Kirīmbā, Imīdhī, Malindī

†732 Muḥammad bin Aḥmad bin Muḥammad bin Sulaymān

(f.7) 'Umar bin Muḥammad bin Aḥmad bin Muḥammad bin
†749 Sulaymān

Muḥammad bin 'Umar bin Muḥammad
†797 bin Aḥmad bin Muḥammad bin Sulaymān

B(w)ānah Mkuh bin Aḥmad and Abū Bakr and 'Umar

Aḥmad bin 'Umar bin Muḥammad bin Aḥmad bin
Muḥammad bin Sulaymān

Abu Bakr bin Muḥammad bin 'Umar bin Muḥammad bin
875 Aḥmad bin Muḥammad bin Sulaymān
[Muḥammad and Aḥmad]

Muḥammad bin Abū Bakr bin Muḥammad bin 'Umar bin
Muḥammad bin Aḥmad bin Muḥammad bin
Sulaymān
900 [Europeans]
(f.8) [B(w)ānah Mkūh]

Abū Bakr bin Muḥammad bin Abū Bakr bin Muḥammad
940 bin Aḥmad bin Muḥammad bin Sulaymān
[Muḥammad + Aḥmad]

B(w)ānah Mkūh bin Muḥammad bin Abū Bakr bin
973 Muḥammad bin 'Umar bin Muḥammad bin Aḥmad
bin Muḥammad bin Sulaymān

Muḥammad bin Abū Bakr bin Muḥammad bin 'Umar bin
Muḥammad bin Aḥmad
1002 bin Muḥammad bin Sulaymān

Abū Bakr bin B(w)ānah Mkūh bin Muḥammad bin Abū
1030 Bakr bin Muḥammad bin 'Umar bin Muḥammad
bin Aḥmad bin Muḥammad bin Sulaymān

Abū Bakr bin Muḥammad bin Abū Bakr bin Muḥammad
bin Abū Bakr bin Muḥammad bin 'Umar bin
Aḥmad bin Muḥammad
1061 bin Sulaymān
[B(w)ānah Mkūh & Aḥmad]

B(w)ānah Mkūh wa B(w)ānah Bakr wa B(w)ānah Mkūh
bin Muḥammad bin Abū Bakr bin Muḥammad bin
'Umar bin Muḥammad
1100 bin Aḥmad bin Muḥammad bin Sulaymān
(f.9) [B(w)ānah Mādī & B(w)ānah Bakr]
Siu, WaFamau

Abū Bakr bin B(w)ānah Mkūh bin Abū Bakr bin
B(w)ānah Mkūh bin Abū Bakr bin Muḥammad bin
Abū Bakr bin Muḥammad bin 'Umar bin
1103 Muḥammad bin Aḥmad bin Muḥammad bin
Sulaymān

Aḥmad bin Abū Bakr bin Muḥammad bin Muḥammad
[*sic*] bin Abū Bakr bin Muḥammad bin 'Umar bin
Aḥmad bin Muḥammad bin Sulaymān
[M(w)ānah Darīni binti B(w)ānah Mkūh]
B(w)ānah Mtiti & B(w)ānah Tamu - Pate

(f.10)

Abū Bakr bin B(w)ānah Tamu Mkūh wa B(w)ānah Mtiti
bin Aḥmad bin Abū Bakr bin 'Umar bin Aḥmad
bin 'Umar bin Muḥammad bin Aḥmad bin
1153 Sulaymān [*sic*]
[al-Imām Sēfu bin Nabahānī l-'Arubī - Maskat]
'Alī bin 'Uthmān & Muḥammad bin 'Uthmān

Aḥmad bin Abū Bakr bin Muḥammad bin Abū Bakr bin
1160 'Umar bin Aḥmad bin 'Umar bin Muḥammad bin
Aḥmad bin Muḥammad bin Sulaymān
[B(w)ānah Mkūh & B(w)ānah Gō(n)go]

Abū Bakr bin [Abū Bakr] bin B(w)ānah Mkū bin Abū
Bakr bin Muḥammad bin Abū Bakr bin Muḥammad
bin Abū Bakr bin Muḥammad bin 'Umar
1177 bin Muḥammad bin Sulaymān

[his sibling] M(w)ānah Mkū Sultān *M(w)ānah Khadīja*
binti B(w)ānah Mkūh bin Abū Bakr bin Muḥammad
bin Abū Bakr bin Muḥammad bin Abū Bakr bin

Bakr bin Muḥammad bin 'Umar bin Muḥammad bin Aḥmad
1187 bin Muḥammad bin Sulaymān

1191 B(w)ānah Mkūh wa Sheye wa B(w)ānah Tamu Mkūh - subjects

(f.12) B(w)ānah Fūmo Mādi, named Sultan Muḥammad bin Abū Bakr bin B(w)ānah Mkūh bin Abū Bakr bin Muḥammad bin Abū Bakr bin Muḥammad bin Abu
1223 Bakr bin Muḥammad bin 'Umar bin Muḥammad bin Aḥmad bin Muḥammad bin Sulaymān

Aḥmad bin Shaykh Fūmo Lūṭi bin Shaykh bin B(w)ānah Mkūh

81 So-and-so, sons of So-and-so [killed]

1228 Sa'īd bin Sulṭān bin al-Imām...Lāmūh

[called] Fūmo Lūṭi & B(w)āna Fūmo Mādī

(f.13)

1230 Fūmo Lūṭi wa B(w)ānah Fūmo Mādī

1236 [Warshaykh]

1237 Fūmo Lūṭi bin Shaykh bin Fūmo Lūṭi wa B(w)ānah Tamu Mkūh

[Mazru'ī]

B(w)ānah Shaykh bin B(w)ānah Fūmo Mādī

1239 [Sayyid bin *(sic)* Sa'īd bin Sulṭān]

1237 B(w)ānah Fūmo Lūti bin Shaykh

B(w)ānah Wazīri

B(w)ānah Tamu - Pate

(f.14) Shaykh Matāka bin Shaykh Mubārak and Fūmo Lūṭi

B(w)ānah Wazīri

Sayyid Sa'īd bin Sulṭān

Sulṭān B(w)ānah Wazīri and Fūmo Bakr wa-B(w)ānah Shaykh wa B(w)ānah Fūmo Mādī

1251 Fūmo Bakr bin Shaykh bin B(w)ānah Fūmo Madī

Shaykh Matāka bin Shaykh Mubārak

Sayyid bin [*sic*] Sa'īd bin Sulṭān

Ḥamādi al-Samār al-Bū Sa'īd

Binti Fūmo Bakr

Muḥammad bin Aḥmad wa B(w)ānah Fūmo Madī

Sayyid Sa'īd bin Sulṭān

Muḥammad bin Aḥmad - sent him away

1262 Aḥmad bin Shaykh Fūmo Lūṭi bin Shaykh wa B(w)ānah

Tamu Mkūh

Fumo Bakr

(f.15) Amir of Shaykh Matāka called Bin Mubārak, Ḥamad 'Umar

Second Amir called Ḥamed (N)goma

Amir Ḥamādi

Fūmo Bakr

Sayyid Sa'īd - Abū Bakr and Muḥammad - children of Shaykh Matāka

(f.16) Shaykh Muḥammad bin Shaykh Matāka

1273 [Sulṭān Aḥmad]

Sulṭān Aḥmad bin Shaykh at Kāu, father of Fūmo Bakr

Fūmo Bakr bin Shaykh driven out of Pate

Muḥammad bin Mkūh Nabahānī

B(w)ānah Reḥema bin Aḥmad Nabahānī [Zanzibar]

Nāṣir bin 'Abd Allāh bin 'Abd Salām

Grand Amīr

Muḥammad bin B(w)ānah Mkūh al-Nabahāni = Muḥammad bin Mkūh [Siyū]

1273 [Sayyid] Sulṭān Mājid bin Sa'īd bin Sulṭān

Sayyid Sulaymān bin Aḥmad

Sulṭān Aḥmad Abū Bakr bin Ḥasan al-Būrī

Nāsir bin 'Abd Allāh [bin] 'Abd Salām

(f.17) Shaykh Muḥuī al-Din

Shaykh Aḥmad

Shaykh 'Abd al-Salām

(f.18) Sharīf Mawlanā bin Abū Bakr

'Īsā bin Aḥmad al-Somālī

Sulṭān Aḥmad, Shaykh Muḥammad bin Shaykh

Sayyid Mājid bin Sa'īd, and Sayyid Mājid...

Sayyid seized him

(f.19)

al-Wālī Sa'ūd bin Ḥamad

Sulṭān Aḥmad

Sayyid Barghash bin Sa'īd

1306 Fūmo Bakr bin Sulṭān Aḥmad bin Shaykh al-Nabahānī

Layla 11 Rabi' al-Awwalā Ūlā 1308

[Europeans]

28 Jumād al-Ūlā 1308

B(w)ānah Shaykh bin Sulṭān Aḥmad bin Shaykh Nabahānī

Fūmo 'Umar Nabahānī

Sulaymān bin Sulaymān al-Muẓaffar Nabahānī
[Sawaḥili]
Muḥammad bin B(w)ānah Mkūh Nabahāni

(f.20) Thirty-one kings and one woman, the total of thirty-two

Ṣafar
1318
Wrote Ṣāliḥ bin Sālim bin Aḥmad bin 'Abd Allāh. This was copied [for] the Honorable Infant Muḥammad bin Aḥmad bin Sulṭān bin [*sic*] Fūmo Bakr bin Shaykh bin B(w)ānah Fūmo Madī wa Simba, Sulṭān Muḥammad bin Abū Bakr bin B(w)ānah Mkūh bin Abū Bakr bin Aḥmad bin Abū Bakr bin Muḥammad bin Abū Bakr bin Muḥammad bin 'Umar bin Muḥammad bin Aḥmad bin Muḥammad bin Sulaymān bin Sulaymān bin Muḍaffer [*sic*] Nabahāni. This copy made 1 Rajab 1333 = 3 February 1925

Wrote the humble Ṣāliḥ bin Sālim bin Aḥmad [bin 'Abd] Allāh.

SULTANS OF PATE

	Bwana Kitini A.			*Bwana Kitini B.*			*Mshahame bin Kombo.*		
		A.H.	A.D.		A.H.	A.D.		A.H.	A.D.
1	Seleman bin Seleman ...	600	1203	Suleiman bin Suleiman ...	601	1204	Suliman bin Suliman ...	600	1203
2	Muhammad bin Seleman...	625	1227	Muhammad bin Suleiman..	625	1227	Muhammad bin Suliman ...	626	1228
3	Ahmad bin Seleman... ...	650	1252	Ahmad bin Muhammad ...	650	1252	Ahmad bin Muhammad ...	666	1267
4	Ahmad bin Muhammad ...	670	1271	Muhammad bin Ahmad ...	690	1291	Muhammad bin Ahmad ...	690	1291
5	Muhammad bin Ahmad bin Muhammad	?	?	Omar bin Muhammad ...	740	1339	Omar bin Muhammad ...	705	1306
6	Omar bin Muhammad ...	732	1331	Muhammad bin Omar ...	795	1392	Muhammad bin Omar ...	745	1344
7	Muhammad bin Omar ...	749	1348	Abubakar bin Omar	825	1422	Ahmad bin Omar	781	1378
8	Ahmad bin Omar	797	1394	Bwana Mkuu	855	1441	Abubakar bin Muhammad	805	1403
9	Abubakar bin Muhammad	840	1436	Muhammad bin Bwana Mkuu	903	1497	Muhammad b. Abubakar .	883	1430
10	Muhammad bin Abubakar	875	1470	Abubakar bin Bwana Mkuu	945	1538	Bwana Mkuu b. Abubakar	856	1454
11	Abubakar bin Muhammad	900	1494	Bwana Mkuu bin Abubakar	995	1587	Abubakar b. Muhammad...	895	1489
12	Bwana Mkuu bin Muhammad	945	1538	Ahmad bin ?	1010	1601	Bwana Bakari	920	1514
13	Muhammad bin Abubakar	973	1565	Muhammad bin Abubakar	1017	1608	Muhammad b. Abubakar...	938	1531
14	Abubakar bin Mkuu... ...	1002	1593	Abubakar bin Bwana Mkuu	1018	1609	Ahmad bin Abubakar ...	978	1570
15	Abubakar bin Muhammad	1041	1631	Muhammad bin ?	1040	1630	Abubakar b. Muhammad...	983	1575
16	Bwana Mkuu bin Muhammad	1061	1650	Abubakar (Bwana Tamu Mkuu)	1060	1649	Abubakar b. Bwana Tamu Mkuu	995	1587

SULTANS OF PATE—*continued*

	Bwana Kitini A.	A.H.	A.D.	*Bwana Kitini B.*	A.H.	A.D.	*Mshahame bin Kombo.*	A.H.	A.D.
17	Abubakar bin Bwana Mkuu	1100	1688	Bwana Mkuu bin Abubakar	1100	1688	Bwana Mkuu b. Abubakar	1034	1626
18	Ahmad bin Abubakar ...	1103	1691	Bwana Tamu Mutiti... ...	1125	1714	Ahmad b. Abubakar... ...	1063	1652
19	Abubakar (Bwana Tamu Mkuu)	1111	1700	Bwana Bakari bin B. Tamu	1135	1722	Muhammad b. Abubakar	(?)	(?)
20	Ahmad bin Abubakar ...	1152	1739	Ahmad bin BwanaTamu...	1150	1737	Ahmad bin Abubakar ...	(?)	(?)
21	Bwana Tamu Mtoto... ...	1160	1747	Mwana Khadija...	1177	1763	Bwana Mkuu bin Muhammad	(?)	(?)
22	Mwana Khadija...	1176	1762	Fumo Luti	1187	1773	Abubakar bin Bwana Mkuu	(?)	(?)
23	Bwana Mkuu	1187	1773	Fumo Madi	1190	1776	Mwana Khadija...	1182	1768
24	Muhammad bin Abubakar	1191	1777	Ahmad bin Sheikh	1224	1809	Fumo Luti	1189	1775
25	Ahmad bin Sheikh	1224	1809	Fumo Luti Kipunga	1229	1813	Muh : b. Abubakar ... ... (= Bwana Fumo Madi)	1192	1778
26	Fumo Luti...	1230	1814	Sheikh wa Fumo Madi ...	1233	1817	Ahmad bin Sheikh	1224	1809
27	Bwana Sheikh	1236	1820	Bwana Wazir	1236	1820	Fumo Luti	1228	1812
28	Bwana Sheikh wa Fumo Madi	1236	1820	Bwana Sheikh (restored) ...	1239	1823	Fumo Luti bin Ahmad ...	1233	1817
29	Ahmad	1237	1821	Bwana Wazir (restored) ...	1240	1824	Bwana Sheikh	(?)	(?)
30	Waziri...	1249	1833	Fumo Bakari bin Sheikh...	[1245]	1829	Bwana Wazir	1238	1822
31	Fumo Bakari bin Sheikh...	1250	1834	Bwana Madi bin Sheikh ... (= Ahmad)	1259	1843	Fumo Bakari	1245	1829
32	Ahmad Simba	1262	1845	Ahmad Simba	1280	1863	Ahmad Fumo Bakari ...	1255	1839
							Ahmad bin Fumo Luti } Simba Balla (?) ... ... }	1255	1839

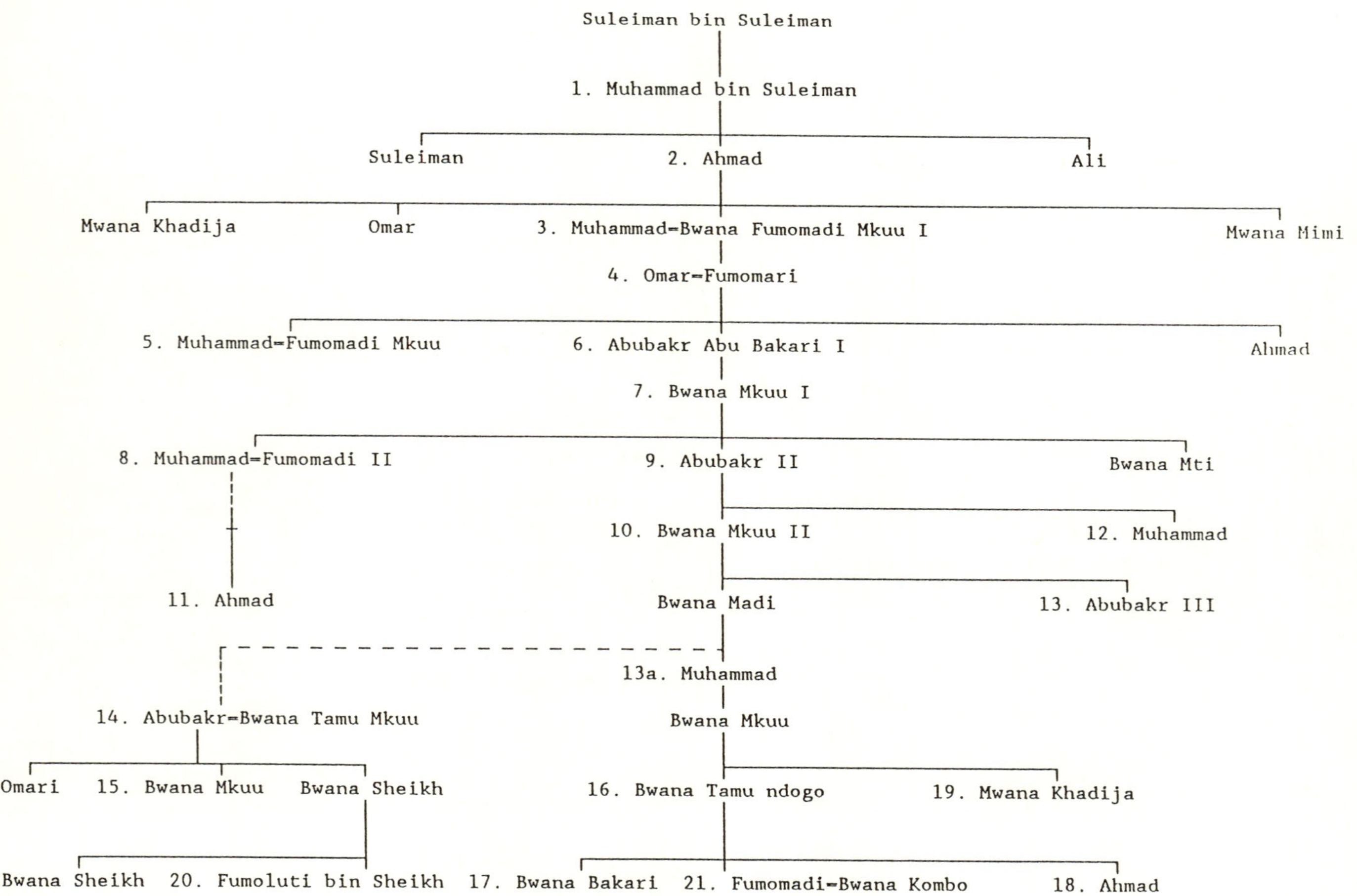
Genealogical Table of the Rulers of Witu
Suleiman bin Suleiman
1. Muhammad bin Suleiman
Suleiman
2. Ahmad
Ali
Mwana Khadija
Omar
3. Muhammad=Bwana Fumomadi Mkuu I
Mwana Mimi
4. Omar=Fumomari
5. Muhammad=Fumomadi Mkuu
6. Abubakr Abu Bakari I
Ahmad
7. Bwana Mkuu I
8. Muhammad=Fumomadi II
9. Abubakr II
Bwana Mti
10. Bwana Mkuu II
12. Muhammad
11. Ahmad
Bwana Madi
13. Abubakr III
13a. Muhammad
14. Abubakr=Bwana Tamu Mkuu
Bwana Mkuu
Omari
15. Bwana Mkuu
Bwana Sheikh
16. Bwana Tamu ndogo
19. Mwana Khadija
Bwana Sheikh
20. Fumoluti bin Sheikh
17. Bwana Bakari
21. Fumomadi=Bwana Kombo
18. Ahmad

Ahmad bin Sheikh — Bwana Sheikh — 23. Fumoluti Kipunga — Bwana Sheikh — Bwana Hamad — Bwana Tamu — Ahmad — Bwana Mkuu

24a. Fumoluti bin Sheikh — 25. Fumobakari — 26. Bwana Madi=Ahmad — Bwana Kitini — 24b. Bwana Wasir — Bwana Kitini — Bwana Simba=Muhammad

27. Ahmad Simba — 28. Fumobakari — 29. Fumomari — Bwana Sheikh — 30. Fumo Amari

CHRONOLOGY OF THE RULERS OF WITU

	A.H.	
	601- 625	Suleiman bin Suleiman. Migrated from Oman, married the daughter of the Pate chief Is-hak and received the reign of Pate as a wedding gift.
1	625- 650	Muhammad bin Suleiman. The first to bear the title of Sultan of Pate.
2	650- 690	Ahmad bin Muhammad.
3	690- 740	Muhammad bin Ahmad = Bwana Fumomadi Mkuu. Pressed all of Pate into submission and spread his authority as far north as Mogadisho.
4	740- 795	Omar = Fumomari. Conquered all of the Swahili coast from Malindi to Kerimba, south of Kilwa.
5	795- 825	Muhammad bin Omar, named Fumomadi Mkuu I. Established many plantations and built ships.
6	825- 855	Abubakr bin Omar = Abu Bakari I. Under him the Portuguese established footholds at Pate and in Dondo.
7	855- 903	Bwana Mkuu bin Abubakr. Under him the country highly prospered through expanded trade.
8	903- 945	Muhammad bin Bwana Mkuu = Bana Fumomadi II. Siu was built up by him, but later put down again; however,

		the prisoners were released at the intercession of the Portuguese.
9	945- 995	Abubakr II bin Bwana Mkuu. The Portuguese attacked Pate, blocked the harbor and besieged the town.
10	995-1010	Bwana Mkuu II bin Sultan Abu Bakari
11	1010-1017	Ahmad, son of Bwana Mkuu's cousin, also uncle to Muhammad bin Bwana Mkuu. Reigned for seven years and then abdicated voluntarily.
12	1017-1018	Muhammad bin Abubakr. Ran into conflict with the Portuguese and was unseated by them after only one year's reign.
13	1018-1060	Abubakr III bin Bwana Mkuu. Murdered.
14	1060-1100	Abubakr bin Muhammad = Bwana Tamu Mkuu. Made a treaty with Portugal in 1728, died about 1733.
15	1100-1125	Bwana Mkuu bin Bwana Tamu Mkuu. Often stayed in Lamu and built a mosque there.
16	1125-1135	Bwana Tamu Ndogo bin Bwana Mkuu bin Muhammad.
17	1135-1150	Bwana Bakri bin Bwana Tamu Ndogo. Resided at Lamu.
18	1150-1177	Ahmad bin Bwana Tamu Ndogo.
19	1177-1187	Mwana Khadija binti Bwana Tamu Ndogo.
19a		Omari, son of Bwana Tamu Mkuu. At the instigation of the Mazrui rose against Mwana Khadija but was killed after five years of joint rule.
20	1187-1190	Fumoluti bin Sheikh, son of Sultan Omari's brother. Killed in 1774.
21	1190-1224	Fumomadi bin Bwana Tamu Ndogo, named Bwana

Kombo (1774-1807). He was the last great sultan of the Nabhan; under him Pate achieved independence from Mombasa.

22 1224-1229 Ahmad bin Sheikh (1807-1812). Nephew of Fumoluti, who was killed in 1774, and son-in-law of Fumomadi. The Mazrui attacked Lamu with Pate's support but were defeated at Shela.

23 1229-1233 Fumoluti Kipunga bin Fumomadi (1812-1816).

24 1233-1240 Bwana Sheikh bin Fumomadi (1817-1823).

24a 1233-1245 Fumoluti bin Sheikh. He was set up against Bwana Sheikh by the Mazrui and fell in 1826.

24b 1236-1245 Bwana Wazir bin Bwana Tamu. Set up against Bwana Sheikh as Ahmad es-Serir but killed soon afterwards.

25 1245-1272 Fumobakari bin Sheikh (1826-1853). Declared independence in 1841.

26 1259-1280 Bwana Madi bin Sheikh. Moved back to the mainland, founded Kau and Kipini and died at Ozi (1840-1856).

27 1280-1306 Ahmad Simba bin Fumoluti. Finally abandoned Pate; moved to Kau on the Ozi and later founded Witu (1856-1889).

28 1306-1308 Fumobakari bin Muhammad (1889-1890). Died soon after the English punitive expedition following the murder of the German national Küntzel and his companions.

29 Fumomari bin Muhammad (1890-1893). Rose in revolt against English authority but submitted in 1893 and died in 1896 in Zanzibar.

Fumo Amari bin Sultan Ahmad. Installed by the English on 7 July 1895.

GENEALOGY OF THE NABHANI RULERS OF PATE

I. Seliman bin Seliman bin Mudhaffar 600-625

II. Muhammad 625-650 III. Ahmad 650-670

IV. Ahmad 670-705

V. Muhammad 705-732

VI. Umari 732-759

VII. Muhammad 749-797

IX. Abu Bakari 840-875 Bwana Mkuu Ahmad Umari

X. Muhammad 875-900 Ahmad

XI. Abu Bakari 900-945 XII. Bwana Mkuu 945-973

XIII. Muhammad 973-1002 Ahmad XIV. Bwana Bakari 1002-1041

XV. Abu Bakari 1041-1061 XVI. Bwana Mkuu 1061-1100

XVIII. Ahmad 1103-1111 Bwana Mkuu Mwana Darini Bwana Madi XVII. Bwana Bakari 1100-1103

XXI. Bwana Tamu Mtoto 1160-1177 (=Abu Bakari, Imamu-l'hudā) XXII. Mwana Hadija 1177-1187

XXIV. Muhammad (=Bwana Fumu Madi) 1191-1224

XXVI. Fumu Lut Kipunga 1230-1236 XXVIII. Bwana Shehe 1236-39; 1242-47 Ahmad

Mwana Jaha XXX. Fumu Bakari 1250-62; 1264-? Muhammad

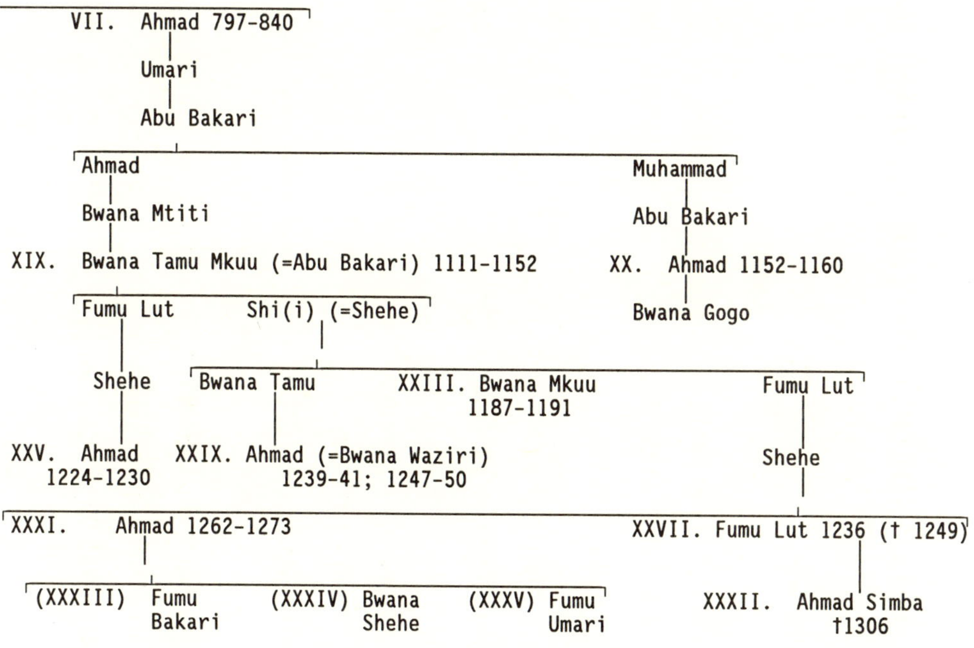
VII. Ahmad 797-840
Umari
Abu Bakari
Ahmad
Muhammad
Bwana Mtiti
Abu Bakari
XIX. Bwana Tamu Mkuu (=Abu Bakari) 1111-1152
XX. Ahmad 1152-1160
Fumu Lut
Shi(i) (=Shehe)
Bwana Gogo
Shehe
Bwana Tamu
XXIII. Bwana Mkuu 1187-1191
Fumu Lut
XXV. Ahmad 1224-1230
XXIX. Ahmad (=Bwana Waziri) 1239-41; 1247-50
Shehe
XXXI. Ahmad 1262-1273
XXVII. Fumu Lut 1236 († 1249)
(XXXIII) Fumu Bakari
(XXXIV) Bwana Shehe
(XXXV) Fumu Umari
XXXII. Ahmad Simba †1306

CHRONOLOGY OF THE NABHANI RULERS OF PATE

Chronicle	Stigand & Voeltzkow	
I. Seliman 600-625 (1203/04-1227/28 Chr.)	Suleiman	601-625
II. Muhammad 625-650 (-1252/53)	Muhammad[1]	625-650
III. Ahmad 650-670 (-1271/72)		
	Ahmad[2]	650-670
IV. Ahmad 670-705 (-1305/06)		
V. Muhammad 705-732 (-1331/32)	Muhammad[3]	690-740
VI. Umari 732-749 (-1348/49)	Omar[4]	740-795
VII. Muhammad 749-797 (-1394/95)	Muhammad[5]	795-825
VIII. Ahmad 797-840 (-1436/37)		
IX. Abu Bakari 840-875 (-1470/71)	→ Abubakr[6](I)	825-855
	Bwana Mkuu[7](I)	855-903
X. Muhammad 875-900 (-1494/95)	Muhammad[8]	903-945
XI. Abu Bakari 900-945 (-1538/39)	→ Abubakr[9](II)	945-995
XII. Bwana Mkuu 945-973 (-1565/66)	Bwana Mkuu[10](II)	995-1010
	→ Ahmad[11]	1010-1017

XIII.	Muhammad 973-1002 (-1593/94)	Muhammad[12]	1017-1018
XIV.	Bwana Bakari 1002-1041 (-1631/32)	Abubakr[13](III)	1018-1060
XV.	Abu Bakari 1041-1061 (-1650/51)		
XVI.	Bwana Mkuu 1061-1100 (-1688/89)		
XVII.	Bwana Bakari 1100-1103 (-1691/92)		
XVIII.	Ahmad 1103-1111 (-1689/1700)		
XIX.	Abu Bakari 1111-1152 (1739/40)	Abubakr[14]	1060-1100
		Bwana Mkuu[15]	1100-1125
XX.	Ahmad 1152-1160 (-1747)		
XXI.	Bwana Tamu Mtoto 1160-1167 (-1763/64)	Bwana Tamu Ndogo[16]	1125-1135
		Bwana Bakari[17]	1135-1150
		Ahmad[18]	1150-1177
XXII.	Mwana Hadiji Umari 1177-1187 (-1773/74)	Mwana Khadija[19]	1177-1178
		Omar[19a]	
XXIII.	Bwana Mkuu 1187-1191 (-1777)	Fumoluti bin Sheikh[20]	1187-1190
XXIV.	Muhammad 1191-1224 (-1809/10)	Fumo Madi[21] =	
		Bwana Kombo	1190-1224
XXV.	Ahmad bin Shehe 1224-1230 (-1814/15)	Ahmad bin Sheikh[22]	1224-1229

XXVI.	Fumu Lut Kipunga 1230-1236 (-1820/21)		Fumoluti Kipunga[23]	1229-1233
XXVII.	Fumu Lut bin Shehe 1236; 1247-1249 (-1833/34)		Fumoluti bin Sheikh[24a]	1233-1245
XXVIII.	Bwana Shehe 1236-1239; 1242-1247 (-1831/32)		Bwana Sheikh[24]	1233-1240
XXIX.	Ahmad==Bwana Waziri 1239-41, 47-50 (-1834/35)		Bwana Waziri[24b]	1236-1245
XXX.	Fumu Bakari 1250-1262, (-1846)		Fumo Bakari[25]	1245-1272
XXXI.	Ahmad bin Shehe 1262-1273 (-1856/57)		Bwana Madi bin Sheikh[26]	1259-1280
XXXII.	Ahmad Simba -1306 (-1888/9)		Ahmad Simba[27]	1280-1306
XXXIII.	Fumu Bakari		Fumobakari[28]	1306-1308
XXXIV.	Bwana Shehe			
XXXV.	Fumu Umari		Fumomari[29]	1890-1893

IMÂMS AND SEYYIDS OF OMAN

Imâms		A.H.	A.D.
Julanda bin Masûd	began to reign	135	751
Muhammad bin Affân	" "	-	-
el Warîth bin Ka'âb	" "	185	801
Ghassân bin 'Abdallah	" "	192	807
'Abdu'l Malik bin Hamîd	" "	208	824
el-Muhenna bin Jaifar	" "	226	840
es-Salt bin Mâlik	" "	237	851
Râshid bin En-Nadhr	" "	273	886
'Azzân bin Temûn	" "	277	890
Muhammad bin el-Hasan	" "	284	897
'Azzân bin el-Hezr	" "	285	898
'Abdallah bin Muhammad	" "	286	899
es-Salt bin el-Kânun	" "	287	900
Hasan bin Sa'id	" "	287	900
el-Hawâry bin Matraf	" "	292	904
'Omar bin Muhammad	" "	300	912
Muhammad bin Yezîd	" "	-	-
Mullah el-Bahary	" "	-	-
Sa'id bin 'Abdallah	died	328	939
Râshid bin el-Walîd		-	-
el-Khalîl bin Shadzân	began to reign	400	1009
Râshid bin Sa'id	died	445	1053

Hafs bin Râshid	began to reign	445	1053
Râshid bin 'Ali	" "	446	1054
Ibn Jâbir Mûsa	died	549	1154

Maliks of the Benu Nebhân	A.H.	A.D.
el Fellah bin el-Muhsin	549	1154
Arâr bin Fellah	?	?
Muzhaffar bin Suleimân	?	?
Makhzûm bin el Fellah reigned till	809	1406

[If this Muzhaffar is the grandfather of the Suleimân bin Suleimân who escaped to Pate A.H. 600--which seems improbable--there is a long gap between him and Makhzûm. It is more likely that he belonged to a later generation. In any case there is a gap in the history, insufficiently bridged by these few names, and "Seleman" of Pate is never mentioned.]

	A.H.	A.D.	
Abu'l Hasan (Azdî)	839	1435	
'Omar bin Khattab	855	1451	
'Omar esh-Sherif	896	1490	
Ahmad bin Muhammad	?	?	
Abu'l Hasan (Yahmadi)	?	?	
Muhammad bin Ismael	906	1500	
Barakât bin Muhammad	936	1529	
'Abdallah bin Muhammad	967	1560	
Nasir bin Murshid	1034	1624	Imâms

Sultan bin Seif I.	1059	1649	of the
Bel 'arab bin Sultan	1079	1688	Ya'arubi
Seif bin Sultan I.	1123	1711	
Sultan bin Seif II.	1123	1711	
Seif bin Sultan II.	1131	1718	
Muhensa bin Sultan	1131	1718	
Ya 'arab bin Bel 'arab	1134	1721	
Muhammad bin Nasir el-Ghafiry	1137	1724	
Seif bin Sultan II. (restored)	1140	1728	
Sultan bin Murshid	1151	1738	
Ahmad bin Sa'id	1154	1741	
Sa'id bin Ahmad	1188	1775	Imâms of
Hamad bin Sa'id	1193	1779	the Al-bû-
Sultan bin Ahmad	1206	1792	Saidi
Salim bin Sultan}			Sayyids
}	1219	1804	
Sa'id bin Sultan }			
Thuwainy bin Sa'id	1273	1856	
Salim bin Thuwainy	1283	1864	
Azzân bin Kais	1285	1868	

Sayyid Sa'id bin Sultan was the last who reigned both at Maskat and Zanzibar in the latter place he was succeeded by:--

	A.H.	A.D.
Mâjid bin Sa'id	1273	1856
Barghash bin Sa'id	1287	1870

Khalifa bin Sa'id	1305	1888
'Ali bin Said	1307	1890
Hamad bin Thuwaini bin Sultan	1310	1893
Hamûd bin Muhammad bin Sa'id..............	1314	1896
'Ali bin Hamûd Albu-Said	1319	1902
Khalifa bin Harb bin Thuwaini bin Said	1329	1911 (end of)Dec.

SELECTED BIBLIOGRAPHY

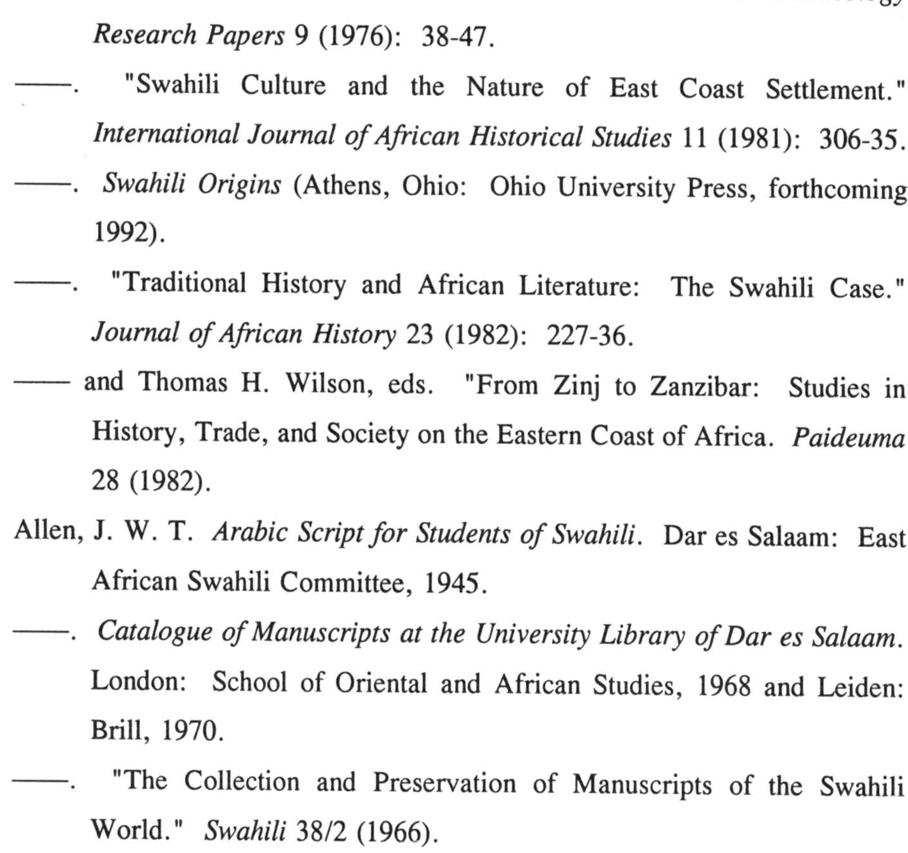

Allen, James de Vere. "The *Siwas* of Pate and Lamu: Two Antique Sideblown Horns from the Swahili Coast." *Art and Archaeology Research Papers* 9 (1976): 38-47.

——. "Swahili Culture and the Nature of East Coast Settlement." *International Journal of African Historical Studies* 11 (1981): 306-35.

——. *Swahili Origins* (Athens, Ohio: Ohio University Press, forthcoming 1992).

——. "Traditional History and African Literature: The Swahili Case." *Journal of African History* 23 (1982): 227-36.

—— and Thomas H. Wilson, eds. "From Zinj to Zanzibar: Studies in History, Trade, and Society on the Eastern Coast of Africa. *Paideuma* 28 (1982).

Allen, J. W. T. *Arabic Script for Students of Swahili*. Dar es Salaam: East African Swahili Committee, 1945.

——. *Catalogue of Manuscripts at the University Library of Dar es Salaam*. London: School of Oriental and African Studies, 1968 and Leiden: Brill, 1970.

——. "The Collection and Preservation of Manuscripts of the Swahili World." *Swahili* 38/2 (1966).

Badger, George Percy, ed. *History of the Imâms and Seyyids of Oman, by Salîl-ibn-Razîk, from A.D. 661-1856.* London: Hakluyt Society, 1871.

al-Bakari al Lamuy/Hichens, C. "Khabari Lamu." *Bantu Studies* 12 (1938): 3-33.

Bennett, Norman R. *A History of the Arab State of Zanzibar.* London: Methuen & Co, 1978.

Chittick, Neville. "Discoveries in the Lamu Archipelago." *Azania* 2 (1965).

——. *Manda: Excavations at an Island Port on the Kenya Coast.* Nairobi: East African Publishing House, 1984.

——. "A New Look at the History of Pate." *Journal of African History* 10 (1969): 375-91.

——. "The 'Shirazi' Colonization of East Africa." *Journal of African History* 6 (1965): 275-94.

—— and Robert I. Rotberg, eds. *East Africa and the Orient.* New York: Africana Publishing Co., 1975.

Coupland, Reginald. *East Africa and Its Invaders.* Oxford: Clarendon Press, 1938.

Cusack, J.W., trans. *History of the Nabahan Sultans of Pate*, Kenya National Archives (Lamu District Record, Vol. I).

Freeman-Grenville, G.S.P. *The East African Coast: Select Documents from the First Century to the Early Nineteenth Century.* Oxford: Clarendon Press, 1962.

——. "Swahili Literature and the History and Archaeology of the East African Coast." *Journal of the East African Swahili Commitee* 28 (1958): 7-25.

Gray, John M. *History of Zanzibar from the Middle Ages to 1856*. London: Oxford University Press, 1962.

Guillain, Charles. *Documents sur l'histoire, la géographie et le commerce de la côte orientale d'Afrique*. 3 vols. Paris: A. Bertrand, 1856-57.

Heepe, M. "Suaheli-Chronik von Pate." *Mitteilungen des Seminars für orientalische Sprachen*, 3. Abteilung: Afrikanische Studien 31 (1928): 145-92.

Henige, David P. *The Chronology of Oral Tradition; Quest for a Chimera*. Oxford: Clarendon Press, 1974.

——. *Oral Historiography*. London, New York: Longman, 1982.

Horton, Mark. "Asiatic Colonization of the East African Coast: Manda Evidence." *Journal of the Royal Asiatic Society* 2 (1986): 201-13.

——. "Early Muslim Trading Settlements on the East African Coast: New Evidence from Shanga." *Antiquaries Journal* 67 (1987): 290-323.

——. *The Early Settlement of the Northern Swahili Coast*. Unpublished Ph.D. Thesis: University of Cambridge, 1984.

——. *Shanga, 1980: An Interim Report*. Nairobi: National Museums of Kenya, 1981.

Kirkman, James S. *Men and Monuments on the East African Coast*. London, 1964 and New York: Praeger, 1966.

Martin, Bradford G. "Arab Migrations to East Africa in Medieval Times." *International Journal of African Historical Studies* 7/3 (1974).

Ma'amiry, Ahmed Hamoud al-. *Oman and East Africa*. New Delhi: Lancers, 1979.

Middleton, John. *The World of the Swahili: an African Mercantile*

Civilization. New Haven: Yale University Press, 1992.

Miller, Joseph V., ed. *The African Past Speaks*. Folkestone, 1980.

Misiugin, V. M. "Notes on Swahili Place Names in the Pate Chronicle" (in Russian). *Africana* 9 (Leningrad, 1972): 51-88.

——. "The Swahili Chronicle of the Medieval State of Pate" (in Russian). *Africana* 6 (Leningrad, 1966).

Nicholls, Christine S. *The Swahili Coast: Politics Diplomacy and Trade on the East African Littoral, 1789-1856*. London: George Allen & Unwin, 1971.

Nurse, Derek and Thomas Spear. *The Swahili: Reconstructing the History and Language of an African Society, 800-1500*. Philadelphia: University of Pennsylvania Press, 1985.

Oliver, Roland and Gervase Mathew, eds. *History of East Africa*. Vol. I. Oxford: Clarendon Press, 1963.

Omar, Ali Yahya and P.J.L. Frankl. "The Mombasa Chronicle." *Afrika und Übersee* 73 (1990): 101-28.

Pouwels, Randall L. *Horn and Crescent: Cultural Change and Traditional Islam on the East African Coast, 800-1900*. Cambridge: University Press, 1987.

——. "Oral Historiography and the Problem of the Shirazi on the East African Coast." *History in Africa* 11 (1984): 237-67.

——. "The Battle of Shela: The Climax of an Era and a Point of Departure in the Modern History of the Kenya Coast." *Cahiers d'Études africaines* 123, XXXI-3 (1991): 363-389.

——. "Swahili Literature and History in the Post-Structuralist Era: A Revisit and Riposte to Allen *et al.*" Forthcoming in the *International Journal of African Historical Studies* 31.

Prins A.H.J. "On Swahili Historiography." *Journal of the East African Swahili Committee* 28 (1958), 26-40.

Reusch, Richard. *History of East Africa.* New York: Ungar, 1961.

Rollins, Jack D. *A History of Swahili Prose.* 2 vols. Leiden: Brill, 1983.

Rugoiyo, Elizabeth. "Some Traditional Histories of Pate, Siu and Shanga." In Mark Horton, *Shanga, 1980: An Interim Report (q.v.)*, Appendix 5.

Schaffer, L. "A Historiographic Appraisal of Kenyan Coastal History." *Ufahamu* 9 (1979): 61-77.

Spear, Thomas. "Oral Traditions: Whose History?" *History in Africa* 8 (1981): 163-79.

——. "The Shirazi in Swahili Traditions, Culture, and History." *History in Africa* 11 (1984): 291-305.

——. "The Interpretation of Evidence in African History." *African Studies Review* 30 (1987): 17-24.

Stigand, C.H. *Land of Zinj.* London, 1913.

Strandes, Justus. *Die Portugiesenzeit von Deutschund Englisch-Ostafika.* Berlin, 1899. English translation by J. F. Wallwork, edited by J.S. Kirkman, *The Portuguese Period in East Africa.* Nairobi: Kenya History Society, 1961. 2nd ed., East African Literature Bureau, 1968.

Tolmacheva, Marina. "The Arabic Influence on Swahili Literature: A Historian's View." *Journal of African Studies* 5 (1978): 223-43.

——. "Group Identity in the Swahili Chronicles." Paper presented at the 1991 Annual Meeting of the American Anthropological Association,

Chicago (forthcoming in print).

——. "'They Came from Damascus in Syria': A Note on Traditional Lamu Historiography." *International Journal of African Historical Studies* 12/2 (1979), 259-269.

Vansina, Jan. *Oral Tradition: A Study in Historical Methodology*. Chicago: Aldine Publishing Co., 1965.

——. *Oral Tradition as History*. Madison, Wis.: University of Wisconsin Press, 1985.

Voeltzkow, Alfred. *Reise in Ostafrika in den Jahren 1903-1905*. 2 vols. Stuttgart, Schweizerbart (Nagele & Sprosser), 1914-1923.

Werner, Alice. "Swahili History of Pate." *Journal of the African Society* 14 (1914): 148-61, 15 (1915) 278-97, 392-413.

Wilkinson, John C. *The Imamate Tradition of Oman*. Cambridge: University Press, 1987.

Ylvisaker, Marguerite. *Lamu in the Nineteenth Century: Land, Trade and Politics*. Boston: Boston University African Studies Center, 1979.

Zein, Abdul Hamid M. el. *The Sacred Meadows: A Structural Analysis of Religious Symbolism in an East African Town*. Evanston, Ill.: Northwestern University Press, 1974.

Zhukov, A. A. *Kul'tura, iagyk i literatura suakhili (dokolonial'nyi period)* [*Swahili Culture, Language, and Literature: Pre-Colonial Period*. In Russian]. Leningrad: Universisty Press, 1983. Reviewed in *African Studies Review* 27 (1987): 114-6.

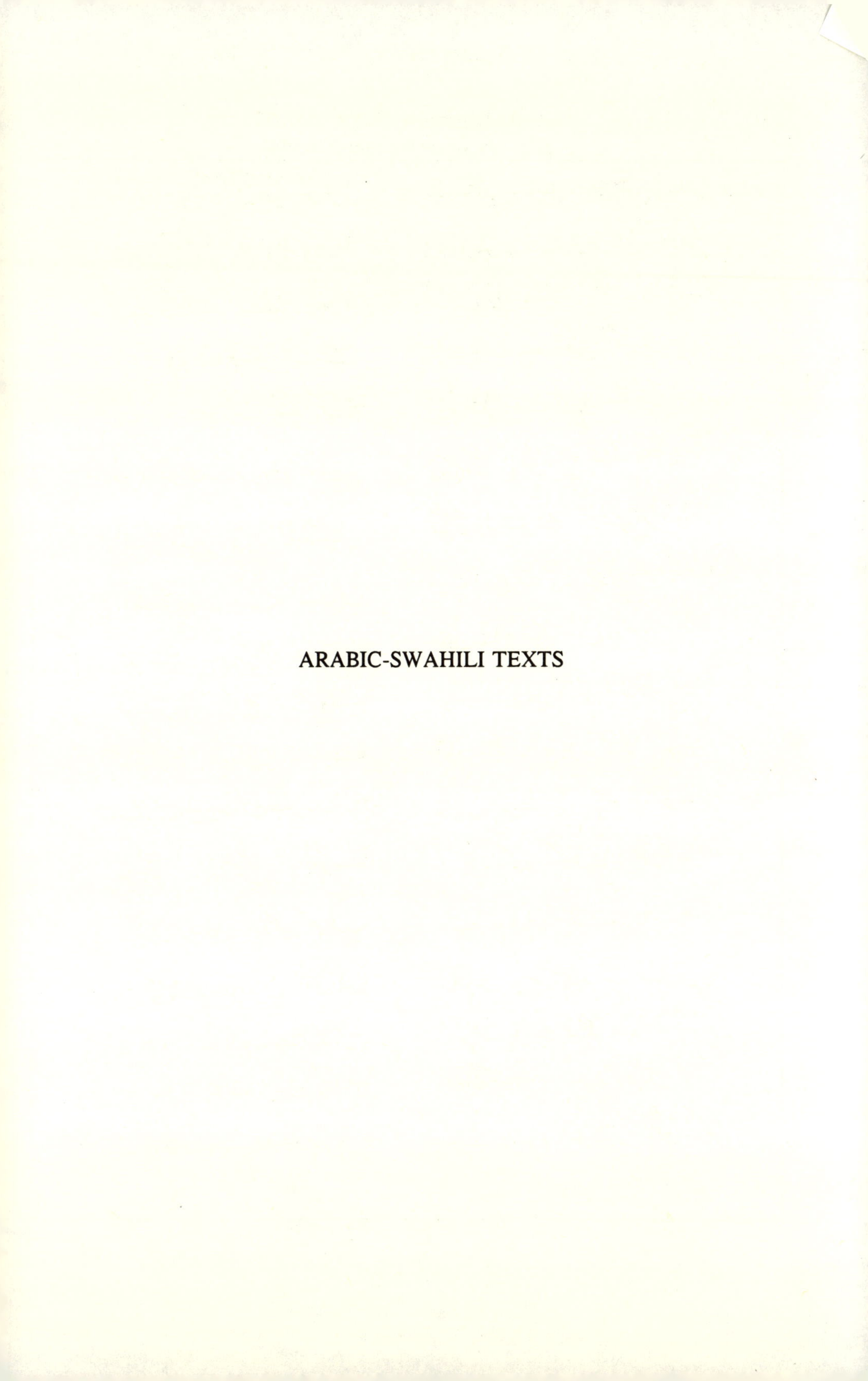

ARABIC-SWAHILI TEXTS

خبار يا اول ينبهاني كوج سواحل
نخبر زاو زوت ومتوال وفلم
واحد وثلاثين نمنمكر مموج
نري وثنين وثلاثين ٣٢
نبار زاو نهير زت تمنقل كمحمد بن فوم
عمر اتواي بانه كتين ناي
اليكي نبي محمد بن بانه مكو
اتواي بان سمبه النبهاني
الظبيت خبار زكال ننسب زاو
كم هيز بليز تاج منت وكوانز
كوج كتكد النبهاني يات
سليمان بن سليمان بن مظفر ندو زوول
علي بن سليمان نعثمان بن سليمان الكو سلطان
سليمان بن سليمان المذكور نري
الي كو معلم عربون اكتلو
نل اليعرب اكاج يات كتكد راش
سنة ٦٠٠ هجرية اكوو كتكد قبل
يبتاويتون بنت ومفلم ويات

M 1

ندستور يسواحل يواسواحل حتى ساس
منت اكولي منت واك اكش سبع هوج
ككغلي يل ببناك مك واك همب
كيت الب كينر كمغلي المبيش يبي
افلم تغ هاب كتوال سليمان بن سليمان المذكور
نكتاك الكو موج كتكد مطلع يبات
نبار ولكواك نوقت هو هوتاس
كوك موج وسينو كول نموج جين
لاك شاغ كتكد مطلع يبات نبار
ولكواك وبيو وبازه المغاريون الكيت
افلم وبات نينج هي كتاك نبات
نمانزه يلكو نمفلم واك ومانزه بن سليمان
بن سليمان المذكور اكزء نجان محمد ناحمد اكاف
سلطان سليمان سنة ٦٢٥ وقت هو
الكو عمر و محمد بن سليمان نيكد عشرين
ناحمد عمر واك نيكد خمسة عشر
كتوال محمد بن سليمان بعد يبباك كبجان
نوات وشاغ الكوشنز الكو فند

M 2

مُوْجِ اَكُوْتَكُوْ وَاتُ وَشَاغَ وَكَاجِ بَاتِ
نَبَعْضِ وَكَمِبِي كَتِكَ وَاتُ وَلَكُوْجِ
بَاتِ نَبَعْضِ يُوْكُنِ وَاتُ قَبِلَ
يُوْكِنْدَ اغُوْ وَكَمِبِي وَسِلَحَالِكَانِ
وَلِبُ كِنْدَ حَتَّى سِكُ زِكَبِيْتَ
اِكَاجِ خَبَارِ كَمَغَنِلْمِ محمد سليمان نَوَوِيْدَا
وَكَمِبِي وَالِ وَلِي كِبِي تِمُوَوُنَ
كَتِكَ مِيتُ اَكِلِنِكَ وَاتُ كُوْغَلِي
وَكُوَوُنَ نْزَانِ مَمِيتُ وَمِفَايِ
مُحَمَّبَ وَمِكِيتِ هَابُ وَكُوتَكُوْ وَكَاجِ
نَاوُ بَاتِ كِيشَ اَكُوْرُدِيْشَ بَابُ
اَلِبُ وَتَكُوْ نْزِيِ اَصْلِ يَسِيُوْكِيْشَ
وَكَاجِ نَوَاتُ وَغِنِ وَسَوَاحِلِ وَكِكِيتِ
سِيُوْ كِيْشَ وَكَاجِ وَفَمَاوُ وَكَاوُ وَكُوْ
وَسِيُوْ كَتِكَ طَاعَ يَمْفَلِمْ وَبَاتِ
نِسِكُ يِغِ كَتِكَ سنة ٦٥٠ اَكَافَ
نْسُلْطَانِ محمد سليمان اَكْتَوَالِ نْزُوْيِ
سلطان احمد بن سليمان اَكْعَرِيْشَ سَانَ

M 3

كَتِكَ نْتِ يَبَاتِ اَكَفَايِ مَشَمْبَ
نَكَجُنْغَ مُحَمَّبَ اَسِيْنِج مَهَالَ حَتَّى
نَ سنة ٦٧٠ اَكَافَ اَكْتَوَالِ كِجَانَ وَسُلْطَا
محمد بن سليمان جِيْنَ لَاكِ احمد بن محمد بن سليمان
اَكِكِيتِ كَمَ سِيَارَ زَعَمِيَاكِ كِتِكَ عِمَارَ
يَمُوْجِ وَبَاتِ اَكِبَاتَ فِجَانَ وَاغَ اَلِبُ
كُوْفَ سنة ٧٠٥ اَكْتَاءُ اُفَلْمِ كِتِكَ فِجَانَ
فَاكِ اجِيْنَ لَاكِ محمد احمد بن محمد بن سليمان
اَكِكِيتِ اَكْفَتَاجِ مِيْجِ يَسَوَاحِلِ بَازَهْ
نَمَانْزَهْ كُوْفِيْتَ فِنْغِ كَتِكَ نْتِ يَبَازَهْ
وَاَمَّا مَانْزَهْ وَلَانْغِي كُوْفِيْتَ فِجِيْلِ
وَكَفِنْدَ كِبِيْسَ نَوَاتُ اَكُوْلِيْتَ بَاتِ
نَبَعْضِ وَكَمِبِي وَكِنْزَ كِلَّ مَهَالَ وَكَاجِ
شِيْلَ نَمِلِنْدِي نَمِيْجِ مِغِيْنِ نَوَلِي
كِنْزَ شِيْلَ وَكَغِي كِتِكَ جَايِ يُوَاتُ
وَاَمْ مْفَلِمْ اَكُوْتَاكَ كُوَاتُ وَاَمْ اَكَكْتَاءُ
كُوْتُوْ وَلِكُوْ كِتِكَ مِنِيْنُ هَايِ مْفَلِمْ
اَكَافَ سنة ٧٣٢ اَكُوَاتَ كِجَانَ كُوْجِ

M 4

جِيْنَ لَاكِ سُلْطَانِ عُمَرَ اَكَتَوَالَ بَعَدَ
يَبَبَاكِ اَكَرَاجِعِ مَنِيْنَ يَبَبَاكِ كُوَاتُ
وَاَمُ كُتَاكَ وَاتُ وَمَانْزَ وَكَكَنَاءِ وَاتُ
وَاَمُ كُوَنْتُوَ اَلَوَ پِيْنْجَ وَكَتَاكَ اَمَانِ
وَاتُ وَاَمُ وَكَوَكَتِكَ طَاعَ بِسُلْطَانِ
عُمَرَ بن محمد بن احمد بن محمد بن سليمان اَكَپَاتَ غُوْفُ
سَانَ اَكَپِيْنْجَ جُمْلَ يِمِيْجِ يَسَوَاحِلِ اُزِيْوَ
نَمَلِنْدِيْ نَكِوَيُوْهِ نَكِتَاوُ نَمِيْنِيَ ،،،
نَامِيْدِيْ نُوَتَامُ حَتَّى اَلَفِيْكَ كِرِمْبَهْ
رِمْبِجِ يُتِّ اَكِتَمَلِكِ تَغُ پَاتِ حَتَّى
كِرِمْبَه كُلَّ مُوْجِ اَكِوِيْكَ مُنْتُ وَلِكِ
بُحُكُوْمُ نْزِيْ اَصْلِ يَهُوْ مُجِمْبِ وَلِيْ
كَتِكَ مِرِيْمَا وُتِّ مَعَنَ نِوُنُوْمُ وَيُمْبِ
نِهِيْ يُمْبِ نِجِيْنَ لِيُمْبَ يُوُ فَلِمْ وَپَاتَ
بُجِنْبِ يَهُوْكِ اَكِتَمَلِكِ حَتَّى وَنْشِيْجِ
كَفِيْتَ اَلِكُوْنْزُ كُيْنْجَ تَغُ كِوَيُوْهْ
نَطُوْلَا نَطُوَالَ نَشُغَايَ نَبَنَادِرِزُتِّ
بَرَا وَمُزْكَا مُقْدِشُوْ هَاپُ مُقْدِشُوْ

M 5

اَكِوَكَ لُوَانِيْ حُكُمُ يِبَنَادِرِ زُتِّ زِكَاوَ مُقْدِشُوْ
اَكَعِيْشِ نَنْتِ هِيْزُ زُتِّ زِكَتِكَ طَاعَ يَاكِ
اِلَّا وُغُوْجَ هَكُتَوَالَ وَقْتِ هُوُ اُغُوْجَ هَيْكُوَ
نْتِ كُوُ نَمْفَلِمْ هِيْ اَلِ اَكِيْدَ فِيْتَ مُنْ نَكِبُدَ
زِعِيَ نَزِعِيَ وَكَوُنَ رَاحَ وَكَپَاتَ نَمَالِ مَاغِ
اِكِسْنَاوِ مُنْ نْتِ يَپَاتِ اَكَافَ سنه ٧٤٩
اَكَوَاتَ وَنُوْتُ وَوِلِ محمد نا احمد اَكَتَوَالَ
محمد بن عمر بن محمد بن احمد بن محمد بن سليمان وَلَهَپَكُوَ نَفِيْتَ
اَكَتَوَالَ اُفَلِمْ وَبَبَاكِ وُتِّ كَامَانِ نَايِ
اَلِمُكِسِنْدَ مَالِ سَانَ نَبِيَشَارَ اَكِسَفِرِشَ
نَمَجَهَازِ اَكِلِيْكَ اِلْهِنْدِيْ كُفِيَ بِبِيَشَارَ نَايِ
*مَالِكُوَ نَبُحْتِ سَانَ يَمَالِ نَمَرَمُوْجَ مَنَاوِ
اَلِسَفِرِ اَكَپَاتَ كِسِيْوَ بُحَرِيْنِ اَكَشُوْكَ اَكُوُنَ
مَعْدِنِ يَفِيْضَ اَكِپِلِيْكَ وَاتُ وَكَغَايَ كَازِ كَپَاتَ
مَالِ مَاغِ سَانَ ‡ يَكَزِبْدِ مُنْ مَالِ كَتِكَ نْتِ
يَپَاتِ حَتَّى وَكَغَايَ فِتَنْدَ فَفِضَ نَغَازِ
زُفِضَ نَفُمْبَ فِنْغِ فَفِضَ اَكَپَاتَ نُوُنْتُ
وَانْتِّ بَانْدُمْكُوُ نَاحُمَدَ نَابُوْبَكِرِ نَعُمَرِ اَكَافَ

M 6

مُعَلِّمِ سنة ٢٩٧ اَكَتَوَالَ نَرُغُ يَاكِ
احمد بن عمر بن محمد بن احمد بن محمد بن سليمان اَگَكِيْتِ
كَامَانِ كَتِكَ نتِ زَاكِ سنة ٨٤٠

اَكَافَ اَكَتَوَالَ ابو بكر بن محمد بن عمر بن محمد بن احمد
بن محمد بن سليمان اَگَكِيْتِ كَسِيَارَ نَجِيْمَ
نَمِيْنِجِ يِتِ كَتِكَ طَاعَ يَاكِ
اَكِيئَمَتِنِيْشَ مِيْجِ يَاكِ يُوْتِ
اَكَافَ كَتِكَ حَالِ پَسِيْنَ كُهَرِبِكِيْوَ
سنة ٨٧٥ اَكَوَاتَ وَنْتُ وَوِلِ
محمد نا احمد اَكَتَوَالَ محمد بن ابي بكر بن محمد بن عمر
بن محمد بن احمد بن محمد بن سليمان وَفَتِ وَاكِ
وَكَاجَ وَزُغُ بُرْتُغَالِ مِيْجِ يَسَوَاحِلِ
يُوْتِ وَكَكِيْتِ مُمْبَاسَهْ وَكَفَايِ
غُوْمِ نَجَنِبُ يَپَاتِ وَكَجِنْغَ دُنْدُوُ
نَوَاتُ وَبَارَ وَكَوَ فُوَاتَ كَكُوَابَ
مَالِ وَكَعِيبَ كَتِكَ طَاعَ يَاوُ وَكَمُعَرِضْ
نَمْفَلْمِ كَتِكَ مُوْجِ وَپَاتِ وَمْپِيْجَ

نَجَنِبُ يَشِيْنْزَ كَاسِ وَكَجِنْغَ نَنِبَاتِ

M 7

قَصْدِ يَكَپِيْجَ بُوْمْبَهْ مُوْجِ وَپَاتِ وَسِوِزِ
كِيْشَ وَكَپِيتَانَ كَامَانِ وَكَفِيَ مْكَاتَبَ
وُشَرْطِ زَاوُ وَكَكِيْتِ پَاتِ وَزُغُ وَكَفِيَ فُرُوْضَ
كُوَجِيْنَ لَاوُ وَزُغُ وَكِئِيْتَ اِلِ فُرُوْضَ فَنْدِ يْكَ
وَكَفِيَ نَمَابُ مَغِ كَتِكَ كِسِوَ تَبَاتِ
بَعَدَ يَهَايِ اَكَفَ مْفَلْمِ سنة ٩٠٠
اَكَوَاتَ وَتُوْتُ بُوَانَهْ مْكُوُ نَا ابُوْبَكَرِ
اَكَتَوَالَ ابو بكر بن محمد بن ابي بكر بن محمد بن عمر بن محمد بن احمد بن محمد بن سليمان
اَگَكِيْتِ كَامَانِ نُوزُغُ وَكَپِيتَانَ كَمَ قَاعِدَ
يَبَاكِ اَكَفَ سنة ٩٤٥ كَوَاتَ وَنْتُ احمد
نَا محمد اَكَتَوَلَ نْتُغُ يَاكِ بَانَ مْكُوُ بن محمد بن ابي بكر
بن محمد بن عمر بن محمد بن احمد بن محمد بن سليمان وَكَوَ نَخْتِلَافُ
نُوزُغُ لَكِنْ پَسِوِ نَفِيْتَ اَكَفَ كَتِكَ فِتِيْنَ
يَسِكَ يِغِ سنة ٩٧٣ اَكَوَاتَ كِجَانَ بَانَ بَكَرِ
اَكَتَوَلَ محمد بن ابي بكر بن محمد بن ابي بكر بن محمد بن عمر بن محمد بن احمد بن محمد
بن سليمان اَكَصَلِحِيَانَ نُوزُغُ نَوُ وَكَتُوَاءِ بَعْضِ
لَمِيْجِ اَكَافَ اَكَوَاتَ كِجَانَ ابو بكر سنة ١٠٠٢

اَكَتَوَلَ بَانَ بَكَرِ وَبَانَ مْكُوُ بن محمد بن ابي بكر بن محمد بن عمر

M 8

بن محمد بن أحمد بن محمد بن سليمان كسيار كم

زبابك لكن أفلم واو واصل

أمپغو أكاف أكوات بات

مكوه وبكر سنه ١٠٤١

اكتوال ابو بكر بن محمد بن ابي بكر بن محمد ابو بكر

بن محمد بن عمر بن محمد بن أحمد بن محمد بن سليمان

اكختلفيان نوزغ اكيلينده وات

كتاك نت يپات وكوپيج وزغ

فكاج فيت فوزغ وكپيج موج

كومزغ وكزوي ندي زنجار

وكپات مشاك وات وپات

وكفي امان بعد يهاي اكاف

معلم اكوات فجان وول بانه

ناحمد سنه ١٠٦١ اكتوال بانه

مكو وبانه بكر وبانه مكو بن محمد بن ابي بكر

بن محمد بن عمر بن محمد بن احمد بن محمد سليمان اكبتان

نوزغ ناي اكپد ككيت ام

حتى موسم اكويت ام اكؤوو

M 9

كوات وام نوفما ومتك وسيو مد

هو ولتكه كتكطاع ياك اكبجان

نو اكوفند موج وسيو اكتكو

نوات وت وسيو اكوليت پات

مكو وسيو اككمبي اكند دوند

كوبرتغال وكطاء حمايه مكو

ولوزغ پرتغال اكاج پات

كوتاك وات وسيو اكپا و

اكور جيز سيو وكيكيت كامان

بعد ياك پرتغال اكفاي جبل

اكاج پات كمركاب اكمتاك

معلم انز مركبون معلم اسند

اكمبلينده بن عم ياك بان مكو

نبي نوات وپات وزغ وكوتكو

كيند مركاب وكوپليند كواو

نوزغون اسر رحت ممنوج

بعد يهاب وكپيج وزغ كل

مهال وليب (واث) بران نفسوان

M 10

وكوتو وكمبي ممباسه بعد يهاي
مفلم اكاف سنه ١١٠٠ الوات فجان وول
نينت ممزج بانه بكار نبات مد نمان
درين التوال منو بات بكر بانه مكو
بن بانه بكار وبانه مكو بن محمد بن عمر بن محمد بن احمد
بن محمد بن سليمان اكيج مفلم غفل ناحمد نزي
بات مكو التكلو نوزغ برتغال المتو
كوا باغ التوال ييي احمد بن ابي بكر بن محمد
بن ابي بكر بن محمد بن عمر بن محمد بن احمد بن محمد بن سليمان سنه ١١٠٣
اكوندم برتغال كوتو ولسلي نوقت
هومات درين بنت بانه مكو وبانه بكار
وبانه مكو بن ابي بكر امكند غووا كتكد
زمان يسلطان احمد اكش كاواو
ندغز وول بات بكار بن بانه مكو نبات
مد بن بات مكو التكلو غو زمان
اكبات حزون سات يموزم واك نكولو
ندغ زاك حتى بعض يسكد كيت
الغزم كفاي عروس كمنتهر مناو

M 11

بات تام منت الاتواي سلطان ابوبكر
امام الهدى وبات امكند غو مفلم
سلطان احمد اكبات خبار ناي كعزم
عروس ال قصد يكمهن سيو اكش
كجو مات درين خبار يكهنو سيو
اكمكو مني بائي مكو شريف
كتكد جمال الليل الكو الجو كازيوجوم
سات اكممبي خبار ياك اكتكد كاك
امفيزي سيو يول القبال اكتاك
اجار ياك اكپاو ريال مبا وعشرين
نپيب زند وثووا اتكاز اپات
كتغو زلز نجيم زفاء ز اكتميز
شرط زاك زت مات درين
اكفاي سيو كو ميز سيبت
الب كينش اكيظهرش غفل كيبليك
كتكد ماجوب ينادغ زاك كمتز
مكو وكيتوز مال ماغ اكممبي
مي بئي الفاي سيو وتاك

M 12

اجاريَاكُ اوْاُتَنَاءَ تُوْزُ اكُنَاءَ تُوْزُ

كَسَبَبُ اَلِوُنَ نِمَالِمَاغَ اكَتَقَبَضِ سِوَ

يَكِ اِكَفِيزِوَ عَرُوْسِ يَاكِ يَمَنَاوِ

حَتّىٰ زَمَانِ يَبَانَ تَامُ مْكُوُ وَاتُ وَامَ

وَكَاجَ كُازِيْمَ سِيْوَ يَاصْلِ اكَوَاپِ

وَكِيَاتَ بَحْرِيْنِ شُمْبُ كِكَافَ مَاجِ

اِكَيْتِي سِوَ بَانَ تَامُ مْكُوُ اكَيْتَاكُ

سِيْوَ يَمَانَ دَرِيْنِ اكَمَمْبِيَ تُبِ

بِسِسِ تُنِمِي كَتِكَ مِيْجِ اكَمَبِيَ كُلَ

قَبَائِلَ اَلِي تُوْزَ سِوَ يَاغَ نَنِمِي بَسِ

مَانَ دَرِيْنِ اكَوَاتَ مْتُوْمَ حُرِ اَجُوَاي

كُپِيْجَ سِوَ هِي نِپِي نَنَسْلِ يَاكِ

نَعَدَ يَاكِ نَپَاوِ رِيَالِ تَانُ نَغُوُ

يَكُتُكُلِيَ سِيْوَ نَسَمْلِ يَكُوْنَ

مِي كُقُثِيَا سِوَ نِتُوْزُ كُلَ مْتُ

قِيَاسِ اَوِزَافُ وَكَاتُوَ نَسْلَ هِي

مُجُمْبِ وَسِيْوَ حَتّىٰ لِيُوُ وَاكُ

وَاتُ وِيِوِ بَاسِ اِكَاوَ نَغُ وَقَتِ

M 13

هُوُ هُنِمِيَا قَبَائِلَ وَپَاتِ وُتِ نَوَمِي

مِغِيْنِ هِنْدَ كُئِزِيمَ كَشَرْطِ هِيْزَ

نَمُفَلِمُ اَكَكِيْتِ مْدَ وَمِيَاكَ سَبَعَ

هَيْكُوْجَ مْفُوَ اكَجِعُزُوْلُ كَتِكَ اُفَلْمِ

نَوَاكِ ـــــــ ١١١١ اكَتَوَالَ سُلْطَانِ

اَبِيْ بَكَرِ بَانُ تَامُ مْكُوُ وَبَانَهْ مْتِيْتِ

بِنْ اَحمد بن ابي بكر بن عمر بن احمد بن عمر بن محمد بن احمد بن محمد

بِنْ سُلَيمَان وَكَتُرَاي نَمْفَلْمِ وَسَسْكَتِ اِمَامُ

الْيَعْرُبْ هِيُ مْفَلِمُ وَپَاتِ كِنْدَ عَرَبُوْنِ

وَكَاغَانَ اَرُدِپُ مْفَلِمِ وَپَاتِ اُوَتُوِ

پُرْتُغَالْ مَمْبَاسَهْ اَلِپُ رُدِ مْفَلِمُ

وَپَاتِ كَپِغَ فِيْتَ مَمْبَاسَ اكَوَپِيْجَ

وَزُوْغُ پُرْتُغَالْ سِكُ بُجُمَ يَبِلِ

اِكَوَاُوَ كَتِكَ غُوْمِ بِمَمْبَاسَ اكَمُعَرِفُ

اِمَامَ الْيَعْرُبْ اكَلِيْتَ الْوَالِي كَتِكَ

بِمَزَارِيْعِ وَنَاتُ نْزِغُ مُوْجَ مُحَمَّد

بِنْ عثمان نَعَلِيْ بِنْ عثمان نَقَضِيْبُ بِنْ عثمان

نَاوُ وَلِكُوْجَ پِمُوْجَ لَعَسْكَرِ طَرَفُ

M 14

يالإمام اليعرب نري أصل يمنزارنع
كوج ممباسه ناي هى مفلم وپات
الكيت نرعي كوزور سان الغيش
الكتميز كتك أفلم وال يكا ازبعين
اكاف سنه ١١٥٢ اكوات وتوت
واغ بعد ياك استوال مناو
الكتوال سلطان احمد ز ابي بكر ز محمد
ز ابي بكر ز عمر ز احمد ز عمر ز محمد ز احمد ز محمد
ز سليمان الكيت كنعم يغ اكيد
كوك غومب واغ سان اكاف
سنه ١١٦٠ اكوات كجان بانه
غوغ بعد ياك الكتوال بانه تام
منت اا توا امام الهدى
وبانه مكوم الككلو نير تغال كين
لاك ابوبكر ز بانه مكوم ز ابي بكر ز محمد
ز ابي بكر ز محمد ز ابي بكر ز محمد ز عمر ز محمد ز احمد
ز محمد ز سليمان اكليت فيت امام اليعرب
كپنج پات وسوز وكاف وعراب

M 15

واغ وكرود وكفاي امان بعد يهاپ
وات وام وكپغو نمفلم وپات ولخلف
وكپجان اسوز نوات وام وكاج پات
كپنج كجانب يكتاك وكفلوز وكرجي
ام بعداي مفلم وپات اكاف فيت
كبار نبحر اكوكپنج وات وام اكونملك
كيش اكووا ومفلم وپات نوات وپات
يموج نوات وامام اليعرب سنه ١١٧٧
الكتوال نزغ ياك سلطان ما نه خدنجه
بنت بانه مكوم ز ابي بكر ز محمد ز ابي بكر ز محمد ز ابي بكر ز محمد
ز عمر ز محمد ز احمد ز محمد سليمان اكپاتو نفتين يغ
كتك نت يپات اكو كتك موج وپات
وفلم وول ييي مان خدنجه المذكوره
نسلطان عمر وكپجان كتك موج مياك
متان الكمبي سلطان عمر اكند براو
كيش اكرود كغوفوا يغ اكغلو اسك
الووا نوات ومانه خدنجه المذكوره
بعد ياك كسك يدوغ اكاف مان

M 16

Khabāri ya-awali ya-Nabhānī

خَبَرِ يَاوَلِ يَنَبْهَانِي كِي سَوَاحِلِ نَخَبَارِ
زَاوُزُوتِ وَمِتَوَالَ وَفَلْمِ وَاحِدِ ...
وَثَلَاثِينِ نَمْنَمْكِ اُمُوِيَ رِيِّ
وَاثْنَيْنِ وَثَلَاثِينِ ٣٢ نَخَبَارِ زَاوُ
نِهِيْزِ زُتِ تُمْنَقِلِ كَمُحَمَّدِ زُفُومِ عُمَرِ
اَمْكُلُوَاوُ بَانَ كِتِيْنِ نَايِ اَلْبِكِي
نَبِي مُحَمَّدُ زُبَانَهُ نَكُوهُ اَمْكُلُوَاوُ ..
بَانَ سِمْبَ النَّبْهَانِي اَلظِّبْتِي
خَبَارِ زَكَالِ نَنَسَبَ زَاوُكَمُ هِيْزِ
مِيْزِ تَايِ مُتُ وَكَنْدُ كُوِيَ كِتِكَ
النَّبْهَانِي يَاهِ سُلَيْمَانْ بِنْ سُلَيْمَانْ بِنْ مُظَفَّرْ
نَرُوزِ وَوِلِ عَلِي بِنْ سُلَيْمَان نَعُثْمَان بِنْ سُلَيْمَان
اَلْكُوُ سُلْطَانِ سُلَيْمَان بِنْ سُلَيْمَان المذكور
رِي اَلْكُومْفَلْمِ عَرَبُونِ اَكِتَلِوَ
نَلْ اَلْيَعْرُبِ اَكِي يَاتِ كِتِكَ رَاسْ
سَنَة ٦٠٠ هِجْرِيَّة اَكُوُ كِتِكَ

A 1

قَبلَ يَبتَتَاوِيُّوْنَ بِنْتِ وَمْفَلْمِ وَيَاتِ
نَدَسْتُوْرِ يَوَاسَوَاحِلِ حَتَّى سَاسَ مُتُ
كِكُولِيَ مَانَ اَكِس سِكَ سَبَعَ هُوْيَ
كُكَغَلِيَ اِلِيْ بَبَاكِ مَنْكِ وَاكَ هُمْبَ
كِنِيتُ اَلِبَ كِيْزِ كَمْغَلِيَ كَمْپِسَ يِيِ
اُفَلْمِ تَغُ هَابُ كَتَوَلَ سُلَيْمَانْ بِنْ سُلَيْمَان
اَلْمَذْكُوْر نَكِتَاكَ وَلِكُوْمَ مُوْيِ كِتِكَ
مَطْلَعِ يَيَاتِ وَقَتِ هُوْنُ هَتَاسَ
كُوكِ مُوْيِ وَسِيْو كَلِيْنِ نَمُوْيِ ...
وَلِتَمْكُلُو شَاغَ كَتِكَ مَطْلَعِ يَيَاتِ نَيَازِ
وَلِكُوكُ وِيِيُو وَپَازِهِ المغَازِيُوْنْ
اَلْكِيتِ اُفَلْمِ وَيَاتِ نِمِي هِنِ كِتَاكَ
نَيَاتِ نَمَانْزَهَ يَلِيْنَ مْفَلْمِ وَاكِ
وَمَانْزَهَ نِسُلَيْمَانِ بِنْ سُلَيْمَانِ المذكور ...
اَكِزَهِ زِحَانَ مُحَمَّد نَاَحْمَد اَكَافَ
سُلْطَان سُلَيْمَان سَنَة ٦٢٥

A 2

وقت هن يلكو عمر ومحمد بن سليمان
يكا عشرين ناحمد عمر واك يك
خمسة عشر كتوال محمد بن سليمان
بعد يبباك كيجان نوات وشاغ
كوشيره كوقونده موي كبيس
وات وشاغ وكي يات نبعض
وكمبي كتك ولكي يات نبعض
يوكن وات قبل يوكندا اغوا
وكمبي وسيوكان ومزب نيره
حتى سد زكبيت اكاي خبار كمغلم
محمد بن سليمان نوويدا وكممبي
ولي وشيو تموون كتك ميت
كميك وات كوغلي وكودرك نران
مميت ومغي زجومبه ومكيت
هاب وكوتكو وكبناو يات كيس
كوردريش باب رب اصل يسيو

A 3

كيس وكاي نوات وغين وسواحل
وكليت سو كيس وكاي وفماو وكو
وكو وسيو كتك طاع يمفلم وبات
سك يغ حتى كتك سنة ٦٥٠ اكاف
سلطان محمد بن سليمان اكتوال نزوي
سلطان أحمد بن سليمان اكعرش سان
كتك نت يبات ككتي مشامبه
نكواك مجومبه اسيبيج مهال حتى
سنة ٦٧٠ اكاف اكتوال كجان وسلطان
محمد بن سليمان اين لاك احمد بن محمد بن سليمان اكليت
كم سيار زعمباك كتك عمار يموي
وبات ناي اكيات زجان واغ الب
كوف سنة ٧٠٥ اكتاء افلم كتك
زجان زاك امكلواو محمد بن أحمد بن محمد بن سليمان
اكليت اكفتاح مي يسواحل بازة
نماثره كزنيت زغ كتك نت بيبازة

A 4

وَاَمَّا مَانْزَةْ وَلِا نْغِي كَزِةَ زَحِلَ ....
وَكَاڤُوْنْدَ كَبِيْسَ نَوَاتُ اَكَوَاِيْتَ
بَاتِ نَبَعْضِ وَنَكِمْبِيَ وَكِرَكُلَ
مَهَالَ وَكَيَ شِيْلَ نَمَلِنْدِيْ
نَمِي مِعِيْنِ وَلكِرَشِيْلَ وَكَنْغِي
كَتِدَ جَاي يَوَاتُ وَاَمُ مْفَلِمَ اَكُوتَاكَ
كَوَاةُ وَاَمُ وَكَاِيْزَ كُوتُوْ وَكَتِكَ ...
مَنِيْنُ هَايُ مْفَلِمُ اَكَافَ سنه ٧٣٢
اَكَوَاتَ كِجَانَ كِمُوْيَ هَمْكُلِوَ سلطان
عُمَرِ اَكَتَوَالَ بَعَدَ يَبَبَاكِ كَرَاجِعِ
مَانِنُ يَبَبَاكِ كَوَاتُ وَاَمُ كُتَاكَ
وَاتُ وَمَانْزَةْ وَكَازَوَاتُ وَاَمُ كُتُوَ
كَوَ پِيْجَ وَكَتِكَ اَمَانِ وَاتُ وَاَمَ
وَكُوَ كَتِكَ طَاعَ يَسلطان عمر بن محمد
بن احمد بن محمد بن سليمان اَكَپَاتَ غُوْقُ ....
سَانَ اَكَپِيْجَ جُمْلَ يَمِي يَسَوَاحِلِ

A 5

اُزِنْوَ نَمَلِنْدِيْ نَكَوِيُوْةْ نَكِتَاوُ نَمِيْيَ
نَامِبْذِيْ نَوَتَامُ حَتَّى كَسِكِلِيَ كِرِيْمْبَهْ
مِيْ يُوْنْتِ كَاتَمَلَكِ تَغُ پَاتِ حَتَّى
كِرِيْمْبَا كُلَ مُوْيِ كَوِكَ مْتُ وَاكِ
اِلِكَمُكُوْمُ زِيُ اَصْلِ يَهُوَ مْجُوْمْبِهْ
وَلِيكُ مْرِيْمَا وُتِّ مَعَنَ نِوَتُوْ مَ
وَنْيُوْمْبِهْ هِيُ يُوْمْبِهْ نِانَ لَيُوْمْبَه
يَوُغَلِمُ وَپَاتِ نَجَنَبُ يَهُكُ اَكَتَمَلَكِ
حَتَّى وَزْشِيْغِ كَزِيْتَ اَلِكَدَ كُپِيْجَ
تَغُ كِوَيُوْه نَطُوْلَا نَطُوَالَا نَشْغَايَ
نَبَنَادِرِ زُتِ بَرَاوَ مْرْكَا مُقْدِشُوْ
هَابُ مُقْدِشُوْ كَوِكَ لُوَالِيْ حُكْمُ
يَبَنَادِرِ زُتِّ زِكَاوَ مُقْدِشُوْ اَكَعِيْشِ
نَنْتِ هِيْزُنْتِ زِكَتِّكَ طَاعَ يَكِ
اِسْكُوَ اُغُوْجَ هَكُتَوَالَ وَقَتِ هُنُ
اُغُوْجَ هَيْكُوَنْتِ كُوُ نَمْفَلِمُ هِيُ

A 6

اَلِكِبِدَ زِيْتَ مْنُ نَكُبِدَ رَعِي نَرَعِيَ
وَكَوْنَ رَاحَ وَكَپَاتَ نَمَالِ مَاغِ اِكَسِتَوِ
مْنُ نْتِ يَپَاتِ اَكَافَ سنة ٧٤٩
اَكَوَتَ زِجَانَ وَوِلِ محمد نَاَحمدَ اَكَتَوَالَ
محمد بن عمر بن محمد بن احمد بن محمد بن سليمان وَلَهَپِكُوَ
نَزِيْتَ كَتَوَلَ اُفَلِمُ وَبَبَاكِ وُتِ
كَامَانِ نَايِ كِبِدَ مَالِ سَانَ نَبِيَشَارَ
اَكِسَفِرِشَ نَزُوْمُسُه كُپِكَ اِلْهِنْدِيْ
كُفِيَ بِيَشَارَ نَايِ اَلِنَ بَخْتِ سَانَ
يَمَالِ نَمَرَ مُوْيَّ مَانِ اَلِسَفِرِ كَپَاتَ
كِسِنِوَ بَحْرِيْنِ كَشُوْكَ كَپَاتَ مَعْدِنِ
يَفِيْضَ اَكِپِكَ وَاتُ وَكَفَيَ كَازِ كَبَاتَ
مَالِ مَاغِ اِكَزِدِ مْنُ مَالِ كَتِكَ نْتِ يَپَاةِ
حَتَّى وَكَفِيَ زِتَانْزَةَ زَفِيْضَ نَغَازِ -
زَفِيْضَ نَزُوْمْبُ زِيْغِ زَفِيْضَ كَپَاتَ
نَزِجَانَ وَانْتِ بَانَ مْكُوُ نَاَحمدَ نَابُوْبَكَرَ

A 7

نَعُمِرَ اَكَافَ مْعَلِمُ سنة ٧٩٧
اَكَتَوَالَ رُيِ احمد بن عمر بن محمد بن احمد بن محمد بن سليمان
اَكَكِيْتِ كَامَانِ كَتِكَ نْتِ زَاكِ حَتَّى
سنة ٨٤٠ اَكَافَ اَكَتَوَالَ ابوبكر بن محمد
بن عمر بن محمد بن احمد بن محمد بن سليمان كَكِيْتِ
كَسِيَارَ نْجِيْمَ نِمِي يُوْتِ كَتِكَ طَاعَ
يَاكِ نَكُامَنِشَ مِي يَاكِ اَكَفَ كَتِكَ
حَالِ پَسِيْنَ كُهَرِ بَكِيْوَ حَتَّى سنة ٨٧٥
اَكَوَاتَ زِجَانَ وَوِلِ محمد نَاحمد ....
اَكَتَوَالَ محمد بن ابي بكر بن محمد بن عمر بن محمد بن احمد بن محمد
بن سليمان وَقَتِ وَاكِ وَكِيَ وَزُغُ بَرُتُغَالِ
مِي يَسَوَاحِلِ يُوْتِ وَكَكِيْتِ مْمْبَاسَةَ
وَكَفِيَ غُوْمِ نْجَنِبُ يَپَاتِ وَكِجِنْغَ ..
نْدُوْدُ نَوَاتُ وَبَرَ وَكَوفُوَاتَ كَكُوَابُ
مَالِ وَكَغِيَ كَتِكَ طَاعَ يَاوُ وَكَمْعَرِضِ
نَمْضَلِمُ كَتِكَ مْمِيِ وَيَاتِ وَكَمْپِجَ

A 8

كجنب يشير كاس وكواك نتيات

قصد يكپيج بومبه موي وبات

وسوز كس وكبتان كامان وكغي

مكاتب وشرط زاو وكگيت پات

وزغ وكغي فروض كان لاو وزغ

ولتمكو فند يك وكغي نماب مغ

كتك كسو تپات بعد يهاي

اكف مفلم سنه ٩٠٠ اكوت زجان

بان مكوم نابوبكر اكتوال ابوبكر

بن محمد بن ابي بكر بن محمد بن عمر بن محمد بن احمد بن محمد بن سليمان

اكگيت كامان نوزغ وپتين كم

قاعد يبباك اكف سنه ٩٤٥

كوت زجان احمد نا محمد اكتوال نتري

بان مكو بن محمد بن ابي بكر بن محمد بن عمر بن محمد بن احمد .

بن محمد بن سليمان وكو نجتلاف نوزغ

لكن يسو نزيت اكف كتك فتين

A 9

يسك يغ سنه ٩٧٣ اكوت زجان

بان بكر اكتوال محمد بن ابي بكر بن محمد بن ابي بكر

بن محمد بن عمر بن محمد بن احمد بن محمد بن سليمان اكصلحيات

نوزغ نو وكتاء بعض يمي اكف كوت

زجان ابوبكر سنه ١٠٠٢ اكتوال بان

بكر وبانه مكو بن محمد بن ابي بكر بن محمد بن عمر بن محمد بن احمد.

بن محمد بن سليمان كسيا ركم زبباك لكن

افلم واو واصل امپغو اكاف اكوت

بانه مكو وبكر سنه ١٠٤١ اكتول ابوبكر

بن محمد بن ابي بكر بن محمد بن ابوبكر بن محمد بن عمر بن محمد بن احمد بن محمد

بن سليمان اكختلفيان نوزغ كپك وات

كتك نت يپات وكوپيج وزغ زكي

زيت زوزغ وكپيج موي كمزغ

وكزوي ندي زحر وكپات مشاك

وات وپات وكغي اماني بعد يهي

اكاف مفلم اكوت زجان ول ..

A 10

بانه مكو ناحمد سنة ١٠٦١ اكتوال بان مكو
وبانه بكر وبان مكو بن محمد بن ابي بكر بن محمد بن عمر
بن محمد بن احمد بن محمد بن سليمان اكيتان نوزغ ناي
اكبد كو كبيت ام حتى موسم الكويت
ام اكوو وكوات وام نوفماو....
وسيو مدهن ولتك طاع يك اكيجا
ناو اكاقوند موي وسو اكتكو...
نوات وت وسو اكوايت پات
مكو وسيو كمبي كنز دوندو...
كوبر تغال وكطاء حايه مكو وو زغ
پرتغال كاي پات كتك وات وسيو
اكپو وكو رحيز سو وكبيت كاماني
بعد يك پرتغال كفي حبل اكي پات
كمركاب اكمتك مفلم كنز مركبون
اسنير مفلم اكمپك بن عميك
بان مكو يپ نوات وبات وزغ

A 11

وكوتكو كتك مركاب كو پيك كاو
ازغون اسرد تن حتى مت اموي
بعد يهاب وكپيج وزغ كل
مهال وليب براڽ نرسوان كوتو
وكمبي وكنز ممباسه بعد يهاي
مفلم اكف سنة ١١٠٠ اكوات
زجان ول نبنت بانه بكر نبان
مد نمان درين اكتوال مات
بانه بكر بن بانه مكو بن بانه بكار وبانه مكو
بن محمد بن ابي بكر بن محمد بن عمر بن محمد بن احمد بن محمد بن سليمان
اكپيج مفلم غفل ناحمد ري بانه مكو
اكتكلو نوزغ پرتغال اكمو وكو باغ
اكتوال يپ احمد بن ابي بكر بن محمد بن ابي بكر بن محمد
بن عمر بن محمد بن احمد بن محمد بن سليمان سنة ١١٠٣
اكوندام وپرتغال كوتو ولسلي
نوقت هومان درين بنت

A 12

بانه مكو وبانه بكار وبانه مكو زابي بكر..
ميترغو وا كتك زمان يسلطان احمد
اكس كاوا و رز و ول بات بكار زبانه
مكو نبان مد بن بان مكو التكلو
مپك غو سابق اكيات حزون سات
يموم واك نكولو نزوز حتى بعض
يسك زكپيت كعزم كغي عروس
كمتهر مان بات تام متت امكلواو
سلطان ابو بكر امام الهدى
وبانه مكو ميترغو مفلم سلطان
احمد اكبهت خبر ناي كعزم عروس
ال قصد يكمهن سيو اكس كيو
مات درين خبار يكهنو سيو اكممكو
مي بابي مكو شريف كتك جمال
الليل الكيو كاز يوجوم سات
اكممبي خبر يك اكتك كاك امغيزي

A 13

سيو اشير ياو الي اكقبال اكتاك
اجار يك كپو ريال مي وعشرين
نپيب زند وقوا انكاز اپات
كتو وزل نجيم زفاز اكتمير شرط
زاك زت مانه درين اكغي سيو
كيز سيت الپ كيس اكيظهرش
غفل كيپك كتك ماجوب يتز
نوند لمتز مالوا وكيتوز مال ماغ
اكممبي مي بمبي الغي سو وتك
اجار يك او اتتاء توز اكتاء توز
كسبب الوت نمال ماغ اكتقبض سو
يك اكفيلز عروس بك يمان حتى
زمان يبان تام مكوم وات وام
وكي كازيم سيو ياصل كواپ
اكبات بحرين تومبو اكلف ماي
اكپتي سو بات تام مكوم اكيتاك

A 14

سِوَ يَمَانَ دَرِيْنِ اَكَمَبِيَ تُبِ سِرِس
تُتِمِي كَتِكَ رِمِيْ اَكَمَبِي كُل قَبَائِلَ
اَلُتُرَ سِوَ يَغُ نَتِمِي بَسِ مَنَادَرِيْنِ
اَكَوَتَ مْتُوْمَ حُرِ اَيُوَاوُ كِپِيْجَ
سِوَ هِنِ يِبِي نَنَسْلِ يَكِ نَغَدَ يَكِ
نَپِوُ رِيَالِ تَانَ نَغُوُ يَكُتَكُلِيَ سِوَ
نَسَمْلِ يَكُوْتَ مِي كُفُزِيَ سِوَ نَتُوْزُ
بُكَلَ مْتَ قِيَاسِ اَوِزَاوُ وَكَامْكَلِوَ نَسْلَ
هِيُ مُيُوْمْبِهْ وَسِيْوَ حَتَّى يِوُوَاكُ
وَاتُوُ بِسِ اِكُوَ وَقَتِ هُنُ هُتِمِيَ
قَبَائِلَ وَپَاتِ وُتِ نُوَمِي مِغِيْنِ
هِيْتَ كَزِيْمَ كُشَرُطِ هِيْزُ نَمْفَلِمِ
اَكِيْتِ مُدَ وَيَكَ سَبَعَ هِيِ كِيَّ
مْقُوَا اَكَ اِعُزُلَ كُتَكَ اُفَلِمِ وَاكِ
سـ ١١١ـنه اَكَتَوَلَ سُلْطَانِ اَبِي بَكَرِ
بَانَ نَامُ مْكُوُمُ وَبَانَ مْتِنِ بْنِ اَحْمَدِ

A 15

بن ابي بكر بن عمر بن احمد بن عمر بن محمد بن أحمد بن محمد بن سليمان
اَكَتُزِيَ نَمْفَلِمِ وَمَسِكَتِ اِمَامُ اَلْيَعْرَبْ
هِيُ مْفَلِمُ وَبَاتِ كِنِزَ عَرَبُوْنِ مْفَلِمِ
وَعَرَبُوْنِ وَكَاغَانَ اَرُدِپَ مْفَلِمُ
وَپَاتِ اَوَنُوُ پُرْتُغَالِ مَمْبَاسَهْ اَلِبُ
رُدِ مْفَلِمُ وَپَاتِ كَپِكَ زِيْتَ مَمْبَاسَهْ
كَمُوَپِيْجَ وَزُغُ پُرْتُغَالِ سِكُ بُجُمَ يَپِلِ
كَمَوَاُوَ كَشِكَ غُوْمَ يَمَمْبَاسَهْ كَمُعَرِفُ
اِمَامُ اَلْيَعْرَبِ اَكَيِتَ اَلْوَالِيْ كُتِكَ مْزَارِعِ
وَاتُ وَتَاتُ رُغُ مُحَمَّدْ بِنْ عُثْمَانِ نَعَلِي بِنْ عُثْمَانِ
نَقَضِيْبُ بِنْ عُثْمَانِ نَاوُ وَلِكُي يَمُوْيَ
نَعَسْكَرِ طَرَفُ يَا اِمَامُ اَلْيَعْرَبِ زَيِ اَصْلِ
يَمَزَارِعِ كُيَ مَمْبَاسَهْ نَايِ هِيُ مْفَلِمُ
وَپَاتِ اَلكِيْتِ نَزَعِيَ كُوُزُوُ رِسَانَ
اَكَعِيْشِ اَكَتِمِيْزِ كُتَكَ اُفَلِمِ وَاكِ يَكَ
اَرْبَعِيْنِ ٤٠ اَلَفَ ـــــ ١١٥٢ ســنه

A 16

اكوت رجان رغ بعد ياك استوال
مان اكتول سلطان احمد ز ابي بكر
بن محمد ز ابي بكر ز عمر ز احمد ز عمر ز محمد ز احمد ز محمد
ز سليمان اكيت كنغم يغ اكيد كوك
غومب واغ سان اكف سنة ١١٦٠
اكوت كجان باند غوغ بعد ياك
اكتول بان تام منت امكلو وا امام
المهدي وباند مكو التكلو نبر تغال
نان لاك ابو بكر ز باند مكو ز ابي بكر
ز محمد ز ابي بكر ز محمد ز ابي بكر ز محمد ز عمر ز محمد ز احمد
ز محمد ز سليمان اكيت زيت امام اليعرب
كپيج پات وسيوز وكاف وعرب
ويغ وكرود وكفاي امان بعد
يهاپ وات وام وكپيج نمفلم
وپات وخلف وكيجان اسيوز
نوات وام وكي پات كپيج كجانب

A 17

يكتاك وكغنكوز وكرجبي ام بعدي
مفلم وپات اكغبي زيت كبار نبحر
كوپيج وات وام كوتملك كس
اكوواو مفلم وپات نوات وپات
پموي نوات وامام اليعرب سنة ١١٧٧
اكتول زي سلطان مانه خدبجه
بنت بان مكو ز ابي بكر ز محمد ز ابي بكر ز محمد -
ز ابي بكر ز محمد ز عمر ز محمد ز احمد ز محمد ز سليمان
اكبات فتن يغ كتك نت يبات
اكوكتك موي وپات وفلم وول
ييي مان خدبجه المذكوره نسلطان
عمر وكيجان كتك موي يكد متان
گكمبي سلطان عمر كنز براو كس
كرجبي كغوقوا كغلو اسكد اكوواو
نوات ومان خدبجه المذكوره بعد
يك كسك كتنبت اكف مان خدبجه

A 18

١١٨٧ سنه اكتول بان مكو وشي
وبانه تام مكو نرعي وكم اذ اكغي
فتن اسپات راح حتى سنه ١١٩١
وكغي وات وموي وكمو وكتاريخ
هن كتول بان فوم مد ان لاك
سلطان محمد ز ابي بكر ز بانه مكو ز ابي بكر ز محمد
ز ابي بكر ز محمد ز ابي بكر ز محمد ز عمر ز محمد ز احمد ز محمد ز سليمان
كس كتول رعي وكتك كغني فتن
اكو پيبج كزيت كوشر اكوشك
وات اربعين ٤٠ وكو نكنك هو
وات اربعين المذكورون وات
وول نرز اكو تيد وت ككو
امان اسپات مت وكموزن تن
كتول كراح نا امان نعم نرعي
وكون راح سان حتى سنه ١٢٢٤
اكف بعد يك هكتول تن كم ببي

A 19

ناي الوت زحابن زغ اكتول سلطان
احمد بن شيخ بن فوم لوط بن تام مكو
اكزد فتن كتك نت يام اگي كوپيج
تاريخ سنه ١٢٢٧ ببي نوات وممباسه
مزارع وكايت وات وكشك شيل
جيش يغ يوات وبات نوات وممباسه
وات وام وكتك وكيجان نو وكغوند
وات وبات نو ممباسه وكتاك
گكمبي مجهز ول الي زمپو وكيجان
زت زكو وكؤاو وات واغ وبات
نو ممباسه هپان عدد كتك
وات وپات ولمعروف اسكو
وتوم نوسيو كان نوات واحد
وثمانين عدد ٨١ ولؤواو نو ممباسه
مبال بعد يهاب وات وام
وكرعر بون وكمنك سيد سعيد

A 20

بَبَاكِ سَيِّدْ بَرْغَشْ وَكَمْبَ نْتِ
سنة ١٢٢٨ رِبُ سَيِّدْ سَعِيْدِ اَلِپُ
تَوَالَ اَمُ اُفَلِمُ وَيَاتِ اُكَسِلِيَ كَتِدَ
كِسِوَ تَيَاتِ نَبَنَادِرِ اُكِزِدِ فِتِنَ كَتِكَ
نْتِ يَيَاتِ اَكَشُكَ مْتُ وَبِلِ كَتِكَ زِجَانَ
وَبَانَه فُوْمُ مَدِ هَمْكُلِوَ فُوْمُ لُوْطِ اِكِيُغَ
اَكِيَجَانَ نَسُلْطَانِ اَحْمَدِ كِسَ سُلْطَانِ
اَحْمَدِ اَكِيَاتَ مَرَضِ اَكَفَ سنة ١٢٢٠
اَكَتَوَلَ سُلْطَانِ فُوْمُ لُوْطِ وَبَابَ
فُوْمُ مَدِ نَايِ اَلِكُومْتُ هُدَرِ سَانَ
شُجَاعَ سَخِيْ نَزَمَانِ هِيْزِ شُيْخِ مْتَاكَ
بِنْ مْبَارَكَ رِبُ اَلِپُ تَوَلَ اُشِيْخِ
وَسِوُ اَكَفِيَ عَسْكَرِ نَبُدُ وْكِ نَايِ
كَتِكَ طَاعَ يَسُلْطَانِ وَيَاتِ نَايِ
اَلِپَتَانَ سَانَ نَمَزَارِعِ حَتَّى سنة ١٢٣٦
اِكَزِدِ فِتِنَ بَيِنِيَاكِ نَسُلْطَانِ زِنْجَبَارِ

A 21

سَيِّدْ سَعِيْدِ اَكَفَ سُلْطَانِ فُوْمُ لُوْطِ
سَنَةَ الْمَذْكُوْرَة بَعَدَ يَكِ اَكَتَوَالَ
فُوْمُ لُوْطِ بِنْ شَيْخِ بِنْ فُوْمُ لُوْطِ بِنْ شَيْخِ
وَبَانَهْ تَامُ مْكُوُ نَهُيُ رِبِي بَبَاكِ
سُلْطَانِ اَحْمَدْ سُلْطَانِ وَوِيتُوْ
اَكَتَوَلَ اَصُبُحِ حَتَّى بَعْدَ الْعَصْرِ
وَاتُ وَمْوُيِ وَكَمْتُوَ اَكِنِرِ سِوُ پُمْوِيَ
نَمَزَارِعِ كِسَ وَكَنِزِ مَمْبَاسَهْ اَكَتَوَلَ
سُلْطَانِ بَانَهْ شَيْخِ وَبَانَه فُوْمُ مَدِ
اَكِپَتَانَ نَسَيِّدْ سَعِيْدِ اَكَتِيَ
وَعَرَابُ يَاتِ وَكَكِيْتِ يَكَ مِتَاتُ
بَعَدَ اِيِ وَاتُ وَمْوِيِ وَكَمْعَزِلُ پُمْوِيَ
نَشُوُرِ لَسَيِّدِ سَعِيْدِ سُلْطَانِ زِنْجَبَارِ
كَتَارِخِ سنة ١٢٣٩ وَكَمْتَاوَلِشَ..
سُلْطَانِ اَحْمَدَ اَمْكُلِوَاوُ بَانَ وَزِيْرِ
وَبَانَه تَامُ وَبَانَ شَيْخِ وَبَانَ تَامُ مْكُوُ

A 22

b•

اكيتان نسيد سعيد اكتول يك
مول بعداي وات وموي وكمعزل
وكمرجيز بان شيخ وباند فوم مد
اكليت كتكد عز كشور لسيد ....
سعيد يكد متان اكف سنه ١٢٤٧
اكرجيز باند وزير كتكد افلم اكاي
فوم لوط بن شيخ الكبير ممباسه
ييي نمزارع وكشكد سو وكيجان
نبان وزير وبان تام پات نبان
وزير پموي نسيد سعيد نفوم
لوط پموي نمزارع نشيخ متاكا
مت وسو كشور موي وكشير فوم
لوط اكشكد موي وسو اكفند و
اكوت وموي فوم لوط نشيخ
متاك وككمبي بران وكليت بران
سكد كتبت وكرجبي سو كزبت

A 23

وكشكد موي وسيو وكواك اكوت
وكيجان پات كسو كس فوم لوط
اكف سو اكتغاي بان وزير وبان
تام سو نپات اكو كتكد طاع ياك
پموي نشور لسيد سعيد بعد
يمكد اكووا وسلطان بان وزير
وبان تام نفوم بكار وبان شيخ
وبان فوم مد اكتول ييي سلطان
فوم بكار بشيخ وباند فوم مد
سنه ١٢٥٠ اكيتان نسيد سعيد
ماندو وكتول كس كخالف
پموي ييي نشيخ متاكا سيد
سعيد كميت امير حماد كپيج
پات نسو اسوز اكفي امان
بعد يهاپ سلطان وپات
اكتكي فتن بين يكد نبن عمياك

A 24

محمد بن احمد وبانه فوم مدِ اكشك ....
يومبه يوفلم كزيت كس وكي وات
وام يموي نمت وسيد سعيد
وكصلحيش محمد بن احمد كيك سيو ....
كويت فوم بكار ككيت پات بعدي
وكتيت وكپجان يك متان سيوكپات
كس وكپتنيش نسيد سعيد اكي
پات محمد بن احمد وكوشور موي نبن
عمياك فوم بكار كس كمشك غفل
كما او كشور لمت وسو كس سيد
سعيد كممكو فوم بكار كنز اغوج
سيد سعيد كمفغ فوم بكار كشور
لواة وام نكسبب يكمو وبن عميك
نكوات كفوات اماني الفي سيد
سعيد كتك ١٢٦٢ سنه اكشك نت
يپات سلطان احمد بن شيخ بن فوم

A 25

لوط بن شيخ وبانه تام ملكو كشور لسيد
سعيد اككيت كتك شور لسيد ...
سعيد يك مول وكتيت اكي سيد
سعيد كمپنج اكشك امير حماد پازه
كنز كپنج سو نسيد سعيد المغفو
سلطان فوم بكار اكمب زيت يموي
نوات وام وككيت متاغ واند
كتك زوب بپي سيد سعيد
ككيت مهل همكلو كجاغ تمپوغا
فرنب يپاز امير حماد اكي سو كوك
ميوم كتك ندي بين يپاز نسو
امير حماد كنز سو كزيت حتى ككشك
متيپ اليك بند رين يسو ....
كيپندو وكفي مبوم كپنج نت
يسو كون اذي مد ولپكو منغ
كرد كنز كتاء مزغ اليوك بمان

A 26

كِيَاتَ نْدِيَانِ وَاتُ وَسِوُ وَكَمْتَكِيَ
غَفُلَ امِيْرِ وَشِيْخِ مَتَاكَا اَمْكُلِوَاوُ
بَانَدَحَادِ وَاُمَارِيْ اَكَمْپِيجَ كَمَاُوَامِيْرِ
حَادِ نَاَمِيْرِ وَپِلِ وَشِيْخِ مَتَاكَا ....
اَمْكُلِوَاوُ بَانَدَحَادِ غُوْمَ كِنِزَ بُوْمَانِ
كَوَپِيْجَ كَتَاءَ مِزِغَ خَبَارِ اِكِسِكِلِيَ
كَسَيِّدِ سَعِيْدِ پَازَهْ كَغِيَ مِرِگَابُوْنِ
اَسِنِ نَمْتُ كِنِزَ زَاكِ مَسِكَاتِ
مَكَ وَپِلِ كَرُدِ كَمُوكَ فُوْمُ بَكَارِ
پَازَهْ اَكَپِيْجَ سِوُ نَپَاتِ گَتِكَ وَقْتِ
هُنُ اَكَافَ شِيْخِ مَتَاكَ كَمَرَاضِ
اِكَوَخِتِلَافَ كَزِجَانَ زَاكِ كُتَاكَ
اُشِيْخِ وَسِوُ وَكَغِيَ كَتِكَ طَاعَ يَسَيِّدِ
سَعِيْدِ اَبُوْبَكَرِ نَمُحَمَّدَ سَيِّدْ سَعِيْدِ
كَمْبَ اَبُوْبَكَرِ زِيْتَ پَمُوْيَ نَسُلْطَانِ
فُوْمُ بَكَرِ كِنِدَ كُمْپِيجَ سُلْطَانِ

A 27

اَحْمَدْ اَكِنِزَ اَبُوْبَكَرِ شِيْخِ مَتَاكَ
پَمُوْيَ نَاَمِيْرِ وَسُلْطَانِ فُوْمُ بَكَرِ
اَمْكُلِوَاوُ بَانَ مْكُوُ وَبَانِ مَدِ وَبَا
نْيُشِ وَكَغِيَ سِوُ اُسِكُ وَكِپِجَانَ
حَتَّى اَصُبُحِ وَكَفُكُوْزَ اَبُوْبَكَرِ اَكِشِكَ
نْدِيَانِ اَكَپِكَ پَاتِ اَكَوُوَاوَ نَسُلْطَانِ
وَپَاتِ بَعَدَ يَاكِ اَكِسِمَامَ شِيْخِ مُحَمَّدَ
بْنِ شِيْخِ مَتَاكَ طَرَفُ يَسَيِّدِ سَعِيْدِ
پَمُوْيَ نَفُوْمُ بَكَارِ سَيِّدِ كَوَاپَ
زِيْتَ عَسِكَرِ نَغَرَامَ وَكَمْپِيجَ سُلْطَانِ
احمد بن شِيْخِ حَتَّى وَكَمْتُوَ پَاتِ كَتِكَ
تَارِيْخِ سنه ١٢٧٣ اَكِرَكَاوُ سِوُ اَكُوَ
بِشِيْخِ مُحَمَّد بن شِيْخِ مَتَاكَ طَرَفُ يَسَيِّدِ
كَمْبَ عَسْكَرِ كَوَكَ غِرِيْزَهْ بَعَدَايِ
وَكَتِيْبَ نَمْتُ وَسَيِّدِ سَعِيْدِ
كَسَبَبُ اَلِقُوْنْدَ بَانْزَ لَمْتِپِ

A 28

اَلُوَاكَ شِيخِ محمد مْبِي يَغرِيزَ بعد
نَشِيخِ محمد نَايِ كَغُنْدَ غِرِيزَ نَكَتِكَ
وَقَتِ هُنُ اَلِكُوفَ سُلْطَانِ اَحْمَدَ
كَاوُ بَبَاكِ غُوْمُ بَكَارِ سُلْطَانِ وَوِيتُو
اَلِكِيتِ مَهَالَ پَاكِ سُلْطَانِ اَحْمَدِ
اَمكِلِوَاوُ وَسِيمْبَه سُلْطَانِ وَوِيتُو
نَقَبْلَ يَشِيخِ محمد بن شيخ مْتَاكَ اَسِيفُوْ وَنِدَ
غِرِيزَ لِسُوَ يَلِتُكِيَ فِتِيْنِ يِبِي نَغُوْمُ
بَكَارِ بِنْ شيخ كُمْتُوَ پَاتِ كِيَازَاكِ
اَمُ كَتَاكَ كِتُمَلَاكِ يِبِي پَاتِ
كَسُوْرَ اَلُوْنَ غُوْفُ زَاكِ نُوْدُوْفُ
وَوَاتُ وَوَپَاتِ وَقَتِ هُنُ وَكُوُ
وَپَاتِ وَسِكِيزِ اَكِيَ كُوَپِيجَ وَكُوُ
وَپَاتِ وَكَسِمَامَ وَلِهُوَنَ مْفَلِمِ
كَشَوْرِ لَاوَاتُ وَتَاتُ وَپَاتِ
محمد بِنْ بَانَه مْكُوُ النَّبْهَانِي نَبَانَه رَحِمَ

A 29

بِنْ اَحْمَدَ النَّبْهَانِي نَنَاصِرِ بِنْ عَبْدَ اللّٰه
بِنْ عَبْدِ السَّلَامِ زِيِ اَلْكُوَمُدَ تِرِ
الْاُمُوْرِ وَمَامْبُ هَايُ وَكُتَاكَ زَانُ
نَبُدُوْكِ وَكِيجَانَ نَشِيخِ مُحَمَّدْ
بِنْ شِيخِ مْتَاكَ وَكَمْشِرَ وَلِمُوْلِيَ
وَاتُ وَاغُ نَمَعْرُوْفُ نِمَامِيزِ وَاكِ
وَاتُ وَوِلِ بَانَ دُمِلَ نَمُوْلَانَ وَشِيِي
كُوْلُ اَكِشَ كُوْنَ شِيخِ مُحَمَّدْ بِنْ شِيخ
مْتَاكَ مَابُ هَايَ اَكِيَ كُتَكَ اَمَانِ
كَمُحَمَّدِ بِنْ بَانَه مْكُوُ المذكور كَانِ زِيِ
اَلْكُوَ بِبَسَوَاوُ كَتِكَ وَاتُ وَتَاتُ
هَاوُ وَكَبَتَانُ وَكُوَحَالِ مْوِيَ كُتَكَ
كُمْبَ يِبِي مُحَمَّدْ بِنْ بَانَ نَمْكُوُ اَفَلِمِ
وَپَاتِ نَسِوُ كَاءِ زَ مُحَمَّدْ بِنْ بَانَ
مْكُوُ اَكَمَمْبِيَ مِمِ نِمْتُ مْزِيمَ
كَمْتَايِ سُلْطَانِ اَحْمَدِ مْفَلِمُ وَوِيتُ

A 30

سيمبه وكينز كمتاء كاپينگ وات
واك شيخ محمد بن شيخ متاكا نياتِ
كينز ناصر بن عبد الله كاو كمتاء سلطان
احمد سيمبه اكسكلي خبار كسلطان
وو غوج سيد ماجد بن سعيد قبل
يهاپ سيد سعيد الكومكوف
اكيت وزير واك سيد ماجد سيد
سليمان بن حمد كمر كاب ال اشكر پات
كقد فتن هي اكوصل مانزپات
امزي كشكد نمت وسلطان احمد
ابوبكر بن حسن امكوي ناي ناصر بن
عبد الله اكس كبات خبار سيد
سليمان بن حمد كرجي اغوج نشيخ
محمد هاپ رپ الپ قند غريز
لسو كس كوصل سلطان احمد
پات اكبا ايو نوات وپات نشيخ

A 31

محمد نوتكوه شيخ مزيه بن سيف
نشيخ شكو نمد موت الكستقر
كاك سلطان احمد افلم كجمل
يوات وليك كتكد كسو تپات
سيد ماجد الكوپك وات وام
پات كنصحه پموي نشيخ ...
محيي الدين كتاك اتاي سلطان
احمد بعض يعسكر وكيت پات
نشيخ محيي الدين هي ري الوتو
عسكر وسيد ماجد كتكد غريز لسو
الپ وپيج شيخ محمد ولندن
اكينز شيخ محيي الدين كونتو كاماني
كان المت وسيد ماجد الپ كينز
ناو كسيد ماجد الكفي حسير سان
اكتاء دراك شيخ محيي الدين
يكر جبز عسكر الپ ان غطب

A 32

كَاٰنِ اَلِمْتُ نَحِيْلَ يِغِ بَعِلْمُ يِغِ بَسِ وَكَيَ
بِيِ نَوَاتُ وَامُ حَتَّىٰ پَاتِ نَوَاتُ وَامُ
وَلُكُيُ پَاتِ نِشَيْخِ اَحْمَدْ نَرُكِ وَكَنِيْنَ
نَسُلْطَانِ اَحْمَدْ اَكَتَاءَ عَسْكَرِ كَبَعْدَ
بَشِدَهْ كَسَبَبُ يَصُحْبُ يَاكِ نَشَيْخِ
اَحْمَدْ نَرُكِ اَلْخَلِفُ شَوُرِ لَوَزِيْرِ
وَاكِ نَاصِرِ بِنْ عَبْدَ اللّٰهْ كَانِ اَلِ اِيْزَ
كُتِيَ عَسْكَرِ حَتَّىٰ اُمُوْيَ وَكِسَ كُغِيَ
وَعَرَابُ پَاتِ وَكُغِيَ شَوُرِ مُوْيَ
نَمَانَ جَاهَ بِنْتِ سُلْطَانِ فُوْمُ لُوْطِ
كِپُغَ وَبَانَهْ فُوْمُ مَدِ مْكِ وَسُلْطَانِ
فُوْمُ بَكَرِ بِنْ شَيْخِ وَقَتِ هُنُ بِيِ
فُوْمُ بَكَرَ اَلِيْكُ اَمُ تِنَ كَشَوُرِ لَسَيِّدْ (مَاجِدْ)
تَغُ اَلِپُ تُلِوَ پَاتِ كُلَّ سِكُ وَكُتِيَ
عَسْكَرِ نَزَانَ اُسِكُ اُسِكُ كَسِيْرِ
كِسَ اَلِپُ يُوَ سُلْطَانِ اَحْمَدْ اِكُوَ
فِتِيْنَ لَعَسْكَرِ وَمِكُوَ وَاغِ پَاتِ

A 33

وَكَمْپِيَ غَفُلَ بَعَدَ يَكِيْسَ جِيْلَ ...
يَكُمْشِكَ وَسِوُزِ كَنِ وَاتُ وُتِ
وَپَاتِ وَلِكُوَ شَوُرِ مُوْيَ نَسَيِّدْ
مَاجِدِ اِسُكُوَ وَزِيْرِ وَاكِ نَاصِرِ بِنْ عَبْدَاللّٰه
وَكِپَجَانَ نَوُرَانِ مَپَاتِ وَكُمْتُوَ
نَشَيْخِ مُحَمَّدْ كَمْتُكُلِيَ سِوُ پَاتِ وَكِيْتِ
وَعَرَابُ نَبَحَرِيْنِ وَكُتِيَ مَرِكَابُ
زِيْتَ زَلِپُ كُوَزِ لُكُوَ اَلِكِيَ بِيِ سَيِّدْ
مَاجِدْ وَكُحُرُصُ كِسِوَ تَپَاتِ كَبَحَارِ
كَتِيَ سِلْسِلَ كَتِكُ كَاتَّ لَمْتُ وَسِوُ
كُوْتِهْ وَكِپَجَانَ بِزِسِتَّهْ كَبَحْرَيْنِ
نَكَپَاتِ نَجَنِبُ يَتِكُوْوُنِ مْزِيَهْ
وَسِيْفُ اَلْخَلِفُ اَكُوَ نِمْتُ وَسَيِّدْ
كَمِيْلَ يِغِ نَمْنِيْنُ مَاغِ وَكُوْنَ
ظِيْقِ سُلْطَانِ اَحْمَدْ نَشَيْخِ مُحَمَّدْ
نَنْتِ يَسِوُ اِكُوَ نِفِتِيْنَ بَغْضِ
وَپِنْدَ كَسَيِّدْ كَسَبَبُ يَمْشَكَ

A 34

ومزيات نوتو نشريف مولانا
بن ابي بكر نعيسى بن احمد ولپ
ان هيو سلطان احمد نشيخ
محمد وكتك امان كسيد كواپ
كتك منين يا امان سلطان احمد
كسفير كسير اسك كنز زاك بران
كركاو نبعد ياك شيخ محمد
كنز مركبون كسيد كمسامح ....
نسيد كنز زاك اغوج كس شيخ
محمد اكنز اغوج كمواجه سيد
كمفغ كمپك غميني ممباسه
نوات واغ الف كبعد يسك
يغ نسلطان احمد الپ كنز
شيخ محمد اغوج اليكيو سعو
بن حمد كمشك كحيل اسوز كنز
زاك ويت سعود اكي بازه المشك
عمر وبان متاك نزجان وشيخ

A 35

محمد وت وكشك سو وكپك
غومیني ممباسه عمر كغ ام
بعد يهاپ اكتملك سيد ماجد
سوحل زت پسو نمت تن
وكمعرض نسلطان (احمد) گكيت
ويت كتك طاع يسيد ماجد
حتى وقت وسيد برغش اكتك
سيد برغش كوك عسكر ويت
نبديره اسكير سلطان احمد
كپك زيت اسوز كفاي اماني
بعد يهاپ سعود بن حمد
اسفراح سيد برغش كسبب
كفي اماني اپس ناي هكمپيج
سان كپيك زيت مر يبيل
زكو نالوالي سعيد بن حمد
سلطان احمد اكتاء حمايه
كجرمن وقت هن زيت زكرد

A 36

زَسَيِّدْ بَرْغَشْ اَكَكِيْتِ سُلْطَانِ
اَحْمَدْ كَتِكَ حِمَايَهْ يَجَرْمَنْ وَكَمْپَ
نَبَعْضِ يَبَرَ يَسَوَاحِلِ اَكَافَ سُلْطَانَ
اَحْمَدْ كَتِكَ حَالِهِيُ سنه ١٣٠٦
اِكَتَوَلَ فُوْمُ بَكَرِ بِنْ سُلْطَانِ
اَحْمَدْ بِنْ شَيْخِ اِكَتُيَ فِتِيْنَ يِي
يَجَرْمَنْ كُنْسِلْ جَرْمَنْ اَكَمُوُ وَا
بَوَابْ وَلَاغُ لَمُوْيِ عَسْكَرِ وَلُكُوَاكَ
وَكَمْپِيْجَ كُنْسِلْ نَوَزُغُ وَلُغُوِتِيْنِ
وَكَوَاُوَ بِغَيْرِ يَكُتَاكَ اَمْرِ كَسُلْطَانِ
عَسْكَرِ كِسَ كُوْنَ اَمِوُوَا وَمَدَانِ
وَاوُ نَوُوَلِوُوَ نَوَاتْ وَوَنَرَمُوْيَ
نَوَمَكْنُوْبِ وَكِسَ كُپَاتَ خَبَارِ نَاوُ
وَكَوَاُوَ وَزُغُ وَلُكُوَاكَ بَعَدَ اِيِ
اِكَايَ دُوْلَ تَكُوْفُ يُوَغِرِيْزَهْ وَكَتِكَ
وَاتْ وَلُوُوَزُغُ وَاتْ وَمَكْنُوْبِ
نَوَوَنْدَمُوْيِ اَسِرِضِكِ كُوَتَوَ

A 37

سُلْطَانِ فُوْمُ بَكَارِ وَكَمْپِيْجَ وَغِزِيْزَ
بِتَارِيْخِ لَيْلَةْ ١١ رَبِيْعِ الْاَوَّلْ سنه ١٣٠٨
حَتَّى اَصْبُحِ يَتَارِيْخِ ١٢ رَبِيْعِ الْاَوَّلْ
سنه ١٣٠٨ وَكَمْتُوَ وِيْتُوْ كَزِيْتَ فُوْمُ
بَكَارِ كِيْزَ جُنْغِيْنِي وِيْتُوْ اِكَتَمَلِكِيُوَ
نَدُوْلَ يُوَغِرِيْزَهْ فُوْمُ بَكَارِ كَكِيْتِ
جُنْغِيْنِي حَتَّى تَارِيْخِ ٢٨ جُمَادِ الْاَوَّلْ
سنه ١٣٠٨ اَكَفَ بَعَدَ يَاكِ اَكَشِكَ مَهَلَ
پُرِيِ بَانَهْ شَيْخِ بِنْ سُلْطَانِ اَحْمَدْ
بَعَدَ يَسِكَ تَاتُ اَكَشِكَ نَرَيِ
فُوْمُ بَكَرِ عُمَرِ نَبَانَ اَقُطُوْلَ
وَكَمْفُغَ بَانَ شَيْخِ اَشِكِ يِيِ فُوْمُ
عُمَرِ بِنْ سُلْطَانِ اَحْمَدْ اِكَوَجِنِس
يَلُ كُوَ بَيْنَ يَاكِ يِيِ نَدُوْلَ تَكُوْفُ
يُوَغِرِيْزَ وَاَمَتَا مْفَلْمِ وَكِيْسَ وَكَتَمَلَكِ
وِبِيْتُوْ نِسُلْطَانِ فُوْمُ بَكَرِ وَاَمَتَا وَپَاتِ

A 38

اخبار بَتِه

مُتُ وَكاند كُيَ بَتِ كَتِكَ نَبَهَانِ سليمان بن سليمان بن مظفر النبهاني نَدُزِ وَاتُ
وَوِلِ علي بن سليمان نعُثمان بن سليمان نَهُوِيُ سليمان بن سليمان المذكور
رِيِ* اَلِيُ كُوَ سلطانِ عَرَبُوْنِ اَلِپُ تَوَلِ اليعربْي اَكَيَ بَتِ سنه ٦٠٠ ستمايه
هجريه اَكَيَ پَتِ كَتَكَ عروسي كَمُفَلْمِ وَپَتِ كَتِكَ هَوَالبتَ وِين نَايِ نِمَعَرُوُف
سلطان سليمان مُفَلْمِ وَبَتِ كَمُوُزَ بنتِ كِكِ* نَدَسْتُوْرِ يَجَمِيْعِ
يَوَ سَوَاحِلِ حَتَي سَاسَ مُتُ كِكُوُ لِيَ بِنْتِ يَكُ سِكُ اِلِيْ
يَسَبَعَ عَروسِيْ هد كُمَغلِيَ مُكِو بَبَ وَمُكِ وَاكِ هُمْبَ كِتُ
كُلَ مُتُ كقَدرِ يَكِ سليمان بن سليمانِ اَلِپُ كَدَ كُمَغَلِيَ بَعَدَ يَكُ *
سَبَعَ اُلِيْ مُفَلْمِ وَپَتِ كَوبِيَ وَاتُ هِيُ سليمان بن سليمان
رِيِ* مُفَلْم مَهَل بَغُ اَكَمْبَ وُفَلْمِ وَاكِ تَغُ هَپُ كتول سليمان بن سليمان
كَلِنَ نَمُجِ كَتِكَ اِيُ جَزِيْرَه يَبَتِ هِتَ كَتِكَ* كَتِكَ مَطِلَعَ يَپَتِ
نَسِيْوُ هَتَسَ كُوَ مْجِ وَلِكُ نَمُجِ مُغِنِ كَتِكَ اِيُ جزيره يَپَتِ
هِتَ شاغَ نَايُ مجِ هِيُ يَلِكُوَ كَتِكَ طَاعَ يَمُفَلْمِ وَپَتِ
نَفَازه وَلِكُ مُجِ وِيِو وَ پَازه المفازيون اُكَكتِ اُفَلْمِ هُنُ
نَمجِ هِنِ* پَتِ نَشَاغَ نَكِتَكَ كَتِكَ طاع يَمُفَلْمِ وَپَتِ
نَمَارَ اَلِيْكُ مُفَلْمِ وَاكِ بَالِ نايِ اَلِنَ غُفُ سَنَ نَهُوِيُ //

سلطان سليمان اَكَبَتَ زِجَنَ وَوِلِ محمد وَ احمد اَكَفَ سلطانِ
سليمان سنه ٦٢٥ نمحمد عُمُرِ وَاكِ يَكَ عِشِرين احمد عمر وَاكِ يَكَ حمسه* عشر
كَتَولِ محمد بن سليمان بَعَدَ يَبَبَاكِ وَاتُ وشَاغَ وكَخَلِفُ كَبِجَانَ
نَوُ كَوَ شِدَ نَمُجِ كَوُ فُدَ كَوُدُوَ اَصلِ بَعَضِ يَوَتُ وَكَجَ
پَتِ نَبَعَضِ يَوَتُ قَبِلَ يَوُ كِنَدَاغُ وَكَكِبِيَ وَسِيُجوكَانِ
وَمِزِپُ كِدَ حَتَّي سِكُ زِكَپِتَ اِكَجَ خَبَرِ كسلطان محمد بن سليمان
نَوَاتُ وِداءُ كُيِدَ وَكَمَبِيَ وَلِيْ وشِيُوُ تُمِوَوُنَ كَتِكَ
مِتُ كَبِكَ وَتُ كُوَ غَلِي وَكَوَدِرِكَ وَمِفَايَ زِجُوْمْپَ
نْدَانِ يَمِتُ وَكُوَ تُكُوَ وَكَجَ نَوُ پَتِ سلطان محمد كَوَ سامِحِ
كَوَرُ دِشَ مَهَلَ پَوُ دِيُ اَصلِ يَمُجِ وسِيُوَ نَوسَوَحِلِ
وَغِنِ وَكَكِتِ وُتِ وَكَجَ نَوَ فَمَاوُ وَك كِتِ وُتِ
وَكَوَ رِوُ* وَكُوپَ وَسِيُوُ كَتِكَ طاعَ يَمُفَلُمِ وَپَتِ اَكَفَ
سلطان محمد بن سليمان كَتَوِلِ رُيِ* احمد بن سليمان اَكَعَمِرِشَ
سَنَ نْتِ يَپَتِ كَتِيَ نَمَشَامْپَ نَكُوكَ مَجُپَ نَنْتِ هِزِ زُتِ
كَتِكَ طاعَ* اَسِبِجِ مَهَلَ اَكَفَ سنه ٦٧٠ كَتَولِ كِجَنَ وَدُيِ جِنَ
لَكِ احمد بن محمد بن سليمان كَكِتِ سِيَارَ يَعَمِيكِ كَتِكَ عَمِارَ يَمُجِ وَبَتِ
كَمُجُب نَمَشَانْپِه نَايِ كَبَتَ زِجَنَ وَغِ اَكَتَاءَ وُفَلُمِ كَتِكَ //

زِجَنَ زَاكِ محمد بن احمد بن محمد بن سليمان اَكَكِتِ نَوَتُ سَنَ وَاتُ وَفَازه وَكَخَلِفُ
كَوَبِجَ كَوَتِيَ كَتَكَ طَاعَ يَكِ بَعد يَزتَ زِغِ سَنَ حَتَّي اَلِپُ وَشِدَ
كَفُتَحِ نَمانْدَ كَيِتَمَلكِ اَمَ مَاراً* اَلِيتَمَلَكِ كَزتَ نَحِيْلَ يِغِ سَنَ
كَانِ لِنَ غُفُ سَنَ سلطان وَمَارَ* يَوَتُ نَمَالِ مَغِ
كَيِفُوْنْدَ كَبِسَ نَوَتُ وَغِنِ كَوَاتَ پَتِ نَبَعَضِ وَكَكِبِيَ
وَكِدَ كُلَ مَهَلَ وَغِنِ وَكَجَ شِيْلَ وَكَغِيَ كَتِكَ حَمَايَ
يَوَتُ وَلَاموه مُفَلُمِ كَوَ تكَ كَوَتُ وَلَاموه وَتُ وَلَاموه
وَكَيِزَ كُوتُوَ نَوَغِنِ وَكِدَ مَلِنْديْ نَبَعَضِ يَبُلُدَانِ
مُفَلُمِ وَبَتِ كَوَءَ دَمَ سَنَ هَوَ وَلِيُ كُجَ شِيْلَ وَتُ وَلَاموه
وَكَيِزَ كُوَ تُوَ قَطَعًا مَنِيْنُ هَيِسَ مُفَلُمِ اَكَفَ سنه ٧٣٢ كَمُوَت
كِجَانَ اُمُوْجَ هِتَ عُمَرِ كَتَولِ وُسلطان عمر بَعَدَ يَبَباكِ كَرَاجِعِ مَنِنُ
يَبَبَاكِ كَوَتُ وَلَاموه كُتَكَ وَاتُ ومَانده وَكَيِزَ وَاتُ وَلَاموه
كُوَ تُوَ كَوَبِجَ زِتَ وكَتَكَ اَمَانِ وَاتُ وَلَاموه وَكَوَ كَتِكَ
طَاعَ يَكِ نسلطان عمر بن محمد بن احمد بن سليمان اَكَبَتَ غُفُ سَنَ كَبِجَ
نَمجِ يَسَوَاحِلِ اُزِيْ ملندي كِوَايُوْ كِتَاوُ مِيَ نَاءِ مِيْذِ
نَوَتَامُ حَتَي اَكَسِكِلِيَ كِرِيْمْپَا مج يُتِ كَتَمَلكِ تَغُ پَتِ حَتَي كِرِيْمْپَا
كُلَ مُجِ كَوِكَ وَاتُ وَاكِ وِيِ كُحُكُمُ رِيُ* اَصِلِ يَهَوَ مَجُبِ وَلِيُكُ //

مِرِيْمَ يُتِ مَعَنَ نِوَ تُوْمَ وَيُوْمْبِ نَهِيُ يُوْمْبِ نِيُوْمْبِ يوُفَلُمِ وپَتِ
نَجَانِبُ يِمَطْلَعِ كَتَملكِ حَتَى وَرْشِيخ كَزِتَ زِغِ اَلكَدَ كُبِجَ زِتَ
تَغْ كِوَ يُوُ نَطُوْلَ نطَوال نَشْغَايَ نَبَنَادِرِ زُتِ بَراوه
مَركَ مُقُدِشُ كَوكَ الوالي جميع احكام زَ بَنَادِرِ زُتِ زِكَوَ
مُقُدِشُ كَعِيْشِ نَتْتِ زُتِ هِزِ كَتِكَ حُكُمُ يِكِ نَطَاعَ يِكِ
اِلاَّ وُغُوْجَ هكُتَولِ وَقَتِ هُنُ نَوُغُجَ هَيِكُوَ نْتِ كُوپَ
نَمُفلُمِ هُيُ سلطان عمر اَلكِبِدَ زِتَ نكُبِدَ رَعِيَ نَرَعِيَ
وَكِمُبِدَ سَنَ اِكتَاءَ غُفُ سَنَ پَتِ اَكَفَ سنه ٧٤٩ كَوتَ
زِجَنَ وَوِلِ محمد ناحمد اَكتَوْلِ محمد بن عمر بن محمد بن احمد بن محمد بن سليمان
وَلاَ هَبَكُوَ نَزِتَ اَكَشِكَ اُفَلُمِ وَبَبَاكِ كَامَانِ نَايِ اَلكِپِدَ
مَالِ سَنَ اَكِسَفِرِشَ نَزُبُ كِپِكَ هند كُفَايَ بِعَشَرَ نَايِ اَلِنُ
بَخَتِ سَنَ يِمَالِ نَمَرَ مُوْجَ اَلسَفِرِ كِجَانَ تَكِ كَبَتَ مَعَدِنِ
يَفِضَ كَيَ نَيُ پَتِ كَفَايَ وَتُ كُيِفَايَ كَزِ كَبَتَ مَالِ مَغِ سَنَ
وَكَفَايَ زِتِرَ زَ فِيْضَ نغَازِ زَ فِيْضَ نَزُپُ زِغِ زَكُتُمِيَ فِضَ
نَايِ كَپَتَ زِجَنَ وَاِنِ بانه مكو ناحمد نابو بكر نعمر
نَايِ مُفَلُمِ اكف سنه ٧٩٧ كَتَولِ رُيِ* احمد بن عمر بن محمد بن احمد بن محمد بن
سليمان كَكِتِ نَوَتُ >>
كَامَانِ نَسَيْرَ جِمَ سَنَ اَكَفَ سته ٨٤٠ كُستَحَركِ يَبُ كَتَوِلِ مُلُكُ //

ابو بكر بن محمد بن عمر بن محمد بن احمد بن محمد بن سليمان كَكِتِ كَسِيَارَ
جِمَ نَمجِ يُتِ كَتِكَ >>
طاع يَكِ اكف سنه ٨٧٥ نَايِ كَخَلِفُ زِجَنَ وَوِلِ محمد ناحمد كتول
محمد بن ابو بكر بن محمد المذكور وَقَتِ وَاكِ وَكَيَ وَزُغُ پُرتُغِيْسِ كَتِكَ
مجِ يَسَوَاحِلِ يُتِ وَكَكِتِ ممباسه وَكَفَايَ غُوْمِ نَجَنِبُ يِپَتِ
وَكَجِغَ اندوْندُ نَوَاتُ وَبَرَ وَكَوَ فُوَات وَكِوپَ* مَالِ
وَكَوَ كَتِكَ طَاعَ يَوُ وَكَمُعَرِضِ مُفَلْمُ وِيَتِ كَتِكَ نْتِ يِپَتِ
وَكَمُبِجَ مُفَلُمِ زِتَ كَجَانِبُ يَشِدَكَاسِ وَكَوكَ نَنْتِ يِبَنِ
كَمعَنِ يَتُتُتُ الي الانَ مَوَاشِ يَپُ قَصدِ يَكُبِجَ يُوْمْپَ زَمُجِ
وِيَتِ وَسِوزِ كِسَ وَكَبَتَانَ كَاءَ مَانِ وَكَفَايَ مِكَاتَبَ يَشُرْطِ
زَاوُ وَكَكِتِ پَتِ وَزُغُ وَكَفَايَ فُرُضَ كَجِنَ لَوَزُغُ
وِلِتَمْكُوَ فَنْدِكَ وَكَفَايَ نَمَپُ مَغِ كَتِكَ كِسِوَ تَبَتِ اَكَفَ
مُفَلُمِ سنه ٩٠٠ كَخَالِفُ زِجَنَ وَوِلِ بانه مكو نا ءَبو بَكَرِ
كَتَوِلِ ابو بكر بن محمد بن ابو بكر بن محمد بن عمر بن محمد بن احمد بن محمد بن سليمان كَكِتِ نَوَزُغُ >>
كَامَانِ كَمَ قَعِدَ يَبَبَاكِ اَكَفَ سنه ٩٤٠ كُستَحَرِكِ يَپُ نَايِ كَخَلِفُ
زِجَانَ وَوِيل احمد ومحمد كَتَوِلِ رُيِ* بانه مكو بن محمد المذكور
وَكَوَ نَختِلاَفُ يِيِ نَوَزُغُ لاَكِنِ بَسِوِ نْزِتَ نِفِتِنَ سِكُ يِغِ
وِلاَ هَوَ كُعَرِضِيَنَ اَكَفَ سنه ٩٧٣ كَخَالِفُ كِجَانَ اُمُوْيَ هِتَ ابو بكر
كَتَوِلِ محمد بن ابو بكر بن محمد بن ابو بكر بن محمد بن عمر بن محمد بن احمد بن محمد بن سليمان >> //

اَكَصِلِحِيَنَ نَوَزُغُ وَكَتَاءَ بَعَضِ يَمجِ اَكَفَ سته ١٠٠٢ كَوَتَ كِجَانَ جِنَ لَكِ

ابو بكر اَستَوِلَ كَتَولِ ابو بكر بن بانه مكو بن محمد بن ابو بكر بن محمد بن عمر بن محمد

بن احمد بن محمد بن سليمان كَكِتِ نَوَزُغُ كَمَ سِيَارَ يَوِلِيُ تَغُلِيَ

وَزِيْ وَاكِ لاَكِنِ يَتِ اِيُغُزِي غُفُ اَكَفَ سنه ١٠٤١

كَوَتَ زِجَنَ وَوِلِ ابو بكر نبان مكو كتول ابو بكر بن محمد بن ابو بكر

بن محمد بن ابو بكر بن محمد بن عمر بن محمد بن احمد بن محمد بن سليمان اِكَوَ

اِختِلاَفُ نَوَزُغُ >>

پُرُتغِيْسِ كَبِجَانَ نَوُ كَوَ فُدَ وَزُغُ بَعَدَ يَزِتَ زِغِ سَنَ

بَعَداَيِ زِكَجَ تِنَ زِتَ زَوَزُغُ وَكَبجَ مُجِ وِيَتِ كَمزِغَ

وَكَزِوِيَ نَدِيَ بَحَرِنِ كُسِبتِ تُوْپُ وَاتُ وَكَوُنَ مَشَكَ سَنَ

وَكَفَايَ امانِ اَكَفَ مُفَلُمِ سنه ١٠٦١ كَوَتَ زِجَنَ وَوِلِ

بانه مكو ناحمد كَتَولِ بانه مكو بن ابو بكر بن مانه* مكو بن محمد بن ابو بكر بن

محمد بن عمر >>

بن محمد بن احمد بن محمد بن سليمان اَكَبَتَ نَ نَوَزُغُ سَنَ نَايِ اَلِپِدَ سَنَ

كَكِتِ لاموه حَتَي مُوْسِمُ كُوِيَتَ لاموه كَفَايَ عروس كَوَتُ

وَلاموه نَكَتِكَ وَقَتِ هُنُ وَفَمَاوُ وَتُ وَسِيُوْ وِلِتُكَ

كَتِكَ طَاعَ يَكِ اَكَوَ بجَ كَفُوْندا نَمجِ وَسِيُوْ كَوُفُدَ بَعَضِ

كَشِكَ نَوَاتُ وَغِنِ كَتِكَ وَتُ وَسِيُوْ كَوِيَتَ يَتِ

مُكُوبَ وَسِيُوْ كَكِبِيَ اَكِدَ نْدُوْنْدُ كِپُرْ تُغَالِ كَتَاكَ //

حمايه مْكُوپَ وَپُرْتُغَالِ اَكَجَ كَتِكَ وَاتُ وَسِيْوُ كَمُفَلْمِ كَوَسَامِحِ
اَكَپُوَ كَوَرِجِزِ مَهَلَ پُوَ سِيْوُ كَتِكَ اَمَانِ بَعَدَايِ پُرتُغَالِ
كَفَايَ حِلَ اَكَجَ پَتِ كَمَرِكَبُ اَكَمُتَكَ مُفَلْمِ كِرَ* مَرِكَبُنِ
اَسِرِ* كَمُبِكَ ابن عَمِيَكِ بانه مكو يِيِ نَوَاتُ وَيَتِ وَزُغُ
وَكَوَ تِكُوَ كَتِكَ مَرِكبُ كَوِبِكَ كَاءُ زُغُنِ اَسِرِدِ حَتَى مُتُ
اُمُوْجَ بَعَدَ يَهَپُ مُفَلْمِ كَوِبجَ وَزُغُ كَجَانِبُ زُتِ كَبَرانِ
زِسوِانِ* كَوَ تُوَ جَانِبُ زَ هُكُ وَكَكَمْبِلِيَ ممباسه بَعَدَ
يَهَبُ اَكَفَ مُفَلْمِ سنه ١١٠٠ كَوَتَ زِجَنَ وَوِلِ بو بكر نبانه مد
نَبِنتِ اُمُوْجَ هِتَ مَانَ دَرِنِ كَتول بانه ابو بكر بن بانه مكو بن ابو بكر
بن مكو بن محمد بن ابى بكر بن محمد بن عمر بن محمد بن احمد بن سليمان اَكَپجُوَ
غَفُلَ نَاحمد>>
رُيِ* بانه مكو اَلِيُ تِكُلِوَ نَوَزُغُ نَايِ الِمبجَ اُبَغَ اكف سنه ١١٠٣ كتولِ يِيِ
احمد بن ابو بكر بن محمد بن ابو بكر بن محمد بن عمر بن محمد بن احمد بن محمد
بن سليمان نكسَ كُتَوِلِ >>
اَكَمُؤَوَ نَبَانَ مَدِ رُيِ* مُفَلْمِ كَوَدَامَ بُرْتُغَالِ كَوَ تُوَ كَتِكَ نْتِ
زَاكِ زُتِ نَوَقَتِ هُنُ مَنَ دَرِينِ بِنتِ بانه مكو بن ابو بكر
مْكِ وَ بانه مُكُو بن ابى بكر اَلِيُ كِدَ غُوَ كَتِكَ زَمَنِ زَ سلطانِ احمد
اَكِسَ كُوُ وِلِوَ رُزِ* وَوِلِ بو بكر نبانَ مَدِي نَمُوْمِ وَاكِ كِدَ غُوَ
كَبَتَ حُزُ نِ سَنَ حَتَي زِكَبِتَ سِكُ يِغ كَتَكَ كُمُتَهِرِ كِجَانَ تَكِ
بان تَامُ مُتُتُ اَلِيُ اَمُكُلِوَ سلطان ابو بكر امام الهدى كِجَانَ وبانه مُكُوُ
اَلِيُ كِدَ غُوَ مُفَلْمِ اَلِيپُ پَتَ خَبَرِ يَحَابَ مَنَ دَرِنِ //

مِعَزِمُ كُفَايَ عَرُوسي كُمُتَهِرِ كِجَانَ تَكِ نَايَ مُفَلِّمِ كَعَزِمُ عَرُوسِي كُوتَهِرِ زِجَنَ
زَكِ مَعَنَ كُمُخنِ مَانَ دَرِنِ سِيْوَ اَكِسَ كُيُوَ خَبَرِ مَانَ
دَرِنِ كَمِتَ مِي بَيَاي بن مكو جمال الليل اَلِكُوَ هُدَرِ سَنَ كَزِ يَوُجُمِ
كَتَكَ اَمُفَيِزِ سِوَ اِشدِ سِوَ يَبَتِ كَرِضِكَ اِجَرَ رِيَال مِيَ عشرين
اَكَمُپ پِپِ زَ دُفُ كَتِؤُوَ مُجَ اَكَفَايَ سِوَ كَسِرِ حَتَي سِكُ
يَلِپُ كِسَ كَيِظِهِرِشَ غَفُل كَبِكَ كَتِكَ مَجُبَ يَجَمَعَ زَاكِ كُلَ مُتُ
كِتُوْزَ حَتَي فُوندي كَسِمَ مِمِ سِتَكِ اُجِرَ نَتَكَ تُزُ كَپُوَ كَبَتَ
مَالِ مَغِ كَتُوْزُ كَفَايَ عروسي يَكِجَانَ تَكِ حَتَي زَمَنِ يَبَانَ
تَامُ مُكُو وَكَجَ وَاتُ وَلَامُوه كَزِمَ سِوَ يَبَتِ يَاصِل كَوَپَ
تُپُ كِكَفَ مَايِ بَحَرِنِ سِوَ اِكَفُتُ بَانَ تَامُ كَيِتَكَ سِيْوَ
يَمَنَ دَرِنِ كَمَبِيَ تُبِ تُتُمِي كَتِكَ مُوْيِ مَانَ دَرِنِ
كَمَبِيَ سِوَ هِنِ زَ كُلَ قَبَايِل اَلِيُ تُزَ نَتُمِي كَوَتَ نَمُتُوْمَ حُرِ
اَيُوَا ءُ كُفُزِيَ سِوَ اَكَسِمَ هُيُ رِيِ* مِي كُبجَ سِوَ هِنِ يِيِ
نَنَسِلَ يَكِ نَعَدَ يَكِ نِرِيَالِ تَنُ نَغُوُ يَكُتُكُلِيَ سِوَ نكُبُوَ
سَمُلِ يَكُوْنَ مِي كُفُزِيَ نَتُوزُ كُلَ مُتُ كَقَدَرِ يَكِ اَوِزَا ءُ
وَكِيْتَ نَسِلَ يَوُ مُيُپِ وَ سِوَ حَتَي يِوُ وَاكُ وَتُوِ اِكَوَ تَغُ //

وَقَتِ هُنُ هُتُمِوَ نَقَبَايِلِ زِيَتِ نَوَتُ وَمِيْ مِغِنِ هِدَ كَزِمَ كَشَرُطِ
هِزُ كُبُوَ مُيُپِ وَسِوَ الي الانَ زِكَزِدِ فِتِنَ داِن يَمُجِ
نكَتِكَ اُفَلُمِ وكِ يَكَ سَبَعَ مِكَفُ هَبَنَ مِفُوَ اَكَيِغُزُلُ
سنه ١١١١ كَتَولِ سلطان ابي بكر بانه تَامُ مكُو وبَان مُتِتِ
بن احمد بن ابي بكر بن عمر بن احمد بن عمر بن محمد بن احمد بن محمد بن
سليمان اَكَبَتَنَ >>
سَنَ نَمُفَلُمِ وَمَسْكَتِ الامام سيف بن نبهان اليعربي نَهُويُ
مُفَلُمِ وپَتِ اَكِدَ عَرَبُونِ وَكَو غَنَ مُفَلُمِ وَعَربُونِ
نَمُفَلُمِ وپَتِ كُوَ تُوَ پُرُتُغَالِ ممباسه اَلِپُ رُدِ عَرَبُوْنِ
مُفَلُمِ وپَتِ كَبِكَ زِتَ ممباسه كَوَبِجَ پُرُتُغَالِ سِكُ
يَجُوْمَ يَبِلِ وَكَفَ پُرُتُغَالِ واَتُ وَغِ سَنَ كَتَملكِ غُوْمِ
يممباسه كَمُعَرِفُ الامام سيف بن نبهان اليعربي اَكَ ءِيْتَ
الوالي كَتِكَ مزاريع واَتُ وتَتُ محمد بن عثمان نعلي بن عثمان
وتَتُ نِسِمُيَهَوُ* جِنَ نَاوُ وَلِكُوَ دُغُ مُوْيَ وَكَجَ نَعَسْكَرِ طرف
الامام سيف بن نبهان اليعربي رِيُ اَصِلِ يَمَزَارِيع كُجَ ممباسه
نَمُفَلُمِ وپَتِ اَلِكتِ نَرَعِيَ سَنَ كَتِمِزَ يَكِ اربعين كَتِكَ وُفَلُمِ
اَكَفَ سنه ١١٥٢ كَوَتَ زِجَنَ وَغِ بَعَدَ يَكِ وَسِتَولِ زِجَنَ
زَكِ كَتَولِ احمد * ابو بكر بن محمد بن ابي بكر بن عمر بن احمد بن عمر بن محمد
بن احمد بن محمد بن سليمان >>
اَكَكِتِ سَنَ نَوَتُ نَايِ اِكپِدَ سَنَ غُبِ كَوكَ غُپِ وَغِ اَكَف سنه ١١٦٠
كَوَتَ كِجَانَ كَمِتَ بان غُوْغُ اَسِتَولِ اَكَتَولِ بان تَامُ مُتُتُ //

اَمكُلِوَاءُ سلطان ابو بكر امام الهدى كِجَانَ وبانه مْكُوْ اَلِيُ تُكُلِوَ نيرتُغَالِ
اَكَيِتَ زِتَ امامِ العرب سيف بن نبهان اليعربي كُبِجَ بَتِ وَسوزِ
وَكَفَ وَعَربُ وَغِ وَكَفَايَ اَمَانِ بَعَدَ يَهَپُ وَتُ ولاموه
وَكَخَالِفُ كَوَبِجَ زِتَ مُفَلُمِ وَبَتِ اَسوَ وزِ وَاتُ ولاموه
نَوَاتُ وَلاموه وَكَفُغَ زِتَ كُبِجَ بَتِ وَكَيِ نَجِيشِ جَانِبُ يَكِتَكَ
وَكَبِجَانَ نَوَتُ وَيَتِ زِتَ زِكُوپَ سَنَ وَكَفُدِك كَوَتُ
وَلاموه وَكَرَجِيَ لاموه مُفَلُمِ وَيَتِ كَفَايَ زِتَ كَبَحَرِ كَيَ
كُوَبِجِ وَتُ وَلَاموه كَوَ تَمَلَكَ بَعَدَ يَهَپُ وَكَوَ حَالِ مُوْجَ
وَتُ وَيَتِ نَوَاتُ وَلامام* اليعربيْ وَكَفَايَ شَوُرِ* وَكَمُوَوَ
مُفَلُمِ سنه ١١٧٧ كَتَولِ رِيَ* مَنَمُكِ سلطان مانه خديجه بنت بانه مكو بن ابى بكر
بن محمد بن ابى بكر بن محمد بن ابى بكر بن محمد بن عمر بن محمد بن احمد بن
محمد بن سليمانِ اَكَبَتَ فِتِنَ >>
يِغ كَتِكَ نْتِ يَبَتِ اِكَوَ كَتِكَ نْتِ يَبَتِ وَفَلُمِ وَولِ مَانه خديجه
المذكوره سلطان* عمر وَكَبِجَانَ كَتِكَ مْجِ وَبَتِ كَكَبِيَ سلطان
عمر اَكَدَ بَرَاوَه كَرَجِيَ يَتِ كَغُفُ كُوپَ سَنَ
وَكَبِجَانَ نَوَاتُ وَمَنَ خَدِيجه زِتَ زِكُوپَ سنَ كِلَ مْتُ كَكِتِ
مَهَلَ پَكِ بَعَدَ يَهَايُ مَنَ خَدِيجه اَكَفَ سنه ١١٨٧ كَمَرَضِ
كَتَولِ بانه مْكُو وَشِي وبانه تَامُ مْكُوُ رَعِيَ وَكَمُفِيزَ اُذِيَ سَنَ
اَسِتَبِتِ رَاحَ حتي سنه ١١٩١ وَكَمُغَلِيَ وَاتُ وَمُوْيِ وَكَمُوُ و كتاريخ
هِيُ كَتَولِ بَانَ فُوْمُ مَدِ اِنَ لَكِ سلطان محمد بن ابي بكر //

بن محمد بن ابى بكر بن محمد بن ابى بكر بن محمد بن عمر بن محمد بن احمد بن
محمد بن سليمان كِسَ كُتَولِ رَعِيَ >>
وَكَتَكَ كُفَايَ فِتِنَ كَوَبجَ كَزِتَ كَوَ شِدَ اَكَشِكَ وَاتُ اربَعينَ
وَكَاوُ نكَتِكَ اربَعينَ هَوُ وَوِلِ نِدُزِ يِيِ مُفَلُمِ خَصَ كَوَتِدَ كَمَ
بُوْزِ جُوُ يَسَكَفُ دَمُ اِكِشُكَ كَتِكَ مَكُپُ* اِكَوَ امَانِ
اَسِتُكِ مُتُ تِنَ كُتَكَ كُفَايَ فِتِنَ كَتَولِ كَامَانِ نَرَحَ
نَرَعِيَ وَكَوُن رَاحَ سَنَ حَتَي سنه ١٢٢٤ اَكَفَ بَعَدَ يَكِ
هكُتَولِ تِنَ مُفَلُمِ كَراحَ كَمَ يِيِ اَكَخَالِفُ زِجَنَ وَاغِ كَتَول
سلطان احمد بن شيخ بن فوم لوط بن بانه تَامُ مُكُو اِكَزِدِ فِتِنَ
كَتِكَ مُجِ وَلَاَموه اَكيَ كَوَبجَ زِتَ سنه ١٢٢٧ يِيِ نَوَاتُ
وممباسه مُزَاريع وَكَيِتَ نَوَاتُ وَكَشُكَ شِيْلَ جَيِش يِغِ سَنَ
يَوَتُ وَيَتِ نَواتُ وممباسه وَتُ وَلاموه وكَتُكَ وَكَج شِيْلَ
وَكَبِجَانَ نَوُ زِتَ زِكُوپَ سَنَ زِتَ زَوَاتُ وَلاموه
زِكَوَ نَغُفُ سَنَ جَيِش ممباسه نَپَتِ زلِپُ فُدِكَ زِتَ وَكجَ
مَجَهَزِنِ يَوُ مَغِن يَمِجَحَبُ* وَكَسِمَامَ هَپُ وَكَبِجَانَ زِتَ
زِكُوبَ سَنَ وَكَفَ وَتُ وَغِ وممباسه نَوَ پَتِ هَبَنَ
عِدَدِ كَتِكَ وَتُ وَيَتِ وَلِيُ مَعَرُوْفُ اِسُكُوَ
وَتُوْمَ نَوَتُ ضَعِيفُ وَاحِدِ وثمانين فلان بن فلان
وِيِ وكِ يَكِدَ مَعِدَ هَيُ نَوَتُ وممباسه بَالِ بَعَد يَهَپُ
وَاتُ ولاموه وَكِدَ عَرَبُونِ وَكَمُتَكَ سيد سعيد بن سلطان //

وَكَمُبَ نْتِ سنه ١٢٢٨ رِبُ* سيد سعيد بن سلطان بن الامام اَلِپُ توَلِ لاموه نوُفَلْمِ وپَتِ
وُكَسَلِيَ >>
كَتِكَ جزيره يَبَتِ كَتُكَ نَمُتُ وَبِيْلِ كَتِكَ زِجَنَ زَبَنَ فُومُ مَدِ فُومُ لُوْطِ كِپُغَ
كَبِجَانَ نسلطِان احمد اَكَفَ سلطان احمد كَمَرِضِ سنه ١٢٣٠ كَتَولِ فُوْمُ لُوْطِ وبانه
فُوْمُ مَدِ نَايِ اَلِكُوَ مُتُ هُدَرِ سَنَ شُجَاعَ كَرِيُم نَزمَنِ هِزُ نَزَمَنِ هِزُ* دِپُ* اَلِپُ
تَوَلِ وُشيحِ* شيح* متاكا بن شيخ مبارك كُتَولِ سِيْوِ كَفَايَ بُدُكِ نَعَسْكَرِ نَايِ نِكَتَكَ
طَاعَ يسلطان وپَتِ نَايِ اَلِبَتَ نَ سَنَ نَمُزَارِيْعِ وَاتُ وَممباسه
حتى سنه ١٢٣٦ اِكَزِدِ فِتِنَ بَينَ يَكِ سلطان* زنجبار سيد سعيد بن سلطان اكف سلطان
فوم لوط اَكَفَ مَكَ هُن بَعَدَ يَكِ كَتَولِ فوم لوطِ بن شيخ بن فوم لوط بن شيخ وبانه تَامُ
مُكُوُ نَهُويُ رِيِ* پِپَاكِ سلطان احمد سلطانِ وِتُ كَتَولِ اَصْبُحِ حتى بَعَدَ صَلاَةِ
العصرِ وَاتُ وَمُوْيِ وَكَمُتُو كِدَ سِيْوُ بَمُوْجَ نَمُزَرِيْعِ كِسَ اَكِد ممباسه كتول سلطان
بانه شيخ وبانه فُوْمُ مَدِ كَبَتَنَ نَسَيِدِ سعيد بن سلطانِ كَتِيَ وَعَرَبُ بَتِ وَكَكِتِ
يَكَ مِتَتُ بَعَدَيِ وَاتُ وَمُجِ وَكَمُعُزَلُ بَمُويَ نَشَوُرِ لسيد سعيد بن سلطان كتاريخ
سنه ١٢٣٩ وَكَمُتَولِشَ سلطان احمد امُكُلِوَاءُ بانه وزير وبانه تَامُ وبانه
شيخ وبانه تامُ مُكُوُ اَكَبَتَنَ سَنَ سَيد * سعيد كَتَوَلِ يَكَ مِولِ
وَاتُ وَمُجِ وَكَمُعُزُلُ وَكَمُرجِيزَ بانه شيخ و بانه فُوْمُ مَدِ
كَكِتِ كَتِكَ عِزِ كَشَوُرِ سيد سعيد بن سلطانِ يَكَ مِتَانُ
اَكَفَ سنه ١٢٤٧ اَكَرجِيَ بانه وَزِيْرِ كَتِكَ وُفَلْمِ اَكِجَ فُوْمُ
لُوْطِ بن شيخ اَلِيُ كِدَ ممباسه يِيِ نَمُزَارِيع وَكَشِكَ سِيْوُ وَكَبِجَانَ
نَبَانَ وَزِيْرِ وبانه تَام بَتِ نَبَانَ وَزِيْرِ بَمُوجَ نسيد سعيد
بن سلطان نَفُوْمُ لُوْطِ المذكور بَمُوْجَ نَمُزَارِيْعِ //

سيح* متاكا بن شيخ مبارك شيخ وَسِيْوُ وَكَجَ بَتِ كَزتَ وَكَبِجَانَ
وَتُ وِيَتِ وَكَشِكَ نْتِ يَسِوُ وَكَفُوْنَدا نَوُكُتَ
وَمُجِ وَسِيْوُ نشيخ متاكا بن شيخ مبارك نَفُوُم لُوْطِ وَكَتُكَ
سِيْوُ وككِبِلِيَ بَرَانِ بَعَدَ يَسِكُ تَتِ وَكَرجِيَ
سِيْوُ كَزتَ زِكُوْپَ سَنَ وَكَوُ شِكَ* مْجِ وَسِيْوُ
وَكَجغَ وُكُتَ وَكَبِجَانَ بَتِ نَسِوُ بَعَدَيِ اَكَفُ فُوْمُ
لُوْطِ كَتَغَايَ بَانَ وَزِيْرِ سِوُ نَپَتِ اِكَوَ كَتِكَ طَاعَ
يَاكِ بَمُوْجَ نَشَوُرِ سيد سعيد بن سلطان بن الامام بَعَدَ
يَمكَ اُمُوْجَ اَكَؤُوَاءَ سلطانِ بانه وزيرِ و بانه
تَامُ وبانه شيخ وبانه تَامُ مُكُو نسُلطانِ فوم بكر
وبانه شيخ وبانه فُوْمُ مَدِيِ النبهانِى كَتَولِ
يِيِ وُفَلُمِ وِيَتِ سنه ١٢٥٠ الف ومايتين وخمسين
هجريه اَكَبَتَنَ سَنَ يِيِ نسيد سعيد سلطان بن الامام
سلطان زنجبار مُدَ وُلِيْ وَكُتَوَلِ كِيْسَ //

كَخَلِفُ بَمُوِيَ نشيح* متاكا سيد سعيد كَيِتَ زِتَ نَاءَ مير* الجيش نَاءمير
حماد بن حمد السمار كَزِبجَ پَتِ نَسِيْوُ اَسِوزِ كَفَايَ اَمَانِ
بَعَدَ يَهَبُ اِكَوَ فِتِنَ بَيِنِ يسلطان وَبَتِ نَعَمِيَكِ محمد
بن احمد وبانه فوم مدى اَكَشِكَ يُوْبَ يَوُفَلُمِ كَزِيْتَ
كِيْسَ وَكَجَ وَتُ وَلاموه بَمُوِيَ نَمُتُ وسيد سعيد بن سلطانِ
وَكَوَ صِلِحِشَ سلطان فوم بكر نمحمد بن احمد كَبِكَ سِيْوُ
كُكِتِ فُوْمُ بَكَرِ كَكِتِ پَتِ بَعدَي وَكَتِتَ وَكَبِجَانَ
يَكَ مِتَنُ سِوُ نَپَتِ كِسَ كَوَ بَتَنِشَ سيد بن سعيد بن سلطان اَكَجَ پَتِ
محمد بن احمد وَكَوَ شَوُرِ مُجَ نَفُوْمُ بَكَرِ كِسَ فُوْمُ بَكَرِ كَمُشِكَ
غَفُلَ كَمُؤُوَ كَشَوُرِ مُوْجَ يِيِ نَمُتُ وَسِيْوُ كِسَ سعيد بن سلطان
كَمِتَ سلطان فوم بكر اَكِدَ اغُوْجَ سيد كَمُفُوْغَ فُوْمُ بَكَرِ كَشَوُرِ
لَوَاتُ ولاموه نكَسَبَبُ يَكُمُؤُوَ ابن عَمِيَكِ محمد بن احمد نكُوَتَ
كُفُوَاتَ صُلُحُ يَكِ اَلِيُ فَايَ يِيِ سيد سعيد كَتِكَ تاريخ سنه ١٢٦٢
اَكَشِكَ پَتِ سلطان احمد بن شيخ بن فوم لوط بن شيخ وبانه تَام مُكُوُ
كَشَوُرِ سيد سعيد بن سلطان اَكَكِتِ كَتِكَ شَوُرِ لَسَيِدِ سعيد
يَكِ مِولِ وَكَتِكَ* نسيد اَكَجَ سيد سعيد كَمُبجَ اَكَشُكَ امير حماد بن حمد
فازه كَبجَ سِيْوُ نسيد كَمُفُغُوَ سلطان فوم بكر اَكَمُپَ نَزِتَ
بَمُوِيَ نَوَاتُ وَلَاموه وَكَكِتِ مُتَغَ وَاندا كَتِكَ زِبُ*//

يِيِ سيد سعيد نامير حماد وَكِدَ پَزَ سَيِدِ سعيد بن سلطان كَكِتِ مَهَلَ
هِتَ كِجَاغَ تَمُبُوغَ قَربُ يَفاره* اَمير حمادِ اَكَجَ سِيْوُ
كَوكَ مَبُوْمَ كَتِكَ دِيَ يَفَازه نسيوي امير حماد اَكِدَ سِيْوُ
كَزِتَ حَتَى كَشِكَ مِتِپِ اِلِيُكُ بَدَرِنِ سِيُو كَبِدُوَ
كَفَايَ مَبُوْمَ كَبِجَ سِوُ كَوُنَ وُذِيَ سَنَ مُدَ وِلِپُ كُوَ
مغِ سَنَ وَزِتَ كَرُدِ امير حماد نَبَعَضِ يَوَاتُ كِدَ بُمَانِ
كُتَاءَ مْزِغَ كِبَتَ دِيَنِ وَتُ وَسِيْوُ وَكَمُتُكِيَ غَفُلَ
امير وشيخ متاكَ حمد عمر نَاءَ مير وبْيلِ حمد غُوْمَ وَكَبِجَانَ دِيَنِ وَكَمُؤوَ
اَمِرِ حَمادِ وَكِدَ نَمبُمَانِ وَكَوَبِجَ نَوعرابُ وِلِيُكُ بُمَانِ
وَكَتَاءَ مِزغَ نَزَانَ نَجَيِش اِلِيُكُ سِوُ هُبِجَانَ وِلِپُ
پَتِ خَبَرِ يَاءَمِرِ حمادِ كُوَ جَيِش يِسَيِدِ اِكَفُدِكَ نَاوُ وِلكُوَ
وَمِسهُتَمَلِكِ* سِوُ سيد سعيد كِسَ كُبَتَ خَبَرِ يَمَوُتِ يحماد بن حمد
كَغِيَ مَرِكَبُونِ اَسِنِن نِيْنُ كِدَ زَاكِ مَسِكَتِ مَكَ وَيِلِ
كَرُدِ كَمُوكَ فُوْمُ بَكَرِ فَاره* اَكَبِجَ سِيْوُ نَپَتِ كَتِكَ وَقَتِ
هُنُ اَكَفَ شيخ متاكا كَمَرَضِ اِكَوَ خِتِلاَفُ كَزِجَنَ زَاكِ
كَتُكَ* اشيخ وَكَغِيَ كَتِكَ طَاعَ يَسيدِ محمد نابو بكر زِجَنَ
زَ شيخ متاكَ سيد كَمُپَ اَبو بكر بن شيخ متاك زِتَ بَمويَ نسلطان فوم بكر
كِدَ كُمُبِجَ سلطانِ احمد اَكِدَ ابو بكر بن شيخ متاكا بمويَ ناءَمِيْرِ//

وفوم بكر بانه مكو وحمد بن بَيشِ النبهانى وَكَغِيَ سِوُ وُسِكُ وَكَبِجَانَ حَتَى
وَكَفُدِكَ ابو بكر نَواتُ وَاكِ وَاتُ وسِوُ وَكَوَدَمَ يُوْمَ وَكَمُشِكَ
ابو بكر بن شيخ متاكا وَكَمُپِكَ كسلطان احمد بَتِ كَوُوَ نسلطان احمد
بَعَدَايَ كَسِمَامَ شيخ محمد بن شيخ متاكا طَرَفُ يسيد بن سلطان يِيِ
نَفُوم بَكَرِ سيد سعيد كَوَپَ زِتَ نَعَسْكَرِ نَغَرامَ وَكَمُبِجَ سلطان
احمد بن شيخ حَتَى وَكَمُتُوَ پَتِ سنه ١٢٧٣ اَكِدَ كَاوُ سِيْوُ اِكَوَ
نشيخ محمد بن متاكا طرفُ يَسَيِدِ كَمُپَ نَعَسْكَرِ كَوكَ غِرزَ وَكَتِتَ
نَمُت و سيد سعيد كَسَبَبُ مُتُ وَسَيِدِ اَلِفُوْ ندا باندا لَمُتِپ
اَلُوكَ شيخ محمد بن شيخ متاكا بِيْ يَغرزَ نشيخ محمد كفونده غِرِيزه
نكَتِكَ وَقَتِ هُوْنُ اَلِكُفَ سلطان احمد الملقب بانه مدوشي
بَبَكَ فُوُمُ بَكَرِ سلطان وِيْتُوه اَكَكتِ مَهَلَ پَكِ سلطان
احمد الملقب سيمپا سلطان وِيتوه نَقَبُلَ يشيخ محمد متاكا
اَسِيَفُدَ غِرزِ لَسِوُ يَلِتُكَ فِتِنَ يِيِ نَفُوُمُ بكر بن شيخ
كَمُتُوَ [فُوُمُ بَكَر بن شيح*] پَتِ اَكَجَ لاموه كَتَملكِ* پَتِ وَ لِپُ أُن غُفُ زَاكِ
وَكُوپَ وَبَتِ نكتِدُ مِزُ فَايَ شيخ محمد متاكا نَمِسُ اَتَكَ كُوَ
تَوِلِ وَسِكِرِ كَوَبِجَ زِتَ وَكَسِمَامَ وَكُوْپَ وِپَتِ
وَلَاَ هَوَنَ مُفَلُمِ كَشَوُرِ لَوَاتُ وَتَتُ محمد بن بانه مكو النبهانى
نَبَانَ رِحِمَ بن احمد النبهانى نَنَاصر بن عبد الله بن عبد السلام
رِيِ* الِيُ كُوَ مُدَبِرِ الامور وَكَكُسَايَ زَن وَكَبِجَانَ
نشيخ محمد متاكا وَكَمُشِدَ سَنَ وَكَفَ وَاتُ مَعَروفُ كَتِكَ //

مَاءَمِر وشيخ محمد متاكا بانه دمِيْلَ نمولانا وشي كُوْلِ شيخ محمد متاكَ
اكَيَ كُتَكَ امَانِ كمحمد بن بانه مكو كَانِ رِيِ* اَلِيُ كُوَ مُكُوپَ وَاءُ
كَتِكَ هَوَ وَتُ وَتَتُ تِمزُ وتَايَ وَكَبَتَنَ كُمپَ يِيِ محمد بن بانه مكو
اَفَلْمِ* وَسِيْوُ نَپَتِ اكَيِزَ كَسِمَ مِمِ نِمُتُ مْزِمَ وَكَدَ كُمُتَاءَ
سلطانِ احمد الملقب سيمپا [اَلِكُ كاوُ] خَبَرِ اِكَفِكَ كَسُلُطَانِ وَوُغَجَ
سيد ماجد بن سعيد كَمُيِتَ وَزِيْرِ وكِ سيد سليمان بن حمد كَمَرِكَبُ اكَجَ
اِلِ اَجِ پَتِ اُفوْندِ فِتِنَ نَمَرِكَبُ اِكوَ صِلِ مَارَ* پَتِ مكسَ
كُشِكَ مُتُ و سلطانِ احمد ابو بكر بن حسن البورى اَلِكُوجَ
نَايِ نِنَاصر بن عبد الله بن عبد السلام اَكِسَ كُبَتَ خَبَرِ سيد سليمانِ
بن حمد كَرِجِيَ وُغُوْجَ نشيخ محمد متاكا وقَتِ هُنُ رِپ*
اَلِپُ فُدَ غِرِزِ لَسِوُ اَكِسَ كُوَصِلِ سلطان احمد
پَتِ جَمِيْعِ يَواتُ وَكَمُبَاعِ كُوَ رِيِ* مُفَلْمِ نشِيخ محمد متاكا
نَمْزِيْ وَ سيْفُ نشيخ شكوه نمحمد مُوْتِ اُكَستَقِرِ
كُوَ سلطان احمد كُوا ندِيِ مُفَلَمِ* وَكَمُبَاعِ وَاتُ هَوَ وُتِ سيد ماجد
كَبِكَ وَاتُ وَلَامُوه پَتِ كَنُصْحَ بَمُوجَ نشيح* محي الدين
كُتَكَ سلطانِ احمد اَوِكِ عَسْكَرِ پَتِ نهوي شيخ
محي الدين رِيِ* اَلِيُ وَتُوَ عَسْكَرَ* وَسَيِّدْ سِيْوُ اَلِپُ
وَبِجِ زِتَ شيخ محمد متاكا عَسِكَرِ وِلِدَانِ يَغرِزَ
يِسِيْوُ شيخ محي الدين كَوَ تُوَ عَسْكَرِ كَامَانِ كَانِ
هُيُ شيخ محي الدين اَلِكُوَ مُتُ وَسَيِّد ماجد بن سعيد //

زَمَنِ اَلِپُ نَعَسْكَرِ وُغُوْجَ سَيِدِ مَاجِدِ كَفَايَ هَسِرَ سَنَ كُوَ
تُوَ عَسْكَرِ سِيْوُ كَتَاءَ دَرَكَ شيخ محي الدين اَلِپُ مُوُنَ
سَيِدِ مَاجِدِ مِفَايَ غَضَبُ نَهُوِيُ شيخ محي الدين اَلِنَ حِيْلَ
سَنَ نَعِلمُ يغِ اَكَجَ لاموه كَتُكُوَ نَخيَارِ يَواتُ ولاموه
نشيخ احمد نشيخ عبد الرحمن اولاد شيخ بَتهِ كُمُنَاصِحِ سلطان
احمد كَصُحُبَ يَلِيُ كُوَ بَينَ يَوُ كَرِضِكَ كُوكَ عَسْكَرِ
بَعَدَ يَشِدّه سَنَ اَكَخالِفُ شَوُرِ لَوَزِيْرِ وَاكِ ناصر بن عبد الله
كَانِ الِيزَ كُتِيَ وَعَرُبُ* حَتَي مُتُ اُمُوجَ كِيْسَ وَاتُ وِپَتِ
وَكَفَاىَ شَوُرِ نَمَانَ جَاهَ بنت السلطان فوم لوطِ كِبُغَ وَبَانَ
فُومُ مَدِ مُكِ و سلطانِ فووم بكر بن شيخ نَوَقَتِ هُنُ فوم بَكَرِ اُكُ
لاموه تِنِ يَشَوُرِ لَسَيِدِ ماجد بن سعيد تَغُ اَلِپُ تُلِوَ پَتَ* بَسِ
كُلَ سِكُ وَكِتِيَ عَسْكَرِ نزَانَ اُسِكُ كَسِرِ حَتَى اَلِپُ جُوَ خَبَرِ
سلطانِ احمد عَسِكَرِ ومِكُوَ وَغِ پَتِ اِكَوَ فِتِنَ وَكَمُبجَ
سلطان احمد غَفُلَ بَعَدَ يَكُتَكَ كُمُشِكَ كَحِيْلَ وَسِوزِ كَانِ
وَتُ وُتِ وِلِكُو شَوُرِ مُجَ نسيد مَاجد بن سعيد اِسُ كُوَ وَزِيْرِ
وَاكِ ناصر بن عبد الله عبد السلام* وَكَبِجَانَ داِنِ يَمُجِ وِپَتِ زِتَ زِكُوْپَ
سَنَ كَتُكَ سلطان احمد يِيِ نشيخ محمد بن متاكا وَكِدَ سِيْوُ
پَتِ وَكَكِتِ وَعَرَبُ طَرَفُ يسيد مَاجد نَبَحرِنِ كَتِيَ
مَرِكَبُ زِتَ زَلِپُ كُوَ زِ كُوُ سَنَ اَكَجَ يِيِ سيد ماجد بن سعيد //

وَكَحُرُص* كِسِوَ تَپَتِ كَبَحارِ كُسِبِتِ تُپُ كَتِيَ سِلِسِلَ كَتِكَ كَنَ
لَمُتُ وَ سِيْوُ كُوْيُ وَكَبِجَانَ يِزِ ستِه كَبَحرِ نكَجَانِبُ يَيِتِ نَجَنِبُ*
مُزِيْ وسِيْفُ كَخَالِفُ اَكَوَ مُتُ وَسَيِدِ مَاجِدِ كَحِيْلَ يِغِ نَمَنِيْنُ
مَغِ كَوُنَ ضِقِ سلطان احمد نشيخ محمد متاكا نَنْتِ يَسِوُ
اِكَوَ فِتِنِ بَعَضِ يَوَتُ وَبِدَ سيد مَاجِدِ كَسَبَبُ يَمَشَكَ
وَمِزُيَتَ نوَ تُوِ نِشَرِيف مولانا بن ابو بكر نعيسى بن احمد السمالي
وَلِپُ اُنَ هَايَ سلطان احمد نشيخ مَتَاكا وَكَتَكَ امانِ
كَسَيِدِ مَاجِدِ كَوَپَ اَمَانِ كَتِكَ مَنِنُ يَا ءَمَانِ سلطان احمد
كَسَفِرِ كَسِرِ اُ سِكُ اَكِدَ بَرَانِ كَرَجِيَ كَاوُ نشيخ محمد متاكا
اَكَمُبِكَ كَجَان تَكِ مَركبونِ شيخ بن محمد نسيد كمسامح كَمُپَ
نَحِشِمَ سَنَ سَيِدِ كَسَفِرِ اَكِدَ زاكِ اُغُوْجَ بَعَدَاي محمد بن متاك
اَكِدَ اُغُوْجَ كُمُواجِهِ سَيِدِ مَاجِدِ سَيِدِ كَمُفُوغ كَمُبِكَ غُمِنِ ممباسه
نوَتُ وَاغِ اَكَفَ بَعَدَ يَسِكُ تَتِ سلطانِ احمد اَلِكُو كَاوُ
كَبِكَوَ الوالى سعود بن حمد كُمُشِكَ كَحِيْلَ اَسِوزِ كَتُكَ كِدَ وِتُ الوالي
سعود بن حمد كَرَجِيَ لاموه اَكِدَ فازه كَفَايَ تَرَتِبُ كَمُشِكَ عمر متاكِ*
نَزجَنَ وشيخ محمد متاكا وُتِ وَكَشِكُوَ سِيْوُ وَكَجَ لاموه
عمر متاكا كَمُفُغَ لاموه زِجَنَ وُتِ كَوَبِكَ غُمِيْنِ ممباسه بَعَدَ
يَهَپُ كَتملكِ سيد ماجد سَوَاحِلِ زُتِ بَسِوِ نَمُتُ وَكُمُعَرِضِ نسلطان
احمد كَكِتِ وِتُ كَتِكَ طَاعَ يَسَيِدِ مَاجِدِ حَتَى وَقَتِ وسيد
بَرَ غَشِ بن سعيد اَكَتَكَ كُوكِ عَسْكَرِ وِتُ نَبدِرَ سلطان احمد //

اَسِرِضِك كَبِكَ زِتَ سيد برغش كَمُبِجَ سلطان احمد اَسِوزِ كَفَايَ
امانِ الوالي سعود بن حمد سيد برغش هكُمُفرَحِيَ تِنَ الوالي سعود بن حمد كَسَبَبُ
كُفَايَ اَمَانِ اُپِسِ نَايِ هكُمُبِجَ سَنَ زِتَ سيد برغش كَبِكَ تِنَ
زِتَ زَمَنِ نالوالي سعود بن حمد سلطان احمد كَتَاءَ حمايه كَجَرمَنِ
وَقَتِ هُنُ زِكَرُدِ زِتَ زَ سَيِدِ برغش كَكَتِ سلطان احمد كَتِكَ
حمايه يجرمَنِ وَكَمُپَ نَبَعَضِ يَبَرَ يَسَوَاحِلِ اَكَفَ سلطان
احمد حَالِ هِيُ كَتِكَ حمايه سنه ١٣٠٦ كَتَوَلِ فوم بكر بن سلطان احمد بن شيخ
كَتِكَ حَالِ هِيُ اَكَتُكَ فِتِنَ بَينَ يَكِ نَجَرمَنِ مُتُ اُمُوجَ هِتَ
كِنْسِلِ كَمُبِجَ بَوَبُ وَلَاغُ لَمُوْيِ كَرَصَاصِ وَلُكُوكُ نعَسِكَرِ تَاوُ
وَكَمُبِجَ كِنْسِلِ نَوَزُغُ وَلِيُ فُوتِنِ نَايِ وَكَوَاُ وَوُتِ
مِنْ غير اَمْرِ يسلطان فوم بكر عَسْكَرِ وَلِپُ مُوُنَ جَمَعَ يَوُ مِكُفَ
هَوَ كُغُجَ اَمْرِ نَوَتُ وَمُكُنْوبِ نَوَرَ* مُوْيُ وَلِپُ بَتَ خَبَرِ
يَكَاپَ وَزُغُ وَمِبِجَانَ وِتُ* نَوُ وَكَوَ اُوَ وَزُغُ
وَلِيُ كُوكِ بَعَدَايِ اَكَجَ دُوله تُكُفُ يَوَغِرِزَ وَكَتَكَ كُفَايَ
اِنْصَافِ وَكَتَكَ وَاتُ وُمكُنوب نَوَاتُ وَوَرَ* مُوْيُ
مَعَنَ اَوتِيِ كَتِكَ حُكُمُ اَسِرِضِكِ سلطان فوم بكر كُوَ تُوَ
وَكَمُبِجَ زِتَ زِكَيَ مَشُوَ حَتَى مُكُنوبِ نَوَرَ* مُوْيُ نكِلِمَانِ //

نَرَپِ* نَيَدُ زَ بَنِ وَكَزِبجَ كَمِزِغَ وَكَزِ تِيَ مُوْتُ حَتَى ليله ١١
ربيع الاول سنه ١٣٠٩ وَكَبِجَانَ وَاتُ وَوِتُ كَتِكَ نْدِيَ يَكِبِيْنِ
نَوَتُ وَدُله تُكُفُ وَاتُ وَوِتُ وَكَفُدِكَ حَتَى اَصُبُحِ
مِزِ ١٢ ربيع الاول سنه ١٣٠٨ وَكَمُبِجَ سلطانِ فُوْمُ بَكَرِ وِيْتُ
وَكَمُتُوَ كَزِيْتَ سلطان فوم بكر اَكِدَ جُغِيْنِ وِيْتُوه اِكَتَمَلَكِوَ
نَدُوْلَ تُكُفُ فوم بَكَر كَكِتِ جُغِيْنِ حَتَى مِزِ ٢٨ جماد الاول* سنه ١٣٠٨
اَكَفَ اَكَشِكَ مَهَلِ پَكِ رُيِ* بانه شيخ بن سلطان احمد بَعَدَ يَسِكُ
تَتِ اِكَوَ فِتِنَ اَكَشِكُوَه نَرُوْيِ* فُوْمُ عمر نَاءَ فُطول وبخيرُ
وَكَمُفِغَ بانَ شيخ يسلطان احمد كَتَوِلِ فُوْمُ عمر بن سلطان احمد بن شيخ
اِكَوَ كَمَ جِنْسِ يَلُ كُوَ بَيِنَ يَكِ نَدُولَه تُكُفُ اَمَ مُفَلُمِ وَكِسَ
كُتَملَكِ وِتُ نسلطان فوم عمر المذكور نَوَكِسَ كُتَملكِ پَتِ
نسلطان احمد سلطان وتُ الملقب سيمپا نَالِيُ تَمَلكِ كَادَ نسليمان
بن سليمان بن المظفر النبهاني امام العرب
هِنِ رِيُ* خَبَرِ يَنَبهانِ كُجَ سَوَاحِلِ نَخَبَرِ زَاوُ وَمِتَوِلِ وَفَلُمِ واحد وثلاثين
نَمَنَمُكِ اُمْوِجَ كَمَ تُمِزُ تَغُلِيَ كُتَاجَ مْپِلِ نَسِ تَلِنَقِلِ هَايَ كمحمد بن فوم
عمر النبهاني الملقب بانه كتيني نَايِ اَلِبُ كِيَ نَجَدِ يَكِ محمد بن بانه مكو
النبهاني الملقب بانه سيْمپَا كَانِ رِيِ* اَلُضِبِتِيِ سَنَ خَبَرِ زَ كَاي
نَنَسَبَ زَاوُ كَمَ تُمِزُ تَغُلِيَ كُتَايَ كتبه صالح بن سالم بن احمد بن عبد الله بن محمد
با شراحيل بيده >> //

هِزِ يَأَخبارِ زَ پَتِ نَزتَ زَاوُ نَسَبَ زَ نَبَهَانِ نَسِ
تَلِ نَقِلِ هَايَ سابقَا كمحمد بن فوم عمر نَايِ اَلِنَقِلِ كَجَدِ يَكِ
محمد بن بانه مكوُ النبهاني مُكُوْپَ وَ وَزِيْ وِيَتِ
ليعلم قمر* العصر* لله تعالى صالح بن سالم بن احمد بن عبد الله بن محمد بن عبد الله
با شراحيل بيده >> //

الول* المبدي الواصل بندر بته

الهجرة ٦٠٠ اخبار بته هاهنا سليمان بن سليمان * مظفر النباهاني
مْنُد وكنْد كُيَ بتِه نبَهانِيْ نسلِيمانِ بن سليمان بن مظفر نبهانِيْ نَرُزِ* ووِيْلِ
على بن سليمان نا عثمان بن سليمان نا هُيُ سليمان بن سيمان الذكور رِيِ*
اُل كُو سلطان نَيِ الِكُو سلطان اكِس كُتولِ بر يا لعرابُ* العربي*
اكيا بتِ سلطان المذكور كتارِيخ سنة ٦٠٠ من لهجر* كُيا كك بتِ
كتَك عَرُوْسِ كمْفَلُمِ و بته كتِك هوَالِ* بَتَوِيْ نَيِ سلطان سليمان
بن سليمان نِمْتُ معرُفُ مْفلُمِ وبِت اكمُ وزَ بنْتِ ياكِ ندستِر يوُت
يا سوحِيْلِ هت س س مْتُ اكُوُ لِيايِ كِجان
گَكُ اكِس سِكُ سبعه ز هرُوْسِ هِيدَ كُمَ غَلِي مْكِيْوِ يُوْمْبَنهِ ملكِ ببا
ومْكِ وكِ كو مْبِيَ وتُ هُيُ سليمان بن ريِ* مفلُمِ وِيْنُ اك مْبَ
وُفلُمِ وكِ الُ كُو نوُ اك تولِ سليمان كلِنا مُوْي هِيْت كتُكِ اِيُ
ياجَزرَ يا بتِه كتِك مطِلعِ يابتِ نسِوُ هت كُو مْجِ ولِكُ مْج مْغِنِ
هِيتَ شغَ كتِك مطِلعِ يابتِ* نا فَازَ ولِكُ مْجِ وِيوِ ويِز المفازى
اِككتِ مجِ هيُ يُوْت اِك كتِ يُوتِ تَحَتِ يا سلطان سليمان بن سليمان
نا مَانْدَ كلِنا مْفلُمِ مْبَلِ نَيِ اُنَ غُفُ سان اكف سلطان سليمان بن سليمان
سنه ٦٢٥ الهجر اكخَلِف زِجان و وِيْلِ محمد نا احمد محمد عُمْرِ وكِ يك
عِشرِيْنِ نا احمد عُمْرِ وكِ يك خَمُسْةَ* عَشَرَ اكتولِ محمد بن سليمان بن سليمان
بعد يا ببكِ اِكو ختِلَفُ يِيِ نوتُ و شغَ كبِجن نمجِ كِيا فُنْدَ
كبِس نا بعِض يوُ وَكَيَا بتِ نو غِنوِ قبِل يوُ كِنا دغُ وككِمْبِيَا

وسِيُو كَنِ مهالَ ولُ كِمْبِلِيَ هت سِكُ زِكِبِتَ اِكيا خبارِ كا سلطان
محمد بن سليمان نا هو وتُ وِرَوُ* كُونْدَ وكَمَبِيَ ولِ وشِوُ تُمِ وَوُنَ
كتكِ مِيْتُ سلطان كبِك وتُ كو اَغلِيَ كو دِرِك وَمِ فَيَ زِجُوْمْبَ
رَنِ* يا مِيْتُ سلطان محمد بن سليمان كو سَمِحِ كو رُدِش مهالِ بَوُ
رِيُ* اصلِ يا مُوْيِ وسوُ وَكيَا نَوَ سَوَحِيْلِ وَغِنِ وككِتِ وُتِ
وَكَيَا نَوَ فَمَوُ وككِتِ وُتِ وَكَوَ وفَمَوُ رِوُ* وكُ* وسِوُ كتِك طع يا
سلطان محمد بن سليمان اكف سنه ٦٥٠ اكتولِ رُيِ* سلطان احمد بن سليمان //
اَكَ اَمِرِشَ سان ارْضِ يا بتِ اكجغَ مَجُمْبَ كفنْيَ نمشامْبَهَ اسِبجِ
مهالِ كَفَ سنه ٦٦٠ كتولِ كجان گَنْدُيِ اِنَ للكِ احمد بن محمد بن سليمان اككِتِ
نوتُ كَوُزُرِ سان كَمَ سِيْرَ زَ عمِ زاكِ كُعَمِرِشَ مْجِ وبتِ نامَشامْبه
هت سنه ٧٠٠ اكف اكخلِفُ زِجان ونْغِ كتولِ كجان گكِ سلطان محمد
بن احمد بن محمد بن سليمان اككِتِ نوتُ كويْمَ سان وتُ وفَازَه وكخلِفُ
اكو بِجَ كوتِيَ كتِك طاع بعَد يزِت زِنْغِ هت الِبُ وشِدَ اَكَيِ
فُتَحِ نمَرَ* كَيِ تملكِ كِزت نَحِيْلَ كانِ الِن غُفُ سان سلطان وَ
مانْرَ* يمالِ نوتُ اك اِفُنْد كِبس نوتُ وغِنِ كواتِ بتِ نبعضِ وَ
كت و* نْيك وككمْبِلِي كُوْل مهالِ وغِنِ وكج شِيْلَهَ وكغِيا كتِك حِماي
يوتُ ولاموه سلطان محمد بن احمد المذكور كوتك وتُ ولاموْه وكَيِزَ
كُو تُو نوغِنِ وَكَيْدَ مَلِيْدِيْ نبعَضِ يَبُلْدَنِ سلطان محمد بن احمد اكو
اَنْدم سان هو ولِيُ كُوْجَ شِيْلَه وتُ ولاموْ وكيِز كوُ تُو قَطَعاً
منِنُ هي يَشِ يِسَ سلطان محمد اكف سنه ٧٣٢ كتولِ كِجان گكِ اُفَلْمِ
سلطان عمر بن محمد بن احمد بن محمد بن سليمان اكي رِجِي منِنُ يببوكِ كوتُ
ولاموْه كوتك وتُ ومانْر* وتُ ولاموْه وكيز كُوتُو كو بِجَ زِت

وكَتك امانِ وتُ ولاموْ وكو كتِك طع سلطان عمر بن محمد بن زِكَزدِ غُفُ
اكبج جُمْلَ يمج يا سوحِيْلِ اُوْز مَلِيْدِيْ كِوَ يُوْ كِتَوُ مِيَ اِمِيْذِيْ
وتامُ كَسلِكِ لِيَ كرِيمْبا مج يُوْتِ كَيِ تملاكِ تغُ بتِ حت كرِيمْبا كَالَ *
مْج كوك مْتُ اَكحُكمُ رِيُ* اصلِ يهو مجُوْمبِ لِيُ كُمرِيْمَ وُتِ
معَن ياكِ نِو تُوْمَ و يُوْمْبِي نهِيُ يُوْمبِ مع نَ نِيُومْبَ يَمْفلُمِ وبتِ
نجنبُ يمطِلعِ كَتَمَ لَكِ حت وَرْشِيخ اكنْد كُبجَ زِت تغُ كوِيَوْ نا
طُوِلَ نا طُوِلَ نا شُغَيَ نَبَنْدِيْرِ زُتِ بَارَوَ نَامَرِكَ نامُقْدِشُوْ
هبُ مُقْدِشُوْ كوك الوالي جمعِ يا حُكْمُ ز بَنَدرِ زكو مُقْدِشُوْ اك
عِشِ نا نْتِ زُتِ هِز كتِك طع ياكِ اِل وُغُجَ هكُ تولِ نوقتِ
هُوْ وُغُجَ هيكُوَ نْتِ كُوُبَ زمنِ هِزُ نا هُيُ سلطان عمر الكِد* زِتَ
نكُ بْند رَعِيَ نارعِي وَكِمْبد اِكتاءَ غُفُ سان نْتِ يا بتِ اكف سلطان
عمر سنه ٧٤٩ كخلِفُ زِجان ووِيْلِ محمد نا احمد كتولِ كِجانَ مْكُوْه سلطان //
محمد بن عمر بن محمد بن احمد بن محمد بن سليمان ولَ* هبكُو نَزِتَ * وُفَلمِ وبباكِ
كاامَنِ ني اِلكِبنْدَ سان مالِ يا بِيَشْرَ اَكِسفَرِش نازمْبُ زكِ هِندِيْ
كُفِي بِيَشْرَ نَيِ اَلِنَ بهتِ سان يا مالِ نمرَ مُوْيَ اِلْمسَفرِ شَ كِجان
گَكِ كبت كِسوَ كتِك باهرِ كبت معدنِ يا فِضه كيا نَيُ بتِ كفِي وتُ
كُيا فَيَ كزِ معدنِ كبت مالِ مغِ سان ياكزدِ مالِ كتك نْتِ يا بتِ
هت وكفِي زِترَ زَ فِضه نا غزِ زَ فِضه نَزمْبُ زِغِ زَ فِضه نِي
مْفلُمِ اكف سنه ٧٩٧ اكخلِفُ زِجان ونِ بانه مْكُوْه نا احمد نا ابو بكر
نا عمر اكتولِ رُيِ* سلطان احمد بن عمر بن محمد بن احمد بن سليمان اككِت
نوتُ كا اَمانِ نَسِيْرَ نْجِمَ نا جمعِ يوتُ اكف اكتولِ ابو بكر بن محمد
بن عمر بن محمد بن احمد بن محمد بن سليمان ككِتِ سان نا جمعِ يوتُ نامجِ يُوْتِ

كتِك طع ياكِ بِلا خِلَفُ سنه ٨٧٥ نَي اَلِ خَلِفُ زِجان زِويْلِ محمد

نا احمد اكتولِ بعد بباكِ محمد بن ابو بكر بن محمد بن عمر بن محمد بن احمد

بن محمد بن سليمان >>

وكتِ وكِ وكج وزُغُ بُرتُكَ لِ كتِك مْج يسَوَحِلِ يُوْتِ ككِتِ

ممباسه وكفي غُوْمِ نا جنبُ يا بتِ وكجغَ نْدُوْنْدُ وتُ وبرانِ

وكو فُوْتَ وكَوَب مالِ وكو كتِك طع يوُ وكَمُوَ رِضِ نا مْفلُمِ كتِك

نْتِ يا بتِ وك مْبجَ زِت مْفلمِ كجنبُ يا شِدَكَسِ وكو نْتِ يا

بتِ بانِ كمعن يا تُوْبِ كحِيْلِ يا كُبجَ مُوْيِ وبتِ وسِوزِ وكب

تن كا امانِ وكفي مْكتب وشرُتِ زَوُ وككِتِ بتِ وُزغُ و

كَفَيَ فُرُضَ كَجِنَ لوُ وزُغُ ولِ كَمْكُوَ فَنْدِكَ وكفي نَمبُ

مَغِ كتِكَ كِسِوِ كَبَتِ اكف سلطان سنه ٩٠٠ اكخلِفُ زِجان ووِيْلِ

بانه مْكُوُوْه نا ابو بكر اكتولِ وفَلُمِ سلطان ابو بكر بن محمد بن ابو بكر بن محمد بن

احمد بن محمد بن سليمان بعد يا بباكِ المذكور اككِتِ نَوتَُ سان

اكتُزَيَ كا اَمانِ كم قعْديا بباكِ اكف سنه ٩٤٠ كُسبَدِ لِك يبُ

نَيِ كخلِفُ زِجان ووِيْلِ احمد و محمد كتولِ عمِ يوُ وُفَلُمِ بانه

مْكُوْه بن محمد بن ابو بكر بن محمد بن عمر بن محمد بن احمد بن محمد بن

سليمان اِكَوَ >>

خِتِلفُ نوزُغُ لكِنِ بَسِوِ نا زِتَ اِكو فِتِن سكُ يغِ اكف سنه ٩٧٣ //

اكخلِفُ كِجان مْمُوْيِ هِيْتَ ابو بكر اكتولِ محمد بن ابو بكر بن محمد بن عمر بن محمد

بن احمد بن محمد بن سليمان اكصلِحِيْنَ نوزُغُ وكتاء بعضِ يامجِ اكف

سنه ١٠٠٢ اكخلِفُ كِجان مْمُوْيَ هِيْت ابو بكر استولِ كتولِ ابو بكر

بن بانه مْكُوْه بن محمد بن ابو بكر بن محمد بن عمر بن محمد بن احمد بن محمد

بن سليمان اككتِ >>

نوزُغُ كم سِيَرَ يا وَزِيْ وكِ ولُتَغْلِيَ نوُفلُمِ وكُبُغُوَ غُوُ اكَفَ

سنه ١٠٤١ اكخلِفُ بانه مْكُوْه نا ابو بكر كخِيْن* لببكِ اكتولِ ابو بكر بن محمد بن

ابو بكر >>

بن محمد بن ابو بكر بن محمد بن عمر بن احمد بن محمد بن سليمان اِكو خِتلِفُ نوزُغُ

وكبِجن كو فُنْدَ وزُغُ كزت زِكُوْ سان بعْدي* زِكيا تِن

زِت زوزُغُ وكبِجن مْوْيِ وبتِ كمزِغَ وكزوِيَ نا نْدِي كا

باحرنِ كُسبِتِ گُمْبُ وتُ وكوُن مشك وكفي امانِ اكفَ مْفَلُمِ سنه ١٠٦١

اكخلِف زِجان وويْلِ بانه مْكُوْه نا احمد اكتولِ بانه مْكُوْه وبانه بكر

وبَانهَ مْكُوْه بن محمد بن ابو بكر بن محمد بن عمر بن محمد بن احمد بن محمد بن

سليمان اكبتن نوزُغُ >>

سان ني الِكبِدَ سان كُكتِ لاموه هت مُسِمُ كُبِتَ لاموه اكفيا نا هَرُوْسِ

كوتُ ولاموه نكتكِ وقتِ هُنُ وفماوُ وَسِوُ ولِ تُك كتِك طع ياك

اكو بِجَ اكو فُنْدَ نَمْجِ وسِوُ كشِك نوتُ وغِنِ كوتِي بتِ مْكُوْبَ

وسِوُ اك كَمبِيَ اكِد دُوْدُ كَبُرتُغَالْ كت ءَ هماِيَ مْكُوْبَ ووزُغُ اكَجَ

بتِ كا مْفلُمِ اَوَ سَمحِ وتُ وسِوُ مْفَلُمِ كَوَ سَمحِ كو رِجز مهالِ يَوُ سِوُ

كتِك امانِ بعد ياكِ بُرتُغالْ اكفي حِيْلَ اكج بتِ كَمرَكَبُ اكمْتك مْفلُمِ كِدَ

مَركَبُن اَسِندِ اكمْبِك بِنْ عمِ ياكِ بانه مْكُوْه يِيِ نَوتُ وبتِ وَزُغُ وكو

تُكُوَ كَتِك مركبُ اسِردِ مْتُ هت مْمُوْيَ بعَد يا هيُ مْفلُمِ كوبِج

وزُغُ كجَنبُ زُتِ كبرانِ نزِسِونِ كَوَ تُوَ جنبُ ز هُكُ زُتِ وكِك

مْبِلِيَ ممباسه اكف مْفلُمِ سنه ١١٠٠ اكوت زِجان بانه بكر نا بانه مادِيْ نا بِنْتِ

مْمُوْيَ هِيْتَ مَانهَ دَرِيْنِ اكتولِ ابو بكر بن بانه مكوه بن ابو بكر بن محمد بن ابو بكر

بن محمد بن عمر بن محمد بن احمد بن محمد بن سليمان اكبجِ مْفَلُمِ غَفَ ُل نا احمد
رُيِ* بانه مْكُوُ >>
اَلِيُ تُكُوْ لِوَ نوزُغُ بُرتُغالْ كوبَغَ اكف مْفلُمِ سنه ١١٠٣ كتولِ
يِيِ احمد بن ابو بكر بن محمد بن محمد بن ابو بكر بن محمد بن عمر بن محمد
بن احمد بن محمد بن سليمان >> //
الِبُ تولِ كونْدمَ بُرتُغالْ اكِو* تو كتِك نْتِ زكِ نوقتُ هُنُ مانه
دَرِيْنِ بنْتِ بانه مكوه وبانه بكر مْكِه وبَانَه مْكُوه بن ابو بكر اليُ تُكُوْ لِوَ نبُرْ تُغالْ
كتِك زمانِ يا سلطان احمد كوُو دُزِ ووِيْلِ ابو بكر نا بانه مادِيْ سلطان
احمد نِمُمِ* وكِ الِيُ تُكُوْ لِوَ كفي هُزُنِ سان زِكبِتَ سِكُ نْيغِ كتِك* كُوْ
طهِرِ كِجان گكِ بانه تمُ مْتُتُ الِيُ مْتُكُوَ سلطان ابو بكر اِمَمُ هُدَ كِجان
وبانه مْكُوْه الِيُ تِدَ غُوَ مْفلُمِ الِبُ بت خبارِ اكعزِمُ يِيِ كُفي هرُوْسِ
يا زِجان زكِ سببُ كُمُ خِنِ سو يا شَبَ اكبت خبارِ مانه درِيْنِ اكمِت
مِيِ بَيِي بن مْكُ شَرِيْفُ كتِك جملِ لِيْلِ الِكُو هُدَرِ سان كزِ يا وُ جُمِ
اكتك امْفَيِز سِوَ اِشدِ سِوَ يا بتِ اك رِضيْكَ اِجار رِيَلِ مِيَه و عِشرِيْنِ
كَمُبَ بِمْبِ زَ نْدُفُ اَكتَوُوَ مُوْجَ اكفي سِو كسِيْرِ هت يلِبُ كُو
طَيَرِ كَيِظهِرِشَ غفُل كيِ بِك كتِك مجُوْمْب يَجَمَعَ زكِ كاُلَ* مْتُ اكِتُوْزَ
يكو مالِ مغِ سان فُونْدِ كا يِزَ اِجارَ اكتك تُوْزُ اكمْب تُوْزُ اكفيَ
عرُوْسِ يا كِجان گكِ هت زمانِ يبانه تَمُ مْكُوْه وَكَجَ وتُ ولاموه
وك اَزِمَ سِو اَكَوَبَ وكَ اِتُكُوَ سِو يا اصلِ هت بحرِيْنِ گُمْبُ كِكَفَ
مَيِ اِكَغِيْبُ بانه تمُ مْكوْه اكتك سِو يا مانه دَرِيْنِ كممْبِيا تُبِ
سِ يْسِ تُتُمِيِ كتِك مْج يُتِ اكمْجِبُ كلِ قَبِيْل اَلِيُ تُزَ نَتُمِيِ سِوَ يَغُ
نا مانه دَرِيْنِ كوتُ* مْتُمَ حُرِ اَيُوَوُ كُفُزِيَ اَكسِمَ هُيُ رِيِ* مِيِ

كُبجَ سِوَ هِنِ* يِي نَنَسِلَ ياكِ نَعَدَ ياكِ نَبُو رِيالِ تانُ نَغُوُ ياَ

كُتُكُ لِيَ سِوَ تِن اَبُو سَامْلِيْ نَتُزُ كُوْلَ مْتُ اَوِزَوُ

وكَمْكُ لِوَ نَسْلَ هِيُ مُيُوبِ وسِو هت يِوُ وكُ وتُويْ تَغُ

وقتِ هُنُ اِلَ لِاَنَ* هُتُ مِوَ نا جَمعِ يا قبااِلِ يا بَتِ نَمَ

قبااِلِ وَمِيْ مِغنِ هِدَ كَزِمَ كَشَرُتِ هِزُ كُبُوَ مُيُوْبِ وَ

سِوَ زِكَزِدِ فِتِنَ رَنِ* يا مْجِ نكتِك وُفلُمِ وكِ نْيك سَبَعَه اِكوَ

مِيْ مِكفُ هكُنَ مْفُوَ مْفلُمِ كَيا* يُوْزُلُ كتولِ سلطان

ابو بكر بن بانَه تَمُ مْكُ و بَانَه مْتِتِ بن احمد

بن ابو بكر بن عمر بن احمد بن عمر بن محمد بن احمد بن محمد بن سليمان ·

اكبتن سان >> //

نا سلطان وَ مَسكَتِ الى* اِمَمُ سيف بن * نبهاني اليعربي هُيُ

سلطان وبتِ اكد عربُوْنِ وك اَغَنِ نَمْفَلُمِ و عربُونِ نا هُيُ

مْفلُمِ وبتِ كو تُو بُرتُغالْ سِكُ يا جُوْمَ بِيْلِ كوُ ووتُ* كتملكِ

غُمِ يا ممباسه اكُمعرفُ الي * اليعربي اك اِتَ الوالي كتِك

مَزَرِعْ وتُ وتتُ محمد بن عثمان نا علي بن عثمان روُغُ* وَتَتُ سِكُ مُيُوَ

جِنَ لك وكي بمُوْي نا عسكرِ الي* اِمَمُ سيف نبهاني اليعربي

رِيُ* اصِلِ يا مَزَرِعْ نا مْفَلُمِ وبتِ اَلِنا سِيَرَ نْجِمَ نا جمعِ يا وتُ

اك عِشِ نْيَكَ اربُعيْن كَتِك وُفَلُمِ وكِ اكف سنه ١١٥٤ اكوت زِجان

وغِ بعَد ياكِ وستِ ولِ زِجان زك اكتولِ احمد بن ابو بكر بن محمد بن ابو بكر

بن احمد بن عمر بن محمد بن احمد بن محمد بن سليمان اككتِ كا وِم نا رعِيِ ني الِ

كِبِد كُوك غُوْمْبِ وغِ سان اكف سنه ١١٦٠ اكخلفُ كِجان مْمُوْيَ

كَمتِ بانه غُوْغُ استِ ولِ كتولِ بانه تمُ مْتُتُ اَمْكُ لِوَوُ اِمَمُ

لِ هُدَ* وبانه مْكُوْه اَلُ تكُوُ لِوَ نابُرتُغالْ نا اِنَ لكِ

ابو بكر بن بانه مْكُوْه بن ابو بكر بن محمد بن ابو بكر بن محمد بن ابو بكر بن محمد

بن عمر بن محمد >>

بن سليمان كتِك وقتِ هُنُ اِمَمُ اليعربي اكيِ تَ زِتَ كُبجَ بتِ

وسِوزِ وكف وعربُ وِغِ* سَان وكفي امانِ بعد يا هيُ وتُ

وسِوُ وك خلِفُ مْفَلُمِ كوبجَ زِت اسِو وِزِ وتُ و سِوُ نوتُ

ولاموه وكَفُغَ زِت وَكَيَا بتِ كجَنِبُ يا كِتُوْكِ وكبِجن وتُ

وبتِ زِت زِكُوْ سان وكفُنْدِك وتُ ولاموه بعدي مْفَلُمِ

وبتِ اكفُغَ زِت كَبَرَ نا بَحَرِ كَوَ بِجَ وتُ ولاموه كوتم لكِ

بعد يا هيُ اَلِ كُو حَلِ مُوْيَ مْفَلُمِ وَبَتِ نوتُ ولاموه اِمَمُ

اليعربي اكفي شَوُرِ مُوْيَ وك مُوُوَ مَفَلُمِ سنه ١١٧٧

اكتولِ رُيِ* مَان مْكِه سلطان مَانَه خديجه بنت بانه مكوه بن ابو بكر بن محمد

بن ابو بكر بن محمد بن ابو بكر بن محمد بن عمر بن محمد بن احمد بن محمد

بن سليمان اِكو فِتِن يِغِ >> //

كتِك نْتِ يا بتِ اِكو وفلُمِ ووِيْلِ مانه خدِيْجه المذكوره * سلطان عمر وكَ

بِجن كتِك مُوْيِ وبتِ نْيَكَ مِتَتُ سلطان عمر اكِد برانِ وكرِجيَ

بتِ كا غُفُ كُوْ سان وُسِكُ وكِبجن نوتُ ومانه خديجه كُوْلَ

مْتُ مهالِ بَكِ اكف مانه خَدِيْجه سنه ١١٨٧ اكتولِ بانه مَكُوْه وَشِيْ

رَعِيَ وكفي وُذِيَ سان اَسِبَتِ رَحَ كتِك وُفلُمِ وكِ هت سنه ١١٩١ وك

مُغلِيَ وتُ ومُوْيِ وكمُوُو كتاريخ هِيُ كتولِ بانه فُوْمُ مَادِيْ اِنَ

لكِ سلطان محمد بن ابو بكر بن بانه مْكُوْه بن ابو بكر بن محمد بن ابو بكر بن محمد

بن ابو بكر بن محمد بن عمر >>

بن محمد بن احمد بن محمد بن سليمان بعَد يا كُتولِ رعِي وكَتك كُفَيَ فِتِنِ كوبجَ
زِت كو شِدَ كو شِك وتُ آربُعيْنِ وَوِيْلِ نِدُزِ خَصَ كَوَ تِنْدَ كَمَ
مْبُوْزِ يُوْ نَسَكَفُ دامُ اِكشُك نْدِيَنِ كتِك مَكُوْب اِكو اَمانِ
اَسِتُكِ مْتُ تِنَ كُفَيَ فِتِن اكتولِ كرح سان هت اكف سنه ١٢٢٤
ول هكُ تولِ مْفَلُمِ كَمَ يِيِ اكخلِفُ زِجان
وغِ سان اكتولِ سلطان احمد بن شيخ فوم لُطاِ* بن شيخ بن بانه
مْكُوه اِكزدِ فِتِن كتِك مْجِ ولاموه اكو بجِ زِت يِيِ نوتُ
وممباسه مَرَيِغُ* هلِ مُوْجَ وك شُكَ شِيْلهَ جِيْشِ كُوْ سان
ووتُ وبتِ نوتُ وممباسه وتُ ولاموه وك تُك وكَجَ شِيْله
وكبِجن نوتُ وبتِ نوتُ وممباسه زِت زَوَتُ ولاموه
زِكو نَغُفُ سان جِيِشِ يا بتِ نَيَ ممباسه وكفُنْدِك وككِبِيَ
مجاهزِنِ مَوُ* مجاهزِ مَغِ نِ يك جهبُ پانِ وكسِمم هبُ
وكبِجَنَ زِت زِكُوْ سان وكف وتُ وغِ سان وتُ وممباسه
نوتُ وبتِ هبن اِددِ كتِك وتُ وبتِ ولُ معرُفُ اِسُ
كُو وتُوْمَ نوتُ ظَعِفُ* وتُ وحِدِ وثمانِينِ ٨١
فُلانِ بن فُلانِ وِيِ وكِ يكِد مَا اِذَ هَيُ بتِ نوتُ
وممباسه هون اِدادِ بعَد يا هبُ وتُ ولاموه وكِد عربُوْن
وكمْتك سعيد بن سلطان بن لاِمَامْ وكَمْبَ نْتِ يا لاموه سنه ١٢٢٨
البُ تولِ لاموه وُفلُمِ وبتِ وكَسَلِ يَ كتِك گَبَاَتِ نا بَندرِ //
* فِتِنَ اكتُك مْتُ وبِيْلِ كتِك زِجان وبانه فُوْمُ مادِيْ هِيْتَ
فُوْمُ لُوْطِ كِپُغَ اكبِجن سلطان احمد كِسَ سلطان احمد اكف
كمرضِ سنه ١٢٣٠ اكتولِ فُوْمُ لُوْطِ وبانه فُوْمُ مادِيْ نيِ اِلكُوَ

هُدَرِ سان شُجع كرِيْمُ نزمنِ هِزُ شيخ متاك بن شيخ مبارك رِبُ*
اِلبُ تولِ وُشِيخ وسِوُ اكفي عسِكرِ نا بُونْدُكِ ني نِكَتِكَ طع
يا سلطان وبَتِ نَيِ اِلبت نَ سان نمزرُعيْ هت سنه ١٢٣٦
هت اِكزدِ فِتِن بَيِن ياكِ سلطان سعيد بن سلطان زنجبار
اكف سلطان فُوْمُ لُوْطِ المذكور سنه ١٢٧٠ بعَد ياكِ
بعد ياكِ* اكتولِ فُوْمُ لُوطِ بن شيخ بن فُومُ لُوْطِ وبانه تَمُ مْكُوْه نا هُيُ
رِيِ* بباكِ سلطان احمد بن* سلطان وَيْتُوه اكتولِ اصُبُحِ هت بعد
لِعِصرِيْ وتُ ومُوْيِ وكَمْتُوَ اكِدَ سِوُ بَمُوْجَ نامَزرُعيِ اَكِدَ وُتِ
ممباسه اكتولِ سلطان بانه شيخ بن بانه فُوم مادِيْ اكبتن سيد سعيد بن سلطان
اكتِيَ وعربُ يتِ وككتِ نْيَكَ مِتَتُ بعديِ وتُ ومُوْيِ وك مُوُزلُ
بَمُوْيَ ناشَوُرِ لا سيد سعيد بن سلطان بتارخ سنه ١٢٣٩ وكمْتو لِشَ
سلطان احمد امْكُووُ* بانه وزِيْرِ وبانه تمُ وبانه شيخ وبانه تَمُ مْكُوْه
كبتن سيد سعيد بن سلطان كتولِ نْيك مِوِيْلِ وتُ وك مُوُزلُ وكمْرجِيَ
بانه شيخ وبانه فُوْمُ مادِيْ اككِتِ كتِك عِزِ كَشَوُر يا سيد سعيد بن سلطان
نْيك مِتَنْ اكف سنه ١٢٧٨ اكرجِيَ بانه وزِيْرِ كتِك وُ سلطان وكِ كيا
بانه فُوْمُ لُوْطِ بن شيخ اليُ كِدَ ممباسه بمُوْيِ نامزرُعيِْ وك سِك* سِوُ
وكبِجن نا بانه وزِيْرِ وبانه تمُ بتِ بانه وِزِيْرِ نِشَوُرِ مُوْجَ نا سيد سعيد
بن سلطان نا فُوْمُ لُوْطِ بَمُوْيَ نمزرُعيْ نا شيخ متاك مْتُ وسِوُ وك
جَ بتِ كزِت وكبِجن جِيِش يسِوُ اِكفُنْدِك بانه وزِيْرِ اك يِشِك نْتِ
يَسِوُ اكفُنْد نَوُكُت ومُوْيِ شيخ متاك بن شيخ مْبَارَكَ نا فُوْمُ لُوْطِ
وككِ مْبِليَ برانِ بمُوْيِ نَب عضِ ياوتُ بعَد يا سِكُ كتِتِ
اكرجِيَ سِوُ كزِت كُ* سان اكو تُو وتُ وبانه وزِيرِ كا

زِت وك وُ شِكَ ووُ مُوْيِ وسِوُ وك جغَ وُكُتا ومُوْيِ وك
بِجن بتِ نسِوُ اِكو كتِك طع بمُويْ نا شوُرِ يا سيد سعيد بن سلطان //
[. . . . .] //
نْدِيَنِ وتُ وسِوُ وكمْتُكِيَ غَفُ لَ عامِرِ وشِيْ مَتَاكَ هِيْتُوهْ
بن مْبَارَكَ احمد عمر نا عامر وبِيْلِ هِيْتُوْه حمد غُمَ وكبِجَن وكمُوُو
عَامِرِ حَمَادِ وكِدَ نا بُمَنِ وك وِبجَ وعربُ ولِ يُوْكُ بُمَنِ وك
تاء نا مِزِغَ نا جِيْشِ اِلِ يُوْكُ سِوُ هُبِجَنَ ولِبُ بت خبار يا
كمْب عامِرِ حمادِ مِوُ وو جِيْشِ يا سيد سعيد بن سلطان اِكفُنْدِك نوُ ولِ
كُوَ كتِك كُت ملكِ سِوُ سيد سعيد بن سلطان كِسَ كُبت خبارِ يمُوتِ يا
عَامِرْ* حُمَاد* كوُ رُك* كغِي مرِكبُوْنِ اسِنِ نِنُ اكِد زكِ مسكتِ مك وبيْلِ
اكمُوِك سلطان فُوْمُ بَكَرِ فازَه اكبِج سِوُ نبتِ كتِك وقتِ هُنُ اكف شيخ
متاك كمرضِ اِكو خلِفُ كزِجان زكِ كُوْلَ مْتُ اَتك وُشيخ وكَغِيَ
كتك طع يا سيد سعيد ابو بكر نا احمد زِجانِ زَ شيخ متاك سيد اَكمْب
ابو بكر زِتُ* بَموْيَ سلطان فُوْمُ بكر كمْبِجَ سلطان احمد سِوُ اكِد ابو بكر
بن شيخ متاك بمُوْي نا اَمِرِ و سلطان فُوْمُ بكر امْكُلِوَوُ حمد وبَايْشِ
نبهانِيْ كغِي سِوُ وُ سِكُ وكبِجن هت وكفُ ندِك وتُ و سلطان
فُوْمُ بكر وك اَنْدَ مِوَ نْدِ ينِ وك مْشِك ابو بكر بن شيخ متاك وكمْبِك بتِ
كوُ وو نسلطان احمد بَعَدَيِ اكسِمام رُيِ* شيخ محمد شيخ متاك طرفُ
يسيد سعيد بن سلطان يِيْيِ * سلطان فُوْمُ بكر سيد سعيد بن سلطان كوب
زِت نَعَسِكَرِ نَغَرَامَ وَكَمْبِجَ سلطان احمد هت وكمُتُو بتِ سنه ١٢٧٣
اكِد كوُ سِوُ اِكو شِيخ محمد بن شيخ متاك طرفُ يا سيد سعيد بن سلطان اك
مبْ نا عسِكرِ كوك نا غِرزَ وكتِت نَمْتُ و سيد سعيد بن سلطان كسببُ

ال فُنْد پانْدَ لَمْتِبِ الُ وك شيخ محمد متاك اِلوك مْبِيْ يا غِرز نَشِيْخِ
محمد متاك كفُند غِرز نكتِك وقتِ هُنُ اِلكُف سلطان احمد بن شيخ كوُ
ببكِ فُوْمُ بكر سلطان وِيْتُوْه اككتِ مهالَ بكِ احمد امْكُلوُ سِمْبَه
سلطان وِيْتُوْه نقبُل يشيخ محمد اسِي فُنْدَ غِرز لا سِوُ يلِتُك فِتِنَ
سلطان فُومُ بكر بن شيخ اكَمْتُوَ بَتِ كزيْتَ اكيا لَاموه اكتك كُيتملكِ بتِ
اِلبُ وُنَ غُفُ زكِ نوكُوْ وبتِ اِلبُ وُن كِتِدُ مِزُ في شيخ محمد بن شيخ
متاك مِسُوِ اَتَك كُو تولِ وسِكِرِ كو بج زِت وكسِمام وكُوْ بُوْ
وبتِ ولا هبن مْفلْمِ كشوُرِ لا وتُ وتتُ محمد بن مْكوه نَبَهَانِيْ نابانه رِحمَ
بن احمد نبهاني نناصِرِ بن عبد الله بن عبد سلام رِيِ* الُ كُو مْدبِرِ اَلاُمُوْرِ* //
اككُ سَيَ زن وكبِجن شيخ محمد بن شيخ متاك وك مْشِدِ وكف وتُ ما
عرُوفُ ما اَمرِ مَكوُوْه وتُ ووِيْلِ بانه دَميل نا مَوْلنا وَشي
كُوْلِ شيخ محمد بن شيخ متاك كِسَ كُوُن مبُ هي اكي كتاك امانِ
كا محمد بن بانه مْكُوْه نبهانيْ كَنا* رِيِ* الِي كُو مْكُوْب ووُ كتك
هو وت وتتُ تُم زُ تَغلِيَ كُتَيَ اكتك كُمْبَ يِيِ محمد بن مْكُوْه
سلطان وسِوُ نا بتِ اك اِز اكجِبُ مِمِ نِمْتُ مْزم وكدِ كُمْتَ
سلطان احمد وَوِيْتُوْه كبِك وتُ شيخ محمد بن شيخ متاك نوتُ وَ
بتِ و كمْبِك شيخ ناصِرِ بن عبد الله بن عبد سلام كِدَ كاوُ كَمْتَ
سلطان احمد اَلْمُلَقَبُ سِمْبَه كيَ نِي بتِ خبارِ اِكسِكِ لِي
وُغُوْجَ سلطان سيد ماجدِ بن سعيد بن سلطان كنِ سيد سعيد وُتَ
غلِيِ كُف سنه ١٢٧٣ قبُل ياهيُ سيد كمْت* وزير وكِ سيد سليمان
بن حمد كمركبُ اِل كُشِك بتِ كُدُشَ* فِتِن مَركبُ اِكوَصِل مَرَ*
بتِ اِمِ كِسَ كُشِكُوْ مْتُ و سلطان احمد ابو بكر بن حَسَنِ البُورِي

اِمكُيَ نيِ ناصرِ بن عبد الله بن عبد سلام اكِس كُبت خبارِ هِيُ سيد

سليمان حمد اَكَرجيَا وُغُوْجَ نا شيخ محمد بن شيخ متاك وقتِ هُنُ

رِبُ* اِلبُ فُنْد غِرز لا سِوُ اكِس كُوصِلِ سليمان بن حمد بتِ

وتُ وكَمْبَ كُوَ رِيِ* سلطان شيخ محمد بن شيخ متاك كُنَ مْزِيْ

سِيْفُ نا شيخ شِكُوِه نا محمد مُوْتِ اكستِكرِ كا سلطان احمد وُفَلُمِ

وكِ سيد ماجِدِ بن سيد سعيد بن سلطان اكبكَ وتُ ولاموه بتِ كن

صح بمُوْيَ نا شيخ مُحُيِ دِيْنِ كمْتك سلطان احمد اِوِك عسكِرِ

وسيد بتِ نا هُيُ شيخ مُحُيِ دِيْنِ رِيِ* الُ تُو عسكِرِ و سيد كتِك

غِرز لا سِوُ اِلبُ وبج شيخ محمد بن شيخ متاك عسكر ولِ رنِ* يا غِرز

اكِد شيخ مُحُيِ دِيْنُ كو تُو كا امانِ كن ال كُوَ مْتُ و سيد ماجِد

بن سيد سعيد كتِك موزِيْرِ اِلبُ كِد وُغُوْجَ نا عسكِر سيد كفي

هَسِرَ سان يُوْ لا شيخ مُحُيِ دِيْنِ نا شيخ مُحُيِ دِيْنِ كتاء دَرَكَ //

اِلبُ مُوُن سيد ماجد نا غَضبُ رِبُ* ال بُ كِد يا* نوتُ و

لاموه نَيِ شيخ مُحُيِ دِيْنِ اِلنا حِيْلَ سان نعلِمُ نْيغِ اكِد بتِ نا خِيارِ

يوتُ ولامو بمُوْيِ نا شيخ احمد نا شيخ عبد الرحمن اَيِ نَيِ شيخ بتِ

وكنِن نا سلطان احمد اكرضِيْك بعد يا شِد كسببُ يا صُحُبَ يا شيخ بتِ

نا شيخ عبد الرحمن اك خلفُ شوُرِ لوزِيْرِ وكِ ناصرِ بن عبد الله بن عبد سلام كَنِ ولِ

وكنِن نا سلطان احمد اَكَرضِيْك بعد يا شِد*

ولِ اِزَ كُتِيَ وعربُ هت مْتُ مْمُوْيَ وتُ وبتِ وكفي شوُرِ مُوْيِ

مانه جاهَ بِنْتِ فُوْمُ لُوْطِ كِبُغَ وبانه فُوْمُ مادِيْ مْكِ و سلطان فُوْمُ

بكر بن شيخ وقتِ هُنُ سلطان فُوْمُ بكر وُكُ لاموه تِن يا

شوُرِ لَ سيد ماجِدِ بن سعيد تَغُ اِلبُ تُوْ لِوَ بتِ باسِ كُلَ سِكُ وكِتِيَ عَسكَرِ

كسِرِ نَزَنَ وُسِكُ وُسِكُ الِبُوَ خبارِ سلطان احمد اِكو فِتِنَ نعسِكرِ وَمِ
كُو وغِ بتِ وكمْبجَ سلطان احمد غُفُ لَ بَعَدَ ياكِسَ حِلَ كُتك كُمْشِكَ وسِ
وِزِ كَنِ وبتِ وُتِ ولِ كُوَ شوُرِ مُوْيَ نا سيد ماجِدِ بن سعيد اِل وزِيْرِ
وكِ ناصِرِ بن عبد الله بن عبد سلام وكبِجنَ رَنِ* يامُوْيِ وبتِ اكتُك سلطان احمد
يِيِ نا شيخ محمد بن شيخ متاك وكِد سِوُ بَتِ وك شِك وعرب نا بهرِنِ وكتِيَ
مرِكبُ زِت زِلبُ كُو زِكُوْ سان الِبُ كُي سيد ماجِدِ بن سعيد كَيِ حُرُصُ*
سِوُ نبتِ نبهرِ كُسبِتِ كُمْبَ كُكُتِ ما دَوُ مِتِبِ وكبِجن بهرِنِ وكِدَ برانِ
كُتءَ كَكُوْلَ نَمَ جِرَ ياكُرُدِ هُوَانَ حَيِ مَيْتِ سيد ماجِدِ اكتِيَ
سِلِسِلِ كتِك كان لَمْتُ وسِوُ كُوْيُ كُسبِتِ كُمْبُ تِنَ نوُ ولِوَنَ نيْزِ
سِتَ كبهرِ نك بتِ نجانِبُ يا فازَه مْزِيْ سِيفُ اكخلِفُ مْتُ و سيد
ماجِدِ بن سعيد كا حِيْلَ نْيغ نَمَ نِنُ مَغِ اكوُن ظِيْكِ* سان سلطان احمد نا شيخ
محمد بن شيخ متاك نَنْتِ يَسِوُ اِكو فِتِن بعضِ يوتُ ومْبِد سيد ماجِدِ كسببُ
يا مَشَكَ ولُ بت نوتُو نِهو شريْفُ موُلنا بن ابو بكر نا عِسَ بن احمد السمالي
الِبُ وُن سلطان احمد * شيخ بن محمد بن شيخ * كَمَ هَيَ و كتَك اَمانِ كَسَيْدِ ماجِدِ
اَكَوَبَ امانِ كتِك منِنُ يا امانِ سلطان احمد اكسفِرِ وُسِكُ اكِد برانِ
اكرِجِيَ كاوُ بعدِي شيخ محمد بن شيخ متاك اكمْبِك كِجان گکِ شيخ محمد بن شيخ
متاك اكدِ مرِكبُوْنِ كا سيد ماجِدِ نا سيد ماجِدِ كَمْ سِمحِ اكمْب نعطيا
يغِ سيد ماجِدِ كسِفِرِ كرِجِيَ وُغُوْجَ كِسَ شيخ محمد بن شيخ متاك اكِد وُغُوْجَ
كمُ وجِهِ سيد ماجِدِ سيد اكمْشِك كَمْفُغَ كتِك غُوْمِ ياممباسه نوتُ اكف شيخ محمد //
نبعَد يسِكُ سيد ماجِدِ اكمْبِك اكمْبِك* الوالي سعود بن حمد كُمْشِك سلطان احمد
كوُ كا حِيْلَ نْيغَ اسِوزِ كُتُكَ كَوُ كا سِرِ اكِد وِيْتُوْه الوالي سعود بن حمد اكيا فَازَ
كُمْشِكَ عمر متاك فازه نزجان ز شيخ محمد بن شيخ متاك كوشِك سِوُ كوبِك

غُمِنِ ممباسه عمر متاك اَكَ مْفُغَ لاموه بعديِ سيد ماجِدِ اكتمالكِ سَوَحِيْلِ
زُتِ هكُن مْتُ وكُمُ عَرِضِ نسُلُطانِ احمد ككِتِ وِيْتُوْه كتِك طع يا
سيد ماجِدِ هَتَ الِبُ تولِ سيد برغش بن سعيد بن سلطان اكتك سيد برغش
كُوك عسِكرِ وِيْتُوْه نا بِنْدرَ سلطان احمد اَس رِضِكِ كبِك زِتَ كُمُبجَ
اسِوزِ اكفي امانِ نَيِ الوالي سعود بن حمد هَكُ مْبجَ سان
زِتَ سيد برغش كبِك زِت زمانِ زَ لوالي سعيد بن حمد بن سعيد سلطان
احمد اكتءَ حِمَيَ كا جَرُ مَنِ اكمْبَ نبعذِ* يا بر يسوحِيْلِ اكف سلطان
احمد كتِك حلِ هِيُ يا حِمَيَ سنه ١٣٠٦ اكتولِ سلطان فُوْمُ بكر بن سلطان
احمد بن شيخ نبهاني اككِتِ كتِك حلِ هِيُ يا حِمَيَ اِكتُكِيَ فِتِنَ يِي نا
جَرُمَنِ مْتُ مُوْج هِيْت قِسلِ اكمْبج بوبُ ولاغُ كمْبجَ غَفُ لَ رَ
صاصِ ولِ كُوكُ عَسِكَرِ كو بجَ كا ر صاصِ نا عسِكرِ وكمْبجَ قِسلِ نا
وزُغُ ولُ فُوتِنِ نَوُ وك وُوَ ووزُغُ* مغِرِ اَمْرِ يا سلطان
فُوْمُ بكر عسِكرِ ولبُ وَوُنَ جمع زوُ ومِ كُفَ هوكُغُوْجَ امْرِ يا
سلطان وك وبجَ وزُغُ نوتُ ومكُنُومْبِه نونْد مُوْيُ ولِبُ
بت خبارِ وزُغُ ومِ بِجن وكو ووزُغُ* ولِيُ كُوكُ بعديِ
اِكي دُوْلِ يوغرزِ وكتك كُفي اِنْصَفِ اكوتك وتُ وْمكُنُومْبَه
نَوَنْدَ مُوْيُ معَن اوتِيِ كتِك حُكُمُ فُومُ بكر اَس رضِيْكِ كُو تُو
وكمْبجَ زِت سلطان فُوْمُ بكر زِكِيَ مْتُوَ* هت مْكُنُومْبِه نونْد مُوْيُ
نكِ لِمَنِ نيَنْدُ زَ بانِ وزِبجِ كمزِغ وكتيِ نا مُوْتُ هت لِيْلَة
١١ ربع* اولا* سنه ١٣٠٨ وكبِجن وتُ وويتوه كتِك نْديَ يا كِبِيْنِ
نوتُ ودُولَ تُكُفُ وكفُدِك وتُ و ويْتُوه هت اَصُبُح سِكُ يا جُوْمَ تتُ
مزِ ١٢ ربع الاولا سنه ١٣٠٨ وكَمْبج سلطان فُومُ بكر وكمْتُو وِيتوه

كزت گِدَ جُغِنِ وِيْتُوه اِكتملكِ و نا دُولَ تُكُفُ سلطان فُوْمُ بكرِ
ككِتِ جُغِنِ هت جماد اولا سنه ١٣٠٨ اكف اكشِك مهالَ باكِ رُيِ*
بانه شيخ بن سلطان احمد بن شيخ نَبَهَانِيْ بعد سِكُ گگِ اِكو فِتِنِ نَرُيِ*
فُوْمُ عمر نبهاني نا افُ تُوْلَ وباهِرُ وك مْفُغَ بانه شيخ بن سلطان بن* حمد* //
اكتولِ سلطان فُوْمُ عمر نوكِس كُتملكِ بتِ سلطان احمد سلطان ووِيْتُوه
نا اَلُ تملكِ كنْد سليمان بن سليمان بن مضفر* نبهاني اِمامُ لِعَرَبِيْ* هِنِ* رِيُ* خبارِ
يا نبهاني كُيَ سوحِيْلِ ناخبارِ زوُ كم تُمِ زُ تَغْلِيَ كُتي ومِزُ تولِ وَ
فَلْمِ وحِدِ وثلاثِيْنِ نا مانه مْكهِ مْمُوجَ جُمْلَ اِثنِيْنِ وثلاثِيْنِ مِنْ غَيرِ ولُ كِتاَ
ولِ وكِ وُزُلوَ وكرجِيَ كُوْ تولِ* تُم نَقِيْلِ هَيَ كا محمد بن فُوْمُ عمر نبهاني
الملقب بانه كِتِيْنِ نَيِ ال نِقيْلِ كا جَادِ ياكِ محمد بن بانه مْكُوْه نبهاني
امْكُلوَوُ بانه سِمْبه اَلِ ذبِ تِشِ يِ سان خبارِ يا نَسَبَ زوُ كم تُمِ
زُ تَجَ كتبه صالح بن سالم بن عبد الله شرحيل بيده ٦ في صفر سنه ١٣١٨ نقلت
هذا للولد* العزيز محمد بن احمد بن سلطان بن فُوْمُ بكر بن شيخ بن بانه فُوْمُ مادِيْ
وسِمْبَه سلطان* محمد بن ابو بكر بن بانه مْكُوْه بن ابو بكر بن احمد بن ابو بكر بن
محمد بن ابو بكر >>
بن محمد بن عمر بن محمد بن احمد بن محمد بن سليمان بن سليمان بن مضفر*
نبهاني نقلت >>
في ١ رجب سنه ١٣٤٢ كتبه الاقل صالح بن سالم بن احمد بيده في ٣ فبروري سنه
١٩٢٥ >> //

تاريخ الهجرة (٦٠٠)

رِوايَه يَتَوارِيْخْ زَ پَاتِ نَا بعض سِهِيْمُ اِفْرِيْقَه شَرِيقيه
هَاهنا سليمان بن سليمان مطفر* النبهاني الول المبدي نبهاني
مُوَنْدُ وَكُويَ پَتِه نَبْهَاني نِسلِيمانِ بن سليمان بن مظفر
نبهاني نَانْدُزِ وَوِيْل : على بن سليمان نا عثمان بن سليمان
نَهُويُ سليمان بن سليمان المذكور نْدِيِ اَلكُوَ سلطان نَايِ اَكِسَ
كُتَوالِيْ بَارَ لعَرَابُ اَكَايَ پَتِّه سلطان المذكور كتك تاريخ سنة
٦٠٠ (ستمائه) من الهجره كُويَ كُوكِ پَاتِ اَكَتَ كَ عروس
كُوَ مْفَلْمِ وَپَتِه كَتِكَ هَا وَالبتاوين . سلطان سليمان بن سليمان
نِمْتُ مُعَرُفُ مْفَلْمِ وَپَاتِ اَكَمُوْزَ بِنْتِ يَكِ نَدَسْتُوْرِ يوَاتُ
يَا وَسَوَاحِلِ حَتَى سَاسَ مْتُ اَكُؤُ لِيَوُ كِجَانَ شَكُ اَكِسَ سِكُ
سَعَبَه زَهَرُوْسِ هِنْدَ كُمُؤَ نْغَالِيَا مْكُوْ* وِيْ يُمْبَانِ مَكِ بَابَا
وَمْكِ وكِ كَوَمْبِيَ وَتُ : هُوْيَ* سليمان بن سليمان نْدِيِ
مْفَلْمِ وِنُ اَكَمْبَ اُفَلْمِ وكِ اَلْكُوَ نَوُ اَكَتَوَلِ سليمان بن
سليمان كُوَ لِنَ مُويِ هَاَتْوَ كِتَكَ اِيُ جَزِيْره يپَات كَتِكَ مَطلَع
يَپَاتِ : نَا سِوُ حَسَا كُوَ مْج وَلِكُ مْجِ مُوْنْغِنِ هِيْتُوا
شَانْغَ كَتِكَ مَطْلَعِ يَابَتِّه : نَفَازَ وَيكُ مْجِ وِنْيِوِ وَپَازَه
المفازي : اِكَكِيْتُ مجِ هِيُو يُوْتِ نَحْتِ* يَا سُلْطَان سليمان بن سليمان
نَامَنْدَ كُوَ لِينَ مْفَلْمِ مْبَالِيْ نَايِ اُنَ نْغُفُ سَانَ : اَكَفَ سلطان
سليمان بن سليمان تاريخ ٦٢٥ هجره اَكَا خَلِفُ زِجَانَ وَوِيْلِ

محمد نأحمد : محمد عُمر وك مِيَاكَ عشرين نَأحمد عمر وكِ نْيَاكَ خمسه عشره
اَكَتَوِلِ محمد بن سليمان بن سليمان بَعَدَ يَبَ بَكِ اِكَوَ خِتْلَافُ //
يِيِ نَوَاتُ وَ شَانْغَ كَبِجَانَ نَامجِ كائِفُنْدَ كابِس نَبَعْضِ يَوُ وَكايَ
پَته نَا وَنْغِنِيوِ قَبِلَ يَوُ كِنْدَغُ وَكَكِمبِيَ وَسِيُو وكانِ مَها* وَمِزُ
كِمْبِلِيَ حَتَى سِكُ زِكَاپِتَ اِكايَ خَبارِ كُوَ سلطان محمد بن سليمان نَحَاوَ وَاتُ
وِنْداوُ كُونْدَ وَكَمُوَمْبِيَ وَالِيِ وَسِوُ تُمِوَوُنَ كَتِكَ مُوتُ : سلطان
كَبِكَ وَاتُ كُوَ نْغَالِيَا كَوَ دِرِكَ ومِفَانْيَا زِجُومُبَا نْدانِ يا مُوِيْتُ
سلطان محمد بن سليمان كَوَ سَمِحِ كَوَرُدِشَ مَهَالَ يَوُ نْدِيُو اصْلِ يَامُوِيِ
وَسِيُوْ : وَكايَ نَوَ سَوَاحِلِ وَنْغِنِ وَكاكِتِ وُتِ : وكايَ نَوَ وَفَماوُ
وَكا كِتِ وَكَاوَ نْدِوُ وَكُوْ وَسِيُوْ كَتِكَ طاعَ يا سلطان محمد بن سليمان .
سلطان محمد المذكور اكف سنه ٦٥٠ اَكتولِ نْدُيِ احمد بن سليمان اَكَعَمِرِشَ
سان ارض يَبَةِ كا جنْغَ مَجُبَ كَفَا نْيَ مَشَانْبه اَسِبِجِ مَهالِ نأكفُ ٦٦٠
سنه ٦٦٠* كاتولِ كِجانَ شَانْدُيِ اِنَ لَكِ احمد بن محمد بن سليمان اكاكِتِ
نَوَتُ كُوَ اُزُرِ سَانَ كَمَ سِرَ زَ عَمِ زكِ كُعَمِرِشَ مْجِ وَبتِه نَمَشانْبه
حتى سنه ٧٠٠ اكاف اكخلِفُ زجان وَنْعِ كتولِ كِجان شَكِ سلطان
محمد بن احمد بن محمد بن سليمان اَكَكِتِ نَوَاتُ كُوَ وِيْمَ سان
وَاتُ وفازه وَكَخلِفُ اَكَوَ بجَ كَوَ تِيَ كتِكَ طاعه بعْدَ يَزتَ زِنْغِ
حتى اَلِبوُ وَشِنْدَ . اَكَاءِ فُتَاحِ نَمَدَ كَوَكَا تملكِ كُوَزِيتَه* نا حلَه
كُوِ* كنِ* اَلِكُوَ نا نْغُفُ سان مْقَلمِ وَمَدَ كُوَ يمالِ نوتُ اَكا ئفُنْدَ
كابِسَه نَوَتُ وُنْغِينِ* كَوَاِتَ پَتِه نَبَعْضِ وكَاتَوَ نْيِكَ وكا
كِمْبِلِيَ كِلَ مَهالَ وَنْغِينِ وَكَاجَه شِيْله وَكَانْغِيَا كَتِكَ حِمايَةَ يَواتُ
ولامْوُ . سلطان محمد بن احمد المذكور كوتكَ كُوْ واتَ ولامو وكائزَ

كُوَ تُوَ نا ونغِينِ وَكِنْدَ مَلِنْدِيَّ نبعْضِ يَا بِلْدٰانِ* : سلطان محمد
بن احمد المذكور كَوَ نَدامَ سان هاوَ وَلِيوُ كُوجَه شِيْلَه : واتُ ولاموه
وكَأَزَ كُوَ تُوَ قطعا . كِسَ سلطان محمد اكف ٧٣٢ اَكتوالِ كِجانَ
شَاكِ اُفَلُمِ سلطان عُمرِ بن محمد بن احمد بن محمد بن سليمان اَكَي رِجِيَا مَنِنُ //
مَنِنُ* يَبَابَ واكِ كُوَ واتُ ولامُو : كَوَ تَكَ وَاتُ وَمَانْدَ : وتُ ولاموه
وَكَأَزَ كُوَ تُوَ كَوَ بجِ زِتَ وَكاتَكَ اَمانِ وَتُ ولاموه وَكُوَ كَتِكَ
طاعا يا سلطان . سلطان عُمر بن محمد زِكَزِدِ نْغُفُ اَكابِجَ جُمله يا مجِ
يا سَوَحِلِ : اُزِ نَمَلنْدِ كِوَ يُوْ : كِتَا . . . . . *
مجِ يُوْتِ كاَتِمَلاكِ تُوكَ بَتِه حَتَى كرِيمْبا : كلَ مْجِ كَوكَ مْتُ وكِ
كِحُكُمُ نْدِيُ اَصْلِ يَهاوَ مَجُموْمْبِى اِلِيُكُ مْرِيْمَ مَعَنَ نِوَ نُوْ مُوَ
وَيُؤمْبى نَهِيُ يُؤمْبِى مَعَنَى نِنْيُوَ مُتَا* يَمْفَلْمِ وِيَةِ : نَجانِبُ
يَمَطُلَع اَكتملكِ حتى وارْشِيخ : اَلِكُونْدَ كَبِجَ زِتَ نَنْغُ* كِوَ يُوْ نَطُوٰلَه
نَا طُوٰالَ نا شُنْغوٰايَ نَا بَنَ دِرِ زُوتِ بَراوَ مَركَ نا مَقْدِشُوْ
اَكَعِش نانْتِ زُوتِ هِزُ كَتِكَ طاعه يكِ اِلاَ اُونْغُوجَه هاكُتوالِ
نَوَقْتِ هُوُ اُنْغُوجَه هائكُوَ نْتِ كُؤ بُوَ : هُوِيُ سلطان عمر المذكور
اَلشِنْدَ زِتَ نكُبِنْدَ رَعِيَه : نا رَعِيَه وَكِمبندَ اِكَتْوآء نْغُفُ سان نْتِ يَپَةِ
اَكَفَ سلطان عمر سنه ٧٤٩ كاخَلِفَ زِجَانَ وَوِيْلِ محمد ناحْمَد كتوالِ
كِجان مُكُوْ سلطان محمد بن عمر بن محمد بن احمد بن محمد بن سلطان* اُفَلُمِ
وَبَبَاكِ كُوَ اَمانِ >>

هَبَ كُوَ نَزتَ نَاِي اَلكِبِنْدَ مَالِ سَانَ نَبِعَشَرَ اَكِسَفِرش نَزُمْبُ
زَكِ هِنْدَ كُفَانْيَا بِعَشَرَ نَاِي اَلِيْنَ بَخْتِ سَانَ يَمالِ نَامَرَ مُوِى
اَلِمسَفِرشَ كِجَانَ شَكِ كَوتَ* كِسوَ كَتِ كَ بَحْرِ اَكبات مَعَدِنِ يَفِضَه

كَايَ نَايُ بَتِ كَفَ نْيَ واتُ وَكُيَفَانْيَ كَازِ مُعْدِن* هَايُ
كَپاتَ مَالِ سان مَنْغِ ياكازِدِ مالِ كَتِكَ نْتِ يَبَته حتى وَكافِيَ
زِتَارَ زَ فِضَه نَنْغَازِ زَ فِضَه نَزُمْبُ زِنْفغ زَ فِضَه نا مْفَلْمِ اكاف
سنه ٧٩٧ اكاخَلِفُ زِجانَ نن بُوَانَ مُكُوْ : نا حمد نا ابو بكر نا عُمر
اَكا تولِ نْدُيِ سلطانِ احمد بن عمر بن محمد بن احمد
بن محمد بن سليمان بن سليمان اَكاكِتِ نَوَاتُ سانَ كُوَ اَمانِ //
نا سِرَ نْجِمَ كُوَ جميع يَواتُ . اَكَافَ اَكاتولِ ابو بكر بن محمد بن عمر بن محمد بن
احمد بن محمد بن سليمان >>
كاكِتِ سانَ ناجَمِيعِ يَوَاتُ نامجِ يُوْتِ كَتِكَ طاعَ يَكِ بلا خلاف (ناي اكف)* سنه ٨٧٥
اكا خَلِفُ زِجَانَ زِوِيْلِ محمد ناحمد اَكتولِ مهالِ بب يَكِ مْتُتُ وكِ محمد بن ابو بكر
بن محمد بن محمد بن عمر بن محمد بن احمد بن محمد بن سليمان وَقَتِ وكِ وكاجه
وَزُنْغُ پُرتُكِلْ* >>
كَتِكَ مج يَسَواحِلِ وُتِ وَكَاكِتِ ممباسه وكافانْيَ نْغُمِ نا جَنِبُ ياپَتِه
كَجنْغَ نْدُوْ نْدوُ* وَاتُ وَبَرانِ وَكَاوَفُوَاتَ وكاوَپَ مالِ وكاوَ كَتِكَ طاعه
يَوُ وَكَمْعَرِض مْفَلُمِ كَتِكَ نْتِ يَكِ يپَتِه وَكَمْبِجَ زِتَ مْفَلْمِ كُوَ جَانبُ
ياشِدَ كاسِ وَكَوَكَ نْتِ يَا پَت بَوانِ كَمَعَنَ يَتُوْبِ كَصِدِيَا
كُبجَ مُوِي وَيَةِ وَسِوزِ وَكاپَتانَ كُوَ اَمانِ وَكُفَ نْىَ مْكَتَبُه شَرُتِ
زَوُ وكاكِتِ پَتِ وَزُنْغَ* وكفانْيَ فَرْض كُوَ جِنَ لَوُ وَزُنْغُ وَالِ
شَمْكُوَ فَنْدِكَ وَكَافَانْيَ نَمامْبُ مَانْغِ كَتِك كِسِوَ شَا پَتِه
اَكَفَ سلطان سنه ٩٠٠ اَكا خَلِفُ زِجانَ وَوِيْلِ بُوانَ مْكُوْ نا بو* بكر
اَكتوالِ اُفلْمِ سلطان ابو بكر بن محمد بن ابو بكر بن محمد بن احمد بن محمد بن
سليمان بعد يبب ك المذكور >>

اَكاكِتِ نَوَتُ سان كُوَ امانِ كَما قاعِدَه يَبباكِ اكفَ سنه ٩٤٠ .
كُسبَدِ لِكِ يامْبُو نا اَكخلِفُ زِجان زوِيْلِ احمد و محمد اَكتولِ عَمِ يَوُ
وُفَلْمِ بُوَانَ مْكُو بن محمد بن ابو بكر بن محمد بن عمر بن محمد بن احمد بن محمد
بن سليمان اِكَوَ خِتِلافُ >>
نَوَزُنْغُ لَكنْ بَسِو نَزتَ اِكَوَ فِتْنه سِكُ نْيِنْغِ اَكَفَ سنه ٩٧٣
اَكاخلِفُ كِجان مْمويَ : ابو بكر اكتولِ محمد بن ابو بكر بن محمد بن عمر بن محمد
بن احمد >>
بن محمد بن سليمان اكاصلِحِيانَ نَوَزُنْغُ ءَكتُواءَ بَعْضِ يَمجِ
اَكَوفَ سنه ١٠٠٢ اَكَخَلِفُ كِجان مُمُوجَ هِتُوَ ابو بكر استِوالِ التولِ *
ابو بكر بن بُوان مْكو بن محمد بن ابو بكر بن محمد بن عمر بن محمد بن احمد بن
محمد بن سليمان اُكِكتِ نَوَ* >>
كَمَ سِتِرَ* يَوَزِيْ زِك وَلتَ نَغُلِيَ نَوَفَلْمِ* اُكَپُوْ نْغُوَ نْغَفُ* //
اَكف سنه ١٠٤١ اَكَخَلِفُ بوان مْكُو نَابُو بكر كُوَ جِنَ لَبَبَكِ اكتولِ ابو بكر
بن محمد بن ابو بكر بن محمد بن ابو بكر بن محمد بن عمر بن احمد بن محمد
بن سليمانُ* اِكَوَ خِتِلاف >>
نَوَزُنْغُ وَكَبِجانَ كَوَ فُنْدَ وَزُنْغُ كَوْ* زِيْتَه زِكُو سان بَعَدَيِ
زِكايَ زِتَ تِنَ زَ وزُنْغُ وكِبجان : مُوْي وبَتِه كُوَ مِزنْغَه وَكَزوِيَ نَانْدِي
كُوَ بَحَرِينِ كُسِپتِ شُوْمْپُ : وات وكاوُن مَشَقَه وَكُفانْيَ اَمانِ
اَكاف مْفَلْمِ سنه ١٠٦١ اكخالِفُ زِجَانَ وَوِيْلِ بُوَانَ مْكُوْ نَاحْمد اكتولِ
بُوَانَ مْكُوْ وبوان بكر وبوان مْكُو بن محمد بن ابو بكر بن محمد بن عمر بن محمد
بن احمد بن محمد بن سليمان >>
اكپِتان نَوزنغ نَايِ اَلِكِبنْدَ سان كُكِتِ لاموه حتى مُوسِمُ كُبِيْتَ

لاَمْوه اكفانْي عرُوْسِ كُوَ وات ولامُوه : نكتِك وَقْتِ هُونُ وَفَمَاوُ
وَسِيُو وِلِتُكَ كَتَكَ طاعه ياكَ* اَكُوَ* بجَ نَمْجِ وَسِوُ كَشِكَ نوَاتُ وْنغِنِ كَوَتِيَ
پَتِه : مْكُوبْوَ وَسِيُو اَكاكِمْبِيَ اَكِنْدَ دُودُ كُو بُرتُغالِ كَتْوآء حمِايه : مْكُوبْوَ
ووزنغ اَكاج پَتِ كُوَ مُفَلْمِ اَوَسَمحِ وات وسِيوُ : مْفَلْمِ كَوَ سَامحِ
كَوَرِجِزَ مهالِ يَوْ سِيُوْ كتِكَ اَمانِ : بَعَد يكِ بُرتغالِ اكف نْيَ حِلَ اكاج
پتهِ كُو مَرْكَب اَكمْتَاكَ مْفَلْمِ كُونْدَ مَرْكَبْنِ اسِنِدِ اَكَمُبِكَ ابن عَمِ يكِ بُوان مْكُو
يِيِ نَوَاتُ وِپتهِ : وزنغ وكاو تُكُوَ كَتِكَ مرْكبْ اسِرُدِ حتى مْتُ مْمُويَ
بعد يهايُ مْفلُمِ كوبجَ وزُنْغُ كُوَ جانِبُ زُوتِ كُوَ برانِ نَزسِوَانِ
كَو تُو جانبُ زَهُوكُ زُتِ كاكِمبِلِيَ ممباسه : اكاف مْفلْمِ سنه ١١٠٠ اكوت
زِجان بُوان بَكَر نَبُوان مَدِ نَبِنْتِ مْمُويَ هُاَتُوَ مُوان دَرِيْنِ
اكتوالِ ابو بكر بن بوان مْكُو بن ابو بكر بن محمد بن ابو بكر بن محمد بن عمر بن
محمد بن احمد بن محمد بن سليمان >>
اكا بِجْوَ مْفلْمِ غَفْلَه ناحْمَد نْدُيِ بُوانَ مْكُوْ اَلْتُكُوْ لِوَ وَزُنْغُ //
بُرتُغالِ كُوَ اُبَانْغَ اكاف مفلمِ سنه ١١٠٣ كتولِ يِيِ احمد بن ابو بكر بن محمد بن محمد
بن ابو بكر بن محمد >>
بن عمر بن محمد بن احمد بن محمد بن سليمان اَلبُو توالِ كَوَنْدامَ بُرتُغالِ اَكِوتُوَ كتِكَ
نْتِ زكِ >>
نَوقْتِ هُونَ مُوان دَرِين بنت بُوان مْكُو وَبُوان بكر مْكِ وَبُوانَ مْكُو بن ابو بكر
اَلِيُوْ تُكُلِوَ نَبُرتُغالْ كَتِكَ زمانِ يا سلطان احمد كَوُوَ رُزِ* وويلِ : ابو بكر
نابُوان مَديْ ناسُلُطانِ احمد نِمُمِ* وكِ اَلِيُتُكولِوَ : كفانْيَ حَزْنِ سان
زِكَبِيْتَ نْيِنْغِ سِكُ نْيِنْغِ اَكَتاكَ كُ طَهِرُ كِجان شَك بُوَانَ تَمُ مْتُتُ اَلِيُو
مْتُكُوَ سلطان ابو بكر اِمِمُ* هُدَى كجان وَبُوان مْكُوُ اَلِيُو تِنْدَ نْغُوْوَ

مفلم اَلِبُو پَتَ خَبَارِ اَكَعِزِيْمُ* يِي كُفَ يَ عَروس يَزجان زكِ
سبابُ كُمْخنِ سِوَ يَشابَ : اَكَوَاتَ خُبَارِ* موان درِيَن اَكمُوتَ مُونِي بَيايِ
بن مكو شريف كتكَ جمال الليل الِكُوَ هُدارِ سان كَزِ يَوُجُمِ اكَتَ كَ اَمْفانْيِزِي
سِوَ اِشدِ سِوَ يَپاتِ اَكَرضِكَ اِجارَ رِيَالِ مايه وعشرين كَمْپَ پمْبِ زَ نْدُفُ
اَكا تِوُوَ مُوَي اَكَف نيَ سِواَ كُوَ سرِ حتى يالِبُوكُوَ طيارِ كا اَظهرِشَ
غفله كائبِ كَ كَتِكَ مَجُومْبَه يا جماع زكِ كُلَ مُتُ اَكتُوْزَ يَكوَ مالِ مانغِ
سان : فُنْدكاءِ زَ اِجاره اَكت كَ تُزُ اَكَمْپَ تُوْزُ اَكَفَ نيَ عروسِ
حتى زَمانِ يبوان تَمُ مْكُوْ وكاجه واتُ ولامُوْ وكَاازِمَ سِوَ
اَكَوَ وكائتُ كُوَ سِوِيَاصْلِ* حتى بَحَرنِ شُومْپُ كِكَفَ ماي اِكَغِيْبُ
بُوان تَامُ مْكُو اكت ك سِوَ يَمُوانَ دَرِيْن كَمُومْبِيَ تُوبِ سِس
تُتُمِي كَتِكَ مْجِ وُتِ اَكَمْجِبُ كِلَ قبيلَه يالتُوْزَ نَتُمِي سِوَ يَنْغُ نامُوان
دَرِينِ كَوات مْتُومْوَ حُرَ اَيُوَوُ كُفُزِيَ اَكَسِمَ هُوِيُ نْدِي مُونْيِ
كُبِجَ سِوَ هِنِ يِي نَانَسْلَ يَكِ نَاعَدَ يَكِ نَپُو رِيالِ تانُ نَانْغُوُ يا
كُتُكُلِيَ سِوَ : تِنَ اَپُو ناسَمْلِ نَا تُزُ كِلَ مْتُ اَوِزَاوُ : وَكَمْكُوْ لِوَ
نَسْلَه هِيُ مُيُومْپِ وَسِوَ حتى يِوُ وَكُ وَتُو تَنْغُ وَقْتِ //
الي الآن هُتُموَ نَاجميع يا قبائِل وَبَته نَمَقَابَائِلِ وَمِي مِنْغِنِ هُونْدَ كُوَزِمَ
كُوَ شَرْطِ هِزُ كُبُوَ مُيُومْبِيْ : وَسِوِ يِزْ كَزدِ فِتْنَه نْدان يَمْج : نكتك
اُفلْمِ وَكِ نْياكَ سَبَعَه اِكوَ مج مِكافُ هكُونَ مْقُوَ : مْفَلْمِ اكا اِعزُلُ
كَتَوالِ سلطان ابو بكر بن بُوانَ تَمُ مْكُوْ وَبُوَانَ مْتِتِ بن احمد بن ابو بكر بن عمر بن احمد
بن عمر بن محمد بن احمد بن محمد بن سليمان اَكبتَ نَ سَانَ نا سلطان وُمشكَت* الامام
سيف بن نبهانى اليعربي : هُوْيُ سلطان وِيَته اِكوَ عربُونِ* :
وَكَوَجَانَ مْفَلم وَعَرُبُونِ* نَهُوِيُ مفلْم وَبتِ كُوتُوَ پُرتُغالِ

سِكُ يا جُمْعَه بِلِ كُوُوَ وَاتُ كُتَمَلَكِ نْغُومِ اكتملكِ نْغُوم يممباسه

اَكَمْوَفُ* الامام اليعربى اكاءَ لِوَلِي كتِك مزارع وات وتاتُ

محمد بن عثمان نا على بن عثمان نْدُغُ وَتَتُ سِكُمْيَوَ اِنَ لَكِ وكاي بَمُوِيَ نعسكر

والامام سيف نبهاني اليعربي نْدِيُ اَصل يَمزارِع . نا مُفلم وَبَنَهَ اَلِنَ

سِرَ نْجِمَ نا جميع يَواتُ اكاعِشِ نْيَاكَ أربعين كتِكَ اُفَلْمِ وكِ اَكَف سنه ١١٥٤

اَكُوات زِجَان وَنْغ بَعد يَكِ وسِتوالِ زِجان زَكِ : اكتوالِ احمد بن ابو بكر بن محمد بن ابو بكر >>

بن محمد بن عمر بن احمد بن عمر بن محمد بن احمد بن محمد بن سليمان اَكَكِتِ كُوَ وِيْما اكف >>

سنه ١١٦٠ اَكَخلِفُ كِجان كَمِيْتَ بوانَ غُوغُ اسِتوالِ اكتوالِ بوان تَامُ

تُتُ اَمْكُو لِوَاوُ اِمامُ الْهُدَاى* وبوان مْكُو اَلْتُكُوَ لِوَ نَپُرتُغال نَأنَ لَكِ

ابو بكر بن بوان مكو بن ابو بكر بن محمد بن ابو بكر بن محمد بن ابو بكر بن محمد بن عمر بن محمد بن سليمان >>

كَتكَ وقْتِ هُونُ امام اليعربي اَكَاَتَ زِيْتَ كُبِجَ پَتِه وَسِوزِ وَكَافُ وعرابُ

وانْغِ سان وَكَفَانْيَ اَمانِ بعَد يهاي واتُ ولامُو وكخالِفُ مْفَلْمِ

كَوَبِجَ زِتَ اَسِوَ وِيْز وات ولامو : نوات ولامو وكَفُونْغَ زِيْتَه

وَكَايَ پَتِه كُوَ جَانبُ ياكتُكِ وكبِجانَ نَواتُ وَيَتَه زِيْتَه زِكُوْ //

ولفُنْدِكَ* وات ولامو بعدى مفلُم وباتِ اكفُونْغ زِيْتَه كُو بار نابَحْرِ

كابِجَ وات ولامو كو تملكِ : بَعد يهايَ وِلكُو حالِ مُوِيَ مْفَلْمِ وباتِ نوات

ولامو: امام اليعربي اكفانْيَ شَوْرِ مُويَ وكامُؤُوَ مفلْمِ ١١٧٧ سنه اكتوالِ

نْدِي مُوان مْلِ سلطان موان خديجه بنت بوان مْكُو بن ابو بكر بن محمد بن ابو بكر بن محمد >>

بن ابُو بكر بن محمد بن عمر بن محمد بن احمد بن محمد بن سليمان اِكَوَ فِتُنه نْيِنْغِ
كتِكَ نْتِ بَاپاتِ >>

اِكَوَ وفلْم وويلِ موان خديجه المذكوره نا سلطان عمر وكبجِان كتِك مْوِي وَيَاتِ
نْيَاكَ متِاتُ سلطان عمر اَكِنْدَ بَرَاوَ كَرَجِيا پَاتِ كَوْ نْغُفُ كوُ سان : وُسِكُ*
نوات ومْوان خديجه كُلَ مْتُ مهالِ پكِ اكف موان حديجه* سنه ١١٨٧ التوال* بوان
مْكُوْ وُشيِ* وَبُوَان تَام مكُو : رَعِيَ وكَفانْيا أُذِيَ سان اسِبتِ راح كتِك
اُفلْم وَكِ حتى سنه ١١٩١ وَكَمْنغِلِي وات وَمْوِي وَكَمُؤُوَ كُوَ تاريخ هِيُ كتوالِ
بوان فُومُ مادِ ان يَكِ سلطان محمد بن ابو بكر بن بوان مكو بن ابو بكر بن محمد بن
ابو بكر بن محمد >>

بن ابو بكر بن محمد بن عمر بن محمد بن احمد بن محمد بن سليمان بعد يكُتوالِ
رَعِيَه وكَتاك كُفانُيا* >>

فِتْنَه كاوبِجَ زِيْتَه كَوَشِنْدَ كَوَشِيكَ وات اربعين نوويُل*
نِنْدُز خاص اكو تِنْدَ كَمَ مْبوُزِ يُو نَسَقَفُ دَامَ اِكَشُكَ نْديانِ
كتِك مَكُوپُ اِكَوَ اَمانِ استُوكِ تِنَ مْتُ كُفَانْيَا فِتُنَه اكتوالِ كُوَ رَاحَ
سان ١٢٢٤ كاف ولا هكُتوالِ مْفَلمِ تِنَ كَمَ يِيِ اكخالِفُ زِجان وانْغِ
اكتوالِ سلطان احمد بن شيخ فومُ لوط بن شيخ بن بوان مْكُو اِكَزِدِ فِتْنَه
كتِك مْجِ ولامو اكوبجَ زيتَ يِيِ نواتُ وممباسه مَازَرِيْعِ حالِ مْوُجَ*
وَكَشُوكَ شيِلَه جَيش كُوَ سَانَ يَواتُ وباتِ نواتُ وممباسه : وات
ولاموه وكتُك وكاجه شِيله وكبِجان نواتُ وبَتِه نواتُ وممباسه وكَفُندِك*
زِتَ زَواتُ ولامو زِكاوَ نْغُوءفُ سَنَ جَيْش يَپَاتِ
نامباسه وكافُنْدِك وكاكِمبْلِيَ مَجَهَزِنِ مْواوُ مَجهَزِ مَنْغِنِ ياكجهابُ
پُوانِ وَكسِمِ هابُ وكبِجان زِتَ زكُو سان وكو واتُ ونْغِ سان ويَاتِ نو ممباسه //

هبان عِدَدِ : كتِك واتُ وباتِ والُ معرُفُ اِشِكُوَ وتُمْوَ نَوَضَعِفُ واتُ
واحد وثمانين فلان بن فلان وِنيِ* وكِ يَكِنْدَ معِدَ هايُ باتِ نَوَاتُ
وممباسه هوانَ عِدَدِ بعد يهايُ وات ولامؤ وكِنْد عربُون وكُمُتاكَ
سعيد بن سلطان ابن الامام وَكَمْبَ نْتِ يا لاموُه سنه ١٢٢٨ اَلِبُو تَوالِ
لامو اُفلْمِ ويَتِ اكَسلِيَ كَتكَ باتِ نابنادرِ : اِكَزدِ فِتُنَه
اَكَتُوكَ مْتُ وَ بِلِ كَتكَ زِجان وبوان فومُ مادِي هُواِتُوَ فُومُ
لُوطِ كِپُوْنْغَه اكبجان سُلُطان احمد كِسَ سلطان احمد اكف
كُوَ مرض ١٢٣٠ اكتوال فُؤمُ لُوط وبوان فُوم ماديْ نَايِ
اَلِكُوَ هُدارِ سان شجاع كَرِيمُ : نَزمانِ هِزُ شيخ مَتَاكَ بن شيخ
مُبارك نْدِپُ اَلِبُو توالِ اُشخِ وَسِوُ اكفانْيَ عَسْكَر نَبُنْدكِ
نَيِ نِكتِك طاعه سلطان وباتِ نايِ اَلِبَتَانَ سَان نمُزارِع
حتى سنه ١٢٣٦ اِكَزدِ فِتْنَه بَيْن يَكِ نا سلطان سعيد بن سلْطان زنجبار
اكف سلطان فومُ لُوطِ المذكور سنه ١٢٧٠ بعَد يَكِ اكتوال فُومُ لُوط
بن شيخ بن فوم لوط وبوانَ تَمُ مْكُو نَهُؤيُ نْدِيُ بَياكِ* سلطان
احمد بن* سلطان وَوِيْتُ اكتوال اَصُبْح حتى بعْد الْعصر واتُ
وَمُوِى وَكَمْتُوَ اَكِنْدَ سِوُ بَمُوىَ نَمُزَارعي وَكِنْدَ وُوُتِ
ممباسه اكتوال سلطان بوان شيخ بن فوم مادي اكب تَنَ
نا سيد سعيد بن سلطان اَكَتِيَ وعراب بَتِه وكاكِتِ نْياكَ مِتاتُ
بَعَدَيِ وَتُ وَمُوِي وَكَمُعُزُلُ نا شَوُر . . . .* سيد سعيد بن سلطان
سنه ١٢٥٩* وَكَمَتَوَ الِشَ* سلطان احمد اَتكُؤ يَواوُ* بْوانَ وزيرِ
وبوان تَمُ وبوان شيخ وبوان تَمُ مْكُؤ كبتن نا سيد سعيد بن سلطان //
اكتوالِ نْياك مِوِيْلِ وات وَكَمُعُزُلُ وَكَمْرجِيَ بوان شيخ وبوان فوم مَادِى

اكاكيْتِ كَتكَ عِز كُو شو* يا سيد سعيد بن سلطان نْياك مِتاتُ اكف سنه ١٢٤٧
اكرجِيَ بوان وزير كتِك اُسُلْطان وكِ : كَيَ بوان فوم لُوط بن شيخ
اَلِيُ تُونْدَ ممباسه نَموجه* نَمْزَارِعِ وَكَشُكَ سِيُو وكبِجان نبوان وزير
وبُوان تَمُ پَتِه نَبُوَان وَزِيْرِ نِشَوُرِ مُوجَ نا سيد سعيد بن سلطان :
نا فومُ لُوط بَمُوجَ نَمزارعي نا شيخ متاك مُتُ وَسِوَ وَكَجَ باتِ كُوَ
زِيْتَه كَبِجان نا جِيشِ ياسِوُ اِكَفُندكَ بوان وزير اِكا اِشِكَ
نْتِ يَسيوُ اَكَفُنْدَ نَوُكُتَ وَمُي شيخ مَتَاكَ نا فُوم لُوطِ وكاكمْبِلِيَ
بَرَانِ بَمُوجَ نَبَعْض يواتُ بعد يسِكُ كَشِيْتِ* كَرجِيَا سِوُ كُوَ زِتَ
زِكُوْ سان وكَوتُوَ واتُ وبوان وزِيْرِ كُوَ زِيْتَ وكا وشِكَ وَوُ
مُوِي وَسِوُ وَكَجِنْغَه اُكُتَ وُمُوِي وكبِجان باتِ نا سِيوُ اِكَوَ
كتِكَ طاعه نا شور يا سيد سعيد بن سلطان بعد يُمواكَ مْمُوجَه اكاؤَاوَ
سلطان بوان وزيرِ نا فوم بكر وبُوان شيخ وبوان فوم مادى
اكا توالِ يِيِ سلطان فُومُ بكر بن شيخ بن بُوان فومُ مادي سنه ١٢٥٠
اكپتن سان سيد سعيد بن سلطان مُدّ وكُتوالِ كِسَ اكخلِفُ بموجه نا شيخ مَتَكَ
بن شيخ مُبارك : سيد سعيد بن سلطان اَكَبِكَ زِيْتَه نامير حماد السمار
البو سعيدى اكبج باتِ نا سِوُ اسوزِ* اكف نْيا امانِ بعَد يهايُ
اَكِتُوكَ فِتْنَه بيْن يا سلطان وبات فُومَ بكر ناعمِ يكِ محمد بن احمد
وبوان فوم مادي اكشِك نْيوْمبا يَ وُفَلْمِ يا سلطان فُومُ بَكر
غَفْله كُوَ زِيْتَه واتُ ولاموُ بَمُوىَ نَمْتُ وسيد سعيد بن سلطان
وكُو صِلِحِشَ محمد بن احمد اَكَمْبِك سِوُ كُكتِ نا فُوم بَكَر اكاي* پَتهِ
بعَدي وَكَتِيْتَ وكَبجان تِنَ نْياك مِتاتُ نَفُومُ بكَرِ سِيُو نپاتِ //
كِسَ سيد سعيد بن سلطان اكو سِلِحِشَ* اكاي باتِ محمد بن احمد كُوَ شَوُرِ مُوىَ يِيِ

نا بن عمّ يكِ فُومّ* بَكَر اكمْشِك محمد بن احمد غفله اكامُؤَ كُوَ شُور بَ
مُويَ يِيِ نَمْتُ وسِوُ : سيد سعيد بن سلطان اُكُمُويُتَ* فُومُ بكر اكِنْدَ اُغُوجه
سيد سعيد بن سلطان اكَمفونْغَ كو شَورِ ياواتُ ولامُوْ نسببُ يكُمُؤَ
محمد بن احمد نِكُتُفُواتَ امانِ اَلِيُوفَانُيَ سيد سعيد بن سلطان كتك سنه ١٢١٢
اكشِك بَاتِ سلطان احمد بن شيخ * فوم لوط بن شيخ وبوان تامُ مْكُو
كُوَ شور يا سيد سعيد بن سلطان اككتِ نْيَاكَ مِوِيْلِ بَعديِ اكخلفُ اكاي
سيد سعيد بن سلطان اَكَمْفُو نْغُوَ سلطان فوم بكر اَكَمْبَ زِيْتَه بَمُوجَ
ناوتُ ولامو وكاكِيُتِ* مْتانْغَ وَنْدَ كتِكَ مَجَهَازِ يا سيد سعيد
اَلِبُو كُوَ نْدَ فازه اكاكِيتِ مَهالَ هِتُوَ : كِجانْغَه شَا مْپُوْنْغَه
كَربُ نفازه امِير حَماد اكَيِ سِوُ كُوكَ مبُوْم كتِك نْدِيَ يبات
نيا فازه نيا سِوُ : امير حماد اَكِندَ سِوُ كُوَ زِيْتَه زِكُو سان
حتى اكشِك مِتُومْبِى اِلِيُوكَ كتِك بنْدر يا سِوُ كَبِنْدُ و كفانْيا مابُومَ
كبج نْتِ يَسِوُ كَوُنَ اُذِيَ سان مُدّ وَزِّيْتا كُوَ زِنْغِ سان وَزتَ
اَكَرَدِ* امير حماد نبعْضِ يا عَسْكر اكِنْدَ بُمْمانِ* كُتُوا مْزِنْغه اَكِبِيْتَا نْدِيَانِ
وات وسِوُ وَكْمتكيَ غفله امِيرِ وشى متاك هِتُوَايِ بن مبارك حَمَد عمر
نامير وَپِيْلِ هِتْوَاوُ حمادِ نْغُمَ وكبجان وكمؤُوَ امير حماد وكنْد
نا بمانِ وكوبجَ وعربُ ولِيُوكُ بُمَانِ وكتُواء نَمزِنْغَه : نا
جيِشِ اِلِيُوكُ سِوُ هُبِجان ولِبُ بات خبار يا كُوُمْبا امِرِ حمادِ
مِوُ وَاؤ جيِشِ يا سيد بن* سعيد بن سلطان اِكَفُنْدِكَ نَوُ ولِكْوَ* كتِك //
نَوُ وِلكُو كتِك* كتملُك* سِوُ : سيد سعيد بن سلطان اكِسَ كُواتَ خبار
يمُوتِ يا امير حماد كَوُ نْدُك كَنْغِيَ مَرْ كَبُوْن اَسِنِن نينَ اَكِنْدَ زكِ
مسقط مُواك وَبِيلِ اَكَمُوكَ سلطان فوم بكر فازه اكبجَ سِوُ نپاتِ

كتِك وقْتِ هُوْنُو اكف شيخ متاك كُوَ مرض اِكو خِلاَفُ كْوَ زِجان
زكِ كُل مْتُ اتك اُشِيخِ وكاءِ نْغِيَ كتك طاعه يسيد سعيد بن سلطان .
ابو بكر نا محمد زِجان ز شيخ مَتَاكَ . سَيِدِ اَكَمْبَ بُو* بَكر زِيْتا
بَمُوجَ نا سلطان فوم بكر كُمْبجَ سلطان احمد سِوُ : اَكِنْدَ ابو بكر بن شيخ
مَتَاكَ بَمُوْىَ نا امير و سلطان فوم بكر اَمْكُو لِوَ اوُ حمادِ وبائِشِ
نبهانى كانْغِيَ سِوُ اُسِكُ وكِبجان حتى * وكفُنْدِك واتُ وسُلطان
فوم بكر وكانْدَ مِوَ* نْديانِ وكمْشِك ابو بكر بن شيخ متاك وكمبِك پاتِ
كُوُ واو نا سلطان احمد بعَدي اكَسِامِ نْدُيِ شيخ محمد بن شيخ متاك طرف
يا سيد سعيد بن سلطان يِيِ نا سلطان فُومُ بكر : سيد سعيد بن سلطان كواپَ
زِيْتَه نا عَسكر ناغَرامه وكمْبج سلطان احمد حتى وكَمْتُوَ پات سنه ١٢٧٣
اَكِنْدَ كْوَوُ سِوُ :* اِكِوَ* نِشِيخ* محمد بن شيخ متاك طرف يا سيد سعيد بن سلطان
اَكمْپَ >>

نا عسْكر كَوكَ نا غِرز وكتِت نَمْتُ وسيد سعيد بن سلطان كُو سبابُ اكِفُنْد
بانْدَ يَمْتِپِ اَلُوكَ شيخ محمد متاك اَلِوكَ مْپِى يَا غِرِيُزَه* نا شيخ
محمد متاك كفُنْدَ غِريزَ : نكتِك وقْتِ هُونُ اِلكُفَ سلطان احمد بن شيخ
كاوُ بَبَاكِ فومُ بَكَر سلطان وَوِيْتُوْ اككِيْتِ مهالَ پَكِ سلطان
احمد اَمْكُوْ لِوَاوُ سِمْپَا سلطان وَوِيْتُو : نَقَبْلَ يا شيخ محمد
اَسِيَا فُنْدَ غِرِيْزَ لَسِوُ يَلِتُكَ فِتْنَه : سلطان فُومُ بكر بن شيخ
اَكَمْتُوَ باتِ كْوَ زِيْتَه اكايَ لامو اكتاك كاَ تملاك پَتِه : الِپُوْنَ
نْغُفُ زكِ نوَكُو وَ پَات اَلِبُوْنَ كِتِنْدُ مِزُ فَانْيَ شيخ محمد بن شيخ متاك
مَوسُوِ اَتاك كُوَ توالِ وسِكِرِ كَوَ بجَ زيتا وكسِامِ وَكُوْ //
وَكُوُ* وَباتِ ولا هپان مُفلْمِ كُوَ شوُرِ لواتُ وتتُ محمد بن مُكو نبهانى نا بُوان

رِحِمَ بن احمد نبهاني نناصرِ بن عبد الله بن عبد السلام نْدِ ولُكُوَ مُدبَرِ الامور
اكاكُو سانُيا• زانه وكبجان شيخ محمد بن شيخ متاك وكَمْشِنْدَ وكاف واتُ مَعرُفُ
نا ما اَمرِ مَكُوْ وات وويلِ بوانه دُمِيْلِي نامولنا وَشي كُوْلى : شيخ محمد
محمد• بن شيخ متاك كِسَ كُوُنَ مامْبُو هايَ اكيا كُتاك امانِ كُوَ محمد بن بوان
مكو النبهاني كُوَنِ نْدِي اَلِيكُوَ مْكُوْ بْوَ واوُ كتِك هاوَ واتَ وتتُ تُمزُ
تَا نُغْلِيَ كُتَيَ : اكتاك كُمْبَ يِي محمد بن مْكُوْ وُسلْطان وَلسِوُ• ونا پَتِ
اكائز كَجِبُ مِمِ نِمْتُ مْزِمَ : وكِنْدَ كُمْتُوآء سلطان احمد وَوِيْتُو
كَبِكَ وات شيخ محمد بن شيخ متاك نوات وپات وكْمبك نا شيخ ناصر بن عبد الله
بن عبد السلام كاوُ كُمْتُوآء سلطان احمد الملقب سِمْبَا كايَ نَيِ
پَاتِ خبارِ اِكَسِكِلِيَ اُنغوجه : سلطان سيد ماجد بن سعيد بن سلطان كُوَنِ
سيد سعيد بن سلطان اُتانُغُلِيْ• كُفَ سته ١٢٧٣ : قَبْلَ يهاي سيد كامُؤيْتَ
وَزِيْرِ وكِ سيد سليمان بن حمد كُوَ مَرْكَبه• ايْلِي كُشِك پاتِ كُفدُشَ•
فِتْنَه مَزْكَبْ اَلِو وَصِلِ : مار• پتِ امِكُوسَ كُشِك مْتُ وسلطان
احمد (ابو بكر بن حسن البوزى•) اَمِكُوْيَ ناصر بن عبد الله بن عبد السلام
اَكِسَ كُباتَ خبارِ هِيُ سيد سليمان بن احمد اكَرجِيَ اُنْغُوَجه نا شيخ محمد
محمد• بن شيخ متاك وقْتِ هُوْنُ نْدپُ اَلِبُو فُنْدَ غِرزَ وَسِوُ اكِسَ
كُوَصِلِ سلطان احمد پات واتُ واكَمْبَ كُوَ نْدِي سلطان :
شيخ محمد بن شيخ متاك كُنا مْزِيْ سِيفُ نا شيخ شِكُو نا محمد مُوتِ
اَكَسِتَاكِرِ كا سلطان احمد وُفَلْمِ وكِ : سيد ماجد بن سعيد بن سلطان
اكا پِك واتُ ولامو باتِ كُوَ ناصِحَ بمُوي نا شيخ محي الدين كَمْتَكَ //
سلطان احمد اَوكِ عسْكر وسيد بات نهُوىُ شيخ محي الدين نْدي اَلْتُوَ عسْكر وَسيد
كتِك غِرِيْرَ• لا سيوُ وَيِجَ شح• محمد بن شيخ متاك عسكر والى • اكِنْد شيخ محى الدين

كُوَ تُوَ كُو امانِ كُوا الِكُوَ مْتُ وسيد ماجد بن سعيد كتِك مَوَزِيْر الِبُوكُونْد اُنْغُوج
نا عسْكر : سيد كف نْيَ هَسِرَ سان يُؤ لشيخ محي الدين نا شيخ محي الدين
أكت دركِ الِبُو مُؤنَ سيد ماجد نغضبْ نْدبُ كِنْدَ
يِي نواتُ ولامو ناي شيخ محي الدين اَلِنَ حِلَ سان نا علم نْيِنْغِ
اَكِنْدَ پَاتِ نخيارِ يواتُ ولامو بموجه نا شيخ احمد نا شيخ عبد الرحمن
اَي نَي شيخ پت وكنين نا سلطان احمد اَكَرِضِك بعُد يا شِدَ
كُو سببُ يا صحبه يا شيخ احمد نا شيخ عبد الرحمن اكخالِفُ شَوُرِ لَوزيرِ وكِ
ناصر بن عبد الله بن عبد السلام كْوانِ وِلِنِزَ كُتِيَ وعراب حتى مْتُ مْمُوِيَ
وات وپات وكفانْيا شَوُرِ مُوجه موان جَاهَ بنت فوم لوط كِبُغ
وبُوان فوم مادى مْكِ وسلطان فُوم بكر بن شيخ وَقْتِ هونُ سلطان
فوم بَكَر اُوكُ لاموه تِنِ يا شور لا سيد ماجد بن سعيد تانْغُ اكِبُو تُلِوَ
پاتِ باس كِلَ سِكُ وكِتِيَ عسكر كْوَ سِرِ نزان اُسِكُ وُسِكُ : اَلِبُوَ
خبار سلطان احمد اِكَوَ فِتُنَه نعسْكرِ ومِكُو وانْغِ پتِ وكْمبجَ
سلطان احمد غَفُله بعدي كِسَ حَلٌ• كتُك كُمْشِك وسِوِزِ كُوَنِ
وپتِ وُتِ ولِكُو شوُرِ موُجه ناسيدِ ماجد بن سعيد اِلِ وزير وكِ
ناصرِ بن عبد الله بن عبد السلام وكبِجان نْدانِ يَمُوِى وباتِ : اكتُك
سلطان احمد يِي نا شيخ محمد بن شيخ متاك وكِنْدَ سِوُ : باتِ وكشِك
وَعْرابُ• نَبَحْرِنِ وكَتِي مَرْكبْ زِيْتَ زِلبُ كُوَ زِكُوْ سان :
اِلبُكوُي سيد ماجد بن سعيد كُؤ حُصُر سِوُ نَپاتِ نَبَحْر كُسِپت //
كُسِبِدِي• گُوْمْبُ گُگُوْتِ مَدَفُ نَمتِيْپِ وكبِجان نَبَحْرِيْنِ وَكُنِ دَ• بَرانِ
كُتوْا شَكوُله نَمجِرَ يَا كُرُدِ هُوَنَ حَل حَي مَيْتِ : سيد ماجد اكتِي سِلْسِل
كُتِكَ• كانّوَ لامْتُ وسِوُ كُؤيُ كُسِپتِ گُوْمْبُ تِنَ : نَوُ وُلِوَانَ

نْيِز سِةَ كْوَ بحر بَحْرِ* ناكْوَ پُوانِ نا جانِبُ يفازه مْزِيْ سيْف
اكجالِفُ* وسيد ماجد بن سعيد كُوَ حِلَ نْيِغ نَمَانِبُ* مَانْغ اَكَوُنِ* ضِقِ سان
سلطان احمد نا شيخ محمد بن شيخ متاك نانْتِ يا سيوُ اِكَوَ فِتْنَه اِكَوَ بَعْضِ
يوَاتُ وَمْبِنْدَ سيد ماجد كُوَ سبابُ يَمَشَكَ ولُباتَ نَو تُو نهَاوَ
شريف مولانَ بن ابو بكر نا عيسى بن احمد السومالى اَلِبُؤنَ سلطان احمد
نا شيخ محمد بن شيخ * كَمَ هايَ وكَتاك امانِ كْوَ سيد ماجد اَكَوابَ : كتِك
منِنُ يَاَمانِ سلطان احمد اكسِفِرِ كُوَ سِرِ اُسِكُ اَكِنْدَ برانِ
اكرِجِيَ كاوُ بعَدِيِ شيخ محمد بن شيخ متاك اكمْبِكَ كِجان شَكِ :
شيخ محمد بن شيخ متاك اَكِنْدَ مَرْكَبُنِ سيد ماجد بن سعيد نا سيد
ماجد اَكَمَسْمحِ اَكَمْباَ نا عطايا نْيِنْغِ : سيد ماجد كسفِرِ اكرجِي
اُونْغُوجه كِسَ شيخ محمد بن شيخ متا* اَكِنْدَ اونغوجه كُمُوَجِه سيد ماجد
اَكَمُشِكَ اكمْفُؤنْغَه كَتِكَ نْغُوْمِ يَمَمباسه نواتُ : اكف شيخ محمد
نبعْد يَسِكُ اكْمبِك لوالى سعود بن حمد كُمْشِكَ سلطان احمد كُوَ حِلّ
نْيِنْغ اَسِوزِ كَتُك كاوُ كُوَ سِرِ اَكِنْدَ وِيْتُو : الوالى سعود بن حمد
اكايَ فازه كُمْشِكَ عُمَرْ متاك فازه نا زجان زَ شيخ محمد بن شيخ متاك
كُوَ شِكَ سِوُ كوپِكَ نْغُمِينِ ممباسه : عُمر متاك اكمفُوْنْغَ //
لاموه بَعَدى سيد ماجد اكتملكِ سوَاحل زُتِ هكُونَ مْتُ وكُمْرض نا سلطانِ
احمد كاكتِ وِيْتُو كَتَكَ* طاعه سيد ماجد حتى اِلبُو توال سيد برغش
بن سعيد بن سلطان اكتك سيد برغش كُوِك عسكر ويْتُو نا بِنْدِرَ : سلطان
اَسِرِضِكِ كبِك زِت كُمْبِجَه اسِوزِ اكف نْياَ* امانِ ناي سعود بن حمد
هكُمْبِجَ سان زِيُتا* : سيد برغش كبِك زِيْتا زمانِ زَ الوالى سعيد بن حمد بن سعيد :
سلطان احمد كَتاك حِمايه كُوَ جرَمَانِ وَكَمْپَ نبعْضِ يبار يَسَوَاحِلِ

اكف سلطان احمد كَتِك حالِ هِيُ يا حماي سنه ١٣٠٦ اكتوالِ سلطان فُومُ
بَكَرِ بن سلطان بن* احمد بن شيخ النبهاني اككيت كتِك هِيُ يا حِماى اِكُتُكِيَ فِتْنَه
يِيِ نجرمن : متُ مْمُوجَ هُؤتُوَ كُنْشِلْ اَكَمْبِجَ بوابُ ولانْغُ
كَمْبِجَ غَفله كُوَ رصاص وِلكُوكُ عسْكر كوبِجه كُو رصاصِ نعسْكرْ*
وكَمْبِج كِنسِلِ نوتُ ونْغُ ولُفُوٓاتِنِ لوُ وكَأواوَ وزُنْغُ مِنْ
غير امْرِ يا سلطان فُومُ بَكر : عسكرْ وِليُوءَوُنَ جماع زَوُ ومِكُفَ
هاوَكُنْغُوجه امْر يا سلطان وكوابجَ وزُونغَ* نَواتَ* نوات*
وَمْكُنُوَمْبِى* نونْد مُوْنِىُ وِلبُ پات خبار نكُومْبَه لاوزُونْغُ
ومِبِجان وكاو اُوْوَ وزُنْغَ وِلَيُوُ كُوكُ بَعديِ اَكايَ دُوله
يَو نْغِرزَ وكتاك كُفانْيا اِنْصاف اكو تك وتُ ومُكُنُومْبِيْ
نوَنْدَ مُونْيُ مَعَنَ اَوتِيِ كتِك حُكْمُ : فُومُ بَكَر اَسِرضِكِ كُوتُوَ
وَكَمْبِجَ زِيته سلطان فوم بكر زِكِيا مَشُوَ حتى مْكُنُومْبِيْ نَونْدَ مُونْيُ
ناكِلِمانِ نْيَدُ زَ پُوانِ وزِبِجِ كُوَ مِزِنْغَه وكَتِىَ نَمُوْتُ حتى ليلة
١١ ربيع الاول سنه ١٣٠٨ وكِبِجان وتُ وُوِيْتُوْ كتِك نْدِيَ ياكِبِنِ
نَواتُ وَدُلَه تُكُفُ وكا فُندِك واتُ ووِيْتُو حتى اَصُبْح //
سِكُ يا جُمعه تاتُ مُوزِ ١٢ ربيع الاول سنه ١٣٠٨ وَكَمْبِجَ سلطان فُومُ بَكَرْ
وكمْتُوَ وِيْتُو وِيْتُوْ* اَكِنْدَ جُونْغِنِ ويتو اِكتما لِكوَ ندُوله تُكُفَ
سلطان فُومُ بَكَر كاكِتِ جُنْغِينِ حتى ٢٨ جمادى الاول* سنه ١٣٠٨ اكف
كشِك مهالَ يكِ نْدُيِ بُوان شيخ بن سلطان احمد نبهاني بعَد يسِكُ
گَاگِ اِكو فِتْنه اكشِك نْدُوِيِ فوم عمر نبهانى نأَ ڤُ تُوْ له وَ
بَاهِرُ وكمْفُونْغَه بُوان شيخ بن سلطان احمد اكتوال سلطان فُومُ
عُمَر : نواكُوِس كُتملكِ پاتِ سلطان أحمد سُلُطان وَوِيْتُوْ

اَلتَملكِ* كُوَنْدَ (سليمان بن سليمان المظفر نبهاني امام اليعربى[)]
هِنِ* نْدِيُ خبارِ يا نبهاني كُوَ سواحِلِ نخبارِ زَوُ كُمَ* تُمزُ تَنْغُلِيَ
كُتيا : ومِزُ توالَ وَفَلْمِ واحد و ثلاثين نَمْوَان مْكِ مْمُوجه جُمُله اثنان
اِثْنِنِ* وثلاثين مِن غَيْرِ* اَلكِتواله* وكوُزِلوَ وكِرجيا كُتوالئ
تُمِ ناقِلِ هاي كُوَ محمد بن فوم عمر النبهاى الملقب بوان كتِيِنِ نايِ
اَلِن قِلِ گو* جَدِ يكِ محمد بن بوان مكو النبهانى امْكُوِلواوُ بُوان
ستميا* اُلضِبِتِ سان خبار يا نسبْ يَوُ كَمَ تُمزُ تاجه
نَقْلَه يا اولِ منقل صالح بن سالم بن احمد بن عبد الله شراحيل ٦ فى صفر سنه ١٣١٨
نقلت هذا اللولى العزيز محمد بن احمد بن سلطان بن فوم بكر بن شيخ بن بوان
فُوْمُ مَادِي : وسِمْيَ* سلطان محمد بن ابو بكر بن بوان مكُو بن ابو بكر بن حمد*
بن ابو بكر بن محمد بن ابو بكر بن محمد بن عمر بن محمد بن احمد بن محمد بن
سليمان بن سليمان المضفر*>>
النبهانى . نقله الثاني ١ فى رجب سنه ١٣٤٣ وكتبه الاقَل صالح بن سالم بن حمد
نقلت الثالث * فى ذى القعده ١٣٦٣ فى ٣ فبرورى وكتبه على محمد
نقلت ذلك نقلا* حرفا بحرف انا الحقير لله تعالى عبد الله بن على بن محمد المعاوي //

الهجره سنه ٦٠٠

اخبار بته

[ملك احمد بن حسن بن حمد با حسين المرشدي لاموه]

هاهنا سليمان بن سليمان مظفر النبهانى الول* المبدي نبهانى
مَنْدُ وَكَنْدَ كُيَ بَتِ نسليمان بن سليمان بن مظفر نبهانى
نَدُزِ وَوِيْلِ على بن سليمان نا عثمان بن سليمان نَهُيُ سليمان
بن سليمان المذكورِي اُلْكُوَ سلطان نيِ اكِس كُتولى بَرَ
لِعربُ اكي بتِ سلطان المذكور كتِك تاريخ سَنَتِ ٦٠٠ الهجرة
كُيَ ككِيْ بتِ اكتك عَرُوْسِ كَمْفَلُمِ وبتِ كتِك البتويين
سلطان سليمان بن سليمان نِمْتُ معرُفُ مْفلُمِ وبتِ اك
مُوُزَ بنت ياكِ نَدَستُورِ يوتُ* يا وسوحِلِ حتى سس مْتُ اكُ
ولِيَي كِجان گَكُ اكِس سِيْكُ سَبَعَه زَهَرُوْسِ هِنْدَ كُمَغَلِيَ
مْكِو نْيُبانِ مَكِ باب ومْكِ وكِ كومْبِيَ واتُ هُيُ سليمان
بن سليمان رِيِ* مْفَلُمِ ويْنُ اك مْبَ وُفَلُمِ وك الُ كُوَ نَوُ //

اكتولِ سليمان بن* رِيِ* مْفَلُمِ كالِن مُوْيِ هِيْت كِتُكِ* اِيُ
جِزِرَ* يابتِ كتِك مطِلعِ يا بتِ نسِوُ حَتَسَ كُو مُوْيِ ولِكُ
مُوْيِ مْغِنِ هِيْتَ شَغَ كتِك مطِلعِ يا بتِ نفازه ولِكُ مُوْيِ
وِيِو وِپازَ المفازى اِككِتِ مِيْ هِيُ يُتِ اِككِتِ يُوْتِ تحتِ
يا سلطان سليمان بن سليمان نا مَرَّ* كلِنا مْفلُمِ مْبَلِ نَيْ
وُنَ غُفُ سن اكف سلطان سليمان بن سليمان سنه ٦٢٥ هجر*
اك خلِفُ زِجان ووِيْلِ محمد نا احمد عُمْرِ يك عشيرين*
احمد عُمْرِ وكِ خمسة عشر اكتولِ محمد بن سليمان بن سليمان
بعد يا ببكِ اِكو ختِلفُ يِيِ نواتُ وشغ كِبجن نمِيْ كيْفُد
كبِس نبعضِ يوُ وكيا بتِ نوغِنِ وقبِل يوُ كِنَدَغُ ووككِمْبِيا
وسِيُو كَنِ مهالَ ومِزُ كمْبِلِيَ حتى سِيْكُ زِكِپتَ اِكَيِ خبرِ
كا سلطان محمد بن سليمان نحُو واتُ وِروُ* كُونْدِ وكمبِيا
ولِ وسِوُ تُمِوَوُنَ كتِك مِيْتُ سلطان كبِك واتُ كُوغلِي
كودرِك ومِفنْي زِجُوْمْب رانِ* يا مِتُ سلطان محمد بن سليمان //

كو صمحِ كورُدِش مهال بَوُ رِيُ* اصِلِ يا مُوْيِ و سِيوُ
وكيا نوسوحِلِ وغِينِ وككِتِ وُتِ وكيا نوفَمَوُ وككِتِ
وكو وفموُ رِّ* وَكُوُ وسِوُ كتِك طع يا سلطان محمد بن سليمان
اكف سنه ٦٥٠ اكتولِ رُيِ* سلطان احمد بن سليمان اك امرِش
سن ارْضِ يا بتِ كَجغَ مَجُمْبَ نا مشامْب اسِبجِ مهال اكف
سنه ٦٦٠ كتولِ كِجان گَنْدُيِ اِن لكِ احمد بن محمد بن سليمان اككِتِ
نواتُ كوُزُرِ سن كم سِيْر ز عَمِ زاكِ كُعمرِش مُيْ وبتِ نمشا
مْب حتى سنه ٧٠٠ اكف اكخلِفُ زِجان ونْغِ كتولِ كِجان گكِ
سلطان محمد بن احمد بن محمد بن سليمان اككِتِ نواتُ كومِ سن واتُ
وفازه وكخلِفُ اكوبِج كوتِي كتِك طع بعد يزِت زِنْغِ حتى
اِلپُ وشِد اك اِفُتحِ نمرِك* كيْ تملكِ كزِت نَخيْلَ كانِ الِن
غُفُ سن سلطان ومرِك يمالِ نواتُ اكئفُنْد كبِس نواتُ
وغِنِ كويْت بتِ نبعضِ وكتو يِك* وككِمْبِلِيَ كُل مهالَ
وغِنِ وكي شِيْلهَ كغِيَ كتِك هِميا يواتُ ولاموه سلطان //

محمد بن احمد المذكور كوتك واتُ لاموه* وكيْز كُو تُو نوغِنِ وكِيْر*
مَلِنْدِی نبعضِ يبُلْدَنِ سلطان محمد بن احمد اكو انْدم سن هو
وِلِيُ كُوْيِ شِيْله واتُ ولاموه وكيْز كُو تُو قطعاً منِنُ هي
كِس سلطان محمد اكف سنه ٧٣٢ اكتولِ كِجان گَكِ اُفلُمِ سلطان
عمر بن محمد بن احمد بن محمد بن سليمان اكيرِجِي منِنُ يا ببوكِ كواتُ ولاموه
كوتك واتُ ومَانْرَ* وات لاموه* وكيْز كُو تُو كوبِج زِيْتَ وكتك
امانِ واتُ ولامو وكو كتِك طع سلطان عمر بن محمد زِكزدِ غُفُ
اكبج جُمْل يا مِيْءِ يا سَوَحِيْلِ اُوْزِ مَلِنْدِی كِو يُوْ كِتاو مايَه
اِمزِيِ وتَامُ كسكِلِيَ كِرِيْمْبا مِيْ يُوْتِ كيِ تملكِ تغُ بتِ حتى كِرِيْمْبا
كُلَ مُيِ كوكِ مْتُ واكِ كُحكُمُ رِيُ* اصِلِ يهو مجُوْمْبِ ولِيُكَ
مِرِيْمَ معن نِيُوْمُبَ يامْفَلُمِ وبتِ معن يال نِوَ تُمَ ويُوْمْبِيْ
نِهِيُ يُوْمْبِ* نِجانِبُ* يمطِلِع كتملكِ حتى ورْشِيْخِ الِكِنْد
كِبج زِت تغُ كِو يُوْ نطوْل نا طُوْلَ نا شُغَيَ نا بَنَدرِ
زوْتِ بَرَوَ مَرِكَ نا مُقُدِشُوْ كوكِ الوالى جمعِ يا حُكُمُ //

زبنَدْرِ زِكو مُقُدِشُوْ اكِعِش نَنْتِ زُتِ هِزِ كتِك طع ياكِ اِلا
وُغُجَ هكُتولِ نوقَتِ هُوُ وُغُجَ هيْكُو نْتِ كُوْوُ زمنِ هِزُ نا
هُيُ سلطان عمر اِلكِد* زِت نكُبِنْدَ رعِي نا رعِيَ وكِمْبِدَ اِكتاءَ غُفُ
سن نْتِ يا بت اكف سلطان عمر سنه ٧٤٩ كخلِفُ زِجان ووِيْلِ
محمد نا احمد كتولِ كِجان مْكُوْ سلطان محمد بن عمر بن محمد بن احمد بن محمد
بن سليمان ولا هپكُو نزت* وُفلُمِ وببلِكِ كا اَمان ني اِلكِبِد سن
مالِ يا بِعَشَرَ اكِسفرِش نزُمْبُ زكِ هِنْدَ كُفي بِعشر نيِ
اِلنا بختِ سن يا مالِ نمر مُوْيِ اِلمسفرِش كِجان گكِ كبت كِسو
كتِك بحرِ كبت معدنِ يا فِضه كينَيُ بتِ كفيا واتُ كُيفَي
كزِ معدنِ كبت مال مغِ سن يكزدِ مِالِ* كتِك نْتِ يا بتِ
حتى وكفي زِتَرَ زَ فِضه نا غزِ زَ فِضه نِي مْفلُمِ اكف سنه ٧٩٧
اكخلِفُ زِجان ونْنِ بانه مْكُوْ نا احمد نا ابو بكر نا عمر اكتولِ
دُيِ سلطان احمد بن عمر بن محمد بن احمد بن محمد بن سليمان اككِتِ
نواتُ كا اَمانِ نسِيْرَ نْجِمَ نا جمعِ يا واتُ اكف اكتولِ ابو بكر //

بن محمد بن عمر بن محمد بن احمد بن محمد بن سليمان ككتِ سَنَ نا جمعِ يا واتُ
نا مِيْ يُوتِ كتك طع ياكِ بِلَ خِلفُ * سنه ٨٧٥ ني الِخلِفُ زِجان
زِوِيْلِ محمد نا احمد اكتولِ بعد يا ببكِ محمد بن ابو بكر بن محمد
بن عمر بن احمد بن محمد بن سليمان وقتِ وكِ وكَيَ وزُغُ بُرتُكلِ كتك
مِيْ يا سَوَحِيْلِ وُتِ وككت ممباسه وكَفَيَ غُمِ نا جنبُ يا بتِ
كجغَ نْدُونْدُ واتُ وبرانِ وكوفُوتَ وكو* مالِ وكو كتك
طع يوُ وكمُعرضِ مُفلُمِ كتك نْتِ يا بتِ وكمْبجَ زِت مْفلُمِ
كجنبُ يا شِركَس* وكوك نْتِ يا بتِ بوانِ كمعن يتُوْبِ
قصدِ يا كُبجَ مُوْيِ وبتِ و سِوزِ وكبتن كا امانِ وكفنْي
مْكتب وشرُتِ زوُ وككت بتِ وزُغُ وكفي فُرْضَ كا اِن
لوُ وزُغُ وِلگمْكوَ فَنْدكِ وكفي نَمَبُ مغِ كتك كِسِو گبتِ
اكف سلطان سنه ٩٠٠ اكخلف زِجان ووِيْلِ بانه مْكُوْ نا ابو
بكر اكتول وُفَلُمِ سلطان ابو بكر بن محمد بن ابو بكر بن ابو بكر بن
محمد بن احمد بن محمد بن سليمان بعد يا ببكِ المذكور اككتِ //

نواتُ سن اكتُزيِ كا اَمانِ كم قوعِد يا ببكِ اكف سنه ٩٤٠

كُسبَدِ لِكِ يبُ نيِ كخلِفُ زِجان ووِ* احمد و محمد اكتولِ عَمِ يوُ

وُفَلُمِ بانه مْكُوْ بن محمد بن ابو بكر بن محمد بن عمر بن محمد بن احمد بن محمد

بن سليمان اِكو خِتِلفُ نوزُغُ لكِنْ بَسِوِ نزتِ اِكو فِتِن

سِيْكُ يغِ اكف سنه ٩٧٣ اكخلِفُ كِجان مْمُوْيَ هِتَوا* ابو بكر اكتولِ

محمد بن ابو بكر بن محمد بن عمر بن محمد بن احمد بن محمد بن سليمان اكصلِحِيْن

نوزُغُ وكتاءَ بعضِ مِيْ اكف سنه ١٠٠٢ اكخلِفُ كِجان مْمُوْيَ

هِيْتَ ابو بكر استِولِ كتولِ ابو بكر بن بانه مْكُوْ بن محمد بن ابو بكر بن

محمد بن عمر بن محمد بن احمد بن محمد بن سليمان اككتِ نوزُغُ كم سِيْرَ يوزِ

وكِ ولُتغُلِي نوُفلُم وُكبُغُوَ غُفُ اكف سنه ١٠٤١ اكخلِفُ بانه مْكُوْ

نا ابو بكر كِجان* لببكِ* اكتولِ ابو بكر بن محمد بن ابو بكر بن محمد بن ابو بكر

بن محمد بن عمر بن احمد بن محمد بن سليمان اِكو خِتِلفُ نوزُغُ وكبِجن كو

فُنْدَ وزُغُ كزِت زِكُوْ سَنَ بعديِ زِكي تِن زِت زوزُغُ وكبجن

مُيْ وبتِ كمِزغَ وكزِوِيَ نا نْدِيَ كبحرِنِ كُسِبِتِ گُمْبُ وتُ وكونَ //

مَشْكَ وكفي اَمانِ اَكف مْفلُمِ سنه ١٠٦١ اكخلِفُ زِجان ووِيْلِ بانه مْكُوْ
نا احمد اكتولِ بَانه مْكُوْ وبانه بكر وبانه مكو بن محمد بن ابو بكر بن محمد بن عمر
بن محمد بن احمد بن محمد بن سليمان اكبتن نوزُغُ سن نيِ الِكبِدِ سن كُكتِ
لاموه حتى مْسِمُ كُبِتَ لاموه اكفي نا هرُوْسِ كواتُ ولاموه نكتك
وقتِ هُنُ وَفَمَوُ وسِوُ ولِتُك كتك طع ياكِ اكوبج اكوفُنْد
نَمِيُ* وسِوُ كشِك نوات وغِنِ كوتِيَ بتِ مْكُوُ وسِوُ اككِمْبِي اكدَ
دُوْدُ كبُرتُغالِ كتاء حِمي مْكُوُ ووزُغُ اكي بتِ كامْفلُمِ اوصمحِ
واتُ وسِوُ مْفَلُمِ كوصَمعِ كورِجزَ مهال بَوُ سِوُ كتك اَمانِ بعد
ياكِ بُرتُغالِ اكفي خِيْلِ اكي بتِ كمركَبُ اكمْتك مْفلُمِ كد مركبُنِ اَسِنْد
اكمْبِك بِنْ عمِ ياكِ بانه مْكُوْ يِي نواتُ وبتِ وزُغُ وكوتُكُو كتك مركبُ
اسِرُدِ مْتُ حتى مْمُوْي بعد ياهي مفلُمِ كوبجَ وزُغُ كا جنبُ زُتِ
كبران نزِسِوانِ كوتُو جنِبُ زهُكُ زُتِ ككِمْبِلِي ممباسه اكف مْفلُمِ
سنه ١١٠٠ اكوت زِجان بانه بكر نا بانه مادي نا بنت مْمُوْي هِيْتَ مانه
دَرِيْنِ اكتولِ ابو بكر بن بانه مْكُوْ بن ابو بكر بن محمد بن ابو بكر بن محمد بن عمر //

بن محمد بن احمد بن محمد بن سليمان اكبج مْفلُمِ غفْل نا احمد رُيِ* بانه مْكُوْ الِيَ*
تُكُلِو نوزُغُ بُرتُغالِ كوُ بغ اكف مْفلُمِ سنه ١١٠٣ اكتولِ يِيِ احمد بن ابو بكر
بن محمد بن محمد بن ابو بكر بن محمد بن عمر بن محمد بن احمد بن محمد بن
سليمان الِبُ تولِ كوندم >>
بُرتُغالِ اكوِ تُو كتِك نْتِ زكِ نوقتِ هُنُ مانه درِيْن بنت بانه مْكُوْ وَ
بانه بكر مْكِ وبانه مْكُوْ بن ابو بكر الِيُ تُكُلِوَ نبُرتُغالِ كتِك زمانِ يا سلطان
احمد كوُو رُزِ* ووِيْلِ ابو بكر نا بانه مدي نا سلطان احمد نِمُ* واكِ الِيُ
تُكُلِو كفى هُزُنِ سن زِكبِت سيِكُ نْيغَ اكتك كُطهِرِ كِجان گكِ بانه تَمُ
مْتُتُ الِيُ مْتُكُوَ سلطان ابو بكر اِمامُ هُدَ كِجان وبانه مْكُوْ الِيْ تِدَ غُوَ
مْفَلُمِ الِبُ بت خبار اكعزِمُ يِيِ كُفِي هرُوْسِ يِزجان زكِ سببُ
كُمُخنِ سِوَ يا شَبَ اكبت خبارِ مانه درِيْنِ اكمتِ مِي بيِي بن مْكُ
شريف كتِك جمل ليل الِكُو هُدرِ سن كزِ يَوُ* يوُجُمِ اكتك اَمْفَيزِي
سِوَ* يا بتِ اك رِضِيْك اِجار رِيَلِ مِايه و عشيرين كَمْبَ بِمْبِ زَ نْدُفُ
اكتوُ وُمْوِيَ اكفي سِو كسِيْرِ حتى يلِبُ كُو طيرِ كيْظهِرش غَفُل
كَيْبِكَ كتِك مجُمْبَ يجمع زكِ كُل مْتُ اكْتُوْز يكو مالِ مَنْغِ سن //

فُنْدِ كئزِ اِجار اكتك تُوْزُ اكمْب تُوْزُ اكفي عروْسِ يكجان
گكِ حتى زمانِ يا بانه تَمُ مْكُوْ وكي وات ولاموه وكئزم سِو
اكوب وكيْتكُو سِو يا اصِلِ حتى بحرنِ گُمْبُ كِكَفَ ماءِ اِكغبُ
بانه تَمُ مْكُوْ اكتك سِو يا مانه درِيْنِ كمبِي تُبِ سِيْسِ تُتُمِي
كتكِ مِيْ يُتِ اكمْجبُ كُل قبِيْلَ اِلِيُ تُزَ نَتُمِي سِوَ يَنْغُ نا مانه درِيْنِ كوت
مْتُم حُرُ ايُوَوُ كُفُزِيَ اكسِمِ هُيُ رِيِ* مِي كُبجَ سِو هِنِ يِي نا نسِلِ
ياكِ نعد ياكِ نبُو رِيالِ تانُ نغُوُ يكُتُكُلِي سِو تِن ابُو نا سَمْلِ
نا تُزُ كُل مْتُ اوزَوُ وَكمْكُلو نسِل* هِيُ مُيُوْبِ وسِو حتى يِوُ وكُ
وتُو تغُ وقتِ هُوُنَ الا لاْنَ* هُتُموَ نا جمعِ يا مقباءِلِ يا بتِ
نا مقبااِلِ* ونْتِ نْيغِنِ هِد كِزم كا شَرْتِ هِزُ كُبُوَ مُيُوْب و سِوَ
زِكَزِدِ فِتِنِ دنِ يا مُيْ نكتكِ وُفلُمِ وكِ نْيك سبعه اِكو مِيْ مِكَفُ
هكُن مْفُوَ مْفلُمِ كيْيِزلُ كتولِ سلطان ابو بكر بن بانه تَمُ مْكُوْ و بانه
مْتِتِ بن احمد بن ابو بكر بن عمر بن احمد بن عمر بن محمد بن احمد بن محمد بن سليمان اكبتن >>
سن نا سلطان ومسْكتِ اَلامام سيف بن* نبهانى لعربى* هُيُ * //

وبتِ اكِد عربُوْنِ وكوغن مْفلُمِ وعربُوْنِ نا هُيُ مْفلُمِ وبتِ
كُوتُو بُرتْغالِ سِيْكُ جُمعه بِلِ كُوُ و واتُ كُتملكِ غُوْمِ يا ممباسه
اكمعُرفُ الامام اليعربى اكئت الوالى كتِك مزرِع واتُ
وتتُ محمد بن عثمان نا على بن عثمان وتتُ سِكُمُيُوَ اِنلكِ وَكَيَ
بمُوْيِ نا عسْكرِ والامام سيف نبهانى اليعربى رِيُ* اصِلِ يا مَزْرُع
نا مْفلُمِ وبتِ اِلن سِيْر جِم نا جمعِ يا واتُ اكعِيْشِ نْيك اريْعِيْنِ*
كتِك وُفلُمِ وكِ اكف سنه ١١٥٤ اكوت زِجان وغِ بعد ياكِ وسِ
تولِ زِجان زكِ اكتولِ احمد بن ابو بكر بن محمد بن ابو بكر بن عمر بن احمد
بن عمر بن محمد بن احمد بن محمد بن سليمان اككتِ كومِ اكف سنه ١١٦٠ اكخلِفُ
كِجان كمِت بانه غُوْغُ استِولِ كتولِ بانه تمُ مْتُتُ امْكلِوَوُ
امام لْهُدى وبانه مْكُوْ الُتُكلِو نا بُرتُغالِ نا اِن لكِ ابو بكر
بن بانه مْكُو بن ابو بكر بن محمد. بن ابو بكر بن محمد بن ابو بكر بن محمد بن
عمر بن محمد * بن سليمان >>
وقتِ هُنُ امام ليعربى اكئتَ زِتَ كُبج بتِ وسِوزِ وكفا
وعربُ وغِ سن وكفي امانِ بعد يا هي واتُ ولامَوْ وخلِفُ* //

مْفَلُمِ كوبِجَ زِت اسِوَزِ واتُ ولاموه نواتُ لاموه* وكفُغ زِت وكي
بتِ كجنِبُ يكِتُكِ وكبِجن نواتُ وبتِ زِت زِكُوُ سن وكفُنْدِك واتُ
ولاموه بعدِي مْفلُمِ وبتِ اكفُع* زِت كبر نبحرِ كوبِج واتُ ولاموه
كوتملكِ * ياهِي الِكُو حِل مُوْيَ مْفلُمِ وبتِ نواتُ ولاموه اِمام ليعربى*
اكفي شورِ مُوُيَ كَمُوُوَ مْفلُمِ سنه ١١٧٧ اكتولِ رُيِ* مانه مْكِ سلطان
مانه خديجه بنت بانه مْكُوْ بن ابو بكر بن محمد بن ابو بكر بن محمد بن ابو بكر
بن محمد بن عمر >>

بن محمد بن احمد بن محمد بن سليمان اِكو فِتِن نْيغِ كتِك نْتِ يا بتِ اِكو وفلُمِ
ووِيْلِ مانه خديجه المذكور نا سلطان عمر وكبِجن كتِك مُيِ وبتِ نْيَكَ
مِتَتُ سلطان عمر اكِدْ برو كرجِي بت كغُفُ كُوُ سن وُسِيْكُ وكبِجن نواتُ
ومانه خديجه كُل مْتُ مهالِ بَكِ اكف مانه خديجه سنه ١١٨٧ اكتولِ بانه
مْكُوُ وشى وبانه تَمُ مْكُوْ رَعِيَ وكفي وُذِيَ سن اسِبتِ رح كتِك وُفلُمِ
وكِ حتى كيْغِي سنه ١١٩١ وكمْغلِيَ واتُ ومُيْ وكمُوُوَ كتاريخ هِيُ كتولِ
بانه فُوْمُ مادِى اِنِ لكِ سلطان محمد بن ابو بكر بن بانه مْكُوْ بن ابو بكر بن محمد
بن ابو بكر بن محمد بن ابو بكر بن محمد بن عمر بن محمد بن احمد بن محمد بن
سليمان بعد يكُتولِ >> //

رعِيَ وكتك كُفَي فِتِن كوبج زِت كوشِد كو شِك واتُ ارْبعِين ووِيْل
نِرُزِ* خَصَ اكو تِنْد كمَ مْبُوْزِ يُوْ نسكفُ دامُ اِكشُك نْديَن كتِك مَكُوْبُ
اِكو اَمانِ استُكِ مْتُ تِن كُفي فِتِن اكتولِ كرح سن حتى سنه ١٢٢٤
كف ولا هكُتولِ مْفلُمِ تِن كم يِي اكخلِفُ زِجان وغِ سن اكتولِ
سلطان احمد بن شيخ فُومُ لُوطِ بن شيخ بن بانه مكو اِكزدِ فِتِن كتِك مُيْ
ولامو اكوبج زِت نواتُ وممباسه مريغِ* حلِ مُوْيَ و كشُك شيله
جِيْشِ كُوُ سن يا واتُ وبتِ نا وات وممباسه واتُ ولاموه وكتُك
وكي شِيْله وكبِجن نا واتُ وبتُ نا واتُ وممباسه زِت زواتُ ولاموه
زِكو نَغُفُ سن جيْشِ يا بتِ نا* ممباسه وكفُدِك وككِمْبِلِيَ مَجَهَزِنِ
ماوُ مجهزِ مغِنِ يكجهبُ بَوانِ* وكسِمم هبُ وكبِجن زِت زِكُوُ
سن وكف واتُ وغِ سن واتُ وممباسه نا واتُ وبتِ هبن عِدد
كتِك واتُ وبتِ ولُ معُرفُ اسِكُو وتُمَ نا واتُ ضعِفُ واتُ وحِدِ
وثمنِيْنِ ٨١ فلان بن فلان وِيِ وكِ يَكدَ معِيْد هيُ بتِ ناواتُ و
ممباسه هون عِددِ بعد يا هي واتُ ولامو وكِد عربُوْنِ //

وكمْتك سعيد بن سلطان بن لامام وكمْب نْتِ لاموه* سنه ١٢٢٨ الِبُ تولِ
لاموه وُفلُمِ وبتِ وُكسلِي بتِ نا بنادرِ اِكزدِ فِتِن اكتُك مْتُ
وبِلِ كتِك زجان وبانه فُوْمُ مادي هُئِتَوا* فُوْمُ لُوْطِ كُپِغَ اكبِجن
نا سلطان احمد كِس سلطان احمد اكف كمرض سنه ١٢٣٠ اكتولِ فُوْمُ
لُوْطِ و بان فُوْمُ مادِي نيِ الِكُو هُدِر سن شُجع كرِيْمُ نزمن
هِزُ شيخ متاك بن شيخ مْبارك نْدبُ الِبُ تولِ وُ شيخِ وسوُ اكفي
عسْكرِ نا بُوْ نْدُكِ نيِ نِكتِك طع يا سلطان وبتِ نيِ الِبتن سن
نَمْزَرِعى حتى سنه ١٢٣٢ اِكزدِ فِتِنِ بيْن ياكِ نا سلطان سعيد بن سلطان
زنجبار اكف سلطان فُوْمُ لُوْط المذكور بعد ياكِ اكتولِ فُوْمُ لُوْطِ
بن شيخ بن فُوْمُ لوُط وبانه تَمُ مْكُوْ نا هُيُ رِي* بباكِ سلطان احمد بن*
سلطان ويْتُ اكتولِ اصُبْح حتى بعد لِعصرى واتُ وَمُيْ وَ
كمْتُو اكِد سِوُ بمُوْي نَمْزَرِعى وكِدَ وُتِ ممباسه اكتولِ سلطان
بانه شيخ بن فُوْمُ مادى اكبتن نا سيد سعيد بن سلطان اَكتِيَ و
عرب بتِ وككِتِ نْيك مِتتُ بعديِ واتُ ومُيْ وكمُوْزُلُ نا //

شَوُرِ سيد سعيد بن سلطان تاريخ سنه ١٢٢٤* وكمْتولِش سلطان احمد
امْكلُووُ بانه وزِيْرِ وبانه تُم وبانه شيخ * تمُ مْكُوْ كبتن نا سيد سعيد
بن سلطان اكتولِ نْيك مويْلِ واتُ وكمُعُزُلُ وكمْرجِيَ بانه * و بانه فُوْمُ
مدي اككتِ كتِك عِزِ كشُورِ يا سيد سعيد بن سلطان نْيك مِتتُ اكف
سنه ١٢٤٧ اكرجِيَ بانه وزِيْرِ كتِك وُ سلطان وكِ كي بانه فُوْمُ لُوْط بن
شيخ الِيُ كِد ممباسه بمُوْيَ نَمْزَرِعِى وكشُك سِوُ وكبِجن نا بانه وزِيْرِ
وبانه تمُ بتِ نا بانه وزِيْرِ نِشَوُرِ مُوْي نا سيد سعيد بن سلطان
نا فُوْمُ لُوْطِ بمُوْي نَمْزَرِعى نا شيخ متاك مْتُ وسِوُ وكي بتِ كزت
وكبِجن جِيْشِ يا سِوُ اكِفُنْدِك بانه وزِيْر اكيْشِك نْتِ يا سِوُ اكفُد
نوُكُت ومُيْ شيخ متاك بن شيخ مبارك نا فُوْمُ لُوْط وككِمْبِلِيَ برانِ
بمُوْي نبعضِ يواتُ بعد يا سِيْكُ كتِتِ كرجِي سِوُ كزت زِكُوُ
سن وكوتُوَ واتُ وبانه وزِير كزت وكوُ شِك وٓاوُ مُيْ وسِوُ
وكجغ وُكُت ومُيْ وكبِجَن بتِ نا سِوُ اِكو كتِك طع نا شوُرِ
يا سيد سعيد بن سلطان بعد يا مَكَ مُمْويَ اَكَوُوَ سلطان //

بانه وزير نا فوم بكر وبانه شيخ وبانه فوم مادى اكتولِ يِيِ سلطان
فُوْمُ بكر بن شيخ بن بانه فُوْمُ مدى سنه ١٢٥٠ اكبتن سن نا سيد سعيد
بن سلطان مُوْد و كُتولِ كِس اكخلِفُ بَمُوْي نا شيخ متاك بن شيخ
مبارك سيد سعيد بن سلطان اكبت زِت نا امِرِ حماد السمار البو سعيدى
اكبِج بتِ نا سِوُ اسِوزِ كفي امانِ بعد يا هي اِكتُوْك فِتِنَ بين يا سلطان
وبتِ فُوْمُ بكر نا عَمِ ياكِ غفُل محمد بن احمد و بانه فُوْمُ مدى اكشِك نْيُمْب يوُ
فلُمِ يا سلطان فوم بكر غفُل كزِت واتُ ولاموه بمُوْي نَمْتُ و سيد سعيد
بن سلطان وكوصِلِحِش محمد بن احمد اكمْبِك سِوُ كُكِتِ نا فُوْمُ بكر اكِتِ بتِ
بعديِ وكتِت وكبِجن تِن نْيك مِتتُ نا فوم بكر سُوِ* نا بتِ كِس سيد
سعيد بن سلطان اكوصِلِحِشِ اكي بتِ محمد بن احمد كو شوُرِ مُوْيَ يِيِ نا بن
عمِ ياكِ فُوْمُ بكر اكمْشِك محمد بن احمد غفُل اكمُوُو كشوُرِ مُوْيَ يِيِ نامْتُ
وسِوُ سيد سعيد بن سلطان اكمِت فُوْمُ بكر اكِد وُغُجَ سيد سعيد بن سلطان
اكمْفُغَ كشَوُرِ يا واتُ ولاموه نسببُ يكُمُوُوَ محمد بن احمد نِكُفُ وُوَتَ اَمانِ
الِي فَنْيَ سيد سعيد بن سلطان كتِك سنه ١٢٦٢ اكشِك بتِ سلطان احمد بن //

شيخ فُوْمُ لُوْط بن شيخ وبانه تمُ مْكُو كَوْ* شوُرِ يا سيد سعيد بن سلطان اككِتِ
نْيك موِيْلِ بعديِ اكخلِفُ اكيَ سيد سعيد بن سلطان نزِت زِكُوُ سن نا امِرِ
حماد فازه اكِبج سِوُ نا سيد سعيد بن سلطان اكمْفُغُوَ سلطان فوم بكر
اكمْب زِت بمُوْي نا واتُ ولاموه وككِتِ مْتَغَ ونْد كتِك مجهزِ نا سيد سعيد
البُ كِد فازه اككِتِ مهل هِيْتَ كِجَعَ* گَامْبُغَ كربُ نا فازه امِرِ حماد اكي
سِوُ كُوك مَبُوْمَ كتِك نْدِيَ يا بتِ نا فازه نا سِوُ امِرِ حماد اكِد سِوُ كزِتَ
زِكُوُ سن حتى اكشِك مِتِبِ الِيُوْكُ كتِك بنْدرِ يا سِوُ كُبِدو كفي مَبُوْمَ كبِجَ
نْتِ يا سِوُ كَوُن أُذِيَ سن مُوُد وزِتَ كُوَ زِغِ سن اكرُدِ
امِرِ حماد نبعضِ يا عسْكرِ اكِدَ بُوْمَنِ كُتاءَ مْزِغَ اكِبت نْدِيَنِ واتُ
وسِوُ وكمْتُكِيَ غفُلَ امِرِ وشِي متاك هِتَوا* بن مبارك حمد عمر نا امِرِ
وبِيْلِ هيْتَوا* حمد غُمِ وكبِجن وكمُوُوَ اَمِرِ حماد وكد نا بُوْمَنِ وكوبِج
وعربُ ولِيُكُ بُوْمَنِ وكتاءَ نا مِزِغَ نا جِيْشِ الِيُكُ سِوُ هُبِجن ولِبُ
بت خبارِ يَكَمْبَ امِرِ حماد مِوُ وو جِيْشِ يا سيد سعيد بن سلطان اِكفُدِك
نوُ ولِكُو كتِك كُتَملَكِ سِوُ سيد سعيد بن سلطان كِسَ كُبت خبار يموُتِ //

يا امِرِ حماد كوُدك كغِي مرْكبُونِ اَسِنِيْنِ نِنُ اكِد زكِ مسْقطِ مك
وبِيْلِ اكمُوكِ سلطان فُوْمُ بكر فازه اكِبج سِوُ نا بتِ كتِك وقتِ هُنُ
اكف شيخ متاك كمرضِ اِكو خلِفُ كزِجان زكِ كُل مْتُ اتك وشيخ
وكغِي كتِك طع يا سيد سعيد بن سلطان ابو بكر نا محمد زِجان ز شيخ
متاك سيد اَكَمْبَ ابو بكر زِت بمُوْيَ نا سلطان فُوْمُ بَكَر كُمْبج سلطان
احمد سِوُ اكِد ابو بكر بن شيخ متاك بَمُوْيَ نا امِرِ وسلطان فُوْمُ بكر
امكُلِو وُ حمد و بايْشِ نبهانى كغِي سِوُ وُ سِيْكُ وكبِجن حتى وكفُدِك
وتُ و سلطان فُوْمُ بكر وك اَنْد مِو نْديَنِ وكمْشِك ابو بكر بن شيخ
متاك وكمْبِك بتِ كُوُ وو سلطان احمد بعدِي اكسِمام رُوْيِ* شيخ
محمد بن شيخ متاك طرفُ يا سيد سعيد بن سلطان يِيْيِ * سلطان فُوْمُ
بكر سيد سعيد بن سلطان كوب زِت نعسِكرِ نَغَرَما وكمْبجَ سلطان احمد
حتى وكمْتُوَ بتِ سنه ١٢٧٣ اكِد كَوُ سِوُ اِكو نشيخ محمد بن شيخ متاك
طرفُ يا سيد سعيد بن سلطان اكمْب نعسِكرِ كوك نغِرزِ وكتِتَ
نَمتُ وسيد سعيد بن سلطان كسببُ الِفُدَ بانْدَ لَمْتِبِ الُوك شيخ //

محمد متاك الِوك مْبِي يغرِز نا شيخ محمد متاك كفد غِرز نكتِك
وقتِ هُنُ الِكُفَ سلطان احمد بن شيخ كاوُ ببكِ فُوْمُ بكر سلطان
وِيْتُ اككتِ مهال بكِ سلطان احمد امْكُلِوُو سِمْبَ سلطان وِيْتُ
نا قبُل يا شيخ محمد اسِيَفُدَ غِرز لسِوُ يلِتُك فِتِن سلطان فُوْمُ بكر
بن شيخ اكمْتُوَ بَتِ كزِت اكي لاموه اكتك كُيْتملكِ بتِ الِبُ وُن
غُفُ زاكِ نوكُوُ و بتِ الِبُ وُن كِتِدُ مِزُفَنْي شيخ محمد بن شيخ متاك مِسُو
اتك كُو تولِ وسِكِرِ كوبج زِت وكسِمام وكُوُ وبتِ ولاهبن مْفلُمِ
كشُور لواتُ وتتُ محمد بن مْكُوْ نبهانى نا بانه رِحِمَ بن احمد نبهانى
نا ناصر بن عبد سلام رِيِ* الُكُو مْدَ بِرِ لاْمُوْرِ اككُسنْي زنا وكبِجن
شيخ محمد بن شيخ متاك وكمْشِد وكف واتُ معُروْفُ نا مامِرِ مكُوُ
واتُ ووِيْل بانه دميل نا مَوْلَنا وَشى كُوْلِ شيخ محمد بن شيخ متاك
اكِسَ كُوُنَ مَمْبُ هي اكي كُتك امانِ كا محمد بن بانه مْكُوْ النبهانى
كانِ رِىِ* الِيُكُو مْكُوْ واوُ كتِك هوواتُ وتتُ تُمزُتَغُلِي كُتيا
اكتك كُمْبَ يِيِ [محمد بن مْكُوْ] أُسلطان [وسِوُ نا بتِ اكِيْزَ ك جِبُ مِمِ نِمْتُ مْزِمَ
وكِد كَمْتَ سطان احمد وِيْتُ] احمد ووِيْتُ* كبِك واتُ شيخ محمد بن شيخ //

متاك نواتُ وبتِ وكمْبِك نا شيخ ناصر بن عبد سلام كُمْتااَ سلطان احمد
اَلْمُلَقَبُ سِمْب كي نَيْ بتِ خبارِ اِكسِكِلِي أُغُجَ سلطان سيد ماجد بن سعيد
بن سلطان كانِ سيد سعيد أُتغُلِي كُفَ سنه ١٢٧٣ قبُل يا هيُ سيد كُمُيِتَ
وزِرِ* واكِ سيد سليمان بن حمد كمِركبُ اِلِ كُشِك بتِ كُرُش* فِتِن مِركبُ
اِكوصِلِ مَرَ بتِ اِمِكِسَ كُشِكَ مْتُ وسلطا* احمد ابو بكر بن حسن البورى
اَمِكُيَ نَيْ ناصر بن عبد سلام اكِس كُبت خبار هِيُ سيد سليمان بن حمد
اكرِجِيَ أُغُجَ نا شيخ محمد بن شيخ متاك وقتِ هُنُ رِبُ* اِلبُ فُنْدَ غرزَ
لَ سِوُ اكِس كُوصِلِ احمد بتِ واتُ وكمْبا كُو رِيِ* سلطان شيخ محمد
بن شيخ متاك كُنَ مْزِ سِيْفُ نا شيخ شِكُوِ نا محمد مُوُتِه اكسِت كِر
كا سلطان احمد وُفلُمِ وكِ سيد ماجد بن سعيد بن سلطان اكبِك
واتُ ولاموه بتِ كنصح بمُوْي نا شيخ مُحي الدين كمْتك سلطان
احمد اَوِكِ عسكرِ وسيد بتِ نا هُيُ شيخ مُحُي الدين رِيِ* اُلتُو
عسْكرِ وسيد كتِك غِرزَ لسِوُ اِلبُ وَبجَ شيخ محمد بن شيخ متاك
عسْكر وِلِ نْدانِ يا غِرزِ اكِد شيخ مُحُي الدِين كوتُو كا امانِ //

كانِ الِكو مْتُ و سيد ماجد بن سعيد كتِك موزِرِ الِبُ كِيْد اُغُجَ نا
عسْكرِ سيد كَفَيَ هسِرِ سن يُوُ لشيخ مُحي الدين نا شيخ محي الدين
اكتاً درك الِبُ مُوُنَ سيد ماجد نغضبُ رِبُ* كِد يِيِ نواتُ ولاموه
نيِ شيخ محى الدين الِن خِيْلَ سن نعِلِمُ نْيغِ اكِد بتِ نا خِيْرِ يواتُ
ولاموه بمُوْي نا شيخ احمد نا شيخ عبد الرحمن اَيِ نَيْ شيخ بتِ كنِنَ
نا سلطان احمد اكَرِضِيْك بعديا شِد كسببُ يأُصُحُبَ و شيخ
احمد نا شيخ عبد الرحمن اكخلِفُ شوُرِ لوزِرِ وكِ ناصر بن عبد سلام
كانِ ولِئِزَ كُتِيَ وعربُ حتى مْتُ مْمُوْيَ واتُ وبتِ وكفى شوُرِ
مُوْىَ مانه جَاهَ بنت فُوْمُ لوُطِ كِبُغَ وبانه فُوْمُ مدي* وسلطان
فُوْمُ بَكر بن شيخ وقتِ هُنُ سلطان فُوْمُ بكر وُكُ لاموه تِنِ يا شوُرِ
لسيد ماجد بن سعيد تغُ الِبُ تُلِو بتِ بسِ كُل سِيْكُ وكِتِي عسْكرِ
كسِرِ نزن وُ سِيْكُ وُ سِيْكُ الِبُوَ خبارِ سلطان احمد اكو فِتِنَ نا
عسْكرِ ومُ* كُوَ وغِ بتِ وكمْبجَ سلطان احمد غفُل بعديِ كِسَ
حل كتُك كُمْشِكَ وسِوزِ كانِ وَبَتِ وُتِ ولِكُوَ شَوُرِ مُوْيَ نا سيد //

ماجد بن سعيد اِلِ وزرِ واكِ ناصر بن عبد سلام وكبِجن ندا‌ٰن يا مُيْ
وبتِ اكتُك سلطان احمد يِيِ نا شيخ محمد بن شيخ متاك وكِد سِوُ بتِ
وكشِك وعربُ نبحرِنِ وكتِيَ مرِكبُ زِت زلِبُ كُوَ زِكُوُ سن الِبُكُيَ
سيد ماجد بن سعيد كَيْ خُصُرَ* سِوُ نا بتِ نا بحرِ كُسِبتِ گُمْبُ گُگُتِ مَدَوُ
نامِتِبِ و كبِجن بحرِنِ وگِد برانِ كُتأ گگُلِ نمجِر يكُرُدِ هُوان حيِ حيِ*
مَيِتِ سيد ماجِدِ اكتِي سِلِسِلِ كتِك كان لَمْتُوْ وسِوُ كَوايَ* كُسِبتِ گُمْبُ
تِنَ نَوُ و لِون نْيِزِ سِتَ كبحرِنِ ناكبرانِ نجنِبُ يا فازه مْزِ سيف
اكخلِفُ اكو مْتُ و سيد ماجد بن سعيد كَخِبْلَ* نْيغِ نمنِيْنُ مَغِ اكوُن
ظِيْكِ سن سلطان احمد نا شيخ محمد بن شيخ متاك نا نْتِ يا سِوُ اِكو فِتِن
بعضِ يا واتُ ومْبِدَ سيد ماجد كسببُ يَمَشَكَ ولُبت نو تُوِ نِهَوَ
شريف مولنا بن ابو بكر نا عيسى بن احمد السمالى البُوُنَ سلطان احمد نا
شيخ محمد بن شيخ * كَمَ هي وكتك امانِ كا سيد ماجد اكوب امانِ كتِك
مِنيْنُ يا امانِ سلطان احمد اكسفِرِ كا سِرِ اُسِيْكُ اكِد برانِ اَكَرجِيَ
كو بعدِي شيخ محمد بن شيخ متاك اكمْبِك كِجان گكِ شيخ محمد بن شيخ متاك //

اكِيْد مرِكبُنِ كا سيد ماجد بن سعيد نا سيد ماجد كمْصمحِ* اكمْب نعطيا
نْيغِ سيد ماجد كسفِرِ كرجِي أُغُج كِس شيخ محمد بن شيخ متاك اكِد أُغُج كُ
مُوجِهِ سيد ماجد اكمْشِك كمْفُغَ كتِك غُوْمِ يا ممباسه نواتُ اكف شيخ
محمد نا بعد يا سِيْكُ سيد ماجد اكمْبِك الوالى سعود بن حمد كُمْشِك سلطان
احمد كوا* خِيْل نْيغِ اسِوزِ كُتُك كوُ كسِرِ اكِد وِيْتُ الوالى سعود بن حمد
اكِي فازه نا زِجان ز شيخ محمد متاك كوشِك سِوُ كو بِك غُمِنِ ممباسه
عمر متاك اكمْفُغَ لاموه بعدِي سيد ماجد اكتملكِ سوحِلِ زُتِ هكُن
مْتُ وكُمُعرِضِ نا سلطان احمد ككِتِ وِيْتُ كتِك طع يا سيد ماجد
الِبُ تولِ سيد برغش بن سعيد بن سلطان اكتك سيد برغش كُوكِ
عسْكرِ وِيْتُ نا كبنْدرِ سلطان احمد اسِ رِضِيْكِ كبِك زِت كُمْبجَ
اسِوزِ اكفي امانِ ني سعود بن حمد هكُمْبجَ سن زِت سيد برغش
كبِك زِت زمانِ زا الوالى سعيد بن حمد بن سعيد سلطان احمد اكتااَ
حِمِيَ كا جرْمنِ كوب نبعضِ يا بر يا سَوَحِيْلِ اكف سلطان احمد
كتِك حلِ هِيُ يا حِمِي سنه ١٣٠٦ اكتول سلطان فُوْمُ بكر بن سلطان //

احمد بن شيخ النبهانى نَيْ اككتِ كتِك هِيُ حِمي اِكتكِيَ فِتِن يِيِ نا
جرمنِ مْتُ مُمُوُي هِيْتَ كِسِيْلِ .اكمْبِج بوبُ ولغُ كمْبِج غفْل كر
صاصِ وِلكُوِكُ عسْكرِ كوبِج كا رصاصِ نا عسْكر وكمْبِج كِسِيْل
نوزُغُ ولُفُوتِنِ نوُ وكوُوو وزُغُ مِنْ غيْرِ امْرِ يا سلطان فُوْمُ
بكر عسْكرِ وِلبُ ووُن جمع زوُ ومِكُف هو كُغُوْج امْرِ يا سلطان
وكوبِج وزُغُ نوان نا واتُ ومْكُنُوبِ نونْد مُنْيُ وِلبُ بت خبارِ
يكمْب وزُغُ ومبِجن وكووُو وزُغُ ولِيُ كُوِكُ بعدِي اِكيا دُ
وْله يا وغِرِز وكتك كُفِي اِنْصفُ اكوتك واتُ ومُكُنُوْبِ نونْد
مُنْيُ معن اوتِيِ كتِك حُكُمُ فُوْمُ بكر اسِرضِيْكِ كوتُو وكمْبِج زِت
سلطان فُومُ بكر زِكيا مشُو حتى مْكُنُوبِ نونْد مُنْيُ نكلِمَنِ
نا نْيَدُوْ زبونِ وزِبجِ كا مِزِغِ وكتِيِ نمُتُ حتى ليْلة ١١ ربع*
الاول سنه ١٣٠٨ وكبِجن واتُ ووِيْتُ كتِك نْدِيَ يا كِبِيْنِ نواتُ
ودُوْله تُكُفُ وكفُنْدِك واتُ ووِيْتُ حتى اَصُبُحِ سِيْكُ
يا جُوْم تتُ مِزِ ١٢ ربيع الاول سنه ١٣٠٨ وكمْبِج سلطان //

سلطان* فُوْمُ بكر وكَمْتُو وِيْتُ كزت اكِد جُنْغِنِ وِيْتُ اِكتملكوَ

ندُوْلة تُكُفُ سلطان فُوْمُ بكر ككِتِ جُنْغِنِ حتى ٢٨ جماد الاول*

سنه ١٣٠٨ اكف اكشِك مهال بكِ رُيِ* بانه شيخ بن احمد نبهانى بعديا

سِيْكُ گگِ اِكوَ فِتِنِ اكشِك نَرُيِ* فُوْمُ عمر نبهانى نااف تُوْلَ وباهِرُ

وكمْفُغ بانه شيخ بن سلطان احمد اكتولِ سلطان فُوْمُ عمر نوكِس* كُتَ

مُلْكِ* بتِ سلطان احمد سلطان وِيْتُ اكُ تملكِ كنْد سليمان

بن سليمان المظفر نبهانى امام العربى هِنِ رِيُ* خبارِ يا نبهانى

كُيَ سوحِيْلِ نخبارِ زوُ كم تُمِزُ تغُلِيَ كُتيا ومِزُ تولِ وفلُمِ وحِدِ

وثلاثيْنِ نا مانه مْكِ مْمُوْيِ جُمْل ثِيْنِ* وثلاثين مِنْ غيْرِ و

لِكتولِ وكوزُ لِو وكرِجي كتُولِ تُمِ نِقيْلِ هي كا محمد بن فُوْمُ

عمر نبهانى الملقب بانه كِتِيْنِ نيِ اِلنقِيْلِ كا جدِ ياكِ محمد بن بانه

مْكُوْ نبهانى امكُلوِ بانه سمْبَ اِلضِبتِيِ سن خبارِ يا نسب

زوُ كم تُمِزُ تي نَقِتلِ* يا اولِ صالح بن سالم بن احمد بن عبد الله شراحيل

٧ فى صفر سنه ١٣١٨ نقلت هذا للولد* العزيز محمد بن احمد سلطان //

بن فوم بكر بن شيخ بن بانه فوم مدى و سمب سلطان محمد بن ابو بكر بن بانه

مكو بن ابو بكر >>

بن احمد بن ابو بكر بن محمد بن ابو بكر بن محمد بن عمر بن محمد بن احمد بن

محمد بن سليمان بن سليمان بن >>

مصفر* نبهانى . نقلت الثانى ١ فى رجب سنه ١٣٤٣ لاقل* صالح بن سالم بن حمد

نقلت لربيع* وخمسه ٢٣ شعبان سنه ١٣٦٥ ... على خليف //